Scribner Writers Series
Master Index

Scribner Writers Series
Master Index

Charles Scribner's Sons

Macmillan Library Reference USA
Simon & Schuster Macmillan
New York

Simon & Schuster Prentice Hall International
London   Mexico City   New Delhi   Singapore   Sydney   Toronto

Charles Scribner's Sons
An imprint of Simon & Schuster Macmillan
1633 Broadway
New York, NY 10019

LIBRARY OF CONGRESS CATALOGING-IN-PUBLICATION DATA

Scribner writers series master index.
        p.   cm.
        "This guide indexes all articles in the Scribner Writers Series as of
December 1997"—Galley.
        ISBN 0-684-80557-X (alk. paper)
        1. Authors—Biography—Indexes.
PN451.S35 1998
016.809—dc21
        [B]   97-40439
                                                                CIP

    3 5 7 9 11 13 15 17 19   20 18 16 14 12 10 8 6 4 2

PRINTED IN THE UNITED STATES OF AMERICA

The paper used in this publication meets the minimum requirements of the American National Standard for Information Sciences—Permanence of Paper for Printed Library Materials, ANSI Z39.48–1984.

Contents

Alphabetical List of Subjects   1

Writers   1

Themes, Genres, Collectives, and Works   41

Subjects by Period   46

Subjects by Language   94

Subjects by Nationality   138

Subjects by Genre   187

Poetry   187

Drama   204

Early Prose Fiction   215

The Novel   216

The Short Story   238

Religion   255

Philosophy   258

Criticism   260

Journalism   269

Autobiography   273

Children's Literature   281

Special Subject Categories   289

Women Writers   289

African American Writers   297

Volume-by-Volume Contents of the Individual Sets of the Scribner Writers Series   299

American Literature   299

• AFRICAN AMERICAN WRITERS   299

• AMERICAN NATURE WRITERS   299

• AMERICAN WRITERS   300

• AMERICAN WRITERS: RETROSPECTIVE SUPPLEMENT   303

• MODERN AMERICAN WOMEN WRITERS   303

English and Commonwealth Literature   304

• BRITISH WRITERS   304

• BRITISH WRITERS: SELECTED AUTHORS   307

• WILLIAM SHAKESPEARE: HIS WORLD, HIS WORK, HIS INFLUENCE   308

World Literature   309

• AFRICAN WRITERS   309

• ANCIENT WRITERS   310

• THE BOOKS OF THE BIBLE   311

• EUROPEAN WRITERS   311

• EUROPEAN WRITERS: SELECTED AUTHORS   315

• LATIN AMERICAN WRITERS   316

• SCIENCE FICTION WRITERS   318

• SUPERNATURAL FICTION WRITERS   319

• WRITERS FOR CHILDREN   320

• WRITERS FOR YOUNG ADULTS   321

Publisher's Note

This guide indexes all articles in the Scribner Writers Series as of December 1997:

African American Writers
African Writers   R 896 A257w
American Nature Writers   R 810.9 A512N
American Writers through *Supplement IV* and the *Retrospective Supplement*   R 928.1 A512
Ancient Writers
The Books of the Bible
British Writers through *Supplement IV*   R 820.9 B862
British Writers: Selected Authors*   R 820.9 B862s
European Writers
European Writers: Selected Authors*
Latin American Writers
Modern American Women Writers
Science Fiction Writers   R 809.309 S416c2
Supernatural Fiction Writers
William Shakespeare: His World, His Work, His Influence
Writers for Children
Writers for Young Adults

All of the essays, except those in *American Writers Retrospective Supplement*; *William Shakespeare: His World, His Work, His Influence*; and *Writers for Young Adults,* can be found in the Comprehensive Authors Edition of the *Scribner Writers Series on CD-ROM,* Release 2.0, published in 1997. Sets marked with an asterisk (*) contain selected, unabridged articles from the original *British Writers* and *European Writers.*

Scribner Writers Series
Master Index

Alphabetical List of Subjects

WRITERS

Articles about individual named authors or closely linked pairs of authors.

Abbey, Edward
American Nature Writers, vol. 1: **1–19**

Abrahams, Peter
African Writers, vol. 1: **1–14**

Acevedo Díaz, Eduardo
Latin American Writers, vol. 1: **299–303**

Achebe, Chinua
African Writers, vol. 1: **15–36**

Ackerman, Diane
American Nature Writers, vol. 1: **21–30**

Acosta, Father Joseph de
Latin American Writers, vol. 1: **47–51**

Adam de la Halle
See "Medieval Drama"

Adams, Henry
American Writers, vol. 1: **1–24**

Addams, Jane
American Writers Supp. 1, part 1: **1–27**

Addison, Joseph
See "Steele, Sir Richard, and Joseph Addison"

Ady, Endre
European Writers, vol. 9: **859–880**

Aeschylus
Ancient Writers, vol. 1: **99–155**

Agee, James
American Writers, vol. 1: **25–47**

Agustini, Delmira
Latin American Writers, vol. 2: **649–654**

Aickman, Robert
Supernatural Fiction Writers, vol. 2: **957–964**

Aidoo, Ama Ata
African Writers, vol. 1: **37–48**

Aiken, Conrad
American Writers, vol. 1: **48–70**

Aiken, Joan
Writers for Young Adults, vol. 1: **1–9**

Ainsworth, William Harrison
Supernatural Fiction Writers, vol. 1: **187–193**

Akhmatova, Anna
European Writers, vol. 10: **1521–1542**

Albee, Edward
American Writers, vol. 1: **71–96**

Alberdi, Juan Bautista
Latin American Writers, vol. 1: **153–158**

Alcaeus
See "Greek Lyric Poets" in Themes, Genres, Collectives, and Works

Alcman
See "Greek Lyric Poets" in Themes, Genres, Collectives, and Works

Alcott, Louisa May
American Writers Supp. 1, part 1: **28–46**
Writers for Children: **1–6**
Writers for Young Adults, vol. 1: **11–20**

Aldiss, Brian W.
Science Fiction Writers: **251–258**

Alegría, Ciro
Latin American Writers, vol. 3: **1099–1103**

Alencar, José de
Latin American Writers, vol. 1: **195–203**

Alexander, Lloyd
  Supernatural Fiction Writers, vol. 2: **965–971**
  Writers for Young Adults, vol. 1: **21–33**

Alfieri, Vittorio
  European Writers, vol. 4: **661–689**

Amado, Jorge
  Latin American Writers, vol. 3: **1153–1162**

Ambler, Eric
  British Writers Supp. 4: **1–24**

Amis, Kingsley
  British Writers Supp. 2: **1–19**

Amis, Martin
  British Writers Supp. 4: **25–44**

Ammianus Marcellinus
  Ancient Writers, vol. 2: **1117–1138**

Amoroso Lima, Alceu
  Latin American Writers, vol. 2: **781–790**

Anacreon
  See "Greek Lyric Poets" in Themes, Genres,
    Collectives, and Works

Andersen, Hans Christian
  European Writers, vol. 6: **863–892**
  European Writers Selected Authors, vol. 1: **1–29**
  Writers for Children: **7–13**

Anderson, Poul
  Science Fiction Writers: **259–265**
  Supernatural Fiction Writers, vol. 2: **973–980**

Anderson, Sherwood
  American Writers, vol. 1: **97–120**

Anderson Imbert, Enrique
  Latin American Writers, vol. 3: **1105–1110**

Andrade, Mário de
  Latin American Writers, vol. 2: **771–780**

Andrić, Ivo
  European Writers, vol. 11: **1751–1779**

Angell, Judie
  Writers for Young Adults, vol. 1: **35–42**

Angelou, Maya
  American Writers Supp. 4, part 1: **1–19**
  Modern American Women Writers: **1–8**
  Writers for Young Adults, vol. 1: **43–52**

Anouilh, Jean
  European Writers, vol. 13: **2843–2865**
  European Writers Selected Authors, vol. 1: **31–52**

Anstey, F.
  Supernatural Fiction Writers, vol. 1: **287–292**

Anthony, Piers
  Supernatural Fiction Writers, vol. 2: **981–986**

Antimachus of Colophon
  See "Hellenistic Poetry at Alexandria" in
    Themes, Genres, Collectives, and Works

Apollinaire, Guillaume
  European Writers, vol. 9: **881–903**

Apollonius of Rhodes
  See "Hellenistic Poetry at Alexandria" in
    Themes, Genres, Collectives, and Works

Apuleius
  Ancient Writers, vol. 2: **1099–1116**
  Supernatural Fiction Writers, vol. 1: **3–9**

Aquinas, Saint Thomas, and Scholasticism
  European Writers, vol. 1: **405–430**
  European Writers Selected Authors, vol. 1: **53–77**

Aragon, Louis
  European Writers, vol. 11: **2061–2087**

Arciniegas, Germán
  Latin American Writers, vol. 2: **897–901**

Arden, John
  British Writers Supp. 2: **21–42**

Ardizzone, Edward
  Writers for Children: **15–20**

Arenas, Reinaldo
  Latin American Writers, vol. 3: **1451–1458**

Arguedas, José María
  Latin American Writers, vol. 3: **1131–1138**

Ariosto, Lodovico
  European Writers, vol. 2: **619–644**

Aristophanes
  Ancient Writers, vol. 1: **291–312**

Aristotle
  Ancient Writers, vol. 1: **377–416**

Arlt, Roberto
  Latin American Writers, vol. 2: **881–886**

Armah, Ayi Kwei
  African Writers, vol. 1: **49–62**

Arnold, Matthew
  British Writers, vol. 5: **203–218**

Arp, Jean
  European Writers, vol. 10: **1365–1384**

Arreola, Juan José
Latin American Writers, vol. 3: **1229–1236**

Artaud, Antonin
European Writers, vol. 11: **1961–1985**

Asbjørnsen, Peter Christen
See "Asbjørnsen and Moe"

Asbjørnsen and Moe (Peter Christen
  Asbjørnsen and Jørgen Moe)
Writers for Children: **21–28**

Ascasubi, Hilario
Latin American Writers, vol. 1: **147–151**

Asclepiades
See "Hellenistic Poetry at Alexandria" in
  Themes, Genres, Collectives, and Works

Ashbery, John
American Writers Supp. 3, part 1: **1–29**

Asher, Sandy
Writers for Young Adults, vol. 1: **53–61**

Asimov, Isaac
Science Fiction Writers: **267–276**

Asturias, Miguel Ángel
Latin American Writers, vol. 2: **865–873**

Atherton, Gertrude
Supernatural Fiction Writers, vol. 2: **777–781**

Auchincloss, Louis
American Writers Supp. 4, part 1: **21–38**

Auden, W. H.
American Writers Supp. 2, part 1: **1–28**
British Writers, vol. 7: **379–399**
British Writers Selected Authors, vol. 1: **1–21**

Audubon, John James
See "Early Romantic Natural History Literature"

Augier, Émile
See "Well-Made Play, The" in Themes, Genres,
  Collectives, and Works

Augustine, Saint
European Writers, vol. 1: **23–50**
European Writers Selected Authors, vol. 1: **103–130**

Austen, Jane
British Writers, vol. 4: **101–124**
British Writers Selected Authors, vol. 1: **23–46**

Austin, Mary Hunter
American Nature Writers, vol. 1: **31–51**

Austin, William
Supernatural Fiction Writers, vol. 2: **693–696**

Avi
Writers for Young Adults, vol. 1: **63–72**

Awoonor, Kofi
African Writers, vol. 1: **63–75**

Aymé, Marcel
European Writers, vol. 12: **2433–2456**

Azevedo, Aluísio
Latin American Writers, vol. 1: **333–341**

Azorín
European Writers, vol. 9: **639–661**

Azuela, Mariano
Latin American Writers, vol. 2: **457–464**

Bâ, Mariama
African Writers, vol. 1: **77–82**

Babel, Isaac
European Writers, vol. 11: **1885–1915**
European Writers Selected Authors, vol. 1: **131–160**

Bacchylides
See "Greek Lyric Poets" in Themes, Genres,
  Collectives, and Works

Bacon, Francis
British Writers, vol. 1: **257–275**

Bailey, Florence Merriam
American Nature Writers, vol. 1: **53–62**

Baker, Frank
Supernatural Fiction Writers, vol. 2: **561–567**

Balbuena, Bernardo de
Latin American Writers, vol. 1: **53–57**

Baldwin, James
African American Writers: **1–14**
American Writers Supp. 1, part 1: **47–71**

Ballagas, Emilio
Latin American Writers, vol. 3: **1081–1087**

Ballard, J. G.
Science Fiction Writers: **277–282**

Balzac, Honoré de
European Writers, vol. 5: **635–658**
European Writers Selected Authors, vol. 1: **161–183**
Supernatural Fiction Writers, vol. 1: **37–44**

Bandeira, Manuel
Latin American Writers, vol. 2: **629–641**

Bandello, Matteo
See "Renaissance Short Fiction" in Themes,
  Genres, Collectives, and Works

Bangs, J. K.
  Supernatural Fiction Writers, vol. 2: **725–729**

Baraka, Amiri
  African American Writers: **15–29**
  American Writers Supp. 2, part 1: **29–63**

Barker, Pat
  British Writers Supp. 4: **45–63**

Barlow, Joel
  American Writers Supp. 2, part 1: **65–86**

Barnes, Djuna
  American Writers Supp. 3, part 1: **31–46**

Barnes, Julian
  British Writers Supp. 4: **65–76**

Baroja, Pío
  European Writers, vol. 9: **589–616**

Barrie, J. M.
  British Writers Supp. 3: **1–17**
  Supernatural Fiction Writers, vol. 1: **405–410**
  Writers for Children: **29–35**

Barrios, Eduardo
  Latin American Writers, vol. 2: **611–618**

Barth, John
  American Writers, vol. 1: **121–143**

Barthelme, Donald
  American Writers Supp. 4, part 1: **39–58**

Barthes, Roland
  European Writers, vol. 13: **3079–3104**

Bartram, William
  American Nature Writers, vol. 1: **63–74**

Basile, Giambattista
  See "Renaissance Short Fiction" in Themes,
    Genres, Collectives, and Works

Bass, Rick
  American Nature Writers, vol. 1: **75–88**

Baudelaire, Charles
  European Writers, vol. 7: **1323–1348**

Bauer, Joan
  Writers for Young Adults, vol. 1: **73–80**

Bauer, Marion Dane
  Writers for Young Adults, vol. 1: **81–88**

Bauernfeld, Eduard von
  See "Well-Made Play, The" in Themes, Genres,
    Collectives, and Works

Baum, L. Frank
  Writers for Children: **37–48**

Beagle, Peter S.
  Supernatural Fiction Writers, vol. 2: **987–991**

Beaumarchais, Pierre-Augustin Caron de
  European Writers, vol. 4: **563–585**

Beaumont, Francis
  See "Beaumont, Francis, and John Fletcher"

Beaumont, Francis, and John Fletcher
  British Writers, vol. 2: **42–67**

Beauvoir, Simone de
  European Writers, vol. 12: **2701–2732**
  European Writers Selected Authors, vol. 1: **185–215**

Beckett, Samuel
  British Writers Supp. 1: **43–64**
  British Writers Selected Authors, vol. 1: **47–68**

Beckford, William
  Supernatural Fiction Writers, vol. 1: **139–144**
  See also "Gothic Novel, The" in Themes,
    Genres, Collectives, and Works

Beerbohm, Max
  British Writers Supp. 2: **43–59**

Behan, Brendan
  British Writers Supp. 2: **61–76**

Behn, Aphra
  British Writers Supp. 3: **19–43**

Bello, Andrés
  Latin American Writers, vol. 1: **129–134**

Belloc, Hilaire
  Writers for Children: **49–54**

Bellow, Saul
  American Writers, vol. 1: **144–166**

Bely, Andrey
  European Writers, vol. 9: **905–929**

Bemelmans, Ludwig
  Writers for Children: **55–61**

Benedetti, Mario
  Latin American Writers, vol. 3: **1255–1263**

Benét, Stephen Vincent
  Supernatural Fiction Writers, vol. 2: **797–803**

Benjamin, Walter
  European Writers, vol. 11: **1703–1730**

Bennett, Arnold
  British Writers, vol. 6: **247–268**

Bennett, Jay
  Writers for Young Adults, vol. 1: **89–97**

Benson, E. F.
Supernatural Fiction Writers, vol. 1: **491–496**

Beresford, J. D.
Supernatural Fiction Writers, vol. 1: **457–461**

Berger, John
British Writers Supp. 4: **77–96**

Bergson, Henri
European Writers, vol. 8: **45–66**

Berlioz, Hector
European Writers, vol. 6: **771–812**

Berry, Wendell
American Nature Writers, vol. 1: **89–105**

Berryman, John
American Writers, vol. 1: **167–189**

Bester, Alfred
Science Fiction Writers: **283–290**

Beston, Henry
American Nature Writers, vol. 1: **107–120**

Bethancourt, T. Ernesto
Writers for Young Adults, vol. 1: **99–109**

Beti, Mongo
African Writers, vol. 1: **83–94**

Betjeman, John
British Writers, vol. 7: **355–378**

Bianco, Margery Williams
Writers for Children: **63–67**

Bierce, Ambrose
American Writers, vol. 1: **190–213**
Supernatural Fiction Writers, vol. 2: **731–737**

Bioy Casares, Adolfo
Latin American Writers, vol. 3: **1201–1208**

Bishop, Elizabeth
American Writers Supp. 1, part 1: **72–97**
Modern American Women Writers: **9–22**

Blackmur, R. P.
American Writers Supp. 2, part 1: **87–112**

Blackwood, Algernon
Supernatural Fiction Writers, vol. 1: **463–470**

Blake, William
British Writers, vol. 3: **288–310**
British Writers Selected Authors, vol. 1: **89–110**
Writers for Children: **69–76**

Blanco Fombona, Rufino
Latin American Writers, vol. 2: **503–511**

Blasco Ibáñez, Vicente
European Writers, vol. 8: **355–388**

Blest Gana, Alberto
Latin American Writers, vol. 1: **205–213**

Blish, James
Science Fiction Writers: **291–296**

Bloch, Robert
Supernatural Fiction Writers, vol. 2: **901–907**

Block, Francesca Lia
Writers for Young Adults, vol. 1: **111–119**

Blok, Alexander
European Writers, vol. 9: **959–990**

Blume, Judy
Writers for Young Adults, vol. 1: **121–131**

Bly, Robert
American Writers Supp. 4, part 1: **59–77**

Boccaccio, Giovanni
European Writers, vol. 2: **509–534**
European Writers Selected Authors, vol. 1: **255–280**
See also "Renaissance Pastoral Poetry" in
      Themes, Genres, Collectives, and Works

Bogan, Louise
American Writers Supp. 3, part 1: **47–68**
Modern American Women Writers: **23–36**

Bograd, Larry
Writers for Young Adults, vol. 1: **133–141**

Boileau-Despréaux, Nicolas
European Writers, vol. 3: **177–205**

Böll, Heinrich
European Writers, vol. 13: **3165–3186**

Bombal, María Luisa
Latin American Writers, vol. 3: **1111–1117**

Bond, Edward
British Writers Supp. 1: **421–436**

Bontemps, Arna
Writers for Children: **77–83**

Borges, Jorge Luis
Latin American Writers, vol. 2: **845–864**

Bossuet, Jacques Bénigne
European Writers, vol. 3: **151–175**

Boswell, James
British Writers, vol. 3: **234–251**
British Writers Selected Authors, vol. 1: **111–128**

Bourne, Randolph
American Writers, vol. 1: **214–238**

Bowen, Elizabeth
British Writers Supp. 2: **77–96**
Supernatural Fiction Writers, vol. 2: **569–575**

Bowles, Paul
American Writers Supp. 4, part 1: **79–99**

Brackett, Leigh
Supernatural Fiction Writers, vol. 2: **909–915**

Bradbury, Ray
American Writers Supp. 4, part 1: **101–118**
Science Fiction Writers: **171–178**
Supernatural Fiction Writers, vol. 2: **917–923**

Bradstreet, Anne
American Writers Supp. 1, part 1: **98–123**

Brancato, Robin F.
Writers for Young Adults, vol. 1: **143–152**

Branscum, Robbie
Writers for Young Adults, vol. 1: **153–161**

Brecht, Bertolt
European Writers, vol. 11: **2089–2112**
European Writers Selected Authors, vol. 1: **281–303**

Breton, André
European Writers, vol. 11: **1939–1960**

Bridgers, Sue Ellen
Writers for Young Adults, vol. 1: **163–172**

Bridges, Robert
British Writers, vol. 6: **71–84**

Brieux, Eugène
See "Well-Made Play, The" in Themes, Genres, Collectives, and Works

Brink, André
African Writers, vol. 1: **95–114**

Brink, Carol Ryrie
Writers for Children: **85–90**

Broch, Hermann
European Writers, vol. 10: **1385–1408**

Brontës, The
British Writers, vol. 5: **105–154**
British Writers Selected Authors, vol. 1: **129–177**

Brooke-Rose, Christine
British Writers Supp. 4: **97–118**

Brooke, Rupert
British Writers Supp. 3: **45–61**
See also "Poets of World War I (British)" in Themes, Genres, Collectives, and Works

Brookner, Anita
British Writers Supp. 4: **119–137**

Brooks, Bruce
Writers for Young Adults, vol. 1: **173–182**

Brooks, Gwendolyn
African American Writers: **31–43**
American Writers Supp. 3, part 1: **69–90**
Modern American Women Writers: **37–48**

Brooks, Van Wyck
American Writers, vol. 1: **239–263**

Brown, Charles Brockden
American Writers Supp. 1, part 1: **124–149**

Brown, Sterling
African American Writers: **45–57**

Browne, Sir Thomas
British Writers, vol. 2: **145–157**

Browning, Elizabeth Barrett
British Writers, vol. 4: **310–322**
British Writers Selected Authors, vol. 1: **179–191**

Browning, Robert
British Writers, vol. 4: **354–375**
British Writers Selected Authors, vol. 1: **193–214**

Brunhoff, Jean de
Writers for Children: **91–96**

Brunner, John
Science Fiction Writers: **297–304**

Brutus, Dennis
African Writers, vol. 1: **115–126**

Bryant, William Cullen
American Writers Supp. 1, part 1: **150–173**

Büchner, Georg
European Writers, vol. 6: **1169–1194**

Buck, Pearl S.
American Writers Supp. 2, part 1: **113–134**

Budrys, Algis
Science Fiction Writers: **305–311**

Bulwer-Lytton, Edward
Supernatural Fiction Writers, vol. 1: **195–204**

Bunting, Eve
Writers for Young Adults, vol. 1: **183–189**

Bunyan, John
British Writers, vol. 2: **240–254**
British Writers Selected Authors, vol. 1: **215–229**
Writers for Children: **97–102**

Burckhardt, Jacob
European Writers, vol. 6: **1225–1244**

Burgess, Anthony
British Writers Supp. 1: **185–198**

Burke, Edmund
British Writers, vol. 3: **193–207**

Burke, Kenneth
American Writers, vol. 1: **264–287**

Burnett, Frances Hodgson
Writers for Children: **103–109**

Burney, Frances
British Writers Supp. 3: **63–78**

Burns, Olive Ann
Writers for Young Adults, vol. 1: **191–198**

Burns, Robert
British Writers, vol. 3: **310–323**
British Writers Selected Authors, vol. 1: **231–244**

Burroughs, Edgar Rice
Science Fiction Writers: **59–64**

Burroughs, John
American Nature Writers, vol. 1: **121–138**

Burroughs, William S.
American Writers Supp. 3, part 1: **91–110**

Burton, Virginia Lee
Writers for Children: **111–115**

Butler, Samuel
British Writers Supp. 2: **97–121**

Butor, Michel
European Writers, vol. 13: **3287–3321**

Byars, Betsy
Writers for Young Adults, vol. 1: **199–207**

Byatt, A. S.
British Writers Supp. 4: **139–156**

Byron, Lord
British Writers, vol. 4: **171–194**
British Writers Selected Authors, vol. 1: **245–268**

Cabell, James Branch
Supernatural Fiction Writers, vol. 2: **789–796**

Cabral de Melo Neto, João
Latin American Writers, vol. 3: **1247–1253**

Cabrera Infante, Guillermo
Latin American Writers, vol. 3: **1383–1391**

Caesar
Ancient Writers, vol. 1: **583–599**

Calderón de la Barca, Pedro
European Writers, vol. 2: **871–895**

Caldwell, Erskine
American Writers, vol. 1: **288–311**

Callimachus
See "Hellenistic Poetry at Alexandria" in Themes, Genres, Collectives, and Works

Calvino, Italo
European Writers, vol. 13: **3259–3286**

Cambaceres, Eugenio
Latin American Writers, vol. 1: **269–276**

Camoëns, Luís Vaz de
European Writers, vol. 2: **747–767**

Campbell, John W., Jr.
Science Fiction Writers: **151–159**

Campbell, Ramsey
Supernatural Fiction Writers, vol. 2: **993–999**

Campbell, Roy
African Writers, vol. 1: **127–137**

Campo, Estanislao del
Latin American Writers, vol. 1: **229–233**

Camus, Albert
African Writers, vol. 1: **139–152**
European Writers, vol. 13: **3049–3078**
European Writers Selected Authors, vol. 1: **305–334**

Canetti, Elias
European Writers, vol. 12: **2615–2633**

Čapek, Karel
European Writers, vol. 10: **1565–1590**
Science Fiction Writers: **583–589**

Capote, Truman
American Writers Supp. 3, part 1: **111–133**

Carballido, Emilio
Latin American Writers, vol. 3: **1289–1294**

Carducci, Giosue
European Writers, vol. 7: **1495–1516**

Carew, Thomas
See "Cavalier Poets, The" in Themes, Genres, Collectives, and Works

Carlyle, Thomas
British Writers, vol. 4: **238–250**
British Writers Selected Authors, vol. 1: **269–281**

Caro, Miguel Antonio
Latin American Writers, vol. 1: **277–281**

Carpentier, Alejo
 Latin American Writers, vol. 3: **1019–1031**

Carrasquilla, Tomás
 Latin American Writers, vol. 1: **343–350**

Carrighar, Sally
 American Nature Writers, vol. 1: **139–149**

Carrió de la Vandera, Alonso
 Latin American Writers, vol. 1: **107–111**

Carroll, Lewis
 British Writers, vol. 5: **261–276**
 Supernatural Fiction Writers, vol. 1: **247–253**
 Writers for Children: **117–127**

Carson, Rachel
 American Nature Writers, vol. 1: **151–171**

Carter, Alden R.
 Writers for Young Adults, vol. 1: **209–218**

Carter, Angela
 British Writers Supp. 3: **79–93**

Carver, Raymond
 American Writers Supp. 3, part 1: **135–151**

Cary, Joyce
 British Writers, vol. 7: **185–196**

Casal, Julián del
 Latin American Writers, vol. 1: **365–370**

Castellanos, Rosario
 Latin American Writers, vol. 3: **1295–1302**

Castiglione, Baldesar
 European Writers, vol. 2: **645–667**

Castro Alves, Antônio de
 Latin American Writers, vol. 1: **289–297**

Cather, Willa
 American Writers, vol. 1: **312–334**
 American Writers Retrospective: **1–23**
 Modern American Women Writers: **49–62**

Catullus
 Ancient Writers, vol. 2: **643–667**

Cavafy, Constantin
 European Writers, vol. 8: **205–228**

Cazotte, Jacques
 Supernatural Fiction Writers, vol. 1: **29–35**

Cela, Camilo José
 European Writers, vol. 13: **3105–3129**

Céline, Louis-Ferdinand
 European Writers, vol. 11: **1859–1884**

Cervantes, Miguel de
 European Writers, vol. 2: **819–844**
 European Writers Selected Authors, vol. 1: **335–359**
 See also "Renaissance Short Fiction" in Themes,
 Genres, Collectives, and Works

Chambers, Aidan
 Writers for Young Adults, vol. 1: **219–227**

Chambers, Robert W.
 Supernatural Fiction Writers, vol. 2: **739–745**

Chamisso, Adelbert von
 Supernatural Fiction Writers, vol. 1: **91–95**

Chandler, Raymond
 American Writers Supp. 4, part 1: **119–138**

Chapman, George
 British Writers, vol. 1: **232–256**

Chateaubriand, François René de
 European Writers, vol. 5: **113–140**

Chatwin, Bruce
 British Writers Supp. 4: **157–177**

Chaucer, Geoffrey
 British Writers, vol. 1: **19–47**
 British Writers Selected Authors, vol. 1: **283–311**

Cheever, John
 American Writers Supp. 1, part 1: **174–199**

Chekhov, Anton
 European Writers, vol. 7: **1855–1882**
 European Writers Selected Authors, vol. 1: **361–387**

Chénier, André
 European Writers, vol. 4: **691–718**

Chesnutt, Charles W.
 African American Writers: **59–70**

Chesterton, G. K.
 British Writers, vol. 6: **335–346**
 Supernatural Fiction Writers, vol. 1: **411–414**

Childress, Alice
 Writers for Young Adults, vol. 1: **229–240**

Chocano, José Santos
 Latin American Writers, vol. 2: **543–549**

Chopin, Kate
 American Writers Supp. 1, part 1: **200–226**
 Modern American Women Writers: **63–78**

Chrétien de Troyes
 European Writers, vol. 1: **185–209**
 See also "Arthurian Romances" in Themes,
 Genres, Collectives, and Works

Christie, Agatha
British Writers Supp. 2: **123–137**

Churchill, Caryl
British Writers Supp. 4: **179–200**

Churchill, Winston
British Writers, vol. 6: **347–362**

Cicero
Ancient Writers, vol. 1: **555–581**

Clark, John Pepper
African Writers, vol. 1: **153–166**

Clarke, Arthur C.
Science Fiction Writers: **313–320**

Claudel, Paul
European Writers, vol. 8: **471–494**

Cleaver, Vera and Bill
Writers for Young Adults, vol. 1: **241–248**

Clement, Hal
Science Fiction Writers: **321–327**

Clough, Arthur Hugh
British Writers, vol. 5: **155–172**

Cocteau, Jean
European Writers, vol. 10: **1543–1564**

Coetzee, J. M.
African Writers, vol. 1: **167–183**

Cole, Brock
Writers for Young Adults, vol. 1: **249–256**

Coleridge, Samuel Taylor
British Writers, vol. 4: **41–57**
British Writers Selected Authors, vol. 1: **313–329**

Colette
European Writers, vol. 9: **617–638**
European Writers Selected Authors, vol. 1: **389–410**

Collier, Christopher and James Lincoln
Writers for Young Adults, vol. 1: **257–269**

Collier, John
Supernatural Fiction Writers, vol. 2: **577–583**

Collins, Wilkie
Supernatural Fiction Writers, vol. 1: **233–238**

Collins, William
British Writers, vol. 3: **160–176**

Collodi, C.
Writers for Children: **129–137**

Colman, Hila
Writers for Young Adults, vol. 1: **271–280**

Colum, Padraic
Writers for Children: **139–146**

Compton-Burnett, Ivy
British Writers, vol. 7: **59–70**

Comstock, Anna Botsford
American Nature Writers, vol. 1: **173–185**

Congreve, William
British Writers, vol. 2: **338–350**

Connolly, Cyril
British Writers Supp. 3: **95–113**

Conrad, Joseph
British Writers, vol. 6: **133–150**
British Writers Selected Authors, vol. 1: **331–348**

Constant, Benjamin
See "French Novelists, Three" in Themes,
Genres, Collectives, and Works

Cooney, Caroline B.
Writers for Young Adults, vol. 1: **281–290**

Cooper, James Fenimore
American Writers, vol. 1: **335–357**
Writers for Children: **147–153**

Cooper, Susan Fenimore
American Nature Writers, vol. 1: **187–198**

Coppard, A. E.
Supernatural Fiction Writers, vol. 2: **523–528**

Corelli, Marie
Supernatural Fiction Writers, vol. 1: **293–297**

Cormier, Robert
Writers for Young Adults, vol. 1: **291–301**

Corneille, Pierre
European Writers, vol. 3: **23–49**

Cortázar, Julio
Latin American Writers, vol. 3: **1177–1194**

Costa, Cláudio Manuel da
Latin American Writers, vol. 1: **113–117**

Couto, Mia
African Writers, vol. 1: **185–197**

Coward, Noël
British Writers Supp. 2: **139–158**

Cowley, Abraham
See "Metaphysical Poets, Four" in Themes,
Genres, Collectives, and Works

Cowley, Malcolm
American Writers Supp. 2, part 1: **135–156**

Cowper, William
British Writers, vol. 3: **207–220**

Cozzens, James Gould
American Writers, vol. 1: **358–381**

Crabbe, George
British Writers, vol. 3: **272–287**

Crane, Hart
American Writers, vol. 1: **381–404**

Crane, Stephen
American Writers, vol. 1: **405–427**
Writers for Young Adults, vol. 1: **303–312**

Crashaw, Richard
See "Metaphysical Poets, Four" in Themes, Genres, Collectives, and Works

Crawford, F. Marion
Supernatural Fiction Writers, vol. 2: **747–751**

Creeley, Robert
American Writers Supp. 4, part 1: **139–161**

Crèvecoeur, Hector St. John de
American Writers Supp. 1, part 1: **227–252**
See also "Early Romantic Natural History Literature" in Themes, Genres, Collectives, and Works

Croce, Benedetto
European Writers, vol. 8: **311–329**

Crutcher, Chris
Writers for Young Adults, vol. 1: **313–322**

Cruz e Sousa, João
Latin American Writers, vol. 1: **359–363**

Cullen, Countee
American Writers Supp. 4, part 1: **163–174**

Cummings, E. E.
American Writers, vol. 1: **428–450**

Cunha, Euclides da
Latin American Writers, vol. 1: **387–395**

Dahl, Roald
British Writers Supp. 4: **201–227**

Daly, Maureen
Writers for Young Adults, vol. 1: **323–333**

Daniel, John
See "New Voices in American Nature Writing" in Themes, Genres, Collectives, and Works

D'Annunzio, Gabriele
European Writers, vol. 8: **175–203**

Dante Alighieri
European Writers, vol. 1: **431–450**
European Writers Selected Authors, vol. 1: **411–430**
See also "Renaissance Pastoral Poetry" in Themes, Genres, Collectives, and Works

Danziger, Paula
Writers for Young Adults, vol. 1: **335–344**

Darío, Rubén
Latin American Writers, vol. 1: **397–412**

Daugherty, James Henry
Writers for Children: **155–161**

Davidson, Avram
Supernatural Fiction Writers, vol. 2: **1001–1008**

Davis, H. L.
American Nature Writers, vol. 1: **199–211**

Davis, Terry
Writers for Young Adults, vol. 1: **345–352**

Day Lewis, Cecil
British Writers Supp. 3: **115–132**

De Camp, L. Sprague
Science Fiction Writers: **179–184**
See also "De Camp, L. Sprague, and Fletcher Pratt"

De Camp, L. Sprague, and Fletcher Pratt
Supernatural Fiction Writers, vol. 2: **925–931**

Defoe, Daniel
British Writers, vol. 3: **1–14**
British Writers Selected Authors, vol. 1: **349–362**
Writers for Children: **163–171**

Delacroix, Eugène
European Writers, vol. 5: **513–539**

De la Mare, Walter
Supernatural Fiction Writers, vol. 1: **497–503**
Writers for Children: **173–180**

Delany, Samuel R.
Science Fiction Writers: **329–336**

Demetrius of Phalerum
See "Hellenistic Poetry at Alexandria" in Themes, Genres, Collectives, and Works

Demosthenes
Ancient Writers, vol. 1: **417–433**

Denevi, Marco
Latin American Writers, vol. 3: **1265–1269**

De Quincey, Thomas
British Writers, vol. 4: **141–156**

Derleth, August
  Supernatural Fiction Writers, vol. 2: **883–890**

Descartes, René
  European Writers, vol. 3: **1–22**
  European Writers Selected Authors, vol. 1: **431–452**

Des Périers, Bonaventure
  See "Renaissance Short Fiction" in Themes,
    Genres, Collectives, and Works

Díaz, Jorge
  Latin American Writers, vol. 3: **1393–1397**

Díaz del Castillo, Bernal
  Latin American Writers, vol. 1: **17–21**

Díaz Rodríguez, Manuel
  Latin American Writers, vol. 1: **431–439**

Dib, Mohammed
  African Writers, vol. 1: **199–207**

Dick, Philip K.
  Science Fiction Writers: **337–343**

Dickens, Charles
  British Writers, vol. 5: **41–74**
  British Writers Selected Authors, vol. 1: **363–396**
  Supernatural Fiction Writers, vol. 1: **213–218**
  Writers for Children: **181–191**
  Writers for Young Adults, vol. 1: **353–364**

Dickey, James
  American Writers Supp. 4, part 1: **175–194**

Dickinson, Emily
  American Writers, vol. 1: **451–473**
  American Writers Retrospective: **25–50**
  Modern American Women Writers: **77–89**
  Writers for Young Adults, vol. 1: **365–372**

Dickinson, Peter
  Writers for Young Adults, vol. 1: **375–383**

Dickson, Gordon R.
  Science Fiction Writers: **345–350**

Diderot, Denis
  European Writers, vol. 4: **475–509**

Didion, Joan
  American Writers Supp. 4, part 1: **195–216**
  Modern American Women Writers: **91–102**

Dillard, Annie
  American Nature Writers, vol. 1: **213–230**

Dinesen, Isak
  European Writers, vol. 10: **1281–1306**
  European Writers Selected Authors, vol. 1: **453–477**

Disch, Thomas M.
  Science Fiction Writers: **351–356**

Disraeli, Benjamin
  British Writers, vol. 4: **292–309**

Doctorow, E. L.
  American Writers Supp. 4, part 1: **217–240**

Dodge, Mary Mapes
  Writers for Children: **193–199**

Donaldson, Stephen R.
  Supernatural Fiction Writers, vol. 2: **1009–1013**

Donne, John
  British Writers, vol. 1: **352–369**
  British Writers Selected Authors, vol. 1: **397–414**

Donoso, José
  Latin American Writers, vol. 3: **1277–1288**

Doolittle, Hilda (H.D.)
  American Writers Supp. 1, part 1: **253–275**
  Modern American Women Writers: **103–121**

Dos Passos, John
  American Writers, vol. 1: **474–496**

Dostoevsky, Feodor
  European Writers, vol. 7: **1349–1373**
  European Writers Selected Authors, vol. 1: **479–501**

Douglas, Marjory Stoneman
  American Nature Writers, vol. 1: **231–245**

Douglas, Norman
  British Writers, vol. 6: **293–306**

Douglass, Frederick
  American Writers Supp. 3, part 1: **153–174**
  See also "Slave Narrative in American
    Literature, The" in Themes, Genres,
    Collectives, and Works

Dove, Rita
  American Writers Supp. 4, part 1: **241–258**

Doyle, Sir Arthur Conan
  British Writers Supp. 2: **159–178**
  British Writers Selected Authors, vol. 1: **415–434**
  Science Fiction Writers: **45–50**
  Writers for Children: **201–207**
  Writers for Young Adults, vol. 1: **385–392**

Drabble, Margaret
  British Writers Supp. 4: **229–254**

Dragún, Osvaldo
  Latin American Writers, vol. 3: **1377–1382**

Dreiser, Theodore
American Writers, vol. 1: **497–520**

Drummond de Andrade, Carlos
Latin American Writers, vol. 2: **957–974**

Dryden, John
British Writers, vol. 2: **289–306**

Du Bois, W. E. B.
African American Writers: **71–87**
American Writers Supp. 2, part 1: **157–189**

Dumas, Alexandre (Fils)
See "Well-Made Play, The" in Themes, Genres,
Collectives, and Works

Dumas, Alexandre (Père)
European Writers, vol. 6: **719–745**
European Writers Selected Authors, vol. 1: **503–527**
Writers for Children: **209–213**

Du Maurier, Daphne
British Writers Supp. 3: **133–149**
British Writers Selected Authors, vol. 1: **435–451**

Dunbar, Paul Laurence
African American Writers: **87–102**
American Writers Supp. 2, part 1: **191–219**

Duncan, Lois
Writers for Young Adults, vol. 1: **393–402**

Dunsany, Lord
Supernatural Fiction Writers, vol. 1: **471–478**

Durrell, Lawrence
British Writers Supp. 1: **93–128**

Dürrenmatt, Friedrich
European Writers, vol. 13: **3215–3235**

Eberhart, Richard
American Writers, vol. 1: **521–543**

Eça de Queiroz, José Maria
European Writers, vol. 7: **1683–1708**

Echeverría, Esteban
Latin American Writers, vol. 1: **141–145**

Eddison, E. R.
Supernatural Fiction Writers, vol. 2: **529–534**

Edgeworth, Maria
British Writers Supp. 3: **151–168**

Edwards, Amelia B.
Supernatural Fiction Writers, vol. 1: **255–260**

Edwards, Jonathan
American Writers, vol. 1: **544–566**

Edwards, Jorge
Latin American Writers, vol. 3: **1399–1403**

Egbuna, Obi
African Writers, vol. 1: **209–221**

Eguren, José María
Latin American Writers, vol. 2: **513–518**

Ehrlich, Gretel
American Nature Writers, vol. 1: **247–258**

Eichelbaum, Samuel
Latin American Writers, vol. 2: **797–801**

Eifert, Virginia
American Nature Writers, vol. 1: **259–268**

Eiseley, Loren
American Nature Writers, vol. 1: **269–285**

Ekelöf, Gunnar
European Writers, vol. 12: **2635–2671**

Ekwensi, Cyprian
African Writers, vol. 1: **223–234**

Eliot, George
British Writers, vol. 5: **187–201**
British Writers Selected Authors, vol. 1: **453–467**

Eliot, T. S.
American Writers, vol. 1: **567–591**
American Writers Retrospective: **51–71**
British Writers, vol. 7: **143–170**
British Writers Selected Authors, vol. 1: **469–496**

Ellison, Harlan
Science Fiction Writers: **357–368**
Supernatural Fiction Writers, vol. 2: **1015–1021**

Ellison, Ralph
African American Writers: **103–129**
American Writers Supp. 2, part 1: **221–252**

Elytis, Odysseus
European Writers, vol. 13: **2955–2988**

Emecheta, Buchi
African Writers, vol. 1: **235–247**

Emerson, Ralph Waldo
American Nature Writers, vol. 1: **287–307**
American Writers, vol. 2: **1–24**

Empson, William
British Writers Supp. 2: **179–198**

Enright, Elizabeth
Writers for Children: **215–220**

Epictetus
See "Epictetus and Marcus Aurelius"

Epictetus and Marcus Aurelius
Ancient Writers, vol. 2: **985–1002**

Equiano, Olaudah
See "Slave Narrative in American Literature, The" in Themes, Genres, Collectives, and Works

Erasmus, Desiderius
European Writers, vol. 2: **571–593**
European Writers Selected Authors, vol. 1: **529–551**

Ercilla y Zúñiga, Don Alonso de
Latin American Writers, vol. 1: **23–31**

Erdrich, Louise
American Writers Supp. 4, part 1: **259–278**

Etherege, Sir George
See "Restoration Court Poets, The" in Themes, Genres, Collectives, and Works

Euripides
Ancient Writers, vol. 1: **233–266**

Evelyn, John
See "Evelyn, John, and Samuel Pepys"

Evelyn, John, and Samuel Pepys
British Writers, vol. 2: **274–288**

Ewing, Juliana Horatia
Writers for Children: **221–226**

Eyerly, Jeannette
Writers for Young Adults, vol. 1: **403–411**

Fagundes Telles, Lygia
Latin American Writers, vol. 3: **1271–1275**

Farah, Nuruddin
African Writers, vol. 1: **249–262**

Farjeon, Eleanor
Writers for Children: **227–234**

Farmer, Philip José
Science Fiction Writers: **369–375**

Farquhar, George
British Writers, vol. 2: **351–365**

Farrell, James T.
American Writers, vol. 2: **25–53**

Faulkner, William
American Writers, vol. 2: **54–76**
American Writers Retrospective: **73–95**

Fauset, Jessie
Modern American Women Writers: **123–139**

Fénelon, François de Salignac de la Mothe-
European Writers, vol. 3: **261–291**

Fernández, Macedonio
Latin American Writers, vol. 2: **483–491**

Fernández de Lizardi, José Joaquín
Latin American Writers, vol. 1: **119–128**

Fernández de Oviedo y Valdés, Gonzalo
Latin American Writers, vol. 1: **11–15**

Ferreira de Castro, Jose Maria
European Writers, vol. 11: **2143–2165**

Feydeau, Georges
See "Well-Made Play, The" in Themes, Genres, Collectives, and Works

Field, Rachel Lyman
Writers for Children: **235–240**

Fielding, Henry
British Writers, vol. 3: **94–106**
British Writers Selected Authors, vol. 2: **497–509**

Finch, Robert Charles
American Nature Writers, vol. 1: **309–321**

Finney, Charles
Supernatural Fiction Writers, vol. 2: **821–826**

Firbank, Ronald
British Writers Supp. 2: **199–224**

Fitzgerald, Edward
British Writers, vol. 4: **340–353**

Fitzgerald, F. Scott
American Writers, vol. 2: **77–100**
American Writers Retrospective: **97–120**

Flaubert, Gustave
European Writers, vol. 7: **1373–1394**
European Writers Selected Authors, vol. 1: **553–574**

Fletcher, John
See "Beaumont, Francis, and John Fletcher"

Fontane, Theodor
European Writers, vol. 6: **1299–1322**

Ford, Ford Madox
British Writers, vol. 6: **319–334**

Ford, John
British Writers, vol. 2: **87–102**

Forster, E. M.
British Writers, vol. 6: **397–414**
British Writers Selected Authors, vol. 2: **511–527**
Supernatural Fiction Writers, vol. 1: **479–484**

Fortune, Dion
Supernatural Fiction Writers, vol. 2: **585–590**

Foscolo, Ugo
    European Writers, vol. 5: **313–341**

Foucault, Michel
    European Writers, vol. 13: **3323–3364**

Fouqué, Friedrich de la Motte
    Supernatural Fiction Writers, vol. 1: **97–105**

Fowles, John
    British Writers Supp. 1: **291–311**

Fox, Paula
    Writers for Young Adults, vol. 1: **413–422**

France, Anatole
    Supernatural Fiction Writers, vol. 1: **67–72**

Frank, Anne
    Writers for Young Adults, vol. 1: **423–431**

Franklin, Benjamin
    American Writers, vol. 2: **101–125**

Frazer, James George
    British Writers Supp. 3: **169–190**

Frederic, Harold
    American Writers, vol. 2: **126–149**

Freedman, Russell
    Writers for Young Adults, vol. 2: **1–9**

Freeman, Mary E. Wilkins
    Modern American Women Writers: **141–153**
    Supernatural Fiction Writers, vol. 2: **769–773**

French, Michael
    Writers for Young Adults, vol. 2: **11–20**

Freneau, Philip
    American Writers Supp. 2, part 1: **253–277**

Freud, Sigmund
    European Writers, vol. 8: **1–20**
    European Writers Selected Authors, vol. 1: **575–594**

Freytag, Gustav
    See "Well-Made Play, The" in Themes, Genres, Collectives, and Works

Frisch, Max
    European Writers, vol. 13: **2895–2924**

Frost, Robert
    American Writers, vol. 2: **150–172**
    American Writers Retrospective: **121–144**
    Writers for Young Adults, vol. 2: **21–31**

Fry, Christopher
    British Writers Supp. 3: **191–210**

Fuentes, Carlos
    Latin American Writers, vol. 3: **1353–1376**

Fugard, Athol
    African Writers, vol. 1: **263–275**

Fuller, Margaret
    American Writers Supp. 2, part 1: **279–306**

Gaddis, William
    American Writers Supp. 4, part 1: **279–296**

Gág, Wanda
    Writers for Children: **241–246**

Gaines, Ernest J.
    African American Writers: **129–145**

Gallegos, Rómulo
    Latin American Writers, vol. 2: **603–610**

Galsworthy, John
    British Writers, vol. 6: **269–293**

Gálvez, Manuel
    Latin American Writers, vol. 2: **585–589**

Gambaro, Griselda
    Latin American Writers, vol. 3: **1323–1328**

Gamboa, Federico
    Latin American Writers, vol. 1: **371–375**

García Lorca, Federico
    European Writers, vol. 11: **2167–2203**
    European Writers Selected Authors, vol. 1:
        595–630

García Márquez, Gabriel
    Latin American Writers, vol. 3: **1329–1346**

Garcilaso de la Vega, El Inca
    Latin American Writers, vol. 1: **39–45**

Garfield, Leon
    Writers for Young Adults, vol. 2: **33–45**

Garner, Alan
    Supernatural Fiction Writers, vol. 2: **1023–1029**

Garnett, David
    Supernatural Fiction Writers, vol. 2: **535–539**

Garnett, Richard
    Supernatural Fiction Writers, vol. 1: **317–320**

Gaskell, Elizabeth
    British Writers, vol. 5: **1–16**

Gautier, Théophile
    European Writers, vol. 6: **1033–1059**
    Supernatural Fiction Writers, vol. 1: **45–50**

Gay, John
    British Writers, vol. 3: **54–68**

Genet, Jean
    European Writers, vol. 13: **2865–2892**

Geoffrey of Monmouth
See "Arthurian Romances" in Themes, Genres, Collectives, and Works

George, Jean Craighead
Writers for Young Adults, vol. 2: **47–57**

George, Stefan
European Writers, vol. 8: **447–470**

Ghelderode, Michel de
European Writers, vol. 11: **2113–2141**

Gibbon, Edward
British Writers, vol. 3: **221–233**

Gide, André
European Writers, vol. 8: **495–518**
European Writers Selected Authors, vol. 1: **631–654**

Gilman, Charlotte Perkins
Modern American Women Writers: **155–170**

Ginsberg, Allen
American Writers Supp. 2, part 1: **307–333**

Ginzburg, Natalia
European Writers, vol. 13: **3131–3163**

Giraldi, Giambattista
See "Renaissance Pastoral Poetry" in Themes, Genres, Collectives, and Works

Giraudoux, Jean
European Writers, vol. 9: **1041–1065**

Gissing, George
British Writers, vol. 5: **423–438**

Glasgow, Ellen
American Writers, vol. 2: **173–195**
Modern American Women Writers: **171–180**

Glaspell, Susan
American Writers Supp. 3, part 1: **175–191**
Modern American Women Writers: **181–188**

Goethe, Johann Wolfgang von
European Writers, vol. 5: **1–26**
European Writers Selected Authors, vol. 1: **655–680**

Gogol, Nikolay Vasilievich
European Writers, vol. 6: **971–998**

Golding, William
British Writers Supp. 1: **65–91**
British Writers Selected Authors, vol. 2: **529–555**

Goldoni, Carlo
European Writers, vol. 4: **421–448**

Goldsmith, Oliver
British Writers, vol. 3: **177–192**

Gombrowicz, Witold
European Writers, vol. 12: **2563–2588**

Gómez Carillo, Enrique
Latin American Writers, vol. 2: **465–469**

Gómez de Avellaneda, Gertrudis
Latin American Writers, vol. 1: **175–180**

Gonçalves Dias, Antônio
Latin American Writers, vol. 1: **185–193**

Goncharov, Ivan
European Writers, vol. 6: **1061–1087**

Goncourt, Edmond Louis Antoine de
See "Goncourt, Edmond Louis Antoine de, and Jules Alfred Huot de Goncourt"

Goncourt, Edmond Louis Antoine de, and Jules Alfred Huot de Goncourt
European Writers, vol. 7: **1395–1419**

Goncourt, Jules Alfred Huot de
See "Goncourt, Edmond Louis Antoine de, and Jules Alfred Huot de Goncourt"

González de Eslava, Fernán
Latin American Writers, vol. 1: **33–37**

González Prada, Manuel
Latin American Writers, vol. 1: **283–288**

Gordimer, Nadine
African Writers, vol. 1: **277–290**
British Writers Supp. 2: **225–245**

Gordon, Caroline
American Writers, vol. 2: **196–222**

Gordon, Mary
American Writers Supp. 4, part 1: **297–317**

Gorky, Maxim
European Writers, vol. 8: **417–446**
European Writers Selected Authors, vol. 2: **681–710**

Gorostiza, José
Latin American Writers, vol. 2: **923–931**

Gottfried von Strassburg
European Writers, vol. 1: **237–262**
See also "Arthurian Romances" in Themes, Genres, Collectives, and Works

Gower, John
British Writers, vol. 1: **48–56**

Grahame, Kenneth
Writers for Children: **247–254**

Grass, Günter
European Writers, vol. 13: **3365–3388**
European Writers Selected Authors, vol. 2: **711–734**

Graves, John
  American Nature Writers, vol. 1: **323–336**
Graves, Robert
  British Writers, vol. 7: **257–272**
Gray, Thomas
  British Writers, vol. 3: **136–145**
Green, Henry
  British Writers Supp. 2: **247–266**
Greene, Bette
  Writers for Young Adults, vol. 2: **59–68**
Greene, Graham
  British Writers Supp. 1: **1–20**
  British Writers Selected Authors, vol. 2: **557–576**
Gregory, Lady Augusta
  See "Synge, J. M., and Lady Augusta Gregory"
Grillparzer, Franz
  European Writers, vol. 5: **417–445**
Grimm, Jacob
  See "Grimm, Jacob and Wilhelm"
Grimm, Jacob and Wilhelm
  Writers for Children: **255–263**
Grimm, Wilhelm
  See "Grimm, Jacob and Wilhelm"
Guarini, Giambattista
  See "Renaissance Pastoral Poetry" in Themes,
    Genres, Collectives, and Works
Guillaume de Lorris
  See "*Romance of the Rose*, The, and Medieval
    Allegory" in Themes, Genres, Collectives,
    and Works
Guillén, Nicolás
  Latin American Writers, vol. 2: **947–955**
Guimarães Rosa, João
  Latin American Writers, vol. 3: **1069–1080**
Güiraldes, Ricardo
  Latin American Writers, vol. 2: **619–627**
Gunn, Thom
  British Writers Supp. 4: **255–279**
Gunn Allen, Paula
  American Writers Supp. 4, part 1: **319–340**
Gunnarsson, Gunnar
  European Writers, vol. 10: **1497–1519**
Gutiérrez Nájera, Manuel
  Latin American Writers, vol. 1: **351–357**

Gutzkow, Karl
  See "Well-Made Play, The" in Themes, Genres,
    Collectives, and Works
Guzmán, Martín Luis
  Latin American Writers, vol. 2: **655–662**
Haggard, H. Rider
  British Writers Supp. 3: **211–228**
  Science Fiction Writers: **19–24**
  Supernatural Fiction Writers, vol. 1: **321–327**
Ḥakīm, Tawfīq, al-
  African Writers, vol. 1: **291–301**
Hale, Lucretia P.
  Writers for Children: **265–268**
Hall, Lynn
  Writers for Young Adults, vol. 2: **69–77**
Hamilton, Virginia
  Writers for Young Adults, vol. 2: **79–92**
Hammett, Dashiell
  American Writers Supp. 4, part 1: **341–357**
Hamsun, Knut
  European Writers, vol. 8: **21–43**
Hansberry, Lorraine
  African American Writers: **147–158**
  American Writers Supp. 4, part 1: **359–377**
Hardwick, Elizabeth
  American Writers Supp. 3, part 1: **193–215**
  Modern American Women Writers: **189–196**
Hardy, Thomas
  British Writers, vol. 6: **1–22**
  British Writers Selected Authors, vol. 2: **577–598**
Hare, David
  British Writers Supp. 4: **281–300**
Harper, Frances Ellen Watkins
  African American Writers: **159–175**
  Modern American Women Writers: **197–205**
Harris, Joel Chandler
  Writers for Children: **269–275**
Harte, Bret
  American Writers Supp. 2, part 1: **335–359**
Hartley, L. P.
  Supernatural Fiction Writers, vol. 2: **639–644**
Harvey, William Fryer
  Supernatural Fiction Writers, vol. 2: **591–596**
Hašek, Jaroslav
  European Writers, vol. 9: **1091–1118**

Hasselstrom, Linda
  American Nature Writers, vol. 1: **337–348**
Hauff, William
  Supernatural Fiction Writers, vol. 1: **107–110**
Hauptmann, Gerhart
  European Writers, vol. 8: **147–174**
Hawthorne, Nathaniel
  American Writers, vol. 2: **223–246**
  American Writers Retrospective: **145–167**
  Supernatural Fiction Writers, vol. 2: **707–715**
  Writers for Children: **277–282**
Hay, John
  American Nature Writers, vol. 1: **349–362**
Hayden, Robert Earl
  African American Writers: **177–192**
  American Writers Supp. 2, part 1: **361–383**
Hazlitt, William
  British Writers, vol. 4: **125–140**
Head, Bessie
  African Writers, vol. 1: **303–320**
Heaney, Seamus
  British Writers Supp. 2: **267–282**
Hebbel, Friedrich
  European Writers, vol. 6: **1089–1122**
Heine, Heinrich
  European Writers, vol. 5: **489–512**
Heinlein, Robert A.
  Science Fiction Writers: **185–196**
Heiremans, Luis Alberto
  Latin American Writers, vol. 3: **1347–1352**
Heller, Joseph
  American Writers Supp. 4, part 1: **379–396**
Hellman, Lillian
  American Writers Supp. 1, part 1: **276–298**
  Modern American Women Writers: **207–220**
Hemingway, Ernest
  American Writers, vol. 2: **247–270**
  American Writers Retrospective: **169–191**
  Writers for Young Adults, vol. 2: **93–102**
Henríquez Ureña, Pedro
  Latin American Writers, vol. 2: **597–601**
Henry, O.
  American Writers Supp. 2, part 1: **385–412**
Hentoff, Nat
  Writers for Young Adults, vol. 2: **103–112**

Herbert, Frank
  Science Fiction Writers: **377–385**
Herbert, George
  British Writers, vol. 2: **117–130**
Herder, Johann Gottfried von
  European Writers, vol. 4: **639–660**
Heredia, José Mariá
  Latin American Writers, vol. 1: **135–140**
Hernández, José
  Latin American Writers, vol. 1: **235–247**
Herodotus
  Ancient Writers, vol. 1: **209–232**
Herrera y Reissig, Julio
  Latin American Writers, vol. 2: **519–530**
Herrick, Robert
  British Writers, vol. 2: **102–116**
Hervieu, Paul
  See "Well-Made Play, The" in Themes, Genres,
    Collectives, and Works
Hesiod
  Ancient Writers, vol. 1: **43–73**
Hesse, Hermann
  European Writers, vol. 9: **833–859**
  European Writers Selected Authors, vol. 2: **735–760**
Hichens, Robert
  Supernatural Fiction Writers, vol. 1: **415–420**
Hinton, S. E.
  Writers for Young Adults, vol. 2: **113–120**
Hoagland, Edward
  American Nature Writers, vol. 1: **363–375**
Hobbs, Will
  Writers for Young Adults, vol. 2: **121–129**
Hodgson, William Hope
  Supernatural Fiction Writers, vol. 1: **421–428**
Hoffmann, E. T. A.
  European Writers, vol. 5: **261–289**
  Supernatural Fiction Writers, vol. 1: **111–119**
  Writers for Children: **283–288**
Hoffmann, Heinrich
  Writers for Children: **289–294**
Hofmannsthal, Hugo von
  European Writers, vol. 9: **689–714**
Hogan, Linda
  American Nature Writers, vol. 1: **377–388**
  American Writers Supp. 4, part 1: **397–418**

Hogg, James
    Supernatural Fiction Writers, vol. 1: **177–183**

Hölderlin, Friedrich
    European Writers, vol. 5: **143–173**

Holland, Isabelle
    Writers for Young Adults, vol. 2: **131–140**

Holmes, Oliver Wendell
    American Writers Supp. 1, part 1: **299–319**

Homer
    Ancient Writers, vol. 1: **1–41**

Honwana, Luís Bernardo
    African Writers, vol. 1: **321–329**

Hood, Thomas
    British Writers, vol. 4: **251–267**

Hooker, Richard
    British Writers, vol. 1: **176–190**

Hoover, Helen
    American Nature Writers, vol. 1: **389–399**

Hope, Christopher
    African Writers, vol. 1: **331–343**

Hopkins, Gerard Manley
    British Writers, vol. 5: **361–382**
    British Writers Selected Authors, vol. 2: **599–620**

Horace
    Ancient Writers, vol. 2: **703–731**

Housman, A. E.
    British Writers, vol. 6: **151–164**
    British Writers Selected Authors, vol. 2: **621–634**

Howard, Henry (Earl of Surrey)
    British Writers, vol. 1: **113–120**

Howard, Robert E.
    Supernatural Fiction Writers, vol. 2: **861–868**

Howe, Susan
    American Writers Supp. 4, part 2: **419–438**

Howells, William Dean
    American Writers, vol. 2: **271–294**

Hoyle, Fred
    Science Fiction Writers: **387–392**

Hubbell, Sue
    American Nature Writers, vol. 1: **401–412**

Hughes, Langston
    African American Writers: **193–205**
    American Writers Retrospective: **193–214**
    American Writers Supp. 1, part 1: **320–348**
    Writers for Children: **295–301**

Hughes, Monica
    Writers for Young Adults, vol. 2: **141–148**

Hughes, Ted
    British Writers Supp. 1: **341–366**

Hugo, Victor
    European Writers, vol. 6: **693–718**
    European Writers Selected Authors, vol. 2: **761–786**

Huidobro, Vicente
    Latin American Writers, vol. 2: **755–764**

Hume, David
    British Writers Supp. 3: **229–245**

Hunter, Mollie
    Writers for Young Adults, vol. 2: **149–159**

Hurston, Zora Neale
    African American Writers: **205–218**
    Modern American Women Writers: **221–235**

Huxley, Aldous
    British Writers, vol. 7: **197–208**
    British Writers Selected Authors, vol. 2: **635–646**
    Science Fiction Writers: **101–108**

Huysmans, Joris Karl
    European Writers, vol. 7: **1709–1729**

Ibarbourou, Juana de
    Latin American Writers, vol. 2: **803–807**

Ibsen, Henrik
    European Writers, vol. 7: **1421–1448**
    European Writers Selected Authors, vol. 2: **787–813**

Ibycus
    See "Greek Lyric Poets" in Themes, Genres,
        Collectives, and Works

Icaza, Jorge
    Latin American Writers, vol. 3: **1063–1067**

Idrīs, Yūsuf
    African Writers, vol. 1: **345–365**

Ionesco, Eugène
    European Writers, vol. 13: **2989–3020**
    European Writers Selected Authors, vol. 2: **815–846**

Irving, Washington
    American Writers, vol. 2: **295–318**
    Supernatural Fiction Writers, vol. 2: **685–691**
    Writers for Children: **303–307**

Irwin, Hadley
    Writers for Young Adults, vol. 2: **161–166**

Isaacs, Jorge
    Latin American Writers, vol. 1: **247–251**

Isherwood, Christopher
  British Writers, vol. 7: **309–320**

Ishiguro, Kazuo
  British Writers Supp. 4: **301–317**

Isocrates
  Ancient Writers, vol. 1: **313–329**

Iyayi, Festus
  African Writers, vol. 1: **367–375**

Jackson, Shirley
  Supernatural Fiction Writers, vol. 2: **1031–1036**

Jacobs, Harriet
  See "Slave Narrative in American Literature, The" in Themes, Genres, Collectives, and Works

Jacobs, Joseph
  Writers for Children: **309–316**

Jacobs, W. W.
  Supernatural Fiction Writers, vol. 1: **383–387**

Jacobson, Dan
  African Writers, vol. 1: **377–389**

Jaimes Freyre, Ricardo
  Latin American Writers, vol. 1: **419–423**

James, Henry
  American Writers, vol. 2: **319–341**
  American Writers Retrospective: **215–242**
  British Writers, vol. 6: **23–69**
  Supernatural Fiction Writers, vol. 1: **337–344**

James, M. R.
  Supernatural Fiction Writers, vol. 1: **429–436**

James, P. D.
  British Writers Supp. 4: **319–341**

James, William
  American Writers, vol. 2: **342–366**

Janovy, John, Jr.
  American Nature Writers, vol. 1: **413–424**

Jarrell, Randall
  American Writers, vol. 2: **367–390**

Jarry, Alfred
  European Writers, vol. 9: **665–687**

Jean de Meun
  See "*Romance of the Rose*, The, and Medieval Allegory" in Themes, Genres, Collectives, and Works

Jeffers, Robinson
  American Writers Supp. 2, part 2: **413–440**

Jefferson, Thomas
  See "Early Romantic Natural History Literature" in Themes, Genres, Collectives, and Works

Jewett, Sarah Orne
  American Writers, vol. 2: **391–414**
  Modern American Women Writers: **235–250**

Jiménez, Juan Ramón
  European Writers, vol. 9: **991–1016**

Johnson, Cathy
  American Nature Writers, vol. 1: **425–438**

Johnson, Eyvind
  European Writers, vol. 12: **2361–2385**

Johnson, James Weldon
  African American Writers: **219–233**

Johnson, Josephine
  American Nature Writers, vol. 1: **439–451**

Johnson, Samuel
  British Writers, vol. 3: **107–123**
  British Writers Selected Authors, vol. 2: **647–663**

Johnston, Norma
  Writers for Young Adults, vol. 2: **167–176**

Jones, David
  See "Poets of World War I (British)" in Themes, Genres, Collectives, and Works

Jones, Gayl
  African American Writers: **235–244**

Jones, Henry Arthur
  See "Well-Made Play, The" in Themes, Genres, Collectives, and Works

Jonson, Ben
  British Writers, vol. 1: **335–352**
  British Writers Selected Authors, vol. 2: **665–681**

Jordan, June
  African American Writers: **245–261**

Josephus
  Ancient Writers, vol. 2: **877–885**

Joyce, James
  British Writers, vol. 7: **41–58**
  British Writers Selected Authors, vol. 2: **683–700**

Juana Inéz de La Cruz, Sor
  Latin American Writers, vol. 1: **85–106**

Juvenal
  See "Persius and Juvenal"

Kafka, Franz
  European Writers, vol. 9: **1151–1179**
  European Writers Selected Authors, vol. 2: **847–875**

Kappel-Smith, Diana
  American Nature Writers, vol. 1: **453–463**
Kästner, Erich
  Writers for Children: **317–322**
Kateb, Yacine
  African Writers, vol. 1: **391–400**
Kazantzakis, Nikos
  European Writers, vol. 9: **1067–1091**
Keats, John
  British Writers, vol. 4: **211–238**
  British Writers Selected Authors, vol. 2: **701–727**
Keller, David H.
  Science Fiction Writers: **119–123**
Keller, Gottfried
  See "Poetic Realism" in Themes, Genres,
      Collectives, and Works
Keneally, Thomas
  British Writers Supp. 4: **343–362**
Kerouac, Jack
  American Writers Supp. 3, part 1: **217–234**
Kerr, M. E.
  Writers for Young Adults, vol. 2: **177–185**
Khlebnikov, Velimir
  European Writers, vol. 10: **1331–1364**
Kierkegaard, Søren
  European Writers, vol. 6: **1123–1146**
  European Writers Selected Authors, vol. 2: **877–900**
King, Clarence
  See "Western Geologists and Explorers" in
      Themes, Genres, Collectives, and Works
King, Stephen
  Supernatural Fiction Writers, vol. 2: **1037–1044**
Kingsley, Charles
  Writers for Children: **323–327**
Kingston, Maxine Hong
  Modern American Women Writers: **251–259**
Kinnell, Galway
  American Writers Supp. 3, part 1: **235–256**
Kipling, Rudyard
  British Writers, vol. 6: **165–206**
  British Writers Selected Authors, vol. 2: **729–770**
  Supernatural Fiction Writers, vol. 1: **437–442**
  Writers for Children: **329–336**
Klein, Norma
  Writers for Young Adults, vol. 2: **187–197**

Kleist, Heinrich von
  European Writers, vol. 5: **291–312**
Klopstock, Friedrich Gottlieb
  European Writers, vol. 4: **511–536**
Knight, Damon
  Science Fiction Writers: **393–400**
Koestler, Arthur
  British Writers Supp. 1: **21–41**
Korman, Gordon
  Writers for Young Adults, vol. 2: **199–206**
Kornbluth, C. M.
  Science Fiction Writers: **401–407**
Kosztolányi, Dezsö
  European Writers, vol. 10: **1231–1249**
Krleža, Miroslav
  European Writers, vol. 11: **1807–1834**
Krutch, Joseph Wood
  American Nature Writers, vol. 1: **465–477**
Kumin, Maxine
  American Nature Writers, vol. 1: **479–497**
  American Writers Supp. 4, part 2: **439–457**
Kundera, Milan
  European Writers, vol. 13: **3389–3413**
Kunitz, Stanley
  American Writers Supp. 3, part 1: **257–270**
Kuttner, Henry
  Science Fiction Writers: **161–167**
Kyd, Thomas, and Early Elizabethan Tragedy
  British Writers, vol. 1: **212–231**
LaBastille, Anne
  American Nature Writers, vol. 1: **499–511**
Labiche, Eugène
  See "Well-Made Play, The" in Themes, Genres,
      Collectives, and Works
La Bruyère, Jean de
  European Writers, vol. 3: **229–260**
Laclos, Choderlos de
  See "French Novelists, Three" in Themes,
      Genres, Collectives, and Works
Lafferty, R. A.
  Supernatural Fiction Writers, vol. 2: **1045–1052**
La Fontaine, Jean de
  European Writers, vol. 3: **73–100**
  European Writers Selected Authors, vol. 2: **901–928**

Laforgue, Jules
  European Writers, vol. 7: **1883–1908**

Lagerkvist, Pär
  European Writers, vol. 10: **1677–1702**

Laguerre, Enrique A.
  Latin American Writers, vol. 3: **1049–1055**

La Guma, Alex
  African Writers, vol. 1: **401–411**

Lamb, Charles
  British Writers, vol. 4: **73–86**

Lampedusa, Giuseppe Tomasi di
  European Writers, vol. 11: **2009–2034**

Landor, Walter Savage
  British Writers, vol. 4: **87–100**

Lang, Andrew
  Writers for Children: **337–343**

Langland, William: Piers Plowman
  British Writers, vol. 1: **1–18**

Lanier, Sidney
  American Writers Supp. 1, part 1: **349–373**

Lardner, Ring
  American Writers, vol. 2: **415–438**

Larkin, Phillip
  British Writers Supp. 1: **275–290**

La Rochefoucauld, François VI, Duc de
  European Writers, vol. 3: **51–71**

Larreta, Enrique
  Latin American Writers, vol. 2: **471–476**

Larsen, Nella
  African American Writers: **263–272**

Las Casas, Bartolomé de
  Latin American Writers, vol. 1: **1–9**

Lasky, Kathryn
  Writers for Young Adults, vol. 2: **207–216**

Lawrence, D. H.
  British Writers, vol. 7: **87–126**
  British Writers Selected Authors, vol. 2: **771–810**

Lawrence, T. E.
  British Writers Supp. 2: **283–298**

Lawson, Robert
  Writers for Children: **345–349**

Laxness, Halldór
  European Writers, vol. 12: **2457–2478**

Laye, Camara
  African Writers, vol. 1: **413–425**

Lear, Edward
  British Writers, vol. 5: **75–88**
  Writers for Children: **351–356**

Least Heat-Moon, William
  American Nature Writers, vol. 1: **513–523**

Leavis, F. R.
  British Writers, vol. 7: **233–256**

Le Carré, John
  British Writers Supp. 2: **299–320**
  British Writers Selected Authors, vol. 2: **811–832**

Leconte de Lisle, Charles Marie
  European Writers, vol. 6: **1245–1273**

Lee, Harper
  Writers for Young Adults, vol. 2: **217–225**

Lee, Tanith
  Supernatural Fiction Writers, vol. 2: **1053–1058**

Lee, Vernon
  Supernatural Fiction Writers, vol. 1: **329–335**

Le Fanu, J. S.
  Supernatural Fiction Writers, vol. 1: **219–231**

Le Guin, Ursula K.
  Science Fiction Writers: **409–417**
  Supernatural Fiction Writers, vol. 2: **1059–1066**
  Writers for Young Adults, vol. 2: **227–236**
  See also "Contemporary Ecofiction" in Themes,
    Genres, Collectives, and Works

Leiber, Fritz
  Science Fiction Writers: **419–424**
  Supernatural Fiction Writers, vol. 2: **933–939**

Leinster, Murray
  Science Fiction Writers: **111–117**

Łem, Stanisław
  Science Fiction Writers: **591–598**

L'Engle, Madeleine
  Writers for Young Adults, vol. 2: **237–246**

Leopardi, Giacomo
  European Writers, vol. 5: **541–567**

Leopold, Aldo
  American Nature Writers, vol. 1: **525–547**

Lermontov, Mikhail Yurievich
  European Writers, vol. 6: **1195–1224**

Lesage, Alain-René
  European Writers, vol. 3: **317–344**

Lessing, Doris
  African Writers, vol. 1: **427–449**
  British Writers Supp. 1: **237–257**
  British Writers Selected Authors, vol. 2: **833–853**

Lessing, Gotthold Ephraim
  European Writers, vol. 4: **537–562**

Levertov, Denise
  American Writers Supp. 3, part 1: **271–287**

Lewis, C. S.
  British Writers Supp. 3: **247–268**
  British Writers Selected Authors, vol. 2: **855–876**
  Science Fiction Writers: **243–248**
  Supernatural Fiction Writers, vol. 2: **661–666**
  Writers for Children: **357–364**
  Writers for Young Adults, vol. 2: **247–255**

Lewis, M. G.
  Supernatural Fiction Writers, vol. 1: **153–160**

Lewis, Sinclair
  American Writers, vol. 2: **439–461**

Lewis, Wyndham
  British Writers, vol. 7: **71–86**

Lezama Lima, José
  Latin American Writers, vol. 3: **1125–1130**

Lima, Jorge de
  Latin American Writers, vol. 2: **765–770**

Lima Barreto, Afonso Henriques de
  Latin American Writers, vol. 2: **565–573**

Lindsay, David
  Supernatural Fiction Writers, vol. 2: **541–547**

Lindsay, Vachel
  American Writers Supp. 1, part 2: **374–403**

Lins do Rego, José
  Latin American Writers, vol. 2: **909–913**

Lipsyte, Robert
  Writers for Young Adults, vol. 2: **257–266**

Lispector, Clarice
  Latin American Writers, vol. 3: **1303–1309**

Livy
  Ancient Writers, vol. 2: **733–764**

Lodge, David
  British Writers Supp. 4: **363–387**

Lofting, Hugh
  Writers for Children: **365–371**

London, Jack
  American Writers, vol. 2: **462–485**
  Writers for Young Adults, vol. 2: **267–278**

Long, Frank Belknap
  Supernatural Fiction Writers, vol. 2: **869–874**

Longfellow, Henry Wadsworth
  American Writers, vol. 2: **486–510**

Longinus
  Ancient Writers, vol. 2: **1063–1080**

Lopez, Barry
  American Nature Writers, vol. 1: **549–568**

Lopez Velarde, Ramon
  Latin American Writers, vol. 2: **663–670**

Lorde, Audre
  African American Writers: **273–288**

Lovecraft, H. P.
  Science Fiction Writers: **131–137**
  Supernatural Fiction Writers, vol. 2: **853–859**

Lovelace, Richard
  See "Cavalier Poets, The" in Themes, Genres,
    Collectives, and Works

Lowell, Amy
  American Writers, vol. 2: **511–533**
  Modern American Women Writers: **261–268**

Lowell, James Russell
  American Writers Supp. 1, part 2: **404–426**

Lowell, Robert
  American Writers, vol. 2: **534–557**

Lowry, Lois
  Writers for Young Adults, vol. 2: **279–287**

Lowry, Malcolm
  British Writers Supp. 3: **269–286**

Lucan
  See "Lucan and Statius"

Lucan and Statius
  Ancient Writers, vol. 2: **917–941**

Lucian
  Ancient Writers, vol. 2: **1081–1097**

Lucretius
  Ancient Writers, vol. 2: **601–620**

Lugones, Leopoldo
  Latin American Writers, vol. 2: **493–502**

Lukács, György
  European Writers, vol. 10: **1251–1279**

Luther, Martin
European Writers, vol. 2: **669–692**
European Writers Selected Authors, vol. 2: **929–951**

Lydgate, John
British Writers, vol. 1: **57–66**

Lyly, John
See "Lyly, John, and George Peele"

Lyly, John, and George Peele
British Writers, vol. 1: **191–211**

Lynch, Benito
Latin American Writers, vol. 2: **559–563**

Lynch, Chris
Writers for Young Adults, vol. 2: **289–297**

Macaulay, Thomas Babington
British Writers, vol. 4: **268–292**

McCaffrey, Anne
Writers for Young Adults, vol. 2: **299–306**

McCarthy, Mary
American Writers, vol. 2: **558–584**
Modern American Women Writers: **269–278**

McCullers, Carson
American Writers, vol. 2: **585–608**
Modern American Women Writers: **279–287**

MacDonald, George
Supernatural Fiction Writers, vol. 1: **239–246**
Writers for Children: **373–380**

Macdonald, Ross
American Writers Supp. 4, part 2: **459–477**

McEwan, Ian
British Writers Supp. 4: **389–408**

Machado, Antonio
European Writers, vol. 9: **743–765**

Machado de Assis, Joaquim Maria
Latin American Writers, vol. 1: **253–268**

Machen, Arthur
Supernatural Fiction Writers, vol. 1: **351–359**

Machiavelli, Niccolò
European Writers, vol. 2: **595–618**
European Writers Selected Authors, vol. 2: **953–976**

McKay, Claude
African American Writers: **305–320**

McKibben, Bill
See "New Voices in American Nature Writing" in Themes, Genres, Collectives, and Works

McKillip, Patricia
Supernatural Fiction Writers, vol. 2: **1067–1072**

Maclean, Norman
See "Contemporary Ecofiction" in Themes, Genres, Collectives, and Works

MacLeish, Archibald
American Writers, vol. 3: **1–25**

Macleod, Fiona
Supernatural Fiction Writers, vol. 1: **369–374**

MacNeice, Louis
British Writers, vol. 7: **401–420**

McNulty, Faith
American Nature Writers, vol. 1: **569–581**

McPhee, John
American Nature Writers, vol. 1: **583–598**
American Writers Supp. 3, part 1: **289–316**

Maeterlinck, Maurice
European Writers, vol. 8: **119–146**

Maḥfūẓ, Najīb
African Writers, vol. 2: **451–465**

Mahy, Margaret (May)
Writers for Young Adults, vol. 2: **307–315**

Mailer, Norman
American Writers, vol. 3: **26–49**

Major, Kevin
Writers for Young Adults, vol. 2: **317–326**

Malamud, Bernard
American Writers Supp. 1, part 2: **427–453**

Mallarmé, Stéphane
European Writers, vol. 7: **1567–1595**

Mallea, Eduardo
Latin American Writers, vol. 3: **981–989**

Malory, Sir Thomas
British Writers, vol. 1: **67–80**
British Writers Selected Authors, vol. 2: **877–890**
See also "Arthurian Romances" in Themes, Genres, Collectives, and Works

Malraux, André
European Writers, vol. 12: **2413–2432**
European Writers Selected Authors, vol. 2: **977–996**

Mandelshtam, Osip
European Writers, vol. 10: **1619–1649**

Mann, Heinrich
European Writers, vol. 8: **519–543**

Mann, Thomas
European Writers, vol. 9: **715–743**
European Writers Selected Authors, vol. 2: **997–1024**

Mansfield, Katherine
  British Writers, vol. 7: **171–184**
  British Writers Selected Authors, vol. 2: **891–904**

Manzoni, Alessandro
  European Writers, vol. 5: **367–394**

Mañach Robato, Jorge
  Latin American Writers, vol. 2: **831–836**

Marcus Aurelius
  See "Epictetus and Marcus Aurelius"

Marechal, Leopoldo
  Latin American Writers, vol. 2: **887–896**

Marguerite, Queen of Navarre
  See "Renaissance Short Fiction" in Themes,
  Genres, Collectives, and Works

Mariátegui, José Carlos
  Latin American Writers, vol. 2: **791–796**

Marín Cañas, José
  Latin American Writers, vol. 3: **991–994**

Marinetti, Filippo Tommaso
  European Writers, vol. 9: **797–832**

Marlowe, Christopher
  British Writers, vol. 1: **275–294**

Mármol, José
  Latin American Writers, vol. 1: **181–184**

Marquand, John P.
  American Writers, vol. 3: **50–73**

Marqués, René
  Latin American Writers, vol. 3: **1237–1246**

Marryat, Frederick
  Writers for Children: **381–387**

Marshall, Paule
  African American Writers: **289–304**

Marston, John
  See "Marston, John, and Cyril Tourneur"

Marston, John, and Cyril Tourneur
  British Writers, vol. 2: **24–41**

Martí, José
  Latin American Writers, vol. 1: **311–320**

Martial
  Ancient Writers, vol. 2: **887–915**

Martínez Estrada, Ezequiel
  Latin American Writers, vol. 2: **809–813**

Marvell, Andrew
  British Writers, vol. 2: **204–220**

Masters, Edgar Lee
  American Writers Supp. 1, part 2: **454–478**

Masuccio Salernitano
  See "Renaissance Short Fiction" in Themes,
  Genres, Collectives, and Works

Mather, Cotton
  American Writers Supp. 2, part 2: **441–470**

Matheson, Richard
  Science Fiction Writers: **425–431**
  Supernatural Fiction Writers, vol. 2: **1073–1080**

Matthiessen, Peter
  American Nature Writers, vol. 2: **599–613**

Matto de Turner, Clorinda
  Latin American Writers, vol. 1: **305–309**

Mattos, Gregório de
  Latin American Writers, vol. 1: **65–69**

Maturin, Charles Robert
  Supernatural Fiction Writers, vol. 1: **161–168**

Maugham, W. Somerset
  British Writers, vol. 6: **363–382**
  British Writers Selected Authors, vol. 2: **905–923**

Maupassant, Guy de
  European Writers, vol. 7: **1759–1784**
  European Writers Selected Authors, vol. 2:
    1025–1050
  Supernatural Fiction Writers, vol. 1: **59–65**

Mauriac, François
  European Writers, vol. 10: **1307–1330**

Mayakovsky, Vladimir
  European Writers, vol. 11: **1835–1858**

Mazer, Harry
  Writers for Young Adults, vol. 2: **327–336**

Mazer, Norma Fox
  Writers for Young Adults, vol. 2: **337–346**

Medici, Lorenzo de'
  See "Renaissance Pastoral Poetry" in Themes,
  Genres, Collectives, and Works

Meigs, Cornelia
  Writers for Children: **389–395**

Meinhold, Wilhelm
  Supernatural Fiction Writers, vol. 1: **121–127**

Meireles, Cecília
  Latin American Writers, vol. 2: **915–922**

Meltzer, Milton
  Writers for Young Adults, vol. 2: **347–358**

Melville, Herman
  American Writers, vol. 3: **74–98**
  American Writers Retrospective: **243–262**

Memmi, Albert
  African Writers, vol. 2: **467–477**

Menander
  Ancient Writers, vol. 1: **435–447**

Mencken, H. L.
  American Writers, vol. 3: **99–121**

Meredith, George
  British Writers, vol. 5: **219–234**

Mérimée, Prosper
  European Writers, vol. 6: **745–769**
  Supernatural Fiction Writers, vol. 1: **51–57**

Merril, Judith
  Science Fiction Writers: **433–439**

Merrill, James
  American Writers Supp. 3, part 1: **317–338**

Merritt, A.
  Science Fiction Writers: **65–71**
  Supernatural Fiction Writers, vol. 2: **835–843**

Merwin, W. S.
  American Writers Supp. 3, part 1: **339–360**

Metcalfe, John
  Supernatural Fiction Writers, vol. 2: **597–602**

Meyer, Conrad Ferdinand
  See "Poetic Realism" in Themes, Genres,
    Collectives, and Works

Michelet, Jules
  See "Michelet, Jules, and Romantic
    Historiography"

Michelet, Jules, and Romantic Historiography
  European Writers, vol. 5: **571–606**

Mickiewicz, Adam
  European Writers, vol. 5: **607–634**

Middleton, Thomas
  British Writers, vol. 2: **1–23**

Miklowitz, Gloria D.
  Writers for Young Adults, vol. 2: **359–368**

Millay, Edna St. Vincent
  American Writers, vol. 3: **122–144**
  Modern American Women Writers: **287–302**

Miller, Arthur
  American Writers, vol. 3: **145–169**

Miller, Henry
  American Writers, vol. 3: **170–192**

Miller, Walter M., Jr.
  Science Fiction Writers: **441–448**

Mills, Enos
  American Nature Writers, vol. 2: **615–624**

Milne, A. A.
  Writers for Children: **397–405**

Milosz, Czeslaw
  European Writers, vol. 13: **2929–2952**

Milton, John
  British Writers, vol. 2: **158–178**
  British Writers Selected Authors, vol. 2: **925–945**

Mirrlees, Hope
  Supernatural Fiction Writers, vol. 2: **603–607**

Mistral, Gabriela
  Latin American Writers, vol. 2: **677–692**

Mitchell, John Hanson
  American Nature Writers, vol. 2: **625–638**

Moberg, Vilhelm
  European Writers, vol. 11: **2203–2231**

Moe, Jörgen
  See "Asbjørnsen and Moe"

Mofolo, Thomas Mokopu
  African Writers, vol. 2: **479–493**

Mohr, Nicholasa
  Writers for Young Adults, vol. 2: **369–378**

Molesworth, M. L. S.
  Writers for Children: **407–413**

Molière
  European Writers, vol. 3: **101–124**
  European Writers Selected Authors, vol. 2: **1115–1137**

Molina, Juan Ramón
  Latin American Writers, vol. 2: **539–542**

Molinari, Ricardo E.
  Latin American Writers, vol. 2: **837–844**

Momaday, N. Scott
  American Nature Writers, vol. 2: **639–649**
  American Writers Supp. 4, part 2: **479–495**

Montaigne, Michel de
  European Writers, vol. 2: **769–790**
  European Writers Selected Authors, vol. 2: **1139–1160**

Montale, Eugenio
　European Writers, vol. 11: **1987–2008**

Montalvo, Juan
　Latin American Writers, vol. 1: **215–220**

Montemayor, Jorge de
　See "Renaissance Pastoral Poetry" in Themes,
　Genres, Collectives, and Works

Montesquieu, Charles-Louis de Secondat
　European Writers, vol. 3: **345–366**

Montgomery, L. M.
　Writers for Children: **415–422**
　Writers for Young Adults, vol. 2: **379–386**

Montherlant, Henry de
　European Writers, vol. 11: **1915–1938**

Moorcock, Michael
　Science Fiction Writers: **449–457**
　Supernatural Fiction Writers, vol. 2: **1081–1089**

Moore, C. L.
　Supernatural Fiction Writers, vol. 2: **891–898**
　See also "Moore, C. L., and Henry Kuttner"

Moore, C. L., and Henry Kuttner
　Science Fiction Writers: **161–167**

Moore, George
　British Writers, vol. 6: **85–100**

Moore, Marianne
　American Writers, vol. 3: **193–217**
　Modern American Women Writers: **303–316**

Moravia, Alberto
　European Writers, vol. 12: **2673–2697**

Morison, Samuel Eliot
　American Writers Supp. 1, part 2: **479–500**

Morris, William
　British Writers, vol. 5: **291–308**
　Supernatural Fiction Writers, vol. 1: **299–306**

Morris, Wright
　American Writers, vol. 3: **218–243**

Morrison, Toni
　African American Writers: **321–333**
　American Writers Supp. 3, part 1: **361–381**
　Modern American Women Writers: **317–338**

Mphahlele, Es'kia
　African Writers, vol. 2: **495–510**

Muir, John
　American Nature Writers, vol. 2: **651–669**

Muldoon, Paul
　British Writers Supp. 4: **409–432**

Mumford, Lewis
　American Writers Supp. 2, part 2: **471–501**

Mundy, Talbot
　Supernatural Fiction Writers, vol. 2: **845–851**

Murdoch, Iris
　British Writers Supp. 1: **215–235**

Musaeus, J. K.
　Supernatural Fiction Writers, vol. 1: **75–81**

Musil, Robert
　European Writers, vol. 9: **931–958**

Musset, Alfred de
　European Writers, vol. 6: **999–1033**

Mwangi, Meja
　African Writers, vol. 2: **511–525**

Myers, Walter Dean
　Writers for Young Adults, vol. 2: **387–396**

Nabhan, Gary Paul
　American Nature Writers, vol. 2: **671–681**

Nabokov, Vladimir
　American Writers, vol. 3: **244–266**
　American Writers Retrospective: **263–281**

Naipaul, V. S.
　British Writers Supp. 1: **383–405**

Nathan, Robert
　Supernatural Fiction Writers, vol. 2: **813–819**

Naylor, Gloria
　African American Writers: **335–347**

Naylor, Phyllis Reynolds
　Writers for Young Adults, vol. 2: **397–409**

Nelson, Richard K.
　American Nature Writers, vol. 2: **683–696**

Nemerov, Howard
　American Writers, vol. 3: **267–289**

Neruda, Pablo
　Latin American Writers, vol. 3: **1001–1018**

Nerval, Gérard de
　European Writers, vol. 6: **943–970**

Nervo, Amado
　Latin American Writers, vol. 1: **425–429**

Nesbit, E.
　Writers for Children: **423–430**

Neto, Agostinho
African Writers, vol. 2: **527–535**

Ngũgĩ wa Thiong'o
African Writers, vol. 2: **537–555**

Niebuhr, Reinhold
American Writers, vol. 3: **290–313**

Nietzsche, Friedrich
European Writers, vol. 7: **1645–1682**
European Writers Selected Authors, vol. 2:
    1161–1197

Nin, Anaïs
Modern American Women Writers: **339–351**

Niven, Larry
Science Fiction Writers: **459–465**

Nixon, Joan Lowery
Writers for Young Adults, vol. 2: **411–419**

Norris, Frank
American Writers, vol. 3: **314–336**

Norton, Andre
Supernatural Fiction Writers, vol. 2: **1091–1096**

Novalis
European Writers, vol. 5: **205–231**

Oates, Joyce Carol
American Writers Supp. 2, part 2: **503–527**
Modern American Women Writers: **353–374**

O'Brien, Fitz-James
Supernatural Fiction Writers, vol. 2: **717–722**

O'Brien, Flann
British Writers Supp. 2: **321–339**

Ocampo, Victoria
Latin American Writers, vol. 2: **705–710**

O'Casey, Sean
British Writers, vol. 7: **1–16**

O'Connor, Flannery
American Writers, vol. 3: **337–360**
Modern American Women Writers: **375–388**

O'Dell, Scott
Writers for Young Adults, vol. 2: **421–431**

Odets, Clifford
American Writers Supp. 2, part 2: **529–554**

O'Hara, John
American Writers, vol. 3: **361–384**

Ojaide, Tanure
African Writers, vol. 2: **557–565**

Okara, Gabriel
African Writers, vol. 2: **567–582**

Okigbo, Christopher
African Writers, vol. 2: **583–598**

Okri, Ben
African Writers, vol. 2: **599–608**

Olesha, Yuri
European Writers, vol. 11: **2233–2253**

Oliphant, Mrs.
Supernatural Fiction Writers, vol. 1: **261–268**

Oliver, Chad
Science Fiction Writers: **467–473**

Olson, Charles
American Writers Supp. 2, part 2: **555–587**

Olson, Sigurd F.
American Nature Writers, vol. 2: **697–709**

Omotoso, Kole
African Writers, vol. 2: **609–617**

Oneal, Zibby
Writers for Young Adults, vol. 2: **433–442**

O'Neill, Eugene
American Writers, vol. 3: **385–408**

Onetti, Juan Carlos
Latin American Writers, vol. 3: **1089–1097**

Onions, Oliver
Supernatural Fiction Writers, vol. 1: **505–511**

Oña, Pedro de
Latin American Writers, vol. 1: **59–63**

Ortega y Gasset, José
European Writers, vol. 9: **1119–1150**

Ortiz, Simon J.
American Writers Supp. 4, part 2: **497–515**

Orwell, George
British Writers, vol. 7: **273–288**
British Writers Selected Authors, vol. 2: **947–961**
Science Fiction Writers: **233–241**

Osborne, John
British Writers Supp. 1: **329–340**

Osofisan, Femi
African Writers, vol. 2: **619–629**

Osundare, Niyi
African Writers, vol. 2: **631–640**

Ovid
Ancient Writers, vol. 2: **783–806**

Owen, Wilfred
  British Writers, vol. 6: **443–460**

Oyono, Ferdinand
  African Writers, vol. 2: **641–649**

Pain, Barry
  Supernatural Fiction Writers, vol. 1: **443–448**

Paine, Thomas
  American Writers Supp. 1, part 2: **501–525**

Palés Matos, Luis
  Latin American Writers, vol. 2: **821–830**

Paley, Grace
  Modern American Women Writers: **389–396**

Palma, Ricardo
  Latin American Writers, vol. 1: **221–228**

Parker, Dorothy
  Modern American Women Writers: **397–409**

Parkman, Francis
  American Writers Supp. 2, part 2: **589–616**

Parra, Nicanor
  Latin American Writers, vol. 3: **1195–1200**

Parra Sanojo, Ana Teresa de la
  Latin American Writers, vol. 2: **717–720**

Pascal, Blaise
  European Writers, vol. 3: **125–150**

Pascoli, Giovanni
  European Writers, vol. 7: **1825–1854**

Pasternak, Boris
  European Writers, vol. 10: **1591–1618**
  European Writers Selected Authors, vol. 2:
    1227–1253

Pater, Walter Horatio
  British Writers, vol. 5: **337–360**

Paterson, Katherine
  Writers for Young Adults, vol. 2: **443–454**

Paton, Alan
  African Writers, vol. 2: **651–668**
  British Writers Supp. 2: **341–361**
  British Writers Selected Authors, vol. 2: **963–983**

Paulsen, Gary
  Writers for Young Adults, vol. 2: **455–463**

Pavese, Cesare
  European Writers, vol. 12: **2759–2784**

Payró, Roberto Jorge
  Latin American Writers, vol. 1: **413–417**

Paz, Octavio
  Latin American Writers, vol. 3: **1163–1176**

p'Bitek, Okot
  African Writers, vol. 2: **669–684**

Peacock, Thomas Love
  British Writers, vol. 4: **157–170**

Peck, Richard
  Writers for Young Adults, vol. 3: **1–14**

Peck, Robert Newton
  Writers for Young Adults, vol. 3: **15–26**

Peele, George
  See "Lyly, John, and George Peele"

Pepetela
  African Writers, vol. 2: **685–695**

Pepys, Samuel
  See "Evelyn, John, and Samuel Pepys"

Percy, Walker
  American Writers Supp. 3, part 1: **383–400**

Pérez Galdós, Benito
  European Writers, vol. 7: **1597–1618**

Perrault, Charles
  Writers for Children: **431–437**

Perrin, Noel
  American Nature Writers, vol. 2: **711–720**

Perse, Saint-John
  European Writers, vol. 10: **1429–1452**

Persius
  See "Persius and Juvenal"

Persius and Juvenal
  Ancient Writers, vol. 2: **855–876**

Pessoa, Fernando
  European Writers, vol. 10: **1475–1495**

Peterson, Brenda
  American Nature Writers, vol. 2: **721–731**

Petrarch
  European Writers, vol. 2: **475–507**
  European Writers Selected Authors, vol. 2:
    1255–1287
  See also "Renaissance Pastoral Poetry" in
    Themes, Genres, Collectives, and Works

Petronius
  Ancient Writers, vol. 2: **833–853**

Petry, Ann
  African American Writers: **347–359**

Pevsner, Stella
  Writers for Young Adults, vol. 3: **27–34**

Peyton, K. M.
  Writers for Young Adults, vol. 3: **35–42**

Pfeffer, Susan Beth
  Writers for Young Adults, vol. 3: **43–52**

Philitas of Cos
  See "Hellenistic Poetry at Alexandria" in
    Themes, Genres, Collectives, and Works

Phillpotts, Eden
  Supernatural Fiction Writers, vol. 2: **549–553**

Picón Salas, Mariano
  Latin American Writers, vol. 2: **903–908**

Pindar
  Ancient Writers, vol. 1: **157–177**

Pinero, Arthur Wing
  See "Well-Made Play, The" in Themes, Genres,
    Collectives, and Works

Pinter, Harold
  British Writers Supp. 1: **367–382**
  British Writers Selected Authors, vol. 2: **985–1000**

Pirandello, Luigi
  European Writers, vol. 8: **389–416**
  European Writers Selected Authors, vol. 2:
    1289–1316

Plath, Sylvia
  American Writers Supp. 1, part 2: **526–549**
  Modern American Women Writers: **411–424**

Plato
  Ancient Writers, vol. 1: **353–376**

Platt, Kin
  Writers for Young Adults, vol. 3: **53–60**

Plautus
  Ancient Writers, vol. 1: **501–523**

Pliny the Younger
  Ancient Writers, vol. 2: **1035–1048**

Plomer, William
  African Writers, vol. 2: **697–706**

Plutarch
  Ancient Writers, vol. 2: **961–983**

Poe, Edgar Allan
  American Writers, vol. 3: **409–432**
  Science Fiction Writers: **11–18**
  Supernatural Fiction Writers, vol. 2: **697–705**
  Writers for Young Adults, vol. 3: **61–73**

Pohl, Frederik
  Science Fiction Writers: **475–482**

Polybius
  Ancient Writers, vol. 1: **525–539**

Pope, Alexander
  British Writers, vol. 3: **68–79**
  British Writers Selected Authors, vol. 2: **1001–1012**

Porter, Katherine Anne
  American Writers, vol. 3: **433–455**
  Modern American Women Writers: **425–440**

Posidippus
  See "Hellenistic Poetry at Alexandria" in
    Themes, Genres, Collectives, and Works

Potter, Beatrix
  British Writers Supp. 3: **287–309**
  Writers for Children: **439–446**

Pound, Ezra
  American Writers, vol. 3: **456–479**
  American Writers Retrospective: **283–294**

Powell, Anthony
  British Writers, vol. 7: **343–352**

Powell, John Wesley
  See "Western Geologists and Explorers" in
    Themes, Genres, Collectives, and Works

Powys, John Cowper
  Supernatural Fiction Writers, vol. 2: **609–616**

Powys, T. F.
  Supernatural Fiction Writers, vol. 2: **609–616**

Prado, Pedro
  Latin American Writers, vol. 2: **643–647**

Pratt, Fletcher
  See "De Camp, L. Sprague, and Fletcher Pratt"

Prévost, Antoine-Francois
  See "French Novelists, Three" in Themes,
    Genres, Collectives, and Works

Priestley, J. B.
  British Writers, vol. 7: **209–232**

Pritchett, V. S.
  British Writers Supp. 3: **311–331**

Propertius
  See "Tibullus and Propertius"

Proust, Marcel
  European Writers, vol. 8: **545–568**
  European Writers Selected Authors, vol. 2:
    1317–1340

Prudentius
　European Writers, vol. 1: **1–22**

Puig, Manuel
　Latin American Writers, vol. 3: **1405–1413**

Pushkin, Alexander
　European Writers, vol. 5: **659–691**
　European Writers Selected Authors, vol. 3:
　　1341–1373

Pyle, Howard
　Writers for Children: **447–454**

Pyle, Robert Michael
　American Nature Writers, vol. 2: **733–739**

Pym, Barbara
　British Writers Supp. 2: **363–385**

Pynchon, Thomas
　American Writers Supp. 2, part 2: **617–638**

Quammen, David
　American Nature Writers, vol. 2: **741–750**

Quasimodo, Salvatore
　European Writers, vol. 12: **2387–2411**

Queiroz, Rachel de
　Latin American Writers, vol. 3: **1119–1123**

Queneau, Raymond
　European Writers, vol. 12: **2511–2534**

Quiller-Couch, Arthur
　Supernatural Fiction Writers, vol. 1: **389–395**

Quintilian
　Ancient Writers, vol. 2: **943–959**

Quiroga, Horacio
　Latin American Writers, vol. 2: **551–558**

Rabelais, François
　European Writers, vol. 2: **693–720**
　European Writers Selected Authors, vol. 3:
　　1375–1402

Racine, Jean
　European Writers, vol. 3: **207–228**

Radcliffe, Ann
　Supernatural Fiction Writers, vol. 1: **145–151**

Ralegh (Raleigh), Sir Walter
　British Writers, vol. 1: **145–159**

Ramos, Graciliano
　Latin American Writers, vol. 2: **745–754**

Rand, Ayn
　American Writers Supp. 4, part 2: **517–535**

Ransom, John Crowe
　American Writers, vol. 3: **480–502**

Ransome, Arthur
　Writers for Children: **455–461**

Rawlings, Marjorie Kinnan
　American Nature Writers, vol. 2: **751–765**
　Writers for Children: **463–467**

Raymo, Chet
　American Nature Writers, vol. 2: **767–780**

Read, Herbert
　See "Poets of World War I (British)" in Themes,
　　Genres, Collectives, and Works

Reed, Ishmael
　African American Writers: **361–377**

Reyes, Alfonso
　Latin American Writers, vol. 2: **693–703**

Reynolds, G. W. M.
　Supernatural Fiction Writers, vol. 1: **205–211**

Rhys, Jean
　British Writers Supp. 2: **387–404**

Rich, Adrienne
　American Writers Supp. 1, part 2: **550–578**
　Modern American Women Writers: **441–456**

Richards, I. A.
　British Writers Supp. 2: **405–433**

Richards, Laura E.
　Writers for Children: **469–475**

Richardson, Samuel
　British Writers, vol. 3: **80–94**

Richter, Jean Paul
　European Writers, vol. 5: **53–88**

Riddell, Mrs. J. H.
　Supernatural Fiction Writers, vol. 1: **269–277**

Rilke, Rainer Maria
　European Writers, vol. 9: **767–796**
　European Writers Selected Authors, vol. 3:
　　1461–1489

Rinaldi, Ann
　Writers for Young Adults, vol. 3: **75–85**

Rinbaud, Arthur
　European Writers, vol. 7: **1785–1824**

Ríos, Alberto Álvaro
　American Writers Supp. 4, part 2: **537–556**

Ritsos, Yannis
　European Writers, vol. 12: **2815–2842**

Rivera, José Eustasio
  Latin American Writers, vol. 2: **671–675**

Roa Bastos, Augusto
  Latin American Writers, vol. 3: **1209–1213**

Robbe-Grillet, Alain
  European Writers, vol. 13: **3237–3256**

Roberts, Elizabeth Madox
  Writers for Children: **477–481**

Robertson, Thomas W.
  See "Well-Made Play, The" in Themes, Genres,
    Collectives, and Works

Robinson, Edwin Arlington
  American Writers, vol. 3: **503–526**

Robinson, Marilynne
  See "Contemporary Ecofiction" in Themes,
    Genres, Collectives, and Works

Rodó, José Enrique
  Latin American Writers, vol. 2: **447–455**

Rodowsky, Colby
  Writers for Young Adults, vol. 3: **87–93**

Roethke, Theodore
  American Writers, vol. 3: **527–550**

Rohmer, Sax
  Supernatural Fiction Writers, vol. 2: **555–560**

Rojas, Manuel
  Latin American Writers, vol. 2: **815–820**

Rojas, Ricardo
  Latin American Writers, vol. 2: **591–596**

Romero, José Rubén
  Latin American Writers, vol. 2: **711–715**

Ronsard, Pierre de
  See "Ronsard, Pierre de, and the Pléiade";
    "Renaissance Pastoral Poetry" in Themes,
    Genres, Collectives, and Works

Ronsard, Pierre de, and the Pléiade
  European Writers, vol. 2: **721–746**

Rosenberg, Isaac
  See "Poets of World War I (British)" in Themes,
    Genres, Collectives, and Works

Rossetti, Christina
  British Writers, vol. 5: **247–260**
  Writers for Children: **483–491**

Rossetti, Dante Gabriel
  British Writers, vol. 5: **235–246**

Roth, Philip
  American Writers Supp. 3, part 2: **401–429**

Rotimi, Ola
  African Writers, vol. 2: **707–720**

Rousseau, Jean Jacques
  European Writers, vol. 4: **449–474**
  European Writers Selected Authors, vol. 3:
    1519–1544

Rulfo, Juan
  Latin American Writers, vol. 3: **1215–1229**

Rushdie, Salman
  British Writers Supp. 4: **433–457**

Ruskin, John
  British Writers, vol. 5: **173–186**
  Writers for Children: **493–496**

Russ, Joanna
  Science Fiction Writers: **483–490**

Russell, Eric Frank
  Science Fiction Writers: **197–202**

Russell, Sharman Apt
  See "New Voices in American Nature Writing"
    in Themes, Genres, Collectives, and Works

Ryden, Hope
  American Nature Writers, vol. 2: **781–792**

Sa'adāwī, Nawāl, al-
  African Writers, vol. 2: **721–731**

Sábato, Ernesto
  Latin American Writers, vol. 3: **1139–1143**

Sacchetti, Franco
  See "Renaissance Short Fiction" in Themes,
    Genres, Collectives, and Works

Sachs, Marilyn
  Writers for Young Adults, vol. 3: **95–104**

Sackville, Charles (Earl of Dorset)
  See "Restoration Court Poets, The" in Themes,
    Genres, Collectives, and Works

Sade, Marquis de, and the French Libertine
    Tradition
  European Writers, vol. 4: **615–638**

St. Clair, Margaret
  Science Fiction Writers: **491–495**

Saint-Exupéry, Antoine de
  European Writers, vol. 12: **2307–2332**
  European Writers Selected Authors, vol. 3:
    1545–1569

Sainte-Beuve, Charles-Augustin
  European Writers, vol. 6: **837–861**
Saki
  Supernatural Fiction Writers, vol. 1: **449–455**
Salazar Arrué, Salvador (Salarrué)
  Latin American Writers, vol. 2: **875–879**
Ṣāliḥ, al-Ṭayyib
  African Writers, vol. 2: **733–744**
Salinger, J. D.
  American Writers, vol. 3: **551–574**
  Writers for Young Adults, vol. 3: **105–112**
Salisbury, Graham
  Writers for Young Adults, vol. 3: **113–121**
Sallust
  Ancient Writers, vol. 2: **621–641**
Salten, Felix
  Writers for Children: **497–501**
Sánchez, Florencio
  Latin American Writers, vol. 2: **531–538**
Sand, George
  European Writers, vol. 6: **813–836**
  European Writers Selected Authors, vol. 3:
    1571–1594
Sandburg, Carl
  American Writers, vol. 3: **575–598**
  Writers for Children: **503–510**
  Writers for Young Adults, vol. 3: **123–133**
Sanders, Scott Russell
  American Nature Writers, vol. 2: **793–804**
Sannazaro, Jacopo
  See "Renaissance Pastoral Poetry" in Themes,
    Genres, Collectives, and Works
Santayana, George
  American Writers, vol. 3: **599–622**
Sappho
  See "Greek Lyric Poets" in Themes, Genres,
    Collectives, and Works
Sarban
  Supernatural Fiction Writers, vol. 2: **667–673**
Sardou, Victor
  See "Well-Made Play, The" in Themes, Genres,
    Collectives, and Works
Sarduy, Severo
  Latin American Writers, vol. 3: **1437–1444**

Sarmiento, Domingo Faustino
  Latin American Writers, vol. 1: **159–167**
Sarraute, Nathalie
  European Writers, vol. 12: **2333–2359**
Sartre, Jean-Paul
  European Writers, vol. 12: **2589–2614**
  European Writers Selected Authors, vol. 3:
    1595–1620
Sassoon, Siegfried
  See "Poets of World War I (British)" in Themes,
    Genres, Collectives, and Works
Sawyer, Ruth
  Writers for Children: **511–517**
Sayers, Dorothy L.
  British Writers Supp. 3: **333–353**
Schiller, Friedrich von
  European Writers, vol. 5: **27–52**
Schlegel, Friedrich von
  European Writers, vol. 5: **177–203**
Schnitzler, Arthur
  European Writers, vol. 8: **89–117**
Schopenhauer, Arthur
  European Writers, vol. 5: **395–415**
Schreiner, Olive
  African Writers, vol. 2: **745–763**
  British Writers Supp. 2: **435–458**
Schwartz, Delmore
  American Writers Supp. 2, part 2: **639–668**
Scoppettone, Sandra
  Writers for Young Adults, vol. 3: **135–143**
Scott, Paul
  British Writers Supp. 1: **259–274**
Scott, Sir Walter
  British Writers, vol. 4: **27–40**
  Supernatural Fiction Writers, vol. 1: **169–176**
Scribe, Augustin Eugène
  See "Well-Made Play, The" in Themes, Genres,
    Collectives, and Works
Sebestyen, Ouida
  Writers for Young Adults, vol. 3: **145–153**
Sedley, Sir Charles
  See "Restoration Court Poets, The" in Themes,
    Genres, Collectives, and Works
Seferis, George
  European Writers, vol. 12: **2255–2271**

Sembène Ousmane
   African Writers, vol. 2: **765–774**

Senarens, Luis Philip
   Science Fiction Writers: **53–58**

Seneca the Younger
   Ancient Writers, vol. 2: **807–832**

Senghor, Léopold Sédar
   African Writers, vol. 2: **775–789**

Seredy, Kate
   Writers for Children: **519–524**

Serviss, Garrett P.
   Science Fiction Writers: **39–44**

Seton, Ernest Thompson
   American Nature Writers, vol. 2: **805–816**

Sewell, Anna
   Writers for Children: **525–528**

Sexton, Anne
   American Writers Supp. 2, part 2: **669–700**
   Modern American Women Writers: **457–470**

Shābbī, Abū al-Qāsim, al-
   African Writers, vol. 2: **791–798**

Shaffer, Peter
   British Writers Supp. 1: **313–328**

Shakespeare, William
   British Writers, vol. 1: **295–334**
   British Writers Selected Authors, vol. 2: **1013–1052**
   Writers for Young Adults, vol. 3: **155–172**
   William Shakespeare: His World, His Work, His Influence
      Church, The: Religion and Its Manifestations, vol. 1: **21–40**
      Contemporary Issues in Shakespearean Interpretation, vol. 3: **889–927**
      Cultural Phenomenon of Shakespeare, The, vol. 3: **831–838**
      Daily Life in City, Town, and Country, vol. 1: **215–232**
      Economic Life in Shakespeare's England, vol. 1: **67–74**
      Education and Aprenticeship, vol. 1: **55–66**
      Ethical and Theological Questions in Shakespeare's Dramatic Works, vol. 2: **557–570**
      Forest, Field, and Garden, vol. 1: **257–268**
      Law and Legal Institutions, vol. 1: **41–54**
      Life, The: A Survey, vol. 2: **281–290**

Literate Culture of Shakespeare's Audience, The, vol. 1: **159–174**
Major Shakespearean Institutions, vol. 3: **787–800**
Medicine and Sanitation, vol. 1: **75–84**
Music in Shakespeare's Work, vol. 2: **417–424**
Painting and Other Fine Arts, vol. 1: **241–256**
Patronage of the Arts, vol. 1: **99–106**
Poems, The, vol. 2: **445–452**
Printing and Publishing in the Tudor Age, vol. 1: **129–142**
Publishing and Editing of Shakespeare's Plays, The, vol. 3: **589–602**
Science, Magic, and Folklore, vol. 1: **175–194**
Sense of History in Renaissance England, The, vol. 1: **143–158**
Shakespeare and Foreigners, vol. 1: **233–240**
Shakespeare and His Audiences, vol. 2: **549–556**
Shakespeare and His Contemporaries, vol. 2: **331–342**
Shakespeare and the Humanities, vol. 3: **839–866**
Shakespeare and the Modern Critic, vol. 3: **867–872**
Shakespeare and the Modern Director, vol. 3: **815–822**
Shakespeare and the Modern Playwright, vol. 3: **809–814**
Shakespeare and the Modern Writer, vol. 3: **801–808**
Shakespeare and the Painter and Illustrator, vol. 3: **757–770**
Shakespeare and Warfare, vol. 1: **85–98**
Shakespeare as a World Figure, vol. 3: **663–680**
Shakespeare as a Writer of Comedy, vol. 2: **489–504**
Shakespeare in Music, vol. 3: **771–786**
Shakespeare in the Theater: The United States and Canada, vol. 3: **629–662**
Shakespeare on Film and Television, vol. 3: **681–704**
Shakespeare on the English Stage, vol. 3: **603–628**
Shakespeare's Dramatic Methods, vol. 2: **397–416**
Shakespeare's Language, vol. 2: **343–362**

Shakespeare, William (*continued*)
> Shakespeare's Poetic Techniques, vol. 2: **363–388**
> Shakespeare's Professional Career: Poet and Playwright, vol. 2: **309–330**
> Shakespeare's Psychology, vol. 2: **571–587**
> Shakespeare's Reputation—Then Till Now, vol. 3: **705–716**
> Shakespeare's Tragedies, vol. 2: **505–532**
> Shakespeare's Tragicomedies and Romances, vol. 2: **533–548**
> Shakespeare's Treatment of English History, vol. 2: **453–472**
> Shakespeare's Treatment of Roman History, vol. 2: **473–488**
> Shakespeare's Use of Prose, vol. 2: **389–396**
> Shakespearean Criticism, vol. 3: **733–756**
> Shakespearean Scholarship: From Rowe to the Present, vol. 3: **717–732**
> Sonnets, The, vol. 2: **433–444**
> Sports and Recreations, vol. 1: **269–280**
> State, The: Government and Politics Under Elizabeth and James, vol. 1: **1–20**
> "Style Is the Man": Manners, Dress, and Decorum, vol. 1: **201–214**
> Teaching Shakespeare: Tradition and the Future, vol. 3: **873–888**
> Theaters and the Dramatic Profession, vol. 1: **107–128**
> Thinking About Shakespeare's Thought, vol. 2: **291–308**
> Tradition, Style, and the Shakespearean Actor Today, vol. 3: **823–830**
> Travel by Sea and Land, vol. 1: **195–200**
> Visual Arts in Shakespeare's Work, The, vol. 2: **425–432**

Shange, Ntozake
> *African American Writers:* **379–393**

Shapiro, Karl
> *American Writers Supp. 2,* part 2: **701–724**

Shaw, George Bernard
> *British Writers,* vol. 6: **101–132**
> *British Writers Selected Authors,* vol. 3: **1053–1084**

Sheckley, Robert
> *Science Fiction Writers:* **497–503**

Shelley, Mary
> *British Writers Supp. 3:* **355–373**
> *British Writers Selected Authors,* vol. 3: **1085–1103**

> *Science Fiction Writers:* **3–9**
> See also "Gothic Novel, The" in Themes, Genres, Collectives, and Works

Shelley, Percy Bysshe
> *British Writers,* vol. 4: **195–210**
> *British Writers Selected Authors,* vol. 3: **1105–1120**

Shepard, Sam
> *American Writers Supp. 3,* part 2: **431–450**

Sheridan, Richard Brinsley
> *British Writers,* vol. 3: **252–271**

Shiel, M. P.
> *Science Fiction Writers:* **31–37**
> *Supernatural Fiction Writers,* vol. 1: **361–367**

Sidney, Sir Philip
> *British Writers,* vol. 1: **160–175**

Sigüenza y Góngora, Carlos de
> *Latin American Writers,* vol. 1: **71–77**

Silko, Leslie Marmon
> *American Nature Writers,* vol. 2: **817–827**
> *American Writers Supp. 4,* part 2: **557–572**

Silone, Ignazione
> *European Writers,* vol. 12: **2273–2305**

Silva, José Asunción
> *Latin American Writers,* vol. 1: **377–385**

Silveira de Queiroz, Dinah
> *Latin American Writers,* vol. 3: **1145–1151**

Silverberg, Robert
> *Science Fiction Writers:* **505–511**

Simak, Clifford D.
> *Science Fiction Writers:* **513–518**

Simenon, Georges
> *European Writers,* vol. 12: **2479–2510**

Simon, Claude
> *European Writers,* vol. 13: **3021–3048**

Simon, Neil
> *American Writers Supp. 4,* part 2: **573–594**

Simonides
> See "Greek Lyric Poets" in Themes, Genres, Collectives, and Works

Sinán, Rogelio
> *Latin American Writers,* vol. 2: **941–946**

Sinclair, May
> *Supernatural Fiction Writers,* vol. 1: **513–519**

Singer, Isaac Bashevis
> *American Writers,* vol. 4: **1–24**

Sitwell, Edith
  British Writers, vol. 7: **127–143**

Skelton, John
  British Writers, vol. 1: **81–96**

Sleator, William
  Writers for Young Adults, vol. 3: **173–182**

Smith, Clark Ashton
  Science Fiction Writers: **139–144**
  Supernatural Fiction Writers, vol. 2: **875–881**

Smith, Cordwainer
  Science Fiction Writers: **519–524**

Smith, E. E.
  Science Fiction Writers: **125–130**

Smith, Stevie
  British Writers Supp. 2: **459–479**

Smith, Thorne
  Supernatural Fiction Writers, vol. 2: **805–811**

Smollett, Tobias
  British Writers, vol. 3: **146–159**

Snow, C. P.
  British Writers, vol. 7: **321–342**

Snyder, Gary
  American Nature Writers, vol. 2: **829–846**

Södergran, Edith
  European Writers, vol. 11: **1781–1806**

Solzhenitsyn, Aleksandr
  European Writers, vol. 13: **3187–3214**
  European Writers Selected Authors, vol. 3: **1621–1647**

Sontag, Susan
  American Writers Supp. 3, part 2: **451–473**
  Modern American Women Writers: **471–483**

Sophocles
  Ancient Writers, vol. 1: **179–207**

Soto, Gary
  Writers for Young Adults, vol. 3: **183–191**

Southey, Robert
  British Writers, vol. 4: **58–72**

Sowande, Bode
  African Writers, vol. 2: **799–806**

Soyinka, Wole
  African Writers, vol. 2: **807–831**

Spagnola, Giovanni Battista (Mantovano)
  See "Renaissance Pastoral Poetry" in Themes,
    Genres, Collectives, and Works

Spark, Muriel
  British Writers Supp. 1: **199–214**

Spender, Steven
  British Writers Supp. 2: **481–496**

Spenser, Edmund
  British Writers, vol. 1: **121–144**
  British Writers Selected Authors, vol. 3: **1121–1144**

Spinelli, Jerry
  Writers for Young Adults, vol. 3: **193–201**

Spyri, Johanna
  Writers for Children: **529–533**

Staël, Madame de
  European Writers, vol. 5: **89–111**

Stanwell-Fletcher, Theodora Cope
  American Nature Writers, vol. 2: **847–860**

Stapledon, Olaf
  Science Fiction Writers: **91–100**

Statius
  See "Lucan and Statius"

Stead, Christina
  British Writers Supp. 4: **459–477**

Steele, Sir Richard
  See "Steele, Sir Richard, and Joseph Addison"

Steele, Sir Richard, and Joseph Addison
  British Writers, vol. 3: **38–53**
  British Writers Selected Authors, vol. 3: **1145–1160**

Stegner, Wallace
  American Nature Writers, vol. 2: **861–875**
  American Writers Supp. 4, part 2: **595–618**

Stein, Gertrude
  American Writers, vol. 4: **25–48**
  Modern American Women Writers: **485–498**

Steinbeck, John
  American Writers, vol. 4: **49–72**
  Writers for Young Adults, vol. 3: **203–214**

Stendhal
  European Writers, vol. 5: **343–366**
  European Writers Selected Authors, vol. 3: **1649–1672**

Stephen, Leslie
  British Writers, vol. 5: **277–290**

Stephens, James
  Supernatural Fiction Writers, vol. 1: **485–490**

Sterne, Laurence
  British Writers, vol. 3: **124–136**

Stesichorus
    See "Greek Lyric Poets" in Themes, Genres,
        Collectives, and Works
Stevens, Wallace
    American Writers, vol. 4: **73–96**
    American Writers Retrospective: **295–315**
Stevenson, Robert Louis
    British Writers, vol. 5: **383–399**
    British Writers Selected Authors, vol. 3: **1161–1176**
    Supernatural Fiction Writers, vol. 1: **307–313**
    Writers for Children: **535–543**
    Writers for Young Adults, vol. 3: **215–224**
Stockton, Frank R.
    Supernatural Fiction Writers, vol. 2: **753–759**
    Writers for Children: **545–554**
Stoker, Bram
    British Writers Supp. 3: **375–391**
    Supernatural Fiction Writers, vol. 1: **375–381**
Stoppard, Tom
    British Writers Supp. 1: **437–454**
    British Writers Selected Authors, vol. 3: **1177–1194**
Storey, David
    British Writers Supp. 1: **407–420**
Storm, Theodor
    See "Poetic Realism" in Themes, Genres,
        Collectives, and Works
Storni, Alfonsina
    Latin American Writers, vol. 2: **739–743**
Stowe, Harriet Beecher
    American Writers Supp. 1, part 2: **579–601**
Strachey, Lytton
    British Writers Supp. 2: **497–518**
Strand, Mark
    American Writers Supp. 4, part 2: **619–636**
Straparola, Gianfrancesco
    See "Renaissance Short Fiction" in Themes,
        Genres, Collectives, and Works
Strasser, Todd
    Writers for Young Adults, vol. 3: **225–236**
Stratemeyer, Edward
    Writers for Young Adults, vol. 3: **237–249**
Stratton Porter, Gene
    American Nature Writers, vol. 2: **877–891**
Strindberg, August
    European Writers, vol. 7: **1731–1758**

Sturgeon, Theodore
    Science Fiction Writers: **203–208**
    Supernatural Fiction Writers, vol. 2: **941–945**
Styron, William
    American Writers, vol. 4: **97–119**
Suassuna, Ariano Vilar
    Latin American Writers, vol. 3: **1317–1321**
Suckling, Sir John
    See "Cavalier Poets, The" in Themes, Genres,
        Collectives, and Works
Suetonius
    Ancient Writers, vol. 2: **1049–1061**
Sutcliff, Rosemary
    Writers for Young Adults, vol. 3: **251–261**
Sutherland, Efua Theodora
    African Writers, vol. 2: **833–849**
Svevo, Italo
    European Writers, vol. 8: **67–87**
Swann, Thomas Burnett
    Supernatural Fiction Writers, vol. 2: **1097–1103**
Swenson, May
    American Writers Supp. 4, part 2: **637–655**
Swift, Jonathan
    British Writers, vol. 3: **15–38**
    British Writers Selected Authors, vol. 3: **1195–1217**
    Writers for Children: **555–559**
Swinburne, Algernon Charles
    British Writers, vol. 5: **309–336**
Synge, J. M.
    See "Synge, J. M., and Lady Augusta Gregory"
Synge, J. M., and Lady Augusta Gregory
    British Writers, vol. 6: **307–318**
Tablada, José Juan
    Latin American Writers, vol. 1: **441–446**
Tacitus
    Ancient Writers, vol. 2: **1003–1033**
Ṭāhā Ḥusayn
    African Writers, vol. 2: **851–863**
Taine, Hippolyte
    European Writers, vol. 7: **1449–1469**
Taine, John
    Science Fiction Writers: **75–82**
Talbert, Marc
    Writers for Young Adults, vol. 3: **263–272**

Tasso, Torquato
European Writers, vol. 2: **791–818**

Tate, Allen
American Writers, vol. 4: **120–143**

Taylor, Edward
American Writers, vol. 4: **144–166**

Taylor, Mildred Delois
Writers for Young Adults, vol. 3: **273–282**

Taylor, Theodore
Writers for Young Adults, vol. 3: **283–292**

Teale, Edwin Way
American Nature Writers, vol. 2: **893–904**

Tenn, William
Science Fiction Writers: **525–530**

Tennyson, Alfred Lord
British Writers, vol. 4: **323–339**
British Writers Selected Authors, vol. 3: **1219–1235**

Terence
Ancient Writers, vol. 1: **541–554**

Thackeray, William Makepeace
British Writers, vol. 5: **17–40**
British Writers Selected Authors, vol. 3: **1237–1259**

Thaxter, Celia
American Nature Writers, vol. 2: **905–917**

Theocritus
Ancient Writers, vol. 1: **483–500**

Thomas, D. M.
British Writers Supp. 4: **479–497**

Thomas, Dylan
British Writers Supp. 1: **169–184**
British Writers Selected Authors, vol. 3: **1261–1276**

Thomas, Edward
British Writers Supp. 3: **393–408**

Thomas, Joyce Carol
Writers for Young Adults, vol. 3: **293–301**

Thomas, Lewis
American Nature Writers, vol. 2: **919–931**

Thompson, Francis
British Writers, vol. 5: **439–452**

Thompson, Julian F.
Writers for Young Adults, vol. 3: **303–310**

Thomson, James
British Writers Supp. 3: **409–429**

Thoreau, Henry David
American Nature Writers, vol. 2: **933–950**
American Writers, vol. 4: **167–189**

Thucydides
Ancient Writers, vol. 1: **267–289**

Thurber, James
American Writers Supp. 1, part 2: **602–627**
Supernatural Fiction Writers, vol. 2: **827–831**

Tibullus
See "Tibullus and Propertius"

Tibullus and Propertius
Ancient Writers, vol. 2: **765–782**

Tieck, Ludwig
European Writers, vol. 5: **233–260**
Supernatural Fiction Writers, vol. 1: **83–89**

Tiptree, James, Jr.
Science Fiction Writers: **531–541**

Tocqueville, Alexis de
European Writers, vol. 6: **893–912**
European Writers Selected Authors, vol. 3:
1673–1691

Tolkien, J. R. R.
British Writers Supp. 2: **519–536**
British Writers Selected Authors, vol. 3: **1277–1294**
Supernatural Fiction Writers, vol. 2: **675–682**
Writers for Children: **561–571**
Writers for Young Adults, vol. 3: **311–320**

Tolson, Melvin
African American Writers: **413–427**

Tolstoy, Leo
European Writers, vol. 7: **1471–1494**
European Writers Selected Authors, vol. 3:
1693–1715

Toomer, Jean
African American Writers: **429–440**
American Writers Supp. 3, part 2: **475–491**

Torres Bodet, Jaime
Latin American Writers, vol. 2: **933–939**

Tourneur, Cyril
See "Marston, John, and Cyril Tourneur"

Traherne, Thomas
See "Metaphysical Poets, Four" in Themes,
Genres, Collectives, and Works

Trakl, Georg
European Writers, vol. 10: **1409–1427**

Trevelyan, G. M.
  British Writers, vol. 6: **383–396**

Trevor, William
  British Writers Supp. 4: **499–519**

Triana, José
  Latin American Writers, vol. 3: **1415–1419**

Trilling, Lionel
  American Writers Supp. 3, part 2: **493–515**

Trollope, Anthony
  British Writers, vol. 5: **89–104**
  British Writers Selected Authors, vol. 3: **1295–1309**

Tsvetaeva, Marina
  European Writers, vol. 11: **1731–1750**

Turgenev, Ivan
  European Writers, vol. 6: **1275–1297**
  European Writers Selected Authors, vol. 3: **1717–1739**

Tutuola, Amos
  African Writers, vol. 2: **865–878**

Twain, Mark
  American Writers, vol. 4: **190–213**
  Supernatural Fiction Writers, vol. 2: **761–768**
  Writers for Children: **573–582**
  Writers for Young Adults, vol. 3: **321–328**

Tychyna, Pavlo
  European Writers, vol. 10: **1651–1676**

Tyler, Anne
  American Writers Supp. 4, part 2: **657–675**
  Modern American Women Writers: **499–510**

Tyndale, William
  See "Bible, The English" in Themes, Genres, Collectives, and Works

Unamuno, Miguel de
  European Writers, vol. 8: **283–310**

Undset, Sigrid
  European Writers, vol. 9: **1017–1041**

Ungaretti, Giuseppe
  European Writers, vol. 10: **1453–1473**

Updike, John
  American Writers, vol. 4: **214–235**
  American Writers Retrospective: **317–338**

Urfé, Honoré, d'
  See "Renaissance Pastoral Poetry" in Themes, Genres, Collectives, and Works

Usigli, Rodolfo
  Latin American Writers, vol. 3: **1033–1042**

Uslar Pietri, Arturo
  Latin American Writers, vol. 3: **1057–1062**

Valencia, Guillermo
  Latin American Writers, vol. 2: **477–482**

Valenzuela, Luisa
  Latin American Writers, vol. 3: **1445–1449**

Valéry, Paul
  European Writers, vol. 8: **569–588**

Valle, Rafael Heliodoro
  Latin American Writers, vol. 2: **721–725**

Valle-Inclán, Ramón del
  European Writers, vol. 8: **331–353**

Vallejo, César
  Latin American Writers, vol. 2: **727–738**

Valle y Caviedes, Juan del
  Latin American Writers, vol. 1: **79–83**

Vanbrugh, Sir John
  British Writers, vol. 2: **323–337**

Vance, Jack
  Science Fiction Writers: **543–549**
  Supernatural Fiction Writers, vol. 2: **1105–1111**

van der Post, Laurens
  African Writers, vol. 2: **879–891**

Van Dyke, John C.
  American Nature Writers, vol. 2: **951–962**

Van Loon, Hendrik Willem
  Writers for Children: **583–589**

Van Vechten, Carl
  American Writers Supp. 2, part 2: **725–751**

Van Vogt, A. E.
  Science Fiction Writers: **209–217**

Vargas Llosa, Mario
  Latin American Writers, vol. 3: **1421–1436**

Vasconcelos, José
  Latin American Writers, vol. 2: **575–584**

Vaughan, Henry
  See "Metaphysical Poets, Four" in Themes, Genres, Collectives, and Works

Veblen, Thorstein
  American Writers Supp. 1, part 2: **628–650**

Vega, Lope de
  European Writers, vol. 2: **845–870**

Verga, Giovanni
  European Writers, vol. 7: **1543–1565**

Vergil
Ancient Writers, vol. 2: **669–701**

Veríssimo, Érico
Latin American Writers, vol. 3: **1043–1048**

Verlaine, Paul
European Writers, vol. 7: **1619–1643**

Verne, Jules
Science Fiction Writers: **573–582**
Writers for Children: **591–598**

Vesaas, Tarjei
European Writers, vol. 11: **2035–2059**

Vico, Giovanni Battista
European Writers, vol. 3: **293–316**

Vidal, Gore
American Writers Supp. 4, part 2: **677–697**

Vieira, José Luandino
African Writers, vol. 2: **893–901**

Vigny, Alfred Victor de
European Writers, vol. 5: **447–488**

Villaurrutia, Xavier
Latin American Writers, vol. 3: **975–980**

Villaverde, Cirilo
Latin American Writers, vol. 1: **169–174**

Villon, François
European Writers, vol. 2: **535–570**

Vittorini, Elio
European Writers, vol. 12: **2733–2757**

Voigt, Cynthia
Writers for Young Adults, vol. 3: **329–338**

Voltaire
European Writers, vol. 4: **367–392**
European Writers Selected Authors, vol. 3:
    1741–1766

Vonnegut, Kurt
American Writers Supp. 2, part 2: **753–783**
Science Fiction Writers: **551–561**

Wagner, Richard
European Writers, vol. 6: **1147–1168**
European Writers Selected Authors, vol. 3:
    1767–1787

Wakefield, H. Russell
Supernatural Fiction Writers, vol. 2: **617–622**

Walker, Alice
African American Writers: **441–458**
American Writers Supp. 3, part 2: **517–540**
Modern American Women Writers: **511–520**

Walker, Margaret
African American Writers: **459–471**

Wall, Mervyn
Supernatural Fiction Writers, vol. 2: **645–650**

Wallace, David Rains
American Nature Writers, vol. 2: **963–972**

Waller, Edmund
See "Cavalier Poets, The" in Themes, Genres,
    Collectives, and Works

Walpole, Horace
Supernatural Fiction Writers, vol. 1: **131–137**
See also "Gothic Novel, The" in Themes,
    Genres, Collectives, and Works

Walsh, Jill Paton
Writers for Young Adults, vol. 3: **339–346**

Walther von der Vogelweide
European Writers, vol. 1: **287–308**

Walton, Izaak
British Writers, vol. 2: **131–144**

Warren, Robert Penn
American Writers, vol. 4: **236–259**

Waugh, Evelyn
British Writers, vol. 7: **289–308**
British Writers Selected Authors, vol. 3: **1311–1330**

Webster, John
British Writers, vol. 2: **68–86**

Wedekind, Frank
European Writers, vol. 8: **229–281**

Weil, Simone
European Writers, vol. 12: **2787–2814**

Weinbaum, Stanley G.
Science Fiction Writers: **145–149**

Weldon, Fay
British Writers Supp. 4: **521–539**

Wellman, Manly Wade
Supernatural Fiction Writers, vol. 2: **947–954**

Wells, H. G.
British Writers, vol. 6: **225–246**
British Writers Selected Authors, vol. 3: **1331–1352**
Science Fiction Writers: **25–30**
Supernatural Fiction Writers, vol. 1: **397–402**
Writers for Children: **599–603**

Welty, Eudora
American Writers, vol. 4: **260–284**
American Writers Retrospective: **359–358**
Modern American Women Writers: **521–538**

Wersba, Barbara
    Writers for Young Adults, vol. 3: **349–357**

West, Nathanael
    American Writers, vol. 4: **285–307**

West, Rebecca
    British Writers Supp. 3: **431–445**

Westall, Robert Atkinson
    Writers for Young Adults, vol. 3: **359–369**

Wharton, Edith
    American Writers, vol. 4: **308–330**
    American Writers Retrospective: **359–385**
    Modern American Women Writers: **539–558**
    Supernatural Fiction Writers, vol. 2: **783–788**

Wheatley, Dennis
    Supernatural Fiction Writers, vol. 2: **623–629**

Wheatley, Phillis
    African American Writers: **473–491**

White, E. B.
    American Writers Supp. 1, part 2: **651–681**

White, Patrick
    British Writers Supp. 1: **129–152**

White, T. H.
    Supernatural Fiction Writers, vol. 2: **651–657**

Whitman, Walt
    American Writers, vol. 4: **331–354**
    American Writers Retrospective: **387–410**

Whittier, John Greenleaf
    American Writers Supp. 1, part 2: **682–706**

Wideman, John Edgar
    African American Writers: **493–504**

Wieland, Christoph Martin
    European Writers, vol. 4: **587–614**

Wiggin, Kate Douglas
    Writers for Children: **605–609**

Wilbur, Richard
    American Writers Supp. 3, part 2: **541–565**

Wilde, Oscar
    British Writers, vol. 5: **399–422**
    British Writers Selected Authors, vol. 3: **1353–1376**
    Supernatural Fiction Writers, vol. 1: **345–350**
    Writers for Children: **611–616**

Wilder, Laura Ingalls
    Writers for Children: **617–623**
    Writers for Young Adults, vol. 3: **371–380**

Wilder, Thornton
    American Writers, vol. 4: **355–377**

Wilkinson, Brenda
    Writers for Young Adults, vol. 3: **381–390**

Williams, Charles
    Supernatural Fiction Writers, vol. 2: **631–638**

Williams, Tennessee
    American Writers, vol. 4: **378–401**

Williams, Terry Tempest
    American Nature Writers, vol. 2: **973–988**

Williams, William Carlos
    American Writers, vol. 4: **402–425**
    American Writers Retrospective: **411–433**

Williamson, Jack
    Science Fiction Writers: **225–231**

Wilmot, John (Earl of Rochester)
    See "Restoration Court Poets, The" in Themes,
        Genres, Collectives, and Works

Wilson, Alexander
    See "Early Romantic Natural History Literature"
        in Themes, Genres, Collectives, and Works

Wilson, Angus
    British Writers Supp. 1: **153–168**

Wilson, Edmund
    American Writers, vol. 4: **426–449**

Winters, Yvor
    American Writers Supp. 2, part 2: **785–816**

Winterson, Jeanette
    British Writers Supp. 4: **541–559**

Witkiewicz (Witkacy), Stanisław Ignacy
    European Writers, vol. 10: **1205–1230**

Wodehouse, P. G.
    British Writers Supp. 3: **447–464**
    British Writers Selected Authors, vol. 3: **1377–1394**

Wolfe, Thomas
    American Writers, vol. 4: **450–473**

Wolfe, Tom
    American Writers Supp. 3, part 2: **567–588**

Wolff, Egon
    Latin American Writers, vol. 3: **1311–1315**

Wolff, Virginia Euwer
    Writers for Young Adults, vol. 3: **391–398**

Wolfram von Eschenbach
    European Writers, vol. 1: **263–286**
    See also "Arthurian Romances" in Themes,
        Genres, Collectives, and Works

Wollstonecraft, Mary
    British Writers Supp. 3: **465–482**

Wood, Mrs. Henry
   Supernatural Fiction Writers, vol. 1: **279–286**

Woolf, Virginia
   British Writers, vol. 7: **17–40**
   British Writers Selected Authors, vol. 3: **1395–1417**

Wordsworth, William
   British Writers, vol. 4: **1–26**
   British Writers Selected Authors, vol. 3: **1419–1444**

Wright, James
   American Writers Supp. 3, part 2: **589–607**

Wright, Richard
   African American Writers: **505–523**
   American Writers, vol. 4: **474–497**

Wright, S. Fowler
   Science Fiction Writers: **83–89**

Wyatt, Sir Thomas
   British Writers, vol. 1: **97–112**

Wycherley, William
   British Writers, vol. 2: **307–322**

Wylie, Elinor
   American Writers Supp. 1, part 2: **707–730**

Wyndham, John
   Science Fiction Writers: **219–224**

Xenophon
   Ancient Writers, vol. 1: **331–351**

Yáñez, Agustín
   Latin American Writers, vol. 3: **995–999**

Yeats, William Butler
   British Writers, vol. 6: **207–224**
   British Writers Selected Authors, vol. 3: **1473–1490**

Yep, Laurence
   Writers for Young Adults, vol. 3: **399–408**

Yolen, Jane
   Writers for Young Adults, vol. 3: **409–420**

Yonge, Charlotte Mary
   Writers for Children: **625–631**

Yourcenar, Marguerite
   European Writers, vol. 12: **2535–2561**

Zamyatin, Yevgeny Ivanovich
   European Writers, vol. 10: **1181–1203**

Zelazny, Roger
   Science Fiction Writers: **563–570**
   Supernatural Fiction Writers, vol. 2: **1113–1119**

Zeno Gandía, Manuel
   Latin American Writers, vol. 1: **321–326**

Zindel, Paul
   Writers for Young Adults, vol. 3: **421–430**

Zola, Émile
   European Writers, vol. 7: **1517–1542**
   European Writers Selected Authors, vol. 3: **1789–1813**

Zorrilla de San Martín, Juan
   Latin American Writers, vol. 1: **327–331**

Zukofsky, Louis
   American Writers Supp. 3, part 2: **609–632**

Zwinger, Ann
   American Nature Writers, vol. 2: **989–1001**

Zwinger, Susan
   See "New Voices in American Nature Writing"
   in Themes, Genres, Collectives, and Works

THEMES, GENRES, COLLECTIVES, AND WORKS

Articles about themes (for example, "The Arthurian Legend"), genres ("Medieval Satire," "The Well-Made Play"), collective subjects ("Canadian Nature Writing"), or anonymous or biblical books.

Acts of the Apostles, The
   See "Gospel of Luke and Acts of the Apostles"

African Americans, Writing, and Nature
   American Nature Writers, vol. 2: **1003–1012**

Amos
   The Books of the Bible, vol. 1: **367–374**

Apocrypha, The
   The Books of the Bible, vol. 2: **3–11**

Aquinas, Saint Thomas, and Scholasticism
   European Writers, vol. 1: **405–430**
   European Writers Selected Authors, vol. 1: **53–77**

Arabian Nights
  Supernatural Fiction Writers, vol. 1: **19–26**

Arthurian Legend
  European Writers, vol. 1: **137–160**
  European Writers Selected Authors, vol. 1: **79–102**

Arthurian Romances
  Supernatural Fiction Writers, vol. 1: **11–18**

Asbjørnsen and Moe (Peter Christen
    Asbjørnsen and Jørgen Moe)
  Writers for Children: **21–28**

Baruch, the Letter of Jeremiah, the Prayer of
    Manasseh
  The Books of the Bible, vol. 2: **87–92**

Beaumont, Francis, and John Fletcher
  British Writers, vol. 2: **42–67**

Beowulf and Anglo-Saxon Poetry
  European Writers, vol. 1: **51–88**
  European Writers Selected Authors, vol. 1: **217–253**

Bible, The English
  British Writers, vol. 1: **370–388**
  British Writers Selected Authors, vol. 1: **69–87**

Bible as Sacred Literature, The
  The Books of the Bible, vol. 1: **1–9**

Bioregionalism in Nature Writing
  American Nature Writers, vol. 2: **1013–1024**

Brontës, The
  British Writers, vol. 5: **105–154**
  British Writers Selected Authors, vol. 1: **129–177**

Canadian Nature Writing in English
  American Nature Writers, vol. 2: **1025–1040**

Cavalier Poets, The
  British Writers, vol. 2: **221–239**

Chanson de Roland, The, and the *Chansons de
    Geste*
  European Writers, vol. 1: **89–112**

Chronicles, Ezra, and Nehemiah (1 and 2
    Chronicles, Ezra, and Nehemiah)
  The Books of the Bible, vol. 1: **155–171**

Cid in Epic and Ballad, The
  European Writers, vol. 1: **113–136**

Contemporary Ecofiction
  American Nature Writers, vol. 2: **1041–1058**

Daniel and Additions to Daniel
  The Books of the Bible, vol. 1: **333–347**

De Camp, L. Sprague, and Fletcher Pratt
  Supernatural Fiction Writers, vol. 2: **925–931**

Deuteronomy
  The Books of the Bible, vol. 1: **89–102**

Early Romantic Natural History Literature
  American Nature Writers, vol. 2: **1059–1078**

Ecclesiastes
  The Books of the Bible, vol. 1: **231–239**

Epictetus and Marcus Aurelius
  Ancient Writers, vol. 2: **985–1002**

Epistle of James
  The Books of the Bible, vol. 2: **339–343**

Epistles of John (1, 2, and 3 John)
  The Books of the Bible, vol. 2: **359–365**

Epistle of Jude
  See "Epistles of Peter and Jude (2 Peter and
    Jude)"

Epistle of Peter (1 Peter)
  The Books of the Bible, vol. 2: **345–351**

Epistle of Peter (2 Peter)
  See "Epistles of Peter and Jude (2 Peter and
    Jude)"

Epistles of Peter and Jude (2 Peter and Jude)
  The Books of the Bible, vol. 2: **353–357**

Epistle to the Colossians
  The Books of the Bible, vol. 2: **301–310**

Epistles to the Corinthians (1 and 2
    Corinthians)
  The Books of the Bible, vol. 2: **245–269**

Epistle to the Ephesians
  The Books of the Bible, vol. 2: **285–292**

Epistle to the Galatians
  The Books of the Bible, vol. 2: **271–284**

Epistle to the Hebrews
  The Books of the Bible, vol. 2: **327–338**

Epistle to Philemon
  The Books of the Bible, vol. 2: **325–326**

Epistle to the Philippians
  The Books of the Bible, vol. 2: **293–299**

Epistle to the Romans
  The Books of the Bible, vol. 2: **229–243**

Epistles to the Thessalonians (1 and 2
    Thessalonians)
  The Books of the Bible, vol. 2: **311–318**

Epistles to Timothy (1 and 2 Timothy)
  See "Epistles to Timothy and Titus (1 and 2
    Timothy and Titus)"

Epistles to Timothy and Titus (1 and 2 Timothy and Titus)
The Books of the Bible, vol. 2: **319–324**

Epistles to Titus
See "Epistles to Timothy and Titus (1 and 2 Timothy and Titus)"

Esdras (1 Esdras)
The Books of the Bible, vol. 2: **13–19**

Esdras (2 Esdras)
The Books of the Bible, vol. 2: **21–34**

Esther and Additions to Esther
The Books of the Bible, vol. 1: **173–179**

Evelyn, John, and Samuel Pepys
British Writers, vol. 2: **274–288**

Exodus
The Books of the Bible, vol. 1: **47–62**

Ezekiel
The Books of the Bible, vol. 1: **319–332**

Forms of American Nature Poetry, The
American Nature Writers, vol. 2: **1079–1098**

French Novelists, Three
European Writers, vol. 4: **393–419**

Genesis
The Books of the Bible, vol. 1: **21–46**

Goncourt, Edmond Louis Antoine de, and Jules Alfred Huot de Goncourt
European Writers, vol. 7: **1395–1419**

Gospel of John
The Books of the Bible, vol. 2: **203–228**

Gospel of Luke
See "Gospel of Luke and Acts of the Apostles"

Gospel of Luke and Acts of the Apostles
The Books of the Bible, vol. 2: **171–202**

Gospel of Mark
The Books of the Bible, vol. 2: **149–169**

Gospel of Matthew
The Books of the Bible, vol. 2: **125–147**

Gothic Novel, The
British Writers, vol. 3: **324–346**

Greek Lyric Poets
Ancient Writers, vol. 1: **75–98**

Grimm, Jacob and Wilhelm
Writers for Children: **255–263**

Habakkuk
The Books of the Bible, vol. 1: **391–396**

Haggai
See "Haggai, Zechariah, and Malachi"

Haggai, Zechariah, and Malachi
The Books of the Bible, vol. 1: **405–414**

Hellenistic Poetry at Alexandria
Ancient Writers, vol. 1: **449–482**

Hosea
The Books of the Bible, vol. 1: **349–358**

Isaiah
The Books of the Bible, vol. 1: **247–279**

Jeremiah
The Books of the Bible, vol. 1: **281–301**

Job
The Books of the Bible, vol. 1: **181–201**

Joel
The Books of the Bible, vol. 1: **359–365**

Jonah
The Books of the Bible, vol. 1: **381–384**

Joshua
The Books of the Bible, vol. 1: **103–112**

Judges
The Books of the Bible, vol. 1: **113-121**

Judith
The Books of the Bible, vol. 2: **43–49**

Kings (1 and 2 Kings)
The Books of the Bible, vol. 1: **141–155**

Kyd, Thomas, and Early Elizabethan Tragedy
British Writers, vol. 1: **212–231**

Lamentations
The Books of the Bible, vol. 1: **303–318**

Leviticus
The Books of the Bible, vol. 1: **63–70**

Literary Theory and Nature Writing
American Nature Writers, vol. 2: **1099–1114**

Literature of Mountaineering
American Nature Writers, vol. 2: **1115–1128**

Lyly, John, and George Peele
British Writers, vol. 1: **191–211**

Lucan and Statius
Ancient Writers, vol. 2: **917–941**

Maccabees (1 and 2 Maccabees)
The Books of the Bible, vol. 2: **93–114**

Malachi
See "Haggai, Zechariah, and Malachi"

Marston, John, and Cyril Tourneur
  British Writers, vol. 2: **24–41**

Medieval Drama
  European Writers, vol. 1: **451–474**
  European Writers Selected Authors, vol. 2: **1051–1074**

Medieval Satire
  European Writers, vol. 1: **337–376**
  European Writers Selected Authors, vol. 2: **1075–1113**

Metaphysical Poets, Four
  British Writers, vol. 2: **179–203**

Micah
  The Books of the Bible, vol. 1: **385–390**

Michelet, Jules, and Romantic Historiography
  European Writers, vol. 5: **571–606**

Modern Birdwatching Literature
  American Nature Writers, vol. 2: **1129–1140**

Moore, C. L., and Henry Kuttner
  Science Fiction Writers: **161–167**

Nahum
  See "Obadiah and Nahum"

Nature in Native American Literatures
  American Nature Writers, vol. 2: **1141–1156**

New Testament, The
  The Books of the Bible, vol. 2: **117–124**

New Voices in American Nature Writing
  American Nature Writers, vol. 2: **1157–1173**

Nibelungenlied, The
  European Writers, vol. 1: **211–236**

Norse Sagas
  European Writers, vol. 1: **377–404**
  European Writers Selected Authors, vol. 3: **1199–1226**

Numbers
  The Books of the Bible, vol. 1: **71–87**

Obadiah
  See "Obadiah and Nahum"

Obadiah and Nahum
  The Books of the Bible, vol. 1: **375–380**

Old Testament, The
  The Books of the Bible, vol. 1: **11–19**

Persius and Juvenal
  Ancient Writers, vol. 2: **855–876**

Poetic Realism
  European Writers, vol. 6: **913–942**

Poets of World War I (British)
  British Writers, vol. 6: **415–442**
  British Writers Selected Authors, vol. 3: **1445–1471**

Poets of World War II (British)
  British Writers, vol. 7: **421–450**

Proverbs
  The Books of the Bible, vol. 1: **223–230**

Psalms
  The Books of the Bible, vol. 1: **203–221**

Renaissance Pastoral Poetry
  European Writers, vol. 2: **899–926**
  European Writers Selected Authors, vol. 3: **1403–1430**

Renaissance Short Fiction
  European Writers, vol. 2: **927–956**
  European Writers Selected Authors, vol. 3: **1431–1460**

Restoration Court Poets, The
  British Writers, vol. 2: **255–272**

Revelation
  The Books of the Bible, vol. 2: **367–381**

Romance of the Rose, The, and Medieval Allegory
  European Writers, vol. 1: **309–335**
  European Writers Selected Authors, vol. 3: **1491–1517**

Ronsard, Pierre de, and the Pléiade
  European Writers, vol. 2: **721–746**

Ruth
  The Books of the Bible, vol. 1: **123–126**

Sade, Marquis de, and the French Libertine Tradition
  European Writers, vol. 4: **615–638**

Samuel (1 and 2 Samuel)
  The Books of the Bible, vol. 1: **127–140**

Sirach (Ecclesiasticus)
  The Books of the Bible, vol. 2: **65–86**

Slave Narrative in American Literature, The
  African American Writers: **395–412**

Song of Solomon
  The Books of the Bible, vol. 1: **241–246**

Steele, Sir Richard, and Joseph Addison
  British Writers, vol. 3: **38–53**
  British Writers Selected Authors, vol. 3: **1145–1160**

Tibullus and Propertius
  Ancient Writers, vol. 2: **765–782**

Tobit
  The Books of the Bible, vol. 2: **35–42**

Troubadours and Trouvères
European Writers, vol. 1: **161–184**

Well-Made Play, The
European Writers, vol. 7: **1909–1934**

Western Geologists and Explorers
American Nature Writers, vol. 2: **1173–1188**

Wisdom of Solomon
The Books of the Bible, vol. 2: **51–63**

Zechariah
See "Haggai, Zechariah, and Malachi"

Zephaniah
The Books of the Bible, vol. 1: **397–404**

Subjects by Period

Writers and works are here grouped into the historical periods of their activity (ancient, medieval, Renaissance, 17th, 18th, 19th, 20th century). Some writers flourished in more than one century, and there is considerable overlap between the first three periods. Birth date, publication date, or floruit (fl.), where known, appears in parentheses following the subject's name. Most ancient and medieval dates are approximate.

ANCIENT

Acts of the Apostles, The (ca. 85–100)
  See "Gospel of Luke and Acts of the Apostles"

Aeschylus (ca. 525 B.C.)
  Ancient Writers, vol. 1: **99–155**

Alcaeus (ca. 620 B.C.)
  See "Greek Lyric Poets"

Alcman (7th century B.C.)
  See "Greek Lyric Poets"

Ammianus Marcellinus (ca. 330)
  Ancient Writers, vol. 2: **1117–1138**

Amos (8th–6th centuries B.C.)
  The Books of the Bible, vol. 1: **367–374**

Anacreon (ca. 582 B.C.)
  See "Greek Lyric Poets"

Antimachus of Colophon (fl. ca. 400 B.C.)
  See "Hellenistic Poetry at Alexandria"

Apocrypha, The
  The Books of the Bible, vol. 2: **3–11**

Apollonius of Rhodes (fl. 3rd century B.C.)
  See "Hellenistic Poetry at Alexandria"

Apuleius (ca. 120)
  Ancient Writers, vol. 2: **1099–1116**
  Supernatural Fiction Writers, vol. 1: **3–9**

Aristophanes (445 B.C.)
  Ancient Writers, vol. 1: **291–312**

Aristotle (384 B.C.)
  Ancient Writers, vol. 1: **377–416**

Asclepiades (fl. 3rd century B.C.)
  See "Hellenistic Poetry at Alexandria"

Augustine, Saint (354)
  European Writers, vol. 1: **23–50**
  European Writers Selected Authors, vol. 1: **103–130**

Bacchylides (fl. 5th century B.C.)
  See "Greek Lyric Poets"

Baruch, the Letter of Jeremiah, the Prayer of Manasseh (6th century B.C.–1st century A.D.)
  The Books of the Bible, vol. 2: **87–92**

Bible as Sacred Literature, The
  The Books of the Bible, vol. 1: **1–9**

Caesar (100 B.C.)
  Ancient Writers, vol. 1: **583–599**

Callimachus (ca. 305 B.C.)
  See "Hellenistic Poetry at Alexandria"

Catullus (ca. 84 B.C.)
  Ancient Writers, vol. 2: **643–667**

Chronicles, Ezra, and Nehemiah (1 and 2 Chronicles, Ezra, and Nehemiah) (5th–4th centuries B.C.)
  The Books of the Bible, vol. 1: **155–171**

Cicero (106 B.C.)
  Ancient Writers, vol. 1: **555–581**

Daniel and Additions to Daniel (3rd–2nd centuries B.C.)
  The Books of the Bible, vol. 1: **333–347**

Demetrius of Phalerum (350? B.C.)
See "Hellenistic Poetry at Alexandria"

Demosthenes (ca. 384 B.C.)
Ancient Writers, vol. 1: **417–433**

Deuteronomy (8th–6th centuries B.C.)
The Books of the Bible, vol. 1: **89–102**

Ecclesiastes (5th–2nd centuries B.C.)
The Books of the Bible, vol. 1: **231–239**

Epictetus (ca. 50)
See "Epictetus and Marcus Aurelius"

Epictetus and Marcus Aurelius
Ancient Writers, vol. 2: **985–1002**

Epistle of James (70–120)
The Books of the Bible, vol. 2: **339–343**

Epistles of John (1, 2, and 3 John) (ca. 90–100)
The Books of the Bible, vol. 2: **359–365**

Epistle of Jude (ca. 50–ca. 120)
See "Epistles of Peter and Jude (2 Peter and Jude)"

Epistle of Peter (1 Peter) (ca. 70–100)
The Books of the Bible, vol. 2: **345–351**

Epistle of Peter (2 Peter) (ca. 90–ca. 120)
See "Epistles of Peter and Jude (2 Peter and Jude)"

Epistles of Peter and Jude (2 Peter and Jude) (ca. 50–ca. 120)
The Books of the Bible, vol. 2: **353–357**

Epistle to the Colossians (ca. 75–100)
The Books of the Bible, vol. 2: **301–310**

Epistles to the Corinthians (1 and 2 Corinthians) (ca. 50–60)
The Books of the Bible, vol. 2: **245–269**

Epistle to the Ephesians (ca. 75–100)
The Books of the Bible, vol. 2: **285–292**

Epistle to the Galatians (ca. 50–60)
The Books of the Bible, vol. 2: **271–284**

Epistle to the Hebrews (ca. 60–95)
The Books of the Bible, vol. 2: **327–338**

Epistle to Philemon (ca. 61–63)
The Books of the Bible, vol. 2: **325–326**

Epistle to the Philippians (ca. 60–63)
The Books of the Bible, vol. 2: **293–299**

Epistle to the Romans (ca. 50–60)
The Books of the Bible, vol. 2: **229–243**

Epistles to the Thessalonians (1 and 2 Thessalonians) (ca. 50–60)
The Books of the Bible, vol. 2: **311–318**

Epistles to Timothy (1 and 2 Timothy) (ca. 70–120)
See "Epistles to Timothy and Titus (1 and 2 Timothy and Titus)"

Epistles to Timothy and Titus (1 and 2 Timothy and Titus) (ca. 70–120)
The Books of the Bible, vol. 2: **319–324**

Epistles to Titus (ca. 70–120)
See "Epistles to Timothy and Titus (1 and 2 Timothy and Titus)"

Esdras (1 Esdras) (2nd–1st centuries B.C.)
The Books of the Bible, vol. 2: **13–19**

Esdras (2 Esdras) (70–100)
The Books of the Bible, vol. 2: **21–34**

Esther and Additions to Esther (4th–2nd centuries B.C.)
The Books of the Bible, vol. 1: **173–179**

Euripides (ca. 480 B.C.)
Ancient Writers, vol. 1: **233–266**

Exodus (8th–6th centuries B.C.)
The Books of the Bible, vol. 1: **47–62**

Ezekiel (6th century B.C.)
The Books of the Bible, vol. 1: **319–332**

Genesis (8th–6th centuries B.C.)
The Books of the Bible, vol. 1: **21–46**

Gospel of John (ca. 90–95)
The Books of the Bible, vol. 2: **203–228**

Gospel of Luke (ca. 85–100)
See "Gospel of Luke and Acts of the Apostles"

Gospel of Luke and Acts of the Apostles (ca. 85–100)
The Books of the Bible, vol. 2: **171–202**

Gospel of Mark (ca. 68–70)
The Books of the Bible, vol. 2: **149–169**

Gospel of Matthew (ca. 85–100)
The Books of the Bible, vol. 2: **125–147**

Greek Lyric Poets
Ancient Writers, vol. 1: **75–98**

Habakkuk (7th–6th centuries B.C.)
The Books of the Bible, vol. 1: **391–396**

Haggai (6th century B.C.)
  See "Haggai, Zechariah, and Malachi"

Haggai, Zechariah, and Malachi
  (6th–5th centuries B.C.)
  The Books of the Bible, vol. 1: **405–414**

Hellenistic Poetry at Alexandria
  Ancient Writers, vol. 1: **449–482**

Herodotus (ca. 484 B.C.)
  Ancient Writers, vol. 1: **209–232**

Hesiod (fl. 8th century B.C.)
  Ancient Writers, vol. 1: **43–73**

Homer (fl. 8th century B.C.)
  Ancient Writers, vol. 1: **1–41**

Horace (65 B.C.)
  Ancient Writers, vol. 2: **703–731**

Hosea (8th century B.C.)
  The Books of the Bible, vol. 1: **349–358**

Ibycus (6th century B.C.)
  See "Greek Lyric Poets"

Isaiah (8th–6th centuries B.C.)
  The Books of the Bible, vol. 1: **247–279**

Isocrates (ca. 436 B.C.)
  Ancient Writers, vol. 1: **313–329**

Jeremiah (7th–5th centuries B.C.)
  The Books of the Bible, vol. 1: **281–301**

Job (6th–3rd centuries B.C.)
  The Books of the Bible, vol. 1: **181–201**

Joel (6th–4th centuries B.C.)
  The Books of the Bible, vol. 1: **359–365**

Jonah (6th–4th centuries B.C.)
  The Books of the Bible, vol. 1: **381–384**

Josephus (ca. 37)
  Ancient Writers, vol. 2: **877–885**

Joshua (6th century B.C.)
  The Books of the Bible, vol. 1: **103–112**

Judges
  The Books of the Bible, vol. 1: **113–121**

Judith (4th–2nd centuries B.C.)
  The Books of the Bible, vol. 2: **43–49**

Juvenal (60?)
  See "Persius and Juvenal"

Kings (1 and 2 Kings) (7th–6th centuries B.C.)
  The Books of the Bible, vol. 1: **141–155**

Lamentations (6th century B.C.)
  The Books of the Bible, vol. 1: **303–318**

Leviticus (8th–6th centuries B.C.)
  The Books of the Bible, vol. 1: **63–70**

Livy (ca. 59 B.C.)
  Ancient Writers, vol. 2: **733–764**

Longinus (fl. 1st century)
  Ancient Writers, vol. 2: **1063–1080**

Lucan (39)
  See "Lucan and Statius"

Lucan and Statius
  Ancient Writers, vol. 2: **917–941**

Lucian (ca. 120)
  Ancient Writers, vol. 2: **1081–1097**

Lucretius (94? B.C.)
  Ancient Writers, vol. 2: **601–620**

Maccabees (1 and 2 Maccabees)
  (2nd–1st centuries B.C.)
  The Books of the Bible, vol. 2: **93–114**

Malachi (5th century B.C.)
  See "Haggai, Zechariah, and Malachi"

Marcus Aurelius (121)
  See "Epictetus and Marcus Aurelius"

Martial (ca. 38)
  Ancient Writers, vol. 2: **887–915**

Menander (ca. 342 B.C.)
  Ancient Writers, vol. 1: **435–447**

Micah (8th–6th centuries B.C.)
  The Books of the Bible, vol. 1: **385–390**

Nahum (7th century B.C.)
  See "Obadiah and Nahum"

New Testament, The (50–120)
  The Books of the Bible, vol. 2: **117–124**

Numbers (8th–6th centuries B.C.)
  The Books of the Bible, vol. 1: **71–87**

Obadiah (6th century B.C.)
  See "Obadiah and Nahum"

Obadiah and Nahum (7th–6th centuries B.C.)
  The Books of the Bible, vol. 1: **375–380**

Old Testament, The (12th–2nd centuries B.C.)
  The Books of the Bible, vol. 1: **11–19**

Ovid (43 B.C.)
  Ancient Writers, vol. 2: **783–806**

Persius (34)
  See "Persius and Juvenal"

Persius and Juvenal
  Ancient Writers, vol. 2: **855–876**

Petronius
Ancient Writers, vol. 2: **833–853**

Philitas of Cos (ca. 330 B.C.)
See "Hellenistic Poetry at Alexandria"

Pindar (ca. 518 B.C.)
Ancient Writers, vol. 1: **157–177**

Plato (428)
Ancient Writers, vol. 1: **353–376**

Plautus (ca. 254 B.C.)
Ancient Writers, vol. 1: **501–523**

Pliny the Younger (ca. 61)
Ancient Writers, vol. 2: **1035–1048**

Plutarch (ca. 40)
Ancient Writers, vol. 2: **961–983**

Polybius (205? B.C.)
Ancient Writers, vol. 1: **525–539**

Posidippus (fl. 3rd century B.C.)
See "Hellenistic Poetry at Alexandria"

Propertius (50? B.C.)
See "Tibullus and Propertius"

Proverbs (6th–4th centuries B.C.)
The Books of the Bible, vol. 1: **223–230**

Prudentius (348)
European Writers, vol. 1: **1–22**

Psalms (11th–4th centuries B.C.)
The Books of the Bible, vol. 1: **203–221**

Quintilian (ca. 40)
Ancient Writers, vol. 2: **943–959**

Revelation (ca. 90–95)
The Books of the Bible, vol. 2: **367–381**

Ruth (9th–6th centuries B.C.)
The Books of the Bible, vol. 1: **123–126**

Sallust (ca. 86 B.C.)
Ancient Writers, vol. 2: **621–641**

Samuel (1 and 2 Samuel) (7th–6th centuries B.C.)
The Books of the Bible, vol. 1: **127–140**

Sappho (ca. 610 B.C.)
See "Greek Lyric Poets"

Seneca the Younger (4? B.C.)
Ancient Writers, vol. 2: **807–832**

Simonides (ca. 556 B.C.)
See "Greek Lyric Poets"

Sirach (Ecclesiasticus) (ca. 180 B.C.)
The Books of the Bible, vol. 2: **65–86**

Song of Solomon (10th–4th centuries B.C.)
The Books of the Bible, vol. 1: **241–246**

Sophocles (ca. 497 B.C.)
Ancient Writers, vol. 1: **179–207**

Statius (45?)
See "Lucan and Statius"

Stesichorus (ca. 632 B.C.)
See "Greek Lyric Poets"

Suetonius (ca. 69)
Ancient Writers, vol. 2: **1049–1061**

Tacitus (ca. 55)
Ancient Writers, vol. 2: **1003–1033**

Terence
Ancient Writers, vol. 1: **541–554**

Theocritus (4th century B.C.)
Ancient Writers, vol. 1: **483–500**

Thucydides (ca. 459 B.C.)
Ancient Writers, vol. 1: **267–289**

Tibullus (54? B.C.)
See "Tibullus and Propertius"

Tibullus and Propertius
Ancient Writers, vol. 2: **765–782**

Tobit (3rd–2nd centuries B.C.)
The Books of the Bible, vol. 2: **35–42**

Vergil (70 B.C.)
Ancient Writers, vol. 2: **669–701**

Wisdom of Solomon (1st century B.C.)
The Books of the Bible, vol. 2: **51–63**

Xenophon (ca. 428 B.C.)
Ancient Writers, vol. 1: **331–351**

Zechariah (6th–5th centuries B.C.)
See "Haggai, Zechariah, and Malachi"

Zephaniah (7th century B.C.)
The Books of the Bible, vol. 1: **397–404**

MEDIEVAL

Adam de la Halle (fl. 1250–1300)
    See "Medieval Drama"

Aquinas, Saint Thomas, and Scholasticism
    (1224)
    European Writers, vol. 1: **405–430**
    European Writers Selected Authors, vol. 1: **53–77**

Arabian Nights
    Supernatural Fiction Writers, vol. 1: **19–26**

Arthurian Legend
    European Writers, vol. 1: **137–160**
    European Writers Selected Authors, vol. 1: **79–102**

Arthurian Romances
    Supernatural Fiction Writers, vol. 1: **11–18**

Beowulf and Anglo-Saxon Poetry
    European Writers, vol. 1: **51–88**
    European Writers Selected Authors, vol. 1: **217–253**

Boccaccio, Giovanni (1313)
    European Writers, vol. 2: **509–534**
    European Writers Selected Authors, vol. 1: **255–280**
    See also "Renaissance Pastoral Poetry" in
    Renaissance

Chanson de Roland, The, and the *Chansons de*
    Geste
    European Writers, vol. 1: **89–112**

Chaucer, Geoffrey (1340)
    British Writers, vol. 1: **19–47**
    British Writers Selected Authors, vol. 1: **283–311**

Chrétien de Troyes (fl. 12th century)
    European Writers, vol. 1: **185–209**
    See also "Arthurian Romances"

Cid in Epic and Ballad, The
    European Writers, vol. 1: **113–136**

Dante Alighieri (1265)
    European Writers, vol. 1: **431–450**
    European Writers Selected Authors, vol. 1: **411–430**
    See also "Renaissance Pastoral Poetry" in
    Renaissance

Geoffrey of Monmouth (ca. 1100)
    See "Arthurian Romances"

Gottfried von Strassburg (fl. 1210)
    European Writers, vol. 1: **237–262**
    See also "Arthurian Romances"

Gower, John (1325)
    British Writers, vol. 1: **48–56**

Guillaume de Lorris (fl. ca. 1220–1240)
    See "*Romance of the Rose*, The, and Medieval
    Allegory"

Jean de Meun (ca. 1240–1250)
    See "*Romance of the Rose*, The, and Medieval
    Allegory"

Langland, William: Piers Plowman (1332)
    British Writers, vol. 1: **1–18**

Lydgate, John (1370)
    British Writers, vol. 1: **57–66**

Malory, Sir Thomas (fl. 15th century)
    British Writers, vol. 1: **67–80**
    British Writers Selected Authors, vol. 2: **877–890**
    See also "Arthurian Romances"

Medieval Drama
    European Writers, vol. 1: **451–474**
    European Writers Selected Authors, vol. 2:
    1051–1074

Medieval Satire
    European Writers, vol. 1: **337–376**
    European Writers Selected Authors, vol. 2:
    1075–1113

Nibelungenlied, The (13th century)
    European Writers, vol. 1: **211–236**

Norse Sagas
    European Writers, vol. 1: **377–404**
    European Writers Selected Authors, vol. 3:
    1199–1226

Petrarch (1304)
    European Writers, vol. 2: **475–507**
    European Writers Selected Authors, vol. 2:
    1255–1287
    See also "Renaissance Pastoral Poetry" in
    Renaissance

Romance of the Rose, The, and Medieval Allegory
    (ca. 1225)
    European Writers, vol. 1: **309–335**
    European Writers Selected Authors, vol. 3:
    1491–1517

Troubadours and Trouvères
    European Writers, vol. 1: **161–184**

Villon, François (1431)
European Writers, vol. 2: **535–570**

Walther von der Vogelweide (ca. 1170)
European Writers, vol. 1: **287–308**

Wolfram von Eschenbach (ca. 1170)
European Writers, vol. 1: **263–286**
See also "Arthurian Romances"

RENAISSANCE

Acosta, Father Joseph de (1540)
Latin American Writers, vol. 1: **47–51**

Arabian Nights
Supernatural Fiction Writers, vol. 1: **19–26**

Ariosto, Lodovico (1474)
European Writers, vol. 2: **619–644**

Bacon, Francis (1561)
British Writers, vol. 1: **257–275**

Balbuena, Bernardo de (1561?)
Latin American Writers, vol. 1: **53–57**

Bandello, Matteo (1485)
See "Renaissance Short Fiction"

Basile, Giambattista (1575)
See "Renaissance Short Fiction"

Beaumont, Francis (1584)
See "Beaumont, Francis, and John Fletcher"

Beaumont, Francis, and John Fletcher
British Writers, vol. 2: **42–67**

Bible, The English (1611)
British Writers, vol. 1: **370–388**
British Writers Selected Authors, vol. 1: **69–87**

Camoëns, Luís Vaz de (1524?)
European Writers, vol. 2: **747–767**

Castiglione, Baldesar (1478)
European Writers, vol. 2: **645–667**

Cervantes, Miguel de (1547)
European Writers, vol. 2: **819–844**
European Writers Selected Authors, vol. 1: **335–359**
See also "Renaissance Short Fiction"

Chapman, George (1559)
British Writers, vol. 1: **232–256**

Des Périers, Bonaventure (1510?)
See "Renaissance Short Fiction"

Díaz del Castillo, Bernal (ca. 1496)
Latin American Writers, vol. 1: **17–21**

Donne, John (1572)
British Writers, vol. 1: **352–369**
British Writers Selected Authors, vol. 1: **397–414**

Erasmus, Desiderius (1466)
European Writers, vol. 2: **571–593**
European Writers Selected Authors, vol. 1: **529–551**

Ercilla y Zúñiga, Don Alonso de (1533)
Latin American Writers, vol. 1: **23–31**

Fernández de Oviedo y Valdés, Gonzalo (1478)
Latin American Writers, vol. 1: **11–15**

Fletcher, John (1579)
See "Beaumont, Francis, and John Fletcher"

Ford, John (1586)
British Writers, vol. 2: **87–102**

Garcilaso de la Vega, El Inca (1539)
Latin American Writers, vol. 1: **39–45**

Giraldi, Giambattista (1504)
See "Renaissance Pastoral Poetry"

González de Eslava, Fernán (1534)
Latin American Writers, vol. 1: **33–37**

Guarini, Giambattista (1538)
See "Renaissance Pastoral Poetry"

Herbert, George (1593)
British Writers, vol. 2: **117–130**

Hooker, Richard (1554)
British Writers, vol. 1: **176–190**

Howard, Henry (Earl of Surrey) (1517)
British Writers, vol. 1: **113–120**

Jonson, Ben (1547)
British Writers, vol. 1: **335–352**
British Writers Selected Authors, vol. 2: **665–681**

Kyd, Thomas, and Early Elizabethan Tragedy
(1558)
British Writers, vol. 1: **212–231**

Las Casas, Bartolomé de (1474)
Latin American Writers, vol. 1: **1–9**

Luther, Martin (1483)
European Writers, vol. 2: **669–692**
European Writers Selected Authors, vol. 2: **929–951**

Lyly, John (ca. 1554)
See Lyly, John, and George Peele

Lyly, John, and George Peele
  British Writers, vol. 1: **191–211**

Machiavelli, Niccolò (1469)
  European Writers, vol. 2: **595–618**
  European Writers Selected Authors, vol. 2: **953–976**

Marguerite, Queen of Navarre (1492)
  See "Renaissance Short Fiction"

Marlowe, Christopher (1564)
  British Writers, vol. 1: **275–294**

Marston, John (1576)
  See "Marston, John, and Cyril Tourneur"

Marston, John, and Cyril Tourneur
  British Writers, vol. 2: **24–41**

Masuccio Salernitano (1410–1415)
  See "Renaissance Short Fiction"

Medici, Lorenzo de' (1449)
  See "Renaissance Pastoral Poetry"

Metaphysical Poets, Four
  British Writers, vol. 2: **179–203**

Middleton, Thomas (1580)
  British Writers, vol. 2: **1–23**

Montaigne, Michel de (1533)
  European Writers, vol. 2: **769–790**
  European Writers Selected Authors, vol. 2: **1139–1160**

Montemayor, Jorge de (1520?)
  See "Renaissance Pastoral Poetry"

Oña, Pedro de (1570)
  Latin American Writers, vol. 1: **59–63**

Peele, George (1556)
  See Lyly, John, and George Peele

Petrarch, Francesco (1304)
  European Writers, vol. 2: **475–507**
  European Writers Selected Authors, vol. 2:
    1255–1287
  See also "Renaissance Pastoral Poetry"

Rabelais, François (1494)
  European Writers, vol. 2: **693–720**
  European Writers Selected Authors, vol. 3:
    1375–1402

Ralegh (Raleigh), Sir Walter (1554)
  British Writers, vol. 1: **145–159**

Renaissance Pastoral Poetry
  European Writers, vol. 2: **899–926**
  European Writers Selected Authors, vol. 3: **1403–1430**

Renaissance Short Fiction
  European Writers, vol. 2: **927–956**
  European Writers Selected Authors, vol. 3:
    1431–1460

Ronsard, Pierre de (1524)
  See "Renaissance Pastoral Poetry"

Ronsard, Pierre de, and the Pléiade (1524)
  European Writers, vol. 2: **721–746**

Sacchetti, Franco (1335)
  See "Renaissance Short Fiction"

Sannazaro, Jacopo (1456)
  See "Renaissance Pastoral Poetry"

Shakespeare, William (1564)
  British Writers, vol. 1: **295–334**
  British Writers Selected Authors, vol. 2:
    1013–1052
  Writers for Young Adults, vol. 3: **155–172** (1554)
  See also entries in *William Shakespeare: His
    World, His Work, His Influence*

Sidney, Sir Philip (1460)
  British Writers, vol. 1: **160–175**

Skelton, John (1448)
  British Writers, vol. 1: **81–96**

Spagnola, Giovanni Battista (Mantovano) (1552)
  See "Renaissance Pastoral Poetry"

Spenser, Edmund (late 15th century)
  British Writers, vol. 1: **121–144**
  British Writers Selected Authors, vol. 3: **1121–1144**

Straparola, Gianfrancesco (1544)
  See "Renaissance Short Fiction"

Tasso, Torquato (1575?)
  European Writers, vol. 2: **791–818**

Tourneur, Cyril (1492?)
  See "Marston, John, and Cyril Tourneur"

Tyndale, William (1567)
  See "Bible, The English"

Urfé, Honoré, d' (1562)
  See "Renaissance Pastoral Poetry"

Vega, Lope de (1580)
  European Writers, vol. 2: **845–870**

Webster, John (1503)
  British Writers, vol. 2: **68–86**

Wyatt, Sir Thomas
  British Writers, vol. 1: **97–112**

Seventeenth Century

Arabian Nights
    Supernatural Fiction Writers, vol. 1: **19–26**

Bacon, Francis (1561)
    British Writers, vol. 1: **257–275**

Balbuena, Bernardo de (1561?)
    Latin American Writers, vol. 1: **53–57**

Basile, Giambattista (1575)
    See "Renaissance Short Fiction" in Renaissance

Beaumont, Francis, and John Fletcher
    British Writers, vol. 2: **42–67**

Behn, Aphra (1640)
    British Writers Supp. 3: **19–43**

Bible, The English (1611)
    British Writers, vol. 1: **370–388**
    British Writers Selected Authors, vol. 1: **69–87**

Boileau-Despréaux, Nicolas (1636)
    European Writers, vol. 3: **177–205**

Bossuet, Jacques Bénigne (1627)
    European Writers, vol. 3: **151–175**

Bradstreet, Anne (1612)
    American Writers Supp. 1, part 1: **98–123**

Browne, Sir Thomas (1605)
    British Writers, vol. 2: **145–157**

Bunyan, John (1628)
    British Writers, vol. 2: **240–254**
    British Writers Selected Authors, vol. 1: **215–229**
    Writers for Children: **97–102**

Calderón de la Barca, Pedro (1600)
    European Writers, vol. 2: **871–895**

Carew, Thomas (ca. 1595)
    See "Cavalier Poets, The"

Cavalier Poets, The
    British Writers, vol. 2: **221–239**

Cervantes, Miguel de (1547)
    European Writers, vol. 2: **819–844**
    European Writers Selected Authors, vol. 1: **335–359**
    See also "Renaissance Short Fiction" in Renaissance

Chapman, George (1559)
    British Writers, vol. 1: **232–256**

Corneille, Pierre (1606)
    European Writers, vol. 3: **23–49**

Cowley, Abraham (1618)
    See "Metaphysical Poets, Four"

Crashaw, Richard (ca. 1613)
    See "Metaphysical Poets, Four"

Defoe, Daniel (1660?)
    British Writers, vol. 3: **1–14**
    British Writers Selected Authors, vol. 1: **349–362**
    Writers for Children: **163–171**

Descartes, René (1596)
    European Writers, vol. 3: **1–22**
    European Writers Selected Authors, vol. 1: **431–452**

Donne, John (1572)
    British Writers, vol. 1: **352–369**
    British Writers Selected Authors, vol. 1: **397–414**

Dryden, John (1631)
    British Writers, vol. 2: **289–306**

Etherege, Sir George (1635)
    See "Restoration Court Poets, The"

Evelyn, John (1620)
    See "Evelyn, John, and Samuel Pepys"

Evelyn, John, and Samuel Pepys
    British Writers, vol. 2: **274–288**

Farquhar, George (1678)
    British Writers, vol. 2: **351–365**

Fénelon, François de Salignac de la Mothe-
    (1651)
    European Writers, vol. 3: **261–291**

Fletcher, John (1579)
    See "Beaumont, Francis, and John Fletcher"

Ford, John (1586)
    British Writers, vol. 2: **87–102**

Guarini, Giambattista (1538)
    See "Renaissance Pastoral Poetry" in
    Renaissance

Herbert, George (1593)
    British Writers, vol. 2: **117–130**

Herrick, Robert (1591)
    British Writers, vol. 2: **102–116**

Juana Inéz de La Cruz, Sor (1651)
    Latin American Writers, vol. 1: **85–106**

La Bruyère, Jean de (1645)
    European Writers, vol. 3: **229–260**

La Fontaine, Jean de (1621)
European Writers, vol. 3: **73–100**
European Writers Selected Authors, vol. 2: **901–928**

La Rochefoucauld, François VI, Duc de (1613)
European Writers, vol. 3: **51–71**

Lesage, Alain-René (1668)
European Writers, vol. 3: **317–344**

Lovelace, Richard (ca. 1618)
See "Cavalier Poets, The"

Marston, John (1576)
See "Marston, John, and Cyril Tourneur"

Marston, John, and Cyril Tourneur
British Writers, vol. 2: **24–41**

Marvell, Andrew (1621)
British Writers, vol. 2: **204–220**

Mather, Cotton (1663)
American Writers Supp. 2, part 2: **441–470**

Mattos, Gregório de (1636)
Latin American Writers, vol. 1: **65–69**

Metaphysical Poets, Four
British Writers, vol. 2: **179–203**

Middleton, Thomas (1580)
British Writers, vol. 2: **1–23**

Milton, John (1608)
British Writers, vol. 2: **158–178**
British Writers Selected Authors, vol. 2: **925–945**

Molière (1622)
European Writers, vol. 3: **101–124**
European Writers Selected Authors, vol. 2: **1115–1137**

Montesquieu, Charles-Louis de Secondat (1689)
European Writers, vol. 3: **345–366**

Nature in Native American Literatures
American Nature Writers, vol. 2: **1141–1156**

Oña, Pedro de (1570)
Latin American Writers, vol. 1: **59–63**

Pascal, Blaise (1623)
European Writers, vol. 3: **125–150**

Pepys, Samuel (1620)
See "Evelyn, John, and Samuel Pepys"

Perrault, Charles (1628)
Writers for Children: **431–437**

Racine, Jean (1639)
European Writers, vol. 3: **207–228**

Restoration Court Poets, The
British Writers, vol. 2: **255–272**

Sackville, Charles (Earl of Dorset) (1643)
See "Restoration Court Poets, The"

Sedley, Sir Charles (1639)
See "Restoration Court Poets, The"

Shakespeare, William (1564)
British Writers, vol. 1: **295–334**
British Writers Selected Authors, vol. 2: **1013–1052**
Writers for Young Adults, vol. 3: **155–172**
See also entries in *William Shakespeare: His World, His Work, His Influence*

Sigüenza y Góngora, Carlos de (1645)
Latin American Writers, vol. 1: **71–77**

Suckling, Sir John (1609)
See "Cavalier Poets, The"

Swift, Jonathan (1667)
British Writers, vol. 3: **15–38**
British Writers Selected Authors, vol. 3: **1195–1217**
Writers for Children: **555–559**

Taylor, Edward (1642)
American Writers, vol. 4: **144–166**

Tourneur, Cyril (1575?)
See "Marston, John, and Cyril Tourneur"

Traherne, Thomas (ca. 1637)
See "Metaphysical Poets, Four"

Urfé, Honoré, d' (1567)
See "Renaissance Pastoral Poetry" in Renaissance

Valle y Caviedes, Juan del (1645?)
Latin American Writers, vol. 1: **79–83**

Vaughan, Henry (ca. 1622)
See "Metaphysical Poets, Four"

Vega, Lope de (1562)
European Writers, vol. 2: **845–870**

Vico, Giovanni Battista (1668)
European Writers, vol. 3: **293–316**

Waller, Edmund (1606)
See "Cavalier Poets, The"

Walton, Izaak (1593)
British Writers, vol. 2: **131–144**

Webster, John (1580)
British Writers, vol. 2: **68–86**

Wilmot, John (Earl of Rochester) (1647)
See "Restoration Court Poets, The"

Wycherley, William (1641)
British Writers, vol. 2: **307–322**

EIGHTEENTH CENTURY

Addison, Joseph (1672)
See "Steele, Sir Richard, and Joseph Addison"

Alfieri, Vittorio (1749)
European Writers, vol. 4: **661–689**

Barlow, Joel (1754)
American Writers Supp. 2, part 1: **65–86**

Bartram, William (1739)
American Nature Writers, vol. 1: **63–74**

Beaumarchais, Pierre-Augustin Caron de (1732)
European Writers, vol. 4: **563–585**

Beckford, William (1760)
Supernatural Fiction Writers, vol. 1: **139–144**
See also "Gothic Novel, The"

Blake, William (1757)
British Writers, vol. 3: **288–310**
British Writers Selected Authors, vol. 1: **89–110**
Writers for Children: **69–76**

Boileau-Despréaux, Nicolas (1636)
European Writers, vol. 3: **177–205**

Bossuet, Jacques Bénigne (1627)
European Writers, vol. 3: **151–175**

Boswell, James (1740)
British Writers, vol. 3: **234–251**
British Writers Selected Authors, vol. 1: **111–128**

Burke, Edmund (1729)
British Writers, vol. 3: **193–207**

Burney, Frances (1752)
British Writers Supp. 3: **63–78**

Burns, Robert (1759)
British Writers, vol. 3: **310–323**
British Writers Selected Authors, vol. 1: **231–244**

Canadian Nature Writing in English
American Nature Writers, vol. 2: **1025–1040**

Carrió de la Vandera, Alonso (ca. 1715)
Latin American Writers, vol. 1: **107–111**

Cazotte, Jacques (1719)
Supernatural Fiction Writers, vol. 1: **29–35**

Chateaubriand, François René de (1768)
European Writers, vol. 5: **113–140**

Chénier, André (1762)
European Writers, vol. 4: **691–718**

Collins, William (1721)
British Writers, vol. 3: **160–176**

Congreve, William (1670)
British Writers, vol. 2: **338–350**

Constant, Benjamin (1767)
See "French Novelists, Three"

Costa, Cláudio Manuel da (1729)
Latin American Writers, vol. 1: **113–117**

Cowper, William (1731)
British Writers, vol. 3: **207–220**

Crabbe, George (1754)
British Writers, vol. 3: **272–287**

Crèvecoeur, Hector St. John de (1735)
American Writers Supp. 1, part 1: **227–252**
See also "Early Romantic Natural History Literature"

Defoe, Daniel (1660?)
British Writers, vol. 3: **1–14**
British Writers Selected Authors, vol. 1: **349–362**
Writers for Children: **163–171**

Diderot, Denis (1713)
European Writers, vol. 4: **475–509**

Early Romantic Natural History Literature
American Nature Writers, vol. 2: **1059–1078**

Edgeworth, Maria (1768)
British Writers Supp. 3: **151–168**

Edwards, Jonathan (1703)
American Writers, vol. 1: **544–566**

Equiano, Olaudah (1745)
See "Slave Narrative in American Literature, The"

Fénelon, François de Salignac de la Mothe- (1651)
European Writers, vol. 3: **261–291**

Fielding, Henry (1707)
British Writers, vol. 3: **94–106**
British Writers Selected Authors, vol. 2: **497–509**

Foscolo, Ugo (1778)
European Writers, vol. 5: **313–341**

Franklin, Benjamin (1706)
American Writers, vol. 2: **101–125**

French Novelists, Three
European Writers, vol. 4: **393–419**

Freneau, Philip (1752)
American Writers Supp. 2, part 1: **253–277**

Gay, John (1685)
  British Writers, vol. 3: **54–68**

Gibbon, Edward (1737)
  British Writers, vol. 3: **221–233**

Goethe, Johann Wolfgang von (1749)
  European Writers, vol. 5: **1–26**
  European Writers Selected Authors, vol. 1: **655–680**

Goldoni, Carlo (1707)
  European Writers, vol. 4: **421–448**

Goldsmith, Oliver (1728)
  British Writers, vol. 3: **177–192**

Gothic Novel, The
  British Writers, vol. 3: **324–346**

Gray, Thomas (1716)
  British Writers, vol. 3: **136–145**

Herder, Johann Gottfried von (1744)
  European Writers, vol. 4: **639–660**

Hölderlin, Friedrich (1770)
  European Writers, vol. 5: **143–173**

Hume, David (1711)
  British Writers Supp. 3: **229–245**

Jefferson, Thomas (1743)
  See "Early Romantic Natural History Literature"

Johnson, Samuel (1709)
  British Writers, vol. 3: **107–123**
  British Writers Selected Authors, vol. 2: **647–663**

Kleist, Heinrich von (1777)
  European Writers, vol. 5: **291–312**

Klopstock, Friedrich Gottlieb (1724)
  European Writers, vol. 4: **511–536**

Laclos, Choderlos de (1741)
  See "French Novelists, Three"

Lesage, Alain-René (1668)
  European Writers, vol. 3: **317–344**

Lessing, Gotthold Ephraim (1729)
  European Writers, vol. 4: **537–562**

Lewis, M. G. (1775)
  Supernatural Fiction Writers, vol. 1: **153–160**

Literature of Mountaineering
  American Nature Writers, vol. 2: **1115–1128**

Mather, Cotton (1663)
  American Writers Supp. 2, part 2: **441–470**

Montesquieu, Charles-Louis de Secondat (1689)
  European Writers, vol. 3: **345–366**

Musaeus, J. K. (1735)
  Supernatural Fiction Writers, vol. 1: **75–81**

Nature in Native American Literatures
  American Nature Writers, vol. 2: **1141–1156**

Novalis (1772)
  European Writers, vol. 5: **205–231**

Paine, Thomas (1737)
  American Writers Supp. 1, part 2: **501–525**

Perrault, Charles (1628)
  Writers for Children: **431–437**

Pope, Alexander (1688)
  British Writers, vol. 3: **68–79**
  British Writers Selected Authors, vol. 2: **1001–1012**

Prévost, Antoine-Francois (1697)
  See "French Novelists, Three"

Radcliffe, Ann (1764)
  Supernatural Fiction Writers, vol. 1: **145–151**

Richardson, Samuel (1689)
  British Writers, vol. 3: **80–94**

Richter, Jean Paul (1763)
  European Writers, vol. 5: **53–88**

Rousseau, Jean Jacques (1712)
  European Writers, vol. 4: **449–474**
  European Writers Selected Authors, vol. 3: **1519–1544**

Sade, Marquis de, and the French Libertine Tradition (1740)
  European Writers, vol. 4: **615–638**

Schiller, Friedrich von (1759)
  European Writers, vol. 5: **27–52**

Schlegel, Friedrich von (1772)
  European Writers, vol. 5: **177–203**

Sheridan, Richard Brinsley (1751)
  British Writers, vol. 3: **252–271**

Slave Narrative in American Literature, The
  African American Writers: **395–412**

Smollett, Tobias (1721)
  British Writers, vol. 3: **146–159**

Staël, Madame de (1766)
  European Writers, vol. 5: **89–111**

Steele, Sir Richard (1672)
  See "Steele, Sir Richard, and Joseph Addison"

Steele, Sir Richard, and Joseph Addison
  British Writers, vol. 3: **38–53**
  British Writers Selected Authors, vol. 3: **1145–1160**

Sterne, Laurence (1713)
British Writers, vol. 3: **124–136**

Swift, Jonathan (1667)
British Writers, vol. 3: **15–38**
British Writers Selected Authors, vol. 3: **1195–1217**
Writers for Children: **555–559**

Taylor, Edward (1642)
American Writers, vol. 4: **144–166**

Thomson, James (1700)
British Writers Supp. 3: **409–429**

Tieck, Ludwig (1773)
European Writers, vol. 5: **233–260**
Supernatural Fiction Writers, vol. 1: **83–89**

Vanbrugh, Sir John (1664)
British Writers, vol. 2: **323–337**

Vico, Giovanni Battista (1668)
European Writers, vol. 3: **293–316**

Voltaire (1694)
European Writers, vol. 4: **367–392**
European Writers Selected Authors, vol. 3:
1741–1766

Walpole, Horace (1717)
Supernatural Fiction Writers, vol. 1: **131–137**
See also "Gothic Novel, The"

Wheatley, Phillis (1753)
African American Writers: **473–491**

Wieland, Christoph Martin (1733)
European Writers, vol. 4: **587–614**

Wilson, Alexander (1766)
See "Early Romantic Natural History
Literature"

Wollstonecraft, Mary (1759)
British Writers Supp. 3: **465–482**

Nineteenth Century

Acevedo Díaz, Eduardo (1851)
Latin American Writers, vol. 1: **299–303**

Adams, Henry (1838)
American Writers, vol. 1: **1–24**

Addams, Jane (1860)
American Writers Supp. 1, part 1: **1–27**

Ainsworth, William Harrison (1805)
Supernatural Fiction Writers, vol. 1: **187–193**

Alberdi, Juan Bautista (1810)
Latin American Writers, vol. 1: **153–158**

Alcott, Louisa May (1832)
American Writers Supp. 1, part 1: **28–46**
Writers for Children: **1–6**
Writers for Young Adults, vol. 1: **11–20**

Alencar, José de (1829)
Latin American Writers, vol. 1: **195–203**

Andersen, Hans Christian (1805)
European Writers, vol. 6: **863–892**
European Writers Selected Authors, vol. 1: **1–29**
Writers for Children: **7–13**

Anstey, F. (1856)
Supernatural Fiction Writers, vol. 1: **287–292**

Arnold, Matthew (1822)
British Writers, vol. 5: **203–218**

Arthurian Romances
Supernatural Fiction Writers, vol. 1: **11–18**

Asbjørnsen, Peter Christen (1812)
See "Asbjørnsen and Moe"

Asbjørnsen and Moe (Peter Christen
Asbjørnsen and Jørgen Moe)
Writers for Children: **21–28**

Ascasubi, Hilario (1807)
Latin American Writers, vol. 1: **147–151**

Atherton, Gertrude (1857)
Supernatural Fiction Writers, vol. 2: **777–781**

Audubon, John James (1785)
See "Early Romantic Natural History Literature"

Augier, Émile (1820)
See "Well-Made Play, The"

Austen, Jane (1775)
British Writers, vol. 4: **101–124**
British Writers Selected Authors, vol. 1: **23–46**

Austin, Mary Hunter (1868)
American Nature Writers, vol. 1: **31–51**

Austin, William (1778)
Supernatural Fiction Writers, vol. 2: **693–696**

Azevedo, Aluísio (1857)
Latin American Writers, vol. 1: **333–341**

Azorín (1873)
  European Writers, vol. 9: **639–661**

Azuela, Mariano (1873)
  Latin American Writers, vol. 2: **457–464**

Bailey, Florence Merriam (1863)
  American Nature Writers, vol. 1: **53–62**

Balzac, Honoré de (1799)
  European Writers, vol. 5: **635–658**
  European Writers Selected Authors, vol. 1: **161–183**
  Supernatural Fiction Writers, vol. 1: **37–44**

Bangs, J. K. (1862)
  Supernatural Fiction Writers, vol. 2: **725–729**

Barlow, Joel (1754)
  American Writers Supp. 2, part 1: **65–86**

Baroja, Pío (1872)
  European Writers, vol. 9: **589–616**

Barrie, J. M. (1860)
  British Writers Supp. 3: **1–17**
  Supernatural Fiction Writers, vol. 1: **405–410**
  Writers for Children: **29–35**

Bartram, William (1739)
  American Nature Writers, vol. 1: **63–74**

Baudelaire, Charles (1821)
  European Writers, vol. 7: **1323–1348**

Bauernfeld, Eduard von (1802)
  See "Well-Made Play, The"

Baum, L. Frank (1856)
  Writers for Children: **37–48**

Beckford, William (1760)
  Supernatural Fiction Writers, vol. 1: **139–144**
  See also "Gothic Novel, The"

Beerbohm, Max (1872)
  British Writers Supp. 2: **43–59**

Bello, Andrés (1781)
  Latin American Writers, vol. 1: **129–134**

Belloc, Hilaire (1870)
  Writers for Children: **49–54**

Benson, E. F. (1867)
  Supernatural Fiction Writers, vol. 1: **491–496**

Bergson, Henri (1859)
  European Writers, vol. 8: **45–66**

Berlioz, Hector (1803)
  European Writers, vol. 6: **771–812**

Bierce, Ambrose (1842)
  American Writers, vol. 1: **190–213**
  Supernatural Fiction Writers, vol. 2: **731–737**

Blake, William (1757)
  British Writers, vol. 3: **288–310**
  British Writers Selected Authors, vol. 1: **89–110**
  Writers for Children: **69–76**

Blanco Fombona, Rufino (1874)
  Latin American Writers, vol. 2: **503–511**

Blasco Ibáñez, Vicente (1867)
  European Writers, vol. 8: **355–388**

Blest Gana, Alberto (1830)
  Latin American Writers, vol. 1: **205–213**

Bridges, Robert (1844)
  British Writers, vol. 6: **71–84**

Brieux, Eugène (1858)
  See "Well-Made Play, The"

Brontës, The (1816)
  British Writers, vol. 5: **105–154**
  British Writers Selected Authors, vol. 1:
    129–177

Brown, Charles Brockden (1771)
  American Writers Supp. 1, part 1: **124–149**

Browning, Elizabeth Barrett (1806)
  British Writers, vol. 4: **310–322**
  British Writers Selected Authors, vol. 1: **179–191**

Browning, Robert (1812)
  British Writers, vol. 4: **354–375**
  British Writers Selected Authors, vol. 1: **193–214**

Bryant, William Cullen (1794)
  American Writers Supp. 1, part 1: **150–173**

Büchner, Georg (1813)
  European Writers, vol. 6: **1169–1194**

Bulwer-Lytton, Edward (1803)
  Supernatural Fiction Writers, vol. 1: **195–204**

Burckhardt, Jacob (1818)
  European Writers, vol. 6: **1225–1244**

Burnett, Frances Hodgson (1849)
  Writers for Children: **103–109**

Burney, Frances (1752)
  British Writers Supp. 3: **63–78**

Burroughs, John (1837)
  American Nature Writers, vol. 1: **121–138**

Butler, Samuel (1835)
British Writers Supp. 2: **97–121**

Byron, Lord (1788)
British Writers, vol. 4: **171–194**
British Writers Selected Authors, vol. 1: **245–268**

Cabell, James Branch (1879)
Supernatural Fiction Writers, vol. 2: **789–796**

Cambaceres, Eugenio (1843)
Latin American Writers, vol. 1: **269–276**

Campo, Estanislao del (1834)
Latin American Writers, vol. 1: **229–233**

Canadian Nature Writing in English
American Nature Writers, vol. 2: **1025–1040**

Carducci, Giosue (1835)
European Writers, vol. 7: **1495–1516**

Carlyle, Thomas (1795)
British Writers, vol. 4: **238–250**
British Writers Selected Authors, vol. 1: **269–281**

Caro, Miguel Antonio (1843)
Latin American Writers, vol. 1: **277–281**

Carrasquilla, Tomás (1858)
Latin American Writers, vol. 1: **343–350**

Carroll, Lewis (1832)
British Writers, vol. 5: **261–276**
Supernatural Fiction Writers, vol. 1: **247–253**
Writers for Children: **117–127**

Casal, Julián del (1863)
Latin American Writers, vol. 1: **365–370**

Castro Alves, Antônio de (1847)
Latin American Writers, vol. 1: **289–297**

Cavafy, Constantin (1863)
European Writers, vol. 8: **205–228**

Chambers, Robert W. (1865)
Supernatural Fiction Writers, vol. 2: **739–745**

Chamisso, Adelbert von (1781)
Supernatural Fiction Writers, vol. 1: **91–95**

Chateaubriand, François René de (1768)
European Writers, vol. 5: **113–140**

Chekhov, Anton (1860)
European Writers, vol. 7: **1855–1882**
European Writers Selected Authors, vol. 1:
361–387

Chesnutt, Charles W. (1858)
African American Writers: **59–70**

Chocano, José Santos (1875)
Latin American Writers, vol. 2: **543–549**

Chopin, Kate (1851)
American Writers Supp. 1, part 1: **200–226**
Modern American Women Writers: **63–78**

Claudel, Paul (1868)
European Writers, vol. 8: **471–494**

Clough, Arthur Hugh (1819)
British Writers, vol. 5: **155–172**

Coleridge, Samuel Taylor (1772)
British Writers, vol. 4: **41–57**
British Writers Selected Authors, vol. 1: **313–329**

Collins, Wilkie (1824)
Supernatural Fiction Writers, vol. 1: **233–238**

Collodi, C. (1826)
Writers for Children: **129–137**

Comstock, Anna Botsford (1854)
American Nature Writers, vol. 1: **173–185**

Conrad, Joseph (1857)
British Writers, vol. 6: **133–150**
British Writers Selected Authors, vol. 1: **331–348**

Constant, Benjamin (1767)
See "French Novelists, Three"

Cooper, James Fenimore (1789)
American Writers, vol. 1: **335–357**
Writers for Children: **147–153**

Cooper, Susan Fenimore (1813)
American Nature Writers, vol. 1: **187–198**

Corelli, Marie (1855)
Supernatural Fiction Writers, vol. 1: **293–297**

Crabbe, George (1754)
British Writers, vol. 3: **272–287**

Crane, Stephen (1871)
American Writers, vol. 1: **405–427**
Writers for Young Adults, vol. 1: **303–312**

Crawford, F. Marion (1815)
Supernatural Fiction Writers, vol. 2: **747–751**

Croce, Benedetto (1866)
European Writers, vol. 8: **311–329**

Cruz e Sousa, João (1861)
Latin American Writers, vol. 1: **359–363**

Cunha, Euclides da (1866)
Latin American Writers, vol. 1: **387–395**

D'Annunzio, Gabriele (1863)
  European Writers, vol. 8: **175–203**

Darío, Rubén (1867)
  Latin American Writers, vol. 1: **397–412**

Delacroix, Eugène (1798)
  European Writers, vol. 5: **513–539**

De la Mare, Walter (1873)
  Supernatural Fiction Writers, vol. 1: **497–503**
  Writers for Children: **173–180**

De Quincey, Thomas (1785)
  British Writers, vol. 4: **141–156**

Díaz Rodríguez, Manuel (1871)
  Latin American Writers, vol. 1: **431–439**

Dickens, Charles (1812)
  British Writers, vol. 5: **41–74**
  British Writers Selected Authors, vol. 1: **363–396**
  Supernatural Fiction Writers, vol.1: **213–218**
  Writers for Children: **181–191**
  Writers for Young Adults, vol. 1: **353–364**

Dickinson, Emily (1830)
  American Writers, vol. 1: **451–473**
  American Writers Retrospective: **25–50**
  Modern American Women Writers: **77–89**
  Writers for Young Adults, vol. 1: **365–372**

Disraeli, Benjamin (1804)
  British Writers, vol. 4: **292–309**

Dodge, Mary Mapes (1831)
  Writers for Children: **193–199**

Dostoevsky, Feodor (1821)
  European Writers, vol. 7: **1349–1373**
  European Writers Selected Authors, vol. 1: **479–501**

Douglass, Frederick (1818)
  American Writers Supp. 3, part 1: **153–174**
  See also "Slave Narrative in American
    Literature, The"

Doyle, Sir Arthur Conan (1859)
  British Writers Supp. 2: **159–178**
  British Writers Selected Authors, vol. 1: **415–434**
  Science Fiction Writers: **45–50**
  Writers for Children: **201–207**
  Writers for Young Adults, vol. 1: **385–392**

Du Bois, W. E. B. (1868)
  African American Writers: **71–87**
  American Writers Supp. 2, part 1: **157–189**

Dumas, Alexandre (Fils) (1824)
  See "Well-Made Play, The"

Dumas, Alexandre (Père) (1802)
  European Writers, vol. 6: **719–745**
  European Writers Selected Authors, vol. 1: **503–527**
  Writers for Children: **209–213**

Dunbar, Paul Laurence (1872)
  African American Writers: **87–102**
  American Writers Supp. 2, part 1: **191–219**

Early Romantic Natural History Literature
  American Nature Writers, vol. 2: **1059–1078**

Eça de Queiroz, José Maria (1845)
  European Writers, vol. 7: **1683–1708**

Echeverría, Esteban (1805)
  Latin American Writers, vol. 1: **141–145**

Edgeworth, Maria (1768)
  British Writers Supp. 3: **151–168**

Edwards, Amelia B. (1831)
  Supernatural Fiction Writers, vol. 1: **255–260**

Eliot, George (1819)
  British Writers, vol. 5: **187–201**
  British Writers Selected Authors, vol. 1: **453–467**

Emerson, Ralph Waldo (1803)
  American Nature Writers, vol. 1: **287–307**
  American Writers, vol. 2: **1–24**

Ewing, Juliana Horatia (1841)
  Writers for Children: **221–226**

Fernández, Macedonio (1874)
  Latin American Writers, vol. 2: **483–491**

Fernández de Lizardi, José Joaquín (1776)
  Latin American Writers, vol. 1: **119–128**

Feydeau, Georges (1862)
  See "Well-Made Play, The"

Fitzgerald, Edward (1809)
  British Writers, vol. 4: **340–353**

Flaubert, Gustave (1821)
  European Writers, vol. 7: **1373–1394**
  European Writers Selected Authors, vol. 1:
    553–574

Fontane, Theodor (1819)
  European Writers, vol. 6: **1299–1322**

Ford, Ford Madox (1873)
  British Writers, vol. 2: **87–102**

Forms of American Nature Poetry, The
  American Nature Writers, vol. 2: **1079–1098**

Foscolo, Ugo (1778)
  European Writers, vol. 5: **313–341**

Fouqué, Friedrich de la Motte (1777)
  Supernatural Fiction Writers, vol. 1: **97–105**

France, Anatole (1844)
  Supernatural Fiction Writers, vol. 1: **67–72**

Frazer, James George (1854)
  British Writers Supp. 3: **169–190**

Frederic, Harold (1856)
  American Writers, vol. 2: **126–149**

Freeman, Mary E. Wilkins (1852)
  Modern American Women Writers: **141–153**
  Supernatural Fiction Writers, vol. 2: **769–773**

French Novelists, Three
  European Writers, vol. 4: **393–419**

Freud, Sigmund (1856)
  European Writers, vol. 8: **1–20**
  European Writers Selected Authors, vol. 1: **575–594**

Freytag, Gustav (1816)
  See "Well-Made Play, The"

Fuller, Margaret (1810)
  American Writers Supp. 2, part 1: **279–306**

Gamboa, Federico (1864)
  Latin American Writers, vol. 1: **371–375**

Garnett, Richard (1835)
  Supernatural Fiction Writers, vol. 1: **317–320**

Gaskell, Elizabeth (1810)
  British Writers, vol. 5: **1–16**

Gautier, Théophile (1811)
  European Writers, vol. 6: **1033–1059**
  Supernatural Fiction Writers, vol. 1: **45–50**

George, Stefan (1868)
  European Writers, vol. 8: **447–470**

Gide, André (1869)
  European Writers, vol. 8: **495–518**
  European Writers Selected Authors, vol. 1: **631–654**

Gilman, Charlotte Perkins (1860)
  Modern American Women Writers: **155–170**

Gissing, George (1857)
  British Writers, vol. 5: **423–438**

Glasgow, Ellen (1873)
  American Writers, vol. 2: **173–195**
  Modern American Women Writers: **171–180**

Goethe, Johann Wolfgang von (1749)
  European Writers, vol. 5: **1–26**
  European Writers Selected Authors, vol. 1: **655–680**

Gogol, Nikolay Vasilievich (1809)
  European Writers, vol. 6: **971–998**

Gómez Carillo, Enrique (1873)
  Latin American Writers, vol. 2: **465–469**

Gómez de Avellaneda, Gertrudis (1814)
  Latin American Writers, vol. 1: **175–180**

Gonçalves Dias, Antônio (1823)
  Latin American Writers, vol. 1: **185–193**

Goncharov, Ivan (1812)
  European Writers, vol. 6: **1061–1087**

Goncourt, Edmond Louis Antoine de (1822)
  See "Goncourt, Edmond Louis Antoine de, and
    Jules Alfred Huot de Goncourt"

Goncourt, Edmond Louis Antoine de, and Jules
    Alfred Huot de Goncourt
  European Writers, vol. 7: **1395–1419**

Goncourt, Jules Alfred Huot de (1830)
  See "Goncourt, Edmond Louis Antoine de, and
    Jules Alfred Huot de Goncourt"

González Prada, Manuel (1844)
  Latin American Writers, vol. 1: **283–288**

Gorky, Maxim (1868)
  European Writers, vol. 8: **417–446**
  European Writers Selected Authors, vol. 2: **681–710**

Gothic Novel, The
  British Writers, vol. 3: **324–346**

Grahame, Kenneth (1859)
  Writers for Children: **247–254**

Grillparzer, Franz (1791)
  European Writers, vol. 5: **417–445**

Grimm, Jacob (1785)
  See "Grimm, Jacob and Wilhelm"

Grimm, Jacob and Wilhelm
  Writers for Children: **255–263**

Grimm, Wilhelm (1786)
  See "Grimm, Jacob and Wilhelm"

Gutiérrez Nájera, Manuel (1859)
  Latin American Writers, vol. 1: **351–357**

Gutzkow, Karl (1811)
  See "Well-Made Play, The"

Haggard, H. Rider (1856)
  British Writers Supp. 3: **211–228**
  Science Fiction Writers: **19–24**
  Supernatural Fiction Writers, vol. 1: **321–327**

Hale, Lucretia P. (1820)
  Writers for Children: **265–268**

Hamsun, Knut (1859)
  European Writers, vol. 8: **21–43**

Hardy, Thomas (1840)
  British Writers, vol. 6: **1–22**
  British Writers Selected Authors, vol. 2:
      577–598

Harper, Frances Ellen Watkins (1825)
  African American Writers: **159–175**
  Modern American Women Writers: **197–205**

Harris, Joel Chandler (1848)
  Writers for Children: **269–275**

Harte, Bret (1836)
  American Writers Supp. 2, part 1: **335–359**

Hauff, William (1802)
  Supernatural Fiction Writers, vol. 1: **107–110**

Hauptmann, Gerhart (1862)
  European Writers, vol. 8: **147–174**

Hawthorne, Nathaniel (1804)
  American Writers, vol. 2: **223–246**
  American Writers Retrospective: **145–167**
  Supernatural Fiction Writers, vol. 2: **707–715**
  Writers for Children: **277–282**

Hazlitt, William (1778)
  British Writers, vol. 4: **125–140**

Hebbel, Friedrich (1813)
  European Writers, vol. 6: **1089–1122**

Heine, Heinrich (1797)
  European Writers, vol. 5: **489–512**

Herder, Johann Gottfried von (1744)
  European Writers, vol. 4: **639–660**

Heredia, José Mariá (1803)
  Latin American Writers, vol. 1: **135–140**

Hernández, José (1834)
  Latin American Writers, vol. 1: **235–247**

Herrera y Reissig, Julio (1875)
  Latin American Writers, vol. 2: **519–530**

Hervieu, Paul (1857)
  See "Well-Made Play, The"

Hichens, Robert (1864)
  Supernatural Fiction Writers, vol. 1: **415–420**

Hoffmann, E. T. A. (1776)
  European Writers, vol. 5: **261–289**
  Supernatural Fiction Writers, vol. 1: **111–119**
  Writers for Children: **283–288**

Hoffmann, Heinrich (1809)
  Writers for Children: **289–294**

Hofmannsthal, Hugo von (1874)
  European Writers, vol. 9: **689–714**

Hogg, James (1770)
  Supernatural Fiction Writers, vol. 1: **177–183**

Hölderlin, Friedrich (1770)
  European Writers, vol. 5: **143–173**

Holmes, Oliver Wendell (1809)
  American Writers Supp. 1, part 1: **299–319**

Hood, Thomas (1799)
  British Writers, vol. 4: **251–267**

Hopkins, Gerard Manley (1844)
  British Writers, vol. 5: **361–382**
  British Writers Selected Authors, vol. 2: **599–620**

Housman, A. E. (1859)
  British Writers, vol. 6: **151–164**
  British Writers Selected Authors, vol. 2: **621–634**

Hugo, Victor (1802)
  European Writers, vol. 6: **693–718**
  European Writers Selected Authors, vol. 2:
      761–786

Huysmans, Joris Karl (1847)
  European Writers, vol. 7: **1709–1729**

Ibsen, Henrik (1828)
  European Writers, vol. 7: **1421–1448**
  European Writers Selected Authors, vol. 2: **787–813**

Irving, Washington (1783)
  American Writers, vol. 2: **295–318**
  Supernatural Fiction Writers, vol. 2: **685–691**
  Writers for Children: **303–307**

Isaacs, Jorge (1837)
  Latin American Writers, vol. 1: **247–251**

Jacobs, Harriet (1813)
  See "Slave Narrative in American Literature, The"

Jacobs, Joseph (1854)
  Writers for Children: **309–316**

Jacobs, W. W. (1863)
  Supernatural Fiction Writers, vol. 1: **383–387**

Jaimes Freyre, Ricardo (1868)
  Latin American Writers, vol. 1: **419–423**

James, Henry (1843)
  American Writers, vol. 2: **319–341**
  American Writers Retrospective: **215–242**
  British Writers, vol. 6: **23–69**
  Supernatural Fiction Writers, vol. 1: **337–344**

James, M. R. (1862)
Supernatural Fiction Writers, vol. 1: **429–436**

James, William (1842)
American Writers, vol. 2: **342–366**

Jarry, Alfred (1873)
European Writers, vol. 9: **665–687**

Jefferson, Thomas (1743)
See "Early Romantic Natural History Literature"

Jewett, Sarah Orne (1849)
American Writers, vol. 2: **391–414**
Modern American Women Writers: **235–250**

Jones, Henry Arthur (1851)
See "Well-Made Play, The"

Keats, John (1795)
British Writers, vol. 4: **211–238**
British Writers Selected Authors, vol. 2: **701–727**

Keller, Gottfried (1819)
See "Poetic Realism"

Kierkegaard, Søren (1813)
European Writers, vol. 6: **1123–1146**
European Writers Selected Authors, vol. 2: **877–900**

King, Clarence (1842)
See "Western Geologists and Explorers"

Kingsley, Charles (1819)
Writers for Children: **323–327**

Kipling, Rudyard (1865)
British Writers, vol. 6: **165–206**
British Writers Selected Authors, vol. 2: **729–770**
Supernatural Fiction Writers, vol. 1: **437–442**
Writers for Children: **329–336**

Kleist, Heinrich von (1777)
European Writers, vol. 5: **291–312**

Labiche, Eugène (1815)
See "Well-Made Play, The"

Laforgue, Jules (1860)
European Writers, vol. 7: **1883–1908**

Lamb, Charles (1775)
British Writers, vol. 4: **73–86**

Landor, Walter Savage (1775)
British Writers, vol. 4: **87–100**

Lang, Andrew (1844)
Writers for Children: **337–343**

Lanier, Sidney (1842)
American Writers Supp. 1, part 1: **349–373**

Larreta, Enrique (1873)
Latin American Writers, vol. 2: **471–476**

Lear, Edward (1812)
British Writers, vol. 5: **75–88**
Writers for Children: **351–356**

Leconte de Lisle, Charles Marie (1818)
European Writers, vol. 6: **1245–1273**

Lee, Vernon (1856)
Supernatural Fiction Writers, vol. 1: **329–335**

Le Fanu, J. S. (1814)
Supernatural Fiction Writers, vol. 1: **219–231**

Leopardi, Giacomo (1798)
European Writers, vol. 5: **541–567**

Lermontov, Mikhail Yurievich (1814)
European Writers, vol. 6: **1195–1224**

Lewis, M. G. (1775)
Supernatural Fiction Writers, vol. 1: **153–160**

Literature of Mountaineering
American Nature Writers, vol. 2: **1115–1128**

Longfellow, Henry Wadsworth (1807)
American Writers, vol. 2: **486–510**

Lowell, James Russell (1819)
American Writers Supp. 1, part 2: **404–426**

Lugones, Leopoldo (1874)
Latin American Writers, vol. 2: **493–502**

Macaulay, Thomas Babington (1800)
British Writers, vol. 4: **268–292**

MacDonald, George (1824)
Supernatural Fiction Writers, vol. 1: **239–246**
Writers for Children: **373–380**

Machado, Antonio (1875)
European Writers, vol. 9: **743–765**

Machado de Assis, Joaquim Maria (1839)
Latin American Writers, vol. 1: **253–268**

Macleod, Fiona (1855)
Supernatural Fiction Writers, vol. 1: **369–374**

Maeterlinck, Maurice (1862)
European Writers, vol. 8: **119–146**

Mallarmé, Stéphane (1842)
European Writers, vol. 7: **1567–1595**

Mann, Heinrich (1871)
European Writers, vol. 8: **519–543**

Manzoni, Alessandro (1785)
European Writers, vol. 5: **367–394**

Mármol, José (1817)
Latin American Writers, vol. 1: **181–184**

Marryat, Frederick (1792)
  Writers for Children: **381–387**

Martí, José (1853)
  Latin American Writers, vol. 1: **311–320**

Matto de Turner, Clorinda (1852)
  Latin American Writers, vol. 1: **305–309**

Maturin, Charles Robert (1780)
  Supernatural Fiction Writers, vol. 1: **161–168**

Maupassant, Guy de (1850)
  European Writers, vol. 7: **1759–1784**
  European Writers Selected Authors, vol. 2: **1025–1050**
  Supernatural Fiction Writers, vol. 1: **59–65**

Meinhold, Wilhelm (1797)
  Supernatural Fiction Writers, vol. 1: **121–127**

Melville, Herman (1819)
  American Writers, vol. 3: **74–98**
  American Writers Retrospective: **243–262**

Meredith, George (1828)
  British Writers, vol. 5: **219–234**

Mérimée, Prosper (1803)
  European Writers, vol. 6: **745–769**
  Supernatural Fiction Writers, vol. 1: **51–57**

Meyer, Conrad Ferdinand (1825)
  See "Poetic Realism"

Michelet, Jules (1798)
  See "Michelet, Jules, and Romantic Historiography"

Michelet, Jules, and Romantic Historiography
      (1798)
  European Writers, vol. 5: **571–606**

Mickiewicz, Adam (1798)
  European Writers, vol. 5: **607–634**

Mills, Enos (1870)
  American Nature Writers, vol. 2: **615–624**

Modern Birdwatching Literature
  American Nature Writers, vol. 2: **1129–1140**

Moe, Jörgen (1813)
  See "Asbjørnsen and Moe"

Molesworth, M. L. S. (1839)
  Writers for Children: **407–413**

Molina, Juan Ramón (1875)
  Latin American Writers, vol. 2: **539–542**

Montalvo, Juan (1832)
  Latin American Writers, vol. 1: **215–220**

Montgomery, L. M. (1874)
  Writers for Children: **415–422**
  Writers for Young Adults, vol. 2: **379–386**

Moore, George (1852)
  British Writers, vol. 6: **85–100**

Morris, William (1834)
  British Writers, vol. 5: **291–308**
  Supernatural Fiction Writers, vol. 1: **299–306**

Muir, John (1838)
  American Nature Writers, vol. 2: **651–669**

Musset, Alfred de (1810)
  European Writers, vol. 6: **999–1033**

Nature in Native American Literatures
  American Nature Writers, vol. 2: **1141–1156**

Nerval, Gérard de (1808)
  European Writers, vol. 6: **943–970**

Nervo, Amado (1870)
  Latin American Writers, vol. 1: **425–429**

Nesbit, E. (1858)
  Writers for Children: **423–430**

Nietzsche, Friedrich (1844)
  European Writers, vol. 7: **1645–1682**
  European Writers Selected Authors, vol. 2:
      1161–1197

Norris, Frank (1870)
  American Writers, vol. 3: **314–336**

Novalis (1772)
  European Writers, vol. 5: **205–231**

O'Brien, Fitz-James (1828)
  Supernatural Fiction Writers, vol. 2: **717–722**

Oliphant, Mrs. (1828)
  Supernatural Fiction Writers, vol. 1: **261–268**

Pain, Barry (1864)
  Supernatural Fiction Writers, vol. 1: **443–448**

Palma, Ricardo (1833)
  Latin American Writers, vol. 1: **221–228**

Parkman, Francis (1823)
  American Writers Supp. 2, part 2: **589–616**

Pascoli, Giovanni (1855)
  European Writers, vol. 7: **1825–1854**

Pater, Walter Horatio (1839)
  British Writers, vol. 5: **337–360**

Payró, Roberto Jorge (1867)
  Latin American Writers, vol. 1: **413–417**

Peacock, Thomas Love (1785)
  British Writers, vol. 4: **157–170**

Pérez Galdós, Benito (1843)
  European Writers, vol. 7: **1597–1618**

Phillpotts, Eden (1862)
  Supernatural Fiction Writers, vol. 2: **549–553**

Pinero, Arthur Wing (1855)
  See "Well-Made Play, The"

Pirandello, Luigi (1867)
  European Writers, vol. 8: **389–416**
  European Writers Selected Authors, vol. 2:
    1289–1316

Poe, Edgar Allan (1809)
  American Writers, vol. 3: **409–432**
  Science Fiction Writers: **11–18**
  Supernatural Fiction Writers, vol. 2: **697–705**
  Writers for Young Adults, vol. 3: **61–73**

Poetic Realism
  European Writers, vol. 6: **913–942**

Potter, Beatrix (1866)
  British Writers Supp. 3: **287–309**
  Writers for Children: **439–446**

Powell, John Wesley (1834)
  See "Western Geologists and Explorers"

Proust, Marcel (1871)
  European Writers, vol. 8: **545–568**
  European Writers Selected Authors, vol. 2:
    1317–1340

Pushkin, Alexander (1799)
  European Writers, vol. 5: **659–691**
  European Writers Selected Authors, vol. 3:
    1341–1373

Pyle, Howard (1852)
  Writers for Children: **447–454**

Quiller-Couch, Arthur (1863)
  Supernatural Fiction Writers, vol. 1: **389–395**

Radcliffe, Ann (1764)
  Supernatural Fiction Writers, vol. 1: **145–151**

Reynolds, G. W. M. (1814)
  Supernatural Fiction Writers, vol. 1: **205–211**

Richards, Laura E. (1850)
  Writers for Children: **469–475**

Richter, Jean Paul (1763)
  European Writers, vol. 5: **53–88**

Riddell, Mrs. J. H. (1832)
  Supernatural Fiction Writers, vol. 1: **269–277**

Rinbaud, Arthur (1854)
  European Writers, vol. 7: **1785–1824**

Robertson, Thomas W. (1829)
  See "Well-Made Play, The"

Rodó, José Enrique (1871)
  Latin American Writers, vol. 2: **447–455**

Rossetti, Christina (1830)
  British Writers, vol. 5: **247–260**
  Writers for Children: **483–491**

Rossetti, Dante Gabriel (1828)
  British Writers, vol. 5: **235–246**

Ruskin, John (1819)
  British Writers, vol. 5: **173–186**
  Writers for Children: **493–496**

Sade, Marquis de, and the French Libertine
    Tradition (1740)
  European Writers, vol. 4: **615–638**

Sainte-Beuve, Charles-Augustin (1804)
  European Writers, vol. 6: **837–861**

Salten, Felix (1869)
  Writers for Children: **497–501**

Sánchez, Florencio (1875)
  Latin American Writers, vol. 2: **531–538**

Sand, George (1804)
  European Writers, vol. 6: **813–836**
  European Writers Selected Authors, vol. 3:
    1571–1594

Santayana, George (1863)
  American Writers, vol. 3: **599–622**

Sardou, Victor (1831)
  See "Well-Made Play, The"

Sarmiento, Domingo Faustino (1811)
  Latin American Writers, vol. 1: **159–167**

Schiller, Friedrich von (1759)
  European Writers, vol. 5: **27–52**

Schlegel, Friedrich von (1772)
  European Writers, vol. 5: **177–203**

Schnitzler, Arthur (1862)
  European Writers, vol. 8: **89–117**

Schopenhauer, Arthur (1788)
  European Writers, vol. 5: **395–415**

Schreiner, Olive (1855)
  African Writers, vol. 2: **745–763**
  British Writers Supp. 2: **435–458**

Scott, Sir Walter (1771)
  British Writers, vol. 4: **27–40**
  Supernatural Fiction Writers, vol. 1: **169–176**

Scribe, Augustin Eugène (1791)
  See "Well-Made Play, The"

Senarens, Luis Philip (1863)
Science Fiction Writers: **53–58**

Serviss, Garrett P. (1851)
Science Fiction Writers: **39–44**

Seton, Ernest Thompson (1860)
American Nature Writers, vol. 2: **805–816**

Sewell, Anna (1820)
Writers for Children: **525–528**

Shaw, George Bernard (1856)
British Writers, vol. 6: **101–132**
British Writers Selected Authors, vol. 3: **1053–1084**

Shelley, Mary (1797)
British Writers Supp. 3: **355–373**
British Writers Selected Authors, vol. 3: **1085–1103**
Science Fiction Writers: **3–9**
See also "Gothic Novel, The"

Shelley, Percy Bysshe (1792)
British Writers, vol. 4: **195–210**
British Writers Selected Authors, vol. 3: **1105–1120**

Shiel, M. P. (1865)
Science Fiction Writers: **31–37**
Supernatural Fiction Writers, vol. 1: **361–367**

Silva, José Asunción (1865)
Latin American Writers, vol. 1: **377–385**

Sinclair, May (1863)
Supernatural Fiction Writers, vol. 1: **513–519**

Slave Narrative in American Literature, The
African American Writers: **395–412**

Southey, Robert (1774)
British Writers, vol. 4: **58–72**

Spyri, Johanna (1827)
Writers for Children: **529–533**

Staël, Madame de (1766)
European Writers, vol. 5: **89–111**

Stendhal (1783)
European Writers, vol. 5: **343–366**
European Writers Selected Authors, vol. 3: **1649–1672**

Stephen, Leslie (1832)
British Writers, vol. 5: **277–290**

Stevenson, Robert Louis (1850)
British Writers, vol. 5: **383–399**
British Writers Selected Authors, vol. 3: **1161–1176**
Supernatural Fiction Writers, vol. 1: **307–313**
Writers for Children: **535–543**
Writers for Young Adults, vol. 3: **215–224**

Stockton, Frank R. (1834)
Supernatural Fiction Writers, vol. 2: **753–759**
Writers for Children: **545–554**

Stoker, Bram (1847)
British Writers Supp. 3: **375–391**
Supernatural Fiction Writers, vol. 1: **375–381**

Storm, Theodor (1817)
See "Poetic Realism"

Stowe, Harriet Beecher (1811)
American Writers Supp. 1, part 2: **579–601**

Stratemeyer, Edward (1862)
Writers for Young Adults, vol. 3: **237–249**

Stratton Porter, Gene (1863)
American Nature Writers, vol. 2: **877–891**

Strindberg, August (1849)
European Writers, vol. 7: **1731–1758**

Svevo, Italo (1861)
European Writers, vol. 8: **67–87**

Swinburne, Algernon Charles (1837)
British Writers, vol. 5: **309–336**

Tablada, José Juan (1871)
Latin American Writers, vol. 1: **441–446**

Taine, Hippolyte (1828)
European Writers, vol. 7: **1449–1469**

Tennyson, Alfred Lord (1809)
British Writers, vol. 4: **323–339**
British Writers Selected Authors, vol. 3: **1219–1235**

Thackeray, William Makepeace (1811)
British Writers, vol. 5: **17–40**
British Writers Selected Authors, vol. 3: **1237–1259**

Thaxter, Celia (1835)
American Nature Writers, vol. 2: **905–917**

Thoreau, Henry David (1817)
American Nature Writers, vol. 2: **933–950**
American Writers, vol. 4: **167–189**

Tieck, Ludwig (1773)
European Writers, vol. 5: **233–260**
Supernatural Fiction Writers, vol. 1: **83–89**

Tocqueville, Alexis de (1805)
European Writers, vol. 6: **893–912**
European Writers Selected Authors, vol. 3: **1673–1691**

Tolstoy, Leo (1828)
European Writers, vol. 7: **1471–1494**
European Writers Selected Authors, vol. 3: **1693–1715**

Trollope, Anthony (1815)
  British Writers, vol. 5: **89–104**
  British Writers Selected Authors, vol. 3: **1295–1309**

Turgenev, Ivan (1818)
  European Writers, vol. 6: **1275–1297**
  European Writers Selected Authors, vol. 3: **1717–1739**

Twain, Mark (1835)
  American Writers, vol. 4: **190–213**
  Supernatural Fiction Writers, vol. 2: **761–768**
  Writers for Children: **573–582**
  Writers for Young Adults, vol. 3: **321–328**

Unamuno, Miguel de (1864)
  European Writers, vol. 8: **283–310**

Valencia, Guillermo (1873)
  Latin American Writers, vol. 2: **477–482**

Valéry, Paul (1871)
  European Writers, vol. 8: **569–588**

Valle-Inclán, Ramón del (1866)
  European Writers, vol. 8: **331–353**

Van Dyke, John C. (1856)
  American Nature Writers, vol. 2: **951–962**

Verga, Giovanni (1840)
  European Writers, vol. 7: **1543–1565**

Verlaine, Paul (1844)
  European Writers, vol. 7: **1619–1643**

Verne, Jules (1828)
  Science Fiction Writers: **573–582**
  Writers for Children: **591–598**

Vigny, Alfred Victor de (1797)
  European Writers, vol. 5: **447–488**

Villaverde, Cirilo (1812)
  Latin American Writers, vol. 1: **169–174**

Wagner, Richard (1813)
  European Writers, vol. 6: **1147–1168**
  European Writers Selected Authors, vol. 3: **1767–1787**

Wedekind, Frank (1864)
  European Writers, vol. 8: **229–281**

Well-Made Play, The
  European Writers, vol. 7: **1909–1934**

Wells, H. G. (1866)
  British Writers, vol. 6: **225–246**
  British Writers Selected Authors, vol. 3: **1331–1352**
  Science Fiction Writers: **25–30**
  Supernatural Fiction Writers, vol. 1: **397–402**
  Writers for Children: **599–603**

Western Geologists and Explorers
  American Nature Writers, vol. 2: **1173–1188**

Wharton, Edith (1862)
  American Writers, vol. 4: **308–330**
  American Writers Retrospective: **359–385**
  Modern American Women Writers: **539–558**
  Supernatural Fiction Writers, vol. 2: **783–788**

Whitman, Walt (1819)
  American Writers, vol. 4: **331–354**
  American Writers Retrospective: **387–410**

Whittier, John Greenleaf (1807)
  American Writers Supp. 1, part 2: **682–706**

Wieland, Christoph Martin (1733)
  European Writers, vol. 4: **587–614**

Wiggin, Kate Douglas (1856)
  Writers for Children: **605–609**

Wilde, Oscar (1854)
  British Writers, vol. 5: **399–422**
  British Writers Selected Authors, vol. 3: **1353–1376**
  Supernatural Fiction Writers, vol. 1: **345–350**
  Writers for Children: **611–616**

Wilder, Laura Ingalls (1867)
  Writers for Children: **617–623**
  Writers for Young Adults, vol. 3: **371–380**

Wilson, Alexander (1766)
  See "Early Romantic Natural History
    Literature"

Wood, Mrs. Henry (1814)
  Supernatural Fiction Writers, vol. 1: **279–286**

Wordsworth, William (1770)
  British Writers, vol. 4: **1–26**
  British Writers Selected Authors, vol. 3: **1419–1444**

Yeats, William Butler (1865)
  British Writers, vol. 6: **207–224**
  British Writers Selected Authors, vol. 3: **1473–1490**

Yonge, Charlotte Mary (1823)
  Writers for Children: **625–631**

Zeno Gandía, Manuel (1855)
  Latin American Writers, vol. 1: **321–326**

Zola, Émile (1840)
  European Writers, vol. 7: **1517–1542**
  European Writers Selected Authors, vol. 3:
    1789–1813

Zorrilla de San Martín, Juan (1855)
  Latin American Writers, vol. 1: **327–331**

TWENTIETH CENTURY

Abbey, Edward (1927)
American Nature Writers, vol. 1: **1–19**

Abrahams, Peter (1919)
African Writers, vol. 1: **1–14**

Acevedo Díaz, Eduardo (1851)
Latin American Writers, vol. 1: **299–303**

Achebe, Chinua (1930)
African Writers, vol. 1: **15–36**

Ackerman, Diane (1948)
American Nature Writers, vol. 1: **21–30**

Adams, Henry (1838)
American Writers, vol. 1: **1–24**

Addams, Jane (1860)
American Writers Supp. 1, part 1: **1–27**

Ady, Endre (1877)
European Writers, vol. 9: **859–880**

African Americans, Writing, and Nature
American Nature Writers, vol. 2: **1003–1012**

Agee, James (1909)
American Writers, vol. 1: **25–47**

Agustini, Delmira (1886)
Latin American Writers, vol. 2: **649–654**

Aickman, Robert (1914)
Supernatural Fiction Writers, vol. 2: **957–964**

Aidoo, Ama Ata (1942)
African Writers, vol. 1: **37–48**

Aiken, Conrad (1889)
American Writers, vol. 1: **48–70**

Aiken, Joan (1924)
Writers for Young Adults, vol. 1: **1–9**

Akhmatova, Anna (1899)
European Writers, vol. 10: **1521–1542**

Albee, Edward (1928)
American Writers, vol. 1: **71–96**

Aldiss, Brian W. (1925)
Science Fiction Writers: **251–258**

Alegría, Ciro (1909)
Latin American Writers, vol. 3: **1099–1103**

Alexander, Lloyd (1924)
Supernatural Fiction Writers, vol. 2: **965–971**
Writers for Young Adults, vol. 1: **21–33**

Amado, Jorge (1912)
Latin American Writers, vol. 3: **1153–1162**

Ambler, Eric (1909)
British Writers Supp. 4: **1–24**

Amis, Kingsley (1922)
British Writers Supp. 2: **1–19**

Amis, Martin (1949)
British Writers Supp. 4: **25–44**

Amoroso Lima, Alceu (1893)
Latin American Writers, vol. 2: **781–790**

Anderson, Poul (1926)
Science Fiction Writers: **259–265**
Supernatural Fiction Writers, vol. 2: **973–980**

Anderson, Sherwood (1876)
American Writers, vol. 1: **97–120**

Anderson Imbert, Enrique (1910)
Latin American Writers, vol. 3: **1105–1110**

Andrade, Mário de (1893)
Latin American Writers, vol. 2: **771–780**

Andrić, Ivo (1892)
European Writers, vol. 11: **1751–1779**

Angell, Judie (1937)
Writers for Young Adults, vol. 1: **35–42**

Angelou, Maya (1928)
American Writers Supp. 4, part 1: **1–19**
Modern American Women Writers: **1–8**
Writers for Young Adults, vol. 1: **43–52**

Anouilh, Jean (1910)
European Writers, vol. 13: **2843–2865**
European Writers Selected Authors, vol. 1:
31–52

Anstey, F. (1856)
Supernatural Fiction Writers, vol. 1: **287–292**

Anthony, Piers (1934)
Supernatural Fiction Writers, vol. 2: **981–986**

Apollinaire, Guillaume (1880)
European Writers, vol. 9: **881–903**

Aragon, Louis (1897)
European Writers, vol. 11: **2061–2087**

Arciniegas, Germán (1900)
Latin American Writers, vol. 2: **897–901**

Arden, John (1930)
British Writers Supp. 2: **21–42**

Ardizzone, Edward (1900)
Writers for Children: **15–20**

Arenas, Reinaldo (1943)
Latin American Writers, vol. 3: **1451–1458**

Arguedas, José María (1911)
Latin American Writers, vol. 3: **1131–1138**

Arlt, Roberto (1900)
Latin American Writers, vol. 2: **881–886**

Armah, Ayi Kwei (1939)
African Writers, vol. 1: **49–62**

Arp, Jean (1886)
European Writers, vol. 10: **1365–1384**

Arreola, Juan José (1918)
Latin American Writers, vol. 3: **1229–1236**

Artaud, Antonin (1895)
European Writers, vol. 11: **1961–1985**

Arthurian Romances
Supernatural Fiction Writers, vol. 1: **11–18**

Ashbery, John (1927)
American Writers Supp. 3, part 1: **1–29**

Asher, Sandy (1942)
Writers for Young Adults, vol. 1: **53–61**

Asimov, Isaac (1920)
Science Fiction Writers: **267–276**

Asturias, Miguel Ángel (1899)
Latin American Writers, vol. 2: **865–873**

Atherton, Gertrude (1857)
Supernatural Fiction Writers, vol. 2: **777–781**

Auchincloss, Louis (1917)
American Writers Supp. 4, part 1: **21–38**

Auden, W. H. (1907)
American Writers Supp. 2, part 1: **1–28**
British Writers, vol. 7: **379–399**
British Writers Selected Authors, vol. 1: **1–21**

Austin, Mary Hunter (1868)
American Nature Writers, vol. 1: **31–51**

Avi (1937)
Writers for Young Adults, vol. 1: **63–72**

Awoonor, Kofi (1935)
African Writers, vol. 1: **63–75**

Aymé, Marcel (1902)
European Writers, vol. 12: **2433–2456**

Azevedo, Aluísio (1857)
Latin American Writers, vol. 1: **333–341**

Azorín (1873)
European Writers, vol. 9: **639–661**

Azuela, Mariano (1873)
Latin American Writers, vol. 2: **457–464**

Bâ, Mariama (1929)
African Writers, vol. 1: **77–82**

Babel, Isaac (1894)
European Writers, vol. 11: **1885–1915**
European Writers Selected Authors, vol. 1: **131–160**

Bailey, Florence Merriam (1863)
American Nature Writers, vol. 1: **53–62**

Baker, Frank (1908)
Supernatural Fiction Writers, vol. 2: **561–567**

Baldwin, James (1924)
African American Writers: **1–14**
American Writers Supp. 1, part 1: **47–71**

Ballagas, Emilio (1908)
Latin American Writers, vol. 3: **1081–1087**

Ballard, J. G. (1930)
Science Fiction Writers: **277–282**

Bandeira, Manuel (1886)
Latin American Writers, vol. 2: **629–641**

Bangs, J. K. (1862)
Supernatural Fiction Writers, vol. 2: **725–729**

Baraka, Amiri (1934)
African American Writers: **15–29**
American Writers Supp. 2, part 1: **29–63**

Barker, Pat (1943)
British Writers Supp. 4: **45–63**

Barnes, Djuna (1892)
American Writers Supp. 3, part 1: **31–46**

Barnes, Julian (1946)
British Writers Supp. 4: **65–76**

Baroja, Pío (1872)
European Writers, vol. 9: **589–616**

Barrie, J. M. (1860)
British Writers Supp. 3: **1–17**
Supernatural Fiction Writers, vol. 1: **405–410**
Writers for Children: **29–35**

Barrios, Eduardo (1884)
Latin American Writers, vol. 2: **611–618**

Barth, John (1930)
American Writers, vol. 1: **121–143**

Barthelme, Donald (1931)
American Writers Supp. 4, part 1: **39–58**

Barthes, Roland (1915)
European Writers, vol. 13: **3079–3104**

Bass, Rick (1958)
    American Nature Writers, vol. 1: **75–88**

Bauer, Joan (1951)
    Writers for Young Adults, vol. 1: **73–80**

Bauer, Marion Dane (1938)
    Writers for Young Adults, vol. 1: **81–88**

Baum, L. Frank (1856)
    Writers for Children: **37–48**

Beagle, Peter S. (1939)
    Supernatural Fiction Writers, vol. 2: **987–991**

Beauvoir, Simone de (1908)
    European Writers, vol. 12: **2701–2732**
    European Writers Selected Authors, vol. 1: **185–215**

Beckett, Samuel (1906)
    British Writers Supp. 1: **43–64**
    British Writers Selected Authors, vol. 1: **47–68**

Beerbohm, Max (1872)
    British Writers Supp. 2: **43–59**

Behan, Brendan (1923)
    British Writers Supp. 2: **61–76**

Belloc, Hilaire (1870)
    Writers for Children: **49–54**

Bellow, Saul (1915)
    American Writers, vol. 1: **144–166**

Bely, Andrey (1880)
    European Writers, vol. 9: **905–929**

Bemelmans, Ludwig (1898)
    Writers for Children: **55–61**

Benedetti, Mario (1920)
    Latin American Writers, vol. 3: **1255–1263**

Benét, Stephen Vincent (1898)
    Supernatural Fiction Writers, vol. 2: **797–803**

Benjamin, Walter (1892)
    European Writers, vol. 11: **1703–1730**

Bennett, Arnold (1867)
    British Writers, vol. 6: **247–268**

Bennett, Jay (1912)
    Writers for Young Adults, vol. 1: **89–97**

Benson, E. F. (1867)
    Supernatural Fiction Writers, vol. 1: **491–496**

Beresford, J. D. (1873)
    Supernatural Fiction Writers, vol. 1: **457–461**

Berger, John (1926)
    British Writers Supp. 4: **77–96**

Bergson, Henri (1859)
    European Writers, vol. 8: **45–66**

Berry, Wendell (1934)
    American Nature Writers, vol. 1: **89–105**

Berryman, John (1914)
    American Writers, vol. 1: **167–189**

Bester, Alfred (1913)
    Science Fiction Writers: **283–290**

Beston, Henry (1888)
    American Nature Writers, vol. 1: **107–120**

Bethancourt, T. Ernesto (1932)
    Writers for Young Adults, vol. 1: **99–109**

Beti, Mongo (1932)
    African Writers, vol. 1: **83–94**

Betjeman, John (1906)
    British Writers, vol. 7: **355–378**

Bianco, Margery Williams (1881)
    Writers for Children: **63–67**

Bierce, Ambrose (1842)
    American Writers, vol. 1: **190–213**
    Supernatural Fiction Writers, vol. 2: **731–737**

Bioregionalism in Nature Writing
    American Nature Writers, vol. 2: **1013–1024**

Bioy Casares, Adolfo (1914)
    Latin American Writers, vol. 3: **1201–1208**

Bishop, Elizabeth (1911)
    American Writers Supp. 1, part 1: **72–97**
    Modern American Women Writers: **9–22**

Blackmur, R. P. (1904)
    American Writers Supp. 2, part 1: **87–112**

Blackwood, Algernon (1869)
    Supernatural Fiction Writers, vol. 1: **463–470**

Blanco Fombona, Rufino (1874)
    Latin American Writers, vol. 2: **503–511**

Blasco Ibáñez, Vicente (1867)
    European Writers, vol. 8: **355–388**

Blest Gana, Alberto (1830)
    Latin American Writers, vol. 1: **205–213**

Blish, James (1921)
    Science Fiction Writers: **291–296**

Bloch, Robert (1917)
    Supernatural Fiction Writers, vol. 2: **901–907**

Block, Francesca Lia (1962)
    Writers for Young Adults, vol. 1: **111–119**

Blok, Alexander (1880)
European Writers, vol. 9: **959–990**

Blume, Judy (1938)
Writers for Young Adults, vol. 1: **121–131**

Bly, Robert (1926)
American Writers Supp. 4, part 1: **59–77**

Bogan, Louise (1897)
American Writers Supp. 3, part 1: **47–68**
Modern American Women Writers: **23–36**

Bograd, Larry (1953)
Writers for Young Adults, vol. 1: **133–141**

Böll, Heinrich (1917)
European Writers, vol. 13: **3165–3186**

Bombal, María Luisa (1910)
Latin American Writers, vol. 3: **1111–1117**

Bond, Edward (1934)
British Writers Supp. 1: **421–436**

Bontemps, Arna (1902)
Writers for Children: **77–83**

Borges, Jorge Luis (1899)
Latin American Writers, vol. 2: **845–864**

Bourne, Randolph (1886)
American Writers, vol. 1: **214–238**

Bowen, Elizabeth (1899)
British Writers Supp. 2: **77–96**
Supernatural Fiction Writers, vol. 2: **569–575**

Bowles, Paul (1910)
American Writers Supp. 4, part 1: **79–99**

Brackett, Leigh (1915)
Supernatural Fiction Writers, vol. 2: **909–915**

Bradbury, Ray (1920)
American Writers Supp. 4, part 1: **101–118**
Supernatural Fiction Writers: **171–178**
Supernatural Fiction Writers, vol. 2: **917–923**

Brancato, Robin F. (1936)
Writers for Young Adults, vol. 1: **143–152**

Branscum, Robbie (1937)
Writers for Young Adults, vol. 1: **153–161**

Brecht, Bertolt (1898)
European Writers, vol. 11: **2089–2112**
European Writers Selected Authors, vol. 1: **281–303**

Breton, André (1896)
European Writers, vol. 11: **1939–1960**

Bridgers, Sue Ellen (1942)
Writers for Young Adults, vol. 1: **163–172**

Brieux, Eugène (1858)
See "Well-Made Play, The"

Brink, André (1935)
African Writers, vol. 1: **95–114**

Brink, Carol Ryrie (1895)
Writers for Children: **85–90**

Broch, Hermann (1886)
European Writers, vol. 10: **1385–1408**

Brooke, Rupert (1887)
British Writers Supp. 3: **45–61**
See also "Poets of World War I (British)"

Brooke-Rose, Christine (1926)
British Writers Supp. 4: **97–118**

Brookner, Anita (1928)
British Writers Supp. 4: **119–137**

Brooks, Bruce (1950)
Writers for Young Adults, vol. 1: **173–182**

Brooks, Gwendolyn (1917)
African American Writers: **31–43**
American Writers Supp. 3, part 1: **69–90**
Modern American Women Writers: **37–48**

Brooks, Van Wyck (1886)
American Writers, vol. 1: **239–263**

Brown, Sterling (1901)
African American Writers: **45–57**

Brunhoff, Jean de (1899)
Writers for Children: **91–96**

Brunner, John (1934)
Science Fiction Writers: **297–304**

Brutus, Dennis (1924)
African Writers, vol. 1: **115–126**

Buck, Pearl S. (1892)
American Writers Supp. 2, part 1: **113–134**

Budrys, Algis (1931)
Science Fiction Writers: **305–311**

Bunting, Eve (1928)
Writers for Young Adults, vol. 1: **183–189**

Burgess, Anthony (1917)
British Writers Supp. 1: **185–198**

Burke, Kenneth (1897)
American Writers, vol. 1: **264–287**

Burnett, Frances Hodgson (1849)
Writers for Children: **103–109**

Burns, Olive Ann (1924)
Writers for Young Adults, vol. 1: **191–198**

Burroughs, Edgar Rice (1875)
  Science Fiction Writers: **59–64**

Burroughs, John (1837)
  American Nature Writers, vol. 1: **121–138**

Burroughs, William S. (1914)
  American Writers Supp. 3, part 1: **91–110**

Burton, Virginia Lee (1909)
  Writers for Children: **111–115**

Butor, Michel (1926)
  European Writers, vol. 13: **3287–3321**

Byars, Betsy (1928)
  Writers for Young Adults, vol. 1: **199–207**

Byatt, A. S. (1936)
  British Writers Supp. 4: **139–156**

Cabell, James Branch (1879)
  Supernatural Fiction Writers, vol. 2: **789–796**

Cabral de Melo Neto, João (1920)
  Latin American Writers, vol. 3: **1247–1253**

Cabrera Infante, Guillermo (1929)
  Latin American Writers, vol. 3: **1383–1391**

Caldwell, Erskine (1903)
  American Writers, vol. 1: **288–311**

Calvino, Italo (1923)
  European Writers, vol. 13: **3259–3286**

Campbell, John W., Jr. (1910)
  Science Fiction Writers: **151–159**

Campbell, Ramsey (1946)
  Supernatural Fiction Writers, vol. 2: **993–999**

Campbell, Roy (1901)
  African Writers, vol. 1: **127–137**

Camus, Albert (1913)
  African Writers, vol. 1: **139–152**
  European Writers, vol. 13: **3049–3078**
  European Writers Selected Authors, vol. 1: **305–334**

Canadian Nature Writing in English
  American Nature Writers, vol. 2: **1025–1040**

Canetti, Elias (1905)
  European Writers, vol. 12: **2615–2633**

Čapek, Karel (1890)
  European Writers, vol. 10: **1565–1590**
  Science Fiction Writers: **583–589**

Capote, Truman (1924)
  American Writers Supp. 3, part 1: **111–133**

Carballido, Emilio (1925)
  Latin American Writers, vol. 3: **1289–1294**

Carducci, Giosue (1835)
  European Writers, vol. 7: **1495–1516**

Caro, Miguel Antonio (1843)
  Latin American Writers, vol. 1: **277–281**

Carpentier, Alejo (1904)
  Latin American Writers, vol. 3: **1019–1031**

Carrasquilla, Tomás (1858)
  Latin American Writers, vol. 1: **343–350**

Carrighar, Sally (1898)
  American Nature Writers, vol. 1: **139–149**

Carson, Rachel (1907)
  American Nature Writers, vol. 1: **151–171**

Carter, Alden R. (1947)
  Writers for Young Adults, vol. 1: **209–218**

Carter, Angela (1940)
  British Writers Supp. 3: **79–93**

Carver, Raymond (1938)
  American Writers Supp. 3, part 1: **135–151**

Cary, Joyce (1888)
  British Writers, vol. 7: **185–196**

Castellanos, Rosario (1925)
  Latin American Writers, vol. 3: **1295–1302**

Cather, Willa (1873)
  American Writers, vol. 1: **312–334**
  American Writers Retrospective: **1–23**
  Modern American Women Writers: **49–62**

Cavafy, Constantin (1863)
  European Writers, vol. 8: **205–228**

Cela, Camilo José (1916)
  European Writers, vol. 13: **3105–3129**

Céline, Louis-Ferdinand (1894)
  European Writers, vol. 11: **1859–1884**

Chambers, Aidan (1934)
  Writers for Young Adults, vol. 1: **219–227**

Chambers, Robert W. (1865)
  Supernatural Fiction Writers, vol. 2: **739–745**

Chandler, Raymond (1888)
  American Writers Supp. 4, part 1: **119–138**

Chatwin, Bruce (1940)
  British Writers Supp. 4: **157–177**

Cheever, John (1912)
  American Writers Supp. 1, part 1: **174–199**

Chesnutt, Charles W. (1858)
  African American Writers: **59–70**

Chesterton, G. K. (1874)
  British Writers, vol. 6: **335–346**
  Supernatural Fiction Writers, vol. 1: **411–414**

Childress, Alice (1920)
  Writers for Young Adults, vol. 1: **229–240**

Chocano, José Santos (1875)
  Latin American Writers, vol. 2: **543–549**

Christie, Agatha (1890)
  British Writers Supp. 2: **123–137**

Churchill, Caryl (1938)
  British Writers Supp. 4: **179–200**

Churchill, Winston (1874)
  British Writers, vol. 6: **347–362**

Clark, John Pepper (1935)
  African Writers, vol. 1: **153–166**

Clarke, Arthur C. (1917)
  Science Fiction Writers: **313–320**

Claudel, Paul (1868)
  European Writers, vol. 8: **471–494**

Cleaver, Vera and Bill (1919; 1920)
  Writers for Young Adults, vol. 1: **241–248**

Clement, Hal (1922)
  Science Fiction Writers: **321–327**

Cocteau, Jean (1889)
  European Writers, vol. 10: **1543–1564**

Coetzee, J. M. (1940)
  African Writers, vol. 1: **167–183**

Cole, Brock (1938)
  Writers for Young Adults, vol. 1: **249–256**

Colette (1873)
  European Writers, vol. 9: **617–638**
  European Writers Selected Authors, vol. 1: **389–410**

Collier, Christopher and James Lincoln
    (1930; 1928)
  Writers for Young Adults, vol. 1: **257–269**

Collier, John (1901)
  Supernatural Fiction Writers, vol. 2: **577–583**

Colman, Hila
  Writers for Young Adults, vol. 1: **271–280**

Colum, Padraic (1881)
  Writers for Children: **139–146**

Compton-Burnett, Ivy (1884)
  British Writers, vol. 7: **59–70**

Comstock, Anna Botsford (1854)
  American Nature Writers, vol. 1: **173–185**

Connolly, Cyril (1903)
  British Writers Supp. 3: **95–113**

Conrad, Joseph (1857)
  British Writers, vol. 6: **133–150**
  British Writers Selected Authors, vol. 1: **331–348**

Contemporary Ecofiction
  American Nature Writers, vol. 2: **1041–1058**

Cooney, Caroline B. (1947)
  Writers for Young Adults, vol. 1: **281–290**

Coppard, A. E. (1878)
  Supernatural Fiction Writers, vol. 2: **523–528**

Cormier, Robert (1925)
  Writers for Young Adults, vol. 1: **291–301**

Corelli, Marie (1855)
  Supernatural Fiction Writers, vol. 1: **293–297**

Cortázar, Julio (1914)
  Latin American Writers, vol. 3: **1177–1194**

Couto, Mia (1955)
  African Writers, vol. 1: **185–197**

Coward, Noël (1899)
  British Writers Supp. 2: **139–158**

Cowley, Malcolm (1898)
  American Writers Supp. 2, part 1: **135–156**

Cozzens, James Gould (1903)
  American Writers, vol. 1: **358–381**

Crane, Hart (1899)
  American Writers, vol. 1: **381–404**

Crawford, F. Marion (1815)
  Supernatural Fiction Writers, vol. 2: **747–751**

Creeley, Robert (1926)
  American Writers Supp. 4, part 1: **139–161**

Croce, Benedetto (1866)
  European Writers, vol. 8: **311–329**

Crutcher, Chris (1946)
  Writers for Young Adults, vol. 1: **313–322**

Cullen, Countee (1903)
  American Writers Supp. 4, part 1: **163–174**

Cummings, E. E. (1894)
  American Writers, vol. 1: **428–450**

Cunha, Euclides da (1866)
  Latin American Writers, vol. 1: **387–395**

Dahl, Roald (1916)
  British Writers Supp. 4: **201–227**

Daly, Maureen (1921)
  Writers for Young Adults, vol. 1: **323–333**

Daniel, John (1948)
See "New Voices in American Nature Writing"

D'Annunzio, Gabriele (1863)
European Writers, vol. 8: **175–203**

Danziger, Paula (1944)
Writers for Young Adults, vol. 1: **335–344**

Darío, Rubén (1867)
Latin American Writers, vol. 1: **397–412**

Daugherty, James Henry (1887)
Writers for Children: **155–161**

Davidson, Avram (1923)
Supernatural Fiction Writers, vol. 2: **1001–1008**

Davis, H. L. (1894)
American Nature Writers, vol. 1: **199–211**

Davis, Terry (1946)
Writers for Young Adults, vol. 1: **345–352**

Day Lewis, Cecil (1904)
British Writers Supp. 3: **115–132**

De Camp, L. Sprague (1907)
Science Fiction Writers: **179–184**
See also "De Camp, L. Sprague, and
Fletcher Pratt"

De Camp, L. Sprague, and Fletcher Pratt
Supernatural Fiction Writers, vol. 2: **925–931**

De la Mare, Walter (1873)
Supernatural Fiction Writers, vol. 1: **497–503**
Writers for Children: **173–180**

Delany, Samuel R. (1942)
Science Fiction Writers: **329–336**

Denevi, Marco (1922)
Latin American Writers, vol. 3: **1265–1269**

Derleth, August (1909)
Supernatural Fiction Writers, vol. 2: **883–890**

Díaz, Jorge (1930)
Latin American Writers, vol. 3: **1393–1397**

Díaz Rodríguez, Manuel (1871)
Latin American Writers, vol. 1: **431–439**

Dib, Mohammed (1920)
African Writers, vol. 1: **199–207**

Dick, Philip K. (1928)
Science Fiction Writers: **337–343**

Dickey, James (1923)
American Writers Supp. 4, part 1: **175–194**

Dickinson, Peter (1927)
Writers for Young Adults, vol. 1: **375–383**

Dickson, Gordon R. (1923)
Science Fiction Writers: **345–350**

Didion, Joan (1934)
American Writers Supp. 4, part 1: **195–216**
Modern American Women Writers: **91–102**

Dillard, Annie (1945)
American Nature Writers, vol. 1: **213–230**

Dinesen, Isak (1885)
European Writers, vol. 10: **1281–1306**
European Writers Selected Authors, vol. 1: **453–477**

Disch, Thomas M. (1940)
Science Fiction Writers: **351–356**

Doctorow, E. L. (1931)
American Writers Supp. 4, part 1: **217–240**

Dodge, Mary Mapes (1831)
Writers for Children: **193–199**

Donaldson, Stephen R. (1947)
Supernatural Fiction Writers, vol. 2: **1009–1013**

Donoso, José (1924)
Latin American Writers, vol. 3: **1277–1288**

Doolittle, Hilda (H.D.) (1886)
American Writers Supp. 1, part 1: **253–275**
Modern American Women Writers: **103–121**

Dos Passos, John (1896)
American Writers, vol. 1: **474–496**

Douglas, Marjory Stoneman (1890)
American Nature Writers, vol. 1: **231–245**

Douglas, Norman (1868)
British Writers, vol. 6: **293–306**

Dove, Rita (1952)
American Writers Supp. 4, part 1: **241–258**

Doyle, Sir Arthur Conan (1859)
British Writers Supp. 2: **159–178**
British Writers Selected Authors, vol. 1: **415–434**
Science Fiction Writers: **45–50**
Writers for Children: **201–207**
Writers for Young Adults, vol. 1: **385–392**

Drabble, Margaret (1939)
British Writers Supp. 4: **229–254**

Dragún, Osvaldo (1929)
Latin American Writers, vol. 3: **1377–1382**

Dreiser, Theodore (1871)
American Writers, vol. 1: **497–520**

Drummond de Andrade, Carlos (1902)
Latin American Writers, vol. 2: **957–974**

Du Bois, W. E. B. (1868)
African American Writers: **71–87**
American Writers Supp. 2, part 1: **157–189**

Du Maurier, Daphne (1907)
British Writers Supp. 3: **133–149**
British Writers Selected Authors, vol. 1: **435–451**

Dunbar, Paul Laurence (1872)
African American Writers: **87–102**
American Writers Supp. 2, part 1: **191–219**

Duncan, Lois (1934)
Writers for Young Adults, vol. 1: **393–402**

Dunsany, Lord (1878)
Supernatural Fiction Writers, vol. 1: **471–478**

Durrell, Lawrence (1912)
British Writers Supp. 1: **93–128**

Dürrenmatt, Friedrich (1921)
European Writers, vol. 13: **3215–3235**

Eberhart, Richard (1904)
American Writers, vol. 1: **521–543**

Eddison, E. R. (1882)
Supernatural Fiction Writers, vol. 2: **529–534**

Edwards, Jorge (1931)
Latin American Writers, vol. 3: **1399–1403**

Egbuna, Obi (1938)
African Writers, vol. 1: **209–221**

Eguren, José María (1874)
Latin American Writers, vol. 2: **513–518**

Ehrlich, Gretel (1946)
American Nature Writers, vol. 1: **247–258**

Eichelbaum, Samuel (1894)
Latin American Writers, vol. 2: **797–801**

Eifert, Virginia (1911)
American Nature Writers, vol. 1: **259–268**

Eiseley, Loren (1907)
American Nature Writers, vol. 1: **269–285**

Ekelöf, Gunnar (1907)
European Writers, vol. 12: **2635–2671**

Ekwensi, Cyprian (1921)
African Writers, vol. 1: **223–234**

Eliot, T. S. (1888)
American Writers, vol. 1: **567–591**
American Writers Retrospective: **51–71**
British Writers, vol. 7: **143–170**
British Writers Selected Authors, vol. 1:
469–496

Ellison, Harlan (1934)
Science Fiction Writers: **357–368**
Supernatural Fiction Writers, vol. 2: **1015–1021**

Ellison, Ralph (1914)
African American Writers: **103–129**
American Writers Supp. 2, part 1: **221–252**

Elytis, Odysseus (1911)
European Writers, vol. 13: **2955–2988**

Emecheta, Buchi (1944)
African Writers, vol. 1: **235–247**

Empson, William (1906)
British Writers Supp. 2: **179–198**

Enright, Elizabeth (1909)
Writers for Children: **215–220**

Erdrich, Louise (1954)
American Writers Supp. 4, part 1: **259–278**

Eyerly, Jeannette (1908)
Writers for Young Adults, vol. 1: **403–411**

Fagundes Telles, Lygia (1923)
Latin American Writers, vol. 3: **1271–1275**

Farah, Nuruddin (1945)
African Writers, vol. 1: **249–262**

Farjeon, Eleanor (1881)
Writers for Children: **227–234**

Farmer, Philip José (1918)
Science Fiction Writers: **369–375**

Farrell, James T. (1904)
American Writers, vol. 2: **25–53**

Faulkner, William (1897)
American Writers, vol. 2: **54–76**
American Writers Retrospective: **73–95**

Fauset, Jessie (1882)
Modern American Women Writers: **123–139**

Fernández, Macedonio (1874)
Latin American Writers, vol. 2: **483–491**

Ferreira de Castro, Jose Maria (1898)
European Writers, vol. 11: **2143–2165**

Feydeau, Georges (1862)
See "Well-Made Play, The"

Field, Rachel Lyman (1894)
Writers for Children: **235–240**

Finch, Robert Charles (1943)
American Nature Writers, vol. 1: **309–321**

Finney, Charles (1905)
Supernatural Fiction Writers, vol. 2: **821–826**

Firbank, Ronald (1886)
British Writers Supp. 2: **199–224**

Fitzgerald, F. Scott (1896)
American Writers, vol. 2: **77–100**
American Writers Retrospective: **97–120**

Ford, Ford Madox (1873)
British Writers, vol. 6: **319–334**

Forms of American Nature Poetry, The
American Nature Writers, vol. 2: **1079–1098**

Forster, E. M. (1879)
British Writers, vol. 6: **397–414**
British Writers Selected Authors, vol. 2: **511–527**
Supernatural Fiction Writers, vol. 1: **479–484**

Fortune, Dion (1890)
Supernatural Fiction Writers, vol. 2: **585–590**

Foucault, Michel (1926)
European Writers, vol. 13: **3323–3364**

Fowles, John (1926)
British Writers Supp. 1: **291–311**

Fox, Paula (1923)
Writers for Young Adults, vol. 1: **413–422**

France, Anatole (1844)
Supernatural Fiction Writers, vol. 1: **67–72**

Frank, Anne (1929)
Writers for Young Adults, vol. 1: **423–431**

Frazer, James George (1854)
British Writers Supp. 3: **169–190**

Freedman, Russell (1929)
Writers for Young Adults, vol. 2: **1–9**

Freeman, Mary E. Wilkins (1852)
Modern American Women Writers: **141–153**
Supernatural Fiction Writers, vol. 2: **769–773**

French, Michael (1944)
Writers for Young Adults, vol. 2: **11–20**

Freud, Sigmund (1856)
European Writers, vol. 8: **1–20**
European Writers Selected Authors, vol. 1: **575–594**

Frisch, Max (1911)
European Writers, vol. 13: **2895–2924**

Frost, Robert (1874)
American Writers, vol. 2: **150–172**
American Writers Retrospective: **121–144**
Writers for Young Adults, vol. 2: **21–31**

Fry, Christopher (1907)
British Writers Supp. 3: **191–210**

Fuentes, Carlos (1928)
Latin American Writers, vol. 3: **1353–1376**

Fugard, Athol (1932)
African Writers, vol. 1: **263–275**

Gaddis, William (1922)
American Writers Supp. 4, part 1: **279–296**

Gág, Wanda (1893)
Writers for Children: **241–246**

Gaines, Ernest J. (1933)
African American Writers: **129–145**

Gallegos, Rómulo (1884)
Latin American Writers, vol. 2: **603–610**

Galsworthy, John (1867)
British Writers, vol. 6: **269–293**

Gálvez, Manuel (1882)
Latin American Writers, vol. 2: **585–589**

Gambaro, Griselda (1928)
Latin American Writers, vol. 3: **1323–1328**

Gamboa, Federico (1864)
Latin American Writers, vol. 1: **371–375**

García Lorca, Federico (1898)
European Writers, vol. 11: **2167–2203**
European Writers Selected Authors, vol. 1: **595–630**

García Márquez, Gabriel (1928)
Latin American Writers, vol. 3: **1329–1346**

Garfield, Leon (1921)
Writers for Young Adults, vol. 2: **33–45**

Garner, Alan (1934)
Supernatural Fiction Writers, vol. 2: **1023–1029**

Garnett, David (1892)
Supernatural Fiction Writers, vol. 2: **535–539**

Genet, Jean (1910)
European Writers, vol. 13: **2865–2892**

George, Jean Craighead (1919)
Writers for Young Adults, vol. 2: **47–57**

George, Stefan (1868)
European Writers, vol. 8: **447–470**

Ghelderode, Michel de (1898)
European Writers, vol. 11: **2113–2141**

Gide, André (1869)
European Writers, vol. 8: **495–518**
European Writers Selected Authors, vol. 1: **631–654**

Gilman, Charlotte Perkins (1860)
Modern American Women Writers: **155–170**

Ginsberg, Allen (1926)
  American Writers Supp. 2, part 1: **307–333**
Ginzburg, Natalia (1916)
  European Writers, vol. 13: **3131–3163**
Giraudoux, Jean (1882)
  European Writers, vol. 9: **1041–1065**
Glaspell, Susan (1876)
  American Writers Supp. 3, part 1: **175–191**
  Modern American Women Writers: **181–188**
Golding, William (1911)
  British Writers Supp. 1: **65–91**
  British Writers Selected Authors, vol. 2: **529–555**
Gombrowicz, Witold (1904)
  European Writers, vol. 12: **2563–2588**
Gómez Carillo, Enrique (1873)
  Latin American Writers, vol. 2: **465–469**
González Prada, Manuel (1844)
  Latin American Writers, vol. 1: **283–288**
Gordimer, Nadine (1923)
  African Writers, vol. 1: **277–290**
  British Writers Supp. 2: **225–245**
Gordon, Caroline (1895)
  American Writers, vol. 2: **196–222**
Gordon, Mary (1949)
  American Writers Supp. 4, part 1: **297–317**
Gorky, Maxim (1868)
  European Writers, vol. 8: **417–446**
  European Writers Selected Authors, vol. 2:
    681–710
Gorostiza, José (1901)
  Latin American Writers, vol. 2: **923–931**
Grahame, Kenneth (1859)
  Writers for Children: **247–254**
Grass, Günter (1927)
  European Writers, vol. 13: **3365–3388**
  European Writers Selected Authors, vol. 2: **711–734**
Graves, John (1920)
  American Nature Writers, vol. 1: **323–336**
Graves, Robert (1895)
  British Writers, vol. 7: **257–272**
Green, Henry (1905)
  British Writers Supp. 2: **247–266**
Greene, Bette (1934)
  Writers for Young Adults, vol. 2: **59–68**

Greene, Graham (1904)
  British Writers Supp. 1: **1–20**
  British Writers Selected Authors, vol. 2: **557–576**
Gregory, Lady Augusta (1852)
  See "Synge, J. M., and Lady Augusta Gregory"
Guillén, Nicolás (1902)
  Latin American Writers, vol. 2: **947–955**
Guimarães Rosa, João (1908)
  Latin American Writers, vol. 3: **1069–1080**
Güiraldes, Ricardo (1886)
  Latin American Writers, vol. 2: **619–627**
Gunn, Thom (1929)
  British Writers Supp. 4: **255–279**
Gunn Allen, Paula (1939)
  American Writers Supp. 4, part 1: **319–340**
Gunnarsson, Gunnar (1889)
  European Writers, vol. 10: **1497–1519**
Gutiérrez Nájera, Manuel (1859)
  Latin American Writers, vol. 1: **351–357**
Guzmán, Martín Luis (1887)
  Latin American Writers, vol. 2: **655–662**
Haggard, H. Rider (1856)
  British Writers Supp. 3: **211–228**
  Science Fiction Writers: **19–24**
  Supernatural Fiction Writers, vol. 1: **321–327**
Ḥakīm, Tawfīq, al- (1898)
  African Writers, vol. 1: **291–301**
Hall, Lynn (1937)
  Writers for Young Adults, vol. 2: **69–77**
Hamilton, Virginia (1936)
  Writers for Young Adults, vol. 2: **79–92**
Hammett, Dashiell (1894)
  American Writers Supp. 4, part 1: **341–357**
Hamsun, Knut (1859)
  European Writers, vol. 8: **21–43**
Hansberry, Lorraine (1930)
  African American Writers: **147–158**
  American Writers Supp. 4, part 1: **359–377**
Hardwick, Elizabeth (1916)
  American Writers Supp. 3, part 1: **193–215**
  Modern American Women Writers: **189–196**
Hardy, Thomas (1840)
  British Writers, vol. 6: **1–22**
  British Writers Selected Authors, vol. 2: **577–598**

Hare, David (1947)
  British Writers Supp. 4: **281–300**

Harper, Frances Ellen Watkins (1825)
  African American Writers: **159–175**
  Modern American Women Writers: **197–205**

Harris, Joel Chandler (1848)
  Writers for Children: **269–275**

Hartley, L. P. (1895)
  Supernatural Fiction Writers, vol. 2: **639–644**

Harvey, William Fryer (1885)
  Supernatural Fiction Writers, vol. 2: **591–596**

Hašek, Jaroslav (1883)
  European Writers, vol. 9: **1091–1118**

Hasselstrom, Linda (1943)
  American Nature Writers, vol. 1: **337–348**

Hauptmann, Gerhart (1862)
  European Writers, vol. 8: **147–174**

Hay, John (1915)
  American Nature Writers, vol. 1: **349–362**

Hayden, Robert Earl (1913)
  African American Writers: **177–192**
  American Writers Supp. 2, part 1: **361–383**

Head, Bessie (1937)
  African Writers, vol. 1: **303–320**

Heaney, Seamus (1939)
  British Writers Supp. 2: **267–282**

Heinlein, Robert A. (1907)
  Science Fiction Writers: **185–196**

Heiremans, Luis Alberto (1928)
  Latin American Writers, vol. 3: **1347–1352**

Heller, Joseph (1923)
  American Writers Supp. 4, part 1: **379–396**

Hellman, Lillian (1905)
  American Writers Supp. 1, part 1: **276–298**
  Modern American Women Writers: **207–220**

Hemingway, Ernest (1899)
  American Writers, vol. 2: **247–270**
  American Writers Retrospective: **169–191**
  Writers for Young Adults, vol. 2: **93–102**

Henríquez Ureña, Pedro (1884)
  Latin American Writers, vol. 2: **597–601**

Henry, O. (1862)
  American Writers Supp. 2, part 1: **385–412**

Hentoff, Nat (1925)
  Writers for Young Adults, vol. 2: **103–112**

Herbert, Frank (1920)
  Science Fiction Writers: **377–385**

Herrera y Reissig, Julio (1875)
  Latin American Writers, vol. 2: **519–530**

Hervieu, Paul (1857)
  See "Well-Made Play, The"

Hesse, Hermann (1877)
  European Writers, vol. 9: **833–859**
  European Writers Selected Authors, vol. 2: **735–760**

Hichens, Robert (1864)
  Supernatural Fiction Writers, vol. 1: **415–420**

Hinton, S. E. (1948)
  Writers for Young Adults, vol. 2: **113–120**

Hoagland, Edward (1932)
  American Nature Writers, vol. 1: **363–375**

Hobbs, Will (1947)
  Writers for Young Adults, vol. 2: **121–129**

Hodgson, William Hope (1877)
  Supernatural Fiction Writers, vol. 1: **421–428**

Hofmannsthal, Hugo von (1874)
  European Writers, vol. 9: **689–714**

Hogan, Linda (1947)
  American Nature Writers, vol. 1: **377–388**
  American Writers Supp. 4, part 1: **397–418**

Holland, Isabelle (1920)
  Writers for Young Adults, vol. 2: **131–140**

Honwana, Luís Bernardo (1942)
  African Writers, vol. 1: **321–329**

Hoover, Helen (1910)
  American Nature Writers, vol. 1: **389–399**

Hope, Christopher (1944)
  African Writers, vol. 1: **331–343**

Housman, A. E. (1859)
  British Writers, vol. 6: **151–164**
  British Writers Selected Authors, vol. 2: **621–634**

Howard, Robert E. (1906)
  Supernatural Fiction Writers, vol. 2: **861–868**

Howe, Susan (1937)
  American Writers Supp. 4, part 2: **419–438**

Howells, William Dean (1837)
  American Writers, vol. 2: **271–294**

Hoyle, Fred (1915)
  Science Fiction Writers: **387–392**

Hubbell, Sue (1935)
  American Nature Writers, vol. 1: **401–412**

Hughes, Langston (1902)
African American Writers: **193–205**
American Writers Retrospective: **193–214**
American Writers Supp. 1, part 1: **320–348**
Writers for Children: **295–301**

Hughes, Monica (1925)
Writers for Young Adults, vol. 2: **141–148**

Hughes, Ted (1930)
British Writers Supp. 1: **341–366**

Huidobro, Vicente (1893)
Latin American Writers, vol. 2: **755–764**

Hunter, Mollie (1922)
Writers for Young Adults, vol. 2: **149–159**

Hurston, Zora Neale (1891)
African American Writers: **205–218**
Modern American Women Writers: **221–235**

Huxley, Aldous (1894)
British Writers, vol. 7: **197–208**
British Writers Selected Authors, vol. 2: **635–646**
Science Fiction Writers: **101–108**

Huysmans, Joris Karl (1847)
European Writers, vol. 7: **1709–1729**

Ibarbourou, Juana de (1895)
Latin American Writers, vol. 2: **803–807**

Icaza, Jorge (1906)
Latin American Writers, vol. 3: **1063–1067**

Idrīs, Yūsuf (1927)
African Writers, vol. 1: **345–365**

Ionesco, Eugène (1912)
European Writers, vol. 13: **2989–3020**
European Writers Selected Authors, vol. 2: **815–846**

Irwin, Hadley (1934; 1915)
Writers for Young Adults, vol. 2: **161–166**

Isherwood, Christopher (1904)
British Writers, vol. 7: **309–320**

Ishiguro, Kazuo (1954)
British Writers Supp. 4: **301–317**

Iyayi, Festus (1947)
African Writers, vol. 1: **367–375**

Jackson, Shirley (1919)
Supernatural Fiction Writers, vol. 2: **1031–1036**

Jacobs, Joseph (1854)
Writers for Children: **309–316**

Jacobs, W. W. (1863)
Supernatural Fiction Writers, vol. 1: **383–387**

Jacobson, Dan (1929)
African Writers, vol. 1: **377–389**

Jaimes Freyre, Ricardo (1868)
Latin American Writers, vol. 1: **419–423**

James, Henry (1843)
American Writers, vol. 2: **319–341**
American Writers Retrospective: **215–242**
British Writers, vol. 6: **23–69**
Supernatural Fiction Writers, vol. 1: **337–344**

James, M. R. (1862)
Supernatural Fiction Writers, vol. 1: **429–436**

James, P. D. (1920)
British Writers Supp. 4: **319–341**

James, William (1842)
American Writers, vol. 2: **342–366**

Janovy, John, Jr. (1937)
American Nature Writers, vol. 1: **413–424**

Jarrell, Randall (1914)
American Writers, vol. 2: **367–390**

Jarry, Alfred (1873)
European Writers, vol. 9: **665–687**

Jeffers, Robinson (1887)
American Writers Supp. 2, part 2: **413–440**

Jiménez, Juan Ramón (1881)
European Writers, vol. 9: **991–1016**

Johnson, Cathy (1942)
American Nature Writers, vol. 1: **425–438**

Johnson, Eyvind (1900)
European Writers, vol. 12: **2361–2385**

Johnson, James Weldon (1871)
African American Writers: **219–233**

Johnson, Josephine (1910)
American Nature Writers, vol. 1: **439–451**

Johnston, Norma
Writers for Young Adults, vol. 2: **167–176**

Jones, David (1895)
See "Poets of World War I (British)"

Jones, Gayl (1949)
African American Writers: **235–244**

Jones, Henry Arthur (1851)
See "Well-Made Play, The"

Jordan, June (1936)
African American Writers: **245–261**

Joyce, James (1882)
British Writers, vol. 7: **41–58**
British Writers Selected Authors, vol. 2: **683–700**

Kafka, Franz (1883)
European Writers, vol. 9: **1151–1179**
European Writers Selected Authors, vol. 2: **847–875**

Kappel-Smith, Diana (1951)
American Nature Writers, vol. 1: **453–463**

Kästner, Erich (1899)
Writers for Children: **317–322**

Kateb, Yacine (1929)
African Writers, vol. 1: **391–400**

Kazantzakis, Nikos (1883)
European Writers, vol. 9: **1067–1091**

Keller, David H. (1880)
Science Fiction Writers: **119–123**

Keneally, Thomas (1935)
British Writers Supp. 4: **343–362**

Kerouac, Jack (1922)
American Writers Supp. 3, part 1: **217–234**

Kerr, M. E. (1927)
Writers for Young Adults, vol. 2: **177–185**

Khlebnikov, Velimir (1885)
European Writers, vol. 10: **1331–1364**

King, Stephen (1947)
Supernatural Fiction Writers, vol. 2: **1037–1044**

Kingston, Maxine Hong (1940)
Modern American Women Writers: **251–259**

Kinnell, Galway (1927)
American Writers Supp. 3, part 1: **235–256**

Kipling, Rudyard (1865)
British Writers, vol. 6: **165–206**
British Writers Selected Authors, vol. 2: **729–770**
Supernatural Fiction Writers, vol. 1: **437–442**
Writers for Children: **329–336**

Klein, Norma (1938)
Writers for Young Adults, vol. 2: **187–197**

Knight, Damon (1922)
Science Fiction Writers: **393–400**

Koestler, Arthur (1905)
British Writers Supp. 1: **21–41**

Korman, Gordon (1963)
Writers for Young Adults, vol. 2: **199–206**

Kornbluth, C. M. (1923)
Science Fiction Writers: **401–407**

Kosztolányi, Dezsö (1885)
European Writers, vol. 10: **1231–1249**

Krleža, Miroslav (1893)
European Writers, vol. 11: **1807–1834**

Krutch, Joseph Wood (1893)
American Nature Writers, vol. 1: **465–477**

Kumin, Maxine (1925)
American Nature Writers, vol. 1: **479–497**
American Writers Supp. 4, part 2: **439–457**

Kundera, Milan (1929)
European Writers, vol. 13: **3389–3413**

Kunitz, Stanley (1905)
American Writers Supp. 3, part 1: **257–270**

Kuttner, Henry (1915)
Science Fiction Writers: **161–167**

LaBastille, Anne (1938)
American Nature Writers, vol. 1: **499–511**

Lafferty, R. A. (1914)
Supernatural Fiction Writers, vol. 2: **1045–1052**

Lagerkvist, Pär (1891)
European Writers, vol. 10: **1677–1702**

Laguerre, Enrique A. (1906)
Latin American Writers, vol. 3: **1049–1055**

La Guma, Alex (1925)
African Writers, vol. 1: **401–411**

Lampedusa, Giuseppe Tomasi di (1896)
European Writers, vol. 11: **2009–2034**

Lang, Andrew (1844)
Writers for Children: **337–343**

Lardner, Ring (1885)
American Writers, vol. 2: **415–438**

Larkin, Phillip (1922)
British Writers Supp. 1: **275–290**

Larreta, Enrique (1873)
Latin American Writers, vol. 2: **471–476**

Larsen, Nella (1891)
African American Writers: **263–272**

Lasky, Kathryn (1944)
Writers for Young Adults, vol. 2: **207–216**

Lawrence, D. H. (1885)
British Writers, vol. 7: **87–126**
British Writers Selected Authors, vol. 2: **771–810**

Lawrence, T. E. (1888)
British Writers Supp. 2: **283–298**

Lawson, Robert (1892)
Writers for Children: **345–349**

Laxness, Halldór (1902)
  European Writers, vol. 12: **2457–2478**

Laye, Camara (1928)
  African Writers, vol. 1: **413–425**

Least Heat-Moon, William (1939)
  American Nature Writers, vol. 1: **513–523**

Leavis, F. R. (1895)
  British Writers, vol. 7: **233–256**

Le Carré, John (1931)
  British Writers Supp. 2: **299–320**
  British Writers Selected Authors, vol. 2: **811–832**

Lee, Harper (1926)
  Writers for Young Adults, vol. 2: **217–225**

Lee, Tanith (1947)
  Supernatural Fiction Writers, vol. 2: **1053–1058**

Lee, Vernon (1856)
  Supernatural Fiction Writers, vol. 1: **329–335**

Le Guin, Ursula K. (1929)
  Science Fiction Writers: **409–417**
  Supernatural Fiction Writers, vol. 2: **1059–1066**
  Writers for Young Adults, vol. 2: **227–236**
  See also "Contemporary Ecofiction"

Leiber, Fritz (1910)
  Science Fiction Writers: **419–424**
  Supernatural Fiction Writers, vol. 2: **933–939**

Leinster, Murray (1896)
  Science Fiction Writers: **111–117**

Łem, Stanisław (1921)
  Science Fiction Writers: **591–598**

L'Engle, Madeleine (1918)
  Writers for Young Adults, vol. 2: **237–246**

Leopold, Aldo (1887)
  American Nature Writers, vol. 1: **525–547**

Lessing, Doris (1919)
  African Writers, vol. 1: **427–449**
  British Writers Supp. 1: **237–257**
  British Writers Selected Authors, vol. 2: **833–853**

Levertov, Denise (1923)
  American Writers Supp. 3, part 1: **271–287**

Lewis, C. S. (1898)
  British Writers Supp. 3: **247–268**
  British Writers Selected Authors, vol. 2: **855–876**
  Science Fiction Writers: **243–248**
  Supernatural Fiction Writers, vol. 2: **661–666**
  Writers for Children: **357–364**
  Writers for Young Adults, vol. 2: **247–255**

Lewis, Sinclair (1885)
  American Writers, vol. 2: **439–461**

Lewis, Wyndham (1884)
  British Writers, vol. 7: **71–86**

Lezama Lima, José (1910)
  Latin American Writers, vol. 3: **1125–1130**

Lima, Jorge de (1893)
  Latin American Writers, vol. 2: **765–770**

Lima Barreto, Afonso Henriques de (1881)
  Latin American Writers, vol. 2: **565–573**

Lindsay, David (1878)
  Supernatural Fiction Writers, vol. 2: **541–547**

Lindsay, Vachel (1879)
  American Writers Supp. 1, part 2: **374–403**

Lins do Rego, José (1901)
  Latin American Writers, vol. 2: **909–913**

Lipsyte, Robert (1938)
  Writers for Young Adults, vol. 2: **257–266**

Lispector, Clarice (1925)
  Latin American Writers, vol. 3: **1303–1309**

Literary Theory and Nature Writing
  American Nature Writers, vol. 2: **1099–1114**

Literature of Mountaineering
  American Nature Writers, vol. 2: **1115–1128**

Lodge, David (1935)
  British Writers Supp. 4: **363–387**

Lofting, Hugh (1886)
  Writers for Children: **365–371**

London, Jack (1876)
  American Writers, vol. 2: **462–485**
  Writers for Young Adults, vol. 2: **267–278**

Long, Frank Belknap (1903)
  Supernatural Fiction Writers, vol. 2: **869–874**

Lopez, Barry (1945)
  American Nature Writers, vol. 1: **549–568**

Lopez Velarde, Ramon (1888)
  Latin American Writers, vol. 2: **663–670**

Lorde, Audre (1934)
  African American Writers: **273–288**

Lovecraft, H. P. (1890)
  Science Fiction Writers: **131–137**
  Supernatural Fiction Writers, vol. 2: **853–859**

Lowell, Amy (1874)
  American Writers, vol. 2: **511–533**
  Modern American Women Writers: **261–268**

Lowell, Robert (1917)
    American Writers, vol. 2: **534–557**

Lowry, Lois (1937)
    Writers for Young Adults, vol. 2: **279–287**

Lowry, Malcolm (1909)
    British Writers Supp. 3: **269–286**

Lugones, Leopoldo (1874)
    Latin American Writers, vol. 2: **493–502**

Lukács, György (1885)
    European Writers, vol. 10: **1251–1279**

Lynch, Benito (1880)
    Latin American Writers, vol. 2: **559–563**

Lynch, Chris (1962)
    Writers for Young Adults, vol. 2: **289–297**

McCaffrey, Anne (1926)
    Writers for Young Adults, vol. 2: **299–306**

McCarthy, Mary (1912)
    American Writers, vol. 2: **558–584**
    Modern American Women Writers: **269–278**

McCullers, Carson (1917)
    American Writers, vol. 2: **585–608**
    Modern American Women Writers: **279–287**

Macdonald, Ross (1915)
    American Writers Supp. 4, part 2: **459–477**

McEwan, Ian (1948)
    British Writers Supp. 4: **389–408**

Machado, Antonio (1875)
    European Writers, vol. 9: **743–765**

Machen, Arthur (1863)
    Supernatural Fiction Writers, vol. 1: **351–359**

McKay, Claude (1890)
    African American Writers: **305–320**

McKibben, Bill (1960)
    See "New Voices in American Nature Writing"

McKillip, Patricia (1948)
    Supernatural Fiction Writers, vol. 2: **1067–1072**

Maclean, Norman (1902)
    See "Contemporary Ecofiction"

MacLeish, Archibald (1892)
    American Writers, vol. 3: **1–25**

Macleod, Fiona (1855)
    Supernatural Fiction Writers, vol. 1: **369–374**

MacNeice, Louis (1907)
    British Writers, vol. 7: **401–420**

McNulty, Faith (1918)
    American Nature Writers, vol. 1: **569–581**

McPhee, John (1931)
    American Nature Writers, vol. 1: **583–598**
    American Writers Supp. 3, part 1: **289–316**

Maeterlinck, Maurice (1862)
    European Writers, vol. 8: **119–146**

Maḥfūẓ, Najīb (1911)
    African Writers, vol. 2: **451–465**

Mahy, Margaret (May) (1936)
    Writers for Young Adults, vol. 2: **307–315**

Mailer, Norman (1923)
    American Writers, vol. 3: **26–49**

Major, Kevin (1949)
    Writers for Young Adults, vol. 2: **317–326**

Malamud, Bernard (1914)
    American Writers Supp. 1, part 2: **427–453**

Mallea, Eduardo (1903)
    Latin American Writers, vol. 3: **981–989**

Malraux, André (1901)
    European Writers, vol. 12: **2413–2432**
    European Writers Selected Authors, vol. 2: **977–996**

Mañach Robato, Jorge (1898)
    Latin American Writers, vol. 2: **831–836**

Mandelshtam, Osip (1891)
    European Writers, vol. 10: **1619–1649**

Mann, Heinrich (1871)
    European Writers, vol. 8: **519–543**

Mann, Thomas (1875)
    European Writers, vol. 9: **715–743**
    European Writers Selected Authors, vol. 2:
        997–1024

Mansfield, Katherine (1888)
    British Writers, vol. 7: **171–184**
    British Writers Selected Authors, vol. 2: **891–904**

Marechal, Leopoldo (1900)
    Latin American Writers, vol. 2: **887–896**

Mariátegui, José Carlos (1894)
    Latin American Writers, vol. 2: **791–796**

Marín Cañas, José (1904)
    Latin American Writers, vol. 3: **991–994**

Marinetti, Filippo Tommaso (1876)
    European Writers, vol. 9: **797–832**

Marquand, John P. (1893)
    American Writers, vol. 3: **50–73**

Marqués, René (1919)
Latin American Writers, vol. 3: **1237–1246**

Marshall, Paule (1929)
African American Writers: **289–304**

Martínez Estrada, Ezequiel (1895)
Latin American Writers, vol. 2: **809–813**

Masters, Edgar Lee (1868)
American Writers Supp. 1, part 2: **454–478**

Matheson, Richard (1926)
Science Fiction Writers: **425–431**
Supernatural Fiction Writers, vol. 2: **1073–1080**

Matthiessen, Peter (1927)
American Nature Writers, vol. 2: **599–613**

Matto de Turner, Clorinda (1852)
Latin American Writers, vol. 1: **305–309**

Maugham, W. Somerset (1874)
British Writers, vol. 6: **363–382**
British Writers Selected Authors, vol. 2: **905–923**

Mauriac, François (1885)
European Writers, vol. 10: **1307–1330**

Mayakovsky, Vladimir (1893)
European Writers, vol. 11: **1835–1858**

Mazer, Harry (1925)
Writers for Young Adults, vol. 2: **327–336**

Mazer, Norma Fox (1931)
Writers for Young Adults, vol. 2: **337–346**

Meigs, Cornelia (1884)
Writers for Children: **389–395**

Meireles, Cecília (1901)
Latin American Writers, vol. 2: **915–922**

Meltzer, Milton (1915)
Writers for Young Adults, vol. 2: **347–358**

Memmi, Albert (1920)
African Writers, vol. 2: **467–477**

Mencken, H. L. (1880)
American Writers, vol. 3: **99–121**

Merril, Judith (1923)
Science Fiction Writers: **433–439**

Merrill, James (1926)
American Writers Supp. 3, part 1: **317–338**

Merritt, A. (1884)
Science Fiction Writers: **65–71**
Supernatural Fiction Writers, vol. 2: **835–843**

Merwin, W. S. (1927)
American Writers Supp. 3, part 1: **339–360**

Metcalfe, John (1891)
Supernatural Fiction Writers, vol. 2: **597–602**

Miklowitz, Gloria D. (1927)
Writers for Young Adults, vol. 2: **359–368**

Millay, Edna St. Vincent (1892)
American Writers, vol. 3: **122–144**
Modern American Women Writers: **287–302**

Miller, Arthur (1915)
American Writers, vol. 3: **145–169**

Miller, Henry (1891)
American Writers, vol. 3: **170–192**

Miller, Walter M., Jr. (1923)
Science Fiction Writers: **441–448**

Mills, Enos (1870)
American Nature Writers, vol. 2: **615–624**

Milne, A. A. (1882)
Writers for Children: **397–405**

Milosz, Czeslaw (1911)
European Writers, vol. 13: **2929–2952**

Mirrlees, Hope (1887)
Supernatural Fiction Writers, vol. 2: **603–607**

Mistral, Gabriela (1889)
Latin American Writers, vol. 2: **677–692**

Mitchell, John Hanson (1940)
American Nature Writers, vol. 2: **625–638**

Moberg, Vilhelm (1898)
European Writers, vol. 11: **2203–2231**

Modern Birdwatching Literature
American Nature Writers, vol. 2: **1129–1140**

Mofolo, Thomas Mokopu (1876)
African Writers, vol. 2: **479–493**

Mohr, Nicholasa (1935)
Writers for Young Adults, vol. 2: **369–378**

Molesworth, M. L. S. (1839)
Writers for Children: **407–413**

Molina, Juan Ramón (1875)
Latin American Writers, vol. 2: **539–542**

Molinari, Ricardo E. (1898)
Latin American Writers, vol. 2: **837–844**

Momaday, N. Scott (1934)
American Nature Writers, vol. 2: **639–649**
American Writers Supp. 4, part 2: **479–495**

Montale, Eugenio (1896)
European Writers, vol. 11: **1987–2008**

Montgomery, L. M. (1874)
  Writers for Children: **415–422**
  Writers for Young Adults, vol. 2: **379–386**

Montherlant, Henry de (1895)
  European Writers, vol. 11: **1915–1938**

Moorcock, Michael (1939)
  Science Fiction Writers: **449–457**
  Supernatural Fiction Writers, vol. 2: **1081–1089**

Moore, C. L. (1911)
  Supernatural Fiction Writers, vol. 2: **891–898**
  See also "Moore, C. L., and Henry Kuttner"

Moore, C. L., and Henry Kuttner
  Science Fiction Writers: **161–167**

Moore, Marianne (1887)
  American Writers, vol. 3: **193–217**
  Modern American Women Writers: **303–316**

Moravia, Alberto (1907)
  European Writers, vol. 12: **2673–2697**

Morison, Samuel Eliot (1887)
  American Writers Supp. 1, part 2: **479–500**

Morris, Wright (1910)
  American Writers, vol. 3: **218–243**

Morrison, Toni (1931)
  African American Writers: **321–333**
  American Writers Supp. 3, part 1: **361–381**
  Modern American Women Writers: **317–338**

Mphahlele, Es'kia (1919)
  African Writers, vol. 2: **495–510**

Muir, John (1838)
  American Nature Writers, vol. 2: **651–669**

Muldoon, Paul (1951)
  British Writers Supp. 4: **409–432**

Mumford, Lewis (1895)
  American Writers Supp. 2, part 2: **471–501**

Mundy, Talbot (1879)
  Supernatural Fiction Writers, vol. 2: **845–851**

Murdoch, Iris (1919)
  British Writers Supp. 1: **215–235**

Musil, Robert (1880)
  European Writers, vol. 9: **931–958**

Mwangi, Meja (1948)
  African Writers, vol. 2: **511–525**

Myers, Walter Dean (1937)
  Writers for Young Adults, vol. 2: **387–396**

Nabhan, Gary Paul (1952)
  American Nature Writers, vol. 2: **671–681**

Nabokov, Vladimir (1899)
  American Writers, vol. 3: **244–266**
  American Writers Retrospective: **263–281**

Naipaul, V. S. (1932)
  British Writers Supp. 1: **383–405**

Nathan, Robert (1894)
  Supernatural Fiction Writers, vol. 2: **813–819**

Nature in Native American Literatures
  American Nature Writers, vol. 2: **1141–1156**

Naylor, Gloria (1950)
  African American Writers: **335–347**

Naylor, Phyllis Reynolds (1933)
  Writers for Young Adults, vol. 2: **397–409**

Nelson, Richard K. (1941)
  American Nature Writers, vol. 2: **683–696**

Nemerov, Howard (1920)
  American Writers, vol. 3: **267–289**

Neruda, Pablo (1904)
  Latin American Writers, vol. 3: **1001–1018**

Nervo, Amado (1870)
  Latin American Writers, vol. 1: **425–429**

Nesbit, E. (1858)
  Writers for Children: **423–430**

Neto, Agostinho (1922)
  African Writers, vol. 2: **527–535**

New Voices in American Nature Writing
  American Nature Writers, vol. 2: **1157–1173**

Ngũgĩ wa Thiong'o (1938)
  African Writers, vol. 2: **537–555**

Niebuhr, Reinhold (1892)
  American Writers, vol. 3: **290–313**

Nin, Anaïs (1903)
  Modern American Women Writers: **339–351**

Niven, Larry (1938)
  Science Fiction Writers: **459–465**

Nixon, Joan Lowery (1927)
  Writers for Young Adults, vol. 2: **411–419**

Norton, Andre (1912)
  Supernatural Fiction Writers, vol. 2: **1091–1096**

Oates, Joyce Carol (1938)
  American Writers Supp. 2, part 2: **503–527**
  Modern American Women Writers: **353–374**

O'Brien, Flann (1911)
British Writers Supp. 2: **321–339**

Ocampo, Victoria (1890)
Latin American Writers, vol. 2: **705–710**

O'Casey, Sean (1880)
British Writers, vol. 7: **1–16**

O'Connor, Flannery (1925)
American Writers, vol. 3: **337–360**
Modern American Women Writers: **375–388**

O'Dell, Scott (1903)
Writers for Young Adults, vol. 2: **421–431**

Odets, Clifford (1906)
American Writers Supp. 2, part 2: **529–554**

O'Hara, John (1905)
American Writers, vol. 3: **361–384**

Ojaide, Tanure (1948)
African Writers, vol. 2: **557–565**

Okara, Gabriel (1921)
African Writers, vol. 2: **567–582**

Okigbo, Christopher (1932)
African Writers, vol. 2: **583–598**

Okri, Ben (1959)
African Writers, vol. 2: **599–608**

Olesha, Yuri (1899)
European Writers, vol. 11: **2233–2253**

Oliver, Chad (1928)
Science Fiction Writers: **467–473**

Olson, Charles (1910)
American Writers Supp. 2, part 2: **555–587**

Olson, Sigurd F. (1899)
American Nature Writers, vol. 2: **697–709**

Omotoso, Kole (1943)
African Writers, vol. 2: **609–617**

Oneal, Zibby (1934)
Writers for Young Adults, vol. 2: **433–442**

O'Neill, Eugene (1888)
American Writers, vol. 3: **385–408**

Onetti, Juan Carlos (1909)
Latin American Writers, vol. 3: **1089–1097**

Onions, Oliver (1873)
Supernatural Fiction Writers, vol. 1: **505–511**

Ortega y Gasset, José (1883)
European Writers, vol. 9: **1119–1150**

Ortiz, Simon J. (1941)
American Writers Supp. 4, part 2: **497–515**

Orwell, George (1903)
British Writers, vol. 7: **273–288**
British Writers Selected Authors, vol. 2: **947–961**
Science Fiction Writers: **233–241**

Osborne, John (1929)
British Writers Supp. 1: **329–340**

Osofisan, Femi (1946)
African Writers, vol. 2: **619–629**

Osundare, Niyi (1947)
African Writers, vol. 2: **631–640**

Oyono, Ferdinand (1929)
African Writers, vol. 2: **641–649**

Pain, Barry (1864)
Supernatural Fiction Writers, vol. 1: **443–448**

Palés Matos, Luis (1898)
Latin American Writers, vol. 2: **821–830**

Paley, Grace (1922)
Modern American Women Writers: **389–396**

Palma, Ricardo (1833)
Latin American Writers, vol. 1: **221–228**

Parker, Dorothy (1893)
Modern American Women Writers: **397–409**

Parra, Nicanor (1914)
Latin American Writers, vol. 3: **1195–1200**

Parra Sanojo, Ana Teresa de la (1890)
Latin American Writers, vol. 2: **717–720**

Pascoli, Giovanni (1855)
European Writers, vol. 7: **1825–1854**

Pasternak, Boris (1890)
European Writers, vol. 10: **1591–1618**
European Writers Selected Authors, vol. 2:
  1227–1253

Paterson, Katherine (1932)
Writers for Young Adults, vol. 2: **443–454**

Paton, Alan (1903)
African Writers, vol. 2: **651–668**
British Writers Supp. 2: **341–361**
British Writers Selected Authors, vol. 2: **963–983**

Paulsen, Gary (1939)
Writers for Young Adults, vol. 2: **455–463**

Pavese, Cesare (1908)
European Writers, vol. 12: **2759–2784**

Payró, Roberto Jorge (1867)
Latin American Writers, vol. 1: **413–417**

Paz, Octavio (1914)
Latin American Writers, vol. 3: **1163–1176**

p'Bitek, Okot (1931)
African Writers, vol. 2: **669–684**

Peck, Richard (1934)
Writers for Young Adults, vol. 3: **1–14**

Peck, Robert Newton (1928)
Writers for Young Adults, vol. 3: **15–26**

Pepetela (1941)
African Writers, vol. 2: **685–695**

Percy, Walker (1916)
American Writers Supp. 3, part 1: **383–400**

Pérez Galdós, Benito (1843)
European Writers, vol. 7: **1597–1618**

Perrin, Noel (1927)
American Nature Writers, vol. 2: **711–720**

Perse, Saint-John (1887)
European Writers, vol. 10: **1429–1452**

Pessoa, Fernando (1885)
European Writers, vol. 10: **1475–1495**

Peterson, Brenda (1950)
American Nature Writers, vol. 2: **721–731**

Petry, Ann (1912)
African American Writers: **347–359**

Pevsner, Stella
Writers for Young Adults, vol. 3: **27–34**

Peyton, K. M. (1929)
Writers for Young Adults, vol. 3: **35–42**

Pfeffer, Susan Beth (1948)
Writers for Young Adults, vol. 3: **43–52**

Phillpotts, Eden (1862)
Supernatural Fiction Writers, vol. 2: **549–553**

Picón Salas, Mariano (1901)
Latin American Writers, vol. 2: **903–908**

Pinero, Arthur Wing (1855)
See "Well-Made Play, The"

Pinter, Harold (1930)
British Writers Supp. 1: **367–382**
British Writers Selected Authors, vol. 2: **985–1000**

Pirandello, Luigi (1867)
European Writers, vol. 8: **389–416**
European Writers Selected Authors, vol. 2:
1289–1316

Plath, Sylvia (1932)
American Writers Supp. 1, part 2: **526–549**
Modern American Women Writers: **411–424**

Platt, Kin (1911)
Writers for Young Adults, vol. 3: **53–60**

Plomer, William (1903)
African Writers, vol. 2: **697–706**

Poets of World War I (British)
British Writers, vol. 6: **415–442**
British Writers Selected Authors, vol. 3: **1445–1471**

Poets of World War II (British)
British Writers, vol. 7: **421–450**

Pohl, Frederik (1919)
Science Fiction Writers: **475–482**

Porter, Katherine Anne (1890)
American Writers, vol. 3: **433–355**
Modern American Women Writers: **425–440**

Potter, Beatrix (1866)
British Writers Supp. 3: **287–309**
Writers for Children: **439–446**

Pound, Ezra (1885)
American Writers, vol. 3: **456–479**
American Writers Retrospective: **283–294**

Powell, Anthony (1905)
British Writers, vol. 7: **343–352**

Powys, John Cowper (1872)
Supernatural Fiction Writers, vol. 2: **609–616**

Powys, T. F. (1875)
Supernatural Fiction Writers, vol. 2: **609–616**

Prado, Pedro (1886)
Latin American Writers, vol. 2: **643–647**

Pratt, Fletcher (1897)
See "De Camp, L. Sprague, and Fletcher Pratt"

Priestley, J. B. (1894)
British Writers, vol. 7: **209–232**

Pritchett, V. S. (1900)
British Writers Supp. 3: **311–331**

Proust, Marcel (1871)
European Writers, vol. 8: **545–568**
European Writers Selected Authors, vol. 2:
1317–1340

Puig, Manuel (1932)
Latin American Writers, vol. 3: **1405–1413**

Pyle, Howard (1852)
Writers for Children: **447–454**

Pyle, Robert Michael (1947)
American Nature Writers, vol. 2: **733–739**

Pym, Barbara (1913)
British Writers Supp. 2: **363–385**

Pynchon, Thomas (1937)
American Writers Supp. 2, part 2: **617–638**

Quammen, David (1948)
American Nature Writers, vol. 2: **741–750**

Quasimodo, Salvatore (1901)
European Writers, vol. 12: **2387–2411**

Queiroz, Rachel de (1910)
Latin American Writers, vol. 3: **1119–1123**

Queneau, Raymond (1903)
European Writers, vol. 12: **2511–2534**

Quiller-Couch, Arthur (1863)
Supernatural Fiction Writers, vol. 1: **389–395**

Quiroga, Horacio (1878)
Latin American Writers, vol. 2: **551–558**

Ramos, Graciliano (1892)
Latin American Writers, vol. 2: **745–754**

Rand, Ayn (1905)
American Writers Supp. 4, part 2: **517–535**

Ransom, John Crowe (1888)
American Writers, vol. 3: **480–502**

Ransome, Arthur (1884)
Writers for Children: **455–461**

Rawlings, Marjorie Kinnan (1896)
American Nature Writers, vol. 2: **751–765**
Writers for Children: **463–467**

Raymo, Chet (1936)
American Nature Writers, vol. 2: **767–780**

Read, Herbert (1893)
See "Poets of World War I (British)"

Reed, Ishmael (1938)
African American Writers: **361–377**

Reyes, Alfonso (1889)
Latin American Writers, vol. 2: **693–703**

Rhys, Jean (1890)
British Writers Supp. 2: **387–404**

Rich, Adrienne (1929)
American Writers Supp. 1, part 2: **550–578**
Modern American Women Writers: **441–456**

Richards, I. A. (1893)
British Writers Supp. 2: **405–433**

Richards, Laura E. (1850)
Writers for Children: **469–475**

Rilke, Rainer Maria (1875)
European Writers, vol. 9: **767–796**
European Writers Selected Authors, vol. 3:
   1461–1489

Rinaldi, Ann (1934)
Writers for Young Adults, vol. 3: **75–85**

Ríos, Alberto Álvaro (1952)
American Writers Supp. 4, part 2: **537–556**

Ritsos, Yannis (1909)
European Writers, vol. 12: **2815–2842**

Rivera, José Eustasio (1888)
Latin American Writers, vol. 2: **671–675**

Roa Bastos, Augusto (1917)
Latin American Writers, vol. 3: **1209–1213**

Robbe-Grillet, Alain (1922)
European Writers, vol. 13: **3237–3256**

Roberts, Elizabeth Madox (1881)
Writers for Children: **477–481**

Robinson, Edwin Arlington (1869)
American Writers, vol. 3: **503–526**

Robinson, Marilynne (1944)
See "Contemporary Ecofiction"

Rodó, José Enrique (1871)
Latin American Writers, vol. 2: **447–455**

Rodowsky, Colby (1932)
Writers for Young Adults, vol. 3: **87–93**

Roethke, Theodore (1908)
American Writers, vol. 3: **527–550**

Rohmer, Sax (1883)
Supernatural Fiction Writers, vol. 2: **555–560**

Rojas, Manuel (1896)
Latin American Writers, vol. 2: **815–820**

Rojas, Ricardo (1882)
Latin American Writers, vol. 2: **591–596**

Romero, José Rubén (1890)
Latin American Writers, vol. 2: **711–715**

Rosenberg, Isaac (1890)
See "Poets of World War I (British)"

Roth, Philip (1933)
American Writers Supp. 3, part 2: **401–429**

Rotimi, Ola (1938)
African Writers, vol. 2: **707–720**

Rulfo, Juan (1918)
  Latin American Writers, vol. 3: **1215–1229**

Rushdie, Salman (1947)
  British Writers Supp. 4: **433–457**

Russ, Joanna (1937)
  Science Fiction Writers: **483–490**

Russell, Eric Frank (1905)
  Science Fiction Writers: **197–202**

Russell, Sharman Apt (1954)
  See "New Voices in American Nature Writing"

Ryden, Hope (Undisclosed)
  American Nature Writers, vol. 2: **781–792**

Sa'adāwī, Nawāl, al- (1931)
  African Writers, vol. 2: **721–731**

Sábato, Ernesto (1911)
  Latin American Writers, vol. 3: **1139–1143**

Sachs, Marilyn (1927)
  Writers for Young Adults, vol. 3: **95–104**

St. Clair, Margaret (1911)
  Science Fiction Writers: **491–495**

Saint-Exupéry, Antoine de (1900)
  European Writers, vol. 12: **2307–2332**
  European Writers Selected Authors, vol. 3:
    1545–1569

Saki (1870)
  Supernatural Fiction Writers, vol. 1: **449–455**

Salazar Arrué, Salvador (Salarrué) (1899)
  Latin American Writers, vol. 2: **875–879**

Ṣāliḥ, al-Ṭayyib (1929)
  African Writers, vol. 2: **733–744**

Salinger, J. D. (1919)
  American Writers, vol. 3: **551–574**
  Writers for Young Adults, vol. 3: **105–112**

Salisbury, Graham (1944)
  Writers for Young Adults, vol. 3: **113–121**

Salten, Felix (1869)
  Writers for Children: **497–501**

Sánchez, Florencio (1875)
  Latin American Writers, vol. 2: **531–538**

Sandburg, Carl (1878)
  American Writers, vol. 3: **575–598**
  Writers for Children: **503–510**
  Writers for Young Adults, vol. 3: **123–133**

Sanders, Scott Russell (1945)
  American Nature Writers, vol. 2: **793–804**

Santayana, George (1863)
  American Writers, vol. 3: **599–622**

Sarban (1910)
  Supernatural Fiction Writers, vol. 2: **667–673**

Sardou, Victor (1831)
  See "Well-Made Play, The"

Sarduy, Severo (1936)
  Latin American Writers, vol. 3: **1437–1444**

Sarraute, Nathalie (1900)
  European Writers, vol. 12: **2333–2359**

Sartre, Jean-Paul (1905)
  European Writers, vol. 12: **2589–2614**
  European Writers Selected Authors, vol. 3: **1595–1620**

Sassoon, Siegfried (1886)
  See "Poets of World War I (British)"

Sawyer, Ruth (1880)
  Writers for Children: **511–517**

Sayers, Dorothy L. (1893)
  British Writers Supp. 3: **333–353**

Schnitzler, Arthur (1862)
  European Writers, vol. 8: **89–117**

Schreiner, Olive (1855)
  African Writers, vol. 2: **745–763**
  British Writers Supp. 2: **435–458**

Schwartz, Delmore (1913)
  American Writers Supp. 2, part 2: **639–668**

Scoppettone, Sandra (1936)
  Writers for Young Adults, vol. 3: **135–143**

Scott, Paul (1920)
  British Writers Supp. 1: **259–274**

Sebestyen, Ouida (1924)
  Writers for Young Adults, vol. 3: **145–153**

Seferis, George (1900)
  European Writers, vol. 12: **2255–2271**

Sembène Ousmane (1925)
  African Writers, vol. 2: **765–774**

Senarens, Luis Philip (1863)
  Science Fiction Writers: **53–58**

Senghor, Léopold Sédar (1906)
  African Writers, vol. 2: **775–789**

Seredy, Kate (1896)
  Writers for Children: **519–524**

Serviss, Garrett P. (1851)
  Science Fiction Writers: **39–44**

Seton, Ernest Thompson (1860)
American Nature Writers, vol. 2: **805–816**

Sexton, Anne (1928)
American Writers Supp. 2, part 2: **669–700**
Modern American Women Writers: **457–470**

Shābbī, Abū al-Qāsim, al- (1909)
African Writers, vol. 2: **791–798**

Shaffer, Peter (1926)
British Writers Supp. 1: **313–328**

Shange, Ntozake (1948)
African American Writers: **379–393**

Shapiro, Karl (1913)
American Writers Supp. 2, part 2: **701–724**

Shaw, George Bernard (1856)
British Writers, vol. 6: **101–132**
British Writers Selected Authors, vol. 3: **1053–1084**

Sheckley, Robert (1928)
Science Fiction Writers: **497–503**

Shepard, Sam (1943)
American Writers Supp. 3, part 2: **431–450**

Shiel, M. P. (1865)
Science Fiction Writers: **31–37**
Supernatural Fiction Writers, vol. 1: **361–367**

Silko, Leslie Marmon (1948)
American Nature Writers, vol. 2: **817–827**
American Writers Supp. 4, part 2: **557–572**

Silone, Ignazione (1900)
European Writers, vol. 12: **2273–2305**

Silveira de Queiroz, Dinah (1911)
Latin American Writers, vol. 3: **1145–1151**

Silverberg, Robert (1935)
Science Fiction Writers: **505–511**

Simak, Clifford D. (1904)
Science Fiction Writers: **513–518**

Simenon, Georges (1903)
European Writers, vol. 12: **2479–2510**

Simon, Claude (1913)
European Writers, vol. 13: **3021–3048**

Simon, Neil (1927)
American Writers Supp. 4, part 2: **573–594**

Sinán, Rogelio (1902)
Latin American Writers, vol. 2: **941–946**

Sinclair, May (1863)
Supernatural Fiction Writers, vol. 1: **513–519**

Singer, Isaac Bashevis (1904)
American Writers, vol. 4: **1–24**

Sitwell, Edith (1887)
British Writers, vol. 7: **127–143**

Sleator, William (1945)
Writers for Young Adults, vol. 3: **173–182**

Smith, Clark Ashton (1893)
Science Fiction Writers: **139–144**
Supernatural Fiction Writers, vol. 2: **875–881**

Smith, Cordwainer (1913)
Science Fiction Writers: **519–524**

Smith, E. E. (1890)
Science Fiction Writers: **125–130**

Smith, Stevie (1902)
British Writers Supp. 2: **459–479**

Smith, Thorne (1891)
Supernatural Fiction Writers, vol. 2: **805–811**

Snow, C. P. (1905)
British Writers, vol. 7: **321–342**

Snyder, Gary (1930)
American Nature Writers, vol. 2: **829–846**

Södergran, Edith (1892)
European Writers, vol. 11: **1781–1806**

Solzhenitsyn, Aleksandr (1918)
European Writers, vol. 13: **3187–3214**
European Writers Selected Authors, vol. 3: **1621–1647**

Sontag, Susan (1933)
American Writers Supp. 3, part 2: **451–473**
Modern American Women Writers: **471–483**

Soto, Gary (1952)
Writers for Young Adults, vol. 3: **183–191**

Sowande, Bode (1948)
African Writers, vol. 2: **799–806**

Soyinka, Wole (1934)
African Writers, vol. 2: **807–831**

Spark, Muriel (1918)
British Writers Supp. 1: **199–214**

Spender, Steven (1909)
British Writers Supp. 2: **481–496**

Spinelli, Jerry (1941)
Writers for Young Adults, vol. 3: **193–201**

Spyri, Johanna (1827)
Writers for Children: **529–533**

Stanwell-Fletcher, Theodora Cope (1906)
    American Nature Writers, vol. 2: **847–860**

Stapledon, Olaf (1886)
    Science Fiction Writers: **91–100**

Stead, Christina (1902)
    British Writers Supp. 4: **459–477**

Stegner, Wallace (1909)
    American Nature Writers, vol. 2: **861–875**
    American Writers Supp. 4, part 2: **595–618**

Stein, Gertrude (1874)
    American Writers, vol. 4: **25–48**
    Modern American Women Writers: **485–498**

Steinbeck, John (1902)
    American Writers, vol. 4: **49–72**
    Writers for Young Adults, vol. 3: **203–214**

Stephens, James (1882)
    Supernatural Fiction Writers, vol. 1: **485–490**

Stevens, Wallace (1879)
    American Writers, vol. 4: **73–96**
    American Writers Retrospective: **295–315**

Stockton, Frank R. (1834)
    Supernatural Fiction Writers, vol. 2: **753–759**
    Writers for Children: **545–554**

Stoker, Bram (1847)
    British Writers Supp. 3: **375–391**
    Supernatural Fiction Writers, vol. 1: **375–381**

Stoppard, Tom (1937)
    British Writers Supp. 1: **437–454**
    British Writers Selected Authors, vol. 3: **1177–1194**

Storey, David (1933)
    British Writers Supp. 1: **407–420**

Storni, Alfonsina (1892)
    Latin American Writers, vol. 2: **739–743**

Strachey, Lytton (1880)
    British Writers Supp. 2: **497–518**

Strand, Mark (1934)
    American Writers Supp. 4, part 2: **619–636**

Strasser, Todd (1950)
    Writers for Young Adults, vol. 3: **225–236**

Stratemeyer, Edward (1862)
    Writers for Young Adults, vol. 3: **237–249**

Stratton Porter, Gene (1863)
    American Nature Writers, vol. 2: **877–891**

Sturgeon, Theodore (1918)
    Science Fiction Writers: **203–208**
    Supernatural Fiction Writers, vol. 2: **941–945**

Styron, William (1925)
    American Writers, vol. 4: **97–119**

Suassuna, Ariano Vilar (1927)
    Latin American Writers, vol. 3: **1317–1321**

Sutcliff, Rosemary (1920)
    Writers for Young Adults, vol. 3: **251–261**

Sutherland, Efua Theodora (1924)
    African Writers, vol. 2: **833–849**

Svevo, Italo (1861)
    European Writers, vol. 8: **67–87**

Swann, Thomas Burnett (1928)
    Supernatural Fiction Writers, vol. 2: **1097–1103**

Swenson, May (1913)
    American Writers Supp. 4, part 2: **637–655**

Synge, J. M. (1871)
    See "Synge, J. M., and Lady Augusta Gregory"

Synge, J. M., and Lady Augusta Gregory
    British Writers, vol. 6: **307–318**

Tablada, José Juan (1871)
    Latin American Writers, vol. 1: **441–446**

Ṭāhā Ḥusayn (1889)
    African Writers, vol. 2: **851–863**

Taine, John (1883)
    Science Fiction Writers: **75–82**

Talbert, Marc (1953)
    Writers for Young Adults, vol. 3: **263–272**

Tate, Allen (1899)
    American Writers, vol. 4: **120–143**

Taylor, Mildred Delois (1943)
    Writers for Young Adults, vol. 3: **273–282**

Taylor, Theodore (1921)
    Writers for Young Adults, vol. 3: **283–292**

Teale, Edwin Way (1899)
    American Nature Writers, vol. 2: **893–904**

Tenn, William (1920)
    Science Fiction Writers: **525–530**

Thomas, D. M. (1935)
    British Writers Supp. 4: **479–497**

Thomas, Dylan (1914)
    British Writers Supp. 1: **169–184**
    British Writers Selected Authors, vol. 3: **1261–1276**

Thomas, Edward (1878)
    British Writers Supp. 3: **393–408**

Thomas, Joyce Carol (1938)
    Writers for Young Adults, vol. 3: **293–301**

Thomas, Lewis (1913)
American Nature Writers, vol. 2: **919–931**

Thompson, Francis (1859)
British Writers, vol. 5: **439–452**

Thompson, Julian F. (1927)
Writers for Young Adults, vol. 3: **303–310**

Thurber, James (1894)
American Writers Supp. 1, part 2: **602–627**
Supernatural Fiction Writers, vol. 2: **827–831**

Tiptree, James, Jr. (1915)
Science Fiction Writers: **531–541**

Tolkien, J. R. R. (1892)
British Writers Supp. 2: **519–536**
British Writers Selected Authors, vol. 3: **1277–1294**
Supernatural Fiction Writers, vol. 2: **675–682**
Writers for Children: **561–571**
Writers for Young Adults, vol. 3: **311–320**

Tolson, Melvin (1898)
African American Writers: **413–427**

Toomer, Jean (1894)
African American Writers: **429–440**
American Writers Supp. 3, part 2: **475–491**

Torres Bodet, Jaime (1902)
Latin American Writers, vol. 2: **933–939**

Trakl, Georg (1887)
European Writers, vol. 10: **1409–1427**

Trevelyan, G. M. (1876)
British Writers, vol. 6: **383–396**

Trevor, William (1928)
British Writers Supp. 4: **499–519**

Triana, José (1933)
Latin American Writers, vol. 3: **1415–1419**

Trilling, Lionel (1905)
American Writers Supp. 3, part 2: **493–515**

Tsvetaeva, Marina (1892)
European Writers, vol. 11: **1731–1750**

Tutuola, Amos (1920)
African Writers, vol. 2: **865–878**

Twain, Mark (1835)
American Writers, vol. 4: **190–213**
Supernatural Fiction Writers, vol. 2: **761–768**
Writers for Children: **573–582**
Writers for Young Adults, vol. 3: **321–328**

Tychyna, Pavlo (1891)
European Writers, vol. 10: **1651–1676**

Tyler, Anne (1941)
American Writers Supp. 4, part 2: **657–675**
Modern American Women Writers: **499–510**

Unamuno, Miguel de (1864)
European Writers, vol. 8: **283–310**

Undset, Sigrid (1882)
European Writers, vol. 9: **1017–1041**

Ungaretti, Giuseppe (1888)
European Writers, vol. 10: **1453–1473**

Updike, John (1932)
American Writers, vol. 4: **214–235**
American Writers Retrospective: **317–338**

Usigli, Rodolfo (1905)
Latin American Writers, vol. 3: **1033–1042**

Uslar Pietri, Arturo (1906)
Latin American Writers, vol. 3: **1057–1062**

Valencia, Guillermo (1873)
Latin American Writers, vol. 2: **477–482**

Valenzuela, Luisa (1938)
Latin American Writers, vol. 3: **1445–1449**

Valéry, Paul (1871)
European Writers, vol. 8: **569–588**

Valle, Rafael Heliodoro (1891)
Latin American Writers, vol. 2: **721–725**

Valle-Inclán, Ramón del (1866)
European Writers, vol. 8: **331–353**

Vallejo, César (1892)
Latin American Writers, vol. 2: **727–738**

Vance, Jack (1916)
Science Fiction Writers: **543–549**
Supernatural Fiction Writers, vol. 2: **1105–1111**

van der Post, Laurens (1906)
African Writers, vol. 2: **879–891**

Van Dyke, John C. (1856)
American Nature Writers, vol. 2: **951–962**

Van Loon, Hendrik Willem (1882)
Writers for Children: **583–589**

Van Vechten, Carl (1880)
American Writers Supp. 2, part 2: **725–751**

Van Vogt, A. E. (1912)
Science Fiction Writers: **209–217**

Vargas Llosa, Mario (1936)
Latin American Writers, vol. 3: **1421–1436**

Vasconcelos, José (1882)
Latin American Writers, vol. 2: **575–584**

Veblen, Thorstein (1857)
American Writers Supp. 1, part 2: **628–650**

Verga, Giovanni (1840)
European Writers, vol. 7: **1543–1565**

Veríssimo, Érico (1905)
Latin American Writers, vol. 3: **1043–1048**

Vesaas, Tarjei (1897)
European Writers, vol. 11: **2035–2059**

Vidal, Gore (1925)
American Writers Supp. 4, part 2: **677–697**

Vieira, José Luandino (1935)
African Writers, vol. 2: **893–901**

Villaurrutia, Xavier (1903)
Latin American Writers, vol. 3: **975–980**

Vittorini, Elio (1908)
European Writers, vol. 12: **2733–2757**

Voigt, Cynthia (1942)
Writers for Young Adults, vol. 3: **329–338**

Vonnegut, Kurt (1922)
American Writers Supp. 2, part 2: **753–783**
Science Fiction Writers: **551–561**

Wakefield, H. Russell (1888)
Supernatural Fiction Writers, vol. 2: **617–622**

Walker, Alice (1944)
African American Writers: **441–458**
American Writers Supp. 3, part 2: **517–540**
Modern American Women Writers: **511–520**

Walker, Margaret (1915)
African American Writers: **459–471**

Wall, Mervyn (1908)
Supernatural Fiction Writers, vol. 2: **645–650**

Wallace, David Rains (1945)
American Nature Writers, vol. 2: **963–972**

Walsh, Jill Paton (1937)
Writers for Young Adults, vol. 3: **339–346**

Warren, Robert Penn (1905)
American Writers, vol. 4: **236–259**

Waugh, Evelyn (1903)
British Writers, vol. 7: **289–308**
British Writers Selected Authors, vol. 3: **1311–1330**

Wedekind, Frank (1864)
European Writers, vol. 8: **229–281**

Weil, Simone (1909)
European Writers, vol. 12: **2787–2814**

Weinbaum, Stanley G. (1902)
Science Fiction Writers: **145–149**

Weldon, Fay (1931)
British Writers Supp. 4: **521–539**

Well-Made Play, The
European Writers, vol. 7: **1909–1934**

Wellman, Manly Wade (1903)
Supernatural Fiction Writers, vol. 2: **947–954**

Wells, H. G. (1866)
British Writers, vol. 6: **225–246**
British Writers Selected Authors, vol. 3: **1331–1352**
Science Fiction Writers: **25–30**
Supernatural Fiction Writers, vol. 1: **397–402**
Writers for Children: **599–603**

Welty, Eudora (1909)
American Writers, vol. 4: **260–284**
American Writers Retrospective: **339–358**
Modern American Women Writers: **521–538**

Wersba, Barbara (1932)
Writers for Young Adults, vol. 3: **349–357**

West, Nathanael (1903)
American Writers, vol. 4: **285–307**

West, Rebecca (1892)
British Writers Supp. 3: **431–445**

Westall, Robert Atkinson (1929)
Writers for Young Adults, vol. 3: **359–369**

Western Geologists and Explorers
American Nature Writers, vol. 2: **1173–1188**

Wharton, Edith (1862)
American Writers, vol. 4: **308–330**
American Writers Retrospective: **359–385**
Modern American Women Writers: **539–558**
Supernatural Fiction Writers, vol. 2: **783–788**

Wheatley, Dennis (1897)
Supernatural Fiction Writers, vol. 2: **623–629**

White, E. B. (1899)
American Writers Supp. 1, part 2: **651–681**

White, Patrick (1912)
British Writers Supp. 1: **129–152**

White, T. H. (1906)
Supernatural Fiction Writers, vol. 2: **651–657**

Wideman, John Edgar (1941)
African American Writers: **493–504**

Wiggin, Kate Douglas (1856)
Writers for Children: **605–609**

Wilbur, Richard (1921)
  American Writers Supp. 3, part 2: **541–565**

Wilder, Laura Ingalls (1867)
  Writers for Children: **617–623**
  Writers for Young Adults, vol. 3: **371–380**

Wilder, Thornton (1897)
  American Writers, vol. 4: **355–377**

Wilkinson, Brenda (1946)
  Writers for Young Adults, vol. 3: **381–390**

Williams, Charles (1886)
  Supernatural Fiction Writers, vol. 2: **631–638**

Williams, Tennessee (1911)
  American Writers, vol. 4: **378–401**

Williams, Terry Tempest (1955)
  American Nature Writers, vol. 2: **973–988**

Williams, William Carlos (1883)
  American Writers, vol. 4: **402–425**
  American Writers Retrospective: **411–433**

Williamson, Jack (1908)
  Science Fiction Writers: **225–231**

Wilson, Angus (1913)
  British Writers Supp. 1: **153–168**

Wilson, Edmund (1895)
  American Writers, vol. 4: **426–449**

Winters, Yvor (1900)
  American Writers Supp. 2, part 2: **785–816**

Winterson, Jeanette (1959)
  British Writers Supp. 4: **541–559**

Witkiewicz (Witkacy), Stanisław Ignacy (1885)
  European Writers, vol. 10: **1205–1230**

Wodehouse, P. G. (1881)
  British Writers Supp. 3: **447–464**
  British Writers Selected Authors, vol. 3:
      1377–1394

Wolfe, Thomas (1900)
  American Writers, vol. 4: **450–473**

Wolfe, Tom (1931)
  American Writers Supp. 3, part 2: **567–588**

Wolff, Egon (1926)
  Latin American Writers, vol. 3: **1311–1315**

Wolff, Virginia Euwer (1937)
  Writers for Young Adults, vol. 3: **391–398**

Woolf, Virginia (1882)
  British Writers, vol. 7: **17–40**
  British Writers Selected Authors, vol. 3: **1395–1417**

Wright, James (1927)
  American Writers Supp. 3, part 2: **589–607**

Wright, Richard (1908)
  African American Writers: **505–523**
  American Writers, vol. 4: **474–497**

Wright, S. Fowler (1874)
  Science Fiction Writers: **83–89**

Wylie, Elinor (1885)
  American Writers Supp. 1, part 2: **707–730**

Wyndham, John (1903)
  Science Fiction Writers: **219–224**

Yáñez, Agustín (1904)
  Latin American Writers, vol. 3: **995–999**

Yeats, William Butler (1865)
  British Writers, vol. 6: **207–224**
  British Writers Selected Authors, vol. 3: **1473–1490**

Yep, Laurence (1948)
  Writers for Young Adults, vol. 3: **399–408**

Yolen, Jane (1939)
  Writers for Young Adults, vol. 3: **409–420**

Yourcenar, Marguerite (1903)
  European Writers, vol. 12: **2535–2561**

Zamyatin, Yevgeny Ivanovich (1884)
  European Writers, vol. 10: **1181–1203**

Zelazny, Roger (1937)
  Science Fiction Writers: **563–570**
  Supernatural Fiction Writers, vol. 2: **1113–1119**

Zeno Gandía, Manuel (1855)
  Latin American Writers, vol. 1: **321–326**

Zindel, Paul (1936)
  Writers for Young Adults, vol. 3: **421–430**

Zorrilla de San Martín, Juan (1855)
  Latin American Writers, vol. 1: **327–331**

Zukofsky, Louis (1904)
  American Writers Supp. 3, part 2: **609–632**

Zwinger, Ann (1925)
  American Nature Writers, vol. 2: **989–1001**

Zwinger, Susan (1947)
  See "New Voices in American Nature Writing"

Subjects by Language

Writers and works grouped according to their language. Many writers and some works (such as the biblical books) have embraced more than one tongue and are listed under more than one language. The thirty principal languages include Acholi, Afrikaans, Akan, Arabic, Aramaic, Czech, Danish, Dutch, English, French, German, Gĩkũyũ, Greek, Hebrew, Hungarian, Icelandic, Ijọ, Italian, Latin, Norwegian, Old Norse, Polish, Portuguese, Russian, Serbo-Croatian, Sesotho, Spanish, Swedish, Ukrainian, and Yiddish.

Acholi

p'Bitek, Okot
African Writers, vol. 2: **669–684**

Afrikaans

Brink, André
African Writers, vol. 1: **95–114**

Akan

Sutherland, Efua Theodora
African Writers, vol. 2: **833–849**

Arabic

Arabian Nights
Supernatural Fiction Writers, vol. 1: **19–26**

Ḥakīm, Tawfīq, al-
African Writers, vol. 1: **291–301**

Idrīs, Yūsuf
African Writers, vol. 1: **345–365**

Maḥfūẓ, Najīb
African Writers, vol. 2: **451–465**

Saʿadāwī, Nawāl, al-
African Writers, vol. 2: **721–731**

Ṣāliḥ, al-Ṭayyib
African Writers, vol. 2: **733–744**

Shābbī, Abū al-Qāsim, al-
African Writers, vol. 2: **791–798**

Ṭāhā Ḥusayn
African Writers, vol. 2: **851–863**

Aramaic

Bible as Sacred Literature, The
The Books of the Bible, vol. 1: **1–9**

Czech

Čapek, Karel
European Writers, vol. 10: **1565–1590**
Science Fiction Writers: **583–589**

Hašek, Jaroslav
European Writers, vol. 9: **1091–1118**

Kundera, Milan
European Writers, vol. 13: **3389–3413**

Danish

Andersen, Hans Christian
European Writers, vol. 6: **863–892**
European Writers Selected Authors, vol. 1: **1–29**
Writers for Children: **7–13**

Dinesen, Isak
European Writers, vol. 10: **1281–1306**
European Writers Selected Authors, vol. 1: **453–477**

Gunnarsson, Gunnar
European Writers, vol. 10: **1497–1519**

Kierkegaard, Søren
European Writers, vol. 6: **1123–1146**
European Writers Selected Authors, vol. 2: **877–900**

Dutch

Renaissance Short Fiction
  European Writers, vol. 2: **927–956**
  European Writers Selected Authors, vol. 3:
      1431–1460

English

Abbey, Edward
  American Nature Writers, vol. 1: **1–19**

Abrahams, Peter
  African Writers, vol. 1: **1–14**

Achebe, Chinua
  African Writers, vol. 1: **15–36**

Ackerman, Diane
  American Nature Writers, vol. 1: **21–30**

Adams, Henry
  American Writers, vol. 1: **1–24**

Addams, Jane
  American Writers Supp. 1, part 1: **1–27**

Addison, Joseph
  See "Steele, Sir Richard, and Joseph Addison"

African Americans, Writing, and Nature
  American Nature Writers, vol. 2: **1003–1012**

Agee, James
  American Writers, vol. 1: **25–47**

Aickman, Robert
  Supernatural Fiction Writers, vol. 2: **957–964**

Aidoo, Ama Ata
  African Writers, vol. 1: **37–48**

Aiken, Conrad
  American Writers, vol. 1: **48–70**

Aiken, Joan
  Writers for Young Adults, vol. 1: **1–9**

Ainsworth, William Harrison
  Supernatural Fiction Writers, vol. 1: **187–193**

Albee, Edward
  American Writers, vol. 1: **71–96**

Alcott, Louisa May
  American Writers Supp. 1, part 1: **28–46**
  Writers for Children: **1–6**
  Writers for Young Adults, vol. 1: **11–20**

Aldiss, Brian W.
  Science Fiction Writers: **251–258**

Alexander, Lloyd
  Supernatural Fiction Writers, vol. 2: **965–971**
  Writers for Young Adults, vol. 1: **21–33**

Ambler, Eric
  British Writers Supp. 4: **1–24**

Amis, Kingsley
  British Writers Supp. 2: **1–19**

Amis, Martin
  British Writers Supp. 4: **25–44**

Anderson, Poul
  Science Fiction Writers: **259–265**
  Supernatural Fiction Writers, vol. 2: **973–980**

Anderson, Sherwood
  American Writers, vol. 1: **97–120**

Angell, Judie
  Writers for Young Adults, vol. 1: **35–42**

Angelou, Maya
  American Writers Supp. 4, part 1: **1–19**
  Modern American Women Writers: **1–8**
  Writers for Young Adults, vol. 1: **43–52**

Anstey, F.
  Supernatural Fiction Writers, vol. 1: **287–292**

Anthony, Piers
  Supernatural Fiction Writers, vol. 2: **981–986**

Arden, John
  British Writers Supp. 2: **21–42**

Ardizzone, Edward
  Writers for Children: **15–20**

Armah, Ayi Kwei
  African Writers, vol. 1: **49–62**

Arnold, Matthew
  British Writers, vol. 5: **203–218**

Arthurian Legend
  European Writers, vol. 1: **137–160**
  European Writers Selected Authors, vol. 1: **79–102**

Arthurian Romances
  Supernatural Fiction Writers, vol. 1: **11–18**

Ashbery, John
  American Writers Supp. 3, part 1: **1–29**

Asher, Sandy
  Writers for Young Adults, vol. 1: **53–61**

Asimov, Isaac
  Science Fiction Writers: **267–276**

Atherton, Gertrude
  Supernatural Fiction Writers, vol. 2: **777–781**

Beowulf and Anglo-Saxon Poetry
    European Writers, vol. 1: **51–88**
    European Writers Selected Authors, vol. 1: **217–253**

Beresford, J. D.
    Supernatural Fiction Writers, vol. 1: **457–461**

Berger, John
    British Writers Supp. 4: **77–96**

Berry, Wendell
    American Nature Writers, vol. 1: **89–105**

Berryman, John
    American Writers, vol. 1: **167–189**

Bester, Alfred
    Science Fiction Writers: **283–290**

Beston, Henry
    American Nature Writers, vol. 1: **107–120**

Bethancourt, T. Ernesto
    Writers for Young Adults, vol. 1: **99–109**

Betjeman, John
    British Writers, vol. 7: **355–378**

Bianco, Margery Williams
    Writers for Children: **63–67**

Bible, The English
    British Writers, vol. 1: **370–388**
    British Writers Selected Authors, vol. 1: **69–87**

Bierce, Ambrose
    American Writers, vol. 1: **190–213**
    Supernatural Fiction Writers, vol. 2: **731–737**

Bioregionalism in Nature Writing
    American Nature Writers, vol. 2: **1013–1024**

Bishop, Elizabeth
    American Writers Supp. 1, part 1: **72–97**
    Modern American Women Writers: **9–22**

Blackmur, R. P.
    American Writers Supp. 2, part 1: **87–112**

Blackwood, Algernon
    Supernatural Fiction Writers, vol. 1: **463–470**

Blake, William
    British Writers, vol. 3: **288–310**
    British Writers Selected Authors, vol. 1: **89–110**
    Writers for Children: **69–76**

Blish, James
    Science Fiction Writers: **291–296**

Bloch, Robert
    Supernatural Fiction Writers, vol. 2: **901–907**

Block, Francesca Lia
    Writers for Young Adults, vol. 1: **111–119**

Blume, Judy
    Writers for Young Adults, vol. 1: **121–131**

Bly, Robert
    American Writers Supp. 4, part 1: **59–77**

Bogan, Louise
    American Writers Supp. 3, part 1: **47–68**
    Modern American Women Writers: **23–36**

Bograd, Larry
    Writers for Young Adults, vol. 1: **133–141**

Bond, Edward
    British Writers Supp. 1: **421–436**

Bontemps, Arna
    Writers for Children: **77–83**

Boswell, James
    British Writers, vol. 3: **234–251**
    British Writers Selected Authors, vol. 1: **111–128**

Bourne, Randolph
    American Writers, vol. 1: **214–238**

Bowen, Elizabeth
    British Writers Supp. 2: **77–96**
    Supernatural Fiction Writers, vol. 2: **569–575**

Bowles, Paul
    American Writers Supp. 4, part 1: **79–99**

Brackett, Leigh
    Supernatural Fiction Writers, vol. 2: **909–915**

Bradbury, Ray
    American Writers Supp. 4, part 1: **101–118**
    Supernatural Fiction Writers: **171–178**
    Supernatural Fiction Writers, vol. 2: **917–923**

Bradstreet, Anne
    American Writers Supp. 1, part 1: **98–123**

Brancato, Robin F.
    Writers for Young Adults, vol. 1: **143–152**

Branscum, Robbie
    Writers for Young Adults, vol. 1: **153–161**

Bridgers, Sue Ellen
    Writers for Young Adults, vol. 1: **163–172**

Bridges, Robert
    British Writers, vol. 6: **71–84**

Brink, André
    African Writers, vol. 1: **95–114**

Brink, Carol Ryrie
    Writers for Children: **85–90**

Brontës, The
    British Writers, vol. 5: **105–154**
    British Writers Selected Authors, vol. 1: **129–177**

Brooke, Rupert
  British Writers Supp. 3: **45–61**
  See also "Poets of World War I (British)"

Brooke-Rose, Christine
  British Writers Supp. 4: **97–118**

Brookner, Anita
  British Writers Supp. 4: **119–137**

Brooks, Bruce
  Writers for Young Adults, vol. 1: **173–182**

Brooks, Gwendolyn
  African American Writers: **31–43**
  American Writers Supp. 3, part 1: **69–90**
  Modern American Women Writers: **37–48**

Brooks, Van Wyck
  American Writers, vol. 1: **239–263**

Brown, Charles Brockden
  American Writers Supp. 1, part 1: **124–149**

Brown, Sterling
  African American Writers: **45–57**

Browne, Sir Thomas
  British Writers, vol. 2: **145–157**

Browning, Elizabeth Barrett
  British Writers, vol. 4: **310–322**
  British Writers Selected Authors, vol. 1: **179–191**

Browning, Robert
  British Writers, vol. 4: **354–375**
  British Writers Selected Authors, vol. 1: **193–214**

Brunner, John
  Science Fiction Writers: **297–304**

Brutus, Dennis
  African Writers, vol. 1: **115–126**

Bryant, William Cullen
  American Writers Supp. 1, part 1: **150–173**

Buck, Pearl S.
  American Writers Supp. 2, part 1: **113–134**

Budrys, Algis
  Science Fiction Writers: **305–311**

Bulwer-Lytton, Edward
  Supernatural Fiction Writers, vol. 1: **195–204**

Bunting, Eve
  Writers for Young Adults, vol. 1: **183–189**

Bunyan, John
  British Writers, vol. 2: **240–254**
  British Writers Selected Authors, vol. 1: **215–229**
  Writers for Children: **97–102**

Burgess, Anthony
  British Writers Supp. 1: **185–198**

Burke, Edmund
  British Writers, vol. 3: **193–207**

Burke, Kenneth
  American Writers, vol. 1: **264–287**

Burnett, Frances Hodgson
  Writers for Children: **103–109**

Burney, Frances
  British Writers Supp. 3: **63–78**

Burns, Olive Ann
  Writers for Young Adults, vol. 1: **191–198**

Burns, Robert
  British Writers, vol. 3: **310–323**
  British Writers Selected Authors, vol. 1: **231–244**

Burroughs, Edgar Rice
  Science Fiction Writers: **59–64**

Burroughs, John
  American Nature Writers, vol. 1: **121–138**

Burroughs, William S.
  American Writers Supp. 3, part 1: **91–110**

Burton, Virginia Lee
  Writers for Children: **111–115**

Butler, Samuel
  British Writers Supp. 2: **97–121**

Byars, Betsy
  Writers for Young Adults, vol. 1: **199–207**

Byatt, A. S.
  British Writers Supp. 4: **139–156**

Byron, Lord
  British Writers, vol. 4: **171–194**
  British Writers Selected Authors, vol. 1: **245–268**

Cabell, James Branch
  Supernatural Fiction Writers, vol. 2: **789–796**

Cabrera Infante, Guillermo
  Latin American Writers, vol. 3: **1383–1391**

Caldwell, Erskine
  American Writers, vol. 1: **288–311**

Campbell, John W., Jr.
  Science Fiction Writers: **151–159**

Campbell, Ramsey
  Supernatural Fiction Writers, vol. 2: **993–999**

Campbell, Roy
  African Writers, vol. 1: **127–137**

Canadian Nature Writing in English
  American Nature Writers, vol. 2: **1025–1040**

Capote, Truman
  American Writers Supp. 3, part 1: **111–133**

Carew, Thomas
  See "Cavalier Poets, The"

Carlyle, Thomas
  British Writers, vol. 4: **238–250**
  British Writers Selected Authors, vol. 1: **269–281**

Carrighar, Sally
  American Nature Writers, vol. 1: **139–149**

Carroll, Lewis
  British Writers, vol. 5: **261–276**
  Supernatural Fiction Writers, vol. 1: **247–253**
  Writers for Children: **117–127**

Carson, Rachel
  American Nature Writers, vol. 1: **151–171**

Carter, Alden R.
  Writers for Young Adults, vol. 1: **209–218**

Carter, Angela
  British Writers Supp. 3: **79–93**

Carver, Raymond
  American Writers Supp. 3, part 1: **135–151**

Cary, Joyce
  British Writers, vol. 7: **185–196**

Cather, Willa
  American Writers, vol. 1: **312–334**
  American Writers Retrospective: **1–23**
  Modern American Women Writers: **49–62**

Cavalier Poets, The
  British Writers, vol. 2: **221–239**

Chambers, Aidan
  Writers for Young Adults, vol. 1: **219–227**

Chambers, Robert W.
  Supernatural Fiction Writers, vol. 2: **739–745**

Chandler, Raymond
  American Writers Supp. 4, part 1: **119–138**

Chapman, George
  British Writers, vol. 1: **232–256**

Chatwin, Bruce
  British Writers Supp. 4: **157–177**

Chaucer, Geoffrey
  British Writers, vol. 1: **19–47**
  British Writers Selected Authors, vol. 1: **283–311**

Cheever, John
  American Writers Supp. 1, part 1: **174–199**

Chesnutt, Charles W.
  African American Writers: **59–70**

Chesterton, G. K.
  British Writers, vol. 6: **335–346**
  Supernatural Fiction Writers, vol. 1: **411–414**

Childress, Alice
  Writers for Young Adults, vol. 1: **229–240**

Chopin, Kate
  American Writers Supp. 1, part 1: **200–226**
  Modern American Women Writers: **63–78**

Christie, Agatha
  British Writers Supp. 2: **123–137**

Churchill, Caryl
  British Writers Supp. 4: **179–200**

Churchill, Winston
  British Writers, vol. 6: **347–362**

Clark, John Pepper
  African Writers, vol. 1: **153–166**

Clarke, Arthur C.
  Science Fiction Writers: **313–320**

Cleaver, Vera and Bill
  Writers for Young Adults, vol. 1: **241–248**

Clement, Hal
  Science Fiction Writers: **321–327**

Clough, Arthur Hugh
  British Writers, vol. 5: **155–172**

Coetzee, J. M.
  African Writers, vol. 1: **167–183**

Cole, Brock
  Writers for Young Adults, vol. 1: **249–256**

Coleridge, Samuel Taylor
  British Writers, vol. 4: **41–57**
  British Writers Selected Authors, vol. 1: **313–329**

Collier, Christopher and James Lincoln
  Writers for Young Adults, vol. 1: **257–269**

Collier, John
  Supernatural Fiction Writers, vol. 2: **577–583**

Collins, Wilkie
  Supernatural Fiction Writers, vol. 1: **233–238**

Collins, William
  British Writers, vol. 3: **160–176**

Colman, Hila
  Writers for Young Adults, vol. 1: **271–280**

Colum, Padraic
  Writers for Children: **139–146**

Eddison, E. R.
      Supernatural Fiction Writers, vol. 2: **529–534**

Edgeworth, Maria
      British Writers Supp. 3: **151–168**

Edwards, Amelia B.
      Supernatural Fiction Writers, vol. 1: **255–260**

Edwards, Jonathan
      American Writers, vol. 1: **544–566**

Egbuna, Obi
      African Writers, vol. 1: **209–221**

Ehrlich, Gretel
      American Nature Writers, vol. 1: **247–258**

Eifert, Virginia
      American Nature Writers, vol. 1: **259–268**

Eiseley, Loren
      American Nature Writers, vol. 1: **269–285**

Ekwensi, Cyprian
      African Writers, vol. 1: **223–234**

Eliot, George
      British Writers, vol. 5: **187–201**
      British Writers Selected Authors, vol. 1: **453–467**

Eliot, T. S.
      American Writers, vol. 1: **567–591**
      American Writers Retrospective: **51–71**
      British Writers, vol. 7: **143–170**
      British Writers Selected Authors, vol. 1: **469–496**

Ellison, Harlan
      Science Fiction Writers: **357–368**
      Supernatural Fiction Writers, vol. 2: **1015–1021**

Ellison, Ralph
      African American Writers: **103–129**
      American Writers Supp. 2, part 1: **221–252**

Emecheta, Buchi
      African Writers, vol. 1: **235–247**

Emerson, Ralph Waldo
      American Nature Writers, vol. 1: **287–307**
      American Writers, vol. 2: **1–24**

Empson, William
      British Writers Supp. 2: **179–198**

Enright, Elizabeth
      Writers for Children: **215–220**

Equiano, Olaudah
      See "Slave Narrative in American Literature, The"

Erdrich, Louise
      American Writers Supp. 4, part 1: **259–278**

Etherege, Sir George
      See "Restoration Court Poets, The"

Evelyn, John, and Samuel Pepys
      British Writers, vol. 2: **274–288**

Ewing, Juliana Horatia
      Writers for Children: **221–226**

Eyerly, Jeannette
      Writers for Young Adults, vol. 1: **403–411**

Farah, Nuruddin
      African Writers, vol. 1: **249–262**

Farjeon, Eleanor
      Writers for Children: **227–234**

Farmer, Philip José
      Science Fiction Writers: **369–375**

Farquhar, George
      British Writers, vol. 2: **351–365**

Farrell, James T.
      American Writers, vol. 2: **25–53**

Faulkner, William
      American Writers, vol. 2: **54–76**
      American Writers Retrospective: **73–95**

Fauset, Jessie
      Modern American Women Writers: **123–139**

Field, Rachel Lyman
      Writers for Children: **235–240**

Fielding, Henry
      British Writers, vol. 3: **94–106**
      British Writers Selected Authors, vol. 2: **497–509**

Finch, Robert Charles
      American Nature Writers, vol. 1: **309–321**

Finney, Charles
      Supernatural Fiction Writers, vol. 2: **821–826**

Firbank, Ronald
      British Writers Supp. 2: **199–224**

Fitzgerald, Edward
      British Writers, vol. 4: **340–353**

Fitzgerald, F. Scott
      American Writers, vol. 2: **77–100**
      American Writers Retrospective: **97–120**

Fletcher, John
      See "Beaumont, Francis, and John Fletcher"

Ford, Ford Madox
      British Writers, vol. 6: **319–334**

Ford, John
      British Writers, vol. 2: **87–102**

Forms of American Nature Poetry, The
   American Nature Writers, vol. 2: **1079–1098**

Forster, E. M.
   British Writers, vol. 6: **397–414**
   British Writers Selected Authors, vol. 2: **511–527**
   Supernatural Fiction Writers, vol. 1: **479–484**

Fortune, Dion
   Supernatural Fiction Writers, vol. 2: **585–590**

Fowles, John
   British Writers Supp. 1: **291–311**

Fox, Paula
   Writers for Young Adults, vol. 1: **413–422**

Frank, Anne
   Writers for Young Adults, vol. 1: **423–431**

Franklin, Benjamin
   American Writers, vol. 2: **101–125**

Frazer, James George
   British Writers Supp. 3: **169–190**

Frederic, Harold
   American Writers, vol. 2: **126–149**

Freedman, Russell
   Writers for Young Adults, vol. 2: **1–9**

Freeman, Mary E. Wilkins
   Modern American Women Writers: **141–153**
   Supernatural Fiction Writers, vol. 2: **769–773**

French, Michael
   Writers for Young Adults, vol. 2: **11–20**

Freneau, Philip
   American Writers Supp. 2, part 1: **253–277**

Frost, Robert
   American Writers, vol. 2: **150–172**
   American Writers Retrospective: **121–144**
   Writers for Young Adults, vol. 2: **21–31**

Fry, Christopher
   British Writers Supp. 3: **191–210**

Fugard, Athol
   African Writers, vol. 1: **263–275**

Fuller, Margaret
   American Writers Supp. 2, part 1: **279–306**

Gaddis, William
   American Writers Supp. 4, part 1: **279–296**

Gág, Wanda
   Writers for Children: **241–246**

Gaines, Ernest J.
   African American Writers: **129–145**

Galsworthy, John
   British Writers, vol. 6: **269–293**

Garfield, Leon
   Writers for Young Adults, vol. 2: **33–45**

Garner, Alan
   Supernatural Fiction Writers, vol. 2: **1023–1029**

Garnett, David
   Supernatural Fiction Writers, vol. 2: **535–539**

Garnett, Richard
   Supernatural Fiction Writers, vol. 1: **317–320**

Gaskell, Elizabeth
   British Writers, vol. 5: **1–16**

Gay, John
   British Writers, vol. 3: **54–68**

George, Jean Craighead
   Writers for Young Adults, vol. 2: **47–57**

Gibbon, Edward
   British Writers, vol. 3: **221–233**

Gilman, Charlotte Perkins
   Modern American Women Writers: **155–170**

Ginsberg, Allen
   American Writers Supp. 2, part 1: **307–333**

Gissing, George
   British Writers, vol. 5: **423–438**

Glasgow, Ellen
   American Writers, vol. 2: **173–195**
   Modern American Women Writers: **171–180**

Glaspell, Susan
   American Writers Supp. 3, part 1: **175–191**
   Modern American Women Writers: **181–188**

Golding, William
   British Writers Supp. 1: **65–91**
   British Writers Selected Authors, vol. 2: **529–555**

Goldsmith, Oliver
   British Writers, vol. 3: **177–192**

Gordimer, Nadine
   African Writers, vol. 1: **277–290**
   British Writers Supp. 2: **225–245**

Gordon, Caroline
   American Writers, vol. 2: **196–222**

Gordon, Mary
   American Writers Supp. 4, part 1: **297–317**

Gothic Novel, The
   British Writers, vol. 3: **324–346**

James, Henry
    American Writers, vol. 2: **319–341**
    American Writers Retrospective: **215–242**
    British Writers, vol. 6: **23–69**
    Supernatural Fiction Writers, vol. 1: **337–344**
James, M. R.
    Supernatural Fiction Writers, vol. 1: **429–436**
James, P. D.
    British Writers Supp. 4: **319–341**
James, William
    American Writers, vol. 2: **342–366**
Janovy, John, Jr.
    American Nature Writers, vol. 1: **413–424**
Jarrell, Randall
    American Writers, vol. 2: **367–390**
Jeffers, Robinson
    American Writers Supp. 2, part 2: **413–440**
Jefferson, Thomas
    See "Early Romantic Natural History Literature"
Jewett, Sarah Orne
    American Writers, vol. 2: **391–414**
    Modern American Women Writers: **235–250**
Johnson, Cathy
    American Nature Writers, vol. 1: **425–438**
Johnson, James Weldon
    African American Writers: **219–233**
Johnson, Josephine
    American Nature Writers, vol. 1: **439–451**
Johnson, Samuel
    British Writers, vol. 3: **107–123**
    British Writers Selected Authors, vol. 2: **647–663**
Johnston, Norma
    Writers for Young Adults, vol. 2: **167–176**
Jones, David
    See "Poets of World War I (British)"
Jones, Gayl
    African American Writers: **235–244**
Jones, Henry Arthur
    See "Well-Made Play, The"
Jonson, Ben
    British Writers, vol. 1: **335–352**
    British Writers Selected Authors, vol. 2: **665–681**
Jordan, June
    African American Writers: **245–261**
Joyce, James
    British Writers, vol. 7: **41–58**
    British Writers Selected Authors, vol. 2: **683–700**

Kappel-Smith, Diana
    American Nature Writers, vol. 1: **453–463**
Keats, John
    British Writers, vol. 4: **211–238**
    British Writers Selected Authors, vol. 2: **701–727**
Keller, David H.
    Science Fiction Writers: **119–123**
Keneally, Thomas
    British Writers Supp. 4: **343–362**
Kerouac, Jack
    American Writers Supp. 3, part 1: **217–234**
Kerr, M. E.
    Writers for Young Adults, vol. 2: **177–185**
King, Clarence
    See "Western Geologists and Explorers"
King, Stephen
    Supernatural Fiction Writers, vol. 2: **1037–1044**
Kingsley, Charles
    Writers for Children: **323–327**
Kingston, Maxine Hong
    Modern American Women Writers: **251–259**
Kinnell, Galway
    American Writers Supp. 3, part 1: **235–256**
Kipling, Rudyard
    British Writers, vol. 6: **165–206**
    British Writers Selected Authors, vol. 2: **729–770**
    Supernatural Fiction Writers, vol. 1: **437–442**
    Writers for Children: **329–336**
Klein, Norma
    Writers for Young Adults, vol. 2: **187–197**
Knight, Damon
    Science Fiction Writers: **393–400**
Koestler, Arthur
    British Writers Supp. 1: **21–41**
Korman, Gordon
    Writers for Young Adults, vol. 2: **199–206**
Kornbluth, C. M.
    Science Fiction Writers: **401–407**
Krutch, Joseph Wood
    American Nature Writers, vol. 1: **465–477**
Kumin, Maxine
    American Nature Writers, vol. 1: **479–497**
    American Writers Supp. 4, part 2: **439–457**
Kunitz, Stanley
    American Writers Supp. 3, part 1: **257–270**

Lipsyte, Robert
   Writers for Young Adults, vol. 2: **257–266**

Literary Theory and Nature Writing
   American Nature Writers, vol. 2: **1099–1114**

Literature of Mountaineering
   American Nature Writers, vol. 2: **1115–1128**

Lodge, David
   British Writers Supp. 4: **363–387**

Lofting, Hugh
   Writers for Children: **365–371**

London, Jack
   American Writers, vol. 2: **462–485**
   Writers for Young Adults, vol. 2: **267–278**

Long, Frank Belknap
   Supernatural Fiction Writers, vol. 2: **869–874**

Longfellow, Henry Wadsworth
   American Writers, vol. 2: **486–510**

Lopez, Barry
   American Nature Writers, vol. 1: **549–568**

Lorde, Audre
   African American Writers: **273–288**

Lovecraft, H. P.
   Science Fiction Writers: **131–137**
   Supernatural Fiction Writers, vol. 2: **853–859**

Lovelace, Richard
   See "Cavalier Poets, The"

Lowell, Amy
   American Writers, vol. 2: **511–533**
   Modern American Women Writers: **261–268**

Lowell, James Russell
   American Writers Supp. 1, part 2: **404–426**

Lowell, Robert
   American Writers, vol. 2: **534–557**

Lowry, Lois
   Writers for Young Adults, vol. 2: **279–287**

Lowry, Malcolm
   British Writers Supp. 3: **269–286**

Lydgate, John
   British Writers, vol. 1: **57–66**

Lyly, John, and George Peele
   British Writers, vol. 1: **191–211**

Lynch, Chris
   Writers for Young Adults, vol. 2: **289–297**

Macaulay, Thomas Babington
   British Writers, vol. 4: **268–292**

McCaffrey, Anne
   Writers for Young Adults, vol. 2: **299–306**

McCarthy, Mary
   American Writers, vol. 2: **558–584**
   Modern American Women Writers: **269–278**

McCullers, Carson
   American Writers, vol. 2: **585–608**
   Modern American Women Writers: **279–287**

MacDonald, George
   Supernatural Fiction Writers, vol. 1: **239–246**
   Writers for Children: **373–380**

Macdonald, Ross
   American Writers Supp. 4, part 2: **459–477**

McEwan, Ian
   British Writers Supp. 4: **389–408**

Machen, Arthur
   Supernatural Fiction Writers, vol. 1: **351–359**

McKay, Claude
   African American Writers: **305–320**

McKibben, Bill
   See "New Voices in American Nature
      Writing"

McKillip, Patricia
   Supernatural Fiction Writers, vol. 2: **1067–1072**

Maclean, Norman
   See "Contemporary Ecofiction"

MacLeish, Archibald
   American Writers, vol. 3: **1–25**

Macleod, Fiona
   Supernatural Fiction Writers, vol. 1: **369–374**

MacNeice, Louis
   British Writers, vol. 7: **401–420**

McNulty, Faith
   American Nature Writers, vol. 1: **569–581**

McPhee, John
   American Nature Writers, vol. 1: **583–598**
   American Writers Supp. 3, part 1: **289–316**

Mahy, Margaret (May)
   Writers for Young Adults, vol. 2: **307–315**

Mailer, Norman
   American Writers, vol. 3: **26–49**

Major, Kevin
   Writers for Young Adults, vol. 2: **317–326**

Malamud, Bernard
   American Writers Supp. 1, part 2: **427–453**

Malory, Sir Thomas
  British Writers, vol. 1: **67–80**
  British Writers Selected Authors, vol. 2: **877–890**
  See also "Arthurian Romances"

Mansfield, Katherine
  British Writers, vol. 7: **171–184**
  British Writers Selected Authors, vol. 2: **891–904**

Marlowe, Christopher
  British Writers, vol. 1: **275–294**

Marquand, John P.
  American Writers, vol. 3: **50–73**

Marryat, Frederick
  Writers for Children: **381–387**

Marshall, Paule
  African American Writers: **289–304**

Marston, John, and Cyril Tourneur
  British Writers, vol. 2: **24–41**

Marvell, Andrew
  British Writers, vol. 2: **204–220**

Masters, Edgar Lee
  American Writers Supp. 1, part 2: **454–478**

Mather, Cotton
  American Writers Supp. 2, part 2: **441–470**

Matheson, Richard
  Science Fiction Writers: **425–431**
  Supernatural Fiction Writers, vol. 2: **1073–1080**

Matthiessen, Peter
  American Nature Writers, vol. 2: **599–613**

Maturin, Charles Robert
  Supernatural Fiction Writers, vol. 1: **161–168**

Maugham, W. Somerset
  British Writers, vol. 6: **363–382**
  British Writers Selected Authors, vol. 2: **905–923**

Mazer, Harry
  Writers for Young Adults, vol. 2: **327–336**

Mazer, Norma Fox
  Writers for Young Adults, vol. 2: **337–346**

Medieval Drama
  European Writers, vol. 1: **451–474**
  European Writers Selected Authors, vol. 2: **1051–1074**

Meigs, Cornelia
  Writers for Children: **389–395**

Meltzer, Milton
  Writers for Young Adults, vol. 2: **347–358**

Melville, Herman
  American Writers, vol. 3: **74–98**
  American Writers Retrospective: **243–262**

Mencken, H. L.
  American Writers, vol. 3: **99–121**

Meredith, George
  British Writers, vol. 5: **219–234**

Merril, Judith
  Science Fiction Writers: **433–439**

Merrill, James
  American Writers Supp. 3, part 1: **317–338**

Merritt, A.
  Science Fiction Writers: **65–71**
  Supernatural Fiction Writers, vol. 2: **835–843**

Merwin, W. S.
  American Writers Supp. 3, part 1: **339–360**

Metaphysical Poets, Four
  British Writers, vol. 2: **179–203**

Metcalfe, John
  Supernatural Fiction Writers, vol. 2: **597–602**

Middleton, Thomas
  British Writers, vol. 2: **1–23**

Miklowitz, Gloria D.
  Writers for Young Adults, vol. 2: **359–368**

Millay, Edna St. Vincent
  American Writers, vol. 3: **122–144**
  Modern American Women Writers: **287–302**

Miller, Arthur
  American Writers, vol. 3: **145–169**

Miller, Henry
  American Writers, vol. 3: **170–182**

Miller, Walter M., Jr.
  Science Fiction Writers: **441–448**

Mills, Enos
  American Nature Writers, vol. 2: **615–624**

Milne, A. A.
  Writers for Children: **397–405**

Milton, John
  British Writers, vol. 2: **158–178**
  British Writers Selected Authors, vol. 2: **925–945**

Mirrlees, Hope
  Supernatural Fiction Writers, vol. 2: **603–607**

Mitchell, John Hanson
  American Nature Writers, vol. 2: **625–638**

Pepys, Samuel
    See "Evelyn, John, and Samuel Pepys"
Percy, Walker
    American Writers Supp. 3, part 1: **383–400**
Perrin, Noel
    American Nature Writers, vol. 2: **711–720**
Peterson, Brenda
    American Nature Writers, vol. 2: **721–731**
Petry, Ann
    African American Writers: **347–359**
Pevsner, Stella
    Writers for Young Adults, vol. 3: **27–34**
Peyton, K. M.
    Writers for Young Adults, vol. 3: **35–42**
Pfeffer, Susan Beth
    Writers for Young Adults, vol. 3: **43–52**
Phillpotts, Eden
    Supernatural Fiction Writers, vol. 2: **549–553**
Pinero, Arthur Wing
    See "Well-Made Play, The"
Pinter, Harold
    British Writers Supp. 1: **367–382**
    British Writers Selected Authors, vol. 2: **985–1000**
Plath, Sylvia
    American Writers Supp. 1, part 2: **526–549**
    Modern American Women Writers: **411–424**
Platt, Kin
    Writers for Young Adults, vol. 3: **53–60**
Plomer, William
    African Writers, vol. 2: **697–706**
Poe, Edgar Allan
    American Writers, vol. 3: **409–432**
    Science Fiction Writers: **11–18**
    Supernatural Fiction Writers, vol. 2: **697–705**
    Writers for Young Adults, vol. 3: **61–73**
Poets of World War I (British)
    British Writers, vol. 6: **415–442**
    British Writers Selected Authors, vol. 3: **1445–1471**
Poets of World War II (British)
    British Writers, vol. 7: **421–450**
Pohl, Frederik
    Science Fiction Writers: **475–482**
Pope, Alexander
    British Writers, vol. 3: **68–79**
    British Writers Selected Authors, vol. 2: **1001–1012**

Porter, Katherine Anne
    American Writers, vol. 3: **433–455**
    Modern American Women Writers: **425–440**
Potter, Beatrix
    British Writers Supp. 3: **287–309**
    Writers for Children: **439–446**
Pound, Ezra
    American Writers, vol. 3: **456–479**
    American Writers Retrospective: **283–294**
Powell, Anthony
    British Writers, vol. 7: **343–352**
Powell, John Wesley
    See "Western Geologists and Explorers"
Powys, John Cowper
    Supernatural Fiction Writers, vol. 2: **609–616**
Powys, T. F.
    Supernatural Fiction Writers, vol. 2: **609–616**
Pratt, Fletcher
    See "De Camp, L. Sprague, and Fletcher Pratt"
Priestley, J. B.
    British Writers, vol. 7: **209–232**
Pritchett, V. S.
    British Writers Supp. 3: **311–331**
Pyle, Howard
    Writers for Children: **447–454**
Pyle, Robert Michael
    American Nature Writers, vol. 2: **733–739**
Pym, Barbara
    British Writers Supp. 2: **363–385**
Pynchon, Thomas
    American Writers Supp. 2, part 2: **617–638**
Quammen, David
    American Nature Writers, vol. 2: **741–750**
Quiller-Couch, Arthur
    Supernatural Fiction Writers, vol. 1: **389–395**
Radcliffe, Ann
    Supernatural Fiction Writers, vol. 1: **145–151**
Ralegh (Raleigh), Sir Walter
    British Writers, vol. 1: **145–159**
Rand, Ayn
    American Writers Supp. 4, part 2: **517–535**
Ransom, John Crowe
    American Writers, vol. 3: **480–502**

Ransome, Arthur
  Writers for Children: **455–461**
Rawlings, Marjorie Kinnan
  American Nature Writers, vol. 2: **751–765**
  Writers for Children: **463–467**
Raymo, Chet
  American Nature Writers, vol. 2: **767–780**
Read, Herbert
  See "Poets of World War I (British)"
Reed, Ishmael
  African American Writers: **361–377**
Renaissance Pastoral Poetry
  European Writers, vol. 2: **899–926**
  European Writers Selected Authors, vol. 3:
    1403–1430
Restoration Court Poets, The
  British Writers, vol. 2: **255–272**
Reynolds, G. W. M.
  Supernatural Fiction Writers, vol. 1: **205–211**
Rhys, Jean
  British Writers Supp. 2: **387–404**
Rich, Adrienne
  American Writers Supp. 1, part 2: **550–578**
  Modern American Women Writers: **441–456**
Richards, I. A.
  British Writers Supp. 2: **405–433**
Richards, Laura E.
  Writers for Children: **469–475**
Richardson, Samuel
  British Writers, vol. 3: **80–94**
Riddell, Mrs. J. H.
  Supernatural Fiction Writers, vol. 1: **269–277**
Rinaldi, Ann
  Writers for Young Adults, vol. 3: **75–85**
Ríos, Alberto Álvaro
  American Writers Supp. 4, part 2: **537–556**
Roberts, Elizabeth Madox
  Writers for Children: **477–481**
Robertson, Thomas W.
  See "Well-Made Play, The"
Robinson, Edwin Arlington
  American Writers, vol. 3: **503–526**
Robinson, Marilynne
  See "Contemporary Ecofiction"

Rodowsky, Colby
  Writers for Young Adults, vol. 3: **87–93**
Roethke, Theodore
  American Writers, vol. 3: **527–550**
Rohmer, Sax
  Supernatural Fiction Writers, vol. 2: **555–560**
Romance of the Rose, The, and Medieval Allegory
  European Writers, vol. 1: **309–335**
  European Writers Selected Authors, vol. 3:
    1491–1517
Rosenberg, Isaac
  See "Poets of World War I (British)"
Rossetti, Christina
  British Writers, vol. 5: **247–260**
  Writers for Children: **483–491**
Rossetti, Dante Gabriel
  British Writers, vol. 5: **235–246**
Roth, Philip
  American Writers Supp. 3, part 2: **401–429**
Rotimi, Ola
  African Writers, vol. 2: **707–720**
Rushdie, Salman
  British Writers Supp. 4: **433–457**
Ruskin, John
  British Writers, vol. 5: **173–186**
  Writers for Children: **493–496**
Russ, Joanna
  Science Fiction Writers: **483–490**
Russell, Eric Frank
  Science Fiction Writers: **197–202**
Russell, Sharman Apt
  See "New Voices in American Nature Writing"
Ryden, Hope
  American Nature Writers, vol. 2: **781–792**
Sachs, Marilyn
  Writers for Young Adults, vol. 3: **95–104**
Sackville, Charles (Earl of Dorset)
  See "Restoration Court Poets, The"
St. Clair, Margaret
  Science Fiction Writers: **491–495**
Saki
  Supernatural Fiction Writers, vol. 1: **449–455**
Salinger, J. D.
  American Writers, vol. 3: **551–574**
  Writers for Young Adults, vol. 3: **105–112**

Salisbury, Graham
　Writers for Young Adults, vol. 3: **113–121**

Sandburg, Carl
　American Writers, vol. 3: **575–598**
　Writers for Children: **503–510**
　Writers for Young Adults, vol. 3: **123–133**

Sanders, Scott Russell
　American Nature Writers, vol. 2: **793–804**

Sarban
　Supernatural Fiction Writers, vol. 2: **667–673**

Sassoon, Siegfried
　See "Poets of World War I (British)"

Sawyer, Ruth
　Writers for Children: **511–517**

Sayers, Dorothy L.
　British Writers Supp. 3: **333–353**

Schreiner, Olive
　African Writers, vol. 2: **745–763**
　British Writers Supp. 2: **435–458**

Schwartz, Delmore
　American Writers Supp. 2, part 2: **639–668**

Scoppettone, Sandra
　Writers for Young Adults, vol. 3: **135–143**

Scott, Paul
　British Writers Supp. 1: **259–274**

Scott, Sir Walter
　British Writers, vol. 4: **27–40**
　Supernatural Fiction Writers, vol. 1: **169–176**

Sebestyen, Ouida
　Writers for Young Adults, vol. 3: **145–153**

Sedley, Sir Charles
　See "Restoration Court Poets, The"

Senarens, Luis Philip
　Science Fiction Writers: **53–58**

Seredy, Kate
　Writers for Children: **519–524**

Serviss, Garrett P.
　Science Fiction Writers: **39–44**

Seton, Ernest Thompson
　American Nature Writers, vol. 2: **805–816**

Sewell, Anna
　Writers for Children: **525–528**

Sexton, Anne
　American Writers Supp. 2, part 2: **669–700**
　Modern American Women Writers: **457–470**

Shaffer, Peter
　British Writers Supp. 1: **313–328**

Shakespeare, William
　British Writers, vol. 1: **295–334**
　British Writers Selected Authors, vol. 2: **1013–1052**
　Writers for Young Adults, vol. 3: **155–172**
　See also entries in *William Shakespeare: His
　　World, His Work, His Influence*

Shange, Ntozake
　African American Writers: **379–393**

Shapiro, Karl
　American Writers Supp. 2, part 2: **701–724**

Shaw, George Bernard
　British Writers, vol. 6: **101–132**
　British Writers Selected Authors, vol. 3: **1053–1084**

Sheckley, Robert
　Science Fiction Writers: **497–503**

Shelley, Mary
　British Writers Supp. 3: **355–373**
　British Writers Selected Authors, vol. 3: **1085–1103**
　Science Fiction Writers: **3–9**
　See also "Gothic Novel, The"

Shelley, Percy Bysshe
　British Writers, vol. 4: **195–210**
　British Writers Selected Authors, vol. 3: **1105–1120**

Shepard, Sam
　American Writers Supp. 3, part 2: **431–450**

Sheridan, Richard Brinsley
　British Writers, vol. 3: **252–271**

Shiel, M. P.
　Science Fiction Writers: **31–37**
　Supernatural Fiction Writers, vol. 1: **361–367**

Sidney, Sir Philip
　British Writers, vol. 1: **160–175**

Silko, Leslie Marmon
　American Nature Writers, vol. 2: **817–827**
　American Writers Supp. 4, part 2: **557–572**

Silverberg, Robert
　Science Fiction Writers: **505–511**

Simak, Clifford D.
　Science Fiction Writers: **513–518**

Simon, Neil
　American Writers Supp. 4, part 2: **573–594**

Sinclair, May
　Supernatural Fiction Writers, vol. 1: **513–519**

Toomer, Jean
  African American Writers: **429–440**
  American Writers Supp. 3, part 2: **475–491**

Tourneur, Cyril
  See "Marston, John, and Cyril Tourneur"

Traherne, Thomas
  See "Metaphysical Poets, Four"

Trevelyan, G. M.
  British Writers, vol. 6: **383–396**

Trevor, William
  British Writers Supp. 4: **499–519**

Trilling, Lionel
  American Writers Supp. 3, part 2: **493–515**

Trollope, Anthony
  British Writers, vol. 5: **89–104**
  British Writers Selected Authors, vol. 3: **1295–1309**

Tutuola, Amos
  African Writers, vol. 2: **865–878**

Twain, Mark
  American Writers, vol. 4: **190–213**
  Supernatural Fiction Writers, vol. 2: **761–768**
  Writers for Children: **573–582**
  Writers for Young Adults, vol. 3: **321–328**

Tyler, Anne
  American Writers Supp. 4, part 2: **657–675**
  Modern American Women Writers: **499–510**

Tyndale, William
  See "Bible, The English"

Updike, John
  American Writers, vol. 4: **214–235**
  American Writers Retrospective: **317–338**

Vanbrugh, Sir John
  British Writers, vol. 2: **323–337**

Vance, Jack
  Science Fiction Writers: **543–549**
  Supernatural Fiction Writers, vol. 2: **1105–1111**

van der Post, Laurens
  African Writers, vol. 2: **879–891**

Van Dyke, John C.
  American Nature Writers, vol. 2: **951–962**

Van Loon, Hendrik Willem
  Writers for Children: **583–589**

Van Vechten, Carl
  American Writers Supp. 2, part 2: **725–751**

Van Vogt, A. E.
  Science Fiction Writers: **209–217**

Vaughan, Henry
  See "Metaphysical Poets, Four"

Veblen, Thorstein
  American Writers Supp. 1, part 2: **628–650**

Vidal, Gore
  American Writers Supp. 4, part 2: **677–697**

Voigt, Cynthia
  Writers for Young Adults, vol. 3: **329–338**

Vonnegut, Kurt
  American Writers Supp. 2, part 2: **753–783**
  Science Fiction Writers: **551–561**

Wakefield, H. Russell
  Supernatural Fiction Writers, vol. 2: **617–622**

Walker, Alice
  African American Writers: **441–458**
  American Writers Supp. 3, part 2: **517–540**
  Modern American Women Writers: **511–520**

Walker, Margaret
  African American Writers: **459–471**

Wall, Mervyn
  Supernatural Fiction Writers, vol. 2: **645–650**

Wallace, David Rains
  American Nature Writers, vol. 2: **963–972**

Waller, Edmund
  See "Cavalier Poets, The"

Walpole, Horace
  Supernatural Fiction Writers, vol. 1: **131–137**
  See also "Gothic Novel, The"

Walsh, Jill Paton
  Writers for Young Adults, vol. 3: **339–346**

Walton, Izaak
  British Writers, vol. 2: **131–144**

Warren, Robert Penn
  American Writers, vol. 4: **236–259**

Waugh, Evelyn
  British Writers, vol. 7: **289–308**
  British Writers Selected Authors, vol. 3: **1311–1330**

Webster, John
  British Writers, vol. 2: **68–86**

Weinbaum, Stanley G.
  Science Fiction Writers: **145–149**

Weldon, Fay
  British Writers Supp. 4: **521–539**

Well-Made Play, The
  European Writers, vol. 7: **1909–1934**

Wolfe, Tom
American Writers Supp. 3, part 2: **567–588**

Wolff, Virginia Euwer
Writers for Young Adults, vol. 3: **391–398**

Wollstonecraft, Mary
British Writers Supp. 3: **465–482**

Wood, Mrs. Henry
Supernatural Fiction Writers, vol. 1: **279–286**

Woolf, Virginia
British Writers, vol. 7: **17–40**
British Writers Selected Authors, vol. 3: **1395–1417**

Wordsworth, William
British Writers, vol. 4: **1–26**
British Writers Selected Authors, vol. 3: **1419–1444**

Wright, James
American Writers Supp. 3, part 2: **589–607**

Wright, Richard
African American Writers: **505–523**
American Writers, vol. 4: **474–497**

Wright, S. Fowler
Science Fiction Writers: **83–89**

Wyatt, Sir Thomas
British Writers, vol. 1: **97–112**

Wycherley, William
British Writers, vol. 2: **307–322**

Wylie, Elinor
American Writers Supp. 1, part 2: **707–730**

Wyndham, John
Science Fiction Writers: **219–224**

Yeats, William Butler
British Writers, vol. 6: **207–224**
British Writers Selected Authors, vol. 3: **1473–1490**

Yep, Laurence
Writers for Young Adults, vol. 3: **399–408**

Yolen, Jane
Writers for Young Adults, vol. 3: **409–420**

Yonge, Charlotte Mary
Writers for Children: **625–631**

Zelazny, Roger
Science Fiction Writers: **563–570**
Supernatural Fiction Writers, vol. 2: **1113–1119**

Zindel, Paul
Writers for Young Adults, vol. 3: **421–430**

Zukofsky, Louis
American Writers Supp. 3, part 2: **609–632**

Zwinger, Ann
American Nature Writers, vol. 2: **989–1001**

Zwinger, Susan
See "New Voices in American Nature Writing"

French

Adam de la Halle
See "Medieval Drama"

Anouilh, Jean
European Writers, vol. 13: **2843–2865**
European Writers Selected Authors, vol. 1: **31–52**

Apollinaire, Guillaume
European Writers, vol. 9: **881–903**

Aragon, Louis
European Writers, vol. 11: **2061–2087**

Arp, Jean
European Writers, vol. 10: **1365–1384**

Artaud, Antonin
European Writers, vol. 11: **1961–1985**

Arthurian Legend
European Writers, vol. 1: **137–160**
European Writers Selected Authors, vol. 1: **79–102**

Arthurian Romances
Supernatural Fiction Writers, vol. 1: **11–18**

Augier, Émile
See "Well-Made Play, The"

Aymé, Marcel
European Writers, vol. 12: **2433–2456**

Bâ, Mariama
African Writers, vol. 1: **77–82**

Balzac, Honoré de
European Writers, vol. 5: **635–658**
European Writers Selected Authors, vol. 1: **161–183**
Supernatural Fiction Writers, vol. 1: **37–44**

Barthes, Roland
European Writers, vol. 13: **3079–3104**

Baudelaire, Charles
European Writers, vol. 7: **1323–1348**

Beaumarchais, Pierre-Augustin Caron de
European Writers, vol. 4: **563–585**

Beauvoir, Simone de
European Writers, vol. 12: **2701–2732**
European Writers Selected Authors, vol. 1: **185–215**

Beckett, Samuel
  British Writers Supp. 1: **43–64**
  British Writers Selected Authors, vol. 1: **47–68**
Beckford, William
  Supernatural Fiction Writers, vol. 1: **139–144**
  See also "Gothic Novel, The" in *British Writers*,
    vol. 3: **324–346**
Bergson, Henri
  European Writers, vol. 8: **45–66**
Berlioz, Hector
  European Writers, vol. 6: **771–812**
Beti, Mongo
  African Writers, vol. 1: **83–94**
Boileau-Despréaux, Nicolas
  European Writers, vol. 3: **177–205**
Bossuet, Jacques Bénigne
  European Writers, vol. 3: **151–175**
Breton, André
  European Writers, vol. 11: **1939–1960**
Brieux, Eugène
  See "Well-Made Play, The"
Brunhoff, Jean de
  Writers for Children: **91–96**
Butor, Michel
  European Writers, vol. 13: **3287–3321**
Camus, Albert
  African Writers, vol. 1: **139–152**
  European Writers, vol. 13: **3049–3078**
  European Writers Selected Authors, vol. 1: **305–334**
Cazotte, Jacques
  Supernatural Fiction Writers, vol. 1: **29–35**
Céline, Louis-Ferdinand
  European Writers, vol. 11: **1859–1884**
Chanson de Roland, The, and the *Chansons de
    Geste*
  European Writers, vol. 1: **89–112**
Chateaubriand, François René de
  European Writers, vol. 5: **113–140**
Chénier, André
  European Writers, vol. 4: **691–718**
Chrétien de Troyes
  European Writers, vol. 1: **185–209**
  See also "Arthurian Romances"
Claudel, Paul
  European Writers, vol. 8: **471–494**

Cocteau, Jean
  European Writers, vol. 10: **1543–1564**
Colette
  European Writers, vol. 9: **617–638**
  European Writers Selected Authors, vol. 1: **389–410**
Constant, Benjamin
  See "French Novelists, Three"
Corneille, Pierre
  European Writers, vol. 3: **23–49**
Crèvecoeur, Hector St. John de
  American Writers Supp. 1, part 1: **227–252**
  See also "Early Romantic Natural History
    Literature" in *American Nature Writers*, vol. 2:
    1059–1078
Delacroix, Eugène
  European Writers, vol. 5: **513–539**
Descartes, René
  European Writers, vol. 3: **1–22**
  European Writers Selected Authors, vol. 1: **431–452**
Des Périers, Bonaventure
  See "Renaissance Short Fiction"
Dib, Mohammed
  African Writers, vol. 1: **199–207**
Diderot, Denis
  European Writers, vol. 4: **475–509**
Dumas, Alexandre (Fils)
  See "Well-Made Play, The"
Dumas, Alexandre (Père)
  European Writers, vol. 6: **719–745**
  European Writers Selected Authors, vol. 1: **503–527**
  Writers for Children: **209–213**
Fénelon, François de Salignac de la Mothe-
  European Writers, vol. 3: **261–291**
Feydeau, Georges
  See "Well-Made Play, The"
Flaubert, Gustave
  European Writers, vol. 7: **1373–1394**
  European Writers Selected Authors, vol. 1:
    553–574
Foucault, Michel
  European Writers, vol. 13: **3323–3364**
France, Anatole
  Supernatural Fiction Writers, vol. 1: **67–72**
French Novelists, Three
  European Writers, vol. 4: **393–419**

Gautier, Théophile
  European Writers, vol. 6: **1033–1059**
  Supernatural Fiction Writers, vol. 1: **45–50**

Genet, Jean
  European Writers, vol. 13: **2865–2892**

Ghelderode, Michel de
  European Writers, vol. 11: **2113–2141**

Gide, André
  European Writers, vol. 8: **495–518**
  European Writers Selected Authors, vol. 1: **631–654**

Giraudoux, Jean
  European Writers, vol. 9: **1041–1065**

Goldoni, Carlo
  European Writers, vol. 4: **421–448**

Goncourt, Edmond Louis Antoine de, and Jules Alfred Huot de Goncourt
  European Writers, vol. 7: **1395–1419**

Gower, John
  British Writers, vol. 1: **48–56**

Guillaume de Lorris
  See "*Romance of the Rose*, The, and Medieval Allegory"

Hervieu, Paul
  See "Well-Made Play, The"

Hoffmann, E. T. A.
  European Writers, vol. 5: **261–289**
  Supernatural Fiction Writers, vol. 1: **111–119**
  Writers for Children: **283–288**

Hugo, Victor
  European Writers, vol. 6: **693–718**
  European Writers Selected Authors, vol. 2: **761–786**

Huysmans, Joris Karl
  European Writers, vol. 7: **1709–1729**

Ionesco, Eugène
  European Writers, vol. 13: **2989–3020**
  European Writers Selected Authors, vol. 2: **815–846**

Jarry, Alfred
  European Writers, vol. 9: **665–687**

Jean de Meun
  See "*Romance of the Rose*, The, and Medieval Allegory"

Kateb, Yacine
  African Writers, vol. 1: **391–400**

Kundera, Milan
  European Writers, vol. 13: **3389–3413**

Labiche, Eugène
  See "Well-Made Play, The"

La Bruyère, Jean de
  European Writers, vol. 3: **229–260**

Laclos, Choderlos de
  See "French Novelists, Three"

La Fontaine, Jean de
  European Writers, vol. 3: **73–100**
  European Writers Selected Authors, vol. 2: **901–928**

Laforgue, Jules
  European Writers, vol. 7: **1883–1908**

La Rochefoucauld, François VI, Duc de
  European Writers, vol. 3: **51–71**

Laye, Camara
  African Writers, vol. 1: **413–425**

Leconte de Lisle, Charles Marie
  European Writers, vol. 6: **1245–1273**

Lesage, Alain-René
  European Writers, vol. 3: **317–344**

Maeterlinck, Maurice
  European Writers, vol. 8: **119–146**

Mallarmé, Stéphane
  European Writers, vol. 7: **1567–1595**

Malraux, André
  European Writers, vol. 12: **2413–2432**
  European Writers Selected Authors, vol. 2: **977–996**

Marguerite, Queen of Navarre
  See "Renaissance Short Fiction"

Maupassant, Guy de
  European Writers, vol. 7: **1759–1784**
  European Writers Selected Authors, vol. 2: **1025–1050**
  Supernatural Fiction Writers, vol. 1: **59–65**

Mauriac, François
  European Writers, vol. 10: **1307–1330**

Medieval Drama
  European Writers, vol. 1: **451–474**
  European Writers Selected Authors, vol. 2: **1051–1074**

Medieval Satire
  European Writers, vol. 1: **337–376**
  European Writers Selected Authors, vol. 2: **1075–1113**

Memmi, Albert
  African Writers, vol. 2: **467–477**

Mérimée, Prosper
  European Writers, vol. 6: **745–769**
  Supernatural Fiction Writers, vol. 1: **51–57**

Michelet, Jules, and Romantic Historiography
  European Writers, vol. 5: **571–606**

Molière
  European Writers, vol. 3: **101–124**
  European Writers Selected Authors, vol. 2:
    1115–1137

Montaigne, Michel de
  European Writers, vol. 2: **769–790**
  European Writers Selected Authors, vol. 2:
    1139–1160

Montesquieu, Charles-Louis de Secondat
  European Writers, vol. 3: **345–366**

Montherlant, Henry de
  European Writers, vol. 11: **1915–1938**

Musset, Alfred de
  European Writers, vol. 6: **999–1033**

Nerval, Gérard de
  European Writers, vol. 6: **943–970**

Oyono, Ferdinand
  African Writers, vol. 2: **641–649**

Pascal, Blaise
  European Writers, vol. 3: **125–150**

Perrault, Charles
  Writers for Children: **431–437**

Perse, Saint-John
  European Writers, vol. 10: **1429–1452**

Prévost, Antoine-Francois
  See "French Novelists, Three"

Proust, Marcel
  European Writers, vol. 8: **545–568**
  European Writers Selected Authors, vol. 2:
    1317–1340

Queneau, Raymond
  European Writers, vol. 12: **2511–2534**

Rabelais, François
  European Writers, vol. 2: **693–720**
  European Writers Selected Authors, vol. 3:
    1375–1402

Racine, Jean
  European Writers, vol. 3: **207–228**

Renaissance Pastoral Poetry
  European Writers, vol. 2: **899–926**

  European Writers Selected Authors, vol. 3:
    1403–1430

Renaissance Short Fiction
  European Writers, vol. 2: **927–956**
  European Writers Selected Authors, vol. 3:
    1431–1460

Rilke, Rainer Maria
  European Writers, vol. 9: **767–796**
  European Writers Selected Authors, vol. 3:
    1461–1489

Rinbaud, Arthur
  European Writers, vol. 7: **1785–1824**

Robbe-Grillet, Alain
  European Writers, vol. 13: **3237–3256**

Romance of the Rose, The, and Medieval Allegory
  European Writers, vol. 1: **309–335**
  European Writers Selected Authors, vol. 3:
    1491–1517

Ronsard, Pierre de
  See "Renaissance Pastoral Poetry"

Ronsard, Pierre de, and the Pléiade
  European Writers, vol. 2: **721–746**

Rousseau, Jean Jacques
  European Writers, vol. 4: **449–474**
  European Writers Selected Authors, vol. 3:
    1519–1544

Sade, Marquis de, and the French Libertine
    Tradition
  European Writers, vol. 4: **615–638**

Saint-Exupéry, Antoine de
  European Writers, vol. 12: **2307–2332**
  European Writers Selected Authors, vol. 3:
    1545–1569

Sainte-Beuve, Charles-Augustin
  European Writers, vol. 6: **837–861**

Sand, George
  European Writers, vol. 6: **813–836**
  European Writers Selected Authors, vol. 3:
    1571–1594

Sardou, Victor
  See "Well-Made Play, The"

Sarraute, Nathalie
  European Writers, vol. 12: **2333–2359**

Sartre, Jean-Paul
  European Writers, vol. 12: **2589–2614**
  European Writers Selected Authors, vol. 3: **1595–1620**

Scribe, Augustin Eugène
  See "Well-Made Play, The"
Sembène Ousmane
  African Writers, vol. 2: **765–774**
Senghor, Léopold Sédar
  African Writers, vol. 2: **775–789**
Simenon, Georges
  European Writers, vol. 12: **2479–2510**
Simon, Claude
  European Writers, vol. 13: **3021–3048**
Staël, Madame de
  European Writers, vol. 5: **89–111**
Stendhal
  European Writers, vol. 5: **343–366**
  European Writers Selected Authors, vol. 3:
    1649–1672
Taine, Hippolyte
  European Writers, vol. 7: **1449–1469**
Tocqueville, Alexis de
  European Writers, vol. 6: **893–912**
  European Writers Selected Authors, vol. 3:
    1673–1691
Troubadours and Trouvères
  European Writers, vol. 1: **161–184**
Urfé, Honoré, d'
  See "Renaissance Pastoral Poetry"
Valéry, Paul
  European Writers, vol. 8: **569–588**
Verlaine, Paul
  European Writers, vol. 7: **1619–1643**
Verne, Jules
  Science Fiction Writers: **573–582**
  Writers for Children: **591–598**
Vigny, Alfred Victor de
  European Writers, vol. 5: **447–488**
Villon, François
  European Writers, vol. 2: **535–570**
Voltaire
  European Writers, vol. 4: **367–392**
  European Writers Selected Authors, vol. 3:
    1741–1766
Weil, Simone
  European Writers, vol. 12: **2787–2814**
Well-Made Play, The
  European Writers, vol. 7: **1909–1934**

Yourcenar, Marguerite
  European Writers, vol. 12: **2535–2561**
Zola, Émile
  European Writers, vol. 7: **1517–1542**
  European Writers Selected Authors, vol. 3:
    1789–1813

German

Arp, Jean
  European Writers, vol. 10: **1365–1384**
Arthurian Legend
  European Writers, vol. 1: **137–160**
  European Writers Selected Authors, vol. 1: **79–102**
Arthurian Romances
  Supernatural Fiction Writers, vol. 1: **11–18**
Bauernfeld, Eduard von
  See "Well-Made Play, The"
Benjamin, Walter
  European Writers, vol. 11: **1703–1730**
Böll, Heinrich
  European Writers, vol. 13: **3165–3186**
Brecht, Bertolt
  European Writers, vol. 11: **2089–2112**
  European Writers Selected Authors, vol. 1:
    281–303
Broch, Hermann
  European Writers, vol. 10: **1385–1408**
Büchner, Georg
  European Writers, vol. 6: **1169–1194**
Burckhardt, Jacob
  European Writers, vol. 6: **1225–1244**
Canetti, Elias
  European Writers, vol. 12: **2615–2633**
Chamisso, Adelbert von
  Supernatural Fiction Writers, vol. 1: **91–95**
Dürrenmatt, Friedrich
  European Writers, vol. 13: **3215–3235**
Fontane, Theodor
  European Writers, vol. 6: **1299–1322**
Fouqué, Friedrich de la Motte
  Supernatural Fiction Writers, vol. 1: **97–105**
Freud, Sigmund
  European Writers, vol. 8: **1–20**
  European Writers Selected Authors, vol. 1: **575–594**

Freytag, Gustav
See "Well-Made Play, The"

Frisch, Max
European Writers, vol. 13: **2895–2924**

George, Stefan
European Writers, vol. 8: **447–470**

Goethe, Johann Wolfgang von
European Writers, vol. 5: **1–26**
European Writers Selected Authors, vol. 1: **655–680**

Gottfried von Strassburg
European Writers, vol. 1: **237–262**
See also "Arthurian Romances"

Grass, Günter
European Writers, vol. 13: **3365–3388**
European Writers Selected Authors, vol. 2:
711–734

Grillparzer, Franz
European Writers, vol. 5: **417–445**

Grimm, Jacob and Wilhelm
Writers for Children: **255–263**

Gutzkow, Karl
See "Well-Made Play, The"

Hauff, William
Supernatural Fiction Writers, vol. 1: **107–110**

Hauptmann, Gerhart
European Writers, vol. 8: **147–174**

Hebbel, Friedrich
European Writers, vol. 6: **1089–1122**

Heine, Heinrich
European Writers, vol. 5: **489–512**

Herder, Johann Gottfried von
European Writers, vol. 4: **639–660**

Hesse, Hermann
European Writers, vol. 9: **833–859**
European Writers Selected Authors, vol. 2:
735–760

Hoffmann, E. T. A.
European Writers, vol. 5: **261–289**
Supernatural Fiction Writers, vol. 1: **111–119**
Writers for Children: **283–288**

Hoffmann, Heinrich
Writers for Children: **289–294**

Hofmannsthal, Hugo von
European Writers, vol. 9: **689–714**

Hölderlin, Friedrich
European Writers, vol. 5: **143–173**

Kafka, Franz
European Writers, vol. 9: **1151–1179**
European Writers Selected Authors, vol. 2: **847–875**

Kästner, Erich
Writers for Children: **317–322**

Keller, Gottfried
See "Poetic Realism"

Kleist, Heinrich von
European Writers, vol. 5: **291–312**

Klopstock, Friedrich Gottlieb
European Writers, vol. 4: **511–536**

Lessing, Gotthold Ephraim
European Writers, vol. 4: **537–562**

Lukács, György
European Writers, vol. 10: **1251–1279**

Luther, Martin
European Writers, vol. 2: **669–692**
European Writers Selected Authors, vol. 2: **929–951**

Mann, Heinrich
European Writers, vol. 8: **519–543**

Mann, Thomas
European Writers, vol. 9: **715–743**
European Writers Selected Authors, vol. 2:
997–1024

Meinhold, Wilhelm
Supernatural Fiction Writers, vol. 1: **121–127**

Meyer, Conrad Ferdinand
See "Poetic Realism"

Musaeus, J. K.
Supernatural Fiction Writers, vol. 1: **75–81**

Musil, Robert
European Writers, vol. 9: **931–958**

Nibelungenlied, The
European Writers, vol. 1: **211–236**

Nietzsche, Friedrich
European Writers, vol. 7: **1645–1682**
European Writers Selected Authors, vol. 2:
1161–1197

Novalis
European Writers, vol. 5: **205–231**

Poetic Realism
European Writers, vol. 6: **913–942**

Renaissance Short Fiction
European Writers, vol. 2: **927–956**
European Writers Selected Authors, vol. 3:
1431–1460

Richter, Jean Paul
  European Writers, vol. 5: **53–88**
Rilke, Rainer Maria
  European Writers, vol. 9: **767–796**
  European Writers Selected Authors, vol. 3:
    1461–1489
Salten, Felix
  Writers for Children: **497–501**
Schiller, Friedrich von
  European Writers, vol. 5: **27–52**
Schlegel, Friedrich von
  European Writers, vol. 5: **177–203**
Schnitzler, Arthur
  European Writers, vol. 8: **89–117**
Schopenhauer, Arthur
  European Writers, vol. 5: **395–415**
Spyri, Johanna
  Writers for Children: **529–533**
Storm, Theodor
  See "Poetic Realism"
Tieck, Ludwig
  European Writers, vol. 5: **233–260**
  Supernatural Fiction Writers, vol. 1: **83–89**
Trakl, Georg
  European Writers, vol. 10: **1409–1427**
Wagner, Richard
  European Writers, vol. 6: **1147–1168**
  European Writers Selected Authors, vol. 3:
    1767–1787
Walther von der Vogelweide
  European Writers, vol. 1: **287–308**
Wedekind, Frank
  European Writers, vol. 8: **229–281**
Well-Made Play, The
  European Writers, vol. 7: **1909–1934**
Wieland, Christoph Martin
  European Writers, vol. 4: **587–614**
Wolfram von Eschenbach
  European Writers, vol. 1: **263–286**
  See also "Arthurian Romances"

Gĩkũyũ

Ngũgĩ wa Thiong'o
  African Writers, vol. 2: **537–555**

Greek

Acts of the Apostles, The
  See "Gospel of Luke and Acts of the Apostles"
Aeschylus
  Ancient Writers, vol. 1: **99–155**
Alcaeus
  See "Greek Lyric Poets"
Alcman
  See "Greek Lyric Poets"
Anacreon
  See "Greek Lyric Poets"
Antimachus of Colophon
  See "Hellenistic Poetry at Alexandria"
Apocrypha, The
  The Books of the Bible, vol. 2: **3–11**
Apollonius of Rhodes
  See "Hellenistic Poetry at Alexandria"
Aristophanes
  Ancient Writers, vol. 1: **291–312**
Aristotle
  Ancient Writers, vol. 1: **377–416**
Asclepiades
  See "Hellenistic Poetry at Alexandria"
Bacchylides
  See "Greek Lyric Poets"
Baruch, the Letter of Jeremiah, the Prayer of
    Manasseh
  The Books of the Bible, vol. 2: **87–92**
Bible as Sacred Literature, The
  The Books of the Bible, vol. 1: **1–9**
Callimachus
  See "Hellenistic Poetry at Alexandria"
Cavafy, Constantin
  European Writers, vol. 8: **205–228**
Demetrius of Phalerum
  See "Hellenistic Poetry at Alexandria"
Demosthenes
  Ancient Writers, vol. 1: **417–433**
Elytis, Odysseus
  European Writers, vol. 13: **2955–2988**
Epictetus and Marcus Aurelius
  Ancient Writers, vol. 2: **985–1002**
Epistle of James
  The Books of the Bible, vol. 2: **339–343**

Epistles of John (1, 2, and 3 John)
  The Books of the Bible, vol. 2: **359–365**

Epistle of Jude
  See "Epistles of Peter and Jude (2 Peter and Jude)"

Epistle of Peter (1 Peter)
  The Books of the Bible, vol. 2: **345–351**

Epistles of Peter and Jude (2 Peter and Jude)
  The Books of the Bible, vol. 2: **353–357**

Epistle to the Colossians
  The Books of the Bible, vol. 2: **301–310**

Epistles to the Corinthians (1 and 2 Corinthians)
  The Books of the Bible, vol. 2: **245–269**

Epistle to the Ephesians
  The Books of the Bible, vol. 2: **285–292**

Epistle to the Galatians
  The Books of the Bible, vol. 2: **271–284**

Epistle to the Hebrews
  The Books of the Bible, vol. 2: **327–338**

Epistle to Philemon
  The Books of the Bible, vol. 2: **325–326**

Epistle to the Philippians
  The Books of the Bible, vol. 2: **293–299**

Epistle to the Romans
  The Books of the Bible, vol. 2: **229–243**

Epistles to the Thessalonians (1 and 2 Thessalonians)
  The Books of the Bible, vol. 2: **311–318**

Epistles to Timothy and Titus (1 and 2 Timothy and Titus)
  The Books of the Bible, vol. 2: **319–324**

Esdras (1 Esdras)
  The Books of the Bible, vol. 2: **13–19**

Euripides
  Ancient Writers, vol. 1: **233–266**

Gospel of John
  The Books of the Bible, vol. 2: **203–228**

Gospel of Luke and Acts of the Apostles
  The Books of the Bible, vol. 2: **171–202**

Gospel of Mark
  The Books of the Bible, vol. 2: **149–169**

Gospel of Matthew
  The Books of the Bible, vol. 2: **125–147**

Greek Lyric Poets
  Ancient Writers, vol. 1: **75–98**

Hellenistic Poetry at Alexandria
  Ancient Writers, vol. 1: **449–482**

Herodotus
  Ancient Writers, vol. 1: **209–232**

Hesiod
  Ancient Writers, vol. 1: **43–73**

Homer
  Ancient Writers, vol. 1: **1–41**

Ibycus
  See "Greek Lyric Poets"

Isocrates
  Ancient Writers, vol. 1: **313–329**

Josephus
  Ancient Writers, vol. 2: **877–885**

Judith
  The Books of the Bible, vol. 2: **43–49**

Kazantzakis, Nikos
  European Writers, vol. 9: **1067–1091**

Longinus
  Ancient Writers, vol. 2: **1063–1080**

Lucian
  Ancient Writers, vol. 2: **1081–1097**

Maccabees (1 and 2 Maccabees)
  The Books of the Bible, vol. 2: **93–114**

Marcus Aurelius
  See "Epictetus and Marcus Aurelius"

Menander
  Ancient Writers, vol. 1: **435–447**

New Testament, The
  The Books of the Bible, vol. 2: **117–124**

Philitas of Cos
  See "Hellenistic Poetry at Alexandria"

Pindar
  Ancient Writers, vol. 1: **157–177**

Plato
  Ancient Writers, vol. 1: **353–376**

Plutarch
  Ancient Writers, vol. 2: **961–983**

Polybius
  Ancient Writers, vol. 1: **525–539**

Posidippus
  See "Hellenistic Poetry at Alexandria"

Revelation
The Books of the Bible, vol. 2: **367–381**

Ritsos, Yannis
European Writers, vol. 12: **2815–2842**

Sappho
See "Greek Lyric Poets"

Seferis, George
European Writers, vol. 12: **2255–2271**

Simonides
See "Greek Lyric Poets"

Sirach (Ecclesiasticus)
The Books of the Bible, vol. 2: **65–86**

Sophocles
Ancient Writers, vol. 1: **179–207**

Stesichorus
See "Greek Lyric Poets"

Theocritus
Ancient Writers, vol. 1: **483–500**

Thucydides
Ancient Writers, vol. 1: **267–289**

Tobit
The Books of the Bible, vol. 2: **35–42**

Wisdom of Solomon
The Books of the Bible, vol. 2: **51–63**

Xenophon
Ancient Writers, vol. 1: **331–351**

Hebrew

Amos
The Books of the Bible, vol. 1: **367–374**

Apocrypha, The
The Books of the Bible, vol. 2: **3–11**

Bible as Sacred Literature, The
The Books of the Bible, vol. 1: **1–9**

Chronicles, Ezra, and Nehemiah (1 and 2 Chronicles, Ezra, and Nehemiah)
The Books of the Bible, vol. 1: **155–171**

Daniel and Additions to Daniel
The Books of the Bible, vol. 1: **333–347**

Deuteronomy
The Books of the Bible, vol. 1: **89–102**

Ecclesiastes
The Books of the Bible, vol. 1: **231–239**

Esther and Additions to Esther
The Books of the Bible, vol. 1: **173–179**

Exodus
The Books of the Bible, vol. 1: **47–62**

Ezekiel
The Books of the Bible, vol. 1: **319–332**

Genesis
The Books of the Bible, vol. 1: **21–46**

Habakkuk
The Books of the Bible, vol. 1: **391–396**

Haggai, Zechariah, and Malachi
The Books of the Bible, vol. 1: **405–414**

Hosea
The Books of the Bible, vol. 1: **349–358**

Isaiah
The Books of the Bible, vol. 1: **247–279**

Jeremiah
The Books of the Bible, vol. 1: **281–301**

Job
The Books of the Bible, vol. 1: **181–201**

Joel
The Books of the Bible, vol. 1: **359–365**

Jonah
The Books of the Bible, vol. 1: **381–384**

Joshua
The Books of the Bible, vol. 1: **103–112**

Judges
The Books of the Bible, vol. 1: **113–121**

Kings (1 and 2 Kings)
The Books of the Bible, vol. 1: **141–155**

Lamentations
The Books of the Bible, vol. 1: **303–318**

Leviticus
The Books of the Bible, vol. 1: **63–70**

Malachi
See "Haggai, Zechariah, and Malachi"

Micah
The Books of the Bible, vol. 1: **385–390**

Nahum
See "Obadiah and Nahum"

Numbers
The Books of the Bible, vol. 1: **71–87**

Obadiah and Nahum
The Books of the Bible, vol. 1: **375–380**

Old Testament, The
  The Books of the Bible, vol. 1: **11–19**
Proverbs
  The Books of the Bible, vol. 1: **223–230**
Psalms
  The Books of the Bible, vol. 1: **203–221**
Ruth
  The Books of the Bible, vol. 1: **123–126**
Samuel (1 and 2 Samuel)
  The Books of the Bible, vol. 1: **127–140**
Singer, Isaac Bashevis
  American Writers, vol. 4: **1–24**
Sirach (Ecclesiasticus)
  The Books of the Bible, vol. 2: **65–86**
Song of Solomon
  The Books of the Bible, vol. 1: **241–246**
Zechariah
  See "Haggai, Zechariah, and Malachi"
Zephaniah
  The Books of the Bible, vol. 1: **397–404**

Hungarian

Ady, Endre
  European Writers, vol. 9: **859–880**
Kosztolányi, Dezsö
  European Writers, vol. 10: **1231–1249**

Icelandic

Gunnarsson, Gunnar
  European Writers, vol. 10: **1497–1519**
Laxness, Halldór
  European Writers, vol. 12: **2457–2478**

Ijọ

Okara, Gabriel
  African Writers, vol. 2: **567–582**

Italian

Alfieri, Vittorio
  European Writers, vol. 4: **661–689**
Ariosto, Lodovico
  European Writers, vol. 2: **619–644**
Bandello, Matteo
  See "Renaissance Short Fiction"
Basile, Giambattista
  See "Renaissance Short Fiction"
Boccaccio, Giovanni
  European Writers, vol. 2: **509–534**
  European Writers Selected Authors, vol. 1: **255–280**
  See also "Renaissance Pastoral Poetry"
Calvino, Italo
  European Writers, vol. 13: **3259–3286**
Carducci, Giosue
  European Writers, vol. 7: **1495–1516**
Castiglione, Baldesar
  European Writers, vol. 2: **645–667**
Collodi, C.
  Writers for Children: **129–137**
Croce, Benedetto
  European Writers, vol. 8: **311–329**
D'Annunzio, Gabriele
  European Writers, vol. 8: **175–203**
Dante Alighieri
  European Writers, vol. 1: **431–450**
  European Writers Selected Authors, vol. 1: **411–430**
  See also "Renaissance Pastoral Poetry"
Foscolo, Ugo
  European Writers, vol. 5: **313–341**
Ginzburg, Natalia
  European Writers, vol. 13: **3131–3163**
Giraldi, Giambattista
  See "Renaissance Pastoral Poetry"
Goldoni, Carlo
  European Writers, vol. 4: **421–448**
Guarini, Giambattista
  See "Renaissance Pastoral Poetry"
Lampedusa, Giuseppe Tomasi di
  European Writers, vol. 11: **2009–2034**
Leopardi, Giacomo
  European Writers, vol. 5: **541–567**
Machiavelli, Niccolò
  European Writers, vol. 2: **595–618**
  European Writers Selected Authors, vol. 2: **953–976**
Manzoni, Alessandro
  European Writers, vol. 5: **367–394**
Marinetti, Filippo Tommaso
  European Writers, vol. 9: **797–832**

Masuccio Salernitano
   See "Renaissance Short Fiction"

Medici, Lorenzo de'
   See "Renaissance Pastoral Poetry"

Montale, Eugenio
   European Writers, vol. 11: **1987–2008**

Moravia, Alberto
   European Writers, vol. 12: **2673–2697**

Pascoli, Giovanni
   European Writers, vol. 7: **1825–1854**

Pavese, Cesare
   European Writers, vol. 12: **2759–2784**

Petrarch, Francesco
   European Writers, vol. 2: **475–507**
   European Writers Selected Authors, vol. 2:
      1255–1287
   See also "Renaissance Pastoral Poetry"

Pirandello, Luigi
   European Writers, vol. 8: **389–416**
   European Writers Selected Authors, vol. 2:
      1289–1316

Quasimodo, Salvatore
   European Writers, vol. 12: **2387–2411**

Renaissance Pastoral Poetry
   European Writers, vol. 2: **899–926**
   European Writers Selected Authors, vol. 3:
      1403–1430

Renaissance Short Fiction
   European Writers, vol. 2: **927–956**
   European Writers Selected Authors, vol. 3:
      1431–1460

Romance of the Rose, The, and Medieval Allegory
   European Writers, vol. 1: **309–335**
   European Writers Selected Authors, vol. 3:
      1491–1517

Sacchetti, Franco
   See "Renaissance Short Fiction"

Silone, Ignazione
   European Writers, vol. 12: **2273–2305**

Straparola, Gianfrancesco
   See "Renaissance Short Fiction"

Svevo, Italo
   European Writers, vol. 8: **67–87**

Tasso, Torquato
   European Writers, vol. 2: **791–818**

Ungaretti, Giuseppe
   European Writers, vol. 10: **1453–1473**

Verga, Giovanni
   European Writers, vol. 7: **1543–1565**

Vico, Giovanni Battista
   European Writers, vol. 3: **293–316**

Vittorini, Elio
   European Writers, vol. 12: **2733–2757**

Latin

Ammianus Marcellinus
   Ancient Writers, vol. 2: **1117–1138**

Apuleius
   Ancient Writers, vol. 2: **1099–1116**
   Supernatural Fiction Writers, vol. 1: **3–9**

Aquinas, Saint Thomas, and Scholasticism
   European Writers, vol. 1: **405–430**
   European Writers Selected Authors, vol. 1: **53–77**

Ariosto, Lodovico
   European Writers, vol. 2: **619–644**

Arthurian Legend
   European Writers, vol. 1: **137–160**
   European Writers Selected Authors, vol. 1: **79–102**

Arthurian Romances
   Supernatural Fiction Writers, vol. 1: **11–18**

Augustine, Saint
   European Writers, vol. 1: **23–50**
   European Writers Selected Authors, vol. 1: **103–130**

Boccaccio, Giovanni
   European Writers, vol. 2: **509–534**
   European Writers Selected Authors, vol. 1: **255–280**
   See also "Renaissance Pastoral Poetry"

Caesar
   Ancient Writers, vol. 1: **583–599**

Castiglione, Baldesar
   European Writers, vol. 2: **645–667**

Catullus
   Ancient Writers, vol. 2: **643–667**

Cicero
   Ancient Writers, vol. 1: **555–581**

Dante Alighieri
   European Writers, vol. 1: **431–450**
   European Writers Selected Authors, vol. 1: **411–430**
   See also "Renaissance Pastoral Poetry"

Erasmus, Desiderius
  European Writers, vol. 2: **571–593**
  European Writers Selected Authors, vol. 1: **529–551**
Esdras (2 Esdras)
  The Books of the Bible, vol. 2: **21–34**
Geoffrey of Monmouth
  See "Arthurian Romances"
Gower, John
  British Writers, vol. 1: **48–56**
Horace
  Ancient Writers, vol. 2: **703–731**
Juvenal
  See "Persius and Juvenal"
Livy
  Ancient Writers, vol. 2: **733–764**
Lucan and Statius
  Ancient Writers, vol. 2: **917–941**
Lucretius
  Ancient Writers, vol. 2: **601–620**
Luther, Martin
  European Writers, vol. 2: **669–692**
  European Writers Selected Authors, vol. 2: **929–951**
Martial
  Ancient Writers, vol. 2: **887–915**
Medieval Drama
  European Writers, vol. 1: **451–474**
  European Writers Selected Authors, vol. 2:
    1051–1074
Medieval Satire
  European Writers, vol. 1: **337–376**
  European Writers Selected Authors, vol. 2:
    1075–1113
Ovid
  Ancient Writers, vol. 2: **783–806**
Persius and Juvenal
  Ancient Writers, vol. 2: **855–876**
Petrarch, Francesco
  European Writers, vol. 2: **475–507**
  European Writers Selected Authors, vol. 2:
    1255–1287
  See also "Renaissance Pastoral Poetry"
Petronius
  Ancient Writers, vol. 2: **833–853**
Plautus
  Ancient Writers, vol. 1: **501–523**

Pliny the Younger
  Ancient Writers, vol. 2: **1035–1048**
Propertius
  See "Tibullus and Propertius"
Prudentius
  European Writers, vol. 1: **1–22**
Quintilian
  Ancient Writers, vol. 2: **943–959**
Renaissance Pastoral Poetry
  European Writers, vol. 2: **899–926**
  European Writers Selected Authors, vol. 3:
    1403–1430
Romance of the Rose, The, and Medieval Allegory
  European Writers, vol. 1: **309–335**
  European Writers Selected Authors, vol. 3:
    1491–1517
Sallust
  Ancient Writers, vol. 2: **621–641**
Sannazaro, Jacopo
  See "Renaissance Pastoral Poetry"
Seneca the Younger
  Ancient Writers, vol. 2: **807–832**
Spagnola, Giovanni Battista (Mantovano)
  See "Renaissance Pastoral Poetry"
Statius
  See "Lucan and Statius"
Suetonius
  Ancient Writers, vol. 2: **1049–1061**
Tacitus
  Ancient Writers, vol. 2: **1003–1033**
Terence
  Ancient Writers, vol. 1: **541–554**
Tibullus and Propertius
  Ancient Writers, vol. 2: **765–782**
Vergil
  Ancient Writers, vol. 2: **669–701**

Norwegian

Asbjørnsen and Moe (Peter Christen
    Asbjørnsen and Jørgen Moe)
  Writers for Children: **21–28**
Hamsun, Knut
  European Writers, vol. 8: **21–43**

Ibsen, Henrik
  European Writers, vol. 7: **1421–1448**
  European Writers Selected Authors, vol. 2: **787–813**

Moe, Jörgen
  See "Asbjørnsen and Moe"

Undset, Sigrid
  European Writers, vol. 9: **1017–1041**

Vesaas, Tarjei
  European Writers, vol. 11: **2035–2059**

Old Norse

Norse Sagas
  European Writers, vol. 1: **377–404**
  European Writers Selected Authors, vol. 3:
    1199–1226

Polish

Gombrowicz, Witold
  European Writers, vol. 12: **2563–2588**

Łem, Stanisław
  Science Fiction Writers: **591–598**

Mickiewicz, Adam
  European Writers, vol. 5: **607–634**

Milosz, Czeslaw
  European Writers, vol. 13: **2929–2952**

Witkiewicz (Witkacy), Stanisław Ignacy
  European Writers, vol. 10: **1205–1230**

Portuguese

Alencar, José de
  Latin American Writers, vol. 1: **195–203**

Amado, Jorge
  Latin American Writers, vol. 3: **1153–1162**

Amoroso Lima, Alceu
  Latin American Writers, vol. 2: **781–790**

Andrade, Mário de
  Latin American Writers, vol. 2: **771–780**

Azevedo, Aluísio
  Latin American Writers, vol. 1: **333–341**

Bandeira, Manuel
  Latin American Writers, vol. 2: **629–641**

Cabral de Melo Neto, João
  Latin American Writers, vol. 3: **1247–1253**

Camoëns, Luís Vaz de
  European Writers, vol. 2: **747–767**

Castro Alves, Antônio de
  Latin American Writers, vol. 1: **289–297**

Costa, Cláudio Manuel da
  Latin American Writers, vol. 1: **113–117**

Couto, Mia
  African Writers, vol. 1: **185–197**

Cruz e Sousa, João
  Latin American Writers, vol. 1: **359–363**

Cunha, Euclides da
  Latin American Writers, vol. 1: **387–395**

Drummond de Andrade, Carlos
  Latin American Writers, vol. 2: **957–974**

Eça de Queiroz, José Maria
  European Writers, vol. 7: **1683–1708**

Fagundes Telles, Lygia
  Latin American Writers, vol. 3: **1271–1275**

Ferreira de Castro, Jose Maria
  European Writers, vol. 11: **2143–2165**

Gonçalves Dias, Antônio
  Latin American Writers, vol. 1: **185–193**

Guimarães Rosa, João
  Latin American Writers, vol. 3: **1069–1080**

Honwana, Luís Bernardo
  African Writers, vol. 1: **321–329**

Lima, Jorge de
  Latin American Writers, vol. 2: **765–770**

Lima Barreto, Afonso Henriques de
  Latin American Writers, vol. 2: **565–573**

Lins do Rego, José
  Latin American Writers, vol. 2: **909–913**

Lispector, Clarice
  Latin American Writers, vol. 3: **1303–1309**

Machado de Assis, Joaquim Maria
  Latin American Writers, vol. 1: **253–268**

Mariátegui, José Carlos
  Latin American Writers, vol. 2: **791–796**

Mattos, Gregório de
  Latin American Writers, vol. 1: **65–69**

Meireles, Cecília
  Latin American Writers, vol. 2: **915–922**

Neto, Agostinho
    African Writers, vol. 2: **527–535**

Pepetela
    African Writers, vol. 2: **685–695**

Pessoa, Fernando
    European Writers, vol. 10: **1475–1495**

Queiroz, Rachel de
    Latin American Writers, vol. 3: **1119–1123**

Ramos, Graciliano
    Latin American Writers, vol. 2: **745–754**

Silveira de Queiroz, Dinah
    Latin American Writers, vol. 3: **1145–1151**

Suassuna, Ariano Vilar
    Latin American Writers, vol. 3: **1317–1321**

Veríssimo, Érico
    Latin American Writers, vol. 3: **1043–1048**

Vieira, José Luandino
    African Writers, vol. 2: **893–901**

Russian

Akhmatova, Anna
    European Writers, vol. 10: **1521–1542**

Babel, Isaac
    European Writers, vol. 11: **1885–1915**
    European Writers Selected Authors, vol. 1: **131–160**

Bely, Andrey
    European Writers, vol. 9: **905–929**

Blok, Alexander
    European Writers, vol. 9: **959–990**

Chekhov, Anton
    European Writers, vol. 7: **1855–1882**
    European Writers Selected Authors, vol. 1: **361–387**

Dostoevsky, Feodor
    European Writers, vol. 7: **1349–1373**
    European Writers Selected Authors, vol. 1: **479–501**

Gogol, Nikolay Vasilievich
    European Writers, vol. 6: **971–998**

Goncharov, Ivan
    European Writers, vol. 6: **1061–1087**

Gorky, Maxim
    European Writers, vol. 8: **417–446**
    European Writers Selected Authors, vol. 2: **681–710**

Khlebnikov, Velimir
    European Writers, vol. 10: **1331–1364**

Lermontov, Mikhail Yurievich
    European Writers, vol. 6: **1195–1224**

Mandelshtam, Osip
    European Writers, vol. 10: **1619–1649**

Mayakovsky, Vladimir
    European Writers, vol. 11: **1835–1858**

Nabokov, Vladimir
    American Writers, vol. 3: **244–266**
    American Writers Retrospective: **263–281**

Olesha, Yuri
    European Writers, vol. 11: **2233–2253**

Pasternak, Boris
    European Writers, vol. 10: **1591–1618**
    European Writers Selected Authors, vol. 2: **1227–1253**

Pushkin, Alexander
    European Writers, vol. 5: **659–691**
    European Writers Selected Authors, vol. 3: **1341–1373**

Solzhenitsyn, Aleksandr
    European Writers, vol. 13: **3187–3214**
    European Writers Selected Authors, vol. 3: **1621–1647**

Tolstoy, Leo
    European Writers, vol. 7: **1471–1494**
    European Writers Selected Authors, vol. 3: **1693–1715**

Tsvetaeva, Marina
    European Writers, vol. 11: **1731–1750**

Turgenev, Ivan
    European Writers, vol. 6: **1275–1297**
    European Writers Selected Authors, vol. 3: **1717–1739**

Zamyatin, Yevgeny Ivanovich
    European Writers, vol. 10: **1181–1203**

Serbo-Croatian

Andrić, Ivo
    European Writers, vol. 11: **1751–1779**

Krleža, Miroslav
    European Writers, vol. 11: **1807–1834**

Sesotho

Mofolo, Thomas Mokopu
African Writers, vol. 2: **479–493**

Spanish

Acevedo Díaz, Eduardo
Latin American Writers, vol. 1: **299–303**

Acosta, Father Joseph de
Latin American Writers, vol. 1: **47–51**

Agustini, Delmira
Latin American Writers, vol. 2: **649–654**

Alberdi, Juan Bautista
Latin American Writers, vol. 1: **153–158**

Alegría, Ciro
Latin American Writers, vol. 3: **1099–1103**

Anderson Imbert, Enrique
Latin American Writers, vol. 3: **1105–1110**

Arciniegas, Germán
Latin American Writers, vol. 2: **897–901**

Arenas, Reinaldo
Latin American Writers, vol. 3: **1451–1458**

Arguedas, José María
Latin American Writers, vol. 3: **1131–1138**

Arlt, Roberto
Latin American Writers, vol. 2: **881–886**

Arreola, Juan José
Latin American Writers, vol. 3: **1229–1236**

Ascasubi, Hilario
Latin American Writers, vol. 1: **147–151**

Asturias, Miguel Ángel
Latin American Writers, vol. 2: **865–873**

Azorín
European Writers, vol. 9: **639–661**

Azuela, Mariano
Latin American Writers, vol. 2: **457–464**

Balbuena, Bernardo de
Latin American Writers, vol. 1: **53–57**

Ballagas, Emilio
Latin American Writers, vol. 3: **1081–1087**

Baroja, Pío
European Writers, vol. 9: **589–616**

Barrios, Eduardo
Latin American Writers, vol. 2: **611–618**

Bello, Andrés
Latin American Writers, vol. 1: **129–134**

Benedetti, Mario
Latin American Writers, vol. 3: **1255–1263**

Bioy Casares, Adolfo
Latin American Writers, vol. 3: **1201–1208**

Blanco Fombona, Rufino
Latin American Writers, vol. 2: **503–511**

Blasco Ibáñez, Vicente
European Writers, vol. 8: **355–388**

Blest Gana, Alberto
Latin American Writers, vol. 1: **205–213**

Bombal, María Luisa
Latin American Writers, vol. 3: **1111–1117**

Borges, Jorge Luis
Latin American Writers, vol. 2: **845–864**

Cabrera Infante, Guillermo
Latin American Writers, vol. 3: **1383–1391**

Calderón de la Barca, Pedro
European Writers, vol. 2: **871–895**

Cambaceres, Eugenio
Latin American Writers, vol. 1: **269–276**

Campo, Estanislao del
Latin American Writers, vol. 1: **229–233**

Carballido, Emilio
Latin American Writers, vol. 3: **1289–1294**

Caro, Miguel Antonio
Latin American Writers, vol. 1: **277–281**

Carpentier, Alejo
Latin American Writers, vol. 3: **1019–1031**

Carrasquilla, Tomás
Latin American Writers, vol. 1: **343–350**

Carrió de la Vandera, Alonso
Latin American Writers, vol. 1: **107–111**

Casal, Julián del
Latin American Writers, vol. 1: **365–370**

Castellanos, Rosario
Latin American Writers, vol. 3: **1295–1302**

Cela, Camilo José
European Writers, vol. 13: **3105–3129**

Cervantes, Miguel de
European Writers, vol. 2: **819–844**
European Writers Selected Authors, vol. 1: **335–359**
See also "Renaissance Short Fiction"

Chocano, José Santos
Latin American Writers, vol. 2: **543–549**

Cid in Epic and Ballad, The
European Writers, vol. 1: **113–136**

Cortázar, Julio
Latin American Writers, vol. 3: **1177–1194**

Darío, Rubén
Latin American Writers, vol. 1: **397–412**

Denevi, Marco
Latin American Writers, vol. 3: **1265–1269**

Díaz, Jorge
Latin American Writers, vol. 3: **1393–1397**

Díaz del Castillo, Bernal
Latin American Writers, vol. 1: **17–21**

Díaz Rodríguez, Manuel
Latin American Writers, vol. 1: **431–439**

Donoso, José
Latin American Writers, vol. 3: **1277–1288**

Dragún, Osvaldo
Latin American Writers, vol. 3: **1377–1382**

Echeverría, Esteban
Latin American Writers, vol. 1: **141–145**

Edwards, Jorge
Latin American Writers, vol. 3: **1399–1403**

Eguren, José María
Latin American Writers, vol. 2: **513–518**

Eichelbaum, Samuel
Latin American Writers, vol. 2: **797–801**

Ercilla y Zúñiga, Don Alonso de
Latin American Writers, vol. 1: **23–31**

Fernández, Macedonio
Latin American Writers, vol. 2: **483–491**

Fernández de Lizardi, José Joaquín
Latin American Writers, vol. 1: **119–128**

Fernández de Oviedo y Valdés, Gonzalo
Latin American Writers, vol. 1: **11–15**

Fuentes, Carlos
Latin American Writers, vol. 3: **1353–1376**

Gallegos, Rómulo
Latin American Writers, vol. 2: **603–610**

Gálvez, Manuel
Latin American Writers, vol. 2: **585–589**

Gambaro, Griselda
Latin American Writers, vol. 3: **1323–1328**

Gamboa, Federico
Latin American Writers, vol. 1: **371–375**

García Lorca, Federico
European Writers, vol. 11: **2167–2203**
European Writers Selected Authors, vol. 1: **595–630**

García Márquez, Gabriel
Latin American Writers, vol. 3: **1329–1346**

Garcilaso de la Vega, El Inca
Latin American Writers, vol. 1: **39–45**

Gómez Carillo, Enrique
Latin American Writers, vol. 2: **465–469**

Gómez de Avellaneda, Gertrudis
Latin American Writers, vol. 1: **175–180**

González de Eslava, Fernán
Latin American Writers, vol. 1: **33–37**

González Prada, Manuel
Latin American Writers, vol. 1: **283–288**

Gorostiza, José
Latin American Writers, vol. 2: **923–931**

Guillén, Nicolás
Latin American Writers, vol. 2: **947–955**

Güiraldes, Ricardo
Latin American Writers, vol. 2: **619–627**

Gutiérrez Nájera, Manuel
Latin American Writers, vol. 1: **351–357**

Guzmán, Martín Luis
Latin American Writers, vol. 2: **655–662**

Heiremans, Luis Alberto
Latin American Writers, vol. 3: **1347–1352**

Henríquez Ureña, Pedro
Latin American Writers, vol. 2: **597–601**

Heredia, José Mariá
Latin American Writers, vol. 1: **135–140**

Hernández, José
Latin American Writers, vol. 1: **235–247**

Herrera y Reissig, Julio
Latin American Writers, vol. 2: **519–530**

Huidobro, Vicente
Latin American Writers, vol. 2: **755–764**

Ibarbourou, Juana de
Latin American Writers, vol. 2: **803–807**

Icaza, Jorge
Latin American Writers, vol. 3: **1063–1067**

Isaacs, Jorge
  Latin American Writers, vol. 1: **247–251**

Jaimes Freyre, Ricardo
  Latin American Writers, vol. 1: **419–423**

Jiménez, Juan Ramón
  European Writers, vol. 9: **991–1016**

Juana Inéz de La Cruz, Sor
  Latin American Writers, vol. 1: **85–106**

Laguerre, Enrique A.
  Latin American Writers, vol. 3: **1049–1055**

Larreta, Enrique
  Latin American Writers, vol. 2: **471–476**

Las Casas, Bartolomé de
  Latin American Writers, vol. 1: **1–9**

Lezama Lima, José
  Latin American Writers, vol. 3: **1125–1130**

Lopez Velarde, Ramon
  Latin American Writers, vol. 2: **663–670**

Lugones, Leopoldo
  Latin American Writers, vol. 2: **493–502**

Lynch, Benito
  Latin American Writers, vol. 2: **559–563**

Machado, Antonio
  European Writers, vol. 9: **743–765**

Mallea, Eduardo
  Latin American Writers, vol. 3: **981–989**

Mañach Robato, Jorge
  Latin American Writers, vol. 2: **831–836**

Marechal, Leopoldo
  Latin American Writers, vol. 2: **887–896**

Marín Cañas, José
  Latin American Writers, vol. 3: **991–994**

Mármol, José
  Latin American Writers, vol. 1: **181–184**

Marqués, René
  Latin American Writers, vol. 3: **1237–1246**

Martí, José
  Latin American Writers, vol. 1: **311–320**

Martínez Estrada, Ezequiel
  Latin American Writers, vol. 2: **809–813**

Matto de Turner, Clorinda
  Latin American Writers, vol. 1: **305–309**

Mistral, Gabriela
  Latin American Writers, vol. 2: **677–692**

Molina, Juan Ramón
  Latin American Writers, vol. 2: **539–542**

Molinari, Ricardo E.
  Latin American Writers, vol. 2: **837–844**

Montalvo, Juan
  Latin American Writers, vol. 1: **215–220**

Montemayor, Jorge de
  See "Renaissance Pastoral Poetry"

Neruda, Pablo
  Latin American Writers, vol. 3: **1001–1018**

Nervo, Amado
  Latin American Writers, vol. 1: **425–429**

Ocampo, Victoria
  Latin American Writers, vol. 2: **705–710**

Oña, Pedro de
  Latin American Writers, vol. 1: **59–63**

Onetti, Juan Carlos
  Latin American Writers, vol. 3: **1089–1097**

Ortega y Gasset, José
  European Writers, vol. 9: **1119–1150**

Palés Matos, Luis
  Latin American Writers, vol. 2: **821–830**

Palma, Ricardo
  Latin American Writers, vol. 1: **221–228**

Parra, Nicanor
  Latin American Writers, vol. 3: **1195–1200**

Parra Sanojo, Ana Teresa de la
  Latin American Writers, vol. 2: **717–720**

Payró, Roberto Jorge
  Latin American Writers, vol. 1: **413–417**

Paz, Octavio
  Latin American Writers, vol. 3: **1163–1176**

Pérez Galdós, Benito
  European Writers, vol. 7: **1597–1618**

Picón Salas, Mariano
  Latin American Writers, vol. 2: **903–908**

Prado, Pedro
  Latin American Writers, vol. 2: **643–647**

Puig, Manuel
  Latin American Writers, vol. 3: **1405–1413**

Quiroga, Horacio
  Latin American Writers, vol. 2: **551–558**

Renaissance Pastoral Poetry
  European Writers, vol. 2: **899–926**

Renaissance Pastoral Poetry (*continued*)
European Writers Selected Authors, vol. 3: **1403–1430**

Renaissance Short Fiction
European Writers, vol. 2: **927–956**
European Writers Selected Authors, vol. 3: **1431–1460**

Reyes, Alfonso
Latin American Writers, vol. 2: **693–703**

Rivera, José Eustasio
Latin American Writers, vol. 2: **671–675**

Roa Bastos, Augusto
Latin American Writers, vol. 3: **1209–1213**

Rodó, José Enrique
Latin American Writers, vol. 2: **447–455**

Rojas, Manuel
Latin American Writers, vol. 2: **815–820**

Rojas, Ricardo
Latin American Writers, vol. 2: **591–596**

Romero, José Rubén
Latin American Writers, vol. 2: **711–715**

Rulfo, Juan
Latin American Writers, vol. 3: **1215–1229**

Sábato, Ernesto
Latin American Writers, vol. 3: **1139–1143**

Salazar Arrué, Salvador (Salarrué)
Latin American Writers, vol. 2: **875–879**

Sánchez, Florencio
Latin American Writers, vol. 2: **531–538**

Santayana, George
American Writers, vol. 3: **599–622**

Sarduy, Severo
Latin American Writers, vol. 3: **1437–1444**

Sarmiento, Domingo Faustino
Latin American Writers, vol. 1: **159–167**

Sigüenza y Góngora, Carlos de
Latin American Writers, vol. 1: **71–77**

Silva, José Asunción
Latin American Writers, vol. 1: **377–385**

Sinán, Rogelio
Latin American Writers, vol. 2: **941–946**

Storni, Alfonsina
Latin American Writers, vol. 2: **739–743**

Tablada, José Juan
Latin American Writers, vol. 1: **441–446**

Torres Bodet, Jaime
Latin American Writers, vol. 2: **933–939**

Triana, José
Latin American Writers, vol. 3: **1415–1419**

Unamuno, Miguel de
European Writers, vol. 8: **283–310**

Usigli, Rodolfo
Latin American Writers, vol. 3: **1033–1042**

Uslar Pietri, Arturo
Latin American Writers, vol. 3: **1057–1062**

Valencia, Guillermo
Latin American Writers, vol. 2: **477–482**

Valenzuela, Luisa
Latin American Writers, vol. 3: **1445–1449**

Valle, Rafael Heliodoro
Latin American Writers, vol. 2: **721–725**

Valle-Inclán, Ramón del
European Writers, vol. 8: **331–353**

Vallejo, César
Latin American Writers, vol. 2: **727–738**

Valle y Caviedes, Juan del
Latin American Writers, vol. 1: **79–83**

Vargas Llosa, Mario
Latin American Writers, vol. 3: **1421–1436**

Vasconcelos, José
Latin American Writers, vol. 2: **575–584**

Vega, Lope de
European Writers, vol. 2: **845–870**

Villaurrutia, Xavier
Latin American Writers, vol. 3: **975–980**

Villaverde, Cirilo
Latin American Writers, vol. 1: **169–174**

Wolff, Egon
Latin American Writers, vol. 3: **1311–1315**

Yáñez, Agustín
Latin American Writers, vol. 3: **995–999**

Zeno Gandía, Manuel
Latin American Writers, vol. 1: **321–326**

Zorrilla de San Martín, Juan
Latin American Writers, vol. 1: **327–331**

Swedish

Ekelöf, Gunnar
European Writers, vol. 12: **2635–2671**

Johnson, Eyvind
    European Writers, vol. 12: **2361–2385**

Lagerkvist, Pär
    European Writers, vol. 10: **1677–1702**

Moberg, Vilhelm
    European Writers, vol. 11: **2203–2231**

Södergran, Edith
    European Writers, vol. 11: **1781–1806**

Strindberg, August
    European Writers, vol. 7: **1731–1758**

Ukrainian

Tychyna, Pavlo
    European Writers, vol. 10: **1651–1676**

Yiddish

Singer, Isaac Bashevis
    American Writers, vol. 4: **1–24**

Subjects by Nationaltiy

Writers and works are here grouped according to the author's national identity. Some authors appear under more than one nationality. "British" is here used to embrace all Anglophone writers of the British Isles and the former Commonwealth. Authors are also listed under their individual nationality of English, Scottish, Irish, and so on. The seventy-eight principal nationalities include Algerian, American, Angolan, Arab, Argentine, Australian, Austrian, Belgian, Bohemian, Bolivian, Brazilian, British (including English), Bulgarian, Cameroonian, Canadian, Chilean, Colombian, Costa Rican, Croatian, Cuban, Czech, Danish, Dominican, Dutch, Ecuadoran, Egyptian, Finnish, French, German, Ghanaian, Greek, Guatemalan, Guinean, Hebrew, Honduran, Hungarian, Icelandic, Indian, Irish, Italian, Japanese, Kenyan, Lesotho, Lithuanian, Mexican, Mozambican, New Zealander, Nicaraguan, Nigerian, Norwegian, Panamanian, Paraguayan, Peruvian, Polish, Portuguese, Puerto Rican, Roman, Russian, Salvadoran, Scottish, Senegalese, Serbian, Somalian, South African, Spanish, Sudanese, Swedish, Swiss, Trinidadian, Tunisian, Ugandan, Ukrainian, Uruguayan, Venezuelan, Welsh, and West Indian.

Algerian

Camus, Albert
African Writers, vol. 1: **139–152**
European Writers, vol. 13: **3049–3078**
European Writers Selected Authors, vol. 1: **305–334**

Dib, Mohammed
African Writers, vol. 1: **199–207**

Kateb, Yacine
African Writers, vol. 1: **391–400**

American

Abbey, Edward
American Nature Writers, vol. 1: **1–19**

Ackerman, Diane
American Nature Writers, vol. 1: **21–30**

Adams, Henry
American Writers, vol. 1: **1–24**

Addams, Jane
American Writers Supp. 1, part 1: **1–27**

African Americans, Writing, and Nature
American Nature Writers, vol. 2: **1003–1012**

Agee, James
American Writers, vol. 1: **25–47**

Aiken, Conrad
American Writers, vol. 1: **48–70**

Albee, Edward
American Writers, vol. 1: **71–96**

Alcott, Louisa May
American Writers Supp. 1, part 1: **28–46**
Writers for Children: **1–6**
Writers for Young Adults, vol. 1: **11–20**

Alexander, Lloyd
Supernatural Fiction Writers, vol. 2: **965–971**
Writers for Young Adults, vol. 1: **21–33**

Anderson, Poul
Science Fiction Writers: **259–265**
Supernatural Fiction Writers, vol. 2: **973–980**

Anderson, Sherwood
American Writers, vol. 1: **97–120**

Angell, Judie
Writers for Young Adults, vol. 1: **35–42**

Angelou, Maya
American Writers Supp. 4, part 1: **1–19**
Modern American Women Writers: **1–8**
Writers for Young Adults, vol. 1: **43–52**

Ashbery, John
American Writers Supp. 3, part 1: **1–29**

Asher, Sandy
    Writers for Young Adults, vol. 1: **53–61**

Asimov, Isaac
    Science Fiction Writers: **267–276**

Atherton, Gertrude
    Supernatural Fiction Writers, vol. 2: **777–781**

Auchincloss, Louis
    American Writers Supp. 4, part 1: **21–38**

Auden, W. H.
    American Writers Supp. 2, part 1: **1–28**
    British Writers, vol. 7: **379–399**
    British Writers Selected Authors, vol. 1: **1–21**

Audubon, John James
    See "Early Romantic Natural History Literature"

Austin, Mary Hunter
    American Nature Writers, vol. 1: **31–51**

Austin, William
    Supernatural Fiction Writers, vol. 2: **693–696**

Avi
    Writers for Young Adults, vol. 1: **63–72**

Bailey, Florence Merriam
    American Nature Writers, vol. 1: **53–62**

Baldwin, James
    African American Writers: **1–14**
    American Writers Supp. 1, part 1: **47–71**

Bangs, J. K.
    Supernatural Fiction Writers, vol. 2: **725–729**

Baraka, Amiri
    African American Writers: **15–29**
    American Writers Supp. 2, part 1: **29–63**

Barlow, Joel
    American Writers Supp. 2, part 1: **65–86**

Barnes, Djuna
    American Writers Supp. 3, part 1: **31–46**

Barth, John
    American Writers, vol. 1: **121–143**

Barthelme, Donald
    American Writers Supp. 4, part 1: **39–58**

Bartram, William
    American Nature Writers, vol. 1: **63–74**

Bass, Rick
    American Nature Writers, vol. 1: **75–88**

Bauer, Joan
    Writers for Young Adults, vol. 1: **73–80**

Bauer, Marion Dane
    Writers for Young Adults, vol. 1: **81–88**

Baum, L. Frank
    Writers for Children: **37–48**

Beagle, Peter S.
    Supernatural Fiction Writers, vol. 2: **987–991**

Bellow, Saul
    American Writers, vol. 1: **144–166**

Bemelmans, Ludwig
    Writers for Children: **55–61**

Benét, Stephen Vincent
    Supernatural Fiction Writers, vol. 2: **797–803**

Bennett, Jay
    Writers for Young Adults, vol. 1: **89–97**

Berry, Wendell
    American Nature Writers, vol. 1: **89–105**

Berryman, John
    American Writers, vol. 1: **167–189**

Bester, Alfred
    Science Fiction Writers: **283–290**

Beston, Henry
    American Nature Writers, vol. 1: **107–120**

Bethancourt, T. Ernesto
    Writers for Young Adults, vol. 1: **99–109**

Bianco, Margery Williams
    Writers for Children: **63–67**

Bierce, Ambrose
    American Writers, vol. 1: **190–213**
    Supernatural Fiction Writers, vol. 2: **731–737**

Bioregionalism in Nature Writing
    American Nature Writers, vol. 2: **1013–1024**

Bishop, Elizabeth
    American Writers Supp. 1, part 1: **72–97**
    Modern American Women Writers: **9–22**

Blackmur, R. P.
    American Writers Supp. 2, part 1: **87–112**

Blish, James
    Science Fiction Writers: **291–296**

Bloch, Robert
    Supernatural Fiction Writers, vol. 2: **901–907**

Block, Francesca Lia
    Writers for Young Adults, vol. 1: **111–119**

Blume, Judy
    Writers for Young Adults, vol. 1: **121–131**

Bly, Robert
    American Writers Supp. 4, part 1: **59–77**

Bogan, Louise
    American Writers Supp. 3, part 1: **47–68**
    Modern American Women Writers: **23–36**

Bograd, Larry
    Writers for Young Adults, vol. 1: **133–141**

Bontemps, Arna
    Writers for Children: **77–83**

Bourne, Randolph
    American Writers, vol. 1: **214–238**

Bowles, Paul
    American Writers Supp. 4, part 1: **79–99**

Brackett, Leigh
    Supernatural Fiction Writers, vol. 2: **909–915**

Bradbury, Ray
    American Writers Supp. 4, part 1: **101–118**
    Supernatural Fiction Writers: **171–178**
    Supernatural Fiction Writers, vol. 2: **917–923**

Bradstreet, Anne
    American Writers Supp. 1, part 1: **98–123**

Brancato, Robin F.
    Writers for Young Adults, vol. 1: **143–152**

Branscum, Robbie
    Writers for Young Adults, vol. 1: **153–161**

Bridgers, Sue Ellen
    Writers for Young Adults, vol. 1: **163–172**

Brink, Carol Ryrie
    Writers for Children: **85–90**

Brooks, Bruce
    Writers for Young Adults, vol. 1: **173–182**

Brooks, Gwendolyn
    African American Writers: **31–43**
    American Writers Supp. 3, part 1: **69–90**
    Modern American Women Writers: **37–48**

Brooks, Van Wyck
    American Writers, vol. 1: **239–263**

Brown, Charles Brockden
    American Writers Supp. 1, part 1: **124–149**

Brown, Sterling
    African American Writers: **45–57**

Bryant, William Cullen
    American Writers Supp. 1, part 1: **150–173**

Buck, Pearl S.
    American Writers Supp. 2, part 1: **113–134**

Bunting, Eve
    Writers for Young Adults, vol. 1: **183–189**

Burke, Kenneth
    American Writers, vol. 1: **264–287**

Burnett, Frances Hodgson
    Writers for Children: **103–109**

Burns, Olive Ann
    Writers for Young Adults, vol. 1: **191–198**

Burroughs, Edgar Rice
    Science Fiction Writers: **59–64**

Burroughs, John
    American Nature Writers, vol. 1: **121–138**

Burroughs, William S.
    American Writers Supp. 3, part 1: **91–110**

Burton, Virginia Lee
    Writers for Children: **111–115**

Byars, Betsy
    Writers for Young Adults, vol. 1: **199–207**

Cabell, James Branch
    Supernatural Fiction Writers, vol. 2: **789–796**

Caldwell, Erskine
    American Writers, vol. 1: **288–311**

Campbell, John W., Jr.
    Science Fiction Writers: **151–159**

Capote, Truman
    American Writers Supp. 3, part 1: **111–133**

Carrighar, Sally
    American Nature Writers, vol. 1: **139–149**

Carson, Rachel
    American Nature Writers, vol. 1: **151–171**

Carter, Alden R.
    Writers for Young Adults, vol. 1: **209–218**

Carver, Raymond
    American Writers Supp. 3, part 1: **135–151**

Cather, Willa
    American Writers, vol. 1: **312–334**
    American Writers Retrospective: **1–23**
    Modern American Women Writers: **49–62**

Chambers, Robert W.
    Supernatural Fiction Writers, vol. 2: **739–745**

Chandler, Raymond
    American Writers Supp. 4, part 1: **119–138**

Cheever, John
    American Writers Supp. 1, part 1: **174–199**

Chesnutt, Charles W.
African American Writers: **59–70**

Childress, Alice
Writers for Young Adults, vol. 1: **229–240**

Chopin, Kate
American Writers Supp. 1, part 1: **200–226**
Modern American Women Writers: **63–78**

Cleaver, Vera and Bill
Writers for Young Adults, vol. 1: **241–248**

Clement, Hal
Science Fiction Writers: **321–327**

Cole, Brock
Writers for Young Adults, vol. 1: **249–256**

Collier, Christopher and James Lincoln
Writers for Young Adults, vol. 1: **257–269**

Colman, Hila
Writers for Young Adults, vol. 1: **271–280**

Comstock, Anna Botsford
American Nature Writers, vol. 1: **173–185**

Contemporary Ecofiction
American Nature Writers, vol. 2: **1041–1058**

Cooney, Caroline B.
Writers for Young Adults, vol. 1: **281–290**

Cooper, James Fenimore
American Writers, vol. 1: **335–357**
Writers for Children: **147–153**

Cooper, Susan Fenimore
American Nature Writers, vol. 1: **187–198**

Cormier, Robert
Writers for Young Adults, vol. 1: **291–301**

Cowley, Malcolm
American Writers Supp. 2, part 1: **135–156**

Cozzens, James Gould
American Writers, vol. 1: **358–381**

Crane, Hart
American Writers, vol. 1: **381–404**

Crane, Stephen
American Writers, vol. 1: **405–427**
Writers for Young Adults, vol. 1: **303–312**

Crawford, F. Marion
Supernatural Fiction Writers, vol. 2: **747–751**

Creeley, Robert
American Writers Supp. 4, part 1: **139–161**

Crèvecoeur, Hector St. John de
American Writers Supp. 1, part 1: **227–252**

See also "Early Romantic Natural History
   Literature"

Crutcher, Chris
Writers for Young Adults, vol. 1: **313–322**

Cullen, Countee
American Writers Supp. 4, part 1: **163–174**

Cummings, E. E.
American Writers, vol. 1: **428–450**

Daly, Maureen
Writers for Young Adults, vol. 1: **323–333**

Daniel, John
See "New Voices in American Nature Writing"

Danziger, Paula
Writers for Young Adults, vol. 1: **335–344**

Daugherty, James Henry
Writers for Children: **155–161**

Davidson, Avram
Supernatural Fiction Writers, vol. 2: **1001–1008**

Davis, H. L.
American Nature Writers, vol. 1: **199–211**

Davis, Terry
Writers for Young Adults, vol. 1: **345–352**

De Camp, L. Sprague
Science Fiction Writers: **179–184**
See also "De Camp, L. Sprague, and Fletcher
   Pratt"

De Camp, L. Sprague, and Fletcher Pratt
Supernatural Fiction Writers, vol. 2: **925–931**

Delany, Samuel R.
Science Fiction Writers: **329–336**

Derleth, August
Supernatural Fiction Writers, vol. 2: **883–890**

Dick, Philip K.
Science Fiction Writers: **337–343**

Dickey, James
American Writers Supp. 4, part 1: **175–194**

Dickinson, Emily
American Writers, vol. 1: **451–473**
American Writers Retrospective: **25–50**
Modern American Women Writers: **77–89**
Writers for Young Adults, vol. 1: **365–372**

Dickinson, Peter
Writers for Young Adults, vol. 1: **375–383**

Dickson, Gordon R.
Science Fiction Writers: **345–350**

Didion, Joan
    American Writers Supp. 4, part 1: **195–216**
    Modern American Women Writers: **91–102**

Dillard, Annie
    American Nature Writers, vol. 1: **213–230**

Disch, Thomas M.
    Science Fiction Writers: **351–356**

Doctorow, E. L.
    American Writers Supp. 4, part 1: **217–240**

Dodge, Mary Mapes
    Writers for Children: **193–199**

Donaldson, Stephen R.
    Supernatural Fiction Writers, vol. 2: **1009–1013**

Doolittle, Hilda (H.D.)
    American Writers Supp. 1, part 1: **253–275**
    Modern American Women Writers: **103–121**

Dos Passos, John
    American Writers, vol. 1: **474–496**

Douglas, Marjory Stoneman
    American Nature Writers, vol. 1: **231–245**

Douglass, Frederick
    American Writers Supp. 3, part 1: **153–174**
    See also "Slave Narrative in American
        Literature, The"

Dove, Rita
    American Writers Supp. 4, part 1: **241–258**

Dreiser, Theodore
    American Writers, vol. 1: **497–520**

Du Bois, W. E. B.
    African American Writers: **71–87**
    American Writers Supp. 2, part 1: **157–189**

Dunbar, Paul Laurence
    African American Writers: **87–102**
    American Writers Supp. 2, part 1: **191–219**

Duncan, Lois
    Writers for Young Adults, vol. 1: **393–402**

Early Romantic Natural History Literature
    American Nature Writers, vol. 2: **1059–1078**

Eberhart, Richard
    American Writers, vol. 1: **521–543**

Edwards, Jonathan
    American Writers, vol. 1: **544–566**

Ehrlich, Gretel
    American Nature Writers, vol. 1: **247–258**

Eifert, Virginia
    American Nature Writers, vol. 1: **259–268**

Eiseley, Loren
    American Nature Writers, vol. 1: **269–285**

Eliot, T. S.
    American Writers, vol. 1: **567–591**
    American Writers Retrospective: **51–71**
    British Writers, vol. 7: **143–170**
    British Writers Selected Authors, vol. 1:
        469–496

Ellison, Harlan
    Science Fiction Writers: **357–368**
    Supernatural Fiction Writers, vol. 2: **1015–1021**

Ellison, Ralph
    African American Writers: **103–129**
    American Writers Supp. 2, part 1: **221–252**

Emerson, Ralph Waldo
    American Nature Writers, vol. 1: **287–307**
    American Writers, vol. 2: **1–24**

Enright, Elizabeth
    Writers for Children: **215–220**

Equiano, Olaudah
    See "Slave Narrative in American Literature,
        The"

Erdrich, Louise
    American Writers Supp. 4, part 1: **259–278**

Eyerly, Jeannette
    Writers for Young Adults, vol. 1: **403–411**

Farmer, Philip José
    Science Fiction Writers: **369–375**

Farrell, James T.
    American Writers, vol. 2: **25–53**

Faulkner, William
    American Writers, vol. 2: **54–76**
    American Writers Retrospective: **73–95**

Fauset, Jessie
    Modern American Women Writers: **123–139**

Field, Rachel Lyman
    Writers for Children: **235–240**

Finch, Robert Charles
    American Nature Writers, vol. 1: **309–321**

Finney, Charles
    Supernatural Fiction Writers, vol. 2: **821–826**

Fitzgerald, F. Scott
    American Writers, vol. 2: **77–100**
    American Writers Retrospective: **97–120**

Forms of American Nature Poetry, The
    American Nature Writers, vol. 2: **1079–1098**

Fox, Paula
    Writers for Young Adults, vol. 1: **413–422**

Franklin, Benjamin
    American Writers, vol. 2: **101–125**

Frederic, Harold
    American Writers, vol. 2: **126–149**

Freedman, Russell
    Writers for Young Adults, vol. 2: **1–9**

Freeman, Mary E. Wilkins
    Modern American Women Writers: **141–153**
    Supernatural Fiction Writers, vol. 2: **769–773**

French, Michael
    Writers for Young Adults, vol. 2: **11–20**

Freneau, Philip
    American Writers Supp. 2, part 1: **253–277**

Frost, Robert
    American Writers, vol. 2: **150–172**
    American Writers Retrospective: **121–144**
    Writers for Young Adults, vol. 2: **21–31**

Fuller, Margaret
    American Writers Supp. 2, part 1: **279–306**

Gaddis, William
    American Writers Supp. 4, part 1: **279–296**

Gág, Wanda
    Writers for Children: **241–246**

Gaines, Ernest J.
    African American Writers: **129–145**

George, Jean Craighead
    Writers for Young Adults, vol. 2: **47–57**

Gilman, Charlotte Perkins
    Modern American Women Writers: **155–170**

Ginsberg, Allen
    American Writers Supp. 2, part 1: **307–333**

Glasgow, Ellen
    American Writers, vol. 2: **173–195**
    Modern American Women Writers: **171–180**

Glaspell, Susan
    American Writers Supp. 3, part 1: **175–191**
    Modern American Women Writers: **181–188**

Gordon, Caroline
    American Writers, vol. 2: **196–222**

Gordon, Mary
    American Writers Supp. 4, part 1: **297–317**

Graves, John
    American Nature Writers, vol. 1: **323–336**

Greene, Bette
    Writers for Young Adults, vol. 2: **59–68**

Gunn, Thom
    British Writers Supp. 4: **255–279**

Gunn Allen, Paula
    American Writers Supp. 4, part 1: **319–340**

Hale, Lucretia P.
    Writers for Children: **265–268**

Hall, Lynn
    Writers for Young Adults, vol. 2: **69–77**

Hamilton, Virginia
    Writers for Young Adults, vol. 2: **79–92**

Hammett, Dashiell
    American Writers Supp. 4, part 1: **341–357**

Hansberry, Lorraine
    African American Writers: **147–158**
    American Writers Supp. 4, part 1: **359–377**

Hardwick, Elizabeth
    American Writers Supp. 3, part 1: **193–215**
    Modern American Women Writers: **189–196**

Harper, Frances Ellen Watkins
    African American Writers: **159–175**
    Modern American Women Writers: **197–205**

Harris, Joel Chandler
    Writers for Children: **269–275**

Harte, Bret
    American Writers Supp. 2, part 1: **335–359**

Hasselstrom, Linda
    American Nature Writers, vol. 1: **337–348**

Hawthorne, Nathaniel
    American Writers, vol. 2: **223–246**
    American Writers Retrospective: **145–167**
    Supernatural Fiction Writers, vol. 2: **707–715**
    Writers for Children: **277–282**

Hay, John
    American Nature Writers, vol. 1: **349–362**

Hayden, Robert Earl
    African American Writers: **177–192**
    American Writers Supp. 2, part 1: **361–383**

Heinlein, Robert A.
    Science Fiction Writers: **185–196**

Heller, Joseph
    American Writers Supp. 4, part 1: **379–396**

Hellman, Lillian
    American Writers Supp. 1, part 1: **276–298**
    Modern American Women Writers: **207–220**

Hemingway, Ernest
　　American Writers, vol. 2: **247–270**
　　American Writers Retrospective: **169–191**
　　Writers for Young Adults, vol. 2: **93–102**

Henry, O.
　　American Writers Supp. 2, part 1: **385–412**

Hentoff, Nat
　　Writers for Young Adults, vol. 2: **103–112**

Herbert, Frank
　　Science Fiction Writers: **377–385**

Hinton, S. E.
　　Writers for Young Adults, vol. 2: **113–120**

Hoagland, Edward
　　American Nature Writers, vol. 1: **363–375**

Hobbs, Will
　　Writers for Young Adults, vol. 2: **121–129**

Hogan, Linda
　　American Nature Writers, vol. 1: **377–388**
　　American Writers Supp. 4, part 1: **397–418**

Holland, Isabelle
　　Writers for Young Adults, vol. 2: **131–140**

Holmes, Oliver Wendell
　　American Writers Supp. 1, part 1: **299–319**

Hoover, Helen
　　American Nature Writers, vol. 1: **389–399**

Howard, Robert E.
　　Supernatural Fiction Writers, vol. 2: **861–868**

Howe, Susan
　　American Writers Supp. 4, part 2: **419–438**

Howells, William Dean
　　American Writers, vol. 2: **271–294**

Hubbell, Sue
　　American Nature Writers, vol. 1: **401–412**

Hughes, Langston
　　African American Writers: **193–205**
　　American Writers Retrospective: **193–214**
　　American Writers Supp. 1, part 1: **320–348**
　　Writers for Children: **295–301**

Hurston, Zora Neale
　　African American Writers: **205–218**
　　Modern American Women Writers: **221–235**

Irving, Washington
　　American Writers, vol. 2: **295–318**
　　Supernatural Fiction Writers, vol. 2: **685–691**
　　Writers for Children: **303–307**

Irwin, Hadley
　　Writers for Young Adults, vol. 2: **161–166**

Isherwood, Christopher
　　British Writers, vol. 7: **309–320**

Jackson, Shirley
　　Supernatural Fiction Writers, vol. 2: **1031–1036**

Jacobs, Harriet
　　See "Slave Narrative in American Literature,
　　　The"

James, Henry
　　American Writers, vol. 2: **319–341**
　　American Writers Retrospective: **215–242**
　　British Writers, vol. 6: **23–69**
　　Supernatural Fiction Writers, vol. 1: **337–344**

James, William
　　American Writers, vol. 2: **342–366**

Janovy, John, Jr.
　　American Nature Writers, vol. 1: **413–424**

Jarrell, Randall
　　American Writers, vol. 2: **367–390**

Jeffers, Robinson
　　American Writers Supp. 2, part 2: **413–440**

Jefferson, Thomas
　　See "Early Romantic Natural History Literature"

Jewett, Sarah Orne
　　American Writers, vol. 2: **391–414**
　　Modern American Women Writers: **235–250**

Johnson, Cathy
　　American Nature Writers, vol. 1: **425–438**

Johnson, James Weldon
　　African American Writers: **219–233**

Johnson, Josephine
　　American Nature Writers, vol. 1: **439–451**

Johnston, Norma
　　Writers for Young Adults, vol. 2: **167–176**

Jones, Gayl
　　African American Writers: **235–244**

Jordan, June
　　African American Writers: **245–261**

Kappel-Smith, Diana
　　American Nature Writers, vol. 1: **453–463**

Keller, David H.
　　Science Fiction Writers: **119–123**

Kerouac, Jack
　　American Writers Supp. 3, part 1: **217–234**

Kerr, M. E.
Writers for Young Adults, vol. 2: **177–185**

King, Clarence
See "Western Geologists and Explorers"

King, Stephen
Supernatural Fiction Writers, vol. 2: **1037–1044**

Kingston, Maxine Hong
Modern American Women Writers: **251–259**

Kinnell, Galway
American Writers Supp. 3, part 1: **235–256**

Klein, Norma
Writers for Young Adults, vol. 2: **187–197**

Knight, Damon
Science Fiction Writers: **393–400**

Korman, Gordon
Writers for Young Adults, vol. 2: **199–206**

Kornbluth, C. M.
Science Fiction Writers: **401–407**

Krutch, Joseph Wood
American Nature Writers, vol. 1: **465–477**

Kumin, Maxine
American Nature Writers, vol. 1: **479–497**
American Writers Supp. 4, part 2: **439–457**

Kunitz, Stanley
American Writers Supp. 3, part 1: **257–270**

Kuttner, Henry
Science Fiction Writers: **161–167**

LaBastille, Anne
American Nature Writers, vol. 1: **499–511**

Lafferty, R. A.
Supernatural Fiction Writers, vol. 2: **1045–1052**

Laguerre, Enrique A.
Latin American Writers, vol. 3: **1049–1055**

Lanier, Sidney
American Writers Supp. 1, part 1: **349–373**

Lardner, Ring
American Writers, vol. 2: **415–438**

Larsen, Nella
African American Writers: **263–272**

Lasky, Kathryn
Writers for Young Adults, vol. 2: **207–216**

Lawson, Robert
Writers for Children: **345–349**

Least Heat-Moon, William
American Nature Writers, vol. 1: **513–523**

Lee, Harper
Writers for Young Adults, vol. 2: **217–225**

Le Guin, Ursula K.
Science Fiction Writers: **409–417**
Supernatural Fiction Writers, vol. 2: **1059–1066**
Writers for Young Adults, vol. 2: **227–236**
See also "Contemporary Ecofiction"

Leiber, Fritz
Science Fiction Writers: **419–424**
Supernatural Fiction Writers, vol. 2: **933–939**

Leinster, Murray
Science Fiction Writers: **111–117**

L'Engle, Madeleine
Writers for Young Adults, vol. 2: **237–246**

Leopold, Aldo
American Nature Writers, vol. 1: **525–547**

Levertov, Denise
American Writers Supp. 3, part 1: **271–287**

Lewis, Sinclair
American Writers, vol. 2: **439–461**

Lindsay, Vachel
American Writers Supp. 1, part 2: **374–403**

Lipsyte, Robert
Writers for Young Adults, vol. 2: **257–266**

Literary Theory and Nature Writing
American Nature Writers, vol. 2: **1099–1114**

Literature of Mountaineering
American Nature Writers, vol. 2: **1115–1128**

Lofting, Hugh
Writers for Children: **365–371**

London, Jack
American Writers, vol. 2: **462–485**
Writers for Young Adults, vol. 2: **267–278**

Long, Frank Belknap
Supernatural Fiction Writers, vol. 2: **869–874**

Longfellow, Henry Wadsworth
American Writers, vol. 2: **486–510**

Lopez, Barry
American Nature Writers, vol. 1: **549–568**

Lorde, Audre
African American Writers: **273–288**

Lovecraft, H. P.
  Science Fiction Writers: **131–137**
  Supernatural Fiction Writers, vol. 2: **853–859**

Lowell, Amy
  American Writers, vol. 2: **511–533**
  Modern American Women Writers: **261–268**

Lowell, James Russell
  American Writers Supp. 1, part 2: **404–426**

Lowell, Robert
  American Writers, vol. 2: **534–557**

Lowry, Lois
  Writers for Young Adults, vol. 2: **279–287**

Lynch, Chris
  Writers for Young Adults, vol. 2: **289–297**

McCaffrey, Anne
  Writers for Young Adults, vol. 2: **299–306**

McCarthy, Mary
  American Writers, vol. 2: **558–584**
  Modern American Women Writers: **269–278**

McCullers, Carson
  American Writers, vol. 2: **585–608**
  Modern American Women Writers: **279–287**

Macdonald, Ross
  American Writers Supp. 4, part 2: **459–477**

McKay, Claude
  African American Writers: **305–320**

McKibben, Bill
  See "New Voices in American Nature Writing"

McKillip, Patricia
  Supernatural Fiction Writers, vol. 2: **1067–1072**

Maclean, Norman
  See "Contemporary Ecofiction"

MacLeish, Archibald
  American Writers, vol. 3: **1–25**

McNulty, Faith
  American Nature Writers, vol. 1: **569–581**

McPhee, John
  American Nature Writers, vol. 1: **583–598**
  American Writers Supp. 3, part 1: **289–316**

Mahy, Margaret (May)
  Writers for Young Adults, vol. 2: **307–315**

Mailer, Norman
  American Writers, vol. 3: **26–49**

Malamud, Bernard
  American Writers Supp. 1, part 2: **427–453**

Marquand, John P.
  American Writers, vol. 3: **50–73**

Marqués, René
  Latin American Writers, vol. 3: **1237–1246**

Marshall, Paule
  African American Writers: **289–304**

Masters, Edgar Lee
  American Writers Supp. 1, part 2: **454–478**

Mather, Cotton
  American Writers Supp. 2, part 2: **441–470**

Matheson, Richard
  Science Fiction Writers: **425–431**
  Supernatural Fiction Writers, vol. 2: **1073–1080**

Matthiessen, Peter
  American Nature Writers, vol. 2: **599–613**

Mazer, Harry
  Writers for Young Adults, vol. 2: **327–336**

Mazer, Norma Fox
  Writers for Young Adults, vol. 2: **337–346**

Meigs, Cornelia
  Writers for Children: **389–395**

Meltzer, Milton
  Writers for Young Adults, vol. 2: **347–358**

Melville, Herman
  American Writers, vol. 3: **74–98**
  American Writers Retrospective: **243–262**

Mencken, H. L.
  American Writers, vol. 3: **99–121**

Merril, Judith
  Science Fiction Writers: **433–439**

Merrill, James
  American Writers Supp. 3, part 1: **317–338**

Merritt, A.
  Science Fiction Writers: **65–71**
  Supernatural Fiction Writers, vol. 2: **835–843**

Merwin, W. S.
  American Writers Supp. 3, part 1: **339–360**

Miklowitz, Gloria D.
  Writers for Young Adults, vol. 2: **359–368**

Millay, Edna St. Vincent
  American Writers, vol. 3: **122–144**
  Modern American Women Writers: **287–302**

Miller, Arthur
  American Writers, vol. 3: **145–169**

Miller, Henry
  American Writers, vol. 3: **170–192**

Miller, Walter M., Jr.
  Science Fiction Writers: **441–448**

Mills, Enos
  American Nature Writers, vol. 2: **615–624**

Milne, A. A.
  Writers for Children: **397–405**

Mitchell, John Hanson
  American Nature Writers, vol. 2: **625–638**

Modern Birdwatching Literature
  American Nature Writers, vol. 2: **1129–1140**

Mohr, Nicholasa
  Writers for Young Adults, vol. 2: **369–378**

Momaday, N. Scott
  American Nature Writers, vol. 2: **639–649**
  American Writers Supp. 4, part 2: **479–495**

Moore, C. L.
  Supernatural Fiction Writers, vol. 2: **891–898**
  See also "Moore, C. L., and Henry Kuttner"

Moore, C. L., and Henry Kuttner
  Science Fiction Writers: **161–167**

Moore, Marianne
  American Writers, vol. 3: **193–217**
  Modern American Women Writers: **303–316**

Morison, Samuel Eliot
  American Writers Supp. 1, part 2: **479–500**

Morris, Wright
  American Writers, vol. 3: **218–243**

Morrison, Toni
  African American Writers: **321–333**
  American Writers Supp. 3, part 1: **361–381**
  Modern American Women Writers: **317–338**

Muir, John
  American Nature Writers, vol. 2: **651–669**

Mumford, Lewis
  American Writers Supp. 2, part 2: **471–501**

Mundy, Talbot
  Supernatural Fiction Writers, vol. 2: **845–851**

Myers, Walter Dean
  Writers for Young Adults, vol. 2: **387–396**

Nabhan, Gary Paul
  American Nature Writers, vol. 2: **671–681**

Nabokov, Vladimir
  American Writers, vol. 3: **244–266**
  American Writers Retrospective: **263–281**

Nathan, Robert
  Supernatural Fiction Writers, vol. 2: **813–819**

Nature in Native American Literatures
  American Nature Writers, vol. 2: **1141–1156**

Naylor, Gloria
  African American Writers: **335–347**

Naylor, Phyllis Reynolds
  Writers for Young Adults, vol. 2: **397–409**

Nelson, Richard K.
  American Nature Writers, vol. 2: **683–696**

Nemerov, Howard
  American Writers, vol. 3: **267–289**

New Voices in American Nature Writing
  American Nature Writers, vol. 2: **1157–1173**

Niebuhr, Reinhold
  American Writers, vol. 3: **290–313**

Nin, Anaïs
  Modern American Women Writers: **339–351**

Niven, Larry
  Science Fiction Writers: **459–465**

Nixon, Joan Lowery
  Writers for Young Adults, vol. 2: **411–419**

Norris, Frank
  American Writers, vol. 3: **314–336**

Norton, Andre
  Supernatural Fiction Writers, vol. 2:
    1091–1096

Oates, Joyce Carol
  American Writers Supp. 2, part 2: **503–527**
  Modern American Women Writers: **353–374**

O'Brien, Fitz-James
  Supernatural Fiction Writers, vol. 2: **717–722**

O'Connor, Flannery
  American Writers, vol. 3: **337–360**
  Modern American Women Writers: **375–388**

O'Dell, Scott
  Writers for Young Adults, vol. 2: **421–431**

Odets, Clifford
  American Writers Supp. 2, part 2: **529–554**

O'Hara, John
  American Writers, vol. 3: **361–384**

Oliver, Chad
  Science Fiction Writers: **467–473**

Olson, Charles
  American Writers Supp. 2, part 2: **555–587**

Olson, Sigurd F.
American Nature Writers, vol. 2: **697–709**

Oneal, Zibby
Writers for Young Adults, vol. 2: **433–442**

O'Neill, Eugene
American Writers, vol. 3: **385–408**

Ortiz, Simon J.
American Writers Supp. 4, part 2: **497–515**

Paine, Thomas
American Writers Supp. 1, part 2: **501–525**

Palés Matos, Luis
Latin American Writers, vol. 2: **821–830**

Paley, Grace
Modern American Women Writers: **389–396**

Parker, Dorothy
Modern American Women Writers: **397–409**

Parkman, Francis
American Writers Supp. 2, part 2: **589–616**

Paterson, Katherine
Writers for Young Adults, vol. 2: **443–454**

Paulsen, Gary
Writers for Young Adults, vol. 2: **455–463**

Peck, Richard
Writers for Young Adults, vol. 3: **1–14**

Peck, Robert Newton
Writers for Young Adults, vol. 3: **15–26**

Percy, Walker
American Writers Supp. 3, part 1: **383–400**

Perrin, Noel
American Nature Writers, vol. 2: **711–720**

Peterson, Brenda
American Nature Writers, vol. 2: **721–731**

Petry, Ann
African American Writers: **347–359**

Pevsner, Stella
Writers for Young Adults, vol. 3: **27–34**

Pfeffer, Susan Beth
Writers for Young Adults, vol. 3: **43–52**

Plath, Sylvia
American Writers Supp. 1, part 2: **526–549**
Modern American Women Writers: **411–424**

Platt, Kin
Writers for Young Adults, vol. 3: **53–60**

Poe, Edgar Allan
American Writers, vol. 3: **409–432**

Science Fiction Writers: **11–18**
Supernatural Fiction Writers, vol. 2: **697–705**
Writers for Young Adults, vol. 3: **61–73**

Pohl, Frederik
Science Fiction Writers: **475–482**

Porter, Katherine Anne
American Writers, vol. 3: **433–455**
Modern American Women Writers: **425–440**

Pound, Ezra
American Writers, vol. 3: **456–479**
American Writers Retrospective: **283–294**

Powell, John Wesley
See "Western Geologists and Explorers"

Pratt, Fletcher
See "De Camp, L. Sprague, and Fletcher Pratt"

Pyle, Howard
Writers for Children: **447–454**

Pyle, Robert Michael
American Nature Writers, vol. 2: **733–739**

Pynchon, Thomas
American Writers Supp. 2, part 2: **617–638**

Quammen, David
American Nature Writers, vol. 2: **741–750**

Rand, Ayn
American Writers Supp. 4, part 2: **517–535**

Ransom, John Crowe
American Writers, vol. 3: **480–502**

Rawlings, Marjorie Kinnan
American Nature Writers, vol. 2: **751–765**
Writers for Children: **463–467**

Raymo, Chet
American Nature Writers, vol. 2: **767–780**

Reed, Ishmael
African American Writers: **361–377**

Rich, Adrienne
American Writers Supp. 1, part 2: **550–578**
Modern American Women Writers: **441–456**

Richards, Laura E.
Writers for Children: **469–475**

Rinaldi, Ann
Writers for Young Adults, vol. 3: **75–85**

Ríos, Alberto Álvaro
American Writers Supp. 4, part 2: **537–556**

Roberts, Elizabeth Madox
Writers for Children: **477–481**

Robinson, Edwin Arlington
  American Writers, vol. 3: **503–526**

Robinson, Marilynne
  See "Contemporary Ecofiction"

Rodowsky, Colby
  Writers for Young Adults, vol. 3: **87–93**

Roethke, Theodore
  American Writers, vol. 3: **527–550**

Roth, Philip
  American Writers Supp. 3, part 2: **401–429**

Russ, Joanna
  Science Fiction Writers: **483–490**

Russell, Sharman Apt
  See "New Voices in American Nature Writing"

Ryden, Hope
  American Nature Writers, vol. 2: **781–792**

Sachs, Marilyn
  Writers for Young Adults, vol. 3: **95–104**

St. Clair, Margaret
  Science Fiction Writers: **491–495**

Salinger, J. D.
  American Writers, vol. 3: **551–574**
  Writers for Young Adults, vol. 3: **105–112**

Salisbury, Graham
  Writers for Young Adults, vol. 3: **113–121**

Sandburg, Carl
  American Writers, vol. 3: **575–598**
  Writers for Children: **503–510**
  Writers for Young Adults, vol. 3: **123–133**

Sanders, Scott Russell
  American Nature Writers, vol. 2: **793–804**

Sawyer, Ruth
  Writers for Children: **511–517**

Schwartz, Delmore
  American Writers Supp. 2, part 2: **639–668**

Scoppettone, Sandra
  Writers for Young Adults, vol. 3: **135–143**

Sebestyen, Ouida
  Writers for Young Adults, vol. 3: **145–153**

Senarens, Luis Philip
  Science Fiction Writers: **53–58**

Serviss, Garrett P.
  Science Fiction Writers: **39–44**

Seton, Ernest Thompson
  American Nature Writers, vol. 2: **805–816**

Sexton, Anne
  American Writers Supp. 2, part 2: **669–700**
  Modern American Women Writers: **457–470**

Shange, Ntozake
  African American Writers: **379–393**

Shapiro, Karl
  American Writers Supp. 2, part 2: **701–724**

Sheckley, Robert
  Science Fiction Writers: **497–503**

Shepard, Sam
  American Writers Supp. 3, part 2: **431–450**

Silko, Leslie Marmon
  American Nature Writers, vol. 2: **817–827**
  American Writers Supp. 4, part 2: **557–572**

Silverberg, Robert
  Science Fiction Writers: **505–511**

Simak, Clifford D.
  Science Fiction Writers: **513–518**

Simon, Neil
  American Writers Supp. 4, part 2: **573–594**

Singer, Isaac Bashevis
  American Writers, vol. 4: **1–24**

Slave Narrative in American Literature, The
  African American Writers: **395–412**

Sleator, William
  Writers for Young Adults, vol. 3: **173–182**

Smith, Clark Ashton
  Science Fiction Writers: **139–144**
  Supernatural Fiction Writers, vol. 2: **875–881**

Smith, Cordwainer
  Science Fiction Writers: **519–524**

Smith, E. E.
  Science Fiction Writers: **125–130**

Smith, Thorne
  Supernatural Fiction Writers, vol. 2: **805–811**

Snyder, Gary
  American Nature Writers, vol. 2: **829–846**

Sontag, Susan
  American Writers Supp. 3, part 2: **451–473**
  Modern American Women Writers: **471–483**

Soto, Gary
  Writers for Young Adults, vol. 3: **183–191**

Spinelli, Jerry
  Writers for Young Adults, vol. 3: **193–201**

Stanwell-Fletcher, Theodora Cope
American Nature Writers, vol. 2: **847–860**

Stegner, Wallace
American Nature Writers, vol. 2: **861–875**
American Writers Supp. 4, part 2: **595–618**

Stein, Gertrude
American Writers, vol. 4: **25–48**
Modern American Women Writers: **485–498**

Steinbeck, John
American Writers, vol. 4: **49–72**
Writers for Young Adults, vol. 3: **203–214**

Stevens, Wallace
American Writers, vol. 4: **73–96**
American Writers Retrospective: **295–315**

Stockton, Frank R.
Supernatural Fiction Writers, vol. 2: **753–759**
Writers for Children: **545–554**

Stowe, Harriet Beecher
American Writers Supp. 1, part 2: **579–601**

Strand, Mark
American Writers Supp. 4, part 2: **619–636**

Strasser, Todd
Writers for Young Adults, vol. 3: **225–236**

Stratemeyer, Edward
Writers for Young Adults, vol. 3: **237–249**

Stratton Porter, Gene
American Nature Writers, vol. 2: **877–891**

Sturgeon, Theodore
Science Fiction Writers: **203–208**
Supernatural Fiction Writers, vol. 2: **941–945**

Styron, William
American Writers, vol. 4: **97–119**

Swann, Thomas Burnett
Supernatural Fiction Writers, vol. 2: **1097–1103**

Swenson, May
American Writers Supp. 4, part 2: **637–655**

Taine, John
Science Fiction Writers: **75–82**

Talbert, Marc
Writers for Young Adults, vol. 3: **263–272**

Tate, Allen
American Writers, vol. 4: **120–143**

Taylor, Edward
American Writers, vol. 4: **144–166**

Taylor, Mildred Delois
Writers for Young Adults, vol. 3: **273–282**

Taylor, Theodore
Writers for Young Adults, vol. 3: **283–292**

Teale, Edwin Way
American Nature Writers, vol. 2: **893–904**

Tenn, William
Science Fiction Writers: **525–530**

Thaxter, Celia
American Nature Writers, vol. 2: **905–917**

Thomas, Joyce Carol
Writers for Young Adults, vol. 3: **293–301**

Thomas, Lewis
American Nature Writers, vol. 2: **919–931**

Thompson, Julian F.
Writers for Young Adults, vol. 3: **303–310**

Thoreau, Henry David
American Nature Writers, vol. 2: **933–950**
American Writers, vol. 4: **167–189**

Thurber, James
American Writers Supp. 1, part 2: **602–627**
Supernatural Fiction Writers, vol. 2: **827–831**

Tiptree, James, Jr.
Science Fiction Writers: **531–541**

Tolson, Melvin
African American Writers: **413–427**

Toomer, Jean
African American Writers: **429–440**
American Writers Supp. 3, part 2: **475–491**

Trilling, Lionel
American Writers Supp. 3, part 2: **493–515**

Twain, Mark
American Writers, vol. 4: **190–213**
Supernatural Fiction Writers, vol. 2: **761–768**
Writers for Children: **573–582**
Writers for Young Adults, vol. 3: **321–328**

Tyler, Anne
American Writers Supp. 4, part 2: **657–675**
Modern American Women Writers: **499–510**

Updike, John
American Writers, vol. 4: **214–235**
American Writers Retrospective: **317–338**

Vance, Jack
Science Fiction Writers: **543–549**
Supernatural Fiction Writers, vol. 2: **1105–1111**

Van Dyke, John C.
American Nature Writers, vol. 2: **951–962**

Wright, Richard
African American Writers: **505–523**
American Writers, vol. 4: **474–497**

Wylie, Elinor
American Writers Supp. 1, part 2: **707–730**

Yep, Laurence
Writers for Young Adults, vol. 3: **399–408**

Yolen, Jane
Writers for Young Adults, vol. 3: **409–420**

Zelazny, Roger
Science Fiction Writers: **563–570**
Supernatural Fiction Writers, vol. 2: **1113–1119**

Zeno Gandía, Manuel
Latin American Writers, vol. 1: **321–326**

Zindel, Paul
Writers for Young Adults, vol. 3: **421–430**

Zukofsky, Louis
American Writers Supp. 3, part 2: **609–632**

Zwinger, Ann
American Nature Writers, vol. 2: **989–1001**

Zwinger, Susan
See "New Voices in American Nature Writing"

Angolan

Neto, Agostinho
African Writers, vol. 2: **527–535**

Pepetela
African Writers, vol. 2: **685–695**

Vieira, José Luandino
African Writers, vol. 2: **893–901**

Arab

Arabian Nights
Supernatural Fiction Writers, vol. 1: **19–26**

Argentine

Alberdi, Juan Bautista
Latin American Writers, vol. 1: **153–158**

Anderson Imbert, Enrique
Latin American Writers, vol. 3: **1105–1110**

Arlt, Roberto
Latin American Writers, vol. 2: **881–886**

Ascasubi, Hilario
Latin American Writers, vol. 1: **147–151**

Bioy Casares, Adolfo
Latin American Writers, vol. 3: **1201–1208**

Borges, Jorge Luis
Latin American Writers, vol. 2: **845–864**

Cambaceres, Eugenio
Latin American Writers, vol. 1: **269–276**

Campo, Estanislao del
Latin American Writers, vol. 1: **229–233**

Cortázar, Julio
Latin American Writers, vol. 3: **1177–1194**

Denevi, Marco
Latin American Writers, vol. 3: **1265–1269**

Dragún, Osvaldo
Latin American Writers, vol. 3: **1377–1382**

Echeverría, Esteban
Latin American Writers, vol. 1: **141–145**

Eichelbaum, Samuel
Latin American Writers, vol. 2: **797–801**

Fernández, Macedonio
Latin American Writers, vol. 2: **483–491**

Gálvez, Manuel
Latin American Writers, vol. 2: **585–589**

Gambaro, Griselda
Latin American Writers, vol. 3: **1323–1328**

Güiraldes, Ricardo
Latin American Writers, vol. 2: **619–627**

Hernández, José
Latin American Writers, vol. 1: **235–247**

Larreta, Enrique
Latin American Writers, vol. 2: **471–476**

Lugones, Leopoldo
Latin American Writers, vol. 2: **493–502**

Lynch, Benito
Latin American Writers, vol. 2: **559–563**

Mallea, Eduardo
Latin American Writers, vol. 3: **981–989**

Marechal, Leopoldo
Latin American Writers, vol. 2: **887–896**

Mármol, José
Latin American Writers, vol. 1: **181–184**

Martínez Estrada, Ezequiel
Latin American Writers, vol. 2: **809–813**

Molinari, Ricardo E.
  Latin American Writers, vol. 2: **837–844**

Ocampo, Victoria
  Latin American Writers, vol. 2: **705–710**

Payró, Roberto Jorge
  Latin American Writers, vol. 1: **413–417**

Puig, Manuel
  Latin American Writers, vol. 3: **1405–1413**

Rojas, Manuel
  Latin American Writers, vol. 2: **815–820**

Rojas, Ricardo
  Latin American Writers, vol. 2: **591–596**

Sábato, Ernesto
  Latin American Writers, vol. 3: **1139–1143**

Sarmiento, Domingo Faustino
  Latin American Writers, vol. 1: **159–167**

Storni, Alfonsina
  Latin American Writers, vol. 2: **739–743**

Valenzuela, Luisa
  Latin American Writers, vol. 3: **1445–1449**

Australian

Jacobs, Joseph
  Writers for Children: **309–316**

Keneally, Thomas
  British Writers Supp. 4: **343–362**

Stead, Christina
  British Writers Supp. 4: **459–477**

White, Patrick
  British Writers Supp. 1: **129–152**

Austrian

Bauernfeld, Eduard von
  See "Well-Made Play, The" in *European Writers*,
    vol. 7: **1909–1934**

Broch, Hermann
  European Writers, vol. 10: **1385–1408**

Freud, Sigmund
  European Writers, vol. 8: **1–20**
  European Writers Selected Authors, vol. 1: **575–594**

Grillparzer, Franz
  European Writers, vol. 5: **417–445**

Hofmannsthal, Hugo von
  European Writers, vol. 9: **689–714**

Kafka, Franz
  European Writers, vol. 9: **1151–1179**
  European Writers Selected Authors, vol. 2: **847–875**

Musil, Robert
  European Writers, vol. 9: **931–958**

Rilke, Rainer Maria
  European Writers, vol. 9: **767–796**
  European Writers Selected Authors, vol. 3:
    1461–1489

Salten, Felix
  Writers for Children: **497–501**

Schnitzler, Arthur
  European Writers, vol. 8: **89–117**

Svevo, Italo
  European Writers, vol. 8: **67–87**

Trakl, Georg
  European Writers, vol. 10: **1409–1427**

Belgian

Ghelderode, Michel de
  European Writers, vol. 11: **2113–2141**

Maeterlinck, Maurice
  European Writers, vol. 8: **119–146**

Simenon, Georges
  European Writers, vol. 12: **2479–2510**

Bohemian

Kafka, Franz
  European Writers, vol. 9: **1151–1179**
  European Writers Selected Authors, vol. 2: **847–875**

Bolivian

Jaimes Freyre, Ricardo
  Latin American Writers, vol. 1: **419–423**

Brazilian

Alencar, José de
  Latin American Writers, vol. 1: **195–203**

Amado, Jorge
Latin American Writers, vol. 3: **1153–1162**

Amoroso Lima, Alceu
Latin American Writers, vol. 2: **781–790**

Andrade, Mário de
Latin American Writers, vol. 2: **771–780**

Azevedo, Aluísio
Latin American Writers, vol. 1: **333–341**

Bandeira, Manuel
Latin American Writers, vol. 2: **629–641**

Cabral de Melo Neto, João
Latin American Writers, vol. 3: **1247–1253**

Castro Alves, Antônio de
Latin American Writers, vol. 1: **289–297**

Costa, Cláudio Manuel da
Latin American Writers, vol. 1: **113–117**

Cruz e Sousa, João
Latin American Writers, vol. 1: **359–363**

Cunha, Euclides da
Latin American Writers, vol. 1: **387–395**

Drummond de Andrade, Carlos
Latin American Writers, vol. 2: **957–974**

Fagundes Telles, Lygia
Latin American Writers, vol. 3: **1271–1275**

Gonçalves Dias, Antônio
Latin American Writers, vol. 1: **185–193**

Guimarães Rosa, João
Latin American Writers, vol. 3: **1069–1080**

Lima, Jorge de
Latin American Writers, vol. 2: **765–770**

Lima Barreto, Afonso Henriques de
Latin American Writers, vol. 2: **565–573**

Lins do Rego, José
Latin American Writers, vol. 2: **909–913**

Lispector, Clarice
Latin American Writers, vol. 3: **1303–1309**

Machado de Assis, Joaquim Maria
Latin American Writers, vol. 1: **253–268**

Mariátegui, José Carlos
Latin American Writers, vol. 2: **791–796**

Mattos, Gregório de
Latin American Writers, vol. 1: **65–69**

Meireles, Cecília
Latin American Writers, vol. 2: **915–922**

Queiroz, Rachel de
Latin American Writers, vol. 3: **1119–1123**

Ramos, Graciliano
Latin American Writers, vol. 2: **745–754**

Silveira de Queiroz, Dinah
Latin American Writers, vol. 3: **1145–1151**

Suassuna, Ariano Vilar
Latin American Writers, vol. 3: **1317–1321**

Veríssimo, Érico
Latin American Writers, vol. 3: **1043–1048**

British

Addison, Joseph
See "Steele, Sir Richard, and Joseph Addison"

Aickman, Robert
Supernatural Fiction Writers, vol. 2: **957–964**

Aiken, Joan
Writers for Young Adults, vol. 1: **1–9**

Ainsworth, William Harrison
Supernatural Fiction Writers, vol. 1: **187–193**

Aldiss, Brian W.
Science Fiction Writers: **251–258**

Ambler, Eric
British Writers Supp. 4: **1–24**

Amis, Kingsley
British Writers Supp. 2: **1–19**

Amis, Martin
British Writers Supp. 4: **25–44**

Anstey, F.
Supernatural Fiction Writers, vol. 1: **287–292**

Anthony, Piers
Supernatural Fiction Writers, vol. 2: **981–986**

Aquinas, Saint Thomas, and Scholasticism
European Writers, vol. 1: **405–430**
European Writers Selected Authors, vol. 1: **53–77**

Arden, John
British Writers Supp. 2: **21–42**

Ardizzone, Edward
Writers for Children: **15–20**

Arnold, Matthew
British Writers, vol. 5: **203–218**

Arthurian Legend
European Writers, vol. 1: **137–160**
European Writers Selected Authors, vol. 1: **79–102**

Arthurian Romances
Supernatural Fiction Writers, vol. 1: **11–18**

Auden, W. H.
American Writers Supp. 2, part 1: **1–28**
British Writers, vol. 7: **379–399**
British Writers Selected Authors, vol. 1: **1–21**

Austen, Jane
British Writers, vol. 4: **101–124**
British Writers Selected Authors, vol. 1: **23–46**

Bacon, Francis
British Writers, vol. 1: **257–275**

Baker, Frank
Supernatural Fiction Writers, vol. 2: **561–567**

Ballard, J. G.
Science Fiction Writers: **277–282**

Barker, Pat
British Writers Supp. 4: **45–63**

Barnes, Julian
British Writers Supp. 4: **65–76**

Barrie, J. M.
British Writers Supp. 3: **1–17**
Supernatural Fiction Writers, vol. 1: **405–410**
Writers for Children: **29–35**

Beaumont, Francis, and John Fletcher
British Writers, vol. 2: **42–67**

Beckett, Samuel
British Writers Supp. 1: **43–64**
British Writers Selected Authors, vol. 1: **47–68**

Beckford, William
Supernatural Fiction Writers, vol. 1: **139–144**
See also "Gothic Novel, The"

Beerbohm, Max
British Writers Supp. 2: **43–59**

Behan, Brendan
British Writers Supp. 2: **61–76**

Behn, Aphra
British Writers Supp. 3: **19–43**

Belloc, Hilaire
Writers for Children: **49–54**

Bennett, Arnold
British Writers, vol. 6: **247–268**

Benson, E. F.
Supernatural Fiction Writers, vol. 1: **491–496**

Beowulf and Anglo-Saxon Poetry
European Writers, vol. 1: **51–88**
European Writers Selected Authors, vol. 1: **217–253**

Beresford, J. D.
Supernatural Fiction Writers, vol. 1: **457–461**

Berger, John
British Writers Supp. 4: **77–96**

Betjeman, John
British Writers, vol. 7: **355–378**

Bianco, Margery Williams
Writers for Children: **63–67**

Bible, The English
British Writers, vol. 1: **370–388**
British Writers Selected Authors, vol. 1: **69–87**

Blackwood, Algernon
Supernatural Fiction Writers, vol. 1: **463–470**

Blake, William
British Writers, vol. 3: **288–310**
British Writers Selected Authors, vol. 1: **89–110**
Writers for Children: **69–76**

Bond, Edward
British Writers Supp. 1: **421–436**

Boswell, James
British Writers, vol. 3: **234–251**
British Writers Selected Authors, vol. 1:
    111–128

Bowen, Elizabeth
British Writers Supp. 2: **77–96**
Supernatural Fiction Writers, vol. 2: **569–575**

Bridges, Robert
British Writers, vol. 6: **71–84**

Brontës, The
British Writers, vol. 5: **105–154**
British Writers Selected Authors, vol. 1: **129–177**

Brooke, Rupert
British Writers Supp. 3: **45–61**
See also "Poets of World War I (British)"

Brooke-Rose, Christine
British Writers Supp. 4: **97–118**

Brookner, Anita
British Writers Supp. 4: **119–137**

Browne, Sir Thomas
British Writers, vol. 2: **145–157**

Browning, Elizabeth Barrett
British Writers, vol. 4: **310–322**
British Writers Selected Authors, vol. 1: **179–191**

Browning, Robert
British Writers, vol. 4: **354–375**
British Writers Selected Authors, vol. 1: **193–214**

Brunner, John
 Science Fiction Writers: **297–304**

Bulwer-Lytton, Edward
 Supernatural Fiction Writers, vol. 1: **195–204**

Bunyan, John
 British Writers, vol. 2: **240–254**
 British Writers Selected Authors, vol. 1: **215–229**
 Writers for Children: **97–102**

Burgess, Anthony
 British Writers Supp. 1: **185–198**

Burke, Edmund
 British Writers, vol. 3: **193–207**

Burnett, Frances Hodgson
 Writers for Children: **103–109**

Burney, Frances
 British Writers Supp. 3: **63–78**

Burns, Robert
 British Writers, vol. 3: **310–323**
 British Writers Selected Authors, vol. 1: **231–244**

Butler, Samuel
 British Writers Supp. 2: **97–121**

Byatt, A. S.
 British Writers Supp. 4: **139–156**

Byron, Lord
 British Writers, vol. 4: **171–194**
 British Writers Selected Authors, vol. 1: **245–268**

Campbell, Ramsey
 Supernatural Fiction Writers, vol. 2: **993–999**

Campbell, Roy
 African Writers, vol. 1: **127–137**

Canetti, Elias
 European Writers, vol. 12: **2615–2633**

Carew, Thomas
 See "Cavalier Poets, The"

Carlyle, Thomas
 British Writers, vol. 4: **238–250**
 British Writers Selected Authors, vol. 1: **269–281**

Carroll, Lewis
 British Writers, vol. 5: **261–276**
 Supernatural Fiction Writers, vol. 1: **247–253**
 Writers for Children: **117–127**

Carter, Angela
 British Writers Supp. 3: **79–93**

Cary, Joyce
 British Writers, vol. 7: **185–196**

Cavalier Poets, The
 British Writers, vol. 2: **221–239**

Chambers, Aidan
 Writers for Young Adults, vol. 1: **219–227**

Chapman, George
 British Writers, vol. 1: **232–256**

Chatwin, Bruce
 British Writers Supp. 4: **157–177**

Chaucer, Geoffrey
 British Writers, vol. 1: **19–47**
 British Writers Selected Authors, vol. 1: **283–311**

Chesterton, G. K.
 British Writers, vol. 6: **335–346**
 Supernatural Fiction Writers, vol. 1: **411–414**

Christie, Agatha
 British Writers Supp. 2: **123–137**

Churchill, Caryl
 British Writers Supp. 4: **179–200**

Churchill, Winston
 British Writers, vol. 6: **347–362**

Clarke, Arthur C.
 Science Fiction Writers: **313–320**

Clough, Arthur Hugh
 British Writers, vol. 5: **155–172**

Coleridge, Samuel Taylor
 British Writers, vol. 4: **41–57**
 British Writers Selected Authors, vol. 1: **313–329**

Collier, John
 Supernatural Fiction Writers, vol. 2: **577–583**

Collins, Wilkie
 Supernatural Fiction Writers, vol. 1: **233–238**

Collins, William
 British Writers, vol. 3: **160–176**

Colum, Padraic
 Writers for Children: **139–146**

Compton-Burnett, Ivy
 British Writers, vol. 7: **59–70**

Congreve, William
 British Writers, vol. 2: **338–350**

Connolly, Cyril
 British Writers Supp. 3: **95–113**

Conrad, Joseph
 British Writers, vol. 6: **133–150**
 British Writers Selected Authors, vol. 1: **331–348**

Coppard, A. E.
Supernatural Fiction Writers, vol. 2: **523–528**

Corelli, Marie
Supernatural Fiction Writers, vol. 1: **293–297**

Coward, Noël
British Writers Supp. 2: **139–158**

Cowley, Abraham
See "Metaphysical Poets, Four"

Cowper, William
British Writers, vol. 3: **207–220**

Crabbe, George
British Writers, vol. 3: **272–287**

Crashaw, Richard
See "Metaphysical Poets, Four"

Dahl, Roald
British Writers Supp. 4: **201–227**

Day Lewis, Cecil
British Writers Supp. 3: **115–132**

Defoe, Daniel
British Writers, vol. 3: **1–14**
British Writers Selected Authors, vol. 1: **349–362**
Writers for Children: **163–171**

De la Mare, Walter
Supernatural Fiction Writers, vol. 1: **497–503**
Writers for Children: **173–180**

De Quincey, Thomas
British Writers, vol. 4: **141–156**

Dickens, Charles
British Writers, vol. 5: **41–74**
British Writers Selected Authors, vol. 1: **363–396**
Supernatural Fiction Writers, vol.1: **213–218**
Writers for Children: **181–191**
Writers for Young Adults, vol. 1: **353–364**

Disraeli, Benjamin
British Writers, vol. 4: **292–309**

Donne, John
British Writers, vol. 1: **352–369**
British Writers Selected Authors, vol. 1: **397–414**

Douglas, Norman
British Writers, vol. 6: **293–306**

Doyle, Sir Arthur Conan
British Writers Supp. 2: **159–178**
British Writers Selected Authors, vol. 1: **415–434**
Science Fiction Writers: **45–50**
Writers for Children: **201–207**
Writers for Young Adults, vol. 1: **385–392**

Drabble, Margaret
British Writers Supp. 4: **229–254**

Dryden, John
British Writers, vol. 2: **289–306**

Du Maurier, Daphne
British Writers Supp. 3: **133–149**
British Writers Selected Authors, vol. 1: **435–451**

Dunsany, Lord
Supernatural Fiction Writers, vol. 1: **471–478**

Durrell, Lawrence
British Writers Supp. 1: **93–128**

Eddison, E. R.
Supernatural Fiction Writers, vol. 2: **529–534**

Edgeworth, Maria
British Writers Supp. 3: **151–168**

Edwards, Amelia B.
Supernatural Fiction Writers, vol. 1: **255–260**

Eliot, George
British Writers, vol. 5: **187–201**
British Writers Selected Authors, vol. 1: **453–467**

Eliot, T. S.
American Writers, vol. 1: **567–591**
American Writers Retrospective: **51–71**
British Writers, vol. 7: **143–170**
British Writers Selected Authors, vol. 1: **469–496**

Empson, William
British Writers Supp. 2: **179–198**

Etherege, Sir George
See "Restoration Court Poets, The"

Evelyn, John, and Samuel Pepys
British Writers, vol. 2: **274–288**

Ewing, Juliana Horatia
Writers for Children: **221–226**

Farjeon, Eleanor
Writers for Children: **227–234**

Farquhar, George
British Writers, vol. 2: **351–365**

Fielding, Henry
British Writers, vol. 3: **94–106**
British Writers Selected Authors, vol. 2: **497–509**

Firbank, Ronald
British Writers Supp. 2: **199–224**

Fitzgerald, Edward
British Writers, vol. 4: **340–353**

Fletcher, John
　See "Beaumont, Francis, and John Fletcher"
Ford, Ford Madox
　British Writers, vol. 6: **319–334**
Ford, John
　British Writers, vol. 2: **87–102**
Forster, E. M.
　British Writers, vol. 6: **397–414**
　British Writers Selected Authors, vol. 2: **511–527**
　Supernatural Fiction Writers, vol. 1: **479–484**
Fortune, Dion
　Supernatural Fiction Writers, vol. 2: **585–590**
Fowles, John
　British Writers Supp. 1: **291–311**
Frazer, James George
　British Writers Supp. 3: **169–190**
Fry, Christopher
　British Writers Supp. 3: **191–210**
Galsworthy, John
　British Writers, vol. 6: **269–293**
Garfield, Leon
　Writers for Young Adults, vol. 2: **33–45**
Garner, Alan
　Supernatural Fiction Writers, vol. 2: **1023–1029**
Garnett, David
　Supernatural Fiction Writers, vol. 2: **535–539**
Garnett, Richard
　Supernatural Fiction Writers, vol. 1: **317–320**
Gaskell, Elizabeth
　British Writers, vol. 5: **1–16**
Gay, John
　British Writers, vol. 3: **54–68**
Geoffrey of Monmouth
　See "Arthurian Romances"
Gibbon, Edward
　British Writers, vol. 3: **221–233**
Gissing, George
　British Writers, vol. 5: **423–438**
Golding, William
　British Writers Supp. 1: **65–91**
　British Writers Selected Authors, vol. 2: **529–555**
Goldsmith, Oliver
　British Writers, vol. 3: **177–192**
Gothic Novel, The
　British Writers, vol. 3: **324–346**

Gower, John
　British Writers, vol. 1: **48–56**
Grahame, Kenneth
　Writers for Children: **247–254**
Graves, Robert
　British Writers, vol. 7: **257–272**
Gray, Thomas
　British Writers, vol. 3: **136–145**
Green, Henry
　British Writers Supp. 2: **247–266**
Greene, Graham
　British Writers Supp. 1: **1–20**
　British Writers Selected Authors, vol. 2: **557–576**
Gregory, Lady Augusta
　See "Synge, J. M., and Lady Augusta
　　Gregory"
Gunn, Thom
　British Writers Supp. 4: **255–279**
Haggard, H. Rider
　British Writers Supp. 3: **211–228**
　Science Fiction Writers: **19–24**
　Supernatural Fiction Writers, vol. 1: **321–327**
Hardy, Thomas
　British Writers, vol. 6: **1–22**
　British Writers Selected Authors, vol. 2: **577–598**
Hare, David
　British Writers Supp. 4: **281–300**
Hartley, L. P.
　Supernatural Fiction Writers, vol. 2: **639–644**
Harvey, William Fryer
　Supernatural Fiction Writers, vol. 2: **591–596**
Hazlitt, William
　British Writers, vol. 4: **125–140**
Heaney, Seamus
　British Writers Supp. 2: **267–282**
Herbert, George
　British Writers, vol. 2: **117–130**
Herrick, Robert
　British Writers, vol. 2: **102–116**
Hichens, Robert
　Supernatural Fiction Writers, vol. 1: **415–420**
Hodgson, William Hope
　Supernatural Fiction Writers, vol. 1: **421–428**
Hogg, James
　Supernatural Fiction Writers, vol. 1: **177–183**

Hood, Thomas
  British Writers, vol. 4: **251–267**

Hooker, Richard
  British Writers, vol. 1: **176–190**

Hope, Christopher
  African Writers, vol. 1: **331–343**

Hopkins, Gerard Manley
  British Writers, vol. 5: **361–382**
  British Writers Selected Authors, vol. 2: **599–620**

Housman, A. E.
  British Writers, vol. 6: **151–164**
  British Writers Selected Authors, vol. 2: **621–634**

Howard, Henry (Earl of Surrey)
  British Writers, vol. 1: **113–120**

Hoyle, Fred
  Science Fiction Writers: **387–392**

Hughes, Ted
  British Writers Supp. 1: **341–366**

Hume, David
  British Writers Supp. 3: **229–245**

Hunter, Mollie
  Writers for Young Adults, vol. 2: **149–159**

Huxley, Aldous
  British Writers, vol. 7: **197–208**
  British Writers Selected Authors, vol. 2: **635–646**
  Science Fiction Writers: **101–108**

Isherwood, Christopher
  British Writers, vol. 7: **309–320**

Ishiguro, Kazuo
  British Writers Supp. 4: **301–317**

Jacobs, Joseph
  Writers for Children: **309–316**

Jacobs, W. W.
  Supernatural Fiction Writers, vol. 1: **383–387**

Jacobson, Dan
  African Writers, vol. 1: **377–389**

James, Henry
  American Writers, vol. 2: **319–341**
  American Writers Retrospective: **215–242**
  British Writers, vol. 6: **23–69**
  Supernatural Fiction Writers, vol. 1: **337–344**

James, M. R.
  Supernatural Fiction Writers, vol. 1: **429–436**

James, P. D.
  British Writers Supp. 4: **319–341**

Johnson, Samuel
  British Writers, vol. 3: **107–123**
  British Writers Selected Authors, vol. 2: **647–663**

Jones, David
  See "Poets of World War I (British)"

Jones, Henry Arthur
  See "Well-Made Play, The"

Jonson, Ben
  British Writers, vol. 1: **335–352**
  British Writers Selected Authors, vol. 2: **665–681**

Joyce, James
  British Writers, vol. 7: **41–58**
  British Writers Selected Authors, vol. 2: **683–700**

Keats, John
  British Writers, vol. 4: **211–238**
  British Writers Selected Authors, vol. 2: **701–727**

Kingsley, Charles
  Writers for Children: **323–327**

Kipling, Rudyard
  British Writers, vol. 6: **165–206**
  British Writers Selected Authors, vol. 2: **729–770**
  Supernatural Fiction Writers, vol. 1: **437–442**
  Writers for Children: **329–336**

Koestler, Arthur
  British Writers Supp. 1: **21–41**

Kyd, Thomas, and Early Elizabethan Tragedy
  British Writers, vol. 1: **212–231**

Lamb, Charles
  British Writers, vol. 4: **73–86**

Landor, Walter Savage
  British Writers, vol. 4: **87–100**

Lang, Andrew
  Writers for Children: **337–343**

Langland, William: Piers Plowman
  British Writers, vol. 1: **1–18**

Larkin, Phillip
  British Writers Supp. 1: **275–290**

Lawrence, D. H.
  British Writers, vol. 7: **87–126**
  British Writers Selected Authors, vol. 2: **771–810**

Lawrence, T. E.
  British Writers Supp. 2: **283–298**

Lear, Edward
  British Writers, vol. 5: **75–88**
  Writers for Children: **351–356**

Leavis, F. R.
  British Writers, vol. 7: **233–256**
Le Carré, John
  British Writers Supp. 2: **299–320**
  British Writers Selected Authors, vol. 2: **811–832**
Lee, Tanith
  Supernatural Fiction Writers, vol. 2: **1053–1058**
Lee, Vernon
  Supernatural Fiction Writers, vol. 1: **329–335**
Le Fanu, J. S.
  Supernatural Fiction Writers, vol. 1: **219–231**
Lessing, Doris
  African Writers, vol. 1: **427–449**
  British Writers Supp. 1: **237–257**
  British Writers Selected Authors, vol. 2: **833–853**
Lewis, C. S.
  British Writers Supp. 3: **247–268**
  British Writers Selected Authors, vol. 2: **855–876**
  Science Fiction Writers: **243–248**
  Supernatural Fiction Writers, vol. 2: **661–666**
  Writers for Children: **357–364**
  Writers for Young Adults, vol. 2: **247–255**
Lewis, M. G.
  Supernatural Fiction Writers, vol. 1: **153–160**
Lewis, Wyndham
  British Writers, vol. 7: **71–86**
Lindsay, David
  Supernatural Fiction Writers, vol. 2: **541–547**
Lodge, David
  British Writers Supp. 4: **363–387**
Lofting, Hugh
  Writers for Children: **365–371**
Lovelace, Richard
  See "Cavalier Poets, The"
Lowry, Malcolm
  British Writers Supp. 3: **269–286**
Lydgate, John
  British Writers, vol. 1: **57–66**
Lyly, John, and George Peele
  British Writers, vol. 1: **191–211**
Macaulay, Thomas Babington
  British Writers, vol. 4: **268–292**
MacDonald, George
  Supernatural Fiction Writers, vol. 1: **239–246**
  Writers for Children: **373–380**

McEwan, Ian
  British Writers Supp. 4: **389–408**
Machen, Arthur
  Supernatural Fiction Writers, vol. 1: **351–359**
Macleod, Fiona
  Supernatural Fiction Writers, vol. 1: **369–374**
MacNeice, Louis
  British Writers, vol. 7: **401–420**
Malory, Sir Thomas
  British Writers, vol. 1: **67–80**
  British Writers Selected Authors, vol. 2: **877–890**
  See also "Arthurian Romances"
Marlowe, Christopher
  British Writers, vol. 1: **275–294**
Marryat, Frederick
  Writers for Children: **381–387**
Marston, John, and Cyril Tourneur
  British Writers, vol. 2: **24–41**
Marvell, Andrew
  British Writers, vol. 2: **204–220**
Maturin, Charles Robert
  Supernatural Fiction Writers, vol. 1: **161–168**
Maugham, W. Somerset
  British Writers, vol. 6: **363–382**
  British Writers Selected Authors, vol. 2: **905–923**
Medieval Drama
  European Writers, vol. 1: **451–474**
  European Writers Selected Authors, vol. 2: **1051–1074**
Medieval Satire
  European Writers, vol. 1: **337–376**
  European Writers Selected Authors, vol. 2: **1075–1113**
Meredith, George
  British Writers, vol. 5: **219–234**
Metaphysical Poets, Four
  British Writers, vol. 2: **179–203**
Metcalfe, John
  Supernatural Fiction Writers, vol. 2: **597–602**
Middleton, Thomas
  British Writers, vol. 2: **1–23**
Milton, John
  British Writers, vol. 2: **158–178**
  British Writers Selected Authors, vol. 2: **925–945**

Mirrlees, Hope
  Supernatural Fiction Writers, vol. 2: **603–607**
Molesworth, M. L. S.
  Writers for Children: **407–413**
Moorcock, Michael
  Science Fiction Writers: **449–457**
  Supernatural Fiction Writers, vol. 2: **1081–1089**
Moore, George
  British Writers, vol. 6: **85–100**
Morris, William
  British Writers, vol. 5: **291–308**
  Supernatural Fiction Writers, vol. 1: **299–306**
Muldoon, Paul
  British Writers Supp. 4: **409–432**
Mundy, Talbot
  Supernatural Fiction Writers, vol. 2: **845–851**
Murdoch, Iris
  British Writers Supp. 1: **215–235**
Naipaul, V. S.
  British Writers Supp. 1: **383–405**
Nesbit, E.
  Writers for Children: **423–430**
O'Brien, Fitz-James
  Supernatural Fiction Writers, vol. 2: **717–722**
O'Brien, Flann
  British Writers Supp. 2: **321–339**
O'Casey, Sean
  British Writers, vol. 7: **1–16**
Okri, Ben
  African Writers, vol. 2: **599–608**
Oliphant, Mrs.
  Supernatural Fiction Writers, vol. 1: **261–268**
Onions, Oliver
  Supernatural Fiction Writers, vol. 1: **505–511**
Orwell, George
  British Writers, vol. 7: **273–288**
  British Writers Selected Authors, vol. 2: **947–961**
  Science Fiction Writers: **233–241**
Osborne, John
  British Writers Supp. 1: **329–340**
Owen, Wilfred
  British Writers, vol. 6: **443–460**
Pain, Barry
  Supernatural Fiction Writers, vol. 1: **443–448**

Pater, Walter Horatio
  British Writers, vol. 5: **337–360**
Paton, Alan
  African Writers, vol. 2: **651–668**
  British Writers Supp. 2: **341–361**
  British Writers Selected Authors, vol. 2: **963–983**
Peacock, Thomas Love
  British Writers, vol. 4: **157–170**
Peele, George
  See "Lyly, John, and George Peele"
Pepys, Samuel
  See "Evelyn, John, and Samuel Pepys"
Peyton, K. M.
  Writers for Young Adults, vol. 3: **35–42**
Phillpotts, Eden
  Supernatural Fiction Writers, vol. 2: **549–553**
Pinero, Arthur Wing
  See "Well-Made Play, The"
Pinter, Harold
  British Writers Supp. 1: **367–382**
  British Writers Selected Authors, vol. 2: **985–1000**
Plomer, William
  African Writers, vol. 2: **697–706**
Poets of World War I (British)
  British Writers, vol. 6: **415–442**
  British Writers Selected Authors, vol. 3: **1445–1471**
Poets of World War II (British)
  British Writers, vol. 7: **421–450**
Pope, Alexander
  British Writers, vol. 3: **68–79**
  British Writers Selected Authors, vol. 2:
    1001–1012
Potter, Beatrix
  British Writers Supp. 3: **287–309**
  Writers for Children: **439–446**
Powell, Anthony
  British Writers, vol. 7: **343–352**
Powys, John Cowper
  Supernatural Fiction Writers, vol. 2: **609–616**
Powys, T. F.
  Supernatural Fiction Writers, vol. 2: **609–616**
Priestley, J. B.
  British Writers, vol. 7: **209–232**
Pritchett, V. S.
  British Writers Supp. 3: **311–331**

Pym, Barbara
    British Writers Supp. 2: **363–385**
Quiller-Couch, Arthur
    Supernatural Fiction Writers, vol. 1: **389–395**
Radcliffe, Ann
    Supernatural Fiction Writers, vol. 1: **145–151**
Ralegh (Raleigh), Sir Walter
    British Writers, vol. 1: **145–159**
Ransome, Arthur
    Writers for Children: **455–461**
Read, Herbert
    See "Poets of World War I (British)"
Renaissance Pastoral Poetry
    European Writers, vol. 2: **899–926**
    European Writers Selected Authors, vol. 3:
        1403–1430
Restoration Court Poets, The
    British Writers, vol. 2: **255–272**
Reynolds, G. W. M.
    Supernatural Fiction Writers, vol. 1: **205–211**
Rhys, Jean
    British Writers Supp. 2: **387–404**
Richards, I. A.
    British Writers Supp. 2: **405–433**
Richardson, Samuel
    British Writers, vol. 3: **80–94**
Riddell, Mrs. J. H.
    Supernatural Fiction Writers, vol. 1: **269–277**
Robertson, Thomas W.
    See "Well-Made Play, The"
Rohmer, Sax
    Supernatural Fiction Writers, vol. 2: **555–560**
Romance of the Rose, The, and Medieval Allegory
    European Writers, vol. 1: **309–335**
    European Writers Selected Authors, vol. 3:
        1491–1517
Rosenberg, Isaac
    See "Poets of World War I (British)"
Rossetti, Christina
    British Writers, vol. 5: **247–260**
    Writers for Children: **483–491**
Rossetti, Dante Gabriel
    British Writers, vol. 5: **235–246**
Rushdie, Salman
    British Writers Supp. 4: **433–457**

Ruskin, John
    British Writers, vol. 5: **173–186**
    Writers for Children: **493–496**
Russell, Eric Frank
    Science Fiction Writers: **197–202**
Sackville, Charles (Earl of Dorset)
    See "Restoration Court Poets, The"
Saki
    Supernatural Fiction Writers, vol. 1: **449–455**
Sarban
    Supernatural Fiction Writers, vol. 2: **667–673**
Sassoon, Siegfried
    See "Poets of World War I (British)"
Sayers, Dorothy L.
    British Writers Supp. 3: **333–353**
Schreiner, Olive
    African Writers, vol. 2: **745–763**
    British Writers Supp. 2: **435–458**
Scott, Paul
    British Writers Supp. 1: **259–274**
Scott, Sir Walter
    British Writers, vol. 4: **27–40**
    Supernatural Fiction Writers, vol. 1: **169–176**
Sedley, Sir Charles
    See "Restoration Court Poets, The"
Sewell, Anna
    Writers for Children: **525–528**
Shaffer, Peter
    British Writers Supp. 1: **313–328**
Shakespeare, William
    British Writers, vol. 1: **295–334**
    British Writers Selected Authors, vol. 2: **1013–1052**
    Writers for Young Adults, vol. 3: **155–172**
    See also entries in *William Shakespeare: His
        World, His Work, His Influence*
Shaw, George Bernard
    British Writers, vol. 6: **101–132**
    British Writers Selected Authors, vol. 3: **1053–1084**
Shelley, Mary
    British Writers Supp. 3: **355–373**
    British Writers Selected Authors, vol. 3: **1085–1103**
    Science Fiction Writers: **3–9**
    See also "Gothic Novel, The"
Shelley, Percy Bysshe
    British Writers, vol. 4: **195–210**
    British Writers Selected Authors, vol. 3: **1105–1120**

Sheridan, Richard Brinsley
  British Writers, vol. 3: **252–271**

Shiel, M. P.
  Science Fiction Writers: **31–37**
  Supernatural Fiction Writers, vol. 1: **361–367**

Sidney, Sir Philip
  British Writers, vol. 1: **160–175**

Sinclair, May
  Supernatural Fiction Writers, vol. 1: **513–519**

Sitwell, Edith
  British Writers, vol. 7: **127–143**

Skelton, John
  British Writers, vol. 1: **81–96**

Smith, Stevie
  British Writers Supp. 2: **459–479**

Smollett, Tobias
  British Writers, vol. 3: **146–159**

Snow, C. P.
  British Writers, vol. 7: **321–342**

Southey, Robert
  British Writers, vol. 4: **58–72**

Spark, Muriel
  British Writers Supp. 1: **199–214**

Spender, Steven
  British Writers Supp. 2: **481–496**

Spenser, Edmund
  British Writers, vol. 1: **121–144**
  British Writers Selected Authors, vol. 3:
    1121–1144

Stapledon, Olaf
  Science Fiction Writers: **91–100**

Stead, Christina
  British Writers Supp. 4: **459–477**

Steele, Sir Richard, and Joseph Addison
  British Writers, vol. 3: **38–53**
  British Writers Selected Authors, vol. 3: **1145–1160**

Stephen, Leslie
  British Writers, vol. 5: **277–290**

Stephens, James
  Supernatural Fiction Writers, vol. 1: **485–490**

Sterne, Laurence
  British Writers, vol. 3: **124–136**

Stevenson, Robert Louis
  British Writers, vol. 5: **383–399**
  British Writers Selected Authors, vol. 3: **1161–1176**

Supernatural Fiction Writers, vol. 1: **307–313**
Writers for Children: **535–543**
Writers for Young Adults, vol. 3: **215–224**

Stoker, Bram
  British Writers Supp. 3: **375–391**
  Supernatural Fiction Writers, vol. 1: **375–381**

Stoppard, Tom
  British Writers Supp. 1: **437–454**
  British Writers Selected Authors, vol. 3: **1177–1194**

Storey, David
  British Writers Supp. 1: **407–420**

Strachey, Lytton
  British Writers Supp. 2: **497–518**

Suckling, Sir John
  See "Cavalier Poets, The"

Sutcliff, Rosemary
  Writers for Young Adults, vol. 3: **251–261**

Swift, Jonathan
  British Writers, vol. 3: **15–38**
  British Writers Selected Authors, vol. 3: **1195–1217**
  Writers for Children: **555–559**

Swinburne, Algernon Charles
  British Writers, vol. 5: **309–336**

Synge, J. M., and Lady Augusta Gregory
  British Writers, vol. 6: **307–318**

Taine, John
  Science Fiction Writers: **75–82**

Tennyson, Alfred Lord
  British Writers, vol. 4: **323–339**
  British Writers Selected Authors, vol. 3: **1219–1235**

Thackeray, William Makepeace
  British Writers, vol. 5: **17–40**
  British Writers Selected Authors, vol. 3: **1237–1259**

Thomas, D. M.
  British Writers Supp. 4: **479–497**

Thomas, Dylan
  British Writers Supp. 1: **169–184**
  British Writers Selected Authors, vol. 3:
    1261–1276

Thomas, Edward
  British Writers Supp. 3: **393–408**

Thompson, Francis
  British Writers, vol. 5: **439–452**

Thomson, James
  British Writers Supp. 3: **409–429**

Tolkien, J. R. R.
British Writers Supp. 2: **519–536**
British Writers Selected Authors, vol. 3: **1277–1294**
Supernatural Fiction Writers, vol. 2: **675–682**
Writers for Children: **561–571**
Writers for Young Adults, vol. 3: **311–320**

Tourneur, Cyril
See "Marston, John, and Cyril Tourneur"

Traherne, Thomas
See "Metaphysical Poets, Four"

Trevelyan, G. M.
British Writers, vol. 6: **383–396**

Trevor, William
British Writers Supp. 4: **499–519**

Trollope, Anthony
British Writers, vol. 5: **89–104**
British Writers Selected Authors, vol. 3: **1295–1309**

Tyndale, William
See "Bible, The English"

Vanbrugh, Sir John
British Writers, vol. 2: **323–337**

Vaughan, Henry
See "Metaphysical Poets, Four"

Wakefield, H. Russell
Supernatural Fiction Writers, vol. 2: **617–622**

Wall, Mervyn
Supernatural Fiction Writers, vol. 2: **645–650**

Waller, Edmund
See "Cavalier Poets, The"

Walpole, Horace
Supernatural Fiction Writers, vol. 1: **131–137**
See also "Gothic Novel, The"

Walton, Izaak
British Writers, vol. 2: **131–144**

Waugh, Evelyn
British Writers, vol. 7: **289–308**
British Writers Selected Authors, vol. 3: **1311–1330**

Webster, John
British Writers, vol. 2: **68–86**

Weldon, Fay
British Writers Supp. 4: **521–539**

Well-Made Play, The
European Writers, vol. 7: **1909–1934**

Wells, H. G.
British Writers, vol. 6: **225–246**
British Writers Selected Authors, vol. 3: **1331–1352**

Science Fiction Writers: **25–30**
Supernatural Fiction Writers, vol. 1: **397–402**
Writers for Children: **599–603**

West, Rebecca
British Writers Supp. 3: **431–445**

Wheatley, Dennis
Supernatural Fiction Writers, vol. 2: **623–629**

White, T. H.
Supernatural Fiction Writers, vol. 2: **651–657**

Wilde, Oscar
British Writers, vol. 5: **399–422**
British Writers Selected Authors, vol. 3: **1353–1376**
Supernatural Fiction Writers, vol. 1: **345–350**
Writers for Children: **611–616**

Williams, Charles
Supernatural Fiction Writers, vol. 2: **631–638**

Wilmot, John (Earl of Rochester)
See "Restoration Court Poets, The"

Wilson, Angus
British Writers Supp. 1: **153–168**

Winterson, Jeanette
British Writers Supp. 4: **541–559**

Wodehouse, P. G.
British Writers Supp. 3: **447–464**
British Writers Selected Authors, vol. 3: **1377–1394**

Wollstonecraft, Mary
British Writers Supp. 3: **465–482**

Wood, Mrs. Henry
Supernatural Fiction Writers, vol. 1: **279–286**

Woolf, Virginia
British Writers, vol. 7: **17–40**
British Writers Selected Authors, vol. 3: **1395–1417**

Wordsworth, William
British Writers, vol. 4: **1–26**
British Writers Selected Authors, vol. 3: **1419–1444**

Wright, S. Fowler
Science Fiction Writers: **83–89**

Wyatt, Sir Thomas
British Writers, vol. 1: **97–112**

Wycherley, William
British Writers, vol. 2: **307–322**

Wyndham, John
Science Fiction Writers: **219–224**

Yeats, William Butler
British Writers, vol. 6: **207–224**
British Writers Selected Authors, vol. 3: **1473–1490**

Yonge, Charlotte Mary
  Writers for Children: **625–631**

Bulgarian

Canetti, Elias
  European Writers, vol. 12: **2615–2633**

Cameroonian

Beti, Mongo
  African Writers, vol. 1: **83–94**

Oyono, Ferdinand
  African Writers, vol. 2: **641–649**

Canadian

Canadian Nature Writing in English
  American Nature Writers, vol. 2: **1025–1040**

Dickson, Gordon R.
  Science Fiction Writers: **345–350**

Hughes, Monica
  Writers for Young Adults, vol. 2: **141–148**

Major, Kevin
  Writers for Young Adults, vol. 2: **317–326**

Montgomery, L. M.
  Writers for Children: **415–422**
  Writers for Young Adults, vol. 2: **379–386**

Van Vogt, A. E.
  Science Fiction Writers: **209–217**

Chilean

Barrios, Eduardo
  Latin American Writers, vol. 2: **611–618**

Blest Gana, Alberto
  Latin American Writers, vol. 1: **205–213**

Bombal, María Luisa
  Latin American Writers, vol. 3: **1111–1117**

Díaz, Jorge
  Latin American Writers, vol. 3: **1393–1397**

Donoso, José
  Latin American Writers, vol. 3: **1277–1288**

Edwards, Jorge
  Latin American Writers, vol. 3: **1399–1403**

Ercilla y Zúñiga, Don Alonso de
  Latin American Writers, vol. 1: **23–31**

Heiremans, Luis Alberto
  Latin American Writers, vol. 3: **1347–1352**

Huidobro, Vicente
  Latin American Writers, vol. 2: **755–764**

Mistral, Gabriela
  Latin American Writers, vol. 2: **677–692**

Neruda, Pablo
  Latin American Writers, vol. 3: **1001–1018**

Oña, Pedro de
  Latin American Writers, vol. 1: **59–63**

Parra, Nicanor
  Latin American Writers, vol. 3: **1195–1200**

Prado, Pedro
  Latin American Writers, vol. 2: **643–647**

Wolff, Egon
  Latin American Writers, vol. 3: **1311–1315**

Colombian

Arciniegas, Germán
  Latin American Writers, vol. 2: **897–901**

Caro, Miguel Antonio
  Latin American Writers, vol. 1: **277–281**

Carrasquilla, Tomás
  Latin American Writers, vol. 1: **343–350**

García Márquez, Gabriel
  Latin American Writers, vol. 3: **1329–1346**

Isaacs, Jorge
  Latin American Writers, vol. 1: **247–251**

Rivera, José Eustasio
  Latin American Writers, vol. 2: **671–675**

Silva, José Asunción
  Latin American Writers, vol. 1: **377–385**

Valencia, Guillermo
  Latin American Writers, vol. 2: **477–482**

Costa Rican

Marín Cañas, José
  Latin American Writers, vol. 3: **991–994**

Croatian

Krleža, Miroslav
  European Writers, vol. 11: **1807–1834**

Cuban

Arenas, Reinaldo
Latin American Writers, vol. 3: **1451–1458**

Ballagas, Emilio
Latin American Writers, vol. 3: **1081–1087**

Cabrera Infante, Guillermo
Latin American Writers, vol. 3: **1383–1391**

Carpentier, Alejo
Latin American Writers, vol. 3: **1019–1031**

Casal, Julián del
Latin American Writers, vol. 1: **365–370**

Fernández de Oviedo y Valdés, Gonzalo
Latin American Writers, vol. 1: **11–15**

Gómez de Avellaneda, Gertrudis
Latin American Writers, vol. 1: **175–180**

Guillén, Nicolás
Latin American Writers, vol. 2: **947–955**

Heredia, José Mariá
Latin American Writers, vol. 1: **135–140**

Lezama Lima, José
Latin American Writers, vol. 3: **1125–1130**

Mañach Robato, Jorge
Latin American Writers, vol. 2: **831–836**

Martí, José
Latin American Writers, vol. 1: **311–320**

Sarduy, Severo
Latin American Writers, vol. 3: **1437–1444**

Triana, José
Latin American Writers, vol. 3: **1415–1419**

Villaverde, Cirilo
Latin American Writers, vol. 1: **169–174**

Czech

Čapek, Karel
European Writers, vol. 10: **1565–1590**
Science Fiction Writers: **583–589**

Hašek, Jaroslav
European Writers, vol. 9: **1091–1118**

Kafka, Franz
European Writers, vol. 9: **1151–1179**
European Writers Selected Authors, vol. 2: **847–875**

Kundera, Milan
European Writers, vol. 13: **3389–3413**

Rilke, Rainer Maria
European Writers, vol. 9: **767–796**
European Writers Selected Authors, vol. 3:
1461–1489

Danish

Andersen, Hans Christian
European Writers, vol. 6: **863–892**
European Writers Selected Authors, vol. 1: **1–29**
Writers for Children: **7–13**

Dinesen, Isak
European Writers, vol. 10: **1281–1306**
European Writers Selected Authors, vol. 1: **453–477**

Kierkegaard, Søren
European Writers, vol. 6: **1123–1146**
European Writers Selected Authors, vol. 2:
877–900

Norse Sagas
European Writers, vol. 1: **377–404**
European Writers Selected Authors, vol. 3:
1199–1226

Dominican

Henríquez Ureña, Pedro
Latin American Writers, vol. 2: **597–601**

Las Casas, Bartolomé de
Latin American Writers, vol. 1: **1–9**

Dutch

Erasmus, Desiderius
European Writers, vol. 2: **571–593**
European Writers Selected Authors, vol. 1:
529–551

Frank, Anne
Writers for Young Adults, vol. 1: **423–431**

Medieval Drama
European Writers, vol. 1: **451–474**
European Writers Selected Authors, vol. 2:
1051–1074

Renaissance Short Fiction
European Writers, vol. 2: **927–956**
European Writers Selected Authors, vol. 3:
1431–1460

Ecuadoran

Icaza, Jorge
Latin American Writers, vol. 3: **1063–1067**

Montalvo, Juan
Latin American Writers, vol. 1: **215–220**

Egyptian

Ḥakīm, Tawfīq, al-
African Writers, vol. 1: **291–301**

Idrīs, Yūsuf
African Writers, vol. 1: **345–365**

Maḥfūẓ, Najīb
African Writers, vol. 2: **451–465**

Saʿadāwī, Nawāl, al-
African Writers, vol. 2: **721–731**

Ṭāhā Ḥusayn
African Writers, vol. 2: **851–863**

English. See British

Finnish

Södergran, Edith
European Writers, vol. 11: **1781–1806**

French

Adam de la Halle
See "Medieval Drama"

Anouilh, Jean
European Writers, vol. 13: **2843–2865**
European Writers Selected Authors, vol. 1:
    31–52

Apollinaire, Guillaume
European Writers, vol. 9: **881–903**

Aquinas, Saint Thomas, and Scholasticism
European Writers, vol. 1: **405–430**
European Writers Selected Authors, vol. 1: **53–77**

Aragon, Louis
European Writers, vol. 11: **2061–2087**

Arp, Jean
European Writers, vol. 10: **1365–1384**

Artaud, Antonin
European Writers, vol. 11: **1961–1985**

Arthurian Legend
European Writers, vol. 1: **137–160**
European Writers Selected Authors, vol. 1: **79–102**

Arthurian Romances
Supernatural Fiction Writers, vol. 1: **11–18**

Augier, Émile
See "Well-Made Play, The"

Aymé, Marcel
European Writers, vol. 12: **2433–2456**

Balzac, Honoré de
European Writers, vol. 5: **635–658**
European Writers Selected Authors, vol. 1: **161–183**
Supernatural Fiction Writers, vol. 1: **37–44**

Barthes, Roland
European Writers, vol. 13: **3079–3104**

Baudelaire, Charles
European Writers, vol. 7: **1323–1348**

Beaumarchais, Pierre-Augustin Caron de
European Writers, vol. 4: **563–585**

Beauvoir, Simone de
European Writers, vol. 12: **2701–2732**
European Writers Selected Authors, vol. 1: **185–215**

Bergson, Henri
European Writers, vol. 8: **45–66**

Berlioz, Hector
European Writers, vol. 6: **771–812**

Boileau-Despréaux, Nicolas
European Writers, vol. 3: **177–205**

Bossuet, Jacques Bénigne
European Writers, vol. 3: **151–175**

Breton, André
European Writers, vol. 11: **1939–1960**

Brieux, Eugène
See "Well-Made Play, The"

Brunhoff, Jean de
Writers for Children: **91–96**

Butor, Michel
European Writers, vol. 13: **3287–3321**

Camus, Albert
African Writers, vol. 1: **139–152**
European Writers, vol. 13: **3049–3078**
European Writers Selected Authors, vol. 1: **305–334**

German

Plutarch
Ancient Writers, vol. 2: **961–983**

Polybius
Ancient Writers, vol. 1: **525–539**

Posidippus
See "Hellenistic Poetry at Alexandria"

Revelation
The Books of the Bible, vol. 2: **367–381**

Ritsos, Yannis
European Writers, vol. 12: **2815–2842**

Sappho
See "Greek Lyric Poets"

Seferis, George
European Writers, vol. 12: **2255–2271**

Simonides
See "Greek Lyric Poets"

Sirach (Ecclesiasticus)
The Books of the Bible, vol. 2: **65–86**

Sophocles
Ancient Writers, vol. 1: **179–207**

Stesichorus
See "Greek Lyric Poets"

Theocritus
Ancient Writers, vol. 1: **483–500**

Thucydides
Ancient Writers, vol. 1: **267–289**

Tobit
The Books of the Bible, vol. 2: **35–42**

Xenophon
Ancient Writers, vol. 1: **331–351**

Guatemalan

Asturias, Miguel Ángel
Latin American Writers, vol. 2: **865–873**

Gómez Carillo, Enrique
Latin American Writers, vol. 2: **465–469**

Guinean

Laye, Camara
African Writers, vol. 1: **413–425**

Hebrew

Acts of the Apostles, The
See "Gospel of Luke and Acts of the Apostles"

Amos
The Books of the Bible, vol. 1: **367–374**

Apocrypha, The
The Books of the Bible, vol. 2: **3–11**

Baruch, the Letter of Jeremiah, the Prayer of
Manasseh
The Books of the Bible, vol. 2: **87–92**

Bible as Sacred Literature, The
The Books of the Bible, vol. 1: **1–9**

Chronicles, Ezra, and Nehemiah (1 and 2
Chronicles, Ezra, and Nehemiah)
The Books of the Bible, vol. 1: **155–171**

Daniel and Additions to Daniel
The Books of the Bible, vol. 1: **333–347**

Deuteronomy
The Books of the Bible, vol. 1: **89–102**

Ecclesiastes
The Books of the Bible, vol. 1: **231–239**

Epistle of James
The Books of the Bible, vol. 2: **339–343**

Epistles of John (1, 2, and 3 John)
The Books of the Bible, vol. 2: **359–365**

Epistle of Jude
See "Epistles of Peter and Jude (2 Peter and
Jude)"

Epistle of Peter (1 Peter)
The Books of the Bible, vol. 2: **345–351**

Epistles of Peter and Jude (2 Peter and Jude)
The Books of the Bible, vol. 2: **353–357**

Epistle to the Colossians
The Books of the Bible, vol. 2: **301–310**

Epistles to the Corinthians (1 and 2
Corinthians)
The Books of the Bible, vol. 2: **245–269**

Epistle to the Ephesians
The Books of the Bible, vol. 2: **285–292**

Epistle to the Galatians
The Books of the Bible, vol. 2: **271–284**

Epistle to the Hebrews
The Books of the Bible, vol. 2: **327–338**

Sirach (Ecclesiasticus)
The Books of the Bible, vol. 2: **65–86**

Song of Solomon
The Books of the Bible, vol. 1: **241–246**

Tobit
The Books of the Bible, vol. 2: **35–42**

Wisdom of Solomon
The Books of the Bible, vol. 2: **51–63**

Zechariah
See "Haggai, Zechariah, and Malachi"

Zephaniah
The Books of the Bible, vol. 1: **397–404**

Honduran

Molina, Juan Ramón
Latin American Writers, vol. 2: **539–542**

Valle, Rafael Heliodoro
Latin American Writers, vol. 2: **721–725**

Hungarian

Ady, Endre
European Writers, vol. 9: **859–880**

Kosztolányi, Dezsö
European Writers, vol. 10: **1231–1249**

Lukács, György
European Writers, vol. 10: **1251–1279**

Seredy, Kate
Writers for Children: **519–524**

Icelandic

Gunnarsson, Gunnar
European Writers, vol. 10: **1497–1519**

Laxness, Halldór
European Writers, vol. 12: **2457–2478**

Norse Sagas
European Writers, vol. 1: **377–404**
European Writers Selected Authors, vol. 3: **1199–1226**

Indian

Rushdie, Salman
British Writers Supp. 4: **433–457**

Irish

Addison, Joseph
See "Steele, Sir Richard, and Joseph Addison"

Beckett, Samuel
British Writers Supp. 1: **43–64**
British Writers Selected Authors, vol. 1: **47–68**

Behan, Brendan
British Writers Supp. 2: **61–76**

Bowen, Elizabeth
British Writers Supp. 2: **77–96**
Supernatural Fiction Writers, vol. 2: **569–575**

Burke, Edmund
British Writers, vol. 3: **193–207**

Chambers, Aidan
Writers for Young Adults, vol. 1: **219–227**

Colum, Padraic
Writers for Children: **139–146**

Day Lewis, Cecil
British Writers Supp. 3: **115–132**

Dunsany, Lord
Supernatural Fiction Writers, vol. 1: **471–478**

Goldsmith, Oliver
British Writers, vol. 3: **177–192**

Gregory, Lady Augusta
See "Synge, J. M., and Lady Augusta Gregory"

Heaney, Seamus
British Writers Supp. 2: **267–282**

Joyce, James
British Writers, vol. 7: **41–58**
British Writers Selected Authors, vol. 2: **683–700**

Le Fanu, J. S.
Supernatural Fiction Writers, vol. 1: **219–231**

Lewis, C. S.
British Writers Supp. 3: **247–268**
British Writers Selected Authors, vol. 2: **855–876**
Science Fiction Writers: **243–248**
Supernatural Fiction Writers, vol. 2: **661–666**
Writers for Children: **357–364**
Writers for Young Adults, vol. 2: **247–255**

Maturin, Charles Robert
Supernatural Fiction Writers, vol. 1: **161–168**

Moore, George
British Writers, vol. 6: **85–100**

Muldoon, Paul
  British Writers Supp. 4: **409–432**
Murdoch, Iris
  British Writers Supp. 1: **215–235**
O'Brien, Fitz-James
  Supernatural Fiction Writers, vol. 2: **717–722**
O'Brien, Flann
  British Writers Supp. 2: **321–339**
O'Casey, Sean
  British Writers, vol. 7: **1–16**
Riddell, Mrs. J. H.
  Supernatural Fiction Writers, vol. 1: **269–277**
Shaw, George Bernard
  British Writers, vol. 6: **101–132**
  British Writers Selected Authors, vol. 3: **1053–1084**
Sheridan, Richard Brinsley
  British Writers, vol. 3: **252–271**
Steele, Sir Richard, and Joseph Addison
  British Writers, vol. 3: **38–53**
  British Writers Selected Authors, vol. 3: **1145–1160**
Stephens, James
  Supernatural Fiction Writers, vol. 1: **485–490**
Stoker, Bram
  British Writers Supp. 3: **375–391**
  Supernatural Fiction Writers, vol. 1: **375–381**
Swift, Jonathan
  British Writers, vol. 3: **15–38**
  British Writers Selected Authors, vol. 3: **1195–1217**
  Writers for Children: **555–559**
Synge, J. M., and Lady Augusta Gregory
  British Writers, vol. 6: **307–318**
Trevor, William
  British Writers Supp. 4: **499–519**
Wall, Mervyn
  Supernatural Fiction Writers, vol. 2: **645–650**
Wilde, Oscar
  British Writers, vol. 5: **399–422**
  British Writers Selected Authors, vol. 3: **1353–1376**
  Supernatural Fiction Writers, vol. 1: **345–350**
  Writers for Children: **611–616**
Yeats, William Butler
  British Writers, vol. 6: **207–224**
  British Writers Selected Authors, vol. 3: **1473–1490**

Italian

Alfieri, Vittorio
  European Writers, vol. 4: **661–689**
Aquinas, Saint Thomas, and Scholasticism
  European Writers, vol. 1: **405–430**
  European Writers Selected Authors, vol. 1: **53–77**
Ariosto, Lodovico
  European Writers, vol. 2: **619–644**
Arthurian Legend
  European Writers, vol. 1: **137–160**
  European Writers Selected Authors, vol. 1: **79–102**
Bandello, Matteo
  See "Renaissance Short Fiction"
Basile, Giambattista
  See "Renaissance Short Fiction"
Boccaccio, Giovanni
  European Writers, vol. 2: **509–534**
  European Writers Selected Authors, vol. 1: **255–280**
  See also "Renaissance Pastoral Poetry"
Calvino, Italo
  European Writers, vol. 13: **3259–3286**
Carducci, Giosue
  European Writers, vol. 7: **1495–1516**
Castiglione, Baldesar
  European Writers, vol. 2: **645–667**
Collodi, C.
  Writers for Children: **129–137**
Croce, Benedetto
  European Writers, vol. 8: **311–329**
D'Annunzio, Gabriele
  European Writers, vol. 8: **175–203**
Dante Alighieri
  European Writers, vol. 1: **431–450**
  European Writers Selected Authors, vol. 1: **411–430**
  See also "Renaissance Pastoral Poetry"
Foscolo, Ugo
  European Writers, vol. 5: **313–341**
Ginzburg, Natalia
  European Writers, vol. 13: **3131–3163**
Giraldi, Giambattista
  See "Renaissance Pastoral Poetry"
Goldoni, Carlo
  European Writers, vol. 4: **421–448**

Japanese

Kenyan

Lesotho

Mofolo, Thomas Mokopu
African Writers, vol. 2: **479–493**

Lithuanian

Budrys, Algis
Science Fiction Writers: **305–311**

Mexican

Arreola, Juan José
Latin American Writers, vol. 3: **1229–1236**

Azuela, Mariano
Latin American Writers, vol. 2: **457–464**

Balbuena, Bernardo de
Latin American Writers, vol. 1: **53–57**

Carballido, Emilio
Latin American Writers, vol. 3: **1289–1294**

Castellanos, Rosario
Latin American Writers, vol. 3: **1295–1302**

Díaz del Castillo, Bernal
Latin American Writers, vol. 1: **17–21**

Fernández de Lizardi, José Joaquín
Latin American Writers, vol. 1: **119–128**

Fuentes, Carlos
Latin American Writers, vol. 3: **1353–1376**

Gamboa, Federico
Latin American Writers, vol. 1: **371–375**

González de Eslava, Fernán
Latin American Writers, vol. 1: **33–37**

Gorostiza, José
Latin American Writers, vol. 2: **923–931**

Gutiérrez Nájera, Manuel
Latin American Writers, vol. 1: **351–357**

Guzmán, Martín Luis
Latin American Writers, vol. 2: **655–662**

Juana Inéz de La Cruz, Sor
Latin American Writers, vol. 1: **85–106**

Lopez Velarde, Ramon
Latin American Writers, vol. 2: **663–670**

Nervo, Amado
Latin American Writers, vol. 1: **425–429**

Paz, Octavio
Latin American Writers, vol. 3: **1163–1176**

Reyes, Alfonso
Latin American Writers, vol. 2: **693–703**

Romero, José Rubén
Latin American Writers, vol. 2: **711–715**

Rulfo, Juan
Latin American Writers, vol. 3: **1215–1229**

Sigüenza y Góngora, Carlos de
Latin American Writers, vol. 1: **71–77**

Tablada, José Juan
Latin American Writers, vol. 1: **441–446**

Torres Bodet, Jaime
Latin American Writers, vol. 2: **933–939**

Usigli, Rodolfo
Latin American Writers, vol. 3: **1033–1042**

Vasconcelos, José
Latin American Writers, vol. 2: **575–584**

Villaurrutia, Xavier
Latin American Writers, vol. 3: **975–980**

Yáñez, Agustín
Latin American Writers, vol. 3: **995–999**

Mozambican

Couto, Mia
African Writers, vol. 1: **185–197**

Honwana, Luís Bernardo
African Writers, vol. 1: **321–329**

New Zealander

Mansfield, Katherine
British Writers, vol. 7: **171–184**
British Writers Selected Authors, vol. 2: **891–904**

Nicaraguan

Darío, Rubén
Latin American Writers, vol. 1: **397–412**

Nigerian

Achebe, Chinua
African Writers, vol. 1: **15–36**

Clark, John Pepper
African Writers, vol. 1: **153–166**

Egbuna, Obi
African Writers, vol. 1: **209–221**

Ekwensi, Cyprian
African Writers, vol. 1: **223–234**

Emecheta, Buchi
African Writers, vol. 1: **235–247**

Iyayi, Festus
African Writers, vol. 1: **367–375**

Ojaide, Tanure
African Writers, vol. 2: **557–565**

Okara, Gabriel
African Writers, vol. 2: **567–582**

Okigbo, Christopher
African Writers, vol. 2: **583–598**

Okri, Ben
African Writers, vol. 2: **599–608**

Omotoso, Kole
African Writers, vol. 2: **609–617**

Osofisan, Femi
African Writers, vol. 2: **619–629**

Osundare, Niyi
African Writers, vol. 2: **631–640**

Rotimi, Ola
African Writers, vol. 2: **707–720**

Sowande, Bode
African Writers, vol. 2: **799–806**

Soyinka, Wole
African Writers, vol. 2: **807–831**

Tutuola, Amos
African Writers, vol. 2: **865–878**

Norwegian

Asbjørnsen and Moe (Peter Christen
    Asbjørnsen and Jørgen Moe)
Writers for Children: **21–28**

Hamsun, Knut
European Writers, vol. 8: **21–43**

Ibsen, Henrik
European Writers, vol. 7: **1421–1448**
European Writers Selected Authors, vol. 2: **787–813**

Moe, Jörgen
See "Asbjørnsen and Moe"

Norse Sagas
European Writers, vol. 1: **377–404**
European Writers Selected Authors, vol. 3:
    1199–1226

Undset, Sigrid
European Writers, vol. 9: **1017–1041**

Vesaas, Tarjei
European Writers, vol. 11: **2035–2059**

Panamanian

Sinán, Rogelio
Latin American Writers, vol. 2: **941–946**

Paraguayan

Roa Bastos, Augusto
Latin American Writers, vol. 3: **1209–1213**

Peruvian

Acosta, Father Joseph de
Latin American Writers, vol. 1: **47–51**

Alegría, Ciro
Latin American Writers, vol. 3: **1099–1103**

Arguedas, José María
Latin American Writers, vol. 3: **1131–1138**

Carrió de la Vandera, Alonso
Latin American Writers, vol. 1: **107–111**

Chocano, José Santos
Latin American Writers, vol. 2: **543–549**

Eguren, José María
Latin American Writers, vol. 2: **513–518**

Garcilaso de la Vega, El Inca
Latin American Writers, vol. 1: **39–45**

González Prada, Manuel
Latin American Writers, vol. 1: **283–288**

Matto de Turner, Clorinda
Latin American Writers, vol. 1: **305–309**

Palma, Ricardo
Latin American Writers, vol. 1: **221–228**

Vallejo, César
  Latin American Writers, vol. 2: **727–738**

Valle y Caviedes, Juan del
  Latin American Writers, vol. 1: **79–83**

Vargas Llosa, Mario
  Latin American Writers, vol. 3: **1421–1436**

Polish

Apollinaire, Guillaume
  European Writers, vol. 9: **881–903**

Gombrowicz, Witold
  European Writers, vol. 12: **2563–2588**

Łem, Stanisław
  Science Fiction Writers: **591–598**

Mickiewicz, Adam
  European Writers, vol. 5: **607–634**

Milosz, Czeslaw
  European Writers, vol. 13: **2929–2952**

Witkiewicz (Witkacy), Stanisław Ignacy
  European Writers, vol. 10: **1205–1230**

Portuguese

Camoëns, Luís Vaz de
  European Writers, vol. 2: **747–767**

Eça de Queiroz, José Maria
  European Writers, vol. 7: **1683–1708**

Ferreira de Castro, Jose Maria
  European Writers, vol. 11: **2143–2165**

Montemayor, Jorge de
  See "Renaissance Pastoral Poetry" in *European Writers*, vol. 2: **889–926**

Pessoa, Fernando
  European Writers, vol. 10: **1475–1495**

Puerto Rican

Laguerre, Enrique A.
  Latin American Writers, vol. 3: **1049–1055**

Marqués, René
  Latin American Writers, vol. 3: **1237–1246**

Palés Matos, Luis
  Latin American Writers, vol. 2: **821–830**

Zeno Gandía, Manuel
  Latin American Writers, vol. 1: **321–326**

Roman

Ammianus Marcellinus
  Ancient Writers, vol. 2: **1117–1138**

Apuleius
  Ancient Writers, vol. 2: **1099–1116**
  Supernatural Fiction Writers, vol. 1: **3–9**

Augustine, Saint
  European Writers, vol. 1: **23–50**
  European Writers Selected Authors, vol. 1: **103–130**

Caesar
  Ancient Writers, vol. 1: **583–599**

Catullus
  Ancient Writers, vol. 2: **643–667**

Cicero
  Ancient Writers, vol. 1: **555–581**

Epictetus and Marcus Aurelius
  Ancient Writers, vol. 2: **985–1002**

Horace
  Ancient Writers, vol. 2: **703–731**

Josephus
  Ancient Writers, vol. 2: **877–885**

Juvenal
  See "Persius and Juvenal"

Livy
  Ancient Writers, vol. 2: **733–764**

Lucan and Statius
  Ancient Writers, vol. 2: **917–941**

Lucretius
  Ancient Writers, vol. 2: **601–620**

Marcus Aurelius
  See "Epictetus and Marcus Aurelius"

Martial
  Ancient Writers, vol. 2: **887–915**

Ovid
  Ancient Writers, vol. 2: **783–806**

Persius and Juvenal
  Ancient Writers, vol. 2: **855–876**

Petronius
  Ancient Writers, vol. 2: **833–853**

Salvadoran

Salazar Arrué, Salvador (Salarrué)
Latin American Writers, vol. 2: **875–879**

Scottish

Barrie, J. M.
British Writers Supp. 3: **1–17**
Supernatural Fiction Writers, vol. 1: **405–410**
Writers for Children: **29–35**

Boswell, James
British Writers, vol. 3: **234–251**
British Writers Selected Authors, vol. 1: **111–128**

Burns, Robert
British Writers, vol. 3: **310–323**
British Writers Selected Authors, vol. 1: **231–244**

Carlyle, Thomas
British Writers, vol. 4: **238–250**
British Writers Selected Authors, vol. 1: **269–281**

Doyle, Sir Arthur Conan
British Writers Supp. 2: **159–178**
British Writers Selected Authors, vol. 1: **415–434**
Science Fiction Writers: **45–50**
Writers for Children: **201–207**
Writers for Young Adults, vol. 1: **385–392**

Frazer, James George
British Writers Supp. 3: **169–190**

Grahame, Kenneth
Writers for Children: **247–254**

Hogg, James
Supernatural Fiction Writers, vol. 1: **177–183**

Hume, David
British Writers Supp. 3: **229–245**

Hunter, Mollie
Writers for Young Adults, vol. 2: **149–159**

Lang, Andrew
Writers for Children: **337–343**

Lovelace, Richard
See "Cavalier Poets, The" in *British Writers*,
vol. 2: **221–239**

MacDonald, George
Supernatural Fiction Writers, vol. 1: **239–246**
Writers for Children: **373–380**

McEwan, Ian
British Writers Supp. 4: **389–408**

Macleod, Fiona
Supernatural Fiction Writers, vol. 1: **369–374**

Molesworth, M. L. S.
Writers for Children: **407–413**

Oliphant, Mrs.
Supernatural Fiction Writers, vol. 1: **261–268**

Scott, Sir Walter
British Writers, vol. 4: **27–40**
Supernatural Fiction Writers, vol. 1: **169–176**

Smollett, Tobias
British Writers, vol. 3: **146–159**

Spark, Muriel
British Writers Supp. 1: **199–214**

Stevenson, Robert Louis
British Writers, vol. 5: **383–399**
British Writers Selected Authors, vol. 3:
1161–1176
Supernatural Fiction Writers, vol. 1: **307–313**
Writers for Children: **535–543**
Writers for Young Adults, vol. 3: **215–224**

Taine, John
Science Fiction Writers: **75–82**

Thomson, James
British Writers Supp. 3: **409–429**

Senegalese

Bâ, Mariama
African Writers, vol. 1: **77–82**

Sembène Ousmane
African Writers, vol. 2: **765–774**

Senghor, Léopold Sédar
African Writers, vol. 2: **775–789**

Serbian

Andrić, Ivo
European Writers, vol. 11: **1751–1779**

Somalian

Farah, Nuruddin
African Writers, vol. 1: **249–262**

South African

Abrahams, Peter
  African Writers, vol. 1: **1–14**

Brink, André
  African Writers, vol. 1: **95–114**

Brutus, Dennis
  African Writers, vol. 1: **115–126**

Campbell, Roy
  African Writers, vol. 1: **127–137**

Coetzee, J. M.
  African Writers, vol. 1: **167–183**

Fugard, Athol
  African Writers, vol. 1: **263–275**

Gordimer, Nadine
  African Writers, vol. 1: **277–290**
  British Writers Supp. 2: **225–245**

Head, Bessie
  African Writers, vol. 1: **303–320**

Hope, Christopher
  African Writers, vol. 1: **331–343**

Jacobson, Dan
  African Writers, vol. 1: **377–389**

La Guma, Alex
  African Writers, vol. 1: **401–411**

Mphahlele, Es'kia
  African Writers, vol. 2: **495–510**

Paton, Alan
  African Writers, vol. 2: **651–668**
  British Writers Supp. 2: **341–361**
  British Writers Selected Authors, vol. 2: **963–983**

Plomer, William
  African Writers, vol. 2: **697–706**

Schreiner, Olive
  African Writers, vol. 2: **745–763**
  British Writers Supp. 2: **435–458**

van der Post, Laurens
  African Writers, vol. 2: **879–891**

Spanish

Azorín
  European Writers, vol. 9: **639–661**

Baroja, Pío
  European Writers, vol. 9: **589–616**

Blasco Ibáñez, Vicente
  European Writers, vol. 8: **355–388**

Calderón de la Barca, Pedro
  European Writers, vol. 2: **871–895**

Cela, Camilo José
  European Writers, vol. 13: **3105–3129**

Cervantes, Miguel de
  European Writers, vol. 2: **819–844**
  European Writers Selected Authors, vol. 1: **335–359**
  See also "Renaissance Short Fiction"

Cid in Epic and Ballad, The
  European Writers, vol. 1: **113–136**

García Lorca, Federico
  European Writers, vol. 11: **2167–2203**
  European Writers Selected Authors, vol. 1: **595–630**

Jiménez, Juan Ramón
  European Writers, vol. 9: **991–1016**

Machado, Antonio
  European Writers, vol. 9: **743–765**

Ortega y Gasset, José
  European Writers, vol. 9: **1119–1150**

Pérez Galdós, Benito
  European Writers, vol. 7: **1597–1618**

Renaissance Short Fiction
  European Writers, vol. 2: **927–956**
  European Writers Selected Authors, vol. 3: **1431–1460**

Santayana, George
  American Writers, vol. 3: **599–622**

Unamuno, Miguel de
  European Writers, vol. 8: **283–310**

Valle-Inclán, Ramón del
  European Writers, vol. 8: **331–353**

Vega, Lope de
  European Writers, vol. 2: **845–870**

Sudanese

Ṣāliḥ, al-Ṭayyib
  African Writers, vol. 2: **733–744**

Swedish

Ekelöf, Gunnar
  European Writers, vol. 12: **2635–2671**

Johnson, Eyvind
  European Writers, vol. 12: **2361–2385**

Lagerkvist, Pär
  European Writers, vol. 10: **1677–1702**

Moberg, Vilhelm
  European Writers, vol. 11: **2203–2231**

Norse Sagas
  European Writers, vol. 1: **377–404**
  European Writers Selected Authors, vol. 3:
    1199–1226

Södergran, Edith
  European Writers, vol. 11: **1781–1806**

Strindberg, August
  European Writers, vol. 7: **1731–1758**

Swiss

Burckhardt, Jacob
  European Writers, vol. 6: **1225–1244**

Dürrenmatt, Friedrich
  European Writers, vol. 13: **3215–3235**

Frisch, Max
  European Writers, vol. 13: **2895–2924**

Keller, Gottfried
  See "Poetic Realism"

Meyer, Conrad Ferdinand
  See "Poetic Realism"

Poetic Realism
  European Writers, vol. 6: **913–942**

Rousseau, Jean Jacques
  European Writers, vol. 4: **449–474**
  European Writers Selected Authors, vol. 3: **1519–1544**

Spyri, Johanna
  Writers for Children: **529–533**

Trinidadian

Naipaul, V. S.
  British Writers Supp. 1: **383–405**

Tunisian

Memmi, Albert
  African Writers, vol. 2: **467–477**

Shābbī, Abū al-Qāsim, al-
  African Writers, vol. 2: **791–798**

Ugandan

p'Bitek, Okot
  African Writers, vol. 2: **669–684**

Ukranian

Gogol, Nikolay Vasilievich
  European Writers, vol. 6: **971–998**

Tychyna, Pavlo
  European Writers, vol. 10: **1651–1676**

Uruguayan

Acevedo Díaz, Eduardo
  Latin American Writers, vol. 1: **299–303**

Agustini, Delmira
  Latin American Writers, vol. 2: **649–654**

Benedetti, Mario
  Latin American Writers, vol. 3: **1255–1263**

Herrera y Reissig, Julio
  Latin American Writers, vol. 2: **519–530**

Ibarbourou, Juana de
  Latin American Writers, vol. 2: **803–807**

Onetti, Juan Carlos
  Latin American Writers, vol. 3: **1089–1097**

Quiroga, Horacio
  Latin American Writers, vol. 2: **551–558**

Rodó, José Enrique
  Latin American Writers, vol. 2: **447–455**

Sánchez, Florencio
  Latin American Writers, vol. 2: **531–538**

Zorrilla de San Martín, Juan
  Latin American Writers, vol. 1: **327–331**

Venezuelan

Bello, Andrés
  Latin American Writers, vol. 1: **129–134**

Blanco Fombona, Rufino
  Latin American Writers, vol. 2: **503–511**

Díaz Rodríguez, Manuel
Latin American Writers, vol. 1: **431–439**

Gallegos, Rómulo
Latin American Writers, vol. 2: **603–610**

Parra Sanojo, Ana Teresa de la
Latin American Writers, vol. 2: **717–720**

Picón Salas, Mariano
Latin American Writers, vol. 2: **903–908**

Uslar Pietri, Arturo
Latin American Writers, vol. 3: **1057–1062**

Welsh

Arthurian Legend
European Writers, vol. 1: **137–160**
European Writers Selected Authors, vol. 1: **79–102**

Dahl, Roald
British Writers Supp. 4: **201–227**

Fortune, Dion
Supernatural Fiction Writers, vol. 2: **585–590**

Lawrence, T. E.
British Writers Supp. 2: **283–298**

Machen, Arthur
Supernatural Fiction Writers, vol. 1: **351–359**

Thomas, Dylan
British Writers Supp. 1: **169–184**
British Writers Selected Authors, vol. 3: **1261–1276**

Vaughan, Henry
See "Metaphysical Poets, Four" in *British Writers*, vol. 2: **179–203**

West Indian

Naipaul, V. S.
British Writers Supp. 1: **383–405**

Rhys, Jean
British Writers Supp. 2: **387–404**

Subjects by Genre

These lists identify articles on authors who wrote significantly in the following categories: (1) Poetry, (2) Drama, (3) Early Prose Fiction, (4) the Novel, (5) the Short Story, (6) Religion, (7) Philosophy, (8) Criticism, (9) Journalism, (10) Autobiography, or (11) Children's Literature. The listings are selective and nonexclusive. Many authors contributed to multiple genres, and not all varieties of literature are covered.

POETRY

Lyric, reflective, and narrative verse of all periods and cultures.

Achebe, Chinua
African Writers, vol. 1: **15–36**

Ackerman, Diane
American Nature Writers, vol. 1: **21–30**

Adam de la Halle
See "Medieval Drama"

Addison, Joseph
See "Steele, Sir Richard, and Joseph Addison" in
British Writers, vol. 3: **38–53**; *British Writers Selected Authors*, vol. 3: **1145–1160**

Ady, Endre
European Writers, vol. 9: **859–880**

Aeschylus
Ancient Writers, vol. 1: **99–155**

Agee, James
American Writers, vol. 1: **25–47**

Agustini, Delmira
Latin American Writers, vol. 2: **649–654**

Aidoo, Ama Ata
African Writers, vol. 1: **37–48**

Aiken, Conrad
American Writers, vol. 1: **48–70**

Akhmatova, Anna
European Writers, vol. 10: **1521–1542**

Alcaeus
See "Greek Lyric Poets"

Alcman
See "Greek Lyric Poets"

Alegría, Ciro
Latin American Writers, vol. 3: **1099–1103**

Alfieri, Vittorio
European Writers, vol. 4: **661–689**

Amis, Kingsley
British Writers Supp. 2: **1–19**

Amos
The Books of the Bible, vol. 1: **367–374**

Anacreon
See "Greek Lyric Poets"

Anderson, Sherwood
American Writers, vol. 1: **97–120**

Andrade, Mário de
Latin American Writers, vol. 2: **771–780**

Andrić, Ivo
European Writers, vol. 11: **1751–1779**

Angelou, Maya
American Writers Supp. 4, part 1: **1–19**
Modern American Women Writers: **1–8**
Writers for Young Adults, vol. 1: **43–52**

Antimachus of Colophon
See "Hellenistic Poetry at Alexandria"

Apollinaire, Guillaume
European Writers, vol. 9: **881–903**

Apollonius of Rhodes
See "Hellenistic Poetry at Alexandria"

Aragon, Louis
European Writers, vol. 11: **2061–2087**

Arenas, Reinaldo
Latin American Writers, vol. 3: **1451–1458**

Ariosto, Lodovico
European Writers, vol. 2: **619–644**

Arnold, Matthew
British Writers, vol. 5: **203–218**

Arp, Jean
European Writers, vol. 10: **1365–1384**

Artaud, Antonin
European Writers, vol. 11: **1961–1985**

Arthurian Legend
European Writers, vol. 1: **137–160**
European Writers Selected Authors, vol. 1: **79–102**

Arthurian Romances
Supernatural Fiction Writers, vol. 1: **11–18**

Ascasubi, Hilario
Latin American Writers, vol. 1: **147–151**

Asclepiades
See "Hellenistic Poetry at Alexandria"

Ashbery, John
American Writers Supp. 3, part 1: **1–29**

Asturias, Miguel Ángel
Latin American Writers, vol. 2: **865–873**

Auden, W. H.
American Writers Supp. 2, part 1: **1–28**
British Writers, vol. 7: **379–399**
British Writers Selected Authors, vol. 1: **1–21**

Awoonor, Kofi
African Writers, vol. 1: **63–75**

Bacchylides
See "Greek Lyric Poets"

Balbuena, Bernardo de
Latin American Writers, vol. 1: **53–57**

Ballagas, Emilio
Latin American Writers, vol. 3: **1081–1087**

Bandeira, Manuel
Latin American Writers, vol. 2: **629–641**

Baraka, Amiri
African American Writers: **15–29**
American Writers Supp. 2, part 1: **29–63**

Barlow, Joel
American Writers Supp. 2, part 1: **65–86**

Barnes, Djuna
American Writers Supp. 3, part 1: **31–46**

Baroja, Pío
European Writers, vol. 9: **589–616**

Baudelaire, Charles
European Writers, vol. 7: **1323–1348**

Beckett, Samuel
British Writers Supp. 1: **43–64**
British Writers Selected Authors, vol. 1: **47–68**

Behn, Aphra
British Writers Supp. 3: **19–43**

Bello, Andrés
Latin American Writers, vol. 1: **129–134**

Belloc, Hilaire
Writers for Children: **49–54**

Bely, Andrey
European Writers, vol. 9: **905–929**

Benedetti, Mario
Latin American Writers, vol. 3: **1255–1263**

Benét, Stephen Vincent
Supernatural Fiction Writers, vol. 2: **797–803**

Beowulf and Anglo-Saxon Poetry
European Writers, vol. 1: **51–88**
European Writers Selected Authors, vol. 1: **217–253**

Berger, John
British Writers Supp. 4: **77–96**

Berry, Wendell
American Nature Writers, vol. 1: **89–105**

Berryman, John
American Writers, vol. 1: **167–189**

Betjeman, John
British Writers, vol. 7: **355–378**

Bible, The English
British Writers, vol. 1: **370–388**
British Writers Selected Authors, vol. 1: **69–87**

Bierce, Ambrose
American Writers, vol. 1: **190–213**
Supernatural Fiction Writers, vol. 2: **731–737**

Bishop, Elizabeth
American Writers Supp. 1, part 1: **72–97**
Modern American Women Writers: **9–22**

Blackmur, R. P.
American Writers Supp. 2, part 1: **87–112**

Blake, William
British Writers, vol. 3: **288–310**

British Writers Selected Authors, vol. 1: **89–110**
Writers for Children: **69–76**

Blanco Fombona, Rufino
Latin American Writers, vol. 2: **503–511**

Blok, Alexander
European Writers, vol. 9: **959–990**

Bly, Robert
American Writers Supp. 4, part 1: **59–77**

Boccaccio, Giovanni
European Writers, vol. 2: **509–534**
European Writers Selected Authors, vol. 1: **255–280**
See also "Renaissance Pastoral Poetry"

Bogan, Louise
American Writers Supp. 3, part 1: **47–68**
Modern American Women Writers: **23–36**

Boileau-Despréaux, Nicolas
European Writers, vol. 3: **177–205**

Böll, Heinrich
European Writers, vol. 13: **3165–3186**

Bontemps, Arna
Writers for Children: **77–83**

Borges, Jorge Luis
Latin American Writers, vol. 2: **845–864**

Bowles, Paul
American Writers Supp. 4, part 1: **79–99**

Bradbury, Ray
American Writers Supp. 4, part 1: **101–118**
Supernatural Fiction Writers: **171–178**
Supernatural Fiction Writers, vol. 2: **917–923**

Bradstreet, Anne
American Writers Supp. 1, part 1: **98–123**

Brecht, Bertolt
European Writers, vol. 11: **2089–2112**
European Writers Selected Authors, vol. 1: **281–303**

Breton, André
European Writers, vol. 11: **1939–1960**

Bridges, Robert
British Writers, vol. 6: **71–84**

Brontës, The
British Writers, vol. 5: **105–154**
British Writers Selected Authors, vol. 1: **129–177**

Brooke, Rupert
British Writers Supp. 3: **45–61**
See also "Poets of World War I (British)"

Brooks, Gwendolyn
African American Writers: **31–43**
American Writers Supp. 3, part 1: **69–90**
Modern American Women Writers: **37–48**

Brown, Sterling
African American Writers: **45–57**

Browning, Elizabeth Barrett
British Writers, vol. 4: **310–322**
British Writers Selected Authors, vol. 1: **179–191**

Browning, Robert
British Writers, vol. 4: **354–375**
British Writers Selected Authors, vol. 1: **193–214**

Brutus, Dennis
African Writers, vol. 1: **115–126**

Bryant, William Cullen
American Writers Supp. 1, part 1: **150–173**

Burns, Robert
British Writers, vol. 3: **310–323**
British Writers Selected Authors, vol. 1: **231–244**

Butor, Michel
European Writers, vol. 13: **3287–3321**

Byron, Lord
British Writers, vol. 4: **171–194**
British Writers Selected Authors, vol. 1: **245–268**

Cabell, James Branch
Supernatural Fiction Writers, vol. 2: **789–796**

Cabral de Melo Neto, João
Latin American Writers, vol. 3: **1247–1253**

Calderón de la Barca, Pedro
European Writers, vol. 2: **871–895**

Callimachus
See "Hellenistic Poetry at Alexandria"

Camoëns, Luís Vaz de
European Writers, vol. 2: **747–767**

Campbell, Roy
African Writers, vol. 1: **127–137**

Campo, Estanislao del
Latin American Writers, vol. 1: **229–233**

Carducci, Giosue
European Writers, vol. 7: **1495–1516**

Carew, Thomas
See "Cavalier Poets, The"

Caro, Miguel Antonio
Latin American Writers, vol. 1: **277–281**

Carpentier, Alejo
  Latin American Writers, vol. 3: **1019–1031**

Carroll, Lewis
  British Writers, vol. 5: **261–276**
  Supernatural Fiction Writers, vol. 1: **247–253**
  Writers for Children: **117–127**

Carver, Raymond
  American Writers Supp. 3, part 1: **135–151**

Cary, Joyce
  British Writers, vol. 7: **185–196**

Casal, Julián del
  Latin American Writers, vol. 1: **365–370**

Castellanos, Rosario
  Latin American Writers, vol. 3: **1295–1302**

Castiglione, Baldesar
  European Writers, vol. 2: **645–667**

Castro Alves, Antônio de
  Latin American Writers, vol. 1: **289–297**

Catullus
  Ancient Writers, vol. 2: **643–667**

Cavafy, Constantin
  European Writers, vol. 8: **205–228**

Cavalier Poets, The
  British Writers, vol. 2: **221–239**

Cela, Camilo José
  European Writers, vol. 13: **3105–3129**

Cervantes, Miguel de
  European Writers, vol. 2: **819–844**
  European Writers Selected Authors, vol. 1: **335–359**
  See also "Renaissance Short Fiction"

Chambers, Aidan
  Writers for Young Adults, vol. 1: **219–227**

Chamisso, Adelbert von
  Supernatural Fiction Writers, vol. 1: **91–95**

Chapman, George
  British Writers, vol. 1: **232–256**

Chateaubriand, François René de
  European Writers, vol. 5: **113–140**

Chaucer, Geoffrey
  British Writers, vol. 1: **19–47**
  British Writers Selected Authors, vol. 1: **283–311**

Chénier, André
  European Writers, vol. 4: **691–718**

Chesterton, G. K.
  British Writers, vol. 6: **335–346**
  Supernatural Fiction Writers, vol. 1: **411–414**

Chocano, José Santos
  Latin American Writers, vol. 2: **543–549**

Chrétien de Troyes
  European Writers, vol. 1: **185–209**
  See also "Arthurian Romances"

Cicero
  Ancient Writers, vol. 1: **555–581**

Cid in Epic and Ballad, The
  European Writers, vol. 1: **113–136**

Clark, John Pepper
  African Writers, vol. 1: **153–166**

Claudel, Paul
  European Writers, vol. 8: **471–494**

Clough, Arthur Hugh
  British Writers, vol. 5: **155–172**

Cocteau, Jean
  European Writers, vol. 10: **1543–1564**

Coleridge, Samuel Taylor
  British Writers, vol. 4: **41–57**
  British Writers Selected Authors, vol. 1: **313–329**

Collier, John
  Supernatural Fiction Writers, vol. 2: **577–583**

Collins, William
  British Writers, vol. 3: **160–176**

Colum, Padraic
  Writers for Children: **139–146**

Coppard, A. E.
  Supernatural Fiction Writers, vol. 2: **523–528**

Cortázar, Julio
  Latin American Writers, vol. 3: **1177–1194**

Costa, Cláudio Manuel da
  Latin American Writers, vol. 1: **113–117**

Couto, Mia
  African Writers, vol. 1: **185–197**

Cowley, Abraham
  See "Metaphysical Poets, Four"

Cowper, William
  British Writers, vol. 3: **207–220**

Crabbe, George
  British Writers, vol. 3: **272–287**

Crane, Hart
  American Writers, vol. 1: **381–404**

Crane, Stephen
  American Writers, vol. 1: **405–427**
  Writers for Young Adults, vol. 1: **303–312**

Crashaw, Richard
  See "Metaphysical Poets, Four"

Creeley, Robert
  American Writers Supp. 4, part 1: **139–161**

Cruz e Sousa, João
  Latin American Writers, vol. 1: **359–363**

Cullen, Countee
  American Writers Supp. 4, part 1: **163–174**

Cummings, E. E.
  American Writers, vol. 1: **428–450**

Daniel, John
  See "New Voices in American Nature Writing"

D'Annunzio, Gabriele
  European Writers, vol. 8: **175–203**

Dante Alighieri
  European Writers, vol. 1: **431–450**
  European Writers Selected Authors, vol. 1:
    411–430
  See also "Renaissance Pastoral Poetry"

Darío, Rubén
  Latin American Writers, vol. 1: **397–412**

Daugherty, James Henry
  Writers for Children: **155–161**

Davis, H. L.
  American Nature Writers, vol. 1: **199–211**

Day Lewis, Cecil
  British Writers Supp. 3: **115–132**

Defoe, Daniel
  British Writers, vol. 3: **1–14**
  British Writers Selected Authors, vol. 1: **349–362**
  Writers for Children: **163–171**

De la Mare, Walter
  Supernatural Fiction Writers, vol. 1: **497–503**
  Writers for Children: **173–180**

Derleth, August
  Supernatural Fiction Writers, vol. 2: **883–890**

Dib, Mohammed
  African Writers, vol. 1: **199–207**

Dickey, James
  American Writers Supp. 4, part 1: **175–194**

Dickinson, Emily
  American Writers, vol. 1: **451–473**
  American Writers Retrospective: **25–50**
  Modern American Women Writers: **77–89**
  Writers for Young Adults, vol. 1: **365–372**

Dillard, Annie
  American Nature Writers, vol. 1: **213–230**

Disch, Thomas M.
  Science Fiction Writers: **351–356**

Dodge, Mary Mapes
  Writers for Children: **193–199**

Donne, John
  British Writers, vol. 1: **352–369**
  British Writers Selected Authors, vol. 1: **397–414**

Donoso, José
  Latin American Writers, vol. 3: **1277–1288**

Doolittle, Hilda (H.D.)
  American Writers Supp. 1, part 1: **253–275**
  Modern American Women Writers: **103–121**

Dove, Rita
  American Writers Supp. 4, part 1: **241–258**

Drummond de Andrade, Carlos
  Latin American Writers, vol. 2: **957–974**

Dryden, John
  British Writers, vol. 2: **289–306**

Dunbar, Paul Laurence
  African American Writers: **87–102**
  American Writers Supp. 2, part 1: **191–219**

Dunsany, Lord
  Supernatural Fiction Writers, vol. 1: **471–478**

Durrell, Lawrence
  British Writers Supp. 1: **93–128**

Eberhart, Richard
  American Writers, vol. 1: **521–543**

Ecclesiastes
  The Books of the Bible, vol. 1: **231–239**

Echeverría, Esteban
  Latin American Writers, vol. 1: **141–145**

Edwards, Amelia B.
  Supernatural Fiction Writers, vol. 1: **255–260**

Eguren, José María
  Latin American Writers, vol. 2: **513–518**

Ehrlich, Gretel
  American Nature Writers, vol. 1: **247–258**

Eiseley, Loren
  American Nature Writers, vol. 1: **269–285**

Ekelöf, Gunnar
  European Writers, vol. 12: **2635–2671**

Eliot, George
   British Writers, vol. 5: **187–201**
   British Writers Selected Authors, vol. 1: **453–467**
Eliot, T. S.
   American Writers, vol. 1: **567–591**
   American Writers Retrospective: **51–71**
   British Writers, vol. 7: **143–170**
   British Writers Selected Authors, vol. 1: **469–496**
Elytis, Odysseus
   European Writers, vol. 13: **2955–2988**
Emerson, Ralph Waldo
   American Nature Writers, vol. 1: **287–307**
   American Writers, vol. 2: **1–24**
Empson, William
   British Writers Supp. 2: **179–198**
Ercilla y Zúñiga, Don Alonso de
   Latin American Writers, vol. 1: **23–31**
Erdrich, Louise
   American Writers Supp. 4, part 1: **259–278**
Etherege, Sir George
   See "Restoration Court Poets, The"
Ewing, Juliana Horatia
   Writers for Children: **221–226**
Ezekiel
   The Books of the Bible, vol. 1: **319–332**
Farjeon, Eleanor
   Writers for Children: **227–234**
Faulkner, William
   American Writers, vol. 2: **54–76**
   American Writers Retrospective: **73–95**
Fauset, Jessie
   Modern American Women Writers: **123–139**
Fernández, Macedonio
   Latin American Writers, vol. 2: **483–491**
Fernández de Lizardi, José Joaquín
   Latin American Writers, vol. 1: **119–128**
Field, Rachel Lyman
   Writers for Children: **235–240**
Fitzgerald, Edward
   British Writers, vol. 4: **340–353**
Fontane, Theodor
   European Writers, vol. 6: **1299–1322**
Ford, Ford Madox
   British Writers, vol. 6: **319–334**
Forms of American Nature Poetry, The
   American Nature Writers, vol. 2: **1079–1098**

Fortune, Dion
   Supernatural Fiction Writers, vol. 2: **585–590**
Foscolo, Ugo
   European Writers, vol. 5: **313–341**
Fouqué, Friedrich de la Motte
   Supernatural Fiction Writers, vol. 1: **97–105**
France, Anatole
   Supernatural Fiction Writers, vol. 1: **67–72**
Freneau, Philip
   American Writers Supp. 2, part 1: **253–277**
Frost, Robert
   American Writers, vol. 2: **150–172**
   American Writers Retrospective: **121–144**
   Writers for Young Adults, vol. 2: **21–31**
Fry, Christopher
   British Writers Supp. 3: **191–210**
Gálvez, Manuel
   Latin American Writers, vol. 2: **585–589**
García Lorca, Federico
   European Writers, vol. 11: **2167–2203**
   European Writers Selected Authors, vol. 1: **595–630**
Garnett, Richard
   Supernatural Fiction Writers, vol. 1: **317–320**
Gautier, Théophile
   European Writers, vol. 6: **1033–1059**
   Supernatural Fiction Writers, vol. 1: **45–50**
Gay, John
   British Writers, vol. 3: **54–68**
Genet, Jean
   European Writers, vol. 13: **2865–2892**
George, Stefan
   European Writers, vol. 8: **447–470**
Ghelderode, Michel de
   European Writers, vol. 11: **2113–2141**
Gilman, Charlotte Perkins
   Modern American Women Writers: **155–170**
Ginsberg, Allen
   American Writers Supp. 2, part 1: **307–333**
Goethe, Johann Wolfgang von
   European Writers, vol. 5: **1–26**
   European Writers Selected Authors, vol. 1: **655–680**
Goldsmith, Oliver
   British Writers, vol. 3: **177–192**
Gómez de Avellaneda, Gertrudis
   Latin American Writers, vol. 1: **175–180**

Gonçalves Dias, Antônio
Latin American Writers, vol. 1: **185–193**

González de Eslava, Fernán
Latin American Writers, vol. 1: **33–37**

González Prada, Manuel
Latin American Writers, vol. 1: **283–288**

Gorostiza, José
Latin American Writers, vol. 2: **923–931**

Gottfried von Strassburg
European Writers, vol. 1: **237–262**
See also "Arthurian Romances"

Gower, John
British Writers, vol. 1: **48–56**

Grahame, Kenneth
Writers for Children: **247–254**

Grass, Günter
European Writers, vol. 13: **3365–3388**
European Writers Selected Authors, vol. 2: **711–734**

Graves, Robert
British Writers, vol. 7: **257–272**

Gray, Thomas
British Writers, vol. 3: **136–145**

Greek Lyric Poets
Ancient Writers, vol. 1: **75–98**

Grillparzer, Franz
European Writers, vol. 5: **417–445**

Guillaume de Lorris
See "*Romance of the Rose*, The, and Medieval Allegory"

Guillén, Nicolás
Latin American Writers, vol. 2: **947–955**

Guimarães Rosa, João
Latin American Writers, vol. 3: **1069–1080**

Güiraldes, Ricardo
Latin American Writers, vol. 2: **619–627**

Gunn, Thom
British Writers Supp. 4: **255–279**

Gunn Allen, Paula
American Writers Supp. 4, part 1: **319–340**

Gunnarsson, Gunnar
European Writers, vol. 10: **1497–1519**

Gutiérrez Nájera, Manuel
Latin American Writers, vol. 1: **351–357**

Habakkuk
The Books of the Bible, vol. 1: **391–396**

Haggai, Zechariah, and Malachi
The Books of the Bible, vol. 1: **405–414**

Hardy, Thomas
British Writers, vol. 6: **1–22**
British Writers Selected Authors, vol. 2: **577–598**

Harper, Frances Ellen Watkins
African American Writers: **159–175**
Modern American Women Writers: **197–205**

Harte, Bret
American Writers Supp. 2, part 1: **335–359**

Hašek, Jaroslav
European Writers, vol. 9: **1091–1118**

Hasselstrom, Linda
American Nature Writers, vol. 1: **337–348**

Hauff, William
Supernatural Fiction Writers, vol. 1: **107–110**

Hauptmann, Gerhart
European Writers, vol. 8: **147–174**

Hay, John
American Nature Writers, vol. 1: **349–362**

Hayden, Robert Earl
African American Writers: **177–192**
American Writers Supp. 2, part 1: **361–383**

Heaney, Seamus
British Writers Supp. 2: **267–282**

Hebbel, Friedrich
European Writers, vol. 6: **1089–1122**

Heine, Heinrich
European Writers, vol. 5: **489–512**

Hellenistic Poetry at Alexandria
Ancient Writers, vol. 1: **449–482**

Herbert, George
British Writers, vol. 2: **117–130**

Heredia, José Mariá
Latin American Writers, vol. 1: **135–140**

Hernández, José
Latin American Writers, vol. 1: **235–247**

Herrera y Reissig, Julio
Latin American Writers, vol. 2: **519–530**

Hesiod
Ancient Writers, vol. 1: **43–73**

Hesse, Hermann
European Writers, vol. 9: **833–859**
European Writers Selected Authors, vol. 2: **735–760**

Hodgson, William Hope
  Supernatural Fiction Writers, vol. 1: **421–428**
Hoffmann, Heinrich
  Writers for Children: **289–294**
Hofmannsthal, Hugo von
  European Writers, vol. 9: **689–714**
Hogan, Linda
  American Nature Writers, vol. 1: **377–388**
  American Writers Supp. 4, part 1: **397–418**
Hogg, James
  Supernatural Fiction Writers, vol. 1: **177–183**
Hölderlin, Friedrich
  European Writers, vol. 5: **143–173**
Holmes, Oliver Wendell
  American Writers Supp. 1, part 1: **299–319**
Homer
  Ancient Writers, vol. 1: **1–41**
Hood, Thomas
  British Writers, vol. 4: **251–267**
Hope, Christopher
  African Writers, vol. 1: **331–343**
Hopkins, Gerard Manley
  British Writers, vol. 5: **361–382**
  British Writers Selected Authors, vol. 2: **599–620**
Horace
  Ancient Writers, vol. 2: **703–731**
Hosea
  The Books of the Bible, vol. 1: **349–358**
Housman, A. E.
  British Writers, vol. 6: **151–164**
  British Writers Selected Authors, vol. 2: **621–634**
Howard, Henry (Earl of Surrey)
  British Writers, vol. 1: **113–120**
Howard, Robert E.
  Supernatural Fiction Writers, vol. 2: **861–868**
Howe, Susan
  American Writers Supp. 4, part 2: **419–438**
Howells, William Dean
  American Writers, vol. 2: **271–294**
Hughes, Langston
  African American Writers: **193–205**
  American Writers Retrospective: **193–214**
  American Writers Supp. 1, part 1: **320–348**
  Writers for Children: **295–301**

Hughes, Ted
  British Writers Supp. 1: **341–366**
Hugo, Victor
  European Writers, vol. 6: **693–718**
  European Writers Selected Authors, vol. 2:
    761–786
Huidobro, Vicente
  Latin American Writers, vol. 2: **755–764**
Ibarbourou, Juana de
  Latin American Writers, vol. 2: **803–807**
Ibycus
  See "Greek Lyric Poets"
Isaacs, Jorge
  Latin American Writers, vol. 1: **247–251**
Isaiah
  The Books of the Bible, vol. 1: **247–279**
Jaimes Freyre, Ricardo
  Latin American Writers, vol. 1: **419–423**
Jarrell, Randall
  American Writers, vol. 2: **367–390**
Jarry, Alfred
  European Writers, vol. 9: **665–687**
Jean de Meun
  See "*Romance of the Rose*, The, and Medieval
    Allegory"
Jeffers, Robinson
  American Writers Supp. 2, part 2: **413–440**
Jeremiah
  The Books of the Bible, vol. 1: **281–301**
Jiménez, Juan Ramón
  European Writers, vol. 9: **991–1016**
Job
  The Books of the Bible, vol. 1: **181–201**
Joel
  The Books of the Bible, vol. 1: **359–365**
Johnson, James Weldon
  African American Writers: **219–233**
Johnson, Josephine
  American Nature Writers, vol. 1: **439–451**
Johnson, Samuel
  British Writers, vol. 3: **107–123**
  British Writers Selected Authors, vol. 2: **647–663**
Jones, David
  See "Poets of World War I (British)"

Jones, Gayl
  African American Writers: **235–244**

Jonson, Ben
  British Writers, vol. 1: **335–352**
  British Writers Selected Authors, vol. 2: **665–681**

Jordan, June
  African American Writers: **245–261**

Juana Inéz de La Cruz, Sor
  Latin American Writers, vol. 1: **85–106**

Juvenal
  See "Persius and Juvenal"

Kästner, Erich
  Writers for Children: **317–322**

Keats, John
  British Writers, vol. 4: **211–238**
  British Writers Selected Authors, vol. 2: **701–727**

Keller, Gottfried
  See "Poetic Realism"

Kerouac, Jack
  American Writers Supp. 3, part 1: **217–234**

Khlebnikov, Velimir
  European Writers, vol. 10: **1331–1364**

Kinnell, Galway
  American Writers Supp. 3, part 1: **235–256**

Kipling, Rudyard
  British Writers, vol. 6: **165–206**
  British Writers Selected Authors, vol. 2: **729–770**
  Supernatural Fiction Writers, vol. 1: **437–442**
  Writers for Children: **329–336**

Kleist, Heinrich von
  European Writers, vol. 5: **291–312**

Klopstock, Friedrich Gottlieb
  European Writers, vol. 4: **511–536**

Kosztolányi, Dezsö
  European Writers, vol. 10: **1231–1249**

Krleža, Miroslav
  European Writers, vol. 11: **1807–1834**

Kumin, Maxine
  American Nature Writers, vol. 1: **479–497**
  American Writers Supp. 4, part 2: **439–457**

Kundera, Milan
  European Writers, vol. 13: **3389–3413**

Kunitz, Stanley
  American Writers Supp. 3, part 1: **257–270**

La Fontaine, Jean de
  European Writers, vol. 3: **73–100**
  European Writers Selected Authors, vol. 2: **901–928**

Laforgue, Jules
  European Writers, vol. 7: **1883–1908**

Laguerre, Enrique A.
  Latin American Writers, vol. 3: **1049–1055**

Lamb, Charles
  British Writers, vol. 4: **73–86**

Lamentations
  The Books of the Bible, vol. 1: **303–318**

Lampedusa, Giuseppe Tomasi di
  European Writers, vol. 11: **2009–2034**

Landor, Walter Savage
  British Writers, vol. 4: **87–100**

Lang, Andrew
  Writers for Children: **337–343**

Langland, William: Piers Plowman
  British Writers, vol. 1: **1–18**

Lanier, Sidney
  American Writers Supp. 1, part 1: **349–373**

Larkin, Phillip
  British Writers Supp. 1: **275–290**

Larreta, Enrique
  Latin American Writers, vol. 2: **471–476**

Laxness, Halldór
  European Writers, vol. 12: **2457–2478**

Lear, Edward
  British Writers, vol. 5: **75–88**
  Writers for Children: **351–356**

Leconte de Lisle, Charles Marie
  European Writers, vol. 6: **1245–1273**

Le Fanu, J. S.
  Supernatural Fiction Writers, vol. 1: **219–231**

Leopardi, Giacomo
  European Writers, vol. 5: **541–567**

Lermontov, Mikhail Yurievich
  European Writers, vol. 6: **1195–1224**

Lessing, Gotthold Ephraim
  European Writers, vol. 4: **537–562**

Levertov, Denise
  American Writers Supp. 3, part 1: **271–287**

Lewis, C. S.
  British Writers Supp. 3: **247–268**
  British Writers Selected Authors, vol. 2: **855–876**
  Science Fiction Writers: **243–248**
  Supernatural Fiction Writers, vol. 2: **661–666**
  Writers for Children: **357–364**
  Writers for Young Adults, vol. 2: **247–255**
Lewis, M. G.
  Supernatural Fiction Writers, vol. 1: **153–160**
Lezama Lima, José
  Latin American Writers, vol. 3: **1125–1130**
Lima, Jorge de
  Latin American Writers, vol. 2: **765–770**
Lindsay, Vachel
  American Writers Supp. 1, part 2: **374–403**
Lofting, Hugh
  Writers for Children: **365–371**
Long, Frank Belknap
  Supernatural Fiction Writers, vol. 2: **869–874**
Longfellow, Henry Wadsworth
  American Writers, vol. 2: **486–510**
Lopez Velarde, Ramon
  Latin American Writers, vol. 2: **663–670**
Lorde, Audre
  African American Writers: **273–288**
Lovelace, Richard
  See "Cavalier Poets, The"
Lowell, Amy
  American Writers, vol. 2: **511–533**
  Modern American Women Writers: **261–268**
Lowell, James Russell
  American Writers Supp. 1, part 2: **404–426**
Lowell, Robert
  American Writers, vol. 2: **534–557**
Lowry, Malcolm
  British Writers Supp. 3: **269–286**
Lucretius
  Ancient Writers, vol. 2: **601–620**
Lugones, Leopoldo
  Latin American Writers, vol. 2: **493–502**
Lydgate, John
  British Writers, vol. 1: **57–66**
Macaulay, Thomas Babington
  British Writers, vol. 4: **268–292**

MacDonald, George
  Supernatural Fiction Writers, vol. 1: **239–246**
  Writers for Children: **373–380**
Machado, Antonio
  European Writers, vol. 9: **743–765**
Machado de Assis, Joaquim Maria
  Latin American Writers, vol. 1: **253–268**
Machiavelli, Niccolò
  European Writers, vol. 2: **595–618**
  European Writers Selected Authors, vol. 2: **953–976**
McKay, Claude
  African American Writers: **305–320**
MacLeish, Archibald
  American Writers, vol. 3: **1–25**
Macleod, Fiona
  Supernatural Fiction Writers, vol. 1: **369–374**
MacNeice, Louis
  British Writers, vol. 7: **401–420**
Maeterlinck, Maurice
  European Writers, vol. 8: **119–146**
Mallarmé, Stéphane
  European Writers, vol. 7: **1567–1595**
Mandelshtam, Osip
  European Writers, vol. 10: **1619–1649**
Manzoni, Alessandro
  European Writers, vol. 5: **367–394**
Marechal, Leopoldo
  Latin American Writers, vol. 2: **887–896**
Mariátegui, José Carlos
  Latin American Writers, vol. 2: **791–796**
Marinetti, Filippo Tommaso
  European Writers, vol. 9: **797–832**
Marlowe, Christopher
  British Writers, vol. 1: **275–294**
Mármol, José
  Latin American Writers, vol. 1: **181–184**
Marqués, René
  Latin American Writers, vol. 3: **1237–1246**
Marston, John, and Cyril Tourneur
  British Writers, vol. 2: **24–41**
Martí, José
  Latin American Writers, vol. 1: **311–320**
Martial
  Ancient Writers, vol. 2: **887–915**

Martínez Estrada, Ezequiel
    Latin American Writers, vol. 2: **809–813**

Marvell, Andrew
    British Writers, vol. 2: **204–220**

Masters, Edgar Lee
    American Writers Supp. 1, part 2: **454–478**

Mattos, Gregório de
    Latin American Writers, vol. 1: **65–69**

Mauriac, François
    European Writers, vol. 10: **1307–1330**

Mayakovsky, Vladimir
    European Writers, vol. 11: **1835–1858**

Medieval Drama
    European Writers, vol. 1: **451–474**
    European Writers Selected Authors, vol. 2:
        1051–1074

Medieval Satire
    European Writers, vol. 1: **337–376**
    European Writers Selected Authors, vol. 2:
        1075–1113

Meinhold, Wilhelm
    Supernatural Fiction Writers, vol. 1: **121–127**

Meireles, Cecília
    Latin American Writers, vol. 2: **915–922**

Melville, Herman
    American Writers, vol. 3: **74–98**
    American Writers Retrospective: **243–262**

Memmi, Albert
    African Writers, vol. 2: **467–477**

Menander
    Ancient Writers, vol. 1: **435–447**

Meredith, George
    British Writers, vol. 5: **219–234**

Mérimée, Prosper
    European Writers, vol. 6: **745–769**
    Supernatural Fiction Writers, vol. 1: **51–57**

Merrill, James
    American Writers Supp. 3, part 1: **317–338**

Merwin, W. S.
    American Writers Supp. 3, part 1: **339–360**

Metaphysical Poets, Four
    British Writers, vol. 2: **179–203**

Meyer, Conrad Ferdinand
    See "Poetic Realism"

Mickiewicz, Adam
    European Writers, vol. 5: **607–634**

Millay, Edna St. Vincent
    American Writers, vol. 3: **122–144**
    Modern American Women Writers: **287–302**

Milne, A. A.
    Writers for Children: **397–405**

Milosz, Czeslaw
    European Writers, vol. 13: **2929–2952**

Milton, John
    British Writers, vol. 2: **158–178**
    British Writers Selected Authors, vol. 2: **925–945**

Mirrlees, Hope
    Supernatural Fiction Writers, vol. 2: **603–607**

Mistral, Gabriela
    Latin American Writers, vol. 2: **677–692**

Molesworth, M. L. S.
    Writers for Children: **407–413**

Molina, Juan Ramón
    Latin American Writers, vol. 2: **539–542**

Molinari, Ricardo E.
    Latin American Writers, vol. 2: **837–844**

Momaday, N. Scott
    American Nature Writers, vol. 2: **639–649**
    American Writers Supp. 4, part 2: **479–495**

Montale, Eugenio
    European Writers, vol. 11: **1987–2008**

Montgomery, L. M.
    Writers for Children: **415–422**
    Writers for Young Adults, vol. 2: **379–386**

Montherlant, Henry de
    European Writers, vol. 11: **1915–1938**

Moore, Marianne
    American Writers, vol. 3: **193–217**
    Modern American Women Writers: **303–316**

Morris, William
    British Writers, vol. 5: **291–308**
    Supernatural Fiction Writers, vol. 1: **299–306**

Mphahlele, Es'kia
    African Writers, vol. 2: **495–510**

Musil, Robert
    European Writers, vol. 9: **931–958**

Musset, Alfred de
    European Writers, vol. 6: **999–1033**

Myers, Walter Dean
  Writers for Young Adults, vol. 2: **387–396**

Nahum
  See "Obadiah and Nahum"

Nathan, Robert
  Supernatural Fiction Writers, vol. 2: **813–819**

Nemerov, Howard
  American Writers, vol. 3: **267–289**

Neruda, Pablo
  Latin American Writers, vol. 3: **1001–1018**

Nerval, Gérard de
  European Writers, vol. 6: **943–970**

Nervo, Amado
  Latin American Writers, vol. 1: **425–429**

Nesbit, E.
  Writers for Children: **423–430**

Neto, Agostinho
  African Writers, vol. 2: **527–535**

Nibelungenlied, The
  European Writers, vol. 1: **211–236**

Nietzsche, Friedrich
  European Writers, vol. 7: **1645–1682**
  European Writers Selected Authors, vol. 2:
      1161–1197

Novalis
  European Writers, vol. 5: **205–231**

Oates, Joyce Carol
  American Writers Supp. 2, part 2: **503–527**
  Modern American Women Writers: **353–374**

Obadiah and Nahum
  The Books of the Bible, vol. 1: **375–380**

O'Brien, Fitz-James
  Supernatural Fiction Writers, vol. 2: **717–722**

Ojaide, Tanure
  African Writers, vol. 2: **557–565**

Okara, Gabriel
  African Writers, vol. 2: **567–582**

Okigbo, Christopher
  African Writers, vol. 2: **583–598**

Okri, Ben
  African Writers, vol. 2: **599–608**

Olesha, Yuri
  European Writers, vol. 11: **2233–2253**

Oña, Pedro de
  Latin American Writers, vol. 1: **59–63**

Ortiz, Simon J.
  American Writers Supp. 4, part 2: **497–515**

Osofisan, Femi
  African Writers, vol. 2: **619–629**

Osundare, Niyi
  African Writers, vol. 2: **631–640**

Ovid
  Ancient Writers, vol. 2: **783–806**

Owen, Wilfred
  British Writers, vol. 6: **443–460**

Pain, Barry
  Supernatural Fiction Writers, vol. 1: **443–448**

Palés Matos, Luis
  Latin American Writers, vol. 2: **821–830**

Paley, Grace
  Modern American Women Writers: **389–396**

Palma, Ricardo
  Latin American Writers, vol. 1: **221–228**

Parker, Dorothy
  Modern American Women Writers: **397–409**

Parra, Nicanor
  Latin American Writers, vol. 3: **1195–1200**

Pascoli, Giovanni
  European Writers, vol. 7: **1825–1854**

Pasternak, Boris
  European Writers, vol. 10: **1591–1618**
  European Writers Selected Authors, vol. 2:
      1227–1253

Paton, Alan
  African Writers, vol. 2: **651–668**
  British Writers Supp. 2: **341–361**
  British Writers Selected Authors, vol. 2:
      963–983

Pavese, Cesare
  European Writers, vol. 12: **2759–2784**

Payró, Roberto Jorge
  Latin American Writers, vol. 1: **413–417**

Paz, Octavio
  Latin American Writers, vol. 3: **1163–1176**

p'Bitek, Okot
  African Writers, vol. 2: **669–684**

Peacock, Thomas Love
  British Writers, vol. 4: **157–170**

Peck, Richard
  Writers for Young Adults, vol. 3: **1–14**

Perrault, Charles
  Writers for Children: **431–437**

Perse, Saint-John
  European Writers, vol. 10: **1429–1452**

Pessoa, Fernando
  European Writers, vol. 10: **1475–1495**

Petrarch, Francesco
  European Writers, vol. 2: **475–507**
  European Writers Selected Authors, vol. 2:
    1255–1287
  See also "Renaissance Pastoral Poetry"

Petronius
  Ancient Writers, vol. 2: **833–853**

Philitas of Cos
  See "Hellenistic Poetry at Alexandria"

Phillpotts, Eden
  Supernatural Fiction Writers, vol. 2: **549–553**

Pindar
  Ancient Writers, vol. 1: **157–177**

Pirandello, Luigi
  European Writers, vol. 8: **389–416**
  European Writers Selected Authors, vol. 2:
    1289–1316

Plath, Sylvia
  American Writers Supp. 1, part 2: **526–549**
  Modern American Women Writers: **411–424**

Plomer, William
  African Writers, vol. 2: **697–706**

Poe, Edgar Allan
  American Writers, vol. 3: **409–432**
  Science Fiction Writers: **11–18**
  Supernatural Fiction Writers, vol. 2: **697–705**
  Writers for Young Adults, vol. 3: **61–73**

Poetic Realism
  European Writers, vol. 6: **913–942**

Poets of World War I (British)
  British Writers, vol. 6: **415–442**
  British Writers Selected Authors, vol. 3: **1445–1471**

Poets of World War II (British)
  British Writers, vol. 7: **421–450**

Pope, Alexander
  British Writers, vol. 3: **68–79**
  British Writers Selected Authors, vol. 2: **1001–1012**

Posidippus
  See "Hellenistic Poetry at Alexandria"

Potter, Beatrix
  British Writers Supp. 3: **287–309**
  Writers for Children: **439–446**

Pound, Ezra
  American Writers, vol. 3: **456–479**
  American Writers Retrospective: **283–294**

Powys, John Cowper
  Supernatural Fiction Writers, vol. 2: **609–616**

Prado, Pedro
  Latin American Writers, vol. 2: **643–647**

Propertius
  See "Tibullus and Propertius" in *Ancient Writers*,
    vol. 2: **917–941**

Proverbs
  The Books of the Bible, vol. 1: **223–230**

Prudentius
  European Writers, vol. 1: **1–22**

Psalms
  The Books of the Bible, vol. 1: **203–221**

Pushkin, Alexander
  European Writers, vol. 5: **659–691**
  European Writers Selected Authors, vol. 3:
    1341–1373

Quasimodo, Salvatore
  European Writers, vol. 12: **2387–2411**

Queneau, Raymond
  European Writers, vol. 12: **2511–2534**

Quiller-Couch, Arthur
  Supernatural Fiction Writers, vol. 1: **389–395**

Ralegh (Raleigh), Sir Walter
  British Writers, vol. 1: **145–159**

Ransom, John Crowe
  American Writers, vol. 3: **480–502**

Read, Herbert
  See "Poets of World War I (British)"

Reed, Ishmael
  African American Writers: **361–377**

Renaissance Pastoral Poetry
  European Writers, vol. 2: **899–926**
  European Writers Selected Authors, vol. 3:
    1403–1430

Restoration Court Poets, The
  British Writers, vol. 2: **255–272**

Reyes, Alfonso
  Latin American Writers, vol. 2: **693–703**

Rich, Adrienne
  American Writers Supp. 1, part 2: **550–578**
  Modern American Women Writers: **441–456**
Richards, I. A.
  British Writers Supp. 2: **405–433**
Richards, Laura E.
  Writers for Children: **469–475**
Rilke, Rainer Maria
  European Writers, vol. 9: **767–796**
  European Writers Selected Authors, vol. 3:
      1461–1489
Rinbaud, Arthur
  European Writers, vol. 7: **1785–1824**
Ríos, Alberto Álvaro
  American Writers Supp. 4, part 2: **537–556**
Ritsos, Yannis
  European Writers, vol. 12: **2815–2842**
Rivera, José Eustasio
  Latin American Writers, vol. 2: **671–675**
Roberts, Elizabeth Madox
  Writers for Children: **477–481**
Robinson, Edwin Arlington
  American Writers, vol. 3: **503–526**
Rojas, Manuel
  Latin American Writers, vol. 2: **815–820**
Rojas, Ricardo
  Latin American Writers, vol. 2: **591–596**
Romance of the Rose, The, and Medieval Allegory
  European Writers, vol. 1: **309–335**
  European Writers Selected Authors, vol. 3:
      1491–1517
Romero, José Rubén
  Latin American Writers, vol. 2: **711–715**
Ronsard, Pierre de, and the Pléiade
  European Writers, vol. 2: **721–746**
Rosenberg, Isaac
  See "Poets of World War I (British)"
Rossetti, Christina
  British Writers, vol. 5: **247–260**
  Writers for Children: **483–491**
Rossetti, Dante Gabriel
  British Writers, vol. 5: **235–246**
Sackville, Charles (Earl of Dorset)
  See "Restoration Court Poets, The"

Sainte-Beuve, Charles-Augustin
  European Writers, vol. 6: **813–861**
Salazar Arrué, Salvador (Salarrué)
  Latin American Writers, vol. 2: **875–879**
Sandburg, Carl
  American Writers, vol. 3: **575–598**
  Writers for Children: **503–510**
  Writers for Young Adults, vol. 3: **123–133**
Sannazaro, Jacopo
  See "Renaissance Pastoral Poetry"
Sappho
  See "Greek Lyric Poets"
Sarduy, Severo
  Latin American Writers, vol. 3: **1437–1444**
Sassoon, Siegfried
  See "Poets of World War I (British)"
Sayers, Dorothy L.
  British Writers Supp. 3: **333–353**
Schiller, Friedrich von
  European Writers, vol. 5: **27–52**
Schlegel, Friedrich von
  European Writers, vol. 5: **177–203**
Schwartz, Delmore
  American Writers Supp. 2, part 2: **639–668**
Scott, Sir Walter
  British Writers, vol. 4: **27–40**
  Supernatural Fiction Writers, vol. 1: **169–176**
Sedley, Sir Charles
  See "Restoration Court Poets, The"
Seferis, George
  European Writers, vol. 12: **2255–2271**
Senghor, Léopold Sédar
  African Writers, vol. 2: **775–789**
Sexton, Anne
  American Writers Supp. 2, part 2: **669–700**
  Modern American Women Writers: **457–470**
Shabbi, Abu al-Qasim, al-
  African Writers, vol. 2: **791–798**
Shakespeare, William
  British Writers, vol. 1: **295–334**
  British Writers Selected Authors, vol. 2: **1013–1052**
  Writers for Young Adults, vol. 3: **155–172**
  See also entries in *William Shakespeare: His World,
      His Work, His Influence*

Shange, Ntozake
African American Writers: **379–393**

Shapiro, Karl
American Writers Supp. 2, part 2: **701–724**

Shelley, Percy Bysshe
British Writers, vol. 4: **195–210**
British Writers Selected Authors, vol. 3: **1105–1120**

Sidney, Sir Philip
British Writers, vol. 1: **160–175**

Sigüenza y Góngora, Carlos de
Latin American Writers, vol. 1: **71–77**

Silko, Leslie Marmon
American Nature Writers, vol. 2: **817–827**
American Writers Supp. 4, part 2: **557–572**

Silone, Ignazione
European Writers, vol. 12: **2273–2305**

Silva, José Asunción
Latin American Writers, vol. 1: **377–385**

Simon, Claude
European Writers, vol. 13: **3021–3048**

Simonides
See "Greek Lyric Poets"

Sinán, Rogelio
Latin American Writers, vol. 2: **941–946**

Sinclair, May
Supernatural Fiction Writers, vol. 1: **513–519**

Sirach (Ecclesiasticus)
The Books of the Bible, vol. 2: **65–86**

Sitwell, Edith
British Writers, vol. 7: **127–143**

Skelton, John
British Writers, vol. 1: **81–96**

Smith, Clark Ashton
Science Fiction Writers: **139–144**
Supernatural Fiction Writers, vol. 2: **875–881**

Smith, Stevie
British Writers Supp. 2: **459–479**

Snyder, Gary
American Nature Writers, vol. 2: **829–846**

Södergran, Edith
European Writers, vol. 11: **1781–1806**

Solzhenitsyn, Aleksandr
European Writers, vol. 13: **3187–3214**
European Writers Selected Authors, vol. 3:
1621–1647

Song of Solomon
The Books of the Bible, vol. 1: **241–246**

Southey, Robert
British Writers, vol. 4: **58–72**

Soyinka, Wole
African Writers, vol. 2: **807–831**

Spagnola, Giovanni Battista (Mantovano)
See "Renaissance Pastoral Poetry"

Spender, Steven
British Writers Supp. 2: **481–496**

Spenser, Edmund
British Writers, vol. 1: **121–144**
British Writers Selected Authors, vol. 3: **1121–1144**

Stapledon, Olaf
Science Fiction Writers: **91–100**

Statius
See "Lucan and Statius"

Stein, Gertrude
American Writers, vol. 4: **25–48**
Modern American Women Writers: **485–498**

Stephens, James
Supernatural Fiction Writers, vol. 1: **485–490**

Stesichorus
See "Greek Lyric Poets"

Stevens, Wallace
American Writers, vol. 4: **73–96**
American Writers Retrospective: **295–315**

Stevenson, Robert Louis
British Writers, vol. 5: **383–399**
British Writers Selected Authors, vol. 3: **1161–1176**
Supernatural Fiction Writers, vol. 1: **307–313**
Writers for Children: **535–543**
Writers for Young Adults, vol. 3: **215–224**

Storm, Theodor
See "Poetic Realism"

Storni, Alfonsina
Latin American Writers, vol. 2: **739–743**

Strand, Mark
American Writers Supp. 4, part 2: **619–636**

Stratton Porter, Gene
American Nature Writers, vol. 2: **877–891**

Suassuna, Ariano Vilar
Latin American Writers, vol. 3: **1317–1321**

Suckling, Sir John
See "Cavalier Poets, The"

Sutherland, Efua Theodora
   African Writers, vol. 2: **833–849**

Swenson, May
   American Writers Supp. 4, part 2: **637–655**

Swift, Jonathan
   British Writers, vol. 3: **15–38**
   British Writers Selected Authors, vol. 3: **1195–1217**
   Writers for Children: **555–559**

Swinburne, Algernon Charles
   British Writers, vol. 5: **309–336**

Tablada, José Juan
   Latin American Writers, vol. 1: **441–446**

Taine, John
   Science Fiction Writers: **75–82**

Tasso, Torquato
   European Writers, vol. 2: **791–818**

Tate, Allen
   American Writers, vol. 4: **120–143**

Taylor, Edward
   American Writers, vol. 4: **144–166**

Tennyson, Alfred Lord
   British Writers, vol. 4: **323–339**
   British Writers Selected Authors, vol. 3: **1219–1235**

Terence
   Ancient Writers, vol. 1: **541–554**

Thaxter, Celia
   American Nature Writers, vol. 2: **905–917**

Theocritus
   Ancient Writers, vol. 1: **483–500**

Thomas, D. M.
   British Writers Supp. 4: **479–497**

Thomas, Dylan
   British Writers Supp. 1: **169–184**
   British Writers Selected Authors, vol. 3: **1261–1276**

Thomas, Edward
   British Writers Supp. 3: **393–408**

Thomas, Joyce Carol
   Writers for Young Adults, vol. 3: **293–301**

Thompson, Francis
   British Writers, vol. 5: **439–452**

Thomson, James
   British Writers Supp. 3: **409–429**

Thoreau, Henry David
   American Nature Writers, vol. 2: **933–950**
   American Writers, vol. 4: **167–189**

Tibullus
   See "Tibullus and Propertius" in *Ancient Writers*,
      vol. 2: **765–782**

Tolkien, J. R. R.
   British Writers Supp. 2: **519–536**
   British Writers Selected Authors, vol. 3: **1277–1294**
   Supernatural Fiction Writers, vol. 2: **675–682**
   Writers for Children: **561–571**
   Writers for Young Adults, vol. 3: **311–320**

Tolson, Melvin
   African American Writers: **413–427**

Toomer, Jean
   African American Writers: **429–440**
   American Writers Supp. 3, part 2: **475–491**

Torres Bodet, Jaime
   Latin American Writers, vol. 2: **933–939**

Tourneur, Cyril
   See "Marston, John, and Cyril Tourneur"

Traherne, Thomas
   See "Metaphysical Poets, Four"

Trakl, Georg
   European Writers, vol. 10: **1409–1427**

Troubadours and Trouvères
   European Writers, vol. 1: **161–184**

Tsvetaeva, Marina
   European Writers, vol. 11: **1731–1750**

Tychyna, Pavlo
   European Writers, vol. 10: **1651–1676**

Unamuno, Miguel de
   European Writers, vol. 8: **283–310**

Ungaretti, Giuseppe
   European Writers, vol. 10: **1453–1473**

Updike, John
   American Writers, vol. 4: **214–235**
   American Writers Retrospective: **317–338**

Urfé, Honoré, d'
   See "Renaissance Pastoral Poetry"

Usigli, Rodolfo
   Latin American Writers, vol. 3: **1033–1042**

Valencia, Guillermo
   Latin American Writers, vol. 2: **477–482**

Valéry, Paul
   European Writers, vol. 8: **569–588**

Valle, Rafael Heliodoro
   Latin American Writers, vol. 2: **721–725**

Valle-Inclán, Ramón del
  European Writers, vol. 8: **331–353**
Vallejo, César
  Latin American Writers, vol. 2: **727–738**
Valle y Caviedes, Juan del
  Latin American Writers, vol. 1: **79–83**
Vaughan, Henry
  See "Metaphysical Poets, Four"
Vega, Lope de
  European Writers, vol. 2: **845–870**
Vergil
  Ancient Writers, vol. 2: **669–701**
Verlaine, Paul
  European Writers, vol. 7: **1619–1643**
Vesaas, Tarjei
  European Writers, vol. 11: **2035–2059**
Vigny, Alfred Victor de
  European Writers, vol. 5: **447–488**
Villaurrutia, Xavier
  Latin American Writers, vol. 3: **975–980**
Villon, François
  European Writers, vol. 2: **535–570**
Voltaire
  European Writers, vol. 4: **367–392**
  European Writers Selected Authors, vol. 3:
    1741–1766
Wagner, Richard
  European Writers, vol. 6: **1147–1168**
  European Writers Selected Authors, vol. 3:
    1767–1787
Walker, Alice
  African American Writers: **441–458**
  American Writers Supp. 3, part 2: **517–540**
  Modern American Women Writers: **511–520**
Walker, Margaret
  African American Writers: **459–471**
Waller, Edmund
  See "Cavalier Poets, The"
Walpole, Horace
  Supernatural Fiction Writers, vol. 1: **131–137**
  See also "Gothic Novel, The"
Walther von der Vogelweide
  European Writers, vol. 1: **287–308**
Warren, Robert Penn
  American Writers, vol. 4: **236–259**

Wedekind, Frank
  European Writers, vol. 8: **229–281**
Wharton, Edith
  American Writers, vol. 4: **308–330**
  American Writers Retrospective: **359-385**
  Modern American Women Writers: **539–558**
  Supernatural Fiction Writers, vol. 2: **783–788**
Wheatley, Phillis
  African American Writers: **473–491**
White, E. B.
  American Writers Supp. 1, part 2: **651–681**
White, T. H.
  Supernatural Fiction Writers, vol. 2: **651–657**
Whitman, Walt
  American Writers, vol. 4: **331–354**
  American Writers Retrospective: **387–410**
Whittier, John Greenleaf
  American Writers Supp. 1, part 2: **682–706**
Wieland, Christoph Martin
  European Writers, vol. 4: **587–614**
Wilbur, Richard
  American Writers Supp. 3, part 2: **541–565**
Wilde, Oscar
  British Writers, vol. 5: **399–422**
  British Writers Selected Authors, vol. 3:
    1353–1376
  Supernatural Fiction Writers, vol. 1: **345–350**
  Writers for Children: **611–616**
Williams, Charles
  Supernatural Fiction Writers, vol. 2: **631–638**
Williams, Tennessee
  American Writers, vol. 4: **378–401**
Williams, Terry Tempest
  American Nature Writers, vol. 2: **973–988**
Williams, William Carlos
  American Writers, vol. 4: **402–425**
  American Writers Retrospective: **411–433**
Wilmot, John (Earl of Rochester)
  See "Restoration Court Poets, The"
Wilson, Edmund
  American Writers, vol. 4: **426–449**
Winters, Yvor
  American Writers Supp. 2, part 2: **785–816**
Wisdom of Solomon
  The Books of the Bible, vol. 2: **51–63**

Wodehouse, P. G.
British Writers Supp. 3: **447–464**
British Writers Selected Authors, vol. 3: **1377–1394**

Wolfram von Eschenbach
European Writers, vol. 1: **263–286**
See also "Arthurian Romances"

Wordsworth, William
British Writers, vol. 4: **1–26**
British Writers Selected Authors, vol. 3: **1419–1444**

Wright, James
American Writers Supp. 3, part 2: **589–607**

Wright, S. Fowler
Science Fiction Writers: **83–89**

Wyatt, Sir Thomas
British Writers, vol. 1: **97–112**

Wylie, Elinor
American Writers Supp. 1, part 2: **707–730**

Yeats, William Butler
British Writers, vol. 6: **207–224**
British Writers Selected Authors, vol. 3:
1473–1490

Yolen, Jane
Writers for Young Adults, vol. 3: **409–420**

Yourcenar, Marguerite
European Writers, vol. 12: **2535–2561**

Zeno Gandía, Manuel
Latin American Writers, vol. 1: **321–326**

Zephaniah
The Books of the Bible, vol. 1: **397–404**

Zorrilla de San Martín, Juan
Latin American Writers, vol. 1: **327–331**

Zukofsky, Louis
American Writers Supp. 3, part 2: **609–632**

DRAMA

Dramatic works for the stage and for the page (closet drama).

Adam de la Halle
See "Medieval Drama"

Aeschylus
Ancient Writers, vol. 1: **99–155**

Aidoo, Ama Ata
African Writers, vol. 1: **37–48**

Ainsworth, William Harrison
Supernatural Fiction Writers, vol. 1: **187–193**

Albee, Edward
American Writers, vol. 1: **71–96**

Alberdi, Juan Bautista
Latin American Writers, vol. 1: **153–158**

Alencar, José de
Latin American Writers, vol. 1: **195–203**

Alfieri, Vittorio
European Writers, vol. 4: **661–689**

Andersen, Hans Christian
European Writers, vol. 6: **863–892**
European Writers Selected Authors, vol. 1: **1–29**
Writers for Children: **7–13**

Anouilh, Jean
European Writers, vol. 13: **2843–2865**
European Writers Selected Authors, vol. 1: **31–52**

Anstey, F.
Supernatural Fiction Writers, vol. 1: **287–292**

Apollinaire, Guillaume
European Writers, vol. 9: **881–903**

Arden, John
British Writers Supp. 2: **21–42**

Arenas, Reinaldo
Latin American Writers, vol. 3: **1451–1458**

Ariosto, Lodovico
European Writers, vol. 2: **619–644**

Aristophanes
Ancient Writers, vol. 1: **291–312**

Arlt, Roberto
Latin American Writers, vol. 2: **881–886**

Arreola, Juan José
Latin American Writers, vol. 3: **1229–1236**

Artaud, Antonin
    European Writers, vol. 11: **1961–1985**
Asher, Sandy
    Writers for Young Adults, vol. 1: **53–61**
Asturias, Miguel Ángel
    Latin American Writers, vol. 2: **865–873**
Auden, W. H.
    American Writers Supp. 2, part 1: **1–28**
    British Writers, vol. 7: **379–399**
    British Writers Selected Authors, vol. 1: **1–21**
Augier, Émile
    See "Well-Made Play, The"
Awoonor, Kofi
    African Writers, vol. 1: **63–75**
Aymé, Marcel
    European Writers, vol. 12: **2433–2456**
Azorín
    European Writers, vol. 9: **639–661**
Azuela, Mariano
    Latin American Writers, vol. 2: **457–464**
Babel, Isaac
    European Writers, vol. 11: **1885–1915**
    European Writers Selected Authors, vol. 1: **131–160**
Baraka, Amiri
    African American Writers: **15–29**
    American Writers Supp. 2, part 1: **29–63**
Barnes, Djuna
    American Writers Supp. 3, part 1: **31–46**
Barrie, J. M.
    British Writers Supp. 3: **1–17**
    Supernatural Fiction Writers, vol. 1: **405–410**
    Writers for Children: **29–35**
Barrios, Eduardo
    Latin American Writers, vol. 2: **611–618**
Bauernfeld, Eduard von
    See "Well-Made Play, The"
Baum, L. Frank
    Writers for Children: **37–48**
Beaumarchais, Pierre-Augustin Caron de
    European Writers, vol. 4: **563–585**
Beaumont, Francis
    See "Beaumont, Francis, and John Fletcher"
Beaumont, Francis, and John Fletcher
    British Writers, vol. 2: **42–67**

Beckett, Samuel
    British Writers Supp. 1: **43–64**
    British Writers Selected Authors, vol. 1: **47–68**
Behan, Brendan
    British Writers Supp. 2: **61–76**
Behn, Aphra
    British Writers Supp. 3: **19–43**
Bello, Andrés
    Latin American Writers, vol. 1: **129–134**
Benedetti, Mario
    Latin American Writers, vol. 3: **1255–1263**
Bennett, Arnold
    British Writers, vol. 6: **247–268**
Bioy Casares, Adolfo
    Latin American Writers, vol. 3: **1201–1208**
Blasco Ibáñez, Vicente
    European Writers, vol. 8: **355–388**
Blest Gana, Alberto
    Latin American Writers, vol. 1: **205–213**
Blok, Alexander
    European Writers, vol. 9: **959–990**
Bond, Edward
    British Writers Supp. 1: **421–436**
Bradbury, Ray
    American Writers Supp. 4, part 1: **101–118**
    Supernatural Fiction Writers: **171–178**
    Supernatural Fiction Writers, vol. 2: **917–923**
Brecht, Bertolt
    European Writers, vol. 11: **2089–2112**
    European Writers Selected Authors, vol. 1: **281–303**
Brieux, Eugène
    See "Well-Made Play, The"
Brooke, Rupert
    British Writers Supp. 3: **45–61**
    See also "Poets of World War I (British)"
Browning, Robert
    British Writers, vol. 4: **354–375**
    British Writers Selected Authors, vol. 1: **193–214**
Büchner, Georg
    European Writers, vol. 6: **1169–1194**
Burnett, Frances Hodgson
    Writers for Children: **103–109**
Byron, Lord
    British Writers, vol. 4: **171–194**
    British Writers Selected Authors, vol. 1: **245–268**

Calderón de la Barca, Pedro
  European Writers, vol. 2: **871–895**
Camus, Albert
  African Writers, vol. 1: **139–152**
  European Writers, vol. 13: **3049–3078**
  European Writers Selected Authors, vol. 1: **305–334**
Canetti, Elias
  European Writers, vol. 12: **2615–2633**
Čapek, Karel
  European Writers, vol. 10: **1565–1590**
  Science Fiction Writers: **583–589**
Capote, Truman
  American Writers Supp. 3, part 1: **111–133**
Carballido, Emilio
  Latin American Writers, vol. 3: **1289–1294**
Carew, Thomas
  See "Cavalier Poets, The"
Carter, Alden R.
  Writers for Young Adults, vol. 1: **209–218**
Castellanos, Rosario
  Latin American Writers, vol. 3: **1295–1302**
Castro Alves, Antônio de
  Latin American Writers, vol. 1: **289–297**
Cavalier Poets, The
  British Writers, vol. 2: **221–239**
Cela, Camilo José
  European Writers, vol. 13: **3105–3129**
Céline, Louis-Ferdinand
  European Writers, vol. 11: **1859–1884**
Cervantes, Miguel de
  European Writers, vol. 2: **819–844**
  European Writers Selected Authors, vol. 1:
    335–359
  See also "Renaissance Short Fiction"
Chambers, Robert W.
  Supernatural Fiction Writers, vol. 2: **739–745**
Chapman, George
  British Writers, vol. 1: **232–256**
Chateaubriand, François René de
  European Writers, vol. 5: **113–140**
Chekhov, Anton
  European Writers, vol. 7: **1855–1882**
  European Writers Selected Authors, vol. 1: **361–387**
Childress, Alice
  Writers for Young Adults, vol. 1: **229–240**

Chocano, José Santos
  Latin American Writers, vol. 2: **543–549**
Christie, Agatha
  British Writers Supp. 2: **123–137**
Churchill, Caryl
  British Writers Supp. 4: **179–200**
Clark, John Pepper
  African Writers, vol. 1: **153–166**
Claudel, Paul
  European Writers, vol. 8: **471–494**
Cocteau, Jean
  European Writers, vol. 10: **1543–1564**
Colette
  European Writers, vol. 9: **617–638**
  European Writers Selected Authors, vol. 1: **389–410**
Collodi, C.
  Writers for Children: **129–137**
Colum, Padraic
  Writers for Children: **139–146**
Congreve, William
  British Writers, vol. 2: **338–350**
Corneille, Pierre
  European Writers, vol. 3: **23–49**
Costa, Cláudio Manuel da
  Latin American Writers, vol. 1: **113–117**
Coward, Noël
  British Writers Supp. 2: **139–158**
Cowley, Abraham
  See "Metaphysical Poets, Four"
Crawford, F. Marion
  Supernatural Fiction Writers, vol. 2: **747–751**
D'Annunzio, Gabriele
  European Writers, vol. 8: **175–203**
De la Mare, Walter
  Supernatural Fiction Writers, vol. 1: **497–503**
  Writers for Children: **173–180**
Denevi, Marco
  Latin American Writers, vol. 3: **1265–1269**
Díaz, Jorge
  Latin American Writers, vol. 3: **1393–1397**
Doctorow, E. L.
  American Writers Supp. 4, part 1: **217–240**
Dos Passos, John
  American Writers, vol. 1: **474–496**

Dragún, Osvaldo
  Latin American Writers, vol. 3: **1377–1382**
Dryden, John
  British Writers, vol. 2: **289–306**
Dumas, Alexandre (Fils)
  See "Well-Made Play, The"
Dumas, Alexandre (Père)
  European Writers, vol. 6: **719–745**
  European Writers Selected Authors, vol. 1:
    503–527
  Writers for Children: **209–213**
Du Maurier, Daphne
  British Writers Supp. 3: **133–149**
  British Writers Selected Authors, vol. 1: **435–451**
Dunsany, Lord
  Supernatural Fiction Writers, vol. 1: **471–478**
Durrell, Lawrence
  British Writers Supp. 1: **93–128**
Dürrenmatt, Friedrich
  European Writers, vol. 13: **3215–3235**
Egbuna, Obi
  African Writers, vol. 1: **209–221**
Eichelbaum, Samuel
  Latin American Writers, vol. 2: **797–801**
Eliot, T. S.
  American Writers, vol. 1: **567–591**
  American Writers Retrospective: **51–71**
  British Writers, vol. 7: **143–170**
  British Writers Selected Authors, vol. 1: **469–496**
Etherege, Sir George
  See "Restoration Court Poets, The"
Euripides
  Ancient Writers, vol. 1: **233–266**
Farah, Nuruddin
  African Writers, vol. 1: **249–262**
Farjeon, Eleanor
  Writers for Children: **227–234**
Farquhar, George
  British Writers, vol. 2: **351–365**
Fernández de Lizardi, José Joaquín
  Latin American Writers, vol. 1: **119–128**
Feydeau, Georges
  See "Well-Made Play, The"
Field, Rachel Lyman
  Writers for Children: **235–240**

Fielding, Henry
  British Writers, vol. 3: **94–106**
  British Writers Selected Authors, vol. 2: **497–509**
Fletcher, John
  See "Beaumont, Francis, and John Fletcher"
Ford, John
  British Writers, vol. 2: **87–102**
Foscolo, Ugo
  European Writers, vol. 5: **313–341**
Fouqué, Friedrich de la Motte
  Supernatural Fiction Writers, vol. 1: **97–105**
France, Anatole
  Supernatural Fiction Writers, vol. 1: **67–72**
Freytag, Gustav
  See "Well-Made Play, The"
Frisch, Max
  European Writers, vol. 13: **2895–2924**
Fry, Christopher
  British Writers Supp. 3: **191–210**
Fuentes, Carlos
  Latin American Writers, vol. 3: **1353–1376**
Fugard, Athol
  African Writers, vol. 1: **263–275**
Galsworthy, John
  British Writers, vol. 6: **269–293**
Gálvez, Manuel
  Latin American Writers, vol. 2: **585–589**
Gambaro, Griselda
  Latin American Writers, vol. 3: **1323–1328**
Gamboa, Federico
  Latin American Writers, vol. 1: **371–375**
García Lorca, Federico
  European Writers, vol. 11: **2167–2203**
  European Writers Selected Authors, vol. 1:
    595–630
Garfield, Leon
  Writers for Young Adults, vol. 2: **33–45**
Garnett, Richard
  Supernatural Fiction Writers, vol. 1: **317–320**
Gautier, Théophile
  European Writers, vol. 6: **1033–1059**
  Supernatural Fiction Writers, vol. 1: **45–50**
Gay, John
  British Writers, vol. 3: **54–68**

Genet, Jean
    European Writers, vol. 13: **2865–2892**
Ghelderode, Michel de
    European Writers, vol. 11: **2113–2141**
Gide, André
    European Writers, vol. 8: **495–518**
    European Writers Selected Authors, vol. 1:
        631–654
Gilman, Charlotte Perkins
    Modern American Women Writers: **155–170**
Ginzburg, Natalia
    European Writers, vol. 13: **3131–3163**
Giraudoux, Jean
    European Writers, vol. 9: **1041–1065**
Glaspell, Susan
    American Writers Supp. 3, part 1: **175–191**
    Modern American Women Writers: **181–188**
Goethe, Johann Wolfgang von
    European Writers, vol. 5: **1–26**
    European Writers Selected Authors, vol. 1:
        655–680
Gogol, Nikolay Vasilievich
    European Writers, vol. 6: **971–998**
Goldoni, Carlo
    European Writers, vol. 4: **421–448**
Goldsmith, Oliver
    British Writers, vol. 3: **177–192**
Gombrowicz, Witold
    European Writers, vol. 12: **2563–2588**
Gómez de Avellaneda, Gertrudis
    Latin American Writers, vol. 1: **175–180**
Gonçalves Dias, Antônio
    Latin American Writers, vol. 1: **185–193**
Goncharov, Ivan
    European Writers, vol. 6: **1061–1087**
Goncourt, Edmond Louis Antoine de, and Jules
        Alfred Huot de Goncourt
    European Writers, vol. 7: **1395–1419**
González de Eslava, Fernán
    Latin American Writers, vol. 1: **33–37**
González Prada, Manuel
    Latin American Writers, vol. 1: **283–288**
Gorky, Maxim
    European Writers, vol. 8: **417–446**
    European Writers Selected Authors, vol. 2:
        681–710

Grass, Günter
    European Writers, vol. 13: **3365–3388**
    European Writers Selected Authors, vol. 2: **711–734**
Gregory, Lady Augusta
    See "Synge, J. M., and Lady Augusta Gregory"
Grillparzer, Franz
    European Writers, vol. 5: **417–445**
Gunnarsson, Gunnar
    European Writers, vol. 10: **1497–1519**
Gutzkow, Karl
    See "Well-Made Play, The"
Ḥakīm, Tawfīq, al-
    African Writers, vol. 1: **291–301**
Hansberry, Lorraine
    African American Writers: **147–158**
    American Writers Supp. 4, part 1: **359–377**
Hardy, Thomas
    British Writers, vol. 6: **1–22**
    British Writers Selected Authors, vol. 2: **577–598**
Hare, David
    British Writers Supp. 4: **281–300**
Hauptmann, Gerhart
    European Writers, vol. 8: **147–174**
Hebbel, Friedrich
    European Writers, vol. 6: **1089–1122**
Heiremans, Luis Alberto
    Latin American Writers, vol. 3: **1347–1352**
Heller, Joseph
    American Writers Supp. 4, part 1: **379–396**
Hellman, Lillian
    American Writers Supp. 1, part 1: **276–298**
    Modern American Women Writers: **207–220**
Heredia, José Mariá
    Latin American Writers, vol. 1: **135–140**
Hervieu, Paul
    See "Well-Made Play, The"
Hoffmann, E. T. A.
    European Writers, vol. 5: **261–289**
    Supernatural Fiction Writers, vol. 1: **111–119**
    Writers for Children: **283–288**
Hofmannsthal, Hugo von
    European Writers, vol. 9: **689–714**
Hölderlin, Friedrich
    European Writers, vol. 5: **143–173**
Howells, William Dean
    American Writers, vol. 2: **271–294**

Hughes, Langston
  African American Writers: **193–205**
  American Writers Retrospective: **193–214**
  American Writers Supp. 1, part 1: **320–348**
  Writers for Children: **295–301**

Hughes, Ted
  British Writers Supp. 1: **341–366**

Hugo, Victor
  European Writers, vol. 6: **693–718**
  European Writers Selected Authors, vol. 2:
    761–786

Huidobro, Vicente
  Latin American Writers, vol. 2: **755–764**

Hurston, Zora Neale
  African American Writers: **205–218**
  Modern American Women Writers: **221–235**

Ibsen, Henrik
  European Writers, vol. 7: **1421–1448**
  European Writers Selected Authors, vol. 2: **787–813**

Icaza, Jorge
  Latin American Writers, vol. 3: **1063–1067**

Idrīs, Yūsuf
  African Writers, vol. 1: **345–365**

Ionesco, Eugène
  European Writers, vol. 13: **2989–3020**
  European Writers Selected Authors, vol. 2: **815–846**

Jaimes Freyre, Ricardo
  Latin American Writers, vol. 1: **419–423**

Jarry, Alfred
  European Writers, vol. 9: **665–687**

Jones, Gayl
  African American Writers: **235–244**

Jones, Henry Arthur
  See "Well-Made Play, The"

Jonson, Ben
  British Writers, vol. 1: **335–352**
  British Writers Selected Authors, vol. 2: **665–681**

Jordan, June
  African American Writers: **245–261**

Juana Inéz de La Cruz, Sor
  Latin American Writers, vol. 1: **85–106**

Kateb, Yacine
  African Writers, vol. 1: **391–400**

Kazantzakis, Nikos
  European Writers, vol. 9: **1067–1091**

Keneally, Thomas
  British Writers Supp. 4: **343–362**

Khlebnikov, Velimir
  European Writers, vol. 10: **1331–1364**

Kipling, Rudyard
  British Writers, vol. 6: **165–206**
  British Writers Selected Authors, vol. 2: **729–770**
  Supernatural Fiction Writers, vol. 1: **437–442**
  Writers for Children: **329–336**

Kleist, Heinrich von
  European Writers, vol. 5: **291–312**

Klopstock, Friedrich Gottlieb
  European Writers, vol. 4: **511–536**

Kosztolányi, Dezsö
  European Writers, vol. 10: **1231–1249**

Krleža, Miroslav
  European Writers, vol. 11: **1807–1834**

Kundera, Milan
  European Writers, vol. 13: **3389–3413**

Kyd, Thomas, and Early Elizabethan Tragedy
  British Writers, vol. 1: **212–231**

Labiche, Eugène
  See "Well-Made Play, The"

La Fontaine, Jean de
  European Writers, vol. 3: **73–100**
  European Writers Selected Authors, vol. 2: **901–928**

Lagerkvist, Pär
  European Writers, vol. 10: **1677–1702**

Laguerre, Enrique A.
  Latin American Writers, vol. 3: **1049–1055**

Larreta, Enrique
  Latin American Writers, vol. 2: **471–476**

Laxness, Halldór
  European Writers, vol. 12: **2457–2478**

Lee, Tanith
  Supernatural Fiction Writers, vol. 2: **1053–1058**

Lermontov, Mikhail Yurievich
  European Writers, vol. 6: **1195–1224**

Lesage, Alain-René
  European Writers, vol. 3: **317–344**

Lessing, Gotthold Ephraim
  European Writers, vol. 4: **537–562**

Lewis, M. G.
  Supernatural Fiction Writers, vol. 1: **153–160**

London, Jack
  American Writers, vol. 2: **462–485**
  Writers for Young Adults, vol. 2: **267–278**
Lowell, Robert
  American Writers, vol. 2: **534–557**
Lyly, John, and George Peele
  British Writers, vol. 1: **191–211**
McCullers, Carson
  American Writers, vol. 2: **585–608**
  Modern American Women Writers: **279–287**
Machado, Antonio
  European Writers, vol. 9: **743–765**
Machado de Assis, Joaquim Maria
  Latin American Writers, vol. 1: **253–268**
Machiavelli, Niccolò
  European Writers, vol. 2: **595–618**
  European Writers Selected Authors, vol. 2: **953–976**
MacLeish, Archibald
  American Writers, vol. 3: **1–25**
Macleod, Fiona
  Supernatural Fiction Writers, vol. 1: **369–374**
Maeterlinck, Maurice
  European Writers, vol. 8: **119–146**
Maḥfūẓ, Najīb
  African Writers, vol. 2: **451–465**
Mallea, Eduardo
  Latin American Writers, vol. 3: **981–989**
Mann, Heinrich
  European Writers, vol. 8: **519–543**
Mann, Thomas
  European Writers, vol. 9: **715–743**
  European Writers Selected Authors, vol. 2: **997–1024**
Manzoni, Alessandro
  European Writers, vol. 5: **367–394**
Marechal, Leopoldo
  Latin American Writers, vol. 2: **887–896**
Mariátegui, José Carlos
  Latin American Writers, vol. 2: **791–796**
Marín Cañas, José
  Latin American Writers, vol. 3: **991–994**
Marinetti, Filippo Tommaso
  European Writers, vol. 9: **797–832**
Marlowe, Christopher
  British Writers, vol. 1: **275–294**

Mármol, José
  Latin American Writers, vol. 1: **181–184**
Marqués, René
  Latin American Writers, vol. 3: **1237–1246**
Marryat, Frederick
  Writers for Children: **381–387**
Marston, John
  See "Marston, John, and Cyril Tourneur"
Marston, John, and Cyril Tourneur
  British Writers, vol. 2: **24–41**
Matto de Turner, Clorinda
  Latin American Writers, vol. 1: **305–309**
Maturin, Charles Robert
  Supernatural Fiction Writers, vol. 1: **161–168**
Maugham, W. Somerset
  British Writers, vol. 6: **363–382**
  British Writers Selected Authors, vol. 2: **905–923**
Mauriac, François
  European Writers, vol. 10: **1307–1330**
Mayakovsky, Vladimir
  European Writers, vol. 11: **1835–1858**
Medieval Drama
  European Writers, vol. 1: **451–474**
  European Writers Selected Authors, vol. 2: **1051–1074**
Meigs, Cornelia
  Writers for Children: **389–395**
Meireles, Cecília
  Latin American Writers, vol. 2: **915–922**
Menander
  Ancient Writers, vol. 1: **435–447**
Mérimée, Prosper
  European Writers, vol. 6: **745–769**
  Supernatural Fiction Writers, vol. 1: **51–57**
Merrill, James
  American Writers Supp. 3, part 1: **317–338**
Merwin, W. S.
  American Writers Supp. 3, part 1: **339–360**
Metaphysical Poets, Four
  British Writers, vol. 2: **179–203**
Mickiewicz, Adam
  European Writers, vol. 5: **607–634**
Middleton, Thomas
  British Writers, vol. 2: **1–23**

Millay, Edna St. Vincent
  American Writers, vol. 3: **122–144**
  Modern American Women Writers: **287–302**

Miller, Arthur
  American Writers, vol. 3: **145–169**

Milne, A. A.
  Writers for Children: **397–405**

Moberg, Vilhelm
  European Writers, vol. 11: **2203–2231**

Molière
  European Writers, vol. 3: **101–124**
  European Writers Selected Authors, vol. 2:
    1115–1137

Montherlant, Henry de
  European Writers, vol. 11: **1915–1938**

Moore, George
  British Writers, vol. 6: **85–100**

Moravia, Alberto
  European Writers, vol. 12: **2673–2697**

Musil, Robert
  European Writers, vol. 9: **931–958**

Musset, Alfred de
  European Writers, vol. 6: **999–1033**

Nerval, Gérard de
  European Writers, vol. 6: **943–970**

Ngũgĩ wa Thiong'o
  African Writers, vol. 2: **537–555**

Oates, Joyce Carol
  American Writers Supp. 2, part 2: **503–527**
  Modern American Women Writers: **353–374**

O'Brien, Fitz-James
  Supernatural Fiction Writers, vol. 2: **717–722**

O'Casey, Sean
  British Writers, vol. 7: **1–16**

Odets, Clifford
  American Writers Supp. 2, part 2: **529–554**

Olesha, Yuri
  European Writers, vol. 11: **2233–2253**

Omotoso, Kole
  African Writers, vol. 2: **609–617**

O'Neill, Eugene
  American Writers, vol. 3: **385–408**

Osborne, John
  British Writers Supp. 1: **329–340**

Osofisan, Femi
  African Writers, vol. 2: **619–629**

Palma, Ricardo
  Latin American Writers, vol. 1: **221–228**

Parker, Dorothy
  Modern American Women Writers: **397–409**

Paton, Alan
  African Writers, vol. 2: **651–668**
  British Writers Supp. 2: **341–361**
  British Writers Selected Authors, vol. 2: **963–983**

Payró, Roberto Jorge
  Latin American Writers, vol. 1: **413–417**

Peele, George
  See "Lyly, John, and George Peele"

Pepetela
  African Writers, vol. 2: **685–695**

Pérez Galdós, Benito
  European Writers, vol. 7: **1597–1618**

Phillpotts, Eden
  Supernatural Fiction Writers, vol. 2: **549–553**

Pinero, Arthur Wing
  See "Well-Made Play, The"

Pinter, Harold
  British Writers Supp. 1: **367–382**
  British Writers Selected Authors, vol. 2: **985–1000**

Pirandello, Luigi
  European Writers, vol. 8: **389–416**
  European Writers Selected Authors, vol. 2:
    1289–1316

Plautus
  Ancient Writers, vol. 1: **501–523**

Prado, Pedro
  Latin American Writers, vol. 2: **643–647**

Priestley, J. B.
  British Writers, vol. 7: **209–232**

Puig, Manuel
  Latin American Writers, vol. 3: **1405–1413**

Pushkin, Alexander
  European Writers, vol. 5: **659–691**
  European Writers Selected Authors, vol. 3:
    1341–1373

Queiroz, Rachel de
  Latin American Writers, vol. 3: **1119–1123**

Queneau, Raymond
  European Writers, vol. 12: **2511–2534**

Racine, Jean
   European Writers, vol. 3: **207–228**
Rand, Ayn
   American Writers Supp. 4, part 2: **517–535**
Restoration Court Poets, The
   British Writers, vol. 2: **255–272**
Rich, Adrienne
   American Writers Supp. 1, part 2: **550–578**
   Modern American Women Writers: **441–456**
Richards, I. A.
   British Writers Supp. 2: **405–433**
Rilke, Rainer Maria
   European Writers, vol. 9: **767–796**
   European Writers Selected Authors, vol. 3:
      1461–1489
Ritsos, Yannis
   European Writers, vol. 12: **2815–2842**
Robertson, Thomas W.
   See "Well-Made Play, The"
Rojas, Ricardo
   Latin American Writers, vol. 2: **591–596**
Rotimi, Ola
   African Writers, vol. 2: **707–720**
Russ, Joanna
   Science Fiction Writers: **483–490**
Saʿadāwī, Nawāl, al-
   African Writers, vol. 2: **721–731**
Sade, Marquis de, and the French Libertine
      Tradition
   European Writers, vol. 4: **615–638**
Sánchez, Florencio
   Latin American Writers, vol. 2: **531–538**
Sardou, Victor
   See "Well-Made Play, The"
Sarduy, Severo
   Latin American Writers, vol. 3: **1437–1444**
Sarraute, Nathalie
   European Writers, vol. 12: **2333–2359**
Sartre, Jean-Paul
   European Writers, vol. 12: **2589–2614**
   European Writers Selected Authors, vol. 3: **1595–1620**
Sayers, Dorothy L.
   British Writers Supp. 3: **333–353**
Schiller, Friedrich von
   European Writers, vol. 5: **27–52**

Schlegel, Friedrich von
   European Writers, vol. 5: **177–203**
Schnitzler, Arthur
   European Writers, vol. 8: **89–117**
Scoppettone, Sandra
   Writers for Young Adults, vol. 3: **135–143**
Scribe, Augustin Eugène
   See "Well-Made Play, The"
Sedley, Sir Charles
   See "Restoration Court Poets, The"
Sembène Ousmane
   African Writers, vol. 2: **765–774**
Seneca the Younger
   Ancient Writers, vol. 2: **807–832**
Shaffer, Peter
   British Writers Supp. 1: **313–328**
Shakespeare, William
   British Writers, vol. 1: **295–334**
   British Writers Selected Authors, vol. 2: **1013–1052**
   Writers for Young Adults, vol. 3: **155–172**
   See also entries in *William Shakespeare: His World,
      His Work, His Influence*
Shange, Ntozake
   African American Writers: **379–393**
Shaw, George Bernard
   British Writers, vol. 6: **101–132**
   British Writers Selected Authors, vol. 3: **1053–1084**
Shelley, Percy Bysshe
   British Writers, vol. 4: **195–210**
   British Writers Selected Authors, vol. 3:
      1105–1120
Shepard, Sam
   American Writers Supp. 3, part 2: **431–450**
Sheridan, Richard Brinsley
   British Writers, vol. 3: **252–271**
Silone, Ignazione
   European Writers, vol. 12: **2273–2305**
Silveira de Queiroz, Dinah
   Latin American Writers, vol. 3: **1145–1151**
Simon, Neil
   American Writers Supp. 4, part 2: **573–594**
Sinán, Rogelio
   Latin American Writers, vol. 2: **941–946**
Sophocles
   Ancient Writers, vol. 1: **179–207**

Sowande, Bode
    African Writers, vol. 2: **799–806**

Soyinka, Wole
    African Writers, vol. 2: **807–831**

Steele, Sir Richard
    See "Steele, Sir Richard, and Joseph Addison" in
    British Writers, vol. 3: **38–53**; *British Writers
    Selected Authors*, vol. 3: **1145–1160**

Stein, Gertrude
    American Writers, vol. 4: **25–48**
    Modern American Women Writers: **485–498**

Steinbeck, John
    American Writers, vol. 4: **49–72**
    Writers for Young Adults, vol. 3: **203–214**

Stoppard, Tom
    British Writers Supp. 1: **437–454**
    British Writers Selected Authors, vol. 3: **1177–1194**

Storey, David
    British Writers Supp. 1: **407–420**

Storni, Alfonsina
    Latin American Writers, vol. 2: **739–743**

Strindberg, August
    European Writers, vol. 7: **1731–1758**

Suassuna, Ariano Vilar
    Latin American Writers, vol. 3: **1317–1321**

Suckling, Sir John
    See "Cavalier Poets, The"

Sutherland, Efua Theodora
    African Writers, vol. 2: **833–849**

Svevo, Italo
    European Writers, vol. 8: **67–87**

Swenson, May
    American Writers Supp. 4, part 2: **637–655**

Swinburne, Algernon Charles
    British Writers, vol. 5: **309–336**

Synge, J. M.
    See "Synge, J. M., and Lady Augusta Gregory"

Synge, J. M., and Lady Augusta Gregory
    British Writers, vol. 6: **307–318**

Tablada, José Juan
    Latin American Writers, vol. 1: **441–446**

Tasso, Torquato
    European Writers, vol. 2: **791–818**

Tennyson, Alfred Lord
    British Writers, vol. 4: **323–339**
    British Writers Selected Authors, vol. 3: **1219–1235**

Terence
    Ancient Writers, vol. 1: **541–554**

Thomas, Dylan
    British Writers Supp. 1: **169–184**
    British Writers Selected Authors, vol. 3: **1261–1276**

Thomas, Joyce Carol
    Writers for Young Adults, vol. 3: **293–301**

Thomson, James
    British Writers Supp. 3: **409–429**

Thurber, James
    American Writers Supp. 1, part 2: **602–627**
    Supernatural Fiction Writers, vol. 2: **827–831**

Tieck, Ludwig
    European Writers, vol. 5: **233–260**
    Supernatural Fiction Writers, vol. 1: **83–89**

Tolstoy, Leo
    European Writers, vol. 7: **1471–1494**
    European Writers Selected Authors, vol. 3:
        1693–1715

Toomer, Jean
    African American Writers: **429–440**
    American Writers Supp. 3, part 2: **475–491**

Tourneur, Cyril
    See "Marston, John, and Cyril Tourneur"

Triana, José
    Latin American Writers, vol. 3: **1415–1419**

Tsvetaeva, Marina
    European Writers, vol. 11: **1731–1750**

Unamuno, Miguel de
    European Writers, vol. 8: **283–310**

Usigli, Rodolfo
    Latin American Writers, vol. 3: **1033–1042**

Uslar Pietri, Arturo
    Latin American Writers, vol. 3: **1057–1062**

Valle-Inclán, Ramón del
    European Writers, vol. 8: **331–353**

Valle y Caviedes, Juan del
    Latin American Writers, vol. 1: **79–83**

Vanbrugh, Sir John
    British Writers, vol. 2: **323–337**

Vasconcelos, José
    Latin American Writers, vol. 2: **575–584**

Vega, Lope de
    European Writers, vol. 2: **845–870**

Verga, Giovanni
 European Writers, vol. 7: **1543–1565**

Verne, Jules
 Science Fiction Writers: **573–582**
 Writers for Children: **591–598**

Vesaas, Tarjei
 European Writers, vol. 11: **2035–2059**

Vidal, Gore
 American Writers Supp. 4, part 2: **677–697**

Villaurrutia, Xavier
 Latin American Writers, vol. 3: **975–980**

Voltaire
 European Writers, vol. 4: **367–392**
 European Writers Selected Authors, vol. 3:
  1741–1766

Vonnegut, Kurt
 American Writers Supp. 2, part 2: **753–783**
 Science Fiction Writers: **551–561**

Wagner, Richard
 European Writers, vol. 6: **1147–1168**
 European Writers Selected Authors, vol. 3:
  1767–1787

Wakefield, H. Russell
 Supernatural Fiction Writers, vol. 2: **617–622**

Wall, Mervyn
 Supernatural Fiction Writers, vol. 2: **645–650**

Webster, John
 British Writers, vol. 2: **68–86**

Wedekind, Frank
 European Writers, vol. 8: **229–281**

Weldon, Fay
 British Writers Supp. 4: **521–539**

Well-Made Play, The
 European Writers, vol. 7: **1909–1934**

White, Patrick
 British Writers Supp. 1: **129–152**

Wieland, Christoph Martin
 European Writers, vol. 4: **587–614**

Wilde, Oscar
 British Writers, vol. 5: **399–422**
 British Writers Selected Authors, vol. 3: **1353–1376**
 Supernatural Fiction Writers, vol. 1: **345–350**
 Writers for Children: **611–616**

Wilder, Thornton
 American Writers, vol. 4: **355–377**

Williams, Charles
 Supernatural Fiction Writers, vol. 2: **631–638**

Williams, Tennessee
 American Writers, vol. 4: **378–401**

Wilson, Edmund
 American Writers, vol. 4: **426–449**

Witkiewicz (Witkacy), Stanisław Ignacy
 European Writers, vol. 10: **1205–1230**

Wodehouse, P. G.
 British Writers Supp. 3: **447–464**
 British Writers Selected Authors, vol. 3: **1377–1394**

Wolfe, Thomas
 American Writers, vol. 4: **450–473**

Wolff, Egon
 Latin American Writers, vol. 3: **1311–1315**

Wycherley, William
 British Writers, vol. 2: **307–322**

Yeats, William Butler
 British Writers, vol. 6: **207–224**
 British Writers Selected Authors, vol. 3: **1473–1490**

Yourcenar, Marguerite
 European Writers, vol. 12: **2535–2561**

Zamyatin, Yevgeny Ivanovich
 European Writers, vol. 10: **1181–1203**

Zindel, Paul
 Writers for Young Adults, vol. 3: **421–430**

EARLY PROSE FICTION

Romances, sagas, fables, fairy tales, biblical narratives, and other prose stories written before ca. 1700.

Apuleius
  Ancient Writers, vol. 2: **1099–1116**
  Supernatural Fiction Writers, vol. 1: **3–9**

Arthurian Legend
  European Writers, vol. 1: **137–160**
  European Writers Selected Authors, vol. 1: **79–102**

Arthurian Romances
  Supernatural Fiction Writers, vol. 1: **11–18**

Bandello, Matteo
  See "Renaissance Short Fiction"

Basile, Giambattista
  See "Renaissance Short Fiction"

Boccaccio, Giovanni
  European Writers, vol. 2: **509–534**
  European Writers Selected Authors, vol. 1: **255–280**
  See also "Renaissance Pastoral Poetry"

Bunyan, John
  British Writers, vol. 2: **240–254**
  British Writers Selected Authors, vol. 1: **215–229**
  Writers for Children: **97–102**

Cervantes, Miguel de
  European Writers, vol. 2: **819–844**
  European Writers Selected Authors, vol. 1: **335–359**
  See also "Renaissance Short Fiction"

Dante Alighieri
  European Writers, vol. 1: **431–450**
  European Writers Selected Authors, vol. 1: **411–430**
  See also "Renaissance Pastoral Poetry"

Des Périers, Bonaventure
  See "Renaissance Short Fiction"

Geoffrey of Monmouth
  See "Arthurian Romances"

Job
  The Books of the Bible, vol. 1: **181–201**

Jonah
  The Books of the Bible, vol. 1: **381–384**

Judith
  The Books of the Bible, vol. 2: **43–49**

La Fontaine, Jean de
  European Writers, vol. 3: **73–100**
  European Writers Selected Authors, vol. 2: **901–928**

Lucian
  Ancient Writers, vol. 2: **1081–1097**

Lyly, John, and George Peele
  British Writers, vol. 1: **191–211**

Malory, Sir Thomas
  British Writers, vol. 1: **67–80**
  British Writers Selected Authors, vol. 2: **877–890**
  See also "Arthurian Romances"

Masuccio Salernitano
  See "Renaissance Short Fiction"

Medieval Satire
  European Writers, vol. 1: **337–376**
  European Writers Selected Authors, vol. 2: **1075–1113**

Montemayor, Jorge de
  See "Renaissance Pastoral Poetry"

Norse Sagas
  European Writers, vol. 1: **377–404**
  European Writers Selected Authors, vol. 3: **1199–1226**

Petrarch
  European Writers, vol. 2: **475–507**
  European Writers Selected Authors, vol. 2: **1255–1287**
  See also "Renaissance Pastoral Poetry"

Petronius
  Ancient Writers, vol. 2: **833–853**

Renaissance Short Fiction
  European Writers, vol. 2: **927–956**
  European Writers Selected Authors, vol. 3: **1431–1460**

Ruth
  The Books of the Bible, vol. 1: **123–126**

Sacchetti, Franco
  See "Renaissance Short Fiction"

Sigüenza y Góngora, Carlos de
  Latin American Writers, vol. 1: **71–77**

Straparola, Gianfrancesco
  See "Renaissance Short Fiction"

Tobit
  The Books of the Bible, vol. 2: **35–42**

Xenophon
  Ancient Writers, vol. 1: **331–351**

THE NOVEL

Extended prose fictions after ca. 1700. "Novel" here is defined broadly to include works of science fiction and fantasy and full-length children's stories.

Abbey, Edward
American Nature Writers, vol. 1: **1–19**

Abrahams, Peter
African Writers, vol. 1: **1–14**

Acevedo Díaz, Eduardo
Latin American Writers, vol. 1: **299–303**

Achebe, Chinua
African Writers, vol. 1: **15–36**

Adams, Henry
American Writers, vol. 1: **1–24**

Agee, James
American Writers, vol. 1: **25–47**

Aickman, Robert
Supernatural Fiction Writers, vol. 2: **957–964**

Aidoo, Ama Ata
African Writers, vol. 1: **37–48**

Aiken, Conrad
American Writers, vol. 1: **48–70**

Aiken, Joan
Writers for Young Adults, vol. 1: **1–9**

Ainsworth, William Harrison
Supernatural Fiction Writers, vol. 1: **187–193**

Alcott, Louisa May
American Writers Supp. 1, part 1: **28–46**
Writers for Children: **1–6**
Writers for Young Adults, vol. 1: **11–20**

Aldiss, Brian W.
Science Fiction Writers: **251–258**

Alegría, Ciro
Latin American Writers, vol. 3: **1099–1103**

Alencar, José de
Latin American Writers, vol. 1: **195–203**

Alexander, Lloyd
Supernatural Fiction Writers, vol. 2: **965–971**
Writers for Young Adults, vol. 1: **21–33**

Alfieri, Vittorio
European Writers, vol. 4: **661–689**

Amado, Jorge
Latin American Writers, vol. 3: **1153–1162**

Ambler, Eric
British Writers Supp. 4: **1–24**

Amis, Kingsley
British Writers Supp. 2: **1–19**

Amis, Martin
British Writers Supp. 4: **25–44**

Andersen, Hans Christian
European Writers, vol. 6: **863–892**
European Writers Selected Authors, vol. 1: **1–29**
Writers for Children: **7–13**

Anderson, Poul
Science Fiction Writers: **259–265**
Supernatural Fiction Writers, vol. 2: **973–980**

Anderson, Sherwood
American Writers, vol. 1: **97–120**

Anderson Imbert, Enrique
Latin American Writers, vol. 3: **1105–1110**

Andrade, Mário de
Latin American Writers, vol. 2: **771–780**

Andrić, Ivo
European Writers, vol. 11: **1751–1779**

Angell, Judie
Writers for Young Adults, vol. 1: **35–42**

Anstey, F.
Supernatural Fiction Writers, vol. 1: **287–292**

Anthony, Piers
Supernatural Fiction Writers, vol. 2: **981–986**

Aragon, Louis
European Writers, vol. 11: **2061–2087**

Arden, John
British Writers Supp. 2: **21–42**

Arenas, Reinaldo
Latin American Writers, vol. 3: **1451–1458**

Arguedas, José María
Latin American Writers, vol. 3: **1131–1138**

Arlt, Roberto
Latin American Writers, vol. 2: **881–886**

Armah, Ayi Kwei
African Writers, vol. 1: **49–62**

Arreola, Juan José
  Latin American Writers, vol. 3: **1229–1236**

Arthurian Legend
  European Writers, vol. 1: **137–160**
  European Writers Selected Authors, vol. 1: **79–102**

Arthurian Romances
  Supernatural Fiction Writers, vol. 1: **11–18**

Asher, Sandy
  Writers for Young Adults, vol. 1: **53–61**

Asimov, Isaac
  Science Fiction Writers: **267–276**

Asturias, Miguel Ángel
  Latin American Writers, vol. 2: **865–873**

Atherton, Gertrude
  Supernatural Fiction Writers, vol. 2: **777–781**

Auchincloss, Louis
  American Writers Supp. 4, part 1: **21–38**

Austen, Jane
  British Writers, vol. 4: **101–124**
  British Writers Selected Authors, vol. 1: **23–46**

Austin, Mary Hunter
  American Nature Writers, vol. 1: **31–51**

Avi
  Writers for Young Adults, vol. 1: **63–72**

Awoonor, Kofi
  African Writers, vol. 1: **63–75**

Aymé, Marcel
  European Writers, vol. 12: **2433–2456**

Azevedo, Aluísio
  Latin American Writers, vol. 1: **333–341**

Azorín
  European Writers, vol. 9: **639–661**

Azuela, Mariano
  Latin American Writers, vol. 2: **457–464**

Bâ, Mariama
  African Writers, vol. 1: **77–82**

Baker, Frank
  Supernatural Fiction Writers, vol. 2: **561–567**

Balbuena, Bernardo de
  Latin American Writers, vol. 1: **53–57**

Baldwin, James
  African American Writers: **1–14**
  American Writers Supp. 1, part 1: **47–71**

Ballard, J. G.
  Science Fiction Writers: **277–282**

Balzac, Honoré de
  European Writers, vol. 5: **635–658**
  European Writers Selected Authors, vol. 1: **161–183**
  Supernatural Fiction Writers, vol. 1: **37–44**

Bangs, J. K.
  Supernatural Fiction Writers, vol. 2: **725–729**

Barker, Pat
  British Writers Supp. 4: **45–63**

Barnes, Djuna
  American Writers Supp. 3, part 1: **31–46**

Barnes, Julian
  British Writers Supp. 4: **65–76**

Baroja, Pío
  European Writers, vol. 9: **589–616**

Barrie, J. M.
  British Writers Supp. 3: **1–17**
  Supernatural Fiction Writers, vol. 1: **405–410**
  Writers for Children: **29–35**

Barrios, Eduardo
  Latin American Writers, vol. 2: **611–618**

Barth, John
  American Writers, vol. 1: **121–143**

Barthelme, Donald
  American Writers Supp. 4, part 1: **39–58**

Bass, Rick
  American Nature Writers, vol. 1: **75–88**

Bauer, Joan
  Writers for Young Adults, vol. 1: **73–80**

Bauer, Marion Dane
  Writers for Young Adults, vol. 1: **81–88**

Baum, L. Frank
  Writers for Children: **37–48**

Beagle, Peter S.
  Supernatural Fiction Writers, vol. 2: **987–991**

Beauvoir, Simone de
  European Writers, vol. 12: **2701–2732**
  European Writers Selected Authors, vol. 1: **185–215**

Beckett, Samuel
  British Writers Supp. 1: **43–64**
  British Writers Selected Authors, vol. 1: **47–68**

Beckford, William
  Supernatural Fiction Writers, vol. 1: **139–144**
  See also "Gothic Novel, The"

Beerbohm, Max
  British Writers Supp. 2: **43–59**

Behan, Brendan
British Writers Supp. 2: **61–76**

Behn, Aphra
British Writers Supp. 3: **19–43**

Belloc, Hilaire
Writers for Children: **49–54**

Bellow, Saul
American Writers, vol. 1: **144–166**

Bely, Andrey
European Writers, vol. 9: **905–929**

Bemelmans, Ludwig
Writers for Children: **55–61**

Benedetti, Mario
Latin American Writers, vol. 3: **1255–1263**

Benét, Stephen Vincent
Supernatural Fiction Writers, vol. 2: **797–803**

Bennett, Arnold
British Writers, vol. 6: **247–268**

Bennett, Jay
Writers for Young Adults, vol. 1: **89–97**

Benson, E. F.
Supernatural Fiction Writers, vol. 1: **491–496**

Beresford, J. D.
Supernatural Fiction Writers, vol. 1: **457–461**

Berger, John
British Writers Supp. 4: **77–96**

Berry, Wendell
American Nature Writers, vol. 1: **89–105**

Bester, Alfred
Science Fiction Writers: **283–290**

Bethancourt, T. Ernesto
Writers for Young Adults, vol. 1: **99–109**

Beti, Mongo
African Writers, vol. 1: **83–94**

Bioy Casares, Adolfo
Latin American Writers, vol. 3: **1201–1208**

Blackwood, Algernon
Supernatural Fiction Writers, vol. 1: **463–470**

Blanco Fombona, Rufino
Latin American Writers, vol. 2: **503–511**

Blasco Ibáñez, Vicente
European Writers, vol. 8: **355–388**

Blest Gana, Alberto
Latin American Writers, vol. 1: **205–213**

Blish, James
Science Fiction Writers: **291–296**

Bloch, Robert
Supernatural Fiction Writers, vol. 2: **901–907**

Block, Francesca Lia
Writers for Young Adults, vol. 1: **111–119**

Blume, Judy
Writers for Young Adults, vol. 1: **121–131**

Bograd, Larry
Writers for Young Adults, vol. 1: **133–141**

Böll, Heinrich
European Writers, vol. 13: **3165–3186**

Bombal, María Luisa
Latin American Writers, vol. 3: **1111–1117**

Bontemps, Arna
Writers for Children: **77–83**

Borges, Jorge Luis
Latin American Writers, vol. 2: **845–864**

Bowen, Elizabeth
British Writers Supp. 2: **77–96**
Supernatural Fiction Writers, vol. 2: **569–575**

Bowles, Paul
American Writers Supp. 4, part 1: **79–99**

Brackett, Leigh
Supernatural Fiction Writers, vol. 2: **909–915**

Bradbury, Ray
American Writers Supp. 4, part 1: **101–118**
Supernatural Fiction Writers: **171–178**
Supernatural Fiction Writers, vol. 2: **917–923**

Brancato, Robin F.
Writers for Young Adults, vol. 1: **143–152**

Branscum, Robbie
Writers for Young Adults, vol. 1: **153–161**

Brecht, Bertolt
European Writers, vol. 11: **2089–2112**
European Writers Selected Authors, vol. 1: **281–303**

Breton, André
European Writers, vol. 11: **1939–1960**

Bridgers, Sue Ellen
Writers for Young Adults, vol. 1: **163–172**

Brink, André
African Writers, vol. 1: **95–114**

Brink, Carol Ryrie
Writers for Children: **85–90**

Broch, Hermann
  European Writers, vol. 10: **1385–1408**
Brontës, The
  British Writers, vol. 5: **105–154**
  British Writers Selected Authors, vol. 1: **129–177**
Brooke-Rose, Christine
  British Writers Supp. 4: **97–118**
Brookner, Anita
  British Writers Supp. 4: **119–137**
Brooks, Bruce
  Writers for Young Adults, vol. 1: **173–182**
Brooks, Gwendolyn
  African American Writers: **31–43**
  American Writers Supp. 3, part 1: **69–90**
  Modern American Women Writers: **37–48**
Brown, Charles Brockden
  American Writers Supp. 1, part 1: **124–149**
Brunner, John
  Science Fiction Writers: **297–304**
Büchner, Georg
  European Writers, vol. 6: **1169–1194**
Buck, Pearl S.
  American Writers Supp. 2, part 1: **113–134**
Budrys, Algis
  Science Fiction Writers: **305–311**
Bulwer-Lytton, Edward
  Supernatural Fiction Writers, vol. 1: **195–204**
Bunting, Eve
  Writers for Young Adults, vol. 1: **183–189**
Burgess, Anthony
  British Writers Supp. 1: **185–198**
Burnett, Frances Hodgson
  Writers for Children: **103–109**
Burney, Frances
  British Writers Supp. 3: **63–78**
Burns, Olive Ann
  Writers for Young Adults, vol. 1: **191–198**
Burroughs, Edgar Rice
  Science Fiction Writers: **59–64**
Burroughs, William S.
  American Writers Supp. 3, part 1: **91–110**
Butler, Samuel
  British Writers Supp. 2: **97–121**
Butor, Michel
  European Writers, vol. 13: **3287–3321**

Byars, Betsy
  Writers for Young Adults, vol. 1: **199–207**
Byatt, A. S.
  British Writers Supp. 4: **139–156**
Cabell, James Branch
  Supernatural Fiction Writers, vol. 2: **789–796**
Cabrera Infante, Guillermo
  Latin American Writers, vol. 3: **1383–1391**
Caldwell, Erskine
  American Writers, vol. 1: **288–311**
Calvino, Italo
  European Writers, vol. 13: **3259–3286**
Cambaceres, Eugenio
  Latin American Writers, vol. 1: **269–276**
Campbell, John W., Jr.
  Science Fiction Writers: **151–159**
Campbell, Ramsey
  Supernatural Fiction Writers, vol. 2: **993–999**
Camus, Albert
  African Writers, vol. 1: **139–152**
  European Writers, vol. 13: **3049–3078**
  European Writers Selected Authors, vol. 1: **305–334**
Canetti, Elias
  European Writers, vol. 12: **2615–2633**
Čapek, Karel
  European Writers, vol. 10: **1565–1590**
  Science Fiction Writers: **583–589**
Capote, Truman
  American Writers Supp. 3, part 1: **111–133**
Carballido, Emilio
  Latin American Writers, vol. 3: **1289–1294**
Carducci, Giosue
  European Writers, vol. 7: **1495–1516**
Carpentier, Alejo
  Latin American Writers, vol. 3: **1019–1031**
Carrasquilla, Tomás
  Latin American Writers, vol. 1: **343–350**
Carroll, Lewis
  British Writers, vol. 5: **261–276**
  Supernatural Fiction Writers, vol. 1: **247–253**
  Writers for Children: **117–127**
Carter, Alden R.
  Writers for Young Adults, vol. 1: **209–218**
Carter, Angela
  British Writers Supp. 3: **79–93**

Cary, Joyce
  British Writers, vol. 7: **185–196**

Castellanos, Rosario
  Latin American Writers, vol. 3: **1295–1302**

Cather, Willa
  American Writers, vol. 1: **312–334**
  American Writers Retrospective: **1–23**
  Modern American Women Writers: **49–62**

Cela, Camilo José
  European Writers, vol. 13: **3105–3129**

Céline, Louis-Ferdinand
  European Writers, vol. 11: **1859–1884**

Cervantes, Miguel de
  European Writers, vol. 2: **819–844**
  European Writers Selected Authors, vol. 1: **335–359**
  See also "Renaissance Short Fiction"

Chambers, Aidan
  Writers for Young Adults, vol. 1: **219–227**

Chambers, Robert W.
  Supernatural Fiction Writers, vol. 2: **739–745**

Chamisso, Adelbert von
  Supernatural Fiction Writers, vol. 1: **91–95**

Chandler, Raymond
  American Writers Supp. 4, part 1: **119–138**

Chatwin, Bruce
  British Writers Supp. 4: **157–177**

Cheever, John
  American Writers Supp. 1, part 1: **174–199**

Chesnutt, Charles W.
  African American Writers: **59–70**

Chesterton, G. K.
  British Writers, vol. 6: **335–346**
  Supernatural Fiction Writers, vol. 1: **411–414**

Childress, Alice
  Writers for Young Adults, vol. 1: **229–240**

Chopin, Kate
  American Writers Supp. 1, part 1: **200–226**
  Modern American Women Writers: **63–78**

Christie, Agatha
  British Writers Supp. 2: **123–137**

Clarke, Arthur C.
  Science Fiction Writers: **313–320**

Cleaver, Vera and Bill
  Writers for Young Adults, vol. 1: **241–248**

Clement, Hal
  Science Fiction Writers: **321–327**

Cocteau, Jean
  European Writers, vol. 10: **1543–1564**

Coetzee, J. M.
  African Writers, vol. 1: **167–183**

Cole, Brock
  Writers for Young Adults, vol. 1: **249–256**

Colette
  European Writers, vol. 9: **617–638**
  European Writers Selected Authors, vol. 1: **389–410**

Collier, Christopher and James Lincoln
  Writers for Young Adults, vol. 1: **257–269**

Collier, John
  Supernatural Fiction Writers, vol. 2: **577–583**

Collins, Wilkie
  Supernatural Fiction Writers, vol. 1: **233–238**

Collodi, C.
  Writers for Children: **129–137**

Colman, Hila
  Writers for Young Adults, vol. 1: **271–280**

Compton-Burnett, Ivy
  British Writers, vol. 7: **59–70**

Connolly, Cyril
  British Writers Supp. 3: **95–113**

Conrad, Joseph
  British Writers, vol. 6: **133–150**
  British Writers Selected Authors, vol. 1: **331–348**

Constant, Benjamin
  See "French Novelists, Three"

Cooney, Caroline B.
  Writers for Young Adults, vol. 1: **281–290**

Cooper, James Fenimore
  American Writers, vol. 1: **335–357**
  Writers for Children: **147–153**

Cooper, Susan Fenimore
  American Nature Writers, vol. 1: **187–198**

Corelli, Marie
  Supernatural Fiction Writers, vol. 1: **293–297**

Cormier, Robert
  Writers for Young Adults, vol. 1: **291–301**

Cortázar, Julio
  Latin American Writers, vol. 3: **1177–1194**

Douglas, Norman
    British Writers, vol. 6: **293–306**

Dove, Rita
    American Writers Supp. 4, part 1: **241–258**

Doyle, Sir Arthur Conan
    British Writers Supp. 2: **159–178**
    British Writers Selected Authors, vol. 1: **415–434**
    Science Fiction Writers: **45–50**
    Writers for Children: **201–207**
    Writers for Young Adults, vol. 1: **385–392**

Drabble, Margaret
    British Writers Supp. 4: **229–254**

Dreiser, Theodore
    American Writers, vol. 1: **497–520**

Du Bois, W. E. B.
    African American Writers: **71–87**
    American Writers Supp. 2, part 1: **157–189**

Dumas, Alexandre (Père)
    European Writers, vol. 6: **719–745**
    European Writers Selected Authors, vol. 1: **503–527**
    Writers for Children: **209–213**

Du Maurier, Daphne
    British Writers Supp. 3: **133–149**
    British Writers Selected Authors, vol. 1: **435–451**

Dunbar, Paul Laurence
    African American Writers: **87–102**
    American Writers Supp. 2, part 1: **191–219**

Duncan, Lois
    Writers for Young Adults, vol. 1: **393–402**

Dunsany, Lord
    Supernatural Fiction Writers, vol. 1: **471–478**

Durrell, Lawrence
    British Writers Supp. 1: **93–128**

Dürrenmatt, Friedrich
    European Writers, vol. 13: **3215–3235**

Eça de Queiroz, José Maria
    European Writers, vol. 7: **1683–1708**

Eddison, E. R.
    Supernatural Fiction Writers, vol. 2: **529–534**

Edgeworth, Maria
    British Writers Supp. 3: **151–168**

Edwards, Amelia B.
    Supernatural Fiction Writers, vol. 1: **255–260**

Edwards, Jorge
    Latin American Writers, vol. 3: **1399–1403**

Egbuna, Obi
    African Writers, vol. 1: **209–221**

Ekwensi, Cyprian
    African Writers, vol. 1: **223–234**

Eliot, George
    British Writers, vol. 5: **187–201**
    British Writers Selected Authors, vol. 1: **453–467**

Ellison, Harlan
    Science Fiction Writers: **357–368**
    Supernatural Fiction Writers, vol. 2: **1015–1021**

Ellison, Ralph
    African American Writers: **103–129**
    American Writers Supp. 2, part 1: **221–252**

Emecheta, Buchi
    African Writers, vol. 1: **235–247**

Enright, Elizabeth
    Writers for Children: **215–220**

Erdrich, Louise
    American Writers Supp. 4, part 1: **259–278**

Ewing, Juliana Horatia
    Writers for Children: **221–226**

Eyerly, Jeannette
    Writers for Young Adults, vol. 1: **403–411**

Fagundes Telles, Lygia
    Latin American Writers, vol. 3: **1271–1275**

Farah, Nuruddin
    African Writers, vol. 1: **249–262**

Farmer, Philip José
    Science Fiction Writers: **369–375**

Farrell, James T.
    American Writers, vol. 2: **25–53**

Faulkner, William
    American Writers, vol. 2: **54–76**
    American Writers Retrospective: **73–95**

Fauset, Jessie
    Modern American Women Writers: **123–139**

Fénelon, François de Salignac de la Mothe-
    European Writers, vol. 3: **261–291**

Fernández, Macedonio
    Latin American Writers, vol. 2: **483–491**

Fernández de Lizardi, José Joaquín
    Latin American Writers, vol. 1: **119–128**

Ferreira de Castro, Jose Maria
    European Writers, vol. 11: **2143–2165**

Field, Rachel Lyman
  Writers for Children: **235–240**

Fielding, Henry
  British Writers, vol. 3: **94–106**
  British Writers Selected Authors, vol. 2: **497–509**

Finney, Charles
  Supernatural Fiction Writers, vol. 2: **821–826**

Firbank, Ronald
  British Writers Supp. 2: **199–224**

Fitzgerald, F. Scott
  American Writers, vol. 2: **77–100**
  American Writers Retrospective: **97–120**

Flaubert, Gustave
  European Writers, vol. 7: **1373–1394**
  European Writers Selected Authors, vol. 1:
    553–574

Fontane, Theodor
  European Writers, vol. 6: **1299–1322**

Ford, Ford Madox
  British Writers, vol. 6: **319–334**

Forster, E. M.
  British Writers, vol. 6: **397–414**
  British Writers Selected Authors, vol. 2: **511–527**
  Supernatural Fiction Writers, vol. 1: **479–484**

Fortune, Dion
  Supernatural Fiction Writers, vol. 2: **585–590**

Foscolo, Ugo
  European Writers, vol. 5: **313–341**

Fouqué, Friedrich de la Motte
  Supernatural Fiction Writers, vol. 1: **97–105**

Fowles, John
  British Writers Supp. 1: **291–311**

Fox, Paula
  Writers for Young Adults, vol. 1: **413–422**

France, Anatole
  Supernatural Fiction Writers, vol. 1: **67–72**

Freeman, Mary E. Wilkins
  Modern American Women Writers: **141–153**
  Supernatural Fiction Writers, vol. 2: **769–773**

French, Michael
  Writers for Young Adults, vol. 2: **11–20**

French Novelists, Three
  European Writers, vol. 4: **393–419**

Frisch, Max
  European Writers, vol. 13: **2895–2924**

Fuentes, Carlos
  Latin American Writers, vol. 3: **1353–1376**

Gaddis, William
  American Writers Supp. 4, part 1: **279–296**

Gaines, Ernest J.
  African American Writers: **129–145**

Gallegos, Rómulo
  Latin American Writers, vol. 2: **603–610**

Galsworthy, John
  British Writers, vol. 6: **269–293**

Gálvez, Manuel
  Latin American Writers, vol. 2: **585–589**

Gambaro, Griselda
  Latin American Writers, vol. 3: **1323–1328**

Gamboa, Federico
  Latin American Writers, vol. 1: **371–375**

García Márquez, Gabriel
  Latin American Writers, vol. 3: **1329–1346**

Garfield, Leon
  Writers for Young Adults, vol. 2: **33–45**

Garner, Alan
  Supernatural Fiction Writers, vol. 2: **1023–1029**

Garnett, David
  Supernatural Fiction Writers, vol. 2: **535–539**

Gaskell, Elizabeth
  British Writers, vol. 5: **1–16**

Gautier, Théophile
  European Writers, vol. 6: **1033–1059**
  Supernatural Fiction Writers, vol. 1: **45–50**

Genet, Jean
  European Writers, vol. 13: **2865–2892**

George, Jean Craighead
  Writers for Young Adults, vol. 2: **47–57**

Gilman, Charlotte Perkins
  Modern American Women Writers: **155–170**

Ginzburg, Natalia
  European Writers, vol. 13: **3131–3163**

Giraudoux, Jean
  European Writers, vol. 9: **1041–1065**

Gissing, George
  British Writers, vol. 5: **423–438**

Glasgow, Ellen
  American Women Writers, vol. 2: **173–195**
  Modern American Women Writers: **171–180**

Glaspell, Susan
   American Writers Supp. 3, part 1: **175–191**
   Modern American Women Writers: **181–188**

Goethe, Johann Wolfgang von
   European Writers, vol. 5: **1–26**
   European Writers Selected Authors, vol. 1: **655–680**

Gogol, Nikolay Vasilievich
   European Writers, vol. 6: **971–998**

Golding, William
   British Writers Supp. 1: **65–91**
   British Writers Selected Authors, vol. 2: **529–555**

Goldoni, Carlo
   European Writers, vol. 4: **421–448**

Goldsmith, Oliver
   British Writers, vol. 3: **177–192**

Gombrowicz, Witold
   European Writers, vol. 12: **2563–2588**

Gómez Carillo, Enrique
   Latin American Writers, vol. 2: **465–469**

Gómez de Avellaneda, Gertrudis
   Latin American Writers, vol. 1: **175–180**

Goncharov, Ivan
   European Writers, vol. 6: **1061–1087**

Goncourt, Edmond Louis Antoine de, and Jules
      Alfred Huot de Goncourt
   European Writers, vol. 7: **1395–1419**

Gordimer, Nadine
   African Writers, vol. 1: **277–290**
   British Writers Supp. 2: **225–245**

Gordon, Caroline
   American Writers, vol. 2: **196–222**

Gordon, Mary
   American Writers Supp. 4, part 1: **297–317**

Gorky, Maxim
   European Writers, vol. 8: **417–446**
   European Writers Selected Authors, vol. 2: **681–710**

Gothic Novel, The
   British Writers, vol. 3: **324–346**

Grahame, Kenneth
   Writers for Children: **247–254**

Grass, Günter
   European Writers, vol. 13: **3365–3388**
   European Writers Selected Authors, vol. 2: **711–734**

Graves, Robert
   British Writers, vol. 7: **257–272**

Green, Henry
   British Writers Supp. 2: **247–266**

Greene, Bette
   Writers for Young Adults, vol. 2: **59–68**

Greene, Graham
   British Writers Supp. 1: **1–20**
   British Writers Selected Authors, vol. 2: **557–576**

Grillparzer, Franz
   European Writers, vol. 5: **417–445**

Guimarães Rosa, João
   Latin American Writers, vol. 3: **1069–1080**

Güiraldes, Ricardo
   Latin American Writers, vol. 2: **619–627**

Gunn Allen, Paula
   American Writers Supp. 4, part 1: **319–340**

Gunnarsson, Gunnar
   European Writers, vol. 10: **1497–1519**

Guzmán, Martín Luis
   Latin American Writers, vol. 2: **655–662**

Haggard, H. Rider
   British Writers Supp. 3: **211–228**
   Science Fiction Writers: **19–24**
   Supernatural Fiction Writers, vol. 1: **321–327**

Ḥakīm, Tawfīq, al-
   African Writers, vol. 1: **291–301**

Hall, Lynn
   Writers for Young Adults, vol. 2: **69–77**

Hamilton, Virginia
   Writers for Young Adults, vol. 2: **79–92**

Hammett, Dashiell
   American Writers Supp. 4, part 1: **341–357**

Hamsun, Knut
   European Writers, vol. 8: **21–43**

Hardwick, Elizabeth
   American Writers Supp. 3, part 1: **193–215**
   Modern American Women Writers: **189–196**

Hardy, Thomas
   British Writers, vol. 6: **1–22**
   British Writers Selected Authors, vol. 2: **577–598**

Harper, Frances Ellen Watkins
   African American Writers: **159–175**
   Modern American Women Writers: **197–205**

Hartley, L. P.
   Supernatural Fiction Writers, vol. 2: **639–644**

Hašek, Jaroslav
  European Writers, vol. 9: **1091–1118**
Hauff, William
  Supernatural Fiction Writers, vol. 1: **107–110**
Hauptmann, Gerhart
  European Writers, vol. 8: **147–174**
Hawthorne, Nathaniel
  American Writers, vol. 2: **223–246**
  American Writers Retrospective: **145–167**
  Supernatural Fiction Writers, vol. 2: **707–715**
  Writers for Children: **277–282**
Head, Bessie
  African Writers, vol. 1: **303–320**
Heinlein, Robert A.
  Science Fiction Writers: **185–196**
Heiremans, Luis Alberto
  Latin American Writers, vol. 3: **1347–1352**
Heller, Joseph
  American Writers Supp. 4, part 1: **379–396**
Hemingway, Ernest
  American Writers, vol. 2: **247–270**
  American Writers Retrospective: **169–191**
  Writers for Young Adults, vol. 2: **93–102**
Hentoff, Nat
  Writers for Young Adults, vol. 2: **103–112**
Herbert, Frank
  Science Fiction Writers: **377–385**
Hernández, José
  Latin American Writers, vol. 1: **235–247**
Hesse, Hermann
  European Writers, vol. 9: **833–859**
  European Writers Selected Authors, vol. 2: **735–760**
Hichens, Robert
  Supernatural Fiction Writers, vol. 1: **415–420**
Hinton, S. E.
  Writers for Young Adults, vol. 2: **113–120**
Hoagland, Edward
  American Nature Writers, vol. 1: **363–375**
Hobbs, Will
  Writers for Young Adults, vol. 2: **121–129**
Hodgson, William Hope
  Supernatural Fiction Writers, vol. 1: **421–428**
Hoffmann, E. T. A.
  European Writers, vol. 5: **261–289**
  Supernatural Fiction Writers, vol. 1: **111–119**
  Writers for Children: **283–288**

Hofmannsthal, Hugo von
  European Writers, vol. 9: **689–714**
Hogan, Linda
  American Nature Writers, vol. 1: **377–388**
  American Writers Supp. 4, part 1: **397–418**
Hogg, James
  Supernatural Fiction Writers, vol. 1: **177–183**
Hölderlin, Friedrich
  European Writers, vol. 5: **143–173**
Holland, Isabelle
  Writers for Young Adults, vol. 2: **131–140**
Holmes, Oliver Wendell
  American Writers Supp. 1, part 1: **299–319**
Hope, Christopher
  African Writers, vol. 1: **331–343**
Howard, Robert E.
  Supernatural Fiction Writers, vol. 2: **861–868**
Howells, William Dean
  American Writers, vol. 2: **271–294**
Hoyle, Fred
  Science Fiction Writers: **387–392**
Hughes, Langston
  African American Writers: **193–205**
  American Writers Retrospective: **193–214**
  American Writers Supp. 1, part 1: **320–348**
  Writers for Children: **295–301**
Hughes, Monica
  Writers for Young Adults, vol. 2: **141–148**
Hugo, Victor
  European Writers, vol. 6: **693–718**
  European Writers Selected Authors, vol. 2:
      761–786
Huidobro, Vicente
  Latin American Writers, vol. 2: **755–764**
Hunter, Mollie
  Writers for Young Adults, vol. 2: **149–159**
Hurston, Zora Neale
  African American Writers: **205–218**
  Modern American Women Writers: **221–235**
Huxley, Aldous
  British Writers, vol. 7: **197–208**
  British Writers Selected Authors, vol. 2:
      635–646
  Science Fiction Writers: **101–108**
Huysmans, Joris Karl
  European Writers, vol. 7: **1709–1729**

Korman, Gordon
  Writers for Young Adults, vol. 2: **199–206**

Kornbluth, C. M.
  Science Fiction Writers: **401–407**

Kosztolányi, Dezsö
  European Writers, vol. 10: **1231–1249**

Krleža, Miroslav
  European Writers, vol. 11: **1807–1834**

Kumin, Maxine
  American Nature Writers, vol. 1: **479–497**
  American Writers Supp. 4, part 2: **439–457**

Kundera, Milan
  European Writers, vol. 13: **3389–3413**

Kuttner, Henry
  Science Fiction Writers: **161–167**

Laclos, Choderlos de
  See "French Novelists, Three"

Lafferty, R. A.
  Supernatural Fiction Writers, vol. 2: **1045–1052**

Lagerkvist, Pär
  European Writers, vol. 10: **1677–1702**

Laguerre, Enrique A.
  Latin American Writers, vol. 3: **1049–1055**

La Guma, Alex
  African Writers, vol. 1: **401–411**

Lampedusa, Giuseppe Tomasi di
  European Writers, vol. 11: **2009–2034**

Lang, Andrew
  Writers for Children: **337–343**

Larkin, Phillip
  British Writers Supp. 1: **275–290**

Larreta, Enrique
  Latin American Writers, vol. 2: **471–476**

Larsen, Nella
  African American Writers: **263–272**

Lasky, Kathryn
  Writers for Young Adults, vol. 2: **207–216**

Lawrence, D. H.
  British Writers, vol. 7: **87–126**
  British Writers Selected Authors, vol. 2: **771–810**

Laxness, Halldór
  European Writers, vol. 12: **2457–2478**

Laye, Camara
  African Writers, vol. 1: **413–425**

Le Carré, John
  British Writers Supp. 2: **299–320**
  British Writers Selected Authors, vol. 2: **811–832**

Lee, Harper
  Writers for Young Adults, vol. 2: **217–225**

Lee, Tanith
  Supernatural Fiction Writers, vol. 2: **1053–1058**

Lee, Vernon
  Supernatural Fiction Writers, vol. 1: **329–335**

Le Fanu, J. S.
  Supernatural Fiction Writers, vol. 1: **219–231**

Le Guin, Ursula K.
  Science Fiction Writers: **409–417**
  Supernatural Fiction Writers, vol. 2: **1059–1066**
  Writers for Young Adults, vol. 2: **227–236**
  See also "Contemporary Ecofiction"

Leiber, Fritz
  Science Fiction Writers: **419–424**
  Supernatural Fiction Writers, vol. 2: **933–939**

Leinster, Murray
  Science Fiction Writers: **111–117**

Łem, Stanisław
  Science Fiction Writers: **591–598**

L'Engle, Madeleine
  Writers for Young Adults, vol. 2: **237–246**

Lermontov, Mikhail Yurievich
  European Writers, vol. 6: **1195–1224**

Lesage, Alain-René
  European Writers, vol. 3: **317–344**

Lessing, Doris
  African Writers, vol. 1: **427–449**
  British Writers Supp. 1: **237–257**
  British Writers Selected Authors, vol. 2: **833–853**

Lewis, C. S.
  British Writers Supp. 3: **247–268**
  British Writers Selected Authors, vol. 2: **855–876**
  Science Fiction Writers: **243–248**
  Supernatural Fiction Writers, vol. 2: **661–666**
  Writers for Children: **357–364**
  Writers for Young Adults, vol. 2: **247–255**

Lewis, M. G.
  Supernatural Fiction Writers, vol. 1: **153–160**

Lewis, Sinclair
  American Writers, vol. 2: **439–461**

Lewis, Wyndham
  British Writers, vol. 7: **71–86**

Mann, Thomas
  European Writers, vol. 9: **715–743**
  European Writers Selected Authors, vol. 2:
    997–1024
Manzoni, Alessandro
  European Writers, vol. 5: **367–394**
Marechal, Leopoldo
  Latin American Writers, vol. 2: **887–896**
Marín Cañas, José
  Latin American Writers, vol. 3: **991–994**
Marinetti, Filippo Tommaso
  European Writers, vol. 9: **797–832**
Mármol, José
  Latin American Writers, vol. 1: **181–184**
Marquand, John P.
  American Writers, vol. 3: **50–73**
Marqués, René
  Latin American Writers, vol. 3: **1237–1246**
Marryat, Frederick
  Writers for Children: **381–387**
Marshall, Paule
  African American Writers: **289–304**
Martí, José
  Latin American Writers, vol. 1: **311–320**
Masters, Edgar Lee
  American Writers Supp. 1, part 2: **454–478**
Matheson, Richard
  Science Fiction Writers: **425–431**
  Supernatural Fiction Writers, vol. 2: **1073–1080**
Matthiessen, Peter
  American Nature Writers, vol. 2: **599–613**
Matto de Turner, Clorinda
  Latin American Writers, vol. 1: **305–309**
Maturin, Charles Robert
  Supernatural Fiction Writers, vol. 1: **161–168**
Maugham, W. Somerset
  British Writers, vol. 6: **363–382**
  British Writers Selected Authors, vol. 2: **905–923**
Maupassant, Guy de
  European Writers, vol. 7: **1759–1784**
  European Writers Selected Authors, vol. 2:
    1025–1050
  Supernatural Fiction Writers, vol. 1: **59–65**
Mauriac, François
  European Writers, vol. 10: **1307–1330**

Mazer, Harry
  Writers for Young Adults, vol. 2: **327–336**
Mazer, Norma Fox
  Writers for Young Adults, vol. 2: **337–346**
Meigs, Cornelia
  Writers for Children: **389–395**
Meinhold, Wilhelm
  Supernatural Fiction Writers, vol. 1: **121–127**
Melville, Herman
  American Writers, vol. 3: **74–98**
  American Writers Retrospective: **243–262**
Memmi, Albert
  African Writers, vol. 2: **467–477**
Meredith, George
  British Writers, vol. 5: **219–234**
Mérimée, Prosper
  European Writers, vol. 6: **745–769**
  Supernatural Fiction Writers, vol. 1: **51–57**
Merril, Judith
  Science Fiction Writers: **433–439**
Merrill, James
  American Writers Supp. 3, part 1: **317–338**
Merritt, A.
  Science Fiction Writers: **65–71**
  Supernatural Fiction Writers, vol. 2: **835–843**
Meyer, Conrad Ferdinand
  See "Poetic Realism"
Miklowitz, Gloria D.
  Writers for Young Adults, vol. 2: **359–368**
Miller, Henry
  American Writers, vol. 3: **170–192**
Miller, Walter M., Jr.
  Science Fiction Writers: **441–448**
Milosz, Czeslaw
  European Writers, vol. 13: **2929–2952**
Mirrlees, Hope
  Supernatural Fiction Writers, vol. 2: **603–607**
Moberg, Vilhelm
  European Writers, vol. 11: **2203–2231**
Mofolo, Thomas Mokopu
  African Writers, vol. 2: **479–493**
Mohr, Nicholasa
  Writers for Young Adults, vol. 2: **369–378**
Molesworth, M. L. S.
  Writers for Children: **407–413**

Okara, Gabriel
  African Writers, vol. 2: **567–582**

Okri, Ben
  African Writers, vol. 2: **599–608**

Olesha, Yuri
  European Writers, vol. 11: **2233–2253**

Oliphant, Mrs.
  Supernatural Fiction Writers, vol. 1: **261–268**

Oliver, Chad
  Science Fiction Writers: **467–473**

Omotoso, Kole
  African Writers, vol. 2: **609–617**

Oneal, Zibby
  Writers for Young Adults, vol. 2: **433–442**

Onetti, Juan Carlos
  Latin American Writers, vol. 3: **1089–1097**

Onions, Oliver
  Supernatural Fiction Writers, vol. 1: **505–511**

Orwell, George
  British Writers, vol. 7: **273–288**
  British Writers Selected Authors, vol. 2: **947–961**
  Science Fiction Writers: **233–241**

Osofisan, Femi
  African Writers, vol. 2: **619–629**

Oyono, Ferdinand
  African Writers, vol. 2: **641–649**

Pain, Barry
  Supernatural Fiction Writers, vol. 1: **443–448**

Palés Matos, Luis
  Latin American Writers, vol. 2: **821–830**

Parra Sanojo, Ana Teresa de la
  Latin American Writers, vol. 2: **717–720**

Pasternak, Boris
  European Writers, vol. 10: **1591–1618**
  European Writers Selected Authors, vol. 2:
    1227–1253

Pater, Walter Horatio
  British Writers, vol. 5: **337–360**

Paterson, Katherine
  Writers for Young Adults, vol. 2: **443–454**

Paton, Alan
  African Writers, vol. 2: **651–668**
  British Writers Supp. 2: **341–361**
  British Writers Selected Authors, vol. 2: **963–983**

Paulsen, Gary
  Writers for Young Adults, vol. 2: **455–463**

Pavese, Cesare
  European Writers, vol. 12: **2759–2784**

Payró, Roberto Jorge
  Latin American Writers, vol. 1: **413–417**

p'Bitek, Okot
  African Writers, vol. 2: **669–684**

Peacock, Thomas Love
  British Writers, vol. 4: **157–170**

Peck, Richard
  Writers for Young Adults, vol. 3: **1–14**

Peck, Robert Newton
  Writers for Young Adults, vol. 3: **15–26**

Pepetela
  African Writers, vol. 2: **685–695**

Percy, Walker
  American Writers Supp. 3, part 1: **383–400**

Pérez Galdós, Benito
  European Writers, vol. 7: **1597–1618**

Peterson, Brenda
  American Nature Writers, vol. 2: **721–731**

Petry, Ann
  African American Writers: **347–359**

Pevsner, Stella
  Writers for Young Adults, vol. 3: **27–34**

Peyton, K. M.
  Writers for Young Adults, vol. 3: **35–42**

Pfeffer, Susan Beth
  Writers for Young Adults, vol. 3: **43–52**

Phillpotts, Eden
  Supernatural Fiction Writers, vol. 2: **549–553**

Picón Salas, Mariano
  Latin American Writers, vol. 2: **903–908**

Pirandello, Luigi
  European Writers, vol. 8: **389–416**
  European Writers Selected Authors, vol. 2:
    1289–1316

Plath, Sylvia
  American Writers Supp. 1, part 2: **526–549**
  Modern American Women Writers: **411–424**

Platt, Kin
  Writers for Young Adults, vol. 3: **53–60**

Plomer, William
  African Writers, vol. 2: **697–706**

Poetic Realism
  European Writers, vol. 6: **913–942**

Robinson, Marilynne
  See "Contemporary Ecofiction"

Rodowsky, Colby
  Writers for Young Adults, vol. 3: **87–93**

Rohmer, Sax
  Supernatural Fiction Writers, vol. 2: **555–560**

Rojas, Manuel
  Latin American Writers, vol. 2: **815–820**

Romero, José Rubén
  Latin American Writers, vol. 2: **711–715**

Roth, Philip
  American Writers Supp. 3, part 2: **401–429**

Rousseau, Jean Jacques
  European Writers, vol. 4: **449–474**
  European Writers Selected Authors, vol. 3:
      1519–1544

Rulfo, Juan
  Latin American Writers, vol. 3: **1215–1229**

Rushdie, Salman
  British Writers Supp. 4: **433–457**

Ruskin, John
  British Writers, vol. 5: **173–186**
  Writers for Children: **493–496**

Russ, Joanna
  Science Fiction Writers: **483–490**

Russell, Eric Frank
  Science Fiction Writers: **197–202**

Saʿadāwī, Nawāl, al-
  African Writers, vol. 2: **721–731**

Sábato, Ernesto
  Latin American Writers, vol. 3: **1139–1143**

Sachs, Marilyn
  Writers for Young Adults, vol. 3: **95–104**

Sade, Marquis de, and the French Libertine
      Tradition
  European Writers, vol. 4: **615–638**

St. Clair, Margaret
  Science Fiction Writers: **491–495**

Saint-Exupéry, Antoine de
  European Writers, vol. 12: **2307–2332**
  European Writers Selected Authors, vol. 3: **1545–1569**

Sainte-Beuve, Charles-Augustin
  European Writers, vol. 6: **837–861**

Saki
  Supernatural Fiction Writers, vol. 1: **449–455**

Salazar Arrué, Salvador (Salarrué)
  Latin American Writers, vol. 2: **875–879**

Ṣāliḥ, al-Ṭayyib
  African Writers, vol. 2: **733–744**

Salinger, J. D.
  American Writers, vol. 3: **551–574**
  Writers for Young Adults, vol. 3: **105–112**

Salisbury, Graham
  Writers for Young Adults, vol. 3: **113–121**

Salten, Felix
  Writers for Children: **497–501**

Sand, George
  European Writers, vol. 6: **813–836**
  European Writers Selected Authors, vol. 3:
      1571–1594

Sandburg, Carl
  American Writers, vol. 3: **575–598**
  Writers for Children: **503–510**
  Writers for Young Adults, vol. 3: **123–133**

Sanders, Scott Russell
  American Nature Writers, vol. 2: **793–804**

Sarban
  Supernatural Fiction Writers, vol. 2: **667–673**

Sarduy, Severo
  Latin American Writers, vol. 3: **1437–1444**

Sarraute, Nathalie
  European Writers, vol. 12: **2333–2359**

Sartre, Jean-Paul
  European Writers, vol. 12: **2589–2614**
  European Writers Selected Authors, vol. 3: **1595–1620**

Sawyer, Ruth
  Writers for Children: **511–517**

Sayers, Dorothy L.
  British Writers Supp. 3: **333–353**

Schlegel, Friedrich von
  European Writers, vol. 5: **177–203**

Schnitzler, Arthur
  European Writers, vol. 8: **89–117**

Schreiner, Olive
  African Writers, vol. 2: **745–763**
  British Writers Supp. 2: **435–458**

Scoppettone, Sandra
  Writers for Young Adults, vol. 3: **135–143**

Scott, Paul
  British Writers Supp. 1: **259–274**

Scott, Sir Walter
   British Writers, vol. 4: **27–40**
   Supernatural Fiction Writers, vol. 1: **169–176**

Sebestyen, Ouida
   Writers for Young Adults, vol. 3: **145–153**

Sembène Ousmane
   African Writers, vol. 2: **765–774**

Senarens, Luis Philip
   Science Fiction Writers: **53–58**

Seredy, Kate
   Writers for Children: **519–524**

Serviss, Garrett P.
   Science Fiction Writers: **39–44**

Seton, Ernest Thompson
   American Nature Writers, vol. 2: **805–816**

Sewell, Anna
   Writers for Children: **525–528**

Shange, Ntozake
   African American Writers: **379–393**

Shaw, George Bernard
   British Writers, vol. 6: **101–132**
   British Writers Selected Authors, vol. 3: **1053–1084**

Sheckley, Robert
   Science Fiction Writers: **497–503**

Shelley, Mary
   British Writers Supp. 3: **355–373**
   British Writers Selected Authors, vol. 3: **1085–1103**
   Science Fiction Writers: **3–9**
   See also "Gothic Novel, The"

Shiel, M. P.
   Science Fiction Writers: **31–37**
   Supernatural Fiction Writers, vol. 1: **361–367**

Sigüenza y Góngora, Carlos de
   Latin American Writers, vol. 1: **71–77**

Silko, Leslie Marmon
   American Nature Writers, vol. 2: **817–827**
   American Writers Supp. 4, part 2: **557–572**

Silone, Ignazione
   European Writers, vol. 12: **2273–2305**

Silva, José Asunción
   Latin American Writers, vol. 1: **377–385**

Silveira de Queiroz, Dinah
   Latin American Writers, vol. 3: **1145–1151**

Silverberg, Robert
   Science Fiction Writers: **505–511**

Simak, Clifford D.
   Science Fiction Writers: **513–518**

Simenon, Georges
   European Writers, vol. 12: **2479–2510**

Simon, Claude
   European Writers, vol. 13: **3021–3048**

Sinán, Rogelio
   Latin American Writers, vol. 2: **941–946**

Sinclair, May
   Supernatural Fiction Writers, vol. 1: **513–519**

Singer, Isaac Bashevis
   American Writers, vol. 4: **1–24**

Sleator, William
   Writers for Young Adults, vol. 3: **173–182**

Smith, Cordwainer
   Science Fiction Writers: **519–524**

Smith, E. E.
   Science Fiction Writers: **125–130**

Smith, Stevie
   British Writers Supp. 2: **459–479**

Smith, Thorne
   Supernatural Fiction Writers, vol. 2: **805–811**

Smollett, Tobias
   British Writers, vol. 3: **146–159**

Snow, C. P.
   British Writers, vol. 7: **321–342**

Solzhenitsyn, Aleksandr
   European Writers, vol. 13: **3187–3214**
   European Writers Selected Authors, vol. 3: **1621–1647**

Sontag, Susan
   American Writers Supp. 3, part 2: **451–473**
   Modern American Women Writers: **471–483**

Soto, Gary
   Writers for Young Adults, vol. 3: **183–191**

Sowande, Bode
   African Writers, vol. 2: **799–806**

Soyinka, Wole
   African Writers, vol. 2: **807–831**

Spark, Muriel
   British Writers Supp. 1: **199–214**

Spinelli, Jerry
   Writers for Young Adults, vol. 3: **193–201**

Stapledon, Olaf
   Science Fiction Writers: **91–100**

Stead, Christina
    British Writers Supp. 4: **459–477**

Stegner, Wallace
    American Nature Writers, vol. 2: **861–875**
    American Writers Supp. 4, part 2: **595–618**

Stein, Gertrude
    American Writers, vol. 4: **25–48**
    Modern American Women Writers: **485–498**

Steinbeck, John
    American Writers, vol. 4: **49–72**
    Writers for Young Adults, vol. 3: **203–214**

Stendhal
    European Writers, vol. 5: **343–366**
    European Writers Selected Authors, vol. 3:
        1649–1672

Stephens, James
    Supernatural Fiction Writers, vol. 1: **485–490**

Sterne, Laurence
    British Writers, vol. 3: **124–136**

Stevenson, Robert Louis
    British Writers, vol. 5: **383–399**
    British Writers Selected Authors, vol. 3: **1161–1176**
    Supernatural Fiction Writers, vol. 1: **307–313**
    Writers for Children: **535–543**
    Writers for Young Adults, vol. 3: **215–224**

Stockton, Frank R.
    Supernatural Fiction Writers, vol. 2: **753–759**
    Writers for Children: **545–554**

Stoker, Bram
    British Writers Supp. 3: **375–391**
    Supernatural Fiction Writers, vol. 1: **375–381**

Storey, David
    British Writers Supp. 1: **407–420**

Storm, Theodor
    See "Poetic Realism"

Stowe, Harriet Beecher
    American Writers Supp. 1, part 2: **579–601**

Strasser, Todd
    Writers for Young Adults, vol. 3: **225–236**

Stratemeyer, Edward
    Writers for Young Adults, vol. 3: **237–249**

Stratton Porter, Gene
    American Nature Writers, vol. 2: **877–891**

Strindberg, August
    European Writers, vol. 7: **1731–1758**

Sturgeon, Theodore
    Science Fiction Writers: **203–208**
    Supernatural Fiction Writers, vol. 2: **941–945**

Styron, William
    American Writers, vol. 4: **97–119**

Suassuna, Ariano Vilar
    Latin American Writers, vol. 3: **1317–1321**

Sutcliff, Rosemary
    Writers for Young Adults, vol. 3: **251–261**

Svevo, Italo
    European Writers, vol. 8: **67–87**

Swann, Thomas Burnett
    Supernatural Fiction Writers, vol. 2: **1097–1103**

Swift, Jonathan
    British Writers, vol. 3: **15–38**
    British Writers Selected Authors, vol. 3: **1195–1217**
    Writers for Children: **555–559**

Swinburne, Algernon Charles
    British Writers, vol. 5: **309–336**

Tablada, José Juan
    Latin American Writers, vol. 1: **441–446**

Ṭāhā Ḥusayn
    African Writers, vol. 2: **851–863**

Taine, John
    Science Fiction Writers: **75–82**

Talbert, Marc
    Writers for Young Adults, vol. 3: **263–272**

Tate, Allen
    American Writers, vol. 4: **120–143**

Taylor, Mildred Delois
    Writers for Young Adults, vol. 3: **273–282**

Taylor, Theodore
    Writers for Young Adults, vol. 3: **283–292**

Tenn, William
    Science Fiction Writers: **525–530**

Thackeray, William Makepeace
    British Writers, vol. 5: **17–40**
    British Writers Selected Authors, vol. 3: **1237–1259**

Thomas, D. M.
    British Writers Supp. 4: **479–497**

Thomas, Joyce Carol
    Writers for Young Adults, vol. 3: **293–301**

Thompson, Julian F.
    Writers for Young Adults, vol. 3: **303–310**

Tieck, Ludwig
  European Writers, vol. 5: **233–260**
  Supernatural Fiction Writers, vol. 1: **83–89**

Tiptree, James, Jr.
  Science Fiction Writers: **531–541**

Tolkien, J. R. R.
  British Writers Supp. 2: **519–536**
  British Writers Selected Authors, vol. 3: **1277–1294**
  Supernatural Fiction Writers, vol. 2: **675–682**
  Writers for Children: **561–571**
  Writers for Young Adults, vol. 3: **311–320**

Tolstoy, Leo
  European Writers, vol. 7: **1471–1494**
  European Writers Selected Authors, vol. 3:
      1693–1715

Torres Bodet, Jaime
  Latin American Writers, vol. 2: **933–939**

Trevor, William
  British Writers Supp. 4: **499–519**

Trollope, Anthony
  British Writers, vol. 5: **89–104**
  British Writers Selected Authors, vol. 3: **1295–1309**

Turgenev, Ivan
  European Writers, vol. 6: **1275–1297**
  European Writers Selected Authors, vol. 3: **1717–1739**

Tutuola, Amos
  African Writers, vol. 2: **865–878**

Twain, Mark
  American Writers, vol. 4: **190–213**
  Supernatural Fiction Writers, vol. 2: **761–768**
  Writers for Children: **573–582**
  Writers for Young Adults, vol. 3: **321–328**

Tyler, Anne
  American Writers Supp. 4, part 2: **657–675**
  Modern American Women Writers: **499–510**

Unamuno, Miguel de
  European Writers, vol. 8: **283–310**

Undset, Sigrid
  European Writers, vol. 9: **1017–1041**

Updike, John
  American Writers, vol. 4: **214–235**
  American Writers Retrospective: **317–338**

Usigli, Rodolfo
  Latin American Writers, vol. 3: **1033–1042**

Uslar Pietri, Arturo
  Latin American Writers, vol. 3: **1057–1062**

Valenzuela, Luisa
  Latin American Writers, vol. 3: **1445–1449**

Valle-Inclán, Ramón del
  European Writers, vol. 8: **331–353**

Vallejo, César
  Latin American Writers, vol. 2: **727–738**

Vance, Jack
  Science Fiction Writers: **543–549**
  Supernatural Fiction Writers, vol. 2: **1105–1111**

van der Post, Laurens
  African Writers, vol. 2: **879–891**

Van Vechten, Carl
  American Writers Supp. 2, part 2: **725–751**

Van Vogt, A. E.
  Science Fiction Writers: **209–217**

Vargas Llosa, Mario
  Latin American Writers, vol. 3: **1421–1436**

Vega, Lope de
  European Writers, vol. 2: **845–870**

Verga, Giovanni
  European Writers, vol. 7: **1543–1565**

Veríssimo, Érico
  Latin American Writers, vol. 3: **1043–1048**

Verne, Jules
  Science Fiction Writers: **573–582**
  Writers for Children: **591–598**

Vesaas, Tarjei
  European Writers, vol. 11: **2035–2059**

Vidal, Gore
  American Writers Supp. 4, part 2: **677–697**

Vieira, José Luandino
  African Writers, vol. 2: **893–901**

Vigny, Alfred Victor de
  European Writers, vol. 5: **447–488**

Villaurrutia, Xavier
  Latin American Writers, vol. 3: **975–980**

Villaverde, Cirilo
  Latin American Writers, vol. 1: **169–174**

Vittorini, Elio
  European Writers, vol. 12: **2733–2757**

Voigt, Cynthia
  Writers for Young Adults, vol. 3: **329–338**

Voltaire
  European Writers, vol. 4: **367–392**

European Writers Selected Authors, vol. 3: **1741–1766**

Vonnegut, Kurt
American Writers Supp. 2, part 2: **753–783**
Science Fiction Writers: **551–561**

Wakefield, H. Russell
Supernatural Fiction Writers, vol. 2: **617–622**

Walker, Alice
African American Writers: **441–458**
American Writers Supp. 3, part 2: **517–540**
Modern American Women Writers: **511–520**

Walker, Margaret
African American Writers: **459–471**

Wall, Mervyn
Supernatural Fiction Writers, vol. 2: **645–650**

Wallace, David Rains
American Nature Writers, vol. 2: **963–972**

Walpole, Horace
Supernatural Fiction Writers, vol. 1: **131–137**
See also "Gothic Novel, The"

Walsh, Jill Paton
Writers for Young Adults, vol. 3: **339–346**

Warren, Robert Penn
American Writers, vol. 4: **236–259**

Waugh, Evelyn
British Writers, vol. 7: **289–308**
British Writers Selected Authors, vol. 3: **1311–1330**

Wedekind, Frank
European Writers, vol. 8: **229–281**

Weinbaum, Stanley G.
Science Fiction Writers: **145–149**

Weldon, Fay
British Writers Supp. 4: **521–539**

Wellman, Manly Wade
Supernatural Fiction Writers, vol. 2: **947–954**

Wells, H. G.
British Writers, vol. 6: **225–246**
British Writers Selected Authors, vol. 3: **1331–1352**
Science Fiction Writers: **25–30**
Supernatural Fiction Writers, vol. 1: **397–402**
Writers for Children: **599–603**

Welty, Eudora
American Writers, vol. 4: **260–284**
American Writers Retrospective: **339–358**
Modern American Women Writers: **521–538**

Wersba, Barbara
Writers for Young Adults, vol. 3: **349–357**

West, Nathanael
American Writers, vol. 4: **285–307**

West, Rebecca
British Writers Supp. 3: **431–445**

Westall, Robert Atkinson
Writers for Young Adults, vol. 3: **359–369**

Wharton, Edith
American Writers, vol. 4: **308–330**
American Writers Retrospective: **359–385**
Modern American Women Writers: **539–558**
Supernatural Fiction Writers, vol. 2: **783–788**

Wheatley, Dennis
Supernatural Fiction Writers, vol. 2: **623–629**

White, Patrick
British Writers Supp. 1: **129–152**

White, T. H.
Supernatural Fiction Writers, vol. 2: **651–657**

Wideman, John Edgar
African American Writers: **493–504**

Wieland, Christoph Martin
European Writers, vol. 4: **587–614**

Wiggin, Kate Douglas
Writers for Children: **605–609**

Wilde, Oscar
British Writers, vol. 5: **399–422**
British Writers Selected Authors, vol. 3: **1353–1376**
Supernatural Fiction Writers, vol. 1: **345–350**
Writers for Children: **611–616**

Wilder, Laura Ingalls
Writers for Children: **617–623**
Writers for Young Adults, vol. 3: **371–380**

Wilder, Thornton
American Writers, vol. 4: **355–377**

Wilkinson, Brenda
Writers for Young Adults, vol. 3: **381–390**

Williams, Charles
Supernatural Fiction Writers, vol. 2: **631–638**

Williams, Tennessee
American Writers, vol. 4: **378–401**

Williams, William Carlos
American Writers, vol. 4: **402–425**
American Writers Retrospective: **411–433**

Williamson, Jack
    Science Fiction Writers: **225–231**

Wilson, Angus
    British Writers Supp. 1: **153–168**

Wilson, Edmund
    American Writers, vol. 4: **426–449**

Winterson, Jeanette
    British Writers Supp. 4: **541–559**

Witkiewicz (Witkacy), Stanisław Ignacy
    European Writers, vol. 10: **1205–1230**

Wodehouse, P. G.
    British Writers Supp. 3: **447–464**
    British Writers Selected Authors, vol. 3: **1377–1394**

Wolfe, Thomas
    American Writers, vol. 4: **450–473**

Wolfe, Tom
    American Writers Supp. 3, part 2: **567–588**

Wolff, Virginia Euwer
    Writers for Young Adults, vol. 3: **391–398**

Wollstonecraft, Mary
    British Writers Supp. 3: **465–482**

Wood, Mrs. Henry
    Supernatural Fiction Writers, vol. 1: **279–286**

Woolf, Virginia
    British Writers, vol. 7: **17–40**
    British Writers Selected Authors, vol. 3: **1395–1417**

Wright, Richard
    African American Writers: **505–523**
    American Writers, vol. 4: **474–497**

Wright, S. Fowler
    Science Fiction Writers: **83–89**

Wylie, Elinor
    American Writers Supp. 1, part 2: **707–730**

Wyndham, John
    Science Fiction Writers: **219–224**

Yáñez, Agustín
    Latin American Writers, vol. 3: **995–999**

Yep, Laurence
    Writers for Young Adults, vol. 3: **399–408**

Yolen, Jane
    Writers for Young Adults, vol. 3: **409–420**

Yonge, Charlotte Mary
    Writers for Children: **625–631**

Yourcenar, Marguerite
    European Writers, vol. 12: **2535–2561**

Zamyatin, Yevgeny Ivanovich
    European Writers, vol. 10: **1181–1203**

Zelazny, Roger
    Science Fiction Writers: **563–570**
    Supernatural Fiction Writers, vol. 2: **1113–1119**

Zeno Gandía, Manuel
    Latin American Writers, vol. 1: **321–326**

Zindel, Paul
    Writers for Young Adults, vol. 3: **421–430**

Zola, Émile
    European Writers, vol. 7: **1517–1542**
    European Writers Selected Authors, vol. 3: **1789–1813**

THE SHORT STORY

The modern short story, including fantasy and science fiction, as practiced after ca. 1840.

Abrahams, Peter
    African Writers, vol. 1: **1–14**

Acevedo Díaz, Eduardo
    Latin American Writers, vol. 1: **299–303**

Achebe, Chinua
    African Writers, vol. 1: **15–36**

Ady, Endre
    European Writers, vol. 9: **859–880**

Aickman, Robert
    Supernatural Fiction Writers, vol. 2: **957–964**

Aidoo, Ama Ata
    African Writers, vol. 1: **37–48**

Aiken, Conrad
    American Writers, vol. 1: **48–70**

Alcott, Louisa May
    American Writers Supp. 1, part 1: **28–46**

Writers for Children: **1–6**
Writers for Young Adults, vol. 1: **11–20**

Aldiss, Brian W.
Science Fiction Writers: **251–258**

Alegría, Ciro
Latin American Writers, vol. 3: **1099–1103**

Alencar, José de
Latin American Writers, vol. 1: **195–203**

Alexander, Lloyd
Supernatural Fiction Writers, vol. 2: **965–971**
Writers for Young Adults, vol. 1: **21–33**

Alfieri, Vittorio
European Writers, vol. 4: **661–689**

Amis, Kingsley
British Writers Supp. 2: **1–19**

Andersen, Hans Christian
European Writers, vol. 6: **863–892**
European Writers Selected Authors, vol. 1: **1–29**
Writers for Children: **7–13**

Anderson, Poul
Science Fiction Writers: **259–265**
Supernatural Fiction Writers, vol. 2: **973–980**

Anderson, Sherwood
American Writers, vol. 1: **97–120**

Anderson Imbert, Enrique
Latin American Writers, vol. 3: **1105–1110**

Andrade, Mário de
Latin American Writers, vol. 2: **771–780**

Andrić, Ivo
European Writers, vol. 11: **1751–1779**

Anstey, F.
Supernatural Fiction Writers, vol. 1: **287–292**

Anthony, Piers
Supernatural Fiction Writers, vol. 2: **981–986**

Apollinaire, Guillaume
European Writers, vol. 9: **881–903**

Arabian Nights
Supernatural Fiction Writers, vol. 1: **19–26**

Aragon, Louis
European Writers, vol. 11: **2061–2087**

Arenas, Reinaldo
Latin American Writers, vol. 3: **1451–1458**

Arguedas, José María
Latin American Writers, vol. 3: **1131–1138**

Arlt, Roberto
Latin American Writers, vol. 2: **881–886**

Armah, Ayi Kwei
African Writers, vol. 1: **49–62**

Arreola, Juan José
Latin American Writers, vol. 3: **1229–1236**

Arthurian Legend
European Writers, vol. 1: **137–160**
European Writers Selected Authors, vol. 1: **79–102**

Arthurian Romances
Supernatural Fiction Writers, vol. 1: **11–18**

Asimov, Isaac
Science Fiction Writers: **267–276**

Asturias, Miguel Ángel
Latin American Writers, vol. 2: **865–873**

Atherton, Gertrude
Supernatural Fiction Writers, vol. 2: **777–781**

Auchincloss, Louis
American Writers Supp. 4, part 1: **21–38**

Austin, Mary Hunter
American Nature Writers, vol. 1: **31–51**

Awoonor, Kofi
African Writers, vol. 1: **63–75**

Aymé, Marcel
European Writers, vol. 12: **2433–2456**

Azevedo, Aluísio
Latin American Writers, vol. 1: **333–341**

Azorín
European Writers, vol. 9: **639–661**

Azuela, Mariano
Latin American Writers, vol. 2: **457–464**

Babel, Isaac
European Writers, vol. 11: **1885–1915**
European Writers Selected Authors, vol. 1: **131–160**

Baker, Frank
Supernatural Fiction Writers, vol. 2: **561–567**

Ballard, J. G.
Science Fiction Writers: **277–282**

Balzac, Honoré de
European Writers, vol. 5: **635–658**
European Writers Selected Authors, vol. 1: **161–183**
Supernatural Fiction Writers, vol. 1: **37–44**

Bangs, J. K.
Supernatural Fiction Writers, vol. 2: **725–729**

Büchner, Georg
  European Writers, vol. 6: **1169–1194**

Buck, Pearl S.
  American Writers Supp. 2, part 1: **113–134**

Budrys, Algis
  Science Fiction Writers: **305–311**

Bulwer-Lytton, Edward
  Supernatural Fiction Writers, vol. 1: **195–204**

Burnett, Frances Hodgson
  Writers for Children: **103–109**

Burroughs, Edgar Rice
  Science Fiction Writers: **59–64**

Burton, Virginia Lee
  Writers for Children: **111–115**

Byars, Betsy
  Writers for Young Adults, vol. 1: **199–207**

Cabell, James Branch
  Supernatural Fiction Writers, vol. 2: **789–796**

Cabrera Infante, Guillermo
  Latin American Writers, vol. 3: **1383–1391**

Caldwell, Erskine
  American Writers, vol. 1: **288–311**

Calvino, Italo
  European Writers, vol. 13: **3259–3286**

Campbell, John W., Jr.
  Science Fiction Writers: **151–159**

Campbell, Ramsey
  Supernatural Fiction Writers, vol. 2: **993–999**

Camus, Albert
  African Writers, vol. 1: **139–152**
  European Writers, vol. 13: **3049–3078**
  European Writers Selected Authors, vol. 1: **305–334**

Čapek, Karel
  European Writers, vol. 10: **1565–1590**
  Science Fiction Writers: **583–589**

Capote, Truman
  American Writers Supp. 3, part 1: **111–133**

Carballido, Emilio
  Latin American Writers, vol. 3: **1289–1294**

Carpentier, Alejo
  Latin American Writers, vol. 3: **1019–1031**

Carrasquilla, Tomás
  Latin American Writers, vol. 1: **343–350**

Carroll, Lewis
  British Writers, vol. 5: **261–276**

  Supernatural Fiction Writers, vol. 1: **247–253**
  Writers for Children: **117–127**

Carter, Alden R.
  Writers for Young Adults, vol. 1: **209–218**

Carter, Angela
  British Writers Supp. 3: **79–93**

Carver, Raymond
  American Writers Supp. 3, part 1: **135–151**

Casal, Julián del
  Latin American Writers, vol. 1: **365–370**

Cather, Willa
  American Writers, vol. 1: **312–334**
  American Writers Retrospective: **1–23**
  Modern American Women Writers: **49–62**

Cazotte, Jacques
  Supernatural Fiction Writers, vol. 1: **29–35**

Cela, Camilo José
  European Writers, vol. 13: **3105–3129**

Cervantes, Miguel de
  European Writers, vol. 2: **819–844**
  European Writers Selected Authors, vol. 1: **335–359**
  See also "Renaissance Short Fiction"

Chambers, Robert W.
  Supernatural Fiction Writers, vol. 2: **739–745**

Chandler, Raymond
  American Writers Supp. 4, part 1: **119–138**

Cheever, John
  American Writers Supp. 1, part 1: **174–199**

Chekhov, Anton
  European Writers, vol. 7: **1855–1882**
  European Writers Selected Authors, vol. 1: **361–387**

Chesnutt, Charles W.
  African American Writers: **59–70**

Chesterton, G. K.
  British Writers, vol. 6: **335–346**
  Supernatural Fiction Writers, vol. 1: **411–414**

Chopin, Kate
  American Writers Supp. 1, part 1: **200–226**
  Modern American Women Writers: **63–78**

Christie, Agatha
  British Writers Supp. 2: **123–137**

Clarke, Arthur C.
  Science Fiction Writers: **313–320**

Clement, Hal
  Science Fiction Writers: **321–327**

Colette
European Writers, vol. 9: **617–638**
European Writers Selected Authors, vol. 1: **389–410**

Collier, John
Supernatural Fiction Writers, vol. 2: **577–583**

Collins, Wilkie
Supernatural Fiction Writers, vol. 1: **233–238**

Collodi, C.
Writers for Children: **129–137**

Colman, Hila
Writers for Young Adults, vol. 1: **271–280**

Colum, Padraic
Writers for Children: **139–146**

Conrad, Joseph
British Writers, vol. 6: **133–150**
British Writers Selected Authors, vol. 1: **331–348**

Coppard, A. E.
Supernatural Fiction Writers, vol. 2: **523–528**

Corelli, Marie
Supernatural Fiction Writers, vol. 1: **293–297**

Cormier, Robert
Writers for Young Adults, vol. 1: **291–301**

Couto, Mia
African Writers, vol. 1: **185–197**

Cozzens, James Gould
American Writers, vol. 1: **358–381**

Crane, Stephen
American Writers, vol. 1: **405–427**
Writers for Young Adults, vol. 1: **303–312**

Crawford, F. Marion
Supernatural Fiction Writers, vol. 2: **747–751**

Dahl, Roald
British Writers Supp. 4: **201–227**

Daly, Maureen
Writers for Young Adults, vol. 1: **323–333**

D'Annunzio, Gabriele
European Writers, vol. 8: **175–203**

Darío, Rubén
Latin American Writers, vol. 1: **397–412**

Daugherty, James Henry
Writers for Children: **155–161**

Davidson, Avram
Supernatural Fiction Writers, vol. 2: **1001–1008**

Davis, H. L.
American Nature Writers, vol. 1: **199–211**

Davis, Terry
Writers for Young Adults, vol. 1: **345–352**

De Camp, L. Sprague
Science Fiction Writers: **179–184**

De la Mare, Walter
Supernatural Fiction Writers, vol. 1: **497–503**
Writers for Children: **173–180**

Delany, Samuel R.
Science Fiction Writers: **329–336**

Denevi, Marco
Latin American Writers, vol. 3: **1265–1269**

Derleth, August
Supernatural Fiction Writers, vol. 2: **883–890**

Díaz Rodríguez, Manuel
Latin American Writers, vol. 1: **431–439**

Dick, Philip K.
Science Fiction Writers: **337–343**

Dickens, Charles
British Writers, vol. 5: **41–74**
British Writers Selected Authors, vol. 1: **363–396**
Supernatural Fiction Writers, vol.1: **213–218**
Writers for Children: **181–191**
Writers for Young Adults, vol. 1: **353–364**

Dickinson, Peter
Writers for Young Adults, vol. 1: **375–383**

Dickson, Gordon R.
Science Fiction Writers: **345–350**

Diderot, Denis
European Writers, vol. 4: **475–509**

Dillard, Annie
American Nature Writers, vol. 1: **213–230**

Dinesen, Isak
European Writers, vol. 10: **1281–1306**
European Writers Selected Authors, vol. 1: **453–477**

Disch, Thomas M.
Science Fiction Writers: **351–356**

Doctorow, E. L.
American Writers Supp. 4, part 1: **217–240**

Dodge, Mary Mapes
Writers for Children: **193–199**

Donaldson, Stephen R.
Supernatural Fiction Writers, vol. 2: **1009–1013**

Donoso, José
Latin American Writers, vol. 3: **1277–1288**

Honwana, Luís Bernardo
  African Writers, vol. 1: **321–329**

Howard, Robert E.
  Supernatural Fiction Writers, vol. 2: **861–868**

Howells, William Dean
  American Writers, vol. 2: **271–294**

Hughes, Langston
  African American Writers: **193–205**
  American Writers Retrospective: **193–214**
  American Writers Supp. 1, part 1: **320–348**
  Writers for Children: **295–301**

Hurston, Zora Neale
  African American Writers: **205–218**
  Modern American Women Writers: **221–235**

Huxley, Aldous
  British Writers, vol. 7: **197–208**
  British Writers Selected Authors, vol. 2: **635–646**
  Science Fiction Writers: **101–108**

Huysmans, Joris Karl
  European Writers, vol. 7: **1709–1729**

Ibarbourou, Juana de
  Latin American Writers, vol. 2: **803–807**

Icaza, Jorge
  Latin American Writers, vol. 3: **1063–1067**

Idrīs, Yūsuf
  African Writers, vol. 1: **345–365**

Irving, Washington
  American Writers, vol. 2: **295–318**
  Supernatural Fiction Writers, vol. 2: **685–691**
  Writers for Children: **303–307**

Jackson, Shirley
  Supernatural Fiction Writers, vol. 2: **1031–1036**

Jacobs, Joseph
  Writers for Children: **309–316**

Jacobs, W. W.
  Supernatural Fiction Writers, vol. 1: **383–387**

Jacobson, Dan
  African Writers, vol. 1: **377–389**

Jaimes Freyre, Ricardo
  Latin American Writers, vol. 1: **419–423**

James, Henry
  American Writers, vol. 2: **319–341**
  American Writers Retrospective: **215–242**
  British Writers, vol. 6: **23–69**
  Supernatural Fiction Writers, vol. 1: **337–344**

James, M. R.
  Supernatural Fiction Writers, vol. 1: **429–436**

Jarry, Alfred
  European Writers, vol. 9: **665–687**

Jewett, Sarah Orne
  American Writers, vol. 2: **391–414**
  Modern American Women Writers: **235–250**

Johnson, Eyvind
  European Writers, vol. 12: **2361–2385**

Johnson, Josephine
  American Nature Writers, vol. 1: **439–451**

Jones, Gayl
  African American Writers: **235–244**

Joyce, James
  British Writers, vol. 7: **41–58**
  British Writers Selected Authors, vol. 2: **683–700**

Kafka, Franz
  European Writers, vol. 9: **1151–1179**
  European Writers Selected Authors, vol. 2: **847–875**

Kästner, Erich
  Writers for Children: **317–322**

Kazantzakis, Nikos
  European Writers, vol. 9: **1067–1091**

Keller, David H.
  Science Fiction Writers: **119–123**

Keller, Gottfried
  See "Poetic Realism"

Kerr, M. E.
  Writers for Young Adults, vol. 2: **177–185**

Khlebnikov, Velimir
  European Writers, vol. 10: **1331–1364**

King, Stephen
  Supernatural Fiction Writers, vol. 2: **1037–1044**

Kingsley, Charles
  Writers for Children: **323–327**

Kingston, Maxine Hong
  Modern American Women Writers: **251–259**

Kipling, Rudyard
  British Writers, vol. 6: **165–206**
  British Writers Selected Authors, vol. 2: **729–770**
  Supernatural Fiction Writers, vol. 1: **437–442**
  Writers for Children: **329–336**

Klein, Norma
  Writers for Young Adults, vol. 2: **187–197**

Knight, Damon
  Science Fiction Writers: **393–400**

Kornbluth, C. M.
  Science Fiction Writers: **401–407**

Lowry, Malcolm
   British Writers Supp. 3: **269–286**

Lugones, Leopoldo
   Latin American Writers, vol. 2: **493–502**

Lynch, Benito
   Latin American Writers, vol. 2: **559–563**

McCarthy, Mary
   American Writers, vol. 2: **558–584**
   Modern American Women Writers: **269–278**

McCullers, Carson
   American Writers, vol. 2: **585–608**
   Modern American Women Writers: **279–287**

MacDonald, George
   Supernatural Fiction Writers, vol. 1: **239–246**
   Writers for Children: **373–380**

Macdonald, Ross
   American Writers Supp. 4, part 2: **459–477**

Machado, Antonio
   European Writers, vol. 9: **743–765**

Machado de Assis, Joaquim Maria
   Latin American Writers, vol. 1: **253–268**

Machen, Arthur
   Supernatural Fiction Writers, vol. 1: **351–359**

McKillip, Patricia
   Supernatural Fiction Writers, vol. 2: **1067–1072**

Macleod, Fiona
   Supernatural Fiction Writers, vol. 1: **369–374**

McPhee, John
   American Nature Writers, vol. 1: **583–598**
   American Writers Supp. 3, part 1: **289–316**

Maḥfūẓ, Najīb
   African Writers, vol. 2: **451–465**

Mailer, Norman
   American Writers, vol. 3: **26–49**

Malamud, Bernard
   American Writers Supp. 1, part 2: **427–453**

Mallea, Eduardo
   Latin American Writers, vol. 3: **981–989**

Mañach Robato, Jorge
   Latin American Writers, vol. 2: **831–836**

Mann, Heinrich
   European Writers, vol. 8: **519–543**

Mann, Thomas
   European Writers, vol. 9: **715–743**
   European Writers Selected Authors, vol. 2:
      997–1024

Mansfield, Katherine
   British Writers, vol. 7: **171–184**
   British Writers Selected Authors, vol. 2: **891–904**

Mariátegui, José Carlos
   Latin American Writers, vol. 2: **791–796**

Marín Cañas, José
   Latin American Writers, vol. 3: **991–994**

Marquand, John P.
   American Writers, vol. 3: **50–73**

Marqués, René
   Latin American Writers, vol. 3: **1237–1246**

Marryat, Frederick
   Writers for Children: **381–387**

Marshall, Paule
   African American Writers: **289–304**

Martínez Estrada, Ezequiel
   Latin American Writers, vol. 2: **809–813**

Matheson, Richard
   Science Fiction Writers: **425–431**
   Supernatural Fiction Writers, vol. 2: **1073–1080**

Matto de Turner, Clorinda
   Latin American Writers, vol. 1: **305–309**

Maugham, W. Somerset
   British Writers, vol. 6: **363–382**
   British Writers Selected Authors, vol. 2: **905–923**

Maupassant, Guy de
   European Writers, vol. 7: **1759–1784**
   European Writers Selected Authors, vol. 2: **1025–1050**
   Supernatural Fiction Writers, vol. 1: **59–65**

Mauriac, François
   European Writers, vol. 10: **1307–1330**

Mayakovsky, Vladimir
   European Writers, vol. 11: **1835–1858**

Meigs, Cornelia
   Writers for Children: **389–395**

Melville, Herman
   American Writers, vol. 3: **74–98**
   American Writers Retrospective: **243–262**

Mérimée, Prosper
   European Writers, vol. 6: **745–769**
   Supernatural Fiction Writers, vol. 1: **51–57**

Merril, Judith
   Science Fiction Writers: **433–439**

Merritt, A.
   Science Fiction Writers: **65–71**
   Supernatural Fiction Writers, vol. 2: **835–843**

Oates, Joyce Carol
  American Writers Supp. 2, part 2: **503–527**
  Modern American Women Writers: **353–374**
O'Brien, Fitz-James
  Supernatural Fiction Writers, vol. 2: **717–722**
O'Connor, Flannery
  American Writers, vol. 3: **337–360**
  Modern American Women Writers: **375–388**
O'Hara, John
  American Writers, vol. 3: **361–384**
Okara, Gabriel
  African Writers, vol. 2: **567–582**
Okri, Ben
  African Writers, vol. 2: **599–608**
Olesha, Yuri
  European Writers, vol. 11: **2233–2253**
Oliphant, Mrs.
  Supernatural Fiction Writers, vol. 1: **261–268**
Oliver, Chad
  Science Fiction Writers: **467–473**
Omotoso, Kole
  African Writers, vol. 2: **609–617**
Onetti, Juan Carlos
  Latin American Writers, vol. 3: **1089–1097**
Onions, Oliver
  Supernatural Fiction Writers, vol. 1: **505–511**
Ortiz, Simon J.
  American Writers Supp. 4, part 2: **497–515**
Osofisan, Femi
  African Writers, vol. 2: **619–629**
Pain, Barry
  Supernatural Fiction Writers, vol. 1: **443–448**
Paley, Grace
  Modern American Women Writers: **389–396**
Palma, Ricardo
  Latin American Writers, vol. 1: **221–228**
Parker, Dorothy
  Modern American Women Writers: **397–409**
Paton, Alan
  African Writers, vol. 2: **651–668**
  British Writers Supp. 2: **341–361**
  British Writers Selected Authors, vol. 2: **963–983**
Pavese, Cesare
  European Writers, vol. 12: **2759–2784**

Payró, Roberto Jorge
  Latin American Writers, vol. 1: **413–417**
Peck, Richard
  Writers for Young Adults, vol. 3: **1–14**
Pepetela
  African Writers, vol. 2: **685–695**
Pérez Galdós, Benito
  European Writers, vol. 7: **1597–1618**
Perrault, Charles
  Writers for Children: **431–437**
Petry, Ann
  African American Writers: **347–359**
Phillpotts, Eden
  Supernatural Fiction Writers, vol. 2: **549–553**
Pirandello, Luigi
  European Writers, vol. 8: **389–416**
  European Writers Selected Authors, vol. 2:
    1289–1316
Plomer, William
  African Writers, vol. 2: **697–706**
Poe, Edgar Allan
  American Writers, vol. 3: **409–432**
  Science Fiction Writers: **11–18**
  Supernatural Fiction Writers, vol. 2: **697–705**
  Writers for Young Adults, vol. 3: **61–73**
Poetic Realism
  European Writers, vol. 6: **913–942**
Pohl, Frederik
  Science Fiction Writers: **475–482**
Porter, Katherine Anne
  American Writers, vol. 3: **433–455**
  Modern American Women Writers: **425–440**
Potter, Beatrix
  British Writers Supp. 3: **287–309**
  Writers for Children: **439–446**
Powys, John Cowper
  Supernatural Fiction Writers, vol. 2: **609–616**
Powys, T. F.
  Supernatural Fiction Writers, vol. 2: **609–616**
Pratt, Fletcher
  See "De Camp, L. Sprague, and Fletcher Pratt"
Pritchett, V. S.
  British Writers Supp. 3: **311–331**
Pushkin, Alexander
  European Writers, vol. 5: **659–691**

European Writers Selected Authors, vol. 3: **1341–1373**

Pyle, Howard
Writers for Children: **447–454**

Pynchon, Thomas
American Writers Supp. 2, part 2: **617–638**

Queiroz, Rachel de
Latin American Writers, vol. 3: **1119–1123**

Queneau, Raymond
European Writers, vol. 12: **2511–2534**

Quiller-Couch, Arthur
Supernatural Fiction Writers, vol. 1: **389–395**

Quiroga, Horacio
Latin American Writers, vol. 2: **551–558**

Ramos, Graciliano
Latin American Writers, vol. 2: **745–754**

Ransome, Arthur
Writers for Children: **455–461**

Rawlings, Marjorie Kinnan
American Nature Writers, vol. 2: **751–765**
Writers for Children: **463–467**

Reed, Ishmael
African American Writers: **361–377**

Reynolds, G. W. M.
Supernatural Fiction Writers, vol. 1: **205–211**

Rhys, Jean
British Writers Supp. 2: **387–404**

Richards, Laura E.
Writers for Children: **469–475**

Riddell, Mrs. J. H.
Supernatural Fiction Writers, vol. 1: **269–277**

Ríos, Alberto Álvaro
American Writers Supp. 4, part 2: **537–556**

Roa Bastos, Augusto
Latin American Writers, vol. 3: **1209–1213**

Robbe-Grillet, Alain
European Writers, vol. 13: **3237–3256**

Roberts, Elizabeth Madox
Writers for Children: **477–481**

Rohmer, Sax
Supernatural Fiction Writers, vol. 2: **555–560**

Rojas, Manuel
Latin American Writers, vol. 2: **815–820**

Rojas, Ricardo
Latin American Writers, vol. 2: **591–596**

Rossetti, Christina
British Writers, vol. 5: **247–260**
Writers for Children: **483–491**

Roth, Philip
American Writers Supp. 3, part 2: **401–429**

Rulfo, Juan
Latin American Writers, vol. 3: **1215–1229**

Ruskin, John
British Writers, vol. 5: **173–186**
Writers for Children: **493–496**

Russ, Joanna
Science Fiction Writers: **483–490**

Russell, Eric Frank
Science Fiction Writers: **197–202**

Sa'adāwī, Nawāl, al-
African Writers, vol. 2: **721–731**

Sade, Marquis de, and the French Libertine Tradition
European Writers, vol. 4: **615–638**

St. Clair, Margaret
Science Fiction Writers: **491–495**

Sainte-Beuve, Charles-Augustin
European Writers, vol. 6: **837–861**

Saki
Supernatural Fiction Writers, vol. 1: **449–455**

Salazar Arrué, Salvador (Salarrué)
Latin American Writers, vol. 2: **875–879**

Ṣāliḥ, al-Ṭayyib
African Writers, vol. 2: **733–744**

Salinger, J. D.
American Writers, vol. 3: **551–574**
Writers for Young Adults, vol. 3: **105–112**

Salisbury, Graham
Writers for Young Adults, vol. 3: **113–121**

Sarban
Supernatural Fiction Writers, vol. 2: **667–673**

Sarraute, Nathalie
European Writers, vol. 12: **2333–2359**

Sawyer, Ruth
Writers for Children: **511–517**

Sayers, Dorothy L.
British Writers Supp. 3: **333–353**

Schnitzler, Arthur
European Writers, vol. 8: **89–117**

Stowe, Harriet Beecher
  American Writers Supp. 1, part 2: **579–601**
Strand, Mark
  American Writers Supp. 4, part 2: **619–636**
Stratemeyer, Edward
  Writers for Young Adults, vol. 3: **237–249**
Strindberg, August
  European Writers, vol. 7: **1731–1758**
Sturgeon, Theodore
  Science Fiction Writers: **203–208**
  Supernatural Fiction Writers, vol. 2: **941–945**
Styron, William
  American Writers, vol. 4: **97–119**
Sutherland, Efua Theodora
  African Writers, vol. 2: **833–849**
Svevo, Italo
  European Writers, vol. 8: **67–87**
Swann, Thomas Burnett
  Supernatural Fiction Writers, vol. 2: **1097–1103**
Swenson, May
  American Writers Supp. 4, part 2: **637–655**
Ṭāhā Ḥusayn
  African Writers, vol. 2: **851–863**
Taine, John
  Science Fiction Writers: **75–82**
Tenn, William
  Science Fiction Writers: **525–530**
Thackeray, William Makepeace
  British Writers, vol. 5: **17–40**
  British Writers Selected Authors, vol. 3: **1237–1259**
Thomas, Dylan
  British Writers Supp. 1: **169–184**
  British Writers Selected Authors, vol. 3: **1261–1276**
Thomas, Edward
  British Writers Supp. 3: **393–408**
Thurber, James
  American Writers Supp. 1, part 2: **602–627**
  Supernatural Fiction Writers, vol. 2: **827–831**
Tieck, Ludwig
  European Writers, vol. 5: **233–260**
  Supernatural Fiction Writers, vol. 1: **83–89**
Tiptree, James, Jr.
  Science Fiction Writers: **531–541**
Tolkien, J. R. R.
  British Writers Supp. 2: **519–536**

British Writers Selected Authors, vol. 3: **1277–1294**
  Supernatural Fiction Writers, vol. 2: **675–682**
  Writers for Children: **561–571**
  Writers for Young Adults, vol. 3: **311–320**
Tolstoy, Leo
  European Writers, vol. 7: **1471–1494**
  European Writers Selected Authors, vol. 3:
    1693–1715
Toomer, Jean
  African American Writers: **429–440**
  American Writers Supp. 3, part 2: **475–491**
Torres Bodet, Jaime
  Latin American Writers, vol. 2: **933–939**
Trevor, William
  British Writers Supp. 4: **499–519**
Turgenev, Ivan
  European Writers, vol. 6: **1275–1297**
  European Writers Selected Authors, vol. 3:
    1717–1739
Tutuola, Amos
  African Writers, vol. 2: **865–878**
Twain, Mark
  American Writers, vol. 4: **190–213**
  Supernatural Fiction Writers, vol. 2: **761–768**
  Writers for Children: **573–582**
  Writers for Young Adults, vol. 3: **321–328**
Tychyna, Pavlo
  European Writers, vol. 10: **1651–1676**
Tyler, Anne
  American Writers Supp. 4, part 2: **657–675**
  Modern American Women Writers: **499–510**
Updike, John
  American Writers, vol. 4: **214–235**
  American Writers Retrospective: **317–338**
Uslar Pietri, Arturo
  Latin American Writers, vol. 3: **1057–1062**
Valenzuela, Luisa
  Latin American Writers, vol. 3: **1445–1449**
Valle-Inclán, Ramón del
  European Writers, vol. 8: **331–353**
Vance, Jack
  Science Fiction Writers: **543–549**
  Supernatural Fiction Writers, vol. 2: **1105–1111**
van der Post, Laurens
  African Writers, vol. 2: **879–891**

Wilson, Edmund
  American Writers, vol. 4: **426–449**

Wodehouse, P. G.
  British Writers Supp. 3: **447–464**
  British Writers Selected Authors, vol. 3: **1377–1394**

Wolfe, Thomas
  American Writers, vol. 4: **450–473**

Wollstonecraft, Mary
  British Writers Supp. 3: **465–482**

Wood, Mrs. Henry
  Supernatural Fiction Writers, vol. 1: **279–286**

Wright, Richard
  African American Writers: **505–523**
  American Writers, vol. 4: **474–497**

Wright, S. Fowler
  Science Fiction Writers: **83–89**

Wyndham, John
  Science Fiction Writers: **219–224**

Yáñez, Agustín
  Latin American Writers, vol. 3: **995–999**

Yep, Laurence
  Writers for Young Adults, vol. 3: **399–408**

Yonge, Charlotte Mary
  Writers for Children: **625–631**

Yourcenar, Marguerite
  European Writers, vol. 12: **2535–2561**

Zamyatin, Yevgeny Ivanovich
  European Writers, vol. 10: **1181–1203**

Zelazny, Roger
  Science Fiction Writers: **563–570**
  Supernatural Fiction Writers, vol. 2: **1113–1119**

Zeno Gandía, Manuel
  Latin American Writers, vol. 1: **321–326**

Zorrilla de San Martín, Juan
  Latin American Writers, vol. 1: **327–331**

RELIGION

Sacred or canonical texts and explicitly theological, polemical, or apologetic prose.

Acevedo Díaz, Eduardo
  Latin American Writers, vol. 1: **299–303**

Acosta, Father Joseph de
  Latin American Writers, vol. 1: **47–51**

Acts of the Apostles, The
  See "Gospel of Luke and Acts of the Apostles"

Amoroso Lima, Alceu
  Latin American Writers, vol. 2: **781–790**

Amos
  The Books of the Bible, vol. 1: **367–374**

Apocrypha, The
  The Books of the Bible, vol. 2: **3–11**

Apuleius
  Ancient Writers, vol. 2: **1099–1116**
  Supernatural Fiction Writers, vol. 1: **3–9**

Aquinas, Saint Thomas, and Scholasticism
  European Writers, vol. 1: **405–430**
  European Writers Selected Authors, vol. 1: **53–77**

Augustine, Saint
  European Writers, vol. 1: **23–50**
  European Writers Selected Authors, vol. 1: **103–130**

Baruch, the Letter of Jeremiah, the Prayer of
    Manasseh
  The Books of the Bible, vol. 2: **87–92**

Bergson, Henri
  European Writers, vol. 8: **45–66**

Bible, The English
  British Writers, vol. 1: **370–388**
  British Writers Selected Authors, vol. 1: **69–87**

Bible as Sacred Literature, The
  The Books of the Bible, vol. 1: **1–9**

Bossuet, Jacques Bénigne
  European Writers, vol. 3: **151–175**

Bunyan, John
  British Writers, vol. 2: **240–254**
  British Writers Selected Authors, vol. 1: **215–229**
  Writers for Children: **97–102**

Calderón de la Barca, Pedro
  European Writers, vol. 2: **871–895**

Chesterton, G. K.
  British Writers, vol. 6: **335–346**
  Supernatural Fiction Writers, vol. 1: **411–414**

Chronicles, Ezra, and Nehemiah (1 and 2
      Chronicles, Ezra, and Nehemiah)
   The Books of the Bible, vol. 1: **155–171**

Claudel, Paul
   European Writers, vol. 8: **471–494**

Daniel and Additions to Daniel
   The Books of the Bible, vol. 1: **333–347**

Dante Alighieri
   European Writers, vol. 1: **431–450**
   European Writers Selected Authors, vol. 1: **411–430**
   See also "Renaissance Pastoral Poetry"

Deuteronomy
   The Books of the Bible, vol. 1: **89–102**

Ecclesiastes
   The Books of the Bible, vol. 1: **231–239**

Edwards, Jonathan
   American Writers, vol. 1: **544–566**

Eliot, T. S.
   American Writers, vol. 1: **567–591**
   American Writers Retrospective: **51–71**
   British Writers, vol. 7: **143–170**
   British Writers Selected Authors, vol. 1: **469–496**

Emerson, Ralph Waldo
   American Nature Writers, vol. 1: **287–307**
   American Writers, vol. 2: **1–24**

Epistle of James
   The Books of the Bible, vol. 2: **339–343**

Epistles of John (1, 2, and 3 John)
   The Books of the Bible, vol. 2: **359–365**

Epistle of Jude
   See "Epistles of Peter and Jude (2 Peter and
      Jude)"

Epistle of Peter (1 Peter)
   The Books of the Bible, vol. 2: **345–351**

Epistles of Peter and Jude (2 Peter and Jude)
   The Books of the Bible, vol. 2: **353–357**

Epistle to the Colossians
   The Books of the Bible, vol. 2: **301–310**

Epistles to the Corinthians (1 and 2
      Corinthians)
   The Books of the Bible, vol. 2: **245–269**

Epistle to the Ephesians
   The Books of the Bible, vol. 2: **285–292**

Epistle to the Galatians
   The Books of the Bible, vol. 2: **271–284**

Epistle to the Hebrews
   The Books of the Bible, vol. 2: **327–338**

Epistle to Philemon
   The Books of the Bible, vol. 2: **325–326**

Epistle to the Philippians
   The Books of the Bible, vol. 2: **293–299**

Epistle to the Romans
   The Books of the Bible, vol. 2: **229–243**

Epistles to the Thessalonians (1 and 2
      Thessalonians)
   The Books of the Bible, vol. 2: **311–318**

Epistles to Timothy and Titus (1 and 2 Timothy
      and Titus)
   The Books of the Bible, vol. 2: **319–324**

Esdras (1 Esdras)
   The Books of the Bible, vol. 2: **13–19**

Esdras (2 Esdras)
   The Books of the Bible, vol. 2: **21–34**

Esther and Additions to Esther
   The Books of the Bible, vol. 1: **173–179**

Exodus
   The Books of the Bible, vol. 1: **47–62**

Ezekiel
   The Books of the Bible, vol. 1: **319–332**

Fénelon, François de Salignac de la Mothe-
   European Writers, vol. 3: **261–291**

Frazer, James George
   British Writers Supp. 3: **169–190**

French Novelists, Three
   European Writers, vol. 4: **393–419**

Genesis
   The Books of the Bible, vol. 1: **21–46**

Gibbon, Edward
   British Writers, vol. 3: **221–233**

Gospel of John
   The Books of the Bible, vol. 2: **203–228**

Gospel of Luke and Acts of the Apostles
   The Books of the Bible, vol. 2: **171–202**

Gospel of Mark
   The Books of the Bible, vol. 2: **149–169**

Gospel of Matthew
   The Books of the Bible, vol. 2: **125–147**

Habakkuk
   The Books of the Bible, vol. 1: **391–396**

Haggai, Zechariah, and Malachi
The Books of the Bible, vol. 1: **405–414**

Herder, Johann Gottfried von
European Writers, vol. 4: **639–660**

Hosea
The Books of the Bible, vol. 1: **349–358**

Hume, David
British Writers Supp. 3: **229–245**

Isaiah
The Books of the Bible, vol. 1: **247–279**

James, William
American Writers, vol. 2: **342–366**

Jeremiah
The Books of the Bible, vol. 1: **281–301**

Job
The Books of the Bible, vol. 1: **181–201**

Joel
The Books of the Bible, vol. 1: **359–365**

Jonah
The Books of the Bible, vol. 1: **381–384**

Joshua
The Books of the Bible, vol. 1: **103–112**

Judges
The Books of the Bible, vol. 1: **113–121**

Judith
The Books of the Bible, vol. 2: **43–49**

Kings (1 and 2 Kings)
The Books of the Bible, vol. 1: **141–155**

Klopstock, Friedrich Gottlieb
European Writers, vol. 4: **511–536**

Lamentations
The Books of the Bible, vol. 1: **303–318**

Lessing, Gotthold Ephraim
European Writers, vol. 4: **537–562**

Leviticus
The Books of the Bible, vol. 1: **63–70**

Lewis, C. S.
British Writers Supp. 3: **247–268**
British Writers Selected Authors, vol. 2: **855–876**
Science Fiction Writers: **243–248**
Supernatural Fiction Writers, vol. 2: **661–666**
Writers for Children: **357–364**
Writers for Young Adults, vol. 2: **247–255**

Maccabees (1 and 2 Maccabees)
The Books of the Bible, vol. 2: **93–114**

MacDonald, George
Supernatural Fiction Writers, vol. 1: **239–246**
Writers for Children: **373–380**

Malachi
See "Haggai, Zechariah, and Malachi"

Manzoni, Alessandro
European Writers, vol. 5: **367–394**

Mariátegui, José Carlos
Latin American Writers, vol. 2: **791–796**

Mauriac, François
European Writers, vol. 10: **1307–1330**

Medieval Drama
European Writers, vol. 1: **451–474**
European Writers Selected Authors, vol. 2: **1051–1074**

Micah
The Books of the Bible, vol. 1: **385–390**

Nahum
See "Obadiah and Nahum"

New Testament, The
The Books of the Bible, vol. 2: **117–124**

Novalis
European Writers, vol. 5: **205–231**

Numbers
The Books of the Bible, vol. 1: **71–87**

Obadiah and Nahum
The Books of the Bible, vol. 1: **375–380**

Old Testament, The
The Books of the Bible, vol. 1: **11–19**

Petrarch, Francesco
European Writers, vol. 2: **475–507**
European Writers Selected Authors, vol. 2: **1255–1287**
See also "Renaissance Pastoral Poetry"

Proverbs
The Books of the Bible, vol. 1: **223–230**

Prudentius
European Writers, vol. 1: **1–22**

Psalms
The Books of the Bible, vol. 1: **203–221**

Revelation
The Books of the Bible, vol. 2: **367–381**

Ruth
The Books of the Bible, vol. 1: **123–126**

Samuel (1 and 2 Samuel)
The Books of the Bible, vol. 1: **127–140**

Sirach (Ecclesiasticus)
  The Books of the Bible, vol. 2: **65–86**

Song of Solomon
  The Books of the Bible, vol. 1: **241–246**

Tobit
  The Books of the Bible, vol. 2: **35–42**

Traherne, Thomas
  See "Metaphysical Poets, Four"

Tyndale, William
  See "Bible, The English"

Weil, Simone
  European Writers, vol. 12: **2787–2814**

Williams, Charles
  Supernatural Fiction Writers, vol. 2: **631–638**

Wisdom of Solomon
  The Books of the Bible, vol. 2: **51–63**

Zechariah
  See "Haggai, Zechariah, and Malachi"

Zephaniah
  The Books of the Bible, vol. 1: **397–404**

PHILOSOPHY

Formal intellectual inquiry as distinct from theological, social, and political discourse.

Alberdi, Juan Bautista
  Latin American Writers, vol. 1: **153–158**

Amoroso Lima, Alceu
  Latin American Writers, vol. 2: **781–790**

Aquinas, Saint Thomas, and Scholasticism
  European Writers, vol. 1: **405–430**
  European Writers Selected Authors, vol. 1: **53–77**

Arciniegas, Germán
  Latin American Writers, vol. 2: **897–901**

Aristotle
  Ancient Writers, vol. 1: **377–416**

Augustine, Saint
  European Writers, vol. 1: **23–50**
  European Writers Selected Authors, vol. 1: **103–130**

Bacon, Francis
  British Writers, vol. 1: **257–275**

Barthes, Roland
  European Writers, vol. 13: **3079–3104**

Beauvoir, Simone de
  European Writers, vol. 12: **2701–2732**
  European Writers Selected Authors, vol. 1: **185–215**

Bely, Andrey
  European Writers, vol. 9: **905–929**

Bergson, Henri
  European Writers, vol. 8: **45–66**

Bible, The English
  British Writers, vol. 1: **370–388**
  British Writers Selected Authors, vol. 1: **69–87**

Bossuet, Jacques Bénigne
  European Writers, vol. 3: **151–175**

Breton, André
  European Writers, vol. 11: **1939–1960**

Broch, Hermann
  European Writers, vol. 10: **1385–1408**

Burckhardt, Jacob
  European Writers, vol. 6: **1225–1244**

Camus, Albert
  African Writers, vol. 1: **139–152**
  European Writers, vol. 13: **3049–3078**
  European Writers Selected Authors, vol. 1: **305–334**

Canetti, Elias
  European Writers, vol. 12: **2615–2633**

Caro, Miguel Antonio
  Latin American Writers, vol. 1: **277–281**

Chateaubriand, François René de
  European Writers, vol. 5: **113–140**

Chénier, André
  European Writers, vol. 4: **691–718**

Cicero
  Ancient Writers, vol. 1: **555–581**

Croce, Benedetto
  European Writers, vol. 8: **311–329**

Descartes, René
  European Writers, vol. 3: **1–22**
  European Writers Selected Authors, vol. 1: **431–452**

Diderot, Denis
European Writers, vol. 4: **475–509**

Drummond de Andrade, Carlos
Latin American Writers, vol. 2: **957–974**

Emerson, Ralph Waldo
American Nature Writers, vol. 1: **287–307**
American Writers, vol. 2: **1–24**

Epictetus and Marcus Aurelius
Ancient Writers, vol. 2: **985–1002**

Fénelon, François de Salignac de la Mothe-
European Writers, vol. 3: **261–291**

Fernández, Macedonio
Latin American Writers, vol. 2: **483–491**

Foucault, Michel
European Writers, vol. 13: **3323–3364**

Henríquez Ureña, Pedro
Latin American Writers, vol. 2: **597–601**

Herder, Johann Gottfried von
European Writers, vol. 4: **639–660**

Hume, David
British Writers Supp. 3: **229–245**

James, William
American Writers, vol. 2: **342–366**

Khlebnikov, Velimir
European Writers, vol. 10: **1331–1364**

Kierkegaard, Søren
European Writers, vol. 6: **1123–1146**
European Writers Selected Authors, vol. 2: **877–900**

Lee, Vernon
Supernatural Fiction Writers, vol. 1: **329–335**

Lessing, Gotthold Ephraim
European Writers, vol. 4: **537–562**

Lucian
Ancient Writers, vol. 2: **1081–1097**

Lucretius
Ancient Writers, vol. 2: **601–620**

Lukács, György
European Writers, vol. 10: **1251–1279**

Machado, Antonio
European Writers, vol. 9: **743–765**

Maḥfūẓ, Najīb
African Writers, vol. 2: **451–465**

Marcus Aurelius
See "Epictetus and Marcus Aurelius"

Marinetti, Filippo Tommaso
European Writers, vol. 9: **797–832**

Mather, Cotton
American Writers Supp. 2, part 2: **441–470**

Memmi, Albert
African Writers, vol. 2: **467–477**

Michelet, Jules, and Romantic Historiography
European Writers, vol. 5: **571–606**

Mickiewicz, Adam
European Writers, vol. 5: **607–634**

Milosz, Czeslaw
European Writers, vol. 13: **2929–2952**

Montaigne, Michel de
European Writers, vol. 2: **769–790**
European Writers Selected Authors, vol. 2: **1139–1160**

Montesquieu, Charles-Louis de Secondat
European Writers, vol. 3: **345–366**

Murdoch, Iris
British Writers Supp. 1: **215–235**

Nerval, Gérard de
European Writers, vol. 6: **943–970**

Nietzsche, Friedrich
European Writers, vol. 7: **1645–1682**
European Writers Selected Authors, vol. 2: **1161–1197**

Ortega y Gasset, José
European Writers, vol. 9: **1119–1150**

Paine, Thomas
American Writers Supp. 1, part 2: **501–525**

Pascal, Blaise
European Writers, vol. 3: **125–150**

Petrarch
European Writers, vol. 2: **475–507**
European Writers Selected Authors, vol. 2: **1255–1287**

Plato
Ancient Writers, vol. 1: **353–376**

Plutarch
Ancient Writers, vol. 2: **961–983**

Powys, John Cowper
Supernatural Fiction Writers, vol. 2: **609–616**

Rand, Ayn
American Writers Supp. 4, part 2: **517–535**

Richter, Jean Paul
  European Writers, vol. 5: **53–88**

Rodó, José Enrique
  Latin American Writers, vol. 2: **447–455**

Ronsard, Pierre de, and the Pléiade
  European Writers, vol. 2: **721–746**

Rousseau, Jean Jacques
  European Writers, vol. 4: **449–474**
  European Writers Selected Authors, vol. 3:
    1519–1544

Sade, Marquis de, and the French Libertine
    Tradition
  European Writers, vol. 4: **615–638**

Sainte-Beuve, Charles-Augustin
  European Writers, vol. 6: **837–861**

Santayana, George
  American Writers, vol. 3: **599–622**

Sartre, Jean-Paul
  European Writers, vol. 12: **2589–2614**
  European Writers Selected Authors, vol. 3:
    1595–1620

Schiller, Friedrich von
  European Writers, vol. 5: **27–52**

Schlegel, Friedrich von
  European Writers, vol. 5: **177–203**

Schopenhauer, Arthur
  European Writers, vol. 5: **395–415**

Seneca the Younger
  Ancient Writers, vol. 2: **807–832**

Silone, Ignazione
  European Writers, vol. 12: **2273–2305**

Sinclair, May
  Supernatural Fiction Writers, vol. 1: **513–519**

Staël, Madame de
  European Writers, vol. 5: **89–111**

Stapledon, Olaf
  Science Fiction Writers: **91–100**

Taine, Hippolyte
  European Writers, vol. 7: **1449–1469**

Valéry, Paul
  European Writers, vol. 8: **569–588**

Vasconcelos, José
  Latin American Writers, vol. 2: **575–584**

Vico, Giovanni Battista
  European Writers, vol. 3: **293–316**

Voltaire
  European Writers, vol. 4: **367–392**
  European Writers Selected Authors, vol. 3:
    1741–1766

Weil, Simone
  European Writers, vol. 12: **2787–2814**

Wieland, Christoph Martin
  European Writers, vol. 4: **587–614**

Witkiewicz (Witkacy), Stanisław Ignacy
  European Writers, vol. 10: **1205–1230**

Xenophon
  Ancient Writers, vol. 1: **331–351**

CRITICISM

Significant collections of writing about literature and the other arts.

Abrahams, Peter
  African Writers, vol. 1: **1–14**

Achebe, Chinua
  African Writers, vol. 1: **15–36**

Agee, James
  American Writers, vol. 1: **25–47**

Aidoo, Ama Ata
  African Writers, vol. 1: **37–48**

Aiken, Conrad
  American Writers, vol. 1: **48–70**

Alberdi, Juan Bautista
  Latin American Writers, vol. 1: **153–158**

Aldiss, Brian W.
  Science Fiction Writers: **251–258**

Alexander, Lloyd
  Supernatural Fiction Writers, vol. 2: **965–971**
  Writers for Young Adults, vol. 1: **21–33**

Amoroso Lima, Alceu
  Latin American Writers, vol. 2: **781–790**

Anderson Imbert, Enrique
Latin American Writers, vol. 3: **1105–1110**

Andrade, Mário de
Latin American Writers, vol. 2: **771–780**

Andrić, Ivo
European Writers, vol. 11: **1751–1779**

Aristotle
Ancient Writers, vol. 1: **377–416**

Armah, Ayi Kwei
African Writers, vol. 1: **49–62**

Arnold, Matthew
British Writers, vol. 5: **203–218**

Artaud, Antonin
European Writers, vol. 11: **1961–1985**

Asimov, Isaac
Science Fiction Writers: **267–276**

Auchincloss, Louis
American Writers Supp. 4, part 1: **21–38**

Auden, W. H.
American Writers Supp. 2, part 1: **1–28**
British Writers, vol. 7: **379–399**
British Writers Selected Authors, vol. 1: **1–21**

Austin, Mary Hunter
American Nature Writers, vol. 1: **31–51**

Awoonor, Kofi
African Writers, vol. 1: **63–75**

Azorín
European Writers, vol. 9: **639–661**

Balbuena, Bernardo de
Latin American Writers, vol. 1: **53–57**

Baldwin, James
African American Writers: **1–14**
American Writers Supp. 1, part 1: **47–71**

Ballagas, Emilio
Latin American Writers, vol. 3: **1081–1087**

Ballard, J. G.
Science Fiction Writers: **277–282**

Bandeira, Manuel
Latin American Writers, vol. 2: **629–641**

Baraka, Amiri
African American Writers: **15–29**
American Writers Supp. 2, part 1: **29–63**

Barnes, Julian
British Writers Supp. 4: **65–76**

Baroja, Pío
European Writers, vol. 9: **589–616**

Barrios, Eduardo
Latin American Writers, vol. 2: **611–618**

Barthes, Roland
European Writers, vol. 13: **3079–3104**

Baudelaire, Charles
European Writers, vol. 7: **1323–1348**

Beaumarchais, Pierre-Augustin Caron de
European Writers, vol. 4: **563–585**

Beerbohm, Max
British Writers Supp. 2: **43–59**

Bello, Andrés
Latin American Writers, vol. 1: **129–134**

Belloc, Hilaire
Writers for Children: **49–54**

Bely, Andrey
European Writers, vol. 9: **905–929**

Benjamin, Walter
European Writers, vol. 11: **1703–1730**

Berger, John
British Writers Supp. 4: **77–96**

Berlioz, Hector
European Writers, vol. 6: **771–812**

Berry, Wendell
American Nature Writers, vol. 1: **89–105**

Beti, Mongo
African Writers, vol. 1: **83–94**

Blackmur, R. P.
American Writers Supp. 2, part 1: **87–112**

Blake, William
British Writers, vol. 3: **288–310**
British Writers Selected Authors, vol. 1:
89–110
Writers for Children: **69–76**

Blanco Fombona, Rufino
Latin American Writers, vol. 2: **503–511**

Blok, Alexander
European Writers, vol. 9: **959–990**

Bogan, Louise
American Writers Supp. 3, part 1: **47–68**
Modern American Women Writers: **23–36**

Boileau-Despréaux, Nicolas
European Writers, vol. 3: **177–205**

Bossuet, Jacques Bénigne
    European Writers, vol. 3: **151–175**
Breton, André
    European Writers, vol. 11: **1939–1960**
Broch, Hermann
    European Writers, vol. 10: **1385–1408**
Brooke-Rose, Christine
    British Writers Supp. 4: **97–118**
Brooks, Van Wyck
    American Writers, vol. 1: **239–263**
Brown, Charles Brockden
    American Writers Supp. 1, part 1: **124–149**
Brown, Sterling
    African American Writers: **45–57**
Burckhardt, Jacob
    European Writers, vol. 6: **1225–1244**
Burgess, Anthony
    British Writers Supp. 1: **185–198**
Burroughs, John
    American Nature Writers, vol. 1: **121–138**
Butor, Michel
    European Writers, vol. 13: **3287–3321**
Byatt, A. S.
    British Writers Supp. 4: **139–156**
Cabell, James Branch
    Supernatural Fiction Writers, vol. 2: **789–796**
Cabral de Melo Neto, João
    Latin American Writers, vol. 3: **1247–1253**
Cabrera Infante, Guillermo
    Latin American Writers, vol. 3: **1383–1391**
Calvino, Italo
    European Writers, vol. 13: **3259–3286**
Camus, Albert
    African Writers, vol. 1: **139–152**
    European Writers, vol. 13: **3049–3078**
    European Writers Selected Authors, vol. 1: **305–334**
Canetti, Elias
    European Writers, vol. 12: **2615–2633**
Carducci, Giosue
    European Writers, vol. 7: **1495–1516**
Caro, Miguel Antonio
    Latin American Writers, vol. 1: **277–281**
Carrasquilla, Tomás
    Latin American Writers, vol. 1: **343–350**

Castellanos, Rosario
    Latin American Writers, vol. 3: **1295–1302**
Chateaubriand, François René de
    European Writers, vol. 5: **113–140**
Chénier, André
    European Writers, vol. 4: **691–718**
Chesterton, G. K.
    British Writers, vol. 6: **335–346**
    Supernatural Fiction Writers, vol. 1: **411–414**
Cicero
    Ancient Writers, vol. 1: **555–581**
Clark, John Pepper
    African Writers, vol. 1: **153–166**
Claudel, Paul
    European Writers, vol. 8: **471–494**
Coetzee, J. M.
    African Writers, vol. 1: **167–183**
Coleridge, Samuel Taylor
    British Writers, vol. 4: **41–57**
    British Writers Selected Authors, vol. 1: **313–329**
Connolly, Cyril
    British Writers Supp. 3: **95–113**
Cowley, Malcolm
    American Writers Supp. 2, part 1: **135–156**
Crawford, F. Marion
    Supernatural Fiction Writers, vol. 2: **747–751**
Creeley, Robert
    American Writers Supp. 4, part 1: **139–161**
Croce, Benedetto
    European Writers, vol. 8: **311–329**
D'Annunzio, Gabriele
    European Writers, vol. 8: **175–203**
Day Lewis, Cecil
    British Writers Supp. 3: **115–132**
De Camp, L. Sprague
    Science Fiction Writers: **179–184**
Delacroix, Eugène
    European Writers, vol. 5: **513–539**
Delany, Samuel R.
    Science Fiction Writers: **329–336**
Demetrius of Phalerum
    See "Hellenistic Poetry at Alexandria"
Demosthenes
    Ancient Writers, vol. 1: **417–433**

De Quincey, Thomas
    British Writers, vol. 4: **141–156**

Dickey, James
    American Writers Supp. 4, part 1: **175–194**

Diderot, Denis
    European Writers, vol. 4: **475–509**

Dillard, Annie
    American Nature Writers, vol. 1: **213–230**

Donoso, José
    Latin American Writers, vol. 3: **1277–1288**

Drabble, Margaret
    British Writers Supp. 4: **229–254**

Egbuna, Obi
    African Writers, vol. 1: **209–221**

Ekwensi, Cyprian
    African Writers, vol. 1: **223–234**

Eliot, T. S.
    American Writers, vol. 1: **567–591**
    American Writers Retrospective: **51–71**
    British Writers, vol. 7: **143–170**
    British Writers Selected Authors, vol. 1:
        469–496

Ellison, Ralph
    African American Writers: **103–129**
    American Writers Supp. 2, part 1: **221–252**

Empson, William
    British Writers Supp. 2: **179–198**

Farrell, James T.
    American Writers, vol. 2: **25–53**

Fénelon, François de Salignac de la Mothe-
    European Writers, vol. 3: **261–291**

Fernández, Macedonio
    Latin American Writers, vol. 2: **483–491**

Fontane, Theodor
    European Writers, vol. 6: **1299–1322**

Forster, E. M.
    British Writers, vol. 6: **397–414**
    British Writers Selected Authors, vol. 2: **511–527**
    Supernatural Fiction Writers, vol. 1: **479–484**

Foscolo, Ugo
    European Writers, vol. 5: **313–341**

Foucault, Michel
    European Writers, vol. 13: **3323–3364**

France, Anatole
    Supernatural Fiction Writers, vol. 1: **67–72**

Frazer, James George
    British Writers Supp. 3: **169–190**

Freud, Sigmund
    European Writers, vol. 8: **1–20**
    European Writers Selected Authors, vol. 1: **575–594**

Frost, Robert
    American Writers, vol. 2: **150–172**
    American Writers Retrospective: **121–144**
    Writers for Young Adults, vol. 2: **21–31**

Fuentes, Carlos
    Latin American Writers, vol. 3: **1353–1376**

Fuller, Margaret
    American Writers Supp. 2, part 1: **279–306**

Garnett, Richard
    Supernatural Fiction Writers, vol. 1: **317–320**

Gautier, Théophile
    European Writers, vol. 6: **1033–1059**
    Supernatural Fiction Writers, vol. 1: **45–50**

George, Stefan
    European Writers, vol. 8: **447–470**

Ginzburg, Natalia
    European Writers, vol. 13: **3131–3163**

Giraudoux, Jean
    European Writers, vol. 9: **1041–1065**

Gissing, George
    British Writers, vol. 5: **423–438**

Gombrowicz, Witold
    European Writers, vol. 12: **2563–2588**

Gómez Carillo, Enrique
    Latin American Writers, vol. 2: **465–469**

Goncourt, Edmond Louis Antoine de, and Jules
        Alfred Huot de Goncourt
    European Writers, vol. 7: **1395–1419**

Gordon, Caroline
    American Writers, vol. 2: **196–222**

Gorostiza, José
    Latin American Writers, vol. 2: **923–931**

Graves, Robert
    British Writers, vol. 7: **257–272**

Green, Henry
    British Writers Supp. 2: **247–266**

Grillparzer, Franz
    European Writers, vol. 5: **417–445**

Grimm, Jacob and Wilhelm
    Writers for Children: **255–263**

Hamsun, Knut
    European Writers, vol. 8: **21–43**

Hardwick, Elizabeth
    American Writers Supp. 3, part 1: **193–215**
    Modern American Women Writers: **189–196**

Hartley, L. P.
    Supernatural Fiction Writers, vol. 2: **639–644**

Hazlitt, William
    British Writers, vol. 4: **125–140**

Heaney, Seamus
    British Writers Supp. 2: **267–282**

Hebbel, Friedrich
    European Writers, vol. 6: **1089–1122**

Henríquez Ureña, Pedro
    Latin American Writers, vol. 2: **597–601**

Herder, Johann Gottfried von
    European Writers, vol. 4: **639–660**

Herodotus
    Ancient Writers, vol. 1: **209–232**

Hoffmann, E. T. A.
    European Writers, vol. 5: **261–289**
    Supernatural Fiction Writers, vol. 1: **111–119**
    Writers for Children: **283–288**

Hofmannsthal, Hugo von
    European Writers, vol. 9: **689–714**

Hogan, Linda
    American Nature Writers, vol. 1: **377–388**
    American Writers Supp. 4, part 1: **397–418**

Hölderlin, Friedrich
    European Writers, vol. 5: **143–173**

Hope, Christopher
    African Writers, vol. 1: **331–343**

Housman, A. E.
    British Writers, vol. 6: **151–164**
    British Writers Selected Authors, vol. 2: **621–634**

Howe, Susan
    American Writers Supp. 4, part 2: **419–438**

Howells, William Dean
    American Writers, vol. 2: **271–294**

Hughes, Langston
    African American Writers: **193–205**
    American Writers Retrospective: **193–214**
    American Writers Supp. 1, part 1: **320–348**
    Writers for Children: **295–301**

Huidobro, Vicente
    Latin American Writers, vol. 2: **755–764**

Huxley, Aldous
    British Writers, vol. 7: **197–208**
    British Writers Selected Authors, vol. 2: **635–646**
    Science Fiction Writers: **101–108**

Idrīs, Yūsuf
    African Writers, vol. 1: **345–365**

Jaimes Freyre, Ricardo
    Latin American Writers, vol. 1: **419–423**

James, Henry
    American Writers, vol. 2: **319–341**
    American Writers Retrospective: **215–242**
    British Writers, vol. 6: **23–69**
    Supernatural Fiction Writers, vol. 1: **337–344**

Jarrell, Randall
    American Writers, vol. 2: **367–390**

Johnson, Eyvind
    European Writers, vol. 12: **2361–2385**

Kinnell, Galway
    American Writers Supp. 3, part 1: **235–256**

Kleist, Heinrich von
    European Writers, vol. 5: **291–312**

Klopstock, Friedrich Gottlieb
    European Writers, vol. 4: **511–536**

Knight, Damon
    Science Fiction Writers: **393–400**

Kosztolányi, Dezsö
    European Writers, vol. 10: **1231–1249**

Krleža, Miroslav
    European Writers, vol. 11: **1807–1834**

Krutch, Joseph Wood
    American Nature Writers, vol. 1: **465–477**

Kundera, Milan
    European Writers, vol. 13: **3389–3413**

La Bruyère, Jean de
    European Writers, vol. 3: **229–260**

Laforgue, Jules
    European Writers, vol. 7: **1883–1908**

Lagerkvist, Pär
    European Writers, vol. 10: **1677–1702**

Lamb, Charles
    British Writers, vol. 4: **73–86**

Lang, Andrew
    Writers for Children: **337–343**

Lanier, Sidney
    American Writers Supp. 1, part 1: **349–373**

La Rochefoucauld, François VI, Duc de
European Writers, vol. 3: **51–71**

Laye, Camara
African Writers, vol. 1: **413–425**

Leavis, F. R.
British Writers, vol. 7: **233–256**

Leconte de Lisle, Charles Marie
European Writers, vol. 6: **1245–1273**

Leopardi, Giacomo
European Writers, vol. 5: **541–567**

Lessing, Gotthold Ephraim
European Writers, vol. 4: **537–562**

Lewis, C. S.
British Writers Supp. 3: **247–268**
British Writers Selected Authors, vol. 2: **855–876**
Science Fiction Writers: **243–248**
Supernatural Fiction Writers, vol. 2: **661–666**
Writers for Children: **357–364**
Writers for Young Adults, vol. 2: **247–255**

Lewis, Sinclair
American Writers, vol. 2: **439–461**

Lezama Lima, José
Latin American Writers, vol. 3: **1125–1130**

Lima Barreto, Afonso Henriques de
Latin American Writers, vol. 2: **565–573**

Lins do Rego, José
Latin American Writers, vol. 2: **909–913**

Lodge, David
British Writers Supp. 4: **363–387**

Longinus
Ancient Writers, vol. 2: **1063–1080**

Lopez Velarde, Ramon
Latin American Writers, vol. 2: **663–670**

Lowell, Amy
American Writers, vol. 2: **511–533**
Modern American Women Writers: **261–268**

Lowell, James Russell
American Writers Supp. 1, part 2: **404–426**

Lucian
Ancient Writers, vol. 2: **1081–1097**

Lugones, Leopoldo
Latin American Writers, vol. 2: **493–502**

Lukács, György
European Writers, vol. 10: **1251–1279**

McCarthy, Mary
American Writers, vol. 2: **558–584**
Modern American Women Writers: **269–278**

Machado, Antonio
European Writers, vol. 9: **743–765**

Machado de Assis, Joaquim Maria
Latin American Writers, vol. 1: **253–268**

Machen, Arthur
Supernatural Fiction Writers, vol. 1: **351–359**

MacLeish, Archibald
American Writers, vol. 3: **1–25**

Macleod, Fiona
Supernatural Fiction Writers, vol. 1: **369–374**

MacNeice, Louis
British Writers, vol. 7: **401–420**

Maḥfūẓ, Najīb
African Writers, vol. 2: **451–465**

Mallarmé, Stéphane
European Writers, vol. 7: **1567–1595**

Malraux, André
European Writers, vol. 12: **2413–2432**
European Writers Selected Authors, vol. 2: **977–996**

Mañach Robato, Jorge
Latin American Writers, vol. 2: **831–836**

Mandelshtam, Osip
European Writers, vol. 10: **1619–1649**

Mann, Heinrich
European Writers, vol. 8: **519–543**

Mann, Thomas
European Writers, vol. 9: **715–743**
European Writers Selected Authors, vol. 2: **997–1024**

Mansfield, Katherine
British Writers, vol. 7: **171–184**
British Writers Selected Authors, vol. 2: **891–904**

Manzoni, Alessandro
European Writers, vol. 5: **367–394**

Mariátegui, José Carlos
Latin American Writers, vol. 2: **791–796**

Marinetti, Filippo Tommaso
European Writers, vol. 9: **797–832**

Marqués, René
Latin American Writers, vol. 3: **1237–1246**

Mauriac, François
European Writers, vol. 10: **1307–1330**

Meireles, Cecília
Latin American Writers, vol. 2: **915–922**

Memmi, Albert
    African Writers, vol. 2: **467–477**

Mencken, H. L.
    American Writers, vol. 3: **99–121**

Mérimée, Prosper
    European Writers, vol. 6: **745–769**
    Supernatural Fiction Writers, vol. 1: **51–57**

Michelet, Jules, and Romantic Historiography
    European Writers, vol. 5: **571–606**

Milne, A. A.
    Writers for Children: **397–405**

Milosz, Czeslaw
    European Writers, vol. 13: **2929–2952**

Montale, Eugenio
    European Writers, vol. 11: **1987–2008**

Montesquieu, Charles-Louis de Secondat
    European Writers, vol. 3: **345–366**

Moore, Marianne
    American Writers, vol. 3: **193–217**
    Modern American Women Writers: **303–316**

Morris, Wright
    American Writers, vol. 3: **218–243**

Morrison, Toni
    African American Writers: **321–333**
    American Writers Supp. 3, part 1: **361–381**
    Modern American Women Writers: **317–338**

Mphahlele, Es'kia
    African Writers, vol. 2: **495–510**

Musil, Robert
    European Writers, vol. 9: **931–958**

Nabokov, Vladimir
    American Writers, vol. 3: **244–266**
    American Writers Retrospective: **263–281**

Nemerov, Howard
    American Writers, vol. 3: **267–289**

Nerval, Gérard de
    European Writers, vol. 6: **943–970**

Ngũgĩ wa Thiong'o
    African Writers, vol. 2: **537–555**

Nin, Anaïs
    Modern American Women Writers: **339–351**

Novalis
    European Writers, vol. 5: **205–231**

Oates, Joyce Carol
    American Writers Supp. 2, part 2: **503–527**
    Modern American Women Writers: **353–374**

Ojaide, Tanure
    African Writers, vol. 2: **557–565**

Okara, Gabriel
    African Writers, vol. 2: **567–582**

Omotoso, Kole
    African Writers, vol. 2: **609–617**

Onetti, Juan Carlos
    Latin American Writers, vol. 3: **1089–1097**

Ortega y Gasset, José
    European Writers, vol. 9: **1119–1150**

Orwell, George
    British Writers, vol. 7: **273–288**
    British Writers Selected Authors, vol. 2: **947–961**
    Science Fiction Writers: **233–241**

Osofisan, Femi
    African Writers, vol. 2: **619–629**

Osundare, Niyi
    African Writers, vol. 2: **631–640**

Parker, Dorothy
    Modern American Women Writers: **397–409**

Pascal, Blaise
    European Writers, vol. 3: **125–150**

Pater, Walter Horatio
    British Writers, vol. 5: **337–360**

Paton, Alan
    African Writers, vol. 2: **651–668**
    British Writers Supp. 2: **341–361**
    British Writers Selected Authors, vol. 2:
        963–983

Paz, Octavio
    Latin American Writers, vol. 3: **1163–1176**

p'Bitek, Okot
    African Writers, vol. 2: **669–684**

Peacock, Thomas Love
    British Writers, vol. 4: **157–170**

Persius and Juvenal
    Ancient Writers, vol. 2: **855–876**

Picón Salas, Mariano
    Latin American Writers, vol. 2: **903–908**

Plato
    Ancient Writers, vol. 1: **353–376**

Pliny the Younger
    Ancient Writers, vol. 2: **1035–1048**

Poe, Edgar Allan
    American Writers, vol. 3: **409–432**
    Science Fiction Writers: **11–18**

Supernatural Fiction Writers, vol. 2: **697–705**
Writers for Young Adults, vol. 3: **61–73**

Pope, Alexander
British Writers, vol. 3: **68–79**
British Writers Selected Authors, vol. 2: **1001–1012**

Pound, Ezra
American Writers, vol. 3: **456–479**
American Writers Retrospective: **283–294**

Powys, John Cowper
Supernatural Fiction Writers, vol. 2: **609–616**

Priestley, J. B.
British Writers, vol. 7: **209–232**

Pritchett, V. S.
British Writers Supp. 3: **311–331**

Quasimodo, Salvatore
European Writers, vol. 12: **2387–2411**

Quiller-Couch, Arthur
Supernatural Fiction Writers, vol. 1: **389–395**

Quintilian
Ancient Writers, vol. 2: **943–959**

Ransom, John Crowe
American Writers, vol. 3: **480–502**

Read, Herbert
See "Poets of World War I (British)"

Reyes, Alfonso
Latin American Writers, vol. 2: **693–703**

Richards, I. A.
British Writers Supp. 2: **405–433**

Richter, Jean Paul
European Writers, vol. 5: **53–88**

Ritsos, Yannis
European Writers, vol. 12: **2815–2842**

Robbe-Grillet, Alain
European Writers, vol. 13: **3237–3256**

Rojas, Manuel
Latin American Writers, vol. 2: **815–820**

Rojas, Ricardo
Latin American Writers, vol. 2: **591–596**

Rousseau, Jean Jacques
European Writers, vol. 4: **449–474**
European Writers Selected Authors, vol. 3: **1519–1544**

Rulfo, Juan
Latin American Writers, vol. 3: **1215–1229**

Rushdie, Salman
British Writers Supp. 4: **433–457**

Ruskin, John
British Writers, vol. 5: **173–186**
Writers for Children: **493–496**

Russ, Joanna
Science Fiction Writers: **483–490**

Sa'adāwī, Nawāl, al-
African Writers, vol. 2: **721–731**

Sade, Marquis de, and the French Libertine Tradition
European Writers, vol. 4: **615–638**

Sainte-Beuve, Charles-Augustin
European Writers, vol. 6: **837–861**

Sanders, Scott Russell
American Nature Writers, vol. 2: **793–804**

Santayana, George
American Writers, vol. 3: **599–622**

Sarduy, Severo
Latin American Writers, vol. 3: **1437–1444**

Sarraute, Nathalie
European Writers, vol. 12: **2333–2359**

Schiller, Friedrich von
European Writers, vol. 5: **27–52**

Schlegel, Friedrich von
European Writers, vol. 5: **177–203**

Schopenhauer, Arthur
European Writers, vol. 5: **395–415**

Schreiner, Olive
African Writers, vol. 2: **745–763**
British Writers Supp. 2: **435–458**

Scott, Sir Walter
British Writers, vol. 4: **27–40**
Supernatural Fiction Writers, vol. 1: **169–176**

Seferis, George
European Writers, vol. 12: **2255–2271**

Senghor, Léopold Sédar
African Writers, vol. 2: **775–789**

Shapiro, Karl
American Writers Supp. 2, part 2: **701–724**

Shelley, Percy Bysshe
British Writers, vol. 4: **195–210**
British Writers Selected Authors, vol. 3: **1105–1120**

Silveira de Queiroz, Dinah
Latin American Writers, vol. 3: **1145–1151**

Simon, Claude
    European Writers, vol. 13: **3021–3048**

Sinán, Rogelio
    Latin American Writers, vol. 2: **941–946**

Sinclair, May
    Supernatural Fiction Writers, vol. 1: **513–519**

Sontag, Susan
    American Writers Supp. 3, part 2: **451–473**
    Modern American Women Writers: **471–483**

Soyinka, Wole
    African Writers, vol. 2: **807–831**

Staël, Madame de
    European Writers, vol. 5: **89–111**

Stein, Gertrude
    American Writers, vol. 4: **25–48**
    Modern American Women Writers: **485–498**

Strachey, Lytton
    British Writers Supp. 2: **497–518**

Strand, Mark
    American Writers Supp. 4, part 2: **619–636**

Styron, William
    American Writers, vol. 4: **97–119**

Sutherland, Efua Theodora
    African Writers, vol. 2: **833–849**

Swann, Thomas Burnett
    Supernatural Fiction Writers, vol. 2: **1097–1103**

Swift, Jonathan
    British Writers, vol. 3: **15–38**
    British Writers Selected Authors, vol. 3: **1195–1217**
    Writers for Children: **555–559**

Swinburne, Algernon Charles
    British Writers, vol. 5: **309–336**

Ṭāhā Ḥusayn
    African Writers, vol. 2: **851–863**

Taine, Hippolyte
    European Writers, vol. 7: **1449–1469**

Tasso, Torquato
    European Writers, vol. 2: **791–818**

Tate, Allen
    American Writers, vol. 4: **120–143**

Thomas, Edward
    British Writers Supp. 3: **393–408**

Tieck, Ludwig
    European Writers, vol. 5: **233–260**
    Supernatural Fiction Writers, vol. 1: **83–89**

Tolkien, J. R. R.
    British Writers Supp. 2: **519–536**
    British Writers Selected Authors, vol. 3: **1277–1294**
    Supernatural Fiction Writers, vol. 2: **675–682**
    Writers for Children: **561–571**
    Writers for Young Adults, vol. 3: **311–320**

Toomer, Jean
    African American Writers: **429–440**
    American Writers Supp. 3, part 2: **475–491**

Torres Bodet, Jaime
    Latin American Writers, vol. 2: **933–939**

Trilling, Lionel
    American Writers Supp. 3, part 2: **493–515**

Updike, John
    American Writers, vol. 4: **214–235**
    American Writers Retrospective: **317–338**

van der Post, Laurens
    African Writers, vol. 2: **879–891**

Van Vechten, Carl
    American Writers Supp. 2, part 2: **725–751**

Vargas Llosa, Mario
    Latin American Writers, vol. 3: **1421–1436**

Verlaine, Paul
    European Writers, vol. 7: **1619–1643**

Vico, Giovanni Battista
    European Writers, vol. 3: **293–316**

Vidal, Gore
    American Writers Supp. 4, part 2: **677–697**

Villaurrutia, Xavier
    Latin American Writers, vol. 3: **975–980**

Vittorini, Elio
    European Writers, vol. 12: **2733–2757**

Voltaire
    European Writers, vol. 4: **367–392**
    European Writers Selected Authors, vol. 3: **1741–1766**

Wagner, Richard
    European Writers, vol. 6: **1147–1168**
    European Writers Selected Authors, vol. 3: **1767–1787**

Walker, Alice
    African American Writers: **441–458**
    American Writers Supp. 3, part 2: **517–540**
    Modern American Women Writers: **511–520**

Warren, Robert Penn
American Writers, vol. 4: **236–259**

Weil, Simone
European Writers, vol. 12: **2787–2814**

Welty, Eudora
American Writers, vol. 4: **260–284**
American Writers Retrospective: **339–358**
Modern American Women Writers: **521–538**

West, Rebecca
British Writers Supp. 3: **431–445**

Wharton, Edith
American Writers, vol. 4: **308–330**
American Writers Retrospective: **359–385**
Modern American Women Writers: **539–558**
Supernatural Fiction Writers, vol. 2: **783–788**

Wieland, Christoph Martin
European Writers, vol. 4: **587–614**

Wilbur, Richard
American Writers Supp. 3, part 2: **541–565**

Wilde, Oscar
British Writers, vol. 5: **399–422**
British Writers Selected Authors, vol. 3: **1353–1376**
Supernatural Fiction Writers, vol. 1: **345–350**
Writers for Children: **611–616**

Williams, Charles
Supernatural Fiction Writers, vol. 2: **631–638**

Williams, William Carlos
American Writers, vol. 4: **402–425**
American Writers Retrospective: **411–433**

Wilson, Edmund
American Writers, vol. 4: **426–449**

Winters, Yvor
American Writers Supp. 2, part 2: **785–816**

Witkiewicz (Witkacy), Stanisław Ignacy
European Writers, vol. 10: **1205–1230**

Wolfe, Tom
American Writers Supp. 3, part 2: **567–588**

Woolf, Virginia
British Writers, vol. 7: **17–40**
British Writers Selected Authors, vol. 3: **1395–1417**

Zamyatin, Yevgeny Ivanovich
European Writers, vol. 10: **1181–1203**

Zola, Émile
European Writers, vol. 7: **1517–1542**
European Writers Selected Authors, vol. 3: **1789–1813**

Zukofsky, Louis
American Writers Supp. 3, part 2: **609–632**

JOURNALISM

The work of career journalists, columnists, and others who left significant collections of periodical writing.

Abrahams, Peter
African Writers, vol. 1: **1–14**

Acevedo Díaz, Eduardo
Latin American Writers, vol. 1: **299–303**

Ady, Endre
European Writers, vol. 9: **859–880**

Agee, James
American Writers, vol. 1: **25–47**

Alencar, José de
Latin American Writers, vol. 1: **195–203**

Anderson, Sherwood
American Writers, vol. 1: **97–120**

Arciniegas, Germán
Latin American Writers, vol. 2: **897–901**

Arlt, Roberto
Latin American Writers, vol. 2: **881–886**

Asimov, Isaac
Science Fiction Writers: **267–276**

Austin, William
Supernatural Fiction Writers, vol. 2: **693–696**

Bangs, J. K.
Supernatural Fiction Writers, vol. 2: **725–729**

Barrie, J. M.
British Writers Supp. 3: **1–17**
Supernatural Fiction Writers, vol. 1: **405–410**
Writers for Children: **29–35**

Barrios, Eduardo
Latin American Writers, vol. 2: **611–618**

Belloc, Hilaire
    Writers for Children: **49–54**

Bierce, Ambrose
    American Writers, vol. 1: **190–213**
    Supernatural Fiction Writers, vol. 2: **731–737**

Blackwood, Algernon
    Supernatural Fiction Writers, vol. 1: **463–470**

Bridgers, Sue Ellen
    Writers for Young Adults, vol. 1: **163–172**

Brooke, Rupert
    British Writers Supp. 3: **45–61**
    See also "Poets of World War I (British)"

Brooks, Bruce
    Writers for Young Adults, vol. 1: **173–182**

Cabell, James Branch
    Supernatural Fiction Writers, vol. 2: **789–796**

Camus, Albert
    African Writers, vol. 1: **139–152**
    European Writers, vol. 13: **3049–3078**
    European Writers Selected Authors, vol. 1:
        305–334

Capote, Truman
    American Writers Supp. 3, part 1: **111–133**

Caro, Miguel Antonio
    Latin American Writers, vol. 1: **277–281**

Carpentier, Alejo
    Latin American Writers, vol. 3: **1019–1031**

Carter, Alden R.
    Writers for Young Adults, vol. 1: **209–218**

Casal, Julián del
    Latin American Writers, vol. 1: **365–370**

Chesterton, G. K.
    British Writers, vol. 6: **335–346**
    Supernatural Fiction Writers, vol. 1: **411–414**

Collier, Christopher and James Lincoln
    Writers for Young Adults, vol. 1: **257–269**

Collodi, C.
    Writers for Children: **129–137**

Cormier, Robert
    Writers for Young Adults, vol. 1: **291–301**

Couto, Mia
    African Writers, vol. 1: **185–197**

Crane, Stephen
    American Writers, vol. 1: **405–427**
    Writers for Young Adults, vol. 1: **303–312**

Cunha, Euclides da
    Latin American Writers, vol. 1: **387–395**

Daly, Maureen
    Writers for Young Adults, vol. 1: **323–333**

Defoe, Daniel
    British Writers, vol. 3: **1–14**
    British Writers Selected Authors, vol. 1: **349–362**
    Writers for Children: **163–171**

De la Mare, Walter
    Supernatural Fiction Writers, vol. 1: **497–503**
    Writers for Children: **173–180**

Denevi, Marco
    Latin American Writers, vol. 3: **1265–1269**

De Quincey, Thomas
    British Writers, vol. 4: **141–156**

Díaz Rodríguez, Manuel
    Latin American Writers, vol. 1: **431–439**

Dickens, Charles
    British Writers, vol. 5: **41–74**
    British Writers Selected Authors, vol. 1: **363–396**
    Supernatural Fiction Writers, vol. 1: **213–218**
    Writers for Children: **181–191**
    Writers for Young Adults, vol. 1: **353–364**

Didion, Joan
    American Writers Supp. 4, part 1: **195–216**
    Modern American Women Writers: **91–102**

Donoso, José
    Latin American Writers, vol. 3: **1277–1288**

Douglas, Marjory Stoneman
    American Nature Writers, vol. 1: **231–245**

Doyle, Sir Arthur Conan
    British Writers Supp. 2: **159–178**
    British Writers Selected Authors, vol. 1: **415–434**
    Science Fiction Writers: **45–50**
    Writers for Children: **201–207**
    Writers for Young Adults, vol. 1: **385–392**

Dreiser, Theodore
    American Writers, vol. 1: **497–520**

Duncan, Lois
    Writers for Young Adults, vol. 1: **393–402**

Eça de Queiroz, José Maria
    European Writers, vol. 7: **1683–1708**

Edwards, Jorge
    Latin American Writers, vol. 3: **1399–1403**

Fernández de Lizardi, José Joaquín
    Latin American Writers, vol. 1: **119–128**

Finney, Charles
  Supernatural Fiction Writers, vol. 2: **821–826**

Fortune, Dion
  Supernatural Fiction Writers, vol. 2: **585–590**

Freedman, Russell
  Writers for Young Adults, vol. 2: **1–9**

Gautier, Théophile
  European Writers, vol. 6: **1033–1059**
  Supernatural Fiction Writers, vol. 1: **45–50**

Ginzburg, Natalia
  European Writers, vol. 13: **3131–3163**

Gómez Carillo, Enrique
  Latin American Writers, vol. 2: **465–469**

Gutiérrez Nájera, Manuel
  Latin American Writers, vol. 1: **351–357**

Guzmán, Martín Luis
  Latin American Writers, vol. 2: **655–662**

Hamilton, Virginia
  Writers for Young Adults, vol. 2: **79–92**

Harper, Frances Ellen Watkins
  African American Writers: **159–175**
  Modern American Women Writers: **197–205**

Harris, Joel Chandler
  Writers for Children: **269–275**

Harte, Bret
  American Writers Supp. 2, part 1: **335–359**

Hazlitt, William
  British Writers, vol. 4: **125–140**

Hemingway, Ernest
  American Writers, vol. 2: **247–270**
  American Writers Retrospective: **169–191**
  Writers for Young Adults, vol. 2: **93–102**

Hentoff, Nat
  Writers for Young Adults, vol. 2: **103–112**

Herbert, Frank
  Science Fiction Writers: **377–385**

Hichens, Robert
  Supernatural Fiction Writers, vol. 1: **415–420**

Hobbs, Will
  Writers for Young Adults, vol. 2: **121–129**

Honwana, Luís Bernardo
  African Writers, vol. 1: **321–329**

Hughes, Langston
  African American Writers: **193–205**
  American Writers Retrospective: **193–214**

American Writers Supp. 1, part 1: **320–348**
  Writers for Children: **295–301**

Hunter, Mollie
  Writers for Young Adults, vol. 2: **149–159**

Idrīs, Yūsuf
  African Writers, vol. 1: **345–365**

Irving, Washington
  American Writers, vol. 2: **295–318**
  Supernatural Fiction Writers, vol. 2: **685–691**
  Writers for Children: **303–307**

Johnson, Eyvind
  European Writers, vol. 12: **2361–2385**

Johnson, Samuel
  British Writers, vol. 3: **107–123**
  British Writers Selected Authors, vol. 2: **647–663**

Kipling, Rudyard
  British Writers, vol. 6: **165–206**
  British Writers Selected Authors, vol. 2: **729–770**
  Supernatural Fiction Writers, vol. 1: **437–442**
  Writers for Children: **329–336**

Lanier, Sidney
  American Writers Supp. 1, part 1: **349–373**

Lardner, Ring
  American Writers, vol. 2: **415–438**

Le Fanu, J. S.
  Supernatural Fiction Writers, vol. 1: **219–231**

L'Engle, Madeleine
  Writers for Young Adults, vol. 2: **237–246**

Lins do Rego, José
  Latin American Writers, vol. 2: **909–913**

Lipsyte, Robert
  Writers for Young Adults, vol. 2: **257–266**

London, Jack
  American Writers, vol. 2: **462–485**
  Writers for Young Adults, vol. 2: **267–278**

Lugones, Leopoldo
  Latin American Writers, vol. 2: **493–502**

Machen, Arthur
  Supernatural Fiction Writers, vol. 1: **351–359**

McNulty, Faith
  American Nature Writers, vol. 1: **569–581**

McPhee, John
  American Nature Writers, vol. 1: **583–598**
  American Writers Supp. 3, part 1: **289–316**

Mailer, Norman
      American Writers, vol. 3: **26–49**

Mann, Thomas
      European Writers, vol. 9: **715–743**
      European Writers Selected Authors, vol. 2:
            997–1024

Mariátegui, José Carlos
      Latin American Writers, vol. 2: **791–796**

Marín Cañas, José
      Latin American Writers, vol. 3: **991–994**

Marryat, Frederick
      Writers for Children: **381–387**

Mauriac, François
      European Writers, vol. 10: **1307–1330**

Meireles, Cecília
      Latin American Writers, vol. 2: **915–922**

Meltzer, Milton
      Writers for Young Adults, vol. 2: **347–358**

Memmi, Albert
      African Writers, vol. 2: **467–477**

Mencken, H. L.
      American Writers, vol. 3: **99–121**

Merritt, A.
      Science Fiction Writers: **65–71**
      Supernatural Fiction Writers, vol. 2: **835–843**

Miklowitz, Gloria D.
      Writers for Young Adults, vol. 2: **359–368**

Moberg, Vilhelm
      European Writers, vol. 11: **2203–2231**

Molina, Juan Ramón
      Latin American Writers, vol. 2: **539–542**

Montale, Eugenio
      European Writers, vol. 11: **1987–2008**

Naylor, Phyllis Reynolds
      Writers for Young Adults, vol. 2: **397–409**

Nerval, Gérard de
      European Writers, vol. 6: **943–970**

Nervo, Amado
      Latin American Writers, vol. 1: **425–429**

Orwell, George
      British Writers, vol. 7: **273–288**
      British Writers Selected Authors, vol. 2: **947–961**
      Science Fiction Writers: **233–241**

Paterson, Katherine
      Writers for Young Adults, vol. 2: **443–454**

Pavese, Cesare
      European Writers, vol. 12: **2759–2784**

Payró, Roberto Jorge
      Latin American Writers, vol. 1: **413–417**

Peck, Richard
      Writers for Young Adults, vol. 3: **1–14**

Poe, Edgar Allan
      American Writers, vol. 3: **409–432**
      Science Fiction Writers: **11–18**
      Supernatural Fiction Writers, vol. 2: **697–705**
      Writers for Young Adults, vol. 3: **61–73**

Pratt, Fletcher
      See "De Camp, L. Sprague, and Fletcher
            Pratt"

Pritchett, V. S.
      British Writers Supp. 3: **311–331**

Queiroz, Rachel de
      Latin American Writers, vol. 3: **1119–1123**

Quiller-Couch, Arthur
      Supernatural Fiction Writers, vol. 1: **389–395**

Reyes, Alfonso
      Latin American Writers, vol. 2: **693–703**

Rohmer, Sax
      Supernatural Fiction Writers, vol. 2: **555–560**

Salten, Felix
      Writers for Children: **497–501**

Sánchez, Florencio
      Latin American Writers, vol. 2: **531–538**

Sarmiento, Domingo Faustino
      Latin American Writers, vol. 1: **159–167**

Schwartz, Delmore
      American Writers Supp. 2, part 2: **639–668**

Serviss, Garrett P.
      Science Fiction Writers: **39–44**

Simak, Clifford D.
      Science Fiction Writers: **513–518**

Tablada, José Juan
      Latin American Writers, vol. 1: **441–446**

Taylor, Theodore
      Writers for Young Adults, vol. 3: **283–292**

Twain, Mark
      American Writers, vol. 4: **190–213**
      Supernatural Fiction Writers, vol. 2: **761–768**
      Writers for Children: **573–582**
      Writers for Young Adults, vol. 3: **321–328**

Valenzuela, Luisa
  Latin American Writers, vol. 3: **1445–1449**

Valle, Rafael Heliodoro
  Latin American Writers, vol. 2: **721–725**

Van Loon, Hendrik Willem
  Writers for Children: **583–589**

Vasconcelos, José
  Latin American Writers, vol. 2: **575–584**

Villaverde, Cirilo
  Latin American Writers, vol. 1: **169–174**

Wells, H. G.
  British Writers, vol. 6: **225–246**
  British Writers Selected Authors, vol. 3: **1331–1352**
  Science Fiction Writers: **25–30**
  Supernatural Fiction Writers, vol. 1: **397–402**
  Writers for Children: **599–603**

West, Rebecca
  British Writers Supp. 3: **431–445**

White, E. B.
  American Writers Supp. 1, part 2: **651–681**

Wilson, Edmund
  American Writers, vol. 4: **426–449**

Wolfe, Tom
  American Writers Supp. 3, part 2: **567–588**

Yolen, Jane
  Writers for Young Adults, vol. 3: **409–420**

Zeno Gandía, Manuel
  Latin American Writers, vol. 1: **321–326**

Zola, Émile
  European Writers, vol. 7: **1517–1542**
  European Writers Selected Authors, vol. 3:
    1789–1813

Zorrilla de San Martín, Juan
  Latin American Writers, vol. 1: **327–331**

AUTOBIOGRAPHY

Authors especially noted for memorable or extensive life stories.

Abrahams, Peter
  African Writers, vol. 1: **1–14**

Adams, Henry
  American Writers, vol. 1: **1–24**

Aickman, Robert
  Supernatural Fiction Writers, vol. 2: **957–964**

Alegría, Ciro
  Latin American Writers, vol. 3: **1099–1103**

Alencar, José de
  Latin American Writers, vol. 1: **195–203**

Alfieri, Vittorio
  European Writers, vol. 4: **661–689**

Amis, Kingsley
  British Writers Supp. 2: **1–19**

Andersen, Hans Christian
  European Writers, vol. 6: **863–892**
  European Writers Selected Authors, vol. 1: **1–29**
  Writers for Children: **7–13**

Angelou, Maya
  American Writers Supp. 4, part 1: **1–19**
  Modern American Women Writers: **1–8**
  Writers for Young Adults, vol. 1: **43–52**

Anstey, F.
  Supernatural Fiction Writers, vol. 1: **287–292**

Artaud, Antonin
  European Writers, vol. 11: **1961–1985**

Asimov, Isaac
  Science Fiction Writers: **267–276**

Augustine, Saint
  European Writers, vol. 1: **23–50**
  European Writers Selected Authors, vol. 1:
    103–130

Azuela, Mariano
  Latin American Writers, vol. 2: **457–464**

Baker, Frank
  Supernatural Fiction Writers, vol. 2: **561–567**

Bandeira, Manuel
  Latin American Writers, vol. 2: **629–641**

Baraka, Amiri
  African American Writers: **15–29**
  American Writers Supp. 2, part 1: **29–63**

Baroja, Pío
  European Writers, vol. 9: **589–616**

Beaumarchais, Pierre-Augustin Caron de
  European Writers, vol. 4: **563–585**

Beauvoir, Simone de
  European Writers, vol. 12: **2701–2732**
  European Writers Selected Authors, vol. 1:
    185–215

Behan, Brendan
  British Writers Supp. 2: **61–76**

Bely, Andrey
  European Writers, vol. 9: **905–929**

Bemelmans, Ludwig
  Writers for Children: **55–61**

Berlioz, Hector
  European Writers, vol. 6: **771–812**

Beston, Henry
  American Nature Writers, vol. 1: **107–120**

Bioy Casares, Adolfo
  Latin American Writers, vol. 3: **1201–1208**

Blackwood, Algernon
  Supernatural Fiction Writers, vol. 1: **463–470**

Blanco Fombona, Rufino
  Latin American Writers, vol. 2: **503–511**

Blok, Alexander
  European Writers, vol. 9: **959–990**

Bombal, María Luisa
  Latin American Writers, vol. 3: **1111–1117**

Bowen, Elizabeth
  British Writers Supp. 2: **77–96**
  Supernatural Fiction Writers, vol. 2: **569–575**

Bowles, Paul
  American Writers Supp. 4, part 1: **79–99**

Brooks, Gwendolyn
  African American Writers: **31–43**
  American Writers Supp. 3, part 1: **69–90**
  Modern American Women Writers: **37–48**

Brooks, Van Wyck
  American Writers, vol. 1: **239–263**

Brunner, John
  Science Fiction Writers: **297–304**

Bunyan, John
  British Writers, vol. 2: **240–254**
  British Writers Selected Authors, vol. 1: **215–229**
  Writers for Children: **97–102**

Burroughs, John
  American Nature Writers, vol. 1: **121–138**

Cabell, James Branch
  Supernatural Fiction Writers, vol. 2: **789–796**

Caesar
  Ancient Writers, vol. 1: **583–599**

Caldwell, Erskine
  American Writers, vol. 1: **288–311**

Campbell, Roy
  African Writers, vol. 1: **127–137**

Canetti, Elias
  European Writers, vol. 12: **2615–2633**

Carrasquilla, Tomás
  Latin American Writers, vol. 1: **343–350**

Carrighar, Sally
  American Nature Writers, vol. 1: **139–149**

Carter, Angela
  British Writers Supp. 3: **79–93**

Céline, Louis-Ferdinand
  European Writers, vol. 11: **1859–1884**

Chateaubriand, François René de
  European Writers, vol. 5: **113–140**

Chesterton, G. K.
  British Writers, vol. 6: **335–346**
  Supernatural Fiction Writers, vol. 1: **411–414**

Christie, Agatha
  British Writers Supp. 2: **123–137**

Churchill, Winston
  British Writers, vol. 6: **347–362**

Clarke, Arthur C.
  Science Fiction Writers: **313–320**

Colette
  European Writers, vol. 9: **617–638**
  European Writers Selected Authors, vol. 1: **389–410**

Connolly, Cyril
  British Writers Supp. 3: **95–113**

Conrad, Joseph
  British Writers, vol. 6: **133–150**
  British Writers Selected Authors, vol. 1: **331–348**

Constant, Benjamin
  See "French Novelists, Three"

Coward, Noël
  British Writers Supp. 2: **139–158**

Cowley, Malcolm
  American Writers Supp. 2, part 1: **135–156**

Creeley, Robert
  American Writers Supp. 4, part 1: **139–161**

Croce, Benedetto
   European Writers, vol. 8: **311–329**

Darío, Rubén
   Latin American Writers, vol. 1: **397–412**

Day Lewis, Cecil
   British Writers Supp. 3: **115–132**

Delacroix, Eugène
   European Writers, vol. 5: **513–539**

Delany, Samuel R.
   Science Fiction Writers: **329–336**

De Quincey, Thomas
   British Writers, vol. 4: **141–156**

Derleth, August
   Supernatural Fiction Writers, vol. 2: **883–890**

Díaz del Castillo, Bernal
   Latin American Writers, vol. 1: **17–21**

Diderot, Denis
   European Writers, vol. 4: **475–509**

Dillard, Annie
   American Nature Writers, vol. 1: **213–230**

Dinesen, Isak
   European Writers, vol. 10: **1281–1306**
   European Writers Selected Authors, vol. 1: **453–477**

Doolittle, Hilda (H.D.)
   American Writers Supp. 1, part 1: **253–275**
   Modern American Women Writers: **103–121**

Dos Passos, John
   American Writers, vol. 1: **474–496**

Douglas, Marjory Stoneman
   American Nature Writers, vol. 1: **231–245**

Douglas, Norman
   British Writers, vol. 6: **293–306**

Douglass, Frederick
   American Writers Supp. 3, part 1: **153–174**
   See also "Slave Narrative in American
      Literature, The"

Dreiser, Theodore
   American Writers, vol. 1: **497–520**

Drummond de Andrade, Carlos
   Latin American Writers, vol. 2: **957–974**

Du Bois, W. E. B.
   African American Writers: **71–87**
   American Writers Supp. 2, part 1: **157–189**

Dumas, Alexandre (Père)
   European Writers, vol. 6: **719–745**

European Writers Selected Authors, vol. 1: **503–527**
Writers for Children: **209–213**

Du Maurier, Daphne
   British Writers Supp. 3: **133–149**
   British Writers Selected Authors, vol. 1: **435–451**

Duncan, Lois
   Writers for Young Adults, vol. 1: **393–402**

Dunsany, Lord
   Supernatural Fiction Writers, vol. 1: **471–478**

Eiseley, Loren
   American Nature Writers, vol. 1: **269–285**

Emecheta, Buchi
   African Writers, vol. 1: **235–247**

Equiano, Olaudah
   See "Slave Narrative in American Literature,
      The"

Evelyn, John, and Samuel Pepys
   British Writers, vol. 2: **274–288**

Farjeon, Eleanor
   Writers for Children: **227–234**

Finney, Charles
   Supernatural Fiction Writers, vol. 2: **821–826**

Ford, Ford Madox
   British Writers, vol. 6: **319–334**

Frank, Anne
   Writers for Young Adults, vol. 1: **423–431**

Franklin, Benjamin
   American Writers, vol. 2: **101–125**

French Novelists, Three
   European Writers, vol. 4: **393–419**

Freud, Sigmund
   European Writers, vol. 8: **1–20**
   European Writers Selected Authors, vol. 1: **575–594**

Frisch, Max
   European Writers, vol. 13: **2895–2924**

Fry, Christopher
   British Writers Supp. 3: **191–210**

Fuller, Margaret
   American Writers Supp. 2, part 1: **279–306**

Gág, Wanda
   Writers for Children: **241–246**

Gálvez, Manuel
   Latin American Writers, vol. 2: **585–589**

Gamboa, Federico
   Latin American Writers, vol. 1: **371–375**

Garnett, David
  Supernatural Fiction Writers, vol. 2: **535–539**
Genet, Jean
  European Writers, vol. 13: **2865–2892**
Gibbon, Edward
  British Writers, vol. 3: **221–233**
Gide, André
  European Writers, vol. 8: **495–518**
  European Writers Selected Authors, vol. 1: **631–654**
Gilman, Charlotte Perkins
  Modern American Women Writers: **155–170**
Ginzburg, Natalia
  European Writers, vol. 13: **3131–3163**
Glasgow, Ellen
  American Writers, vol. 2: **173–195**
  Modern American Women Writers: **171–180**
Goethe, Johann Wolfgang von
  European Writers, vol. 5: **1–26**
  European Writers Selected Authors, vol. 1: **655–680**
Goldoni, Carlo
  European Writers, vol. 4: **421–448**
Gombrowicz, Witold
  European Writers, vol. 12: **2563–2588**
Gómez Carillo, Enrique
  Latin American Writers, vol. 2: **465–469**
Goncourt, Edmond Louis Antoine de, and Jules
    Alfred Huot de Goncourt
  European Writers, vol. 7: **1395–1419**
Gorky, Maxim
  European Writers, vol. 8: **417–446**
  European Writers Selected Authors, vol. 2: **681–710**
Green, Henry
  British Writers Supp. 2: **247–266**
Greene, Graham
  British Writers Supp. 1: **1–20**
  British Writers Selected Authors, vol. 2: **557–576**
Grillparzer, Franz
  European Writers, vol. 5: **417–445**
Gunnarsson, Gunnar
  European Writers, vol. 10: **1497–1519**
Hauptmann, Gerhart
  European Writers, vol. 8: **147–174**
Head, Bessie
  African Writers, vol. 1: **303–320**
Heller, Joseph
  American Writers Supp. 4, part 1: **379–396**

Hellman, Lillian
  American Writers Supp. 1, part 1: **276–298**
  Modern American Women Writers: **207–220**
Hemingway, Ernest
  American Writers, vol. 2: **247–270**
  American Writers Retrospective: **169–191**
  Writers for Young Adults, vol. 2: **93–102**
Hentoff, Nat
  Writers for Young Adults, vol. 2: **103–112**
Hesse, Hermann
  European Writers, vol. 9: **833–859**
  European Writers Selected Authors, vol. 2: **735–760**
Hichens, Robert
  Supernatural Fiction Writers, vol. 1: **415–420**
Hofmannsthal, Hugo von
  European Writers, vol. 9: **689–714**
Holmes, Oliver Wendell
  American Writers Supp. 1, part 1: **299–319**
Hope, Christopher
  African Writers, vol. 1: **331–343**
Howells, William Dean
  American Writers, vol. 2: **271–294**
Hughes, Langston
  African American Writers: **193–205**
  American Writers Retrospective: **193–214**
  American Writers Supp. 1, part 1: **320–348**
  Writers for Children: **295–301**
Hurston, Zora Neale
  African American Writers: **205–218**
  Modern American Women Writers: **221–235**
Ionesco, Eugène
  European Writers, vol. 13: **2989–3020**
  European Writers Selected Authors, vol. 2:
    815–846
Jacobs, Harriet
  See "Slave Narrative in American Literature,
    The"
James, Henry
  American Writers, vol. 2: **319–341**
  American Writers Retrospective: **215–242**
  British Writers, vol. 6: **23–69**
  Supernatural Fiction Writers, vol. 1: **337–344**
Johnson, Josephine
  American Nature Writers, vol. 1: **439–451**
Josephus
  Ancient Writers, vol. 2: **877–885**

Juana Inéz de La Cruz, Sor
  Latin American Writers, vol. 1: **85–106**

Kafka, Franz
  European Writers, vol. 9: **1151–1179**
  European Writers Selected Authors, vol. 2:
    847–875

Kästner, Erich
  Writers for Children: **317–322**

Kazantzakis, Nikos
  European Writers, vol. 9: **1067–1091**

Kerouac, Jack
  American Writers Supp. 3, part 1: **217–234**

Kerr, M. E.
  Writers for Young Adults, vol. 2: **177–185**

Kingston, Maxine Hong
  Modern American Women Writers: **251–259**

Kipling, Rudyard
  British Writers, vol. 6: **165–206**
  British Writers Selected Authors, vol. 2: **729–770**
  Supernatural Fiction Writers, vol. 1: **437–442**
  Writers for Children: **329–336**

Klopstock, Friedrich Gottlieb
  European Writers, vol. 4: **511–536**

Koestler, Arthur
  British Writers Supp. 1: **21–41**

Kosztolányi, Dezsö
  European Writers, vol. 10: **1231–1249**

Krutch, Joseph Wood
  American Nature Writers, vol. 1: **465–477**

La Rochefoucauld, François VI, Duc de
  European Writers, vol. 3: **51–71**

Larreta, Enrique
  Latin American Writers, vol. 2: **471–476**

Lawrence, T. E.
  British Writers Supp. 2: **283–298**

Lawson, Robert
  Writers for Children: **345–349**

Least Heat-Moon, William
  American Nature Writers, vol. 1: **513–523**

L'Engle, Madeleine
  Writers for Young Adults, vol. 2: **237–246**

Leopardi, Giacomo
  European Writers, vol. 5: **541–567**

Lessing, Doris
  African Writers, vol. 1: **427–449**

  British Writers Supp. 1: **237–257**
  British Writers Selected Authors, vol. 2: **833–853**

Lewis, C. S.
  British Writers Supp. 3: **247–268**
  British Writers Selected Authors, vol. 2: **855–876**
  Science Fiction Writers: **243–248**
  Supernatural Fiction Writers, vol. 2: **661–666**
  Writers for Children: **357–364**
  Writers for Young Adults, vol. 2: **247–255**

Lima Barreto, Afonso Henriques de
  Latin American Writers, vol. 2: **565–573**

Lins do Rego, José
  Latin American Writers, vol. 2: **909–913**

Lorde, Audre
  African American Writers: **273–288**

McCarthy, Mary
  American Writers, vol. 2: **558–584**
  Modern American Women Writers: **269–278**

Machen, Arthur
  Supernatural Fiction Writers, vol. 1: **351–359**

McKay, Claude
  African American Writers: **305–320**

Maeterlinck, Maurice
  European Writers, vol. 8: **119–146**

Malraux, André
  European Writers, vol. 12: **2413–2432**
  European Writers Selected Authors, vol. 2:
    977–996

Mann, Thomas
  European Writers, vol. 9: **715–743**
  European Writers Selected Authors, vol. 2:
    997–1024

Masters, Edgar Lee
  American Writers Supp. 1, part 2: **454–478**

Mather, Cotton
  American Writers Supp. 2, part 2: **441–470**

Maugham, W. Somerset
  British Writers, vol. 6: **363–382**
  British Writers Selected Authors, vol. 2: **905–923**

Mauriac, François
  European Writers, vol. 10: **1307–1330**

Mencken, H. L.
  American Writers, vol. 3: **99–121**

Milne, A. A.
  Writers for Children: **397–405**

Momaday, N. Scott
    American Nature Writers, vol. 2: **639–649**
    American Writers Supp. 4, part 2: **479–495**

Montgomery, L. M.
    Writers for Children: **415–422**
    Writers for Young Adults, vol. 2: **379–386**

Moore, George
    British Writers, vol. 6: **85–100**

Moravia, Alberto
    European Writers, vol. 12: **2673–2697**

Morris, William
    British Writers, vol. 5: **291–308**
    Supernatural Fiction Writers, vol. 1: **299–306**

Mphahlele, Es'kia
    African Writers, vol. 2: **495–510**

Muir, John
    American Nature Writers, vol. 2: **651–669**

Mumford, Lewis
    American Writers Supp. 2, part 2: **471–501**

Musil, Robert
    European Writers, vol. 9: **931–958**

Nabokov, Vladimir
    American Writers, vol. 3: **244–266**
    American Writers Retrospective: **263–281**

Naipaul, V. S.
    British Writers Supp. 1: **383–405**

Neruda, Pablo
    Latin American Writers, vol. 3: **1001–1018**

Nietzsche, Friedrich
    European Writers, vol. 7: **1645–1682**
    European Writers Selected Authors, vol. 2: **1161–1197**

Nin, Anaïs
    Modern American Women Writers: **339–351**

Ocampo, Victoria
    Latin American Writers, vol. 2: **705–710**

Olesha, Yuri
    European Writers, vol. 11: **2233–2253**

Orwell, George
    British Writers, vol. 7: **273–288**
    British Writers Selected Authors, vol. 2: **947–961**
    Science Fiction Writers: **233–241**

Osborne, John
    British Writers Supp. 1: **329–340**

Pasternak, Boris
    European Writers, vol. 10: **1591–1618**
    European Writers Selected Authors, vol. 2: **1227–1253**

Paton, Alan
    African Writers, vol. 2: **651–668**
    British Writers Supp. 2: **341–361**
    British Writers Selected Authors, vol. 2: **963–983**

Pavese, Cesare
    European Writers, vol. 12: **2759–2784**

Pepys, Samuel
    See "Evelyn, John, and Samuel Pepys"

Pérez Galdós, Benito
    European Writers, vol. 7: **1597–1618**

Picón Salas, Mariano
    Latin American Writers, vol. 2: **903–908**

Plomer, William
    African Writers, vol. 2: **697–706**

Potter, Beatrix
    British Writers Supp. 3: **287–309**
    Writers for Children: **439–446**

Powys, John Cowper
    Supernatural Fiction Writers, vol. 2: **609–616**

Pritchett, V. S.
    British Writers Supp. 3: **311–331**

Pym, Barbara
    British Writers Supp. 2: **363–385**

Quiller-Couch, Arthur
    Supernatural Fiction Writers, vol. 1: **389–395**

Ramos, Graciliano
    Latin American Writers, vol. 2: **745–754**

Reyes, Alfonso
    Latin American Writers, vol. 2: **693–703**

Rhys, Jean
    British Writers Supp. 2: **387–404**

Richards, Laura E.
    Writers for Children: **469–475**

Richter, Jean Paul
    European Writers, vol. 5: **53–88**

Rinbaud, Arthur
    European Writers, vol. 7: **1785–1824**

Robbe-Grillet, Alain
    European Writers, vol. 13: **3237–3256**

Rojas, Manuel
    Latin American Writers, vol. 2: **815–820**

Rousseau, Jean Jacques
    European Writers, vol. 4: **449–474**

European Writers Selected Authors, vol. 3:
1519–1544

Ruskin, John
British Writers, vol. 5: **173–186**
Writers for Children: **493–496**

Sa'adāwī, Nawāl, al-
African Writers, vol. 2: **721–731**

Sand, George
European Writers, vol. 6: **813–836**
European Writers Selected Authors, vol. 3:
1571–1594

Sandburg, Carl
American Writers, vol. 3: **575–598**
Writers for Children: **503–510**
Writers for Young Adults, vol. 3: **123–133**

Santayana, George
American Writers, vol. 3: **599–622**

Sartre, Jean-Paul
European Writers, vol. 12: **2589–2614**
European Writers Selected Authors, vol. 3: **1595–1620**

Seferis, George
European Writers, vol. 12: **2255–2271**

Seton, Ernest Thompson
American Nature Writers, vol. 2: **805–816**

Silone, Ignazione
European Writers, vol. 12: **2273–2305**

Simenon, Georges
European Writers, vol. 12: **2479–2510**

Singer, Isaac Bashevis
American Writers, vol. 4: **1–24**

Slave Narrative in American Literature, The
African American Writers: **395–412**

Soyinka, Wole
African Writers, vol. 2: **807–831**

Spender, Steven
British Writers Supp. 2: **481–496**

Staël, Madame de
European Writers, vol. 5: **89–111**

Stein, Gertrude
American Writers, vol. 4: **25–48**
Modern American Women Writers: **485–498**

Stendhal
European Writers, vol. 5: **343–366**
European Writers Selected Authors, vol. 3:
1649–1672

Strachey, Lytton
British Writers Supp. 2: **497–518**

Strindberg, August
European Writers, vol. 7: **1731–1758**

Styron, William
American Writers, vol. 4: **97–119**

Tablada, José Juan
Latin American Writers, vol. 1: **441–446**

Ṭāhā Ḥusayn
African Writers, vol. 2: **851–863**

Thomas, Edward
British Writers Supp. 3: **393–408**

Thoreau, Henry David
American Nature Writers, vol. 2: **933–950**
American Writers, vol. 4: **167–189**

Thurber, James
American Writers Supp. 1, part 2: **602–627**
Supernatural Fiction Writers, vol. 2: **827–831**

Tocqueville, Alexis de
European Writers, vol. 6: **893–912**
European Writers Selected Authors, vol. 3:
1673–1691

Torres Bodet, Jaime
Latin American Writers, vol. 2: **933–939**

Trevelyan, G. M.
British Writers, vol. 6: **383–396**

Trollope, Anthony
British Writers, vol. 5: **89–104**
British Writers Selected Authors, vol. 3: **1295–1309**

Tsvetaeva, Marina
European Writers, vol. 11: **1731–1750**

Twain, Mark
American Writers, vol. 4: **190–213**
Supernatural Fiction Writers, vol. 2: **761–768**
Writers for Children: **573–582**
Writers for Young Adults, vol. 3: **321–328**

Unamuno, Miguel de
European Writers, vol. 8: **283–310**

Undset, Sigrid
European Writers, vol. 9: **1017–1041**

Usigli, Rodolfo
Latin American Writers, vol. 3: **1033–1042**

van der Post, Laurens
African Writers, vol. 2: **879–891**

Van Dyke, John C.
    American Nature Writers, vol. 2: **951–962**

Vasconcelos, José
    Latin American Writers, vol. 2: **575–584**

Veríssimo, Érico
    Latin American Writers, vol. 3: **1043–1048**

Vesaas, Tarjei
    European Writers, vol. 11: **2035–2059**

Vico, Giovanni Battista
    European Writers, vol. 3: **293–316**

Vidal, Gore
    American Writers Supp. 4, part 2: **677–697**

Vigny, Alfred Victor de
    European Writers, vol. 5: **447–488**

Voltaire
    European Writers, vol. 4: **367–392**
    European Writers Selected Authors, vol. 3:
        1741–1766

Wagner, Richard
    European Writers, vol. 6: **1147–1168**
    European Writers Selected Authors, vol. 3:
        1767–1787

Walpole, Horace
    Supernatural Fiction Writers, vol. 1: **131–137**
    See also "Gothic Novel, The"

Wells, H. G.
    British Writers, vol. 6: **225–246**
    British Writers Selected Authors, vol. 3: **1331–1352**
    Science Fiction Writers: **25–30**
    Supernatural Fiction Writers, vol. 1: **397–402**
    Writers for Children: **599–603**

Welty, Eudora
    American Writers, vol. 4: **260–284**
    American Writers Retrospective: **339–358**
    Modern American Women Writers: **521–538**

West, Rebecca
    British Writers Supp. 3: **431–445**

Wharton, Edith
    American Writers, vol. 4: **308–330**
    American Writers Retrospective: **359–385**
    Modern American Women Writers: **539–558**
    Supernatural Fiction Writers, vol. 2: **783–788**

Wheatley, Dennis
    Supernatural Fiction Writers, vol. 2: **623–629**

White, Patrick
    British Writers Supp. 1: **129–152**

Wideman, John Edgar
    African American Writers: **493–504**

Wiggin, Kate Douglas
    Writers for Children: **605–609**

Williams, Terry Tempest
    American Nature Writers, vol. 2: **973–988**

Williams, William Carlos
    American Writers, vol. 4: **402–425**
    American Writers Retrospective: **411–433**

Wilson, Edmund
    American Writers, vol. 4: **426–449**

Woolf, Virginia
    British Writers, vol. 7: **17–40**
    British Writers Selected Authors, vol. 3:
        1395–1417

Wright, Richard
    African American Writers: **505–523**
    American Writers, vol. 4: **474–497**

Yep, Laurence
    Writers for Young Adults, vol. 3: **399–408**

Yourcenar, Marguerite
    European Writers, vol. 12: **2535–2561**

Zamyatin, Yevgeny Ivanovich
    European Writers, vol. 10: **1181–1203**

Zindel, Paul
    Writers for Young Adults, vol. 3: **421–430**

CHILDREN'S LITERATURE

Works that have appealed to young readers, regardless of original intent.

Achebe, Chinua
African Writers, vol. 1: **15–36**

Aidoo, Ama Ata
African Writers, vol. 1: **37–48**

Aiken, Joan
Writers for Young Adults, vol. 1: **1–9**

Alcott, Louisa May
American Writers Supp. 1, part 1: **28–46**
Writers for Children: **1–6**
Writers for Young Adults, vol. 1: **11–20**

Alexander, Lloyd
Supernatural Fiction Writers, vol. 2: **965–971**
Writers for Young Adults, vol. 1: **21–33**

Andersen, Hans Christian
European Writers, vol. 6: **863–892**
European Writers Selected Authors, vol. 1: **1–29**
Writers for Children: **7–13**

Anderson, Poul
Science Fiction Writers: **259–265**
Supernatural Fiction Writers, vol. 2: **973–980**

Angell, Judie
Writers for Young Adults, vol. 1: **35–42**

Anstey, F.
Supernatural Fiction Writers, vol. 1: **287–292**

Ardizzone, Edward
Writers for Children: **15–20**

Asbjørnsen and Moe (Peter Christen
　　Asbjørnsen and Jørgen Moe)
Writers for Children: **21–28**

Asher, Sandy
Writers for Young Adults, vol. 1: **53–61**

Avi
Writers for Young Adults, vol. 1: **63–72**

Barrie, J. M.
British Writers Supp. 3: **1–17**
Supernatural Fiction Writers, vol. 1: **405–410**
Writers for Children: **29–35**

Bauer, Joan
Writers for Young Adults, vol. 1: **73–80**

Bauer, Marion Dane
Writers for Young Adults, vol. 1: **81–88**

Baum, L. Frank
Writers for Children: **37–48**

Belloc, Hilaire
Writers for Children: **49–54**

Bemelmans, Ludwig
Writers for Children: **55–61**

Bennett, Jay
Writers for Young Adults, vol. 1: **89–97**

Beston, Henry
American Nature Writers, vol. 1: **107–120**

Bethancourt, T. Ernesto
Writers for Young Adults, vol. 1: **99–109**

Bianco, Margery Williams
Writers for Children: **63–67**

Bible, The English
British Writers, vol. 1: **370–388**
British Writers Selected Authors, vol. 1: **69–87**

Blake, William
British Writers, vol. 3: **288–310**
British Writers Selected Authors, vol. 1: **89–110**
Writers for Children: **69–76**

Block, Francesca Lia
Writers for Young Adults, vol. 1: **111–119**

Blume, Judy
Writers for Young Adults, vol. 1: **121–131**

Bograd, Larry
Writers for Young Adults, vol. 1: **133–141**

Bontemps, Arna
Writers for Children: **77–83**

Bradbury, Ray
American Writers Supp. 4, part 1: **101–118**
Supernatural Fiction Writers: **171–178**
Supernatural Fiction Writers, vol. 2: **917–923**

Brancato, Robin F.
Writers for Young Adults, vol. 1: **143–152**

Branscum, Robbie
Writers for Young Adults, vol. 1: **153–161**

Bridgers, Sue Ellen
    Writers for Young Adults, vol. 1: **163–172**

Brink, Carol Ryrie
    Writers for Children: **85–90**

Brooks, Bruce
    Writers for Young Adults, vol. 1: **173–182**

Brunhoff, Jean de
    Writers for Children: **91–96**

Bunting, Eve
    Writers for Young Adults, vol. 1: **183–189**

Bunyan, John
    British Writers, vol. 2: **240–254**
    British Writers Selected Authors, vol. 1: **215–229**
    Writers for Children: **97–102**

Burnett, Frances Hodgson
    Writers for Children: **103–109**

Burns, Olive Ann
    Writers for Young Adults, vol. 1: **191–198**

Burroughs, Edgar Rice
    Science Fiction Writers: **59–64**

Burton, Virginia Lee
    Writers for Children: **111–115**

Byars, Betsy
    Writers for Young Adults, vol. 1: **199–207**

Campbell, Roy
    African Writers, vol. 1: **127–137**

Carroll, Lewis
    British Writers, vol. 5: **261–276**
    Supernatural Fiction Writers, vol. 1: **247–253**
    Writers for Children: **117–127**

Carter, Alden R.
    Writers for Young Adults, vol. 1: **209–218**

Carter, Angela
    British Writers Supp. 3: **79–93**

Chambers, Aidan
    Writers for Young Adults, vol. 1: **219–227**

Childress, Alice
    Writers for Young Adults, vol. 1: **229–240**

Cleaver, Vera and Bill
    Writers for Young Adults, vol. 1: **241–248**

Clement, Hal
    Science Fiction Writers: **321–327**

Cole, Brock
    Writers for Young Adults, vol. 1: **249–256**

Collier, Christopher and James Lincoln
    Writers for Young Adults, vol. 1: **257–269**

Collodi, C.
    Writers for Children: **129–137**

Colman, Hila
    Writers for Young Adults, vol. 1: **271–280**

Colum, Padraic
    Writers for Children: **139–146**

Cooney, Caroline B.
    Writers for Young Adults, vol. 1: **281–290**

Cooper, James Fenimore
    American Writers, vol. 1: **335–357**
    Writers for Children: **147–153**

Cormier, Robert
    Writers for Young Adults, vol. 1: **291–301**

Crane, Stephen
    American Writers, vol. 1: **405–427**
    Writers for Young Adults, vol. 1: **303–312**

Crutcher, Chris
    Writers for Young Adults, vol. 1: **313–322**

Cullen, Countee
    American Writers Supp. 4, part 1: **163–174**

Dahl, Roald
    British Writers Supp. 4: **201–227**

Daly, Maureen
    Writers for Young Adults, vol. 1: **323–333**

Danziger, Paula
    Writers for Young Adults, vol. 1: **335–344**

Daugherty, James Henry
    Writers for Children: **155–161**

Davis, Terry
    Writers for Young Adults, vol. 1: **345–352**

Day Lewis, Cecil
    British Writers Supp. 3: **115–132**

Defoe, Daniel
    British Writers, vol. 3: **1–14**
    British Writers Selected Authors, vol. 1: **349–362**
    Writers for Children: **163–171**

De la Mare, Walter
    Supernatural Fiction Writers, vol. 1: **497–503**
    Writers for Children: **173–180**

Derleth, August
    Supernatural Fiction Writers, vol. 2: **883–890**

Díaz, Jorge
    Latin American Writers, vol. 3: **1393–1397**

Dickens, Charles
British Writers, vol. 5: **41–74**
British Writers Selected Authors, vol. 1: **363–396**
Supernatural Fiction Writers, vol.1: **213–218**
Writers for Children: **181–191**
Writers for Young Adults, vol. 1: **353–364**

Dickinson, Emily
American Writers, vol. 1: **451–473**
American Writers Retrospective: **25–50**
Modern American Women Writers: **77–89**
Writers for Young Adults, vol. 1: **365–372**

Dickinson, Peter
Writers for Young Adults, vol. 1: **375–383**

Dodge, Mary Mapes
Writers for Children: **193–199**

Doyle, Sir Arthur Conan
British Writers Supp. 2: **159–178**
British Writers Selected Authors, vol. 1: **415–434**
Science Fiction Writers: **45–50**
Writers for Children: **201–207**
Writers for Young Adults, vol. 1: **385–392**

Dumas, Alexandre (Père)
European Writers, vol. 6: **719–745**
European Writers Selected Authors, vol. 1: **503–527**
Writers for Children: **209–213**

Duncan, Lois
Writers for Young Adults, vol. 1: **393–402**

Edgeworth, Maria
British Writers Supp. 3: **151–168**

Eifert, Virginia
American Nature Writers, vol. 1: **259–268**

Ekwensi, Cyprian
African Writers, vol. 1: **223–234**

Emecheta, Buchi
African Writers, vol. 1: **235–247**

Enright, Elizabeth
Writers for Children: **215–220**

Ewing, Juliana Horatia
Writers for Children: **221–226**

Eyerly, Jeannette
Writers for Young Adults, vol. 1: **403–411**

Farjeon, Eleanor
Writers for Children: **227–234**

Field, Rachel Lyman
Writers for Children: **235–240**

Fox, Paula
Writers for Young Adults, vol. 1: **413–422**

Frank, Anne
Writers for Young Adults, vol. 1: **423–431**

Freedman, Russell
Writers for Young Adults, vol. 2: **1–9**

Freeman, Mary E. Wilkins
Modern American Women Writers: **141–153**
Supernatural Fiction Writers, vol. 2: **769–773**

French, Michael
Writers for Young Adults, vol. 2: **11–20**

Fry, Christopher
British Writers Supp. 3: **191–210**

Gág, Wanda
Writers for Children: **241–246**

Garfield, Leon
Writers for Young Adults, vol. 2: **33–45**

Garner, Alan
Supernatural Fiction Writers, vol. 2: **1023–1029**

George, Jean Craighead
Writers for Young Adults, vol. 2: **47–57**

Grahame, Kenneth
Writers for Children: **247–254**

Greene, Bette
Writers for Young Adults, vol. 2: **59–68**

Grimm, Jacob and Wilhelm
Writers for Children: **255–263**

Haggard, H. Rider
British Writers Supp. 3: **211–228**
Science Fiction Writers: **19–24**
Supernatural Fiction Writers, vol. 1: **321–327**

Hale, Lucretia P.
Writers for Children: **265–268**

Hall, Lynn
Writers for Young Adults, vol. 2: **69–77**

Harris, Joel Chandler
Writers for Children: **269–275**

Hawthorne, Nathaniel
American Writers, vol. 2: **223–246**
American Writers Retrospective: **145–167**
Supernatural Fiction Writers, vol. 2: **707–715**
Writers for Children: **277–282**

Heinlein, Robert A.
Science Fiction Writers: **185–196**

Hentoff, Nat
    Writers for Young Adults, vol. 2: **103–112**
Hinton, S. E.
    Writers for Young Adults, vol. 2: **113–120**
Hoffmann, E. T. A.
    European Writers, vol. 5: **261–289**
    Supernatural Fiction Writers, vol. 1: **111–119**
    Writers for Children: **283–288**
Hoffmann, Heinrich
    Writers for Children: **289–294**
Holland, Isabelle
    Writers for Young Adults, vol. 2: **131–140**
Hoover, Helen
    American Nature Writers, vol. 1: **389–399**
Hope, Christopher
    African Writers, vol. 1: **331–343**
Hughes, Langston
    African American Writers: **193–205**
    American Writers Retrospective: **193–214**
    American Writers Supp. 1, part 1: **320–348**
    Writers for Children: **295–301**
Hughes, Monica
    Writers for Young Adults, vol. 2: **141–148**
Hunter, Mollie
    Writers for Young Adults, vol. 2: **149–159**
Irving, Washington
    American Writers, vol. 2: **295–318**
    Supernatural Fiction Writers, vol. 2: **685–691**
    Writers for Children: **303–307**
Irwin, Hadley
    Writers for Young Adults, vol. 2: **161–166**
Jackson, Shirley
    Supernatural Fiction Writers, vol. 2: **1031–1036**
Jacobs, Joseph
    Writers for Children: **309–316**
Johnston, Norma
    Writers for Young Adults, vol. 2: **167–176**
Jordan, June
    African American Writers: **245–261**
Kästner, Erich
    Writers for Children: **317–322**
Keneally, Thomas
    British Writers Supp. 4: **343–362**
Kerr, M. E.
    Writers for Young Adults, vol. 2: **177–185**

Kingsley, Charles
    Writers for Children: **323–327**
Kipling, Rudyard
    British Writers, vol. 6: **165–206**
    British Writers Selected Authors, vol. 2: **729–770**
    Supernatural Fiction Writers, vol. 1: **437–442**
    Writers for Children: **329–336**
Klein, Norma
    Writers for Young Adults, vol. 2: **187–197**
Korman, Gordon
    Writers for Young Adults, vol. 2: **199–206**
Kumin, Maxine
    American Nature Writers, vol. 1: **479–497**
    American Writers Supp. 4, part 2: **439–457**
Lang, Andrew
    Writers for Children: **337–343**
Lasky, Kathryn
    Writers for Young Adults, vol. 2: **207–216**
Lawson, Robert
    Writers for Children: **345–349**
Lear, Edward
    British Writers, vol. 5: **75–88**
    Writers for Children: **351–356**
Lee, Harper
    Writers for Young Adults, vol. 2: **217–225**
Le Guin, Ursula K.
    Science Fiction Writers: **409–417**
    Supernatural Fiction Writers, vol. 2: **1059–1066**
    Writers for Young Adults, vol. 2: **227–236**
    See also "Contemporary Ecofiction"
L'Engle, Madeleine
    Writers for Young Adults, vol. 2: **237–246**
Lewis, C. S.
    British Writers Supp. 3: **247–268**
    British Writers Selected Authors, vol. 2: **855–876**
    Science Fiction Writers: **243–248**
    Supernatural Fiction Writers, vol. 2: **661–666**
    Writers for Children: **357–364**
    Writers for Young Adults, vol. 2: **247–255**
Lipsyte, Robert
    Writers for Young Adults, vol. 2: **257–266**
Lofting, Hugh
    Writers for Children: **365–371**
London, Jack
    American Writers, vol. 2: **462–485**
    Writers for Young Adults, vol. 2: **267–278**

Lowry, Lois
  Writers for Young Adults, vol. 2: **279–287**

Lynch, Chris
  Writers for Young Adults, vol. 2: **289–297**

McCaffrey, Anne
  Writers for Young Adults, vol. 2: **299–306**

MacDonald, George
  Supernatural Fiction Writers, vol. 1: **239–246**
  Writers for Children: **373–380**

McNulty, Faith
  American Nature Writers, vol. 1: **569–581**

Mahy, Margaret (May)
  Writers for Young Adults, vol. 2: **307–315**

Major, Kevin
  Writers for Young Adults, vol. 2: **317–326**

Malory, Sir Thomas
  British Writers, vol. 1: **67–80**
  British Writers Selected Authors, vol. 2: **877–890**
  See also "Arthurian Romances"

Marryat, Frederick
  Writers for Children: **381–387**

Mazer, Harry
  Writers for Young Adults, vol. 2: **327–336**

Mazer, Norma Fox
  Writers for Young Adults, vol. 2: **337–346**

Meigs, Cornelia
  Writers for Children: **389–395**

Meltzer, Milton
  Writers for Young Adults, vol. 2: **347–358**

Metcalfe, John
  Supernatural Fiction Writers, vol. 2: **597–602**

Miklowitz, Gloria D.
  Writers for Young Adults, vol. 2: **359–368**

Milne, A. A.
  Writers for Children: **397–405**

Moe, Jörgen
  See "Asbjørnsen and Moe"

Mohr, Nicholasa
  Writers for Young Adults, vol. 2: **369–378**

Molesworth, M. L. S.
  Writers for Children: **407–413**

Montgomery, L. M.
  Writers for Children: **415–422**
  Writers for Young Adults, vol. 2: **379–386**

Moravia, Alberto
  European Writers, vol. 12: **2673–2697**

Mwangi, Meja
  African Writers, vol. 2: **511–525**

Myers, Walter Dean
  Writers for Young Adults, vol. 2: **387–396**

Naylor, Phyllis Reynolds
  Writers for Young Adults, vol. 2: **397–409**

Nesbit, E.
  Writers for Children: **423–430**

Ngũgĩ wa Thiong'o
  African Writers, vol. 2: **537–555**

Nixon, Joan Lowery
  Writers for Young Adults, vol. 2: **411–419**

Norton, Andre
  Supernatural Fiction Writers, vol. 2: **1091–1096**

Okara, Gabriel
  African Writers, vol. 2: **567–582**

Olesha, Yuri
  European Writers, vol. 11: **2233–2253**

Oliver, Chad
  Science Fiction Writers: **467–473**

Oneal, Zibby
  Writers for Young Adults, vol. 2: **433–442**

Ortiz, Simon J.
  American Writers Supp. 4, part 2: **497–515**

Paterson, Katherine
  Writers for Young Adults, vol. 2: **443–454**

Paulsen, Gary
  Writers for Young Adults, vol. 2: **455–463**

Peck, Richard
  Writers for Young Adults, vol. 3: **1–14**

Peck, Robert Newton
  Writers for Young Adults, vol. 3: **15–26**

Perrault, Charles
  Writers for Children: **431–437**

Petry, Ann
  African American Writers: **347–359**

Pevsner, Stella
  Writers for Young Adults, vol. 3: **27–34**

Peyton, K. M.
  Writers for Young Adults, vol. 3: **35–42**

Pfeffer, Susan Beth
  Writers for Young Adults, vol. 3: **43–52**

Platt, Kin
  Writers for Young Adults, vol. 3: **53–60**
Poe, Edgar Allan
  American Writers, vol. 3: **409–432**
  Science Fiction Writers: **11–18**
  Supernatural Fiction Writers, vol. 2: **697–705**
  Writers for Young Adults, vol. 3: **61–73**
Potter, Beatrix
  British Writers Supp. 3: **287–309**
  Writers for Children: **439–446**
Pyle, Howard
  Writers for Children: **447–454**
Quiller-Couch, Arthur
  Supernatural Fiction Writers, vol. 1: **389–395**
Ramos, Graciliano
  Latin American Writers, vol. 2: **745–754**
Ransome, Arthur
  Writers for Children: **455–461**
Rawlings, Marjorie Kinnan
  American Nature Writers, vol. 2: **751–765**
  Writers for Children: **463–467**
Richards, Laura E.
  Writers for Children: **469–475**
Rinaldi, Ann
  Writers for Young Adults, vol. 3: **75–85**
Roberts, Elizabeth Madox
  Writers for Children: **477–481**
Rodowsky, Colby
  Writers for Young Adults, vol. 3: **87–93**
Rossetti, Christina
  British Writers, vol. 5: **247–260**
  Writers for Children: **483–491**
Rushdie, Salman
  British Writers Supp. 4: **433–457**
Ruskin, John
  British Writers, vol. 5: **173–186**
  Writers for Children: **493–496**
Sachs, Marilyn
  Writers for Young Adults, vol. 3: **95–104**
Saint-Exupéry, Antoine de
  European Writers, vol. 12: **2307–2332**
  European Writers Selected Authors, vol. 3:
    1545–1569
Salisbury, Graham
  Writers for Young Adults, vol. 3: **113–121**

Salten, Felix
  Writers for Children: **497–501**
Sandburg, Carl
  American Writers, vol. 3: **575–598**
  Writers for Children: **503–510**
  Writers for Young Adults, vol. 3: **123–133**
Sawyer, Ruth
  Writers for Children: **511–517**
Sayers, Dorothy L.
  British Writers Supp. 3: **333–353**
Scoppettone, Sandra
  Writers for Young Adults, vol. 3: **135–143**
Sebestyen, Ouida
  Writers for Young Adults, vol. 3: **145–153**
Seredy, Kate
  Writers for Children: **519–524**
Seton, Ernest Thompson
  American Nature Writers, vol. 2: **805–816**
Sewell, Anna
  Writers for Children: **525–528**
Shakespeare, William
  British Writers, vol. 1: **295–334**
  British Writers Selected Authors, vol. 2: **1013–1052**
  Writers for Young Adults, vol. 3: **155–172**
  See also entries in *William Shakespeare: His World,
    His Work, His Influence*
Silveira de Queiroz, Dinah
  Latin American Writers, vol. 3: **1145–1151**
Silverberg, Robert
  Science Fiction Writers: **505–511**
Sleator, William
  Writers for Young Adults, vol. 3: **173–182**
Soto, Gary
  Writers for Young Adults, vol. 3: **183–191**
Spinelli, Jerry
  Writers for Young Adults, vol. 3: **193–201**
Spyri, Johanna
  Writers for Children: **529–533**
Stevenson, Robert Louis
  British Writers, vol. 5: **383–399**
  British Writers Selected Authors, vol. 3:
    1161–1176
  Supernatural Fiction Writers, vol. 1: **307–313**
  Writers for Children: **535–543**
  Writers for Young Adults, vol. 3: **215–224**

Stockton, Frank R.
 Supernatural Fiction Writers, vol. 2: **753–759**
 Writers for Children: **545–554**

Strasser, Todd
 Writers for Young Adults, vol. 3: **225–236**

Stratemeyer, Edward
 Writers for Young Adults, vol. 3: **237–249**

Stratton Porter, Gene
 American Nature Writers, vol. 2: **877–891**

Sutcliff, Rosemary
 Writers for Young Adults, vol. 3: **251–261**

Sutherland, Efua Theodora
 African Writers, vol. 2: **833–849**

Swenson, May
 American Writers Supp. 4, part 2: **637–655**

Swift, Jonathan
 British Writers, vol. 3: **15–38**
 British Writers Selected Authors, vol. 3: **1195–1217**
 Writers for Children: **555–559**

Talbert, Marc
 Writers for Young Adults, vol. 3: **263–272**

Taylor, Mildred Delois
 Writers for Young Adults, vol. 3: **273–282**

Taylor, Theodore
 Writers for Young Adults, vol. 3: **283–292**

Teale, Edwin Way
 American Nature Writers, vol. 2: **893–904**

Thaxter, Celia
 American Nature Writers, vol. 2: **905–917**

Thomas, Joyce Carol
 Writers for Young Adults, vol. 3: **293–301**

Thompson, Julian F.
 Writers for Young Adults, vol. 3: **303–310**

Thurber, James
 American Writers Supp. 1, part 2: **602–627**
 Supernatural Fiction Writers, vol. 2: **827–831**

Tolkien, J. R. R.
 British Writers Supp. 2: **519–536**
 British Writers Selected Authors, vol. 3: **1277–1294**
 Supernatural Fiction Writers, vol. 2: **675–682**
 Writers for Children: **561–571**
 Writers for Young Adults, vol. 3: **311–320**

Twain, Mark
 American Writers, vol. 4: **190–213**
 Supernatural Fiction Writers, vol. 2: **761–768**

Writers for Children: **573–582**
 Writers for Young Adults, vol. 3: **321–328**

Tychyna, Pavlo
 European Writers, vol. 10: **1651–1676**

Tyler, Anne
 American Writers Supp. 4, part 2: **657–675**
 Modern American Women Writers: **499–510**

Van Loon, Hendrik Willem
 Writers for Children: **583–589**

Veríssimo, Érico
 Latin American Writers, vol. 3: **1043–1048**

Verne, Jules
 Science Fiction Writers: **573–582**
 Writers for Children: **591–598**

Voigt, Cynthia
 Writers for Young Adults, vol. 3: **329–338**

Walker, Alice
 African American Writers: **441–458**
 American Writers Supp. 3, part 2: **517–540**
 Modern American Women Writers: **511–520**

Walsh, Jill Paton
 Writers for Young Adults, vol. 3: **339–346**

Wellman, Manly Wade
 Supernatural Fiction Writers, vol. 2: **947–954**

Wells, H. G.
 British Writers, vol. 6: **225–246**
 British Writers Selected Authors, vol. 3: **1331–1352**
 Science Fiction Writers: **25–30**
 Supernatural Fiction Writers, vol. 1: **397–402**
 Writers for Children: **599–603**

Welty, Eudora
 American Writers, vol. 4: **260–284**
 American Writers Retrospective: **339–358**
 Modern American Women Writers: **521–538**

Wersba, Barbara
 Writers for Young Adults, vol. 3: **349–357**

Westall, Robert Atkinson
 Writers for Young Adults, vol. 3: **359–369**

White, E. B.
 American Writers Supp. 1, part 2: **651–681**

White, T. H.
 Supernatural Fiction Writers, vol. 2: **651–657**

Wiggin, Kate Douglas
 Writers for Children: **605–609**

Special Subject Categories

WOMEN WRITERS

Ackerman, Diane
American Nature Writers, vol. 1: **21–30**

Addams, Jane
American Writers Supp. 1, part 1: **1–27**

Agustini, Delmira
Latin American Writers, vol. 2: **649–654**

Aidoo, Ama Ata
African Writers, vol. 1: **37–48**

Aiken, Joan
Writers for Young Adults, vol. 1: **1–9**

Akhmatova, Anna
European Writers, vol. 10: **1521–1542**

Alcott, Louisa May
American Writers Supp. 1, part 1: **28–46**
Writers for Children: **1–6**
Writers for Young Adults, vol. 1: **11–20**

Angell, Judie
Writers for Young Adults, vol. 1: **35–42**

Angelou, Maya
American Writers Supp. 4, part 1: **1–19**
Modern American Women Writers: **1–8**
Writers for Young Adults, vol. 1: **43–52**

Asher, Sandy
Writers for Young Adults, vol. 1: **53–61**

Austen, Jane
British Writers, vol. 4: **101–124**
British Writers Selected Authors, vol. 1: **23–46**

Austin, Mary Hunter
American Nature Writers, vol. 1: **31–51**

Bâ, Mariama
African Writers, vol. 1: **77–82**

Bailey, Florence Merriam
American Nature Writers, vol. 1: **53–62**

Barker, Pat
British Writers Supp. 4: **45–63**

Barnes, Djuna
American Writers Supp. 3, part 1: **31–46**

Bauer, Joan
Writers for Young Adults, vol. 1: **73–80**

Bauer, Marion Dane
Writers for Young Adults, vol. 1: **81–88**

Beauvoir, Simone de
European Writers, vol. 12: **2701–2732**
European Writers Selected Authors, vol. 1: **185–215**

Behn, Aphra
British Writers Supp. 3: **19–43**

Bianco, Margery Williams
Writers for Children: **63–67**

Bishop, Elizabeth
American Writers Supp. 1, part 1: **72–97**
Modern American Women Writers: **9–22**

Block, Francesca Lia
Writers for Young Adults, vol. 1: **111–119**

Blume, Judy
Writers for Young Adults, vol. 1: **121–131**

Bogan, Louise
American Writers Supp. 3, part 1: **47–68**
Modern American Women Writers: **23–36**

Bombal, María Luisa
Latin American Writers, vol. 3: **1111–1117**

Bowen, Elizabeth
British Writers Supp. 2: **77–96**
Supernatural Fiction Writers, vol. 2: **569–575**

Brackett, Leigh
Supernatural Fiction Writers, vol. 2: **909–915**

Bradstreet, Anne
American Writers Supp. 1, part 1: **98–123**

Brancato, Robin F.
Writers for Young Adults, vol. 1: **143–152**

Bridgers, Sue Ellen
   Writers for Young Adults, vol. 1: **163–172**

Brink, Carol Ryrie
   Writers for Children: **85–90**

Brontës, The
   British Writers, vol. 5: **105–154**
   British Writers Selected Authors, vol. 1: **129–177**

Brooke-Rose, Christine
   British Writers Supp. 4: **97–118**

Brookner, Anita
   British Writers Supp. 4: **119–137**

Brooks, Gwendolyn
   African American Writers: **31–43**
   American Writers Supp. 3, part 1: **69–90**
   Modern American Women Writers: **37–48**

Browning, Elizabeth Barrett
   British Writers, vol. 4: **310–322**
   British Writers Selected Authors, vol. 1: **179–191**

Buck, Pearl S.
   American Writers Supp. 2, part 1: **113–134**

Bunting, Eve
   Writers for Young Adults, vol. 1: **183–189**

Burnett, Frances Hodgson
   Writers for Children: **103–109**

Burney, Frances
   British Writers Supp. 3: **63–78**

Burns, Olive Ann
   Writers for Young Adults, vol. 1: **191–198**

Burton, Virginia Lee
   Writers for Children: **111–115**

Byars, Betsy
   Writers for Young Adults, vol. 1: **199–207**

Byatt, A. S.
   British Writers Supp. 4: **139–156**

Carrighar, Sally
   American Nature Writers, vol. 1: **139–149**

Carson, Rachel
   American Nature Writers, vol. 1: **151–171**

Carter, Angela
   British Writers Supp. 3: **79–93**

Castellanos, Rosario
   Latin American Writers, vol. 3: **1295–1302**

Cather, Willa
   American Writers, vol. 1: **312–334**
   American Writers Retrospective: **1–23**
   Modern American Women Writers: **49–62**

Childress, Alice
   Writers for Young Adults, vol. 1: **229–240**

Chopin, Kate
   American Writers Supp. 1, part 1: **200–226**
   Modern American Women Writers: **63–78**

Christie, Agatha
   British Writers Supp. 2: **123–137**

Churchill, Caryl
   British Writers Supp. 4: **179–200**

Cleaver, Vera
   See "Cleaver, Vera and Bill" in *Writers for Young Adults*, vol. 1: **241–248**

Colette
   European Writers, vol. 9: **617–638**
   European Writers Selected Authors, vol. 1: **389–410**

Colman, Hila
   Writers for Young Adults, vol. 1: **271–280**

Compton-Burnett, Ivy
   British Writers, vol. 7: **59–70**

Comstock, Anna Botsford
   American Nature Writers, vol. 1: **173–185**

Cooney, Caroline B.
   Writers for Young Adults, vol. 1: **281–290**

Cooper, Susan Fenimore
   American Nature Writers, vol. 1: **187–198**

Corelli, Marie
   Supernatural Fiction Writers, vol. 1: **293–297**

Daly, Maureen
   Writers for Young Adults, vol. 1: **323–333**

Danziger, Paula
   Writers for Young Adults, vol. 1: **335–344**

Dickinson, Emily
   American Writers, vol. 1: **451–473**
   American Writers Retrospective: **25–50**
   Modern American Women Writers: **77–89**
   Writers for Young Adults, vol. 1: **365–372**

Didion, Joan
   American Writers Supp. 4, part 1: **195–216**
   Modern American Women Writers: **91–102**

Dillard, Annie
   American Nature Writers, vol. 1: **213–230**

Dinesen, Isak
   European Writers, vol. 10: **1281–1306**
   European Writers Selected Authors, vol. 1: **453–477**

Dodge, Mary Mapes
   Writers for Children: **193–199**

Doolittle, Hilda (H.D.)
  American Writers Supp. 1, part 1: **253–275**
  Modern American Women Writers: **103–121**

Douglas, Marjory Stoneman
  American Nature Writers, vol. 1: **231–245**

Dove, Rita
  American Writers Supp. 4, part 1: **241–258**

Drabble, Margaret
  British Writers Supp. 4: **229–254**

Du Maurier, Daphne
  British Writers Supp. 3: **133–149**
  British Writers Selected Authors, vol. 1: **435–451**

Duncan, Lois
  Writers for Young Adults, vol. 1: **393–402**

Edgeworth, Maria
  British Writers Supp. 3: **151–168**

Edwards, Amelia B.
  Supernatural Fiction Writers, vol. 1: **255–260**

Ehrlich, Gretel
  American Nature Writers, vol. 1: **247–258**

Eifert, Virginia
  American Nature Writers, vol. 1: **259–268**

Eliot, George
  British Writers, vol. 5: **187–201**
  British Writers Selected Authors, vol. 1: **453–467**

Emecheta, Buchi
  African Writers, vol. 1: **235–247**

Enright, Elizabeth
  Writers for Children: **215–220**

Erdrich, Louise
  American Writers Supp. 4, part 1: **259–278**

Ewing, Juliana Horatia
  Writers for Children: **221–226**

Eyerly, Jeannette
  Writers for Young Adults, vol. 1: **403–411**

Fagundes Telles, Lygia
  Latin American Writers, vol. 3: **1271–1275**

Farjeon, Eleanor
  Writers for Children: **227–234**

Fauset, Jessie
  Modern American Women Writers: **123–139**

Field, Rachel Lyman
  Writers for Children: **235–240**

Fortune, Dion
  Supernatural Fiction Writers, vol. 2: **585–590**

Fox, Paula
  Writers for Young Adults, vol. 1: **413–422**

Frank, Anne
  Writers for Young Adults, vol. 1: **423–431**

Freeman, Mary E. Wilkins
  Modern American Women Writers: **141–153**
  Supernatural Fiction Writers, vol. 2: **769–773**

Fuller, Margaret
  American Writers Supp. 2, part 1: **279–306**

Gág, Wanda
  Writers for Children: **241–246**

Gambaro, Griselda
  Latin American Writers, vol. 3: **1323–1328**

Gaskell, Elizabeth
  British Writers, vol. 5: **1–16**

George, Jean Craighead
  Writers for Young Adults, vol. 2: **47–57**

Gilman, Charlotte Perkins
  Modern American Women Writers: **155–170**

Ginzburg, Natalia
  European Writers, vol. 13: **3131–3163**

Glasgow, Ellen
  American Writers, vol. 2: **173–195**
  Modern American Women Writers: **171–180**

Glaspell, Susan
  American Writers Supp. 3, part 1: **175–191**
  Modern American Women Writers: **181–188**

Gómez de Avellaneda, Gertrudis
  Latin American Writers, vol. 1: **175–180**

Gordimer, Nadine
  African Writers, vol. 1: **277–290**
  British Writers Supp. 2: **225–245**

Gordon, Caroline
  American Writers, vol. 2: **196–222**

Gordon, Mary
  American Writers Supp. 4, part 1: **297–317**

Greene, Bette
  Writers for Young Adults, vol. 2: **59–68**

Gregory, Lady Augusta
  See "Synge, J. M., and Lady Augusta Gregory"
    in *British Writers*, vol. 6: **307–318**

Gunn Allen, Paula
  American Writers Supp. 4, part 1: **319–340**

Hale, Lucretia P.
  Writers for Children: **265–268**

Hall, Lynn
Writers for Young Adults, vol. 2: **69–77**

Hamilton, Virginia
Writers for Young Adults, vol. 2: **79–92**

Hansberry, Lorraine
African American Writers: **147–158**
American Writers Supp. 4, part 1: **359–377**

Hardwick, Elizabeth
American Writers Supp. 3, part 1: **193–215**
Modern American Women Writers: **189–196**

Harper, Frances Ellen Watkins
African American Writers: **159–175**
Modern American Women Writers: **197–205**

Hasselstrom, Linda
American Nature Writers, vol. 1: **337–348**

Head, Bessie
African Writers, vol. 1: **303–320**

Hellman, Lillian
American Writers Supp. 1, part 1: **276–298**
Modern American Women Writers: **207–220**

Hinton, S. E.
Writers for Young Adults, vol. 2: **113–120**

Hogan, Linda
American Nature Writers, vol. 1: **377–388**
American Writers Supp. 4, part 1: **397–418**

Holland, Isabelle
Writers for Young Adults, vol. 2: **131–140**

Hoover, Helen
American Nature Writers, vol. 1: **389–399**

Howe, Susan
American Writers Supp. 4, part 2: **419–438**

Hubbell, Sue
American Nature Writers, vol. 1: **401–412**

Hughes, Monica
Writers for Young Adults, vol. 2: **141–148**

Hunter, Mollie
Writers for Young Adults, vol. 2: **149–159**

Hurston, Zora Neale
African American Writers: **205–218**
Modern American Women Writers: **221–235**

Ibarbourou, Juana de
Latin American Writers, vol. 2: **803–807**

Irwin, Hadley
Writers for Young Adults, vol. 2: **161–166**

Jackson, Shirley
Supernatural Fiction Writers, vol. 2: **1031–1036**

Jacobs, Harriet
See "Slave Narrative in American Literature,
The" in *African American Writers*: **395–412**

James, P. D.
British Writers Supp. 4: **319–341**

Jewett, Sarah Orne
American Writers, vol. 2: **391–414**
Modern American Women Writers: **235–250**

Johnson, Cathy
American Nature Writers, vol. 1: **425–438**

Johnson, Josephine
American Nature Writers, vol. 1: **439–451**

Johnston, Norma
Writers for Young Adults, vol. 2: **167–176**

Jones, Gayl
African American Writers: **235–244**

Jordan, June
African American Writers: **245–261**

Juana Inéz de La Cruz, Sor
Latin American Writers, vol. 1: **85–106**

Kappel-Smith, Diana
American Nature Writers, vol. 1: **453–463**

Kerr, M. E.
Writers for Young Adults, vol. 2: **177–185**

Kingston, Maxine Hong
Modern American Women Writers: **251–259**

Klein, Norma
Writers for Young Adults, vol. 2: **187–197**

Kumin, Maxine
American Nature Writers, vol. 1: **479–497**
American Writers Supp. 4, part 2: **439–457**

LaBastille, Anne
American Nature Writers, vol. 1: **499–511**

Larsen, Nella
African American Writers: **263–272**

Lasky, Kathryn
Writers for Young Adults, vol. 2: **207–216**

Lee, Harper
Writers for Young Adults, vol. 2: **217–225**

Lee, Tanith
Supernatural Fiction Writers, vol. 2: **1053–1058**

Lee, Vernon
Supernatural Fiction Writers, vol. 1: **329–335**

Le Guin, Ursula K.
  Science Fiction Writers: **409–417**
  Supernatural Fiction Writers, vol. 2: **1059–1066**
  Writers for Young Adults, vol. 2: **227–236**
  See also "Contemporary Ecofiction" in *American Nature Writers*, vol. 2: **1041–1058**

L'Engle, Madeleine
  Writers for Young Adults, vol. 2: **237–246**

Lessing, Doris
  African Writers, vol. 1: **427–449**
  British Writers Supp. 1: **237–257**
  British Writers Selected Authors, vol. 2: **833–853**

Levertov, Denise
  American Writers Supp. 3, part 1: **271–287**

Lispector, Clarice
  Latin American Writers, vol. 3: **1303–1309**

Lorde, Audre
  African American Writers: **273–288**

Lowell, Amy
  American Writers, vol. 2: **511–533**
  Modern American Women Writers: **261–268**

Lowry, Lois
  Writers for Young Adults, vol. 2: **279–287**

McCaffrey, Anne
  Writers for Young Adults, vol. 2: **299–306**

McCarthy, Mary
  American Writers, vol. 2: **558–584**
  Modern American Women Writers: **269–278**

McCullers, Carson
  American Writers, vol. 2: **585–608**
  Modern American Women Writers: **279–287**

McKillip, Patricia
  Supernatural Fiction Writers, vol. 2: **1067–1072**

McNulty, Faith
  American Nature Writers, vol. 1: **569–581**

Mahy, Margaret (May)
  Writers for Young Adults, vol. 2: **307–315**

Mansfield, Katherine
  British Writers, vol. 7: **171–184**
  British Writers Selected Authors, vol. 2: **891–904**

Marguerite, Queen of Navarre
  See "Renaissance Short Fiction" in *European Writers*, vol. 2: **927–956**

Marshall, Paule
  African American Writers: **289–304**

Matto de Turner, Clorinda
  Latin American Writers, vol. 1: **305–309**

Mazer, Norma Fox
  Writers for Young Adults, vol. 2: **337–346**

Meigs, Cornelia
  Writers for Children: **389–395**

Meireles, Cecília
  Latin American Writers, vol. 2: **915–922**

Merril, Judith
  Science Fiction Writers: **433–439**

Miklowitz, Gloria D.
  Writers for Young Adults, vol. 2: **359–368**

Millay, Edna St. Vincent
  American Writers, vol. 3: **122–144**
  Modern American Women Writers: **287–302**

Mirrlees, Hope
  Supernatural Fiction Writers, vol. 2: **603–607**

Mistral, Gabriela
  Latin American Writers, vol. 2: **677–692**

Mohr, Nicholasa
  Writers for Young Adults, vol. 2: **369–378**

Molesworth, M. L. S.
  Writers for Children: **407–413**

Montgomery, L. M.
  Writers for Children: **415–422**
  Writers for Young Adults, vol. 2: **379–386**

Moore, C. L.
  Supernatural Fiction Writers, vol. 2: **891–898**
  See also "Moore, C. L., and Henry Kuttner" in *Science Fiction Writers*: **161–167**

Moore, Marianne
  American Writers, vol. 3: **193–217**
  Modern American Women Writers: **303–316**

Morrison, Toni
  African American Writers: **321–333**
  American Writers Supp. 3, part 1: **361–381**
  Modern American Women Writers: **317–338**

Murdoch, Iris
  British Writers Supp. 1: **215–235**

Naylor, Gloria
  African American Writers: **335–347**

Naylor, Phyllis Reynolds
  Writers for Young Adults, vol. 2: **397–409**

Nesbit, E.
  Writers for Children: **423–430**

Nin, Anaïs
  Modern American Women Writers: **339–351**

Nixon, Joan Lowery
  Writers for Young Adults, vol. 2: **411–419**

Norton, Andre
  Supernatural Fiction Writers, vol. 2: **1091–1096**

Oates, Joyce Carol
  American Writers Supp. 2, part 2: **503–527**
  Modern American Women Writers: **353–374**

Ocampo, Victoria
  Latin American Writers, vol. 2: **705–710**

O'Connor, Flannery
  American Writers, vol. 3: **337–360**
  Modern American Women Writers: **375–388**

Oliphant, Mrs.
  Supernatural Fiction Writers, vol. 1: **261–268**

Oneal, Zibby
  Writers for Young Adults, vol. 2: **433–442**

Paley, Grace
  Modern American Women Writers: **389–396**

Parker, Dorothy
  Modern American Women Writers: **397–409**

Parkman, Francis
  American Writers Supp. 2, part 2: **589–616**

Parra Sanojo, Ana Teresa de la
  Latin American Writers, vol. 2: **717–720**

Paterson, Katherine
  Writers for Young Adults, vol. 2: **443–454**

Peterson, Brenda
  American Nature Writers, vol. 2: **721–731**

Petry, Ann
  African American Writers: **347–359**

Pevsner, Stella
  Writers for Young Adults, vol. 3: **27–34**

Peyton, K. M.
  Writers for Young Adults, vol. 3: **35–42**

Pfeffer, Susan Beth
  Writers for Young Adults, vol. 3: **43–52**

Plath, Sylvia
  American Writers Supp. 1, part 2: **526–549**
  Modern American Women Writers: **411–424**

Porter, Katherine Anne
  American Writers, vol. 3: **433–455**
  Modern American Women Writers: **425–440**

Potter, Beatrix
  British Writers Supp. 3: **287–309**
  Writers for Children: **439–446**

Pym, Barbara
  British Writers Supp. 2: **363–385**

Queiroz, Rachel de
  Latin American Writers, vol. 3: **1119–1123**

Radcliffe, Ann
  Supernatural Fiction Writers, vol. 1: **145–151**

Rand, Ayn
  American Writers Supp. 4, part 2: **517–535**

Rawlings, Marjorie Kinnan
  American Nature Writers, vol. 2: **751–765**
  Writers for Children: **463–467**

Rhys, Jean
  British Writers Supp. 2: **387–404**

Rich, Adrienne
  American Writers Supp. 1, part 2: **550–578**
  Modern American Women Writers: **441–456**

Richards, Laura E.
  Writers for Children: **469–475**

Riddell, Mrs. J. H.
  Supernatural Fiction Writers, vol. 1: **269–277**

Rinaldi, Ann
  Writers for Young Adults, vol. 3: **75–85**

Roberts, Elizabeth Madox
  Writers for Children: **477–481**

Robinson, Marilynne
  See "Contemporary Ecofiction" in *American Nature Writers,* vol. 2: **1041–1058**

Rodowsky, Colby
  Writers for Young Adults, vol. 3: **87–93**

Rossetti, Christina
  British Writers, vol. 5: **247–260**
  Writers for Children: **483–491**

Russ, Joanna
  Science Fiction Writers: **483–490**

Russell, Sharman Apt
  See "New Voices in American Nature Writing" in *American Nature Writers,* vol. 2: **1157–1173**

Ryden, Hope
  American Nature Writers, vol. 2: **781–792**

Saʿadāwī, Nawāl, al-
  African Writers, vol. 2: **721–731**

Sachs, Marilyn
  Writers for Young Adults, vol. 3: **95–104**

St. Clair, Margaret
  Science Fiction Writers: **491–495**

Sand, George
  European Writers, vol. 6: **813–836**
  European Writers Selected Authors, vol. 3:
    1571–1594

Sappho
  See "Greek Lyric Poets" in *Ancient Writers*, vol. 1:
    75–98

Sarraute, Nathalie
  European Writers, vol. 12: **2333–2359**

Sawyer, Ruth
  Writers for Children: **511–517**

Sayers, Dorothy L.
  British Writers Supp. 3: **333–353**

Schreiner, Olive
  African Writers, vol. 2: **745–763**
  British Writers Supp. 2: **435–458**

Scoppettone, Sandra
  Writers for Young Adults, vol. 3: **135–143**

Sebestyen, Ouida
  Writers for Young Adults, vol. 3: **145–153**

Seredy, Kate
  Writers for Children: **519–524**

Sewell, Anna
  Writers for Children: **525–528**

Sexton, Anne
  American Writers Supp. 2, part 2: **669–700**
  Modern American Women Writers: **457–470**

Shange, Ntozake
  African American Writers: **379–393**

Shelley, Mary
  British Writers Supp. 3: **355–373**
  British Writers Selected Authors, vol. 3:
    1085–1103
  Science Fiction Writers: **3–9**
  See also "Gothic Novel, The" in *British Writers*,
    vol. 3: **324–346**

Silko, Leslie Marmon
  American Nature Writers, vol. 2: **817–827**
  American Writers Supp. 4, part 2: **557–572**

Silveira de Queiroz, Dinah
  Latin American Writers, vol. 3: **1145–1151**

Sinclair, May
  Supernatural Fiction Writers, vol. 1: **513–519**

Sitwell, Edith
  British Writers, vol. 7: **127–143**

Smith, Stevie
  British Writers Supp. 2: **459–479**

Södergran, Edith
  European Writers, vol. 11: **1781–1806**

Sontag, Susan
  American Writers Supp. 3, part 2: **451–473**
  Modern American Women Writers: **471–483**

Spark, Muriel
  British Writers Supp. 1: **199–214**

Spyri, Johanna
  Writers for Children: **529–533**

Staël, Madame de
  European Writers, vol. 5: **89–111**

Stanwell-Fletcher, Theodora Cope
  American Nature Writers, vol. 2: **847–860**

Stead, Christina
  British Writers Supp. 4: **459–477**

Stein, Gertrude
  American Writers, vol. 4: **25–48**
  Modern American Women Writers: **485–498**

Storni, Alfonsina
  Latin American Writers, vol. 2: **739–743**

Stowe, Harriet Beecher
  American Writers Supp. 1, part 2: **579–601**

Stratton Porter, Gene
  American Nature Writers, vol. 2: **877–891**

Sutcliff, Rosemary
  Writers for Young Adults, vol. 3: **251–261**

Sutherland, Efua Theodora
  African Writers, vol. 2: **833–849**

Swenson, May
  American Writers Supp. 4, part 2: **637–655**

Taylor, Mildred Delois
  Writers for Young Adults, vol. 3: **273–282**

Thaxter, Celia
  American Nature Writers, vol. 2: **905–917**

Thomas, Joyce Carol
  Writers for Young Adults, vol. 3: **293–301**

Tiptree, James, Jr.
  Science Fiction Writers: **531–541**

Tsvetaeva, Marina
 European Writers, vol. 11: **1731–1750**

Tyler, Anne
 American Writers Supp. 4, part 2: **657–675**
 Modern American Women Writers: **499–510**

Undset, Sigrid
 European Writers, vol. 9: **1017–1041**

Valenzuela, Luisa
 Latin American Writers, vol. 3: **1445–1449**

Voigt, Cynthia
 Writers for Young Adults, vol. 3: **329–338**

Walker, Alice
 African American Writers: **441–458**
 American Writers Supp. 3, part 2: **517–540**
 Modern American Women Writers: **511–520**

Walker, Margaret
 African American Writers: **459–471**

Walsh, Jill Paton
 Writers for Young Adults, vol. 3: **339–346**

Weil, Simone
 European Writers, vol. 12: **2787–2814**

Weldon, Fay
 British Writers Supp. 4: **521–539**

Welty, Eudora
 American Writers, vol. 4: **260–284**
 American Writers Retrospective: **339–358**
 Modern American Women Writers: **521–538**

Wersba, Barbara
 Writers for Young Adults, vol. 3: **349–357**

West, Rebecca
 British Writers Supp. 3: **431–445**

Wharton, Edith
 American Writers, vol. 4: **308–330**
 American Writers Retrospective: **359–385**
 Modern American Women Writers: **539–558**
 Supernatural Fiction Writers, vol. 2: **783–788**

Wheatley, Phillis
 African American Writers: **473–491**

Wiggin, Kate Douglas
 Writers for Children: **605–609**

Wilder, Laura Ingalls
 Writers for Children: **617–623**
 Writers for Young Adults, vol. 3: **371–380**

Wilkinson, Brenda
 Writers for Young Adults, vol. 3: **381–390**

Williams, Terry Tempest
 American Nature Writers, vol. 2: **973–988**

Winterson, Jeanette
 British Writers Supp. 4: **541–559**

Wolff, Virginia Euwer
 Writers for Young Adults, vol. 3: **391–398**

Wollstonecraft, Mary
 British Writers Supp. 3: **465–482**

Wood, Mrs. Henry
 Supernatural Fiction Writers, vol. 1: **279–286**

Woolf, Virginia
 British Writers, vol. 7: **17–40**
 British Writers Selected Authors, vol. 3: **1395–1417**

Wylie, Elinor
 American Writers Supp. 1, part 2: **707–730**

Yolen, Jane
 Writers for Young Adults, vol. 3: **409–420**

Yonge, Charlotte Mary
 Writers for Children: **625–631**

Yourcenar, Marguerite
 European Writers, vol. 12: **2535–2561**

Zwinger, Ann
 American Nature Writers, vol. 2: **989–1001**

Zwinger, Susan
 See "New Voices in American Nature Writing"
  in *American Nature Writers*, vol. 2: **1157–1173**

AFRICAN AMERICAN WRITERS

African Americans, Writing, and Nature
  American Nature Writers, vol. 2: **1003–1012**

Angelou, Maya
  American Writers Supp. 4, part 1: **1–19**
  Modern American Women Writers: **1–8**
  Writers for Young Adults, vol. 1: **43–52**

Baldwin, James
  African American Writers: **1–14**
  American Writers Supp. 1, part 1: **47–71**

Baraka, Amiri
  African American Writers: **15–29**
  American Writers Supp. 2, part 1: **29–63**

Bontemps, Arna
  Writers for Children: **77–83**

Brooks, Gwendolyn
  African American Writers: **31–43**
  American Writers Supp. 3, part 1: **69–90**
  Modern American Women Writers: **37–48**

Brown, Sterling
  African American Writers: **45–57**

Chesnutt, Charles W.
  African American Writers: **59–70**

Cullen, Countee
  American Writers Supp. 4, part 1: **163–174**

Delany, Samuel R.
  Science Fiction Writers: **329–336**

Douglass, Frederick
  American Writers Supp. 3, part 1: **153–174**
  See also "Slave Narrative in American
    Literature, The"

Dove, Rita
  American Writers Supp. 4, part 1: **241–258**

Du Bois, W. E. B.
  African American Writers: **71–87**
  American Writers Supp. 2, part 1: **157–189**

Dunbar, Paul Laurence
  African American Writers: **87–102**
  American Writers Supp. 2, part 1: **191–219**

Ellison, Ralph
  African American Writers: **103–129**
  American Writers Supp. 2, part 1: **221–252**

Equiano, Olaudah
  See "Slave Narrative in American Literature, The"

Fauset, Jessie
  Modern American Women Writers: **123–139**

Gaines, Ernest J.
  African American Writers: **129–145**

Hansberry, Lorraine
  African American Writers: **147–158**
  American Writers Supp. 4, part 1: **359–377**

Harper, Frances Ellen Watkins
  African American Writers: **159–175**
  Modern American Women Writers: **197–205**

Hayden, Robert Earl
  African American Writers: **177–192**
  American Writers Supp. 2, part 1: **361–383**

Hughes, Langston
  African American Writers: **193–205**
  American Writers Retrospective: **193–214**
  American Writers Supp. 1, part 1: **320–348**
  Writers for Children: **295–301**

Hurston, Zora Neale
  African American Writers: **205–218**
  Modern American Women Writers: **221–235**

Jacobs, Harriet
  See "Slave Narrative in American Literature, The"

Johnson, James Weldon
  African American Writers: **219–233**

Jones, Gayl
  African American Writers: **235–244**

Jordan, June
  African American Writers: **245–261**

Larsen, Nella
  African American Writers: **263–272**

Lorde, Audre
  African American Writers: **273–288**

McKay, Claude
  African American Writers: **305–320**

Marshall, Paule
  African American Writers: **289–304**

Morrison, Toni
  African American Writers: **321–333**
  American Writers Supp. 3, part 1: **361–381**
  Modern American Women Writers: **317–338**

Naylor, Gloria
  African American Writers: **335–347**

Palés Matos, Luis
    Latin American Writers, vol. 2: **821–830**

Petry, Ann
    African American Writers: **347–359**

Reed, Ishmael
    African American Writers: **361–377**

Shange, Ntozake
    African American Writers: **379–393**

Slave Narrative in American Literature, The
    African American Writers: **395–412**

Tolson, Melvin
    African American Writers: **413–427**

Toomer, Jean
    African American Writers: **429–440**
    American Writers Supp. 3, part 2: **475–491**

Walker, Alice
    African American Writers: **441–458**
    American Writers Supp. 3, part 2: **517–540**
    Modern American Women Writers: **511–520**

Walker, Margaret
    African American Writers: **459–471**

Wheatley, Phillis
    African American Writers: **473–491**

Wideman, John Edgar
    African American Writers: **493–504**

Wright, Richard
    African American Writers: **505–523**
    American Writers, vol. 4: **474–497**

Volume-by-Volume Contents of the Individual Sets of the Scribner Writers Series

AMERICAN LITERATURE

African American Writers

Baldwin, James: **1–14**
Baraka, Amiri: **15–29**
Brooks, Gwendolyn: **31–43**
Brown, Sterling: **45–57**
Chesnutt, Charles W.: **59–70**
Du Bois, W. E. B.: **71–86**
Dunbar, Paul Laurence: **87–102**
Ellison, Ralph: **103–128**
Gaines, Ernest J.: **129–145**
Hansberry, Lorraine: **147–158**
Harper, Frances Ellen Watkins: **159–175**
Hayden, Robert Earl: **177–192**
Hughes, Langston: **193–204**
Hurston, Zora Neale: **205–218**
Johnson, James Weldon: **219–233**
Jones, Gayl: **235–244**
Jordan, June: **245–261**
Larsen, Nella: **263–272**
Lorde, Audre: **273–288**
Marshall, Paule: **289–304**
McKay, Claude: **305–320**
Morrison, Toni: **321–333**
Naylor, Gloria: **335–346**
Petry, Ann: **347–359**
Reed, Ishmael: **361–377**
Shange, Ntozake: **379–393**
Slave Narrative in American Literature, The: **395–412**
Tolson, Melvin: **413–427**

Toomer, Jean: **429–440**
Walker, Alice: **441–458**
Walker, Margaret: **459–471**
Wheatley, Phillis: **473–491**
Wideman, John Edgar: **493–504**
Wright, Richard: **505–523**

American Nature Writers

VOLUME 1

Abbey, Edward: **1–19**
Ackerman, Diane: **21–30**
Austin, Mary Hunter: **31–51**
Bailey, Florence Merriam: **53–62**
Bartram, William: **63–74**
Bass, Rick: **75–88**
Berry, Wendell: **89–105**
Beston, Henry: **107–120**
Burroughs, John: **121–138**
Carrighar, Sally: **139–149**
Carson, Rachel: **151–171**
Comstock, Anna Botsford: **173–185**
Cooper, Susan Fenimore: **187–198**
Davis, H. L.: **199–211**
Dillard, Annie: **213–230**
Douglas, Marjory Stoneman: **231–245**
Ehrlich, Gretel: **247–258**
Eifert, Virginia: **259–268**
Eiseley, Loren: **269–285**
Emerson, Ralph Waldo: **287–307**

Finch, Robert Charles: **309–321**
Graves, John: **323–336**
Hasselstrom, Linda: **337–348**
Hay, John: **349–362**
Hoagland, Edward: **363–375**
Hogan, Linda: **377–388**
Hoover, Helen: **389–399**
Hubbell, Sue: **401–412**
Janovy, John, Jr.: **413–424**
Johnson, Cathy: **425–438**
Johnson, Josephine: **439–451**
Kappel-Smith, Diana: **453–463**
Krutch, Joseph Wood: **465–477**
Kumin, Maxine: **479–497**
LaBastille, Anne: **499–511**
Least Heat-Moon, William: **513–523**
Leopold, Aldo: **525–547**
Lopez, Barry: **549–568**
McNulty, Faith: **569–581**
McPhee, John: **583–598**

VOLUME 2

Matthiessen, Peter: **599–613**
Mills, Enos: **615–624**
Mitchell, John Hanson: **625–638**
Momaday, N. Scott: **639–649**
Muir, John: **651–669**
Nabhan, Gary Paul: **671–681**
Nelson, Richard K.: **683–696**
Olson, Sigurd F.: **697–709**
Perrin, Noel: **711–720**
Peterson, Brenda: **721–731**
Pyle, Robert Michael: **733–739**
Quammen, David: **741–750**
Rawlings, Marjorie Kinnan: **751–765**
Raymo, Chet: **767–780**
Ryden, Hope: **781–792**
Sanders, Scott Russell: **793–804**
Seton, Ernest Thompson: **805–816**
Silko, Leslie Marmon: **817–827**
Snyder, Gary: **829–846**
Stanwell-Fletcher, Theodora Cope: **847–860**
Stegner, Wallace: **861–875**
Stratton Porter, Gene: **877–891**
Teale, Edwin Way: **893–904**
Thaxter, Celia: **905–917**

Thomas, Lewis: **919–931**
Thoreau, Henry David: **933–950**
Van Dyke, John C.: **951–962**
Wallace, David Rains: **963–972**
Williams, Terry Tempest: **973–988**
Zwinger, Ann: **989–1001**
African Americans, Writing, and Nature:
    1003–1012
Bioregionalism in Nature Writing: **1013–1024**
Canadian Nature Writing in English: **1025–1040**
Contemporary Ecofiction: **1041–1058**
Early Romantic Natural History Literature:
    1059–1078
Forms of American Nature Poetry, The:
    1079–1098
Literary Theory and Nature Writing:
    1099–1114
Literature of Mountaineering: **1115–1128**
Modern Birdwatching Literature: **1129–1140**
Nature in Native American Literatures:
    1141–1156
New Voices in American Nature Writing:
    1157–1172
Western Geologists and Explorers: **1173–1188**

American Writers

VOLUME 1

Adams, Henry: **1–24**
Agee, James: **25–47**
Aiken, Conrad: **48–70**
Albee, Edward: **71–96**
Anderson, Sherwood: **97–120**
Barth, John: **121–143**
Bellow, Saul: **144–166**
Berryman, John: **167–189**
Bierce, Ambrose: **190–213**
Bourne, Randolph: **214–238**
Brooks, Van Wyck: **239–263**
Burke, Kenneth: **264–287**
Caldwell, Erskine: **288–311**
Cather, Willa: **312–334**
Cooper, James Fenimore: **335–357**
Cozzens, James Gould: **358–381**
Crane, Hart: **381–404**

Crane, Stephen: **405–427**
Cummings, E. E.: **428–450**
Dickinson, Emily: **451–473**
Dos Passos, John: **474–496**
Dreiser, Theodore: **497–520**
Eberhart, Richard: **521–543**
Edwards, Jonathan: **544–566**
Eliot, T. S.: **567–591**

VOLUME 2

Emerson, Ralph Waldo: **1–24**
Farrell, James T.: **25–53**
Faulkner, William: **54–76**
Fitzgerald, F. Scott: **77–100**
Franklin, Benjamin: **101–125**
Frederic, Harold: **126–149**
Frost, Robert: **150–172**
Glasgow, Ellen: **173–195**
Gordon, Caroline: **196–222**
Hawthorne, Nathaniel: **223–246**
Hemingway, Ernest: **247–270**
Howells, William Dean: **271–294**
Irving, Washington: **295–318**
James, Henry: **319–341**
James, William: **342–366**
Jarrell, Randall: **367–390**
Jewett, Sarah Orne: **391–414**
Lardner, Ring: **415–438**
Lewis, Sinclair: **439–461**
London, Jack: **462–485**
Longfellow, Henry Wadsworth: **486–510**
Lowell, Amy: **511–533**
Lowell, Robert: **534–557**
McCarthy, Mary: **558–584**
McCullers, Carson: **585–608**

VOLUME 3

MacLeish, Archibald: **1–25**
Mailer, Norman: **26–49**
Marquand, John P.: **50–73**
Melville, Herman: **74–98**
Mencken, H. L.: **99–121**
Millay, Edna St. Vincent: **122–144**
Miller, Arthur: **145–169**
Miller, Henry: **170–192**

Moore, Marianne: **193–217**
Morris, Wright: **218–243**
Nabokov, Vladimir: **244–266**
Nemerov, Howard: **267–289**
Niebuhr, Reinhold: **290–313**
Norris, Frank: **314–336**
O'Connor, Flannery: **337–360**
O'Hara, John: **361–384**
O'Neill, Eugene: **385–408**
Poe, Edgar Allan: **409–432**
Porter, Katherine Anne: **433–455**
Pound, Ezra: **456–479**
Ransom, John Crowe: **480–502**
Robinson, Edwin Arlington: **503–526**
Roethke, Theodore: **527–550**
Salinger, J. D.: **551–574**
Sandburg, Carl: **575–598**
Santayana, George: **599–622**

VOLUME 4

Singer, Isaac Bashevis: **1–24**
Stein, Gertrude: **25–48**
Steinbeck, John: **49–72**
Stevens, Wallace: **73–96**
Styron, William: **97–119**
Tate, Allen: **120–143**
Taylor, Edward: **144–166**
Thoreau, Henry David: **167–189**
Twain, Mark: **190–213**
Updike, John: **214–235**
Warren, Robert Penn: **236–259**
Welty, Eudora: **260–284**
West, Nathanael: **285–307**
Wharton, Edith: **308–330**
Whitman, Walt: **331–354**
Wilder, Thornton: **355–377**
Williams, Tennessee: **378–401**
Williams, William Carlos: **402–425**
Wilson, Edmund: **426–449**
Wolfe, Thomas: **450–473**
Wright, Richard: **474–497**

SUPPLEMENT I, part 1

Addams, Jane: **1–27**
Alcott, Louisa May: **28–46**

Baldwin, James: **47–71**
Bishop, Elizabeth: **72–97**
Bradstreet, Anne: **98–123**
Brown, Charles Brockden: **124–149**
Bryant, William Cullen: **150–173**
Cheever, John: **174–199**
Chopin, Kate: **200–226**
Crèvecoeur, Hector St. John de: **227–252**
Doolittle, Hilda (H.D.): **253–275**
Hellman, Lillian: **276–298**
Holmes, Oliver Wendell: **299–319**
Hughes, Langston: **320–348**
Lanier, Sidney: **349–373**

SUPPLEMENT I, part 2

Lindsay, Vachel: **374–403**
Lowell, James Russell: **404–426**
Malamud, Bernard: **427–453**
Masters, Edgar Lee: **454–478**
Morison, Samuel Eliot: **479–500**
Paine, Thomas: **501–525**
Plath, Sylvia: **526–549**
Rich, Adrienne: **550–578**
Stowe, Harriet Beecher: **579–601**
Thurber, James: **602–627**
Veblen, Thorstein: **628–650**
White, E. B.: **651–681**
Whittier, John Greenleaf: **682–706**
Wylie, Elinor: **707–730**

SUPPLEMENT II, part 1

Auden, W. H.: **1–28**
Baraka, Amiri: **29–63**
Barlow, Joel: **65–86**
Blackmur, R. P.: **87–112**
Buck, Pearl S.: **113–134**
Cowley, Malcolm: **135–156**
Du Bois, W. E. B.: **157–189**
Dunbar, Paul Laurence: **191–219**
Ellison, Ralph: **221–252**
Freneau, Philip: **253–277**
Fuller, Margaret: **279–306**
Ginsberg, Allen: **307–333**
Harte, Bret: **335–359**

Hayden, Robert: **361–383**
Henry, O.: **385–412**

SUPPLEMENT II, part 2

Jeffers, Robinson: **413–440**
Mather, Cotton: **441–470**
Mumford, Lewis: **471–501**
Oates, Joyce Carol: **503–527**
Odets, Clifford: **529–554**
Olson, Charles: **555–587**
Parkman, Francis: **589–616**
Pynchon, Thomas: **617–638**
Schwartz, Delmore: **639–668**
Sexton, Anne: **669–700**
Shapiro, Karl: **701–724**
Van Vechten, Carl: **725–751**
Vonnegut, Kurt: **753–783**
Winters, Yvor: **785–816**

SUPPLEMENT III, part 1

Ashbery, John: **1–29**
Barnes, Djuna: **31–46**
Bogan, Louise: **47–68**
Brooks, Gwendolyn: **69–90**
Burroughs, William S.: **91–110**
Capote, Truman: **111–133**
Carver, Raymond: **135–151**
Douglass, Frederick: **153–174**
Glaspell, Susan: **175–191**
Hardwick, Elizabeth: **193–215**
Kerouac, Jack: **217–234**
Kinnell, Galway: **235–256**
Kunitz, Stanley: **257–270**
Levertov, Denise: **271–287**
McPhee, John: **289–316**
Merrill, James: **317–338**
Merwin, W. S.: **339–360**
Morrison, Toni: **361–381**
Percy, Walker: **383–400**

SUPPLEMENT III, part 2

Roth, Philip: **401–429**
Shepard, Sam: **431–450**

Sontag, Susan: **451–473**
Toomer, Jean: **475–491**
Trilling, Lionel: **493–515**
Walker, Alice: **517–540**
Wilbur, Richard: **541–565**
Wolfe, Tom: **567–588**
Wright, James: **589–607**
Zukofsky, Louis: **609–632**

SUPPLEMENT IV, PART 1

Angelou, Maya: **1–19**
Auchincloss, Louis: **21–38**
Barthelme, Donald: **39–58**
Bly, Robert: **59–77**
Bowles, Paul: **79–99**
Bradbury, Ray: **101–118**
Chandler, Raymond: **119–138**
Creeley, Robert: **139–161**
Cullen, Countee: **163–174**
Dickey, James: **175–194**
Didion, Joan: **195–216**
Doctorow, E. L.: **217–240**
Dove, Rita: **241–258**
Erdrich, Louise: **259–278**
Gaddis, William: **279–296**
Gordon, Mary: **297–317**
Gunn Allen, Paula: **319–340**
Hammett, Dashiell: **341–357**
Hansberry, Lorraine: **359–377**
Heller, Joseph: **379–396**
Hogan, Linda: **397–418**

SUPPLEMENT IV, PART 2

Howe, Susan: **419–438**
Kumin, Maxine: **439–457**
Macdonald, Ross: **459–477**
Momaday, N. Scott: **479–495**
Ortiz, Simon J.: **497–515**
Rand, Ayn: **517–535**
Ríos, Alberto Álvaro: **537–556**
Silko, Leslie Marmon: **557–572**
Simon, Neil: **573–594**
Stegner, Wallace: **595–618**
Strand, Mark: **619–636**

Swenson, May: **637–655**
Tyler, Anne: **657–675**
Vidal, Gore: **677–697**

American Writers: Retrospective Supplement

Cather, Willa: **1–23**
Dickinson, Emily: **25–50**
Eliot, T. S.: **51–71**
Faulkner, William: **73–95**
Fitzgerald, F. Scott: **97–120**
Frost, Robert: **121–144**
Hawthorne, Nathaniel: **145–167**
Hemingway, Ernest: **169–191**
Hughes, Langston: **193–214**
James, Henry: **215–242**
Melville, Herman: **243–262**
Nabokov, Vladimir: **263–281**
Pound, Ezra: **283–294**
Stevens, Wallace: **295–315**
Updike, John: **317–338**
Welty, Eudora: **339–358**
Wharton, Edith: **359–385**
Whitman, Walt: **387–410**
Williams, William Carlos: **411–433**

Modern American Women Writers

Angelou, Maya: **1–8**
Bishop, Elizabeth: **9–22**
Bogan, Louise: **23–36**
Brooks, Gwendolyn: **37–48**
Cather, Willa: **49–62**
Chopin, Kate: **63–78**
Dickinson, Emily: **77–89**
Didion, Joan: **91–102**
Doolittle, Hilda (H.D.): **103–121**
Fauset, Jessie: **123–139**
Freeman, Mary E. Wilkins: **141–153**
Gilman, Charlotte Perkins: **155–170**
Glasgow, Ellen: **171–180**
Glaspell, Susan: **181–188**

Hardwick, Elizabeth: **189–196**
Harper, Frances Ellen Watkins: **197–205**
Hellman, Lillian: **207–220**
Hurston, Zora Neale: **221–234**
Jewett, Sarah Orne: **235–250**
Kingston, Maxine Hong: **251–259**
Lowell, Amy: **261–268**
McCarthy, Mary: **269–278**
McCullers, Carson: **279–286**
Millay, Edna St. Vincent: **287–302**
Moore, Marianne: **303–316**
Morrison, Toni: **317–338**
Nin, Anaïs: **339–351**
Oates, Joyce Carol: **353–374**

O'Connor, Flannery: **375–388**
Paley, Grace: **389–396**
Parker, Dorothy: **397–409**
Plath, Sylvia: **411–424**
Porter, Katherine Anne: **425–440**
Rich, Adrienne: **441–456**
Sexton, Anne: **457–470**
Sontag, Susan: **471–483**
Stein, Gertrude: **485–498**
Tyler, Anne: **499–510**
Walker, Alice: **511–520**
Welty, Eudora: **521–538**
Wharton, Edith: **539–558**

ENGLISH AND COMMONWEALTH LITERATURE

British Writers

* Essays preceded by an asterisk are also available in
BRITISH WRITERS: SELECTED AUTHORS.

VOLUME 1

Langland, William: Piers Plowman: **1–18**
*Chaucer, Geoffrey: **19–47**
Gower, John: **48–56**
Lydgate, John: **57–66**
*Malory, Sir Thomas: **67–80**
Skelton, John: **81–96**
Wyatt, Sir Thomas: **97–112**
Howard, Henry (Earl of Surrey): **113–120**
*Spenser, Edmund: **121–144**
Ralegh (Raleigh), Sir Walter: **145–159**
Sidney, Sir Philip: **160–175**
Hooker, Richard: **176–190**
Lyly, John, and George Peele: **191–211**
Kyd, Thomas, and Early Elizabethan Tragedy:
   212–231
Chapman, George: **232–256**
Bacon, Francis: **257–274**
Marlowe, Christopher: **275–294**
*Shakespeare, William: **295–334**
*Jonson, Ben: **335–352**

*Donne, John: **352–369**
*Bible, The English: **370–388**

VOLUME 2

Middleton, Thomas: **1–23**
Marston, John, and Cyril Tourneur: **24–41**
Beaumont, Francis, and John Fletcher: **42–67**
Webster, John: **68–86**
Ford, John: **87–101**
Herrick, Robert: **102–116**
Herbert, George: **117–130**
Walton, Izaak: **131–144**
Browne, Sir Thomas: **145–157**
*Milton, John: **158–178**
Metaphysical Poets, Four: **179–203**
Marvell, Andrew: **204–220**
Cavalier Poets, The: **221–239**
*Bunyan, John: **240–254**
Restoration Court Poets, The: **255–272**
Evelyn, John, and Samuel Pepys: **274–288**
Dryden, John: **289–306**
Wycherley, William: **307–322**
Vanbrugh, Sir John: **323–337**
Congreve, William: **338–350**
Farquhar, George: **351–365**

VOLUME 3

*Defoe, Daniel: **1–14**
*Swift, Jonathan: **15–37**
*Steele, Sir Richard, and Joseph Addison: **38–53**
 Gay, John: **54–67**
*Pope, Alexander: **68–79**
 Richardson, Samuel: **80–93**
*Fielding, Henry: **94–106**
*Johnson, Samuel: **107–123**
 Sterne, Laurence: **124–135**
 Gray, Thomas: **136–145**
 Smollett, Tobias: **146–159**
 Collins, William: **160–176**
 Goldsmith, Oliver: **177–192**
 Burke, Edmund: **193–206**
 Cowper, William: **207–220**
 Gibbon, Edward: **221–233**
*Boswell, James: **234–251**
 Sheridan, Richard Brinsley: **252–271**
 Crabbe, George: **272–287**
*Blake, William: **288–309**
*Burns, Robert: **310–323**
 Gothic Novel, The: **324–346**

VOLUME 4

*Wordsworth, William: **1–26**
 Scott, Sir Walter: **27–40**
*Coleridge, Samuel Taylor: **41–57**
 Southey, Robert: **58–72**
 Lamb, Charles: **73–86**
 Landor, Walter Savage: **87–100**
*Austen, Jane: **101–124**
 Hazlitt, William: **125–140**
 De Quincey, Thomas: **141–156**
 Peacock, Thomas Love: **157–170**
*Byron, Lord: **171–194**
*Shelley, Percy Bysshe: **195–210**
*Keats, John: **211–237**
*Carlyle, Thomas: **238–250**
 Hood, Thomas: **251–267**
 Macaulay, Thomas Babington: **268–291**
 Disraeli, Benjamin: **292–309**
*Browning, Elizabeth Barrett: **310–322**
*Tennyson, Alfred Lord: **323–339**

Fitzgerald, Edward: **340–353**
*Browning, Robert: **354–375**

VOLUME 5

 Gaskell, Elizabeth: **1–16**
*Thackeray, William Makepeace: **17–40**
*Dickens, Charles: **41–74**
 Lear, Edward: **75–88**
*Trollope, Anthony: **89–104**
*Brontës, The: **105–154**
 Clough, Arthur Hugh: **155–172**
 Ruskin, John: **173–186**
*Eliot, George: **187–201**
 Arnold, Matthew: **203–218**
 Meredith, George: **219–234**
 Rossetti, Dante Gabriel: **235–246**
 Rossetti, Christina: **247–260**
 Carroll, Lewis: **261–276**
 Stephen, Leslie: **277–290**
 Morris, William: **291–308**
 Swinburne, Algernon Charles: **309–336**
 Pater, Walter Horatio: **337–360**
*Hopkins, Gerard Manley: **361–382**
*Stevenson, Robert Louis: **383–398**
*Wilde, Oscar: **399–422**
 Gissing, George: **423–438**
 Thompson, Francis: **439–452**

VOLUME 6

*Hardy, Thomas: **1–22**
 James, Henry: **23–69**
 Bridges, Robert: **71–84**
 Moore, George: **85–100**
*Shaw, George Bernard: **101–132**
*Conrad, Joseph: **133–150**
*Housman, A. E.: **151–164**
*Kipling, Rudyard: **165–206**
*Yeats, William Butler: **207–224**
*Wells, H. G.: **225–246**
 Bennett, Arnold: **247–268**
 Galsworthy, John: **269–292**
 Douglas, Norman: **293–306**
 Synge, J. M., and Lady Augusta Gregory:
  307–318

Ford, Ford Madox: **319–334**
Chesterton, G. K.: **335–346**
Churchill, Winston: **347–362**
*Maugham, W. Somerset: **363–382**
Trevelyan, G. M.: **383–396**
*Forster, E. M.: **397–414**
*Poets of World War I (British): **415–442**
Owen, Wilfred: **443–460**

VOLUME 7

O'Casey, Sean: **1–16**
*Woolf, Virginia: **17–40**
*Joyce, James: **41–58**
Compton-Burnett, Ivy: **59–70**
Lewis, Wyndham: **71–86**
*Lawrence, D. H.: **87–126**
Sitwell, Edith: **127–142**
*Eliot, T. S.: **143–170**
*Mansfield, Katherine: **171–184**
Cary, Joyce: **185–196**
*Huxley, Aldous: **197–208**
Priestley, J. B.: **209–232**
Leavis, F. R.: **233–256**
Graves, Robert: **257–272**
*Orwell, George: **273–288**
*Waugh, Evelyn: **289–308**
Isherwood, Christopher: **309–320**
Snow, C. P.: **321–342**
Powell, Anthony: **343–352**
Betjeman, John: **355–378**
*Auden, W. H.: **379–399**
MacNeice, Louis: **401–420**
Poets of World War II (British): **421–450**

SUPPLEMENT I

*Greene, Graham: **1–20**
Koestler, Arthur: **21–41**
*Beckett, Samuel: **43–64**
*Golding, William: **65–91**
Durrell, Lawrence: **93–128**
White, Patrick: **129–152**
Wilson, Angus: **153–168**
*Thomas, Dylan: **169–184**

Burgess, Anthony: **185–198**
Spark, Muriel: **199–214**
Murdoch, Iris: **215–235**
*Lessing, Doris: **237–257**
Scott, Paul: **259–274**
Larkin, Phillip: **275–290**
Fowles, John: **291–311**
Shaffer, Peter: **313–328**
Osborne, John: **329–340**
Hughes, Ted: **341–366**
*Pinter, Harold: **367–382**
Naipaul, V. S.: **383–405**
Storey, David: **407–420**
Bond, Edward: **421–436**
*Stoppard, Tom: **437–454**

SUPPLEMENT II

Amis, Kingsley: **1–19**
Arden, John: **21–42**
Beerbohm, Max: **43–59**
Behan, Brendan: **61–76**
Bowen, Elizabeth: **77–96**
Butler, Samuel: **97–121**
Christie, Agatha: **123–137**
Coward, Noël: **139–158**
*Doyle, Arthur Conan: **159–178**
Empson, William: **179–198**
Firbank, Ronald: **199–224**
Gordimer, Nadine: **225–245**
Green, Henry: **247–266**
Heaney, Seamus: **267–282**
Lawrence, T. E.: **283–298**
*Le Carré, John: **299–320**
O'Brien, Flann: **321–339**
*Paton, Alan: **341–361**
Pym, Barbara: **363–385**
Rhys, Jean: **387–404**
Richards, I. A.: **405–433**
Schreiner, Olive: **435–458**
Smith, Stevie: **459–479**
Spender, Steven: **481–496**
Strachey, Lytton: **497–518**
*Tolkien, J. R. R.: **519–536**

SUPPLEMENT III

Barrie, James M.: **1–17**
Behn, Aphra: **19–43**
Brooke, Rupert: **45–61**
Burney, Frances: **63–78**
Carter, Angela: **79–93**
Connolly, Cyril: **95–113**
Day Lewis, Cecil: **115–132**
*Du Maurier, Daphne: **133–149**
Edgeworth, Maria: **151–168**
Frazer, James George: **169–190**
Fry, Christopher: **191–210**
Haggard, H. Rider: **211–228**
Hume, David: **229–245**
*Lewis, C. S.: **247–268**
Lowry, Malcolm: **269–286**
Potter, Beatrix: **287–309**
Pritchett, V. S.: **311–331**
Sayers, Dorothy L.: **333–353**
*Shelley, Mary: **355–373**
Stoker, Bram: **375–391**
Thomas, Edward: **393–408**
Thomson, James: **409–429**
West, Rebecca: **431–445**
*Wodehouse, P. G.: **447–464**
Wollstonecraft, Mary: **465–482**

SUPPLEMENT IV

Ambler, Eric: **1–24**
Amis, Martin: **25–44**
Barker, Pat: **45–63**
Barnes, Julian: **65–76**
Berger, John: **77–96**
Brooke-Rose, Christine: **97–118**
Brookner, Anita: **119–137**
Byatt, A. S.: **139–156**
Chatwin, Bruce: **157–177**
Churchill, Caryl: **179–200**
Dahl, Roald: **201–227**
Drabble, Margaret: **229–254**
Gunn, Thom: **255–279**
Hare, David: **281–300**
Ishiguro, Kazuo: **301–317**
James, P. D.: **319–341**
Keneally, Thomas: **343–362**

Lodge, David: **363–387**
McEwan, Ian: **389–408**
Muldoon, Paul: **409–432**
Rushdie, Salman: **433–457**
Stead, Christina: **459–477**
Thomas, D. M.: **479–497**
Trevor, William: **499–519**
Weldon, Fay: **521–539**
Winterson, Jeanette: **541–559**

British Writers: Selected Authors

The following essays were reprinted from British Writers.

VOLUME 1

Auden, W. H.: **1–21**
Austen, Jane: **23–46**
Beckett, Samuel: **47–68**
Bible, The English: **69–87**
Blake, William: **89–110**
Boswell, James: **111–128**
Brontës, The: **129–177**
Browning, Elizabeth Barrett: **179–191**
Browning, Robert: **193–214**
Bunyan, John: **215–229**
Burns, Robert: **231–244**
Byron, Lord: **245–268**
Carlyle, Thomas: **269–281**
Chaucer, Geoffrey: **283–311**
Coleridge, Samuel Taylor: **313–329**
Conrad, Joseph: **331–348**
Defoe, Daniel: **349–362**
Dickens, Charles: **363–396**
Donne, John: **397–414**
Doyle, Arthur Conan: **415–434**
Du Maurier, Daphne: **435–451**
Eliot, George: **453–467**
Eliot, T. S.: **469–496**

VOLUME 2

Fielding, Henry: **497–509**
Forster, E. M.: **511–527**

Golding, William: **529–555**
Greene, Graham: **557–576**
Hardy, Thomas: **577–598**
Hopkins, Gerard Manley: **599–620**
Housman, A. E.: **621–634**
Huxley, Aldous: **635–646**
Johnson, Samuel: **647–663**
Jonson, Ben: **665–681**
Joyce, James: **683–700**
Keats, John: **701–727**
Kipling, Rudyard: **729–770**
Lawrence, D. H.: **771–810**
Le Carré, John: **811–832**
Lessing, Doris: **833–853**
Lewis, C. S.: **855–876**
Malory, Sir Thomas: **877–890**
Mansfield, Katherine: **891–904**
Maugham, W. Somerset: **905–923**
Milton, John: **925–945**
Orwell, George: **947–961**
Paton, Alan: **963–983**
Pinter, Harold: **985–1000**
Pope, Alexander: **1001–1012**
Shakespeare, William: **1013–1052**

VOLUME 3

Shaw, George Bernard: **1053–1084**
Shelley, Mary: **1085–1103**
Shelley, Percy Bysshe: **1105–1120**
Spenser, Edmund: **1121–1144**
Steele, Sir Richard, and Joseph Addison:
    1145–1160
Stevenson, Robert Louis: **1161–1176**
Stoppard, Tom: **1177–1194**
Swift, Jonathan: **1195–1217**
Tennyson, Alfred Lord: **1219–1235**
Thackeray, William Makepeace: **1237–1259**
Thomas, Dylan: **1261–1276**
Tolkien, J. R. R.: **1277–1294**
Trollope, Anthony: **1295–1309**
Waugh, Evelyn: **1311–1330**
Wells, H. G.: **1331–1352**
Wilde, Oscar: **1353–1376**
Wodehouse, P. G.: **1377–1394**
Woolf, Virginia: **1395–1417**
Wordsworth, William: **1419–1444**

Poets of World War I (British): **1445–1471**
Yeats, William Butler: **1473–1490**

William Shakespeare: His World, His Work, His Influence

VOLUME 1

State, The: Government and Politics Under
    Elizabeth and James: **1–20**
Church, The: Religion and Its Manifestations:
    21–40
Law and Legal Institutions: **41–54**
Education and Aprenticeship: **55–66**
Economic Life in Shakespeare's England: **67–74**
Medicine and Sanitation: **75–84**
Shakespeare and Warfare: **85–98**
Patronage of the Arts: **99–106**
Theaters and the Dramatic Profession: **107–128**
Printing and Publishing in the Tudor Age:
    129–142
Sense of History in Renaissance England, The:
    143–158
Literate Culture of Shakespeare's Audience,
    The: **159–174**
Science, Magic, and Folklore: **175–194**
Travel by Sea and Land: **195–200**
"Style Is the Man": Manners, Dress, and
    Decorum: **201–214**
Daily Life in City, Town, and Country: **215–232**
Shakespeare and Foreigners: **233–240**
Painting and Other Fine Arts: **241–256**
Forest, Field, and Garden: **257–268**
Sports and Recreations: **269–280**

VOLUME 2

Life, The: A Survey: **281–290**
Thinking About Shakespeare's Thought:
    291–308
Shakespeare's Professional Career: Poet and
    Playwright: **309–330**
Shakespeare and His Contemporaries: **331–342**
Shakespeare's Language: **343–362**
Shakespeare's Poetic Techniques: **363–388**
Shakespeare's Use of Prose: **389–396**
Shakespeare's Dramatic Methods: **397–416**

Music in Shakespeare's Work: **417–424**

Visual Arts in Shakespeare's Work, The: **425–432**

Sonnets, The: **433–444**

Poems, The: **445–452**

Shakespeare's Treatment of English History: **453–472**

Shakespeare's Treatment of Roman History: **473–488**

Shakespeare as a Writer of Comedy: **489–504**

Shakespeare's Tragedies: **505–532**

Shakespeare's Tragicomedies and Romances: **533–548**

Shakespeare and His Audiences: **549–556**

Ethical and Theological Questions in Shakespeare's Dramatic Works: **557–570**

Shakespeare's Psychology: **571–587**

VOLUME 3

Publishing and Editing of Shakespeare's Plays, The: **589–602**

Shakespeare on the English Stage: **603–628**

Shakespeare in the Theater: The United States and Canada: **629–662**

Shakespeare as a World Figure: **663–680**

Shakespeare on Film and Television: **681–704**

Shakespeare's Reputation—Then Till Now: **705–716**

Shakespearean Scholarship: From Rowe to the Present: **717–732**

Shakespearean Criticism: **733–756**

Shakespeare and the Painter and Illustrator: **757–770**

Shakespeare in Music: **771–786**

Major Shakespearean Institutions: **787–800**

Shakespeare and the Modern Writer: **801–808**

Shakespeare and the Modern Playwright: **809–814**

Shakespeare and the Modern Director: **815–822**

Tradition, Style, and the Shakespearean Actor Today: **823–830**

Cultural Phenomenon of Shakespeare, The: **831–838**

Shakespeare and the Humanities: **839–866**

Shakespeare and the Modern Critic: **867–872**

Teaching Shakespeare: Tradition and the Future: **873–888**

Contemporary Issues in Shakespearean Interpretation: **889–927**

WORLD LITERATURE

African Writers

VOLUME 1

Abrahams, Peter: **1–14**

Achebe, Chinua: **15–36**

Aidoo, Ama Ata: **37–48**

Armah, Ayi Kwei: **49–62**

Awoonor, Kofi: **63–75**

Bâ, Mariama: **77–82**

Beti, Mongo: **83–94**

Brink, André: **95–114**

Brutus, Dennis: **115–126**

Campbell, Roy: **127–137**

Camus, Albert: **139–152**

Clark, John Pepper: **153–166**

Coetzee, J. M.: **167–183**

Couto, Mia: **185–197**

Dib, Mohammed: **199–207**

Egbuna, Obi: **209–221**

Ekwensi, Cyprian: **223–234**

Emecheta, Buchi: **235–247**

Farah, Nuruddin: **249–262**

Fugard, Athol: **263–275**

Gordimer, Nadine: **277–290**

Ḥakīm, Tawfīq, al-: **291–301**

Head, Bessie: **303–320**

Honwana, Luís Bernardo: **321–329**

Hope, Christopher: **331–343**

Idrīs, Yūsuf: **345–365**

Iyayi, Festus: **367–375**

Jacobson, Dan: **377–389**

Kateb, Yacine: **391–400**

La Guma, Alex: **401–411**
Laye, Camara: **413–425**
Lessing, Doris: **427–449**

VOLUME 2

Maḥfūẓ, Najib: **451–465**
Memmi, Albert: **467–477**
Mofolo, Thomas Mokopu: **479–493**
Mphahlele, Es'kia: **495–510**
Mwangi, Meja: **511–525**
Neto, Agostinho: **527–535**
Ngũgĩ wa Thiong'o: **537–555**
Ojaide, Tanure: **557–565**
Okara, Gabriel: **567–582**
Okigbo, Christopher: **583–598**
Okri, Ben: **599–608**
Omotoso, Kole: **609–617**
Osofisan, Femi: **619–629**
Osundare, Niyi: **631–640**
Oyono, Ferdinand: **641–649**
Paton, Alan: **651–668**
p'Bitek, Okot: **669–684**
Pepetela: **685–695**
Plomer, William: **697–706**
Rotimi, Ola: **707–720**
Sa'adāwī, Nawāl, al-: **721–731**
Ṣāliḥ, al-Ṭayyib: **733–744**
Schreiner, Olive: **745–763**
Sembène Ousmane: **765–774**
Senghor, Léopold Sédar: **775–789**
Shābbī, Abū al-Qāsim, al-: **791–798**
Sowande, Bode: **799–806**
Soyinka, Wole: **807–831**
Sutherland, Efua Theodora: **833–849**
Ṭāhā Ḥusayn: **851–863**
Tutuola, Amos: **865–878**
van der Post, Laurens: **879–891**
Vieira, José Luandino: **893–901**

Ancient Writers

VOLUME 1

Homer: **1–41**
Hesiod: **43–73**

Greek Lyric Poets: **75–98**
Aeschylus: **99–155**
Pindar: **157–177**
Sophocles: **179–207**
Herodotus: **209–232**
Euripides: **233–266**
Thucydides: **267–289**
Aristophanes: **291–312**
Isocrates: **313–329**
Xenophon: **331–351**
Plato: **353–376**
Aristotle: **377–416**
Demosthenes: **417–433**
Menander: **435–447**
Hellenistic Poetry at Alexandria: **449–482**
Theocritus: **483–500**
Plautus: **501–523**
Polybius: **525–539**
Terence: **541–554**
Cicero: **555–581**
Caesar: **583–599**

VOLUME 2

Lucretius: **601–620**
Sallust: **621–641**
Catullus: **643–667**
Vergil: **669–701**
Horace: **703–731**
Livy: **733–764**
Tibullus and Propertius: **765–782**
Ovid: **783–806**
Seneca the Younger: **807–832**
Petronius: **833–853**
Persius and Juvenal: **855–876**
Josephus: **877–885**
Martial: **887–915**
Lucan and Statius: **917–941**
Quintilian: **943–959**
Plutarch: **961–983**
Epictetus and Marcus Aurelius: **985–1002**
Tacitus: **1003–1033**
Pliny the Younger: **1035–1048**
Suetonius: **1049–1061**
Longinus: **1063–1080**
Lucian: **1081–1097**

Apuleius: **1099–1116**
Ammianus Marcellinus: **1117–1138**

The Books of the Bible

VOLUME 1

Bible as Sacred Literature, The: **1–9**
Old Testament, The: **11–19**
Genesis: **21–45**
Exodus: **47–62**
Leviticus: **63–70**
Numbers: **71–87**
Deuteronomy: **89–102**
Joshua: **103–112**
Judges: **113–121**
Ruth: **123–126**
Samuel (1 and 2 Samuel): **127–140**
Kings (1 and 2 Kings): **141–153**
Chronicles, Ezra, and Nehemiah (1 and 2 Chronicles, Ezra, and Nehemiah): **155–171**
Esther and Additions to Esther: **173–179**
Job: **181–201**
Psalms: **203–221**
Proverbs: **223–230**
Ecclesiastes: **231–239**
Song of Solomon: **241–246**
Isaiah: **247–279**
Jeremiah: **281–301**
Lamentations: **303–318**
Ezekiel: **319–332**
Daniel and Additions to Daniel: **333–347**
Hosea: **349–358**
Joel: **359–365**
Amos: **367–374**
Obadiah and Nahum: **375–380**
Jonah: **381–384**
Micah: **385–390**
Habakkuk: **391–396**
Zephaniah: **397–404**
Haggai, Zechariah, and Malachi: **405–414**

VOLUME 2

Apocrypha, The: **3–11**
Esdras (1 Esdras): **13–19**

Esdras (2 Esdras): **21–34**
Tobit: **35–42**
Judith: **43–49**
Wisdom of Solomon: **51–63**
Sirach (Ecclesiasticus): **65–86**
Baruch, the Letter of Jeremiah, the Prayer of Manasseh: **87–92**
Maccabees (1 and 2 Maccabees): **93–114**
New Testament, The: **117–124**
Gospel of Matthew: **125–147**
Gospel of Mark: **149–169**
Gospel of Luke and Acts of the Apostles: **171–202**
Gospel of John: **203–228**
Epistle to the Romans: **229–243**
Epistles to the Corinthians (1 and 2 Corinthians): **245–269**
Epistle to the Galatians: **271–284**
Epistle to the Ephesians: **285–292**
Epistle to the Philippians: **293–299**
Epistle to the Colossians: **301–310**
Epistles to the Thessalonians (1 and 2 Thessalonians): **311–318**
Epistles to Timothy and Titus (1 and 2 Timothy and Titus): **319–324**
Epistle to Philemon: **325–326**
Epistle to the Hebrews: **327–338**
Epistle of James: **339–343**
Epistle of Peter (1 Peter): **345–351**
Epistles of Peter and Jude (2 Peter and Jude): **353–357**
Epistles of John (1, 2, and 3 John): **359–365**
Revelation: **367–381**

European Writers

Essays preceded by an asterisk are also available in EUROPEAN WRITERS: SELECTED AUTHORS.

VOLUME 1

Prudentius: **1–22**
* Augustine, Saint: **23–50**
* *Beowulf* and Anglo-Saxon Poetry: **51–88**
  Chanson de Roland, The, and the *Chansons de Geste*: **89–112**

Cid in Epic and Ballad, The: **113–136**
*Arthurian Legend: **137–160**
Troubadours and Trouvères: **161–184**
Chrétien de Troyes: **185–209**
Nibelungenlied, The: **211–236**
Gottfried von Strassburg: **237–262**
Wolfram von Eschenbach: **263–286**
Walther von der Vogelweide: **287–308**
**Romance of the Rose*, The, and Medieval
    Allegory: **309–335**
*Medieval Satire: **337–376**
*Norse Sagas: **377–404**
*Aquinas, Saint Thomas, and Scholasticism:
    405–430
*Dante Alighieri: **431–450**
*Medieval Drama: **451–474**

VOLUME 2

*Petrarch: **475–507**
*Boccaccio, Giovanni: **509–534**
Villon, François: **535–570**
*Erasmus, Desiderius: **571–593**
*Machiavelli, Niccolò: **595–618**
Ariosto, Lodovico: **619–644**
Castiglione, Baldesar: **645–667**
*Luther, Martin: **669–692**
*Rabelais, François: **693–720**
Ronsard, Pierre de, and the Pléiade: **721–746**
Camoëns, Luís Vaz de: **747–767**
*Montaigne, Michel de: **769–790**
Tasso, Torquato: **791–818**
Cervantes, Miguel de: **819–844**
Vega, Lope de: **845–870**
Calderón de la Barca, Pedro: **871–897**
*Renaissance Pastoral Poetry: **899–926**
*Renaissance Short Fiction: **927–956**

VOLUME 3

*Descartes, René: **1–22**
Corneille, Pierre: **23–49**
La Rochefoucauld, François VI, Duc de:
    51–71
*La Fontaine, Jean de: **73–100**

*Molière: **101–124**
Pascal, Blaise: **125–150**
Bossuet, Jacques Bénigne: **151–175**
Boileau-Despréaux, Nicolas: **177–205**
Racine, Jean: **207–228**
La Bruyère, Jean de: **229–260**
Fénelon, François de Salignac de la Mothe-:
    261–291
Vico, Giovanni Battista: **293–316**
Lesage, Alain-René: **317–344**
Montesquieu, Charles-Louis de Secondat:
    345–366

VOLUME 4

*Voltaire: **367–392**
French Novelists, Three: **393–419**
Goldoni, Carlo: **421–448**
*Rousseau, Jean Jacques: **449–474**
Diderot, Denis: **475–509**
Klopstock, Friedrich Gottlieb: **511–536**
Lessing, Gotthold Ephraim: **537–562**
Beaumarchais, Pierre-Augustin Caron de:
    563–585
Wieland, Christoph Martin: **587–614**
Sade, Marquis de, and the French Libertine
    Tradition: **615–638**
Herder, Johann Gottfried von: **639–660**
Alfieri, Vittorio: **661–689**
Chénier, André: **691–718**

VOLUME 5

*Goethe, Johann Wolfgang von: **1–26**
Schiller, Friedrich von: **27–52**
Richter, Jean Paul: **53–88**
Staël, Madame de: **89–111**
Chateaubriand, François René de: **113–141**
Hölderlin, Friedrich: **143–175**
Schlegel, Friedrich von: **177–203**
Novalis: **205–231**
Tieck, Ludwig: **233–260**
Hoffmann, E. T. A.: **261–289**
Kleist, Heinrich von: **291–312**
Foscolo, Ugo: **313–341**

* Stendhal: **343–366**
Manzoni, Alessandro: **367–394**
Schopenhauer, Arthur: **395–415**
Grillparzer, Franz: **417–445**
Vigny, Alfred Victor de: **447–488**
Heine, Heinrich: **489–512**
Delacroix, Eugène: **513–539**
Leopardi, Giacomo: **541–569**
Michelet, Jules, and Romantic Historiography:
   571–606
Mickiewicz, Adam: **607–634**
* Balzac, Honoré de: **635–658**
* Pushkin, Alexander: **659–691**

VOLUME 6

* Hugo, Victor: **693–718**
* Dumas, Alexandre (Père): **719–743**
Mérimée, Prosper: **745–769**
Berlioz, Hector: **771–812**
* Sand, George: **813–836**
Sainte-Beuve, Charles-Augustin: **837–861**
* Andersen, Hans Christian: **863–892**
* Tocqueville, Alexis de: **893–912**
Poetic Realism: **913–942**
Nerval, Gérard de: **943–970**
Gogol, Nikolay Vasilievich: **971–997**
Musset, Alfred de: **999–1032**
Gautier, Théophile: **1033–1060**
Goncharov, Ivan: **1061–1087**
Hebbel, Friedrich: **1089–1122**
* Kierkegaard, Søren: **1123–1146**
* Wagner, Richard: **1147–1167**
Büchner, Georg: **1169–1194**
Lermontov, Mikhail Yurievich: **1195–1224**
Burckhardt, Jacob: **1225–1244**
Leconte de Lisle, Charles Marie:
   1245–1273
* Turgenev, Ivan: **1275–1297**
Fontane, Theodor: **1299–1322**

VOLUME 7

Baudelaire, Charles: **1323–1348**
* Dostoevsky, Feodor: **1349–1371**
* Flaubert, Gustave: **1373–1394**

Goncourt, Edmond Louis Antoine de, and
   Jules Alfred Huot de Goncourt: **1395–1419**
* Ibsen, Henrik: **1421–1447**
Taine, Hippolyte: **1449–1469**
* Tolstoy, Leo: **1471–1493**
Carducci, Giosue: **1495–1516**
* Zola, Émile: **1517–1541**
Verga, Giovanni: **1543–1565**
Mallarmé, Stéphane: **1567–1595**
Pérez Galdós, Benito: **1597–1618**
Verlaine, Paul: **1619–1643**
* Nietzsche, Friedrich: **1645–1681**
Eça de Queiroz, José Maria: **1683–1708**
Huysmans, Joris Karl: **1709–1730**
Strindberg, August: **1731–1757**
* Maupassant, Guy de: **1759–1784**
Rinbaud, Arthur: **1785–1824**
Pascoli, Giovanni: **1825–1854**
* Chekhov, Anton: **1855–1881**
Laforgue, Jules: **1883–1908**
Well-Made Play, The: **1909–1934**

VOLUME 8

* Freud, Sigmund: **1–20**
Hamsun, Knut: **21–43**
Bergson, Henri: **45–66**
Svevo, Italo: **67–87**
Schnitzler, Arthur: **89–117**
Maeterlinck, Maurice: **119–146**
Hauptmann, Gerhart: **147–174**
D'Annunzio, Gabriele: **175–203**
Cavafy, Constantin: **205–228**
Wedekind, Frank: **229–281**
Unamuno, Miguel de: **283–310**
Croce, Benedetto: **311–329**
Valle-Inclán, Ramón del: **331–353**
Blasco Ibáñez, Vicente: **355–388**
* Pirandello, Luigi: **389–416**
* Gorky, Maxim: **417–446**
George, Stefan: **447–470**
Claudel, Paul: **471–494**
* Gide, André: **495–518**
Mann, Heinrich: **519–543**
* Proust, Marcel: **545–568**
Valéry, Paul: **569–588**

VOLUME 9

Baroja, Pío: **589–616**
*Colette: **617–638**
Azorín: **639–663**
Jarry, Alfred: **665–687**
Hofmannsthal, Hugo von: **689–714**
*Mann, Thomas: **715–742**
Machado, Antonio: **743–765**
*Rilke, Rainer Maria: **767–795**
Marinetti, Filippo Tommaso: **797–832**
*Hesse, Hermann: **833–858**
Ady, Endre: **859–880**
Apollinaire, Guillaume: **881–903**
Bely, Andrey: **905–929**
Musil, Robert: **931–958**
Blok, Alexander: **959–990**
Jiménez, Juan Ramón: **991–1016**
Undset, Sigrid: **1017–1040**
Giraudoux, Jean: **1041–1066**
Kazantzakis, Nikos: **1067–1089**
Hašek, Jaroslav: **1091–1118**
Ortega y Gasset, José: **1119–1150**
*Kafka, Franz: **1151–1179**

VOLUME 10

Zamyatin, Yevgeny Ivanovich: **1181–1203**
Witkiewicz (Witkacy), Stanisław Ignacy:
    1205–1230
Kosztolányi, Dezső: **1231–1249**
Lukács, György: **1251–1279**
*Dinesen, Isak: **1281–1305**
Mauriac, François: **1307–1330**
Khlebnikov, Velimir: **1331–1364**
Arp, Jean: **1365–1384**
Broch, Hermann: **1385–1408**
Trakl, Georg: **1409–1427**
Perse, Saint-John: **1429–1452**
Ungaretti, Giuseppe: **1453–1473**
Pessoa, Fernando: **1475–1495**
Gunnarsson, Gunnar: **1497–1519**
Akhmatova, Anna: **1521–1542**
Cocteau, Jean: **1543–1563**
Čapek, Karel: **1565–1589**
*Pasternak, Boris: **1591–1617**

Mandelshtam, Osip: **1619–1649**
Tychyna, Pavlo: **1651–1676**
Lagerkvist, Pär: **1677–1702**

VOLUME 11

Benjamin, Walter: **1703–1730**
Tsvetaeva, Marina: **1731–1750**
Andrić, Ivo: **1751–1779**
Södergran, Edith: **1781–1806**
Krleža, Miroslav: **1807–1834**
Mayakovsky, Vladimir: **1835–1858**
Céline, Louis-Ferdinand: **1859–1884**
*Babel, Isaac: **1885–1914**
Montherlant, Henry de: **1915–1938**
Breton, André: **1939–1960**
Artaud, Antonin: **1961–1985**
Montale, Eugenio: **1987–2008**
Lampedusa, Giuseppe Tomasi di: **2009–2034**
Vesaas, Tarjei: **2035–2059**
Aragon, Louis: **2061–2087**
*Brecht, Bertolt: **2089–2111**
Ghelderode, Michel de: **2113–2141**
Ferreira de Castro, Jose Maria: **2143–2165**
*García Lorca, Federico: **2167–2202**
Moberg, Vilhelm: **2203–2231**
Olesha, Yuri: **2233–2253**

VOLUME 12

Seferis, George: **2255–2271**
Silone, Ignazione: **2273–2305**
*Saint-Exupéry, Antoine de: **2307–2331**
Sarraute, Nathalie: **2333–2359**
Johnson, Eyvind: **2361–2385**
Quasimodo, Salvatore: **2387–2411**
*Malraux, André: **2413–2432**
Aymé, Marcel: **2433–2456**
Laxness, Halldór: **2457–2478**
Simenon, Georges: **2479–2510**
Queneau, Raymond: **2511–2534**
Yourcenar, Marguerite: **2535–2561**
Gombrowicz, Witold: **2563–2588**
*Sartre, Jean-Paul: **2589–2614**
Canetti, Elias: **2615–2633**
Ekelöf, Gunnar: **2635–2671**

Moravia, Alberto: **2673–2699**
*Beauvoir, Simone de: **2701–2731**
Vittorini, Elio: **2733–2757**
Pavese, Cesare: **2759–2786**
Weil, Simone: **2787–2814**
Ritsos, Yannis: **2815–2842**

VOLUME 13

*Anouilh, Jean: **2843–2864**
Genet, Jean: **2865–2893**
Frisch, Max: **2895–2927**
Milosz, Czeslaw: **2929–2953**
Elytis, Odysseus: **2955–2988**
*Ionesco, Eugène: **2989–3020**
Simon, Claude: **3021–3048**
*Camus, Albert: **3049–3078**
Barthes, Roland: **3079–3104**
Cela, Camilo José: **3105–3129**
Ginzburg, Natalia: **3131–3163**
Böll, Heinrich: **3165–3186**
*Solzhenitsyn, Aleksandr: **3187–3213**
Dürrenmatt, Friedrich: **3215–3235**
Robbe-Grillet, Alain: **3237–3257**
Calvino, Italo: **3259–3286**
Butor, Michel: **3287–3321**
Foucault, Michel: **3323–3364**
*Grass, Günter: **3365–3388**
Kundera, Milan: **3389–3413**

European Writers: Selected Authors

The following essays were reprinted from
EUROPEAN WRITERS.

VOLUME 1

Andersen, Hans Christian: **1–29**
Anouilh, Jean: **31–52**
Aquinas, Saint Thomas, and Scholasticism:
  53–77
Arthurian Legend: **79–102**
Augustine, Saint: **103–130**
Babel, Isaac: **131–160**
Balzac, Honoré de: **161–183**

Beauvoir, Simone de: **185–215**
Beowulf and Anglo-Saxon Poetry: **217–253**
Boccaccio, Giovanni: **255–280**
Brecht, Bertolt: **281–303**
Camus, Albert: **305–334**
Chekhov, Anton: **361–387**
Colette: **389–410**
Dante Alighieri: **411–430**
Descartes, René: **431–452**
Dinesen, Isak: **453–477**
Dostoevsky, Feodor: **479–501**
Dumas, Alexandre (Père): **503–527**
Erasmus, Desiderius: **529–551**
Flaubert, Gustave: **553–574**
Freud, Sigmund: **575–594**
García Lorca, Federico: **595–630**
Gide, André: **631–654**
Goethe, Johann Wolfgang von: **655–680**

VOLUME 2

Gorky, Maxim: **681–710**
Grass, Günter: **711–734**
Hesse, Hermann: **735–760**
Hugo, Victor: **761–786**
Ibsen, Henrik: **787–813**
Ionesco, Eugène: **815–846**
Kafka, Franz: **847–875**
Kierkegaard, Søren: **877–900**
La Fontaine, Jean de: **901–928**
Luther, Martin: **929–951**
Machiavelli, Niccolò: **953–976**
Malraux, André: **977–996**
Mann, Thomas: **997–1024**
Maupassant, Guy de: **1025–1050**
Medieval Drama: **1051–1074**
Medieval Satire: **1075–1113**
Molière: **1115–1137**
Montaigne, Michel de: **1139–1160**
Nietzsche, Friedrich: **1161–1197**
Norse Sagas: **1199–1226**
Pasternak, Boris: **1227–1253**
Petrarch: **1255–1287**
Pirandello, Luigi: **1289–1316**
Proust, Marcel: **1317–1340**

VOLUME 3

Pushkin, Alexander: **1341–1373**
Rabelais, François: **1375–1402**
Renaissance Pastoral Poetry: **1403–1430**
Renaissance Short Fiction: **1431–1460**
Rilke, Rainer Maria: **1461–1489**
Romance of the Rose, The, and Medieval
    Allegory: **1491–1517**
Rousseau, Jean Jacques: **1519–1544**
Saint-Exupéry, Antoine de: **1545–1569**
Sand, George: **1571–1594**
Sartre, Jean-Paul: **1595–1620**
Solzhenitsyn, Aleksandr: **1621–1647**
Stendhal: **1649–1672**
Tocqueville, Alexis de: **1673–1691**
Tolstoy, Leo: **1693–1715**
Turgenev, Ivan: **1717–1739**
Voltaire: **1741–1766**
Wagner, Richard: **1767–1787**
Zola, Émile: **1789–1813**

Latin American Writers

VOLUME 1

Las Casas, Bartolomé de: **1–9**
Fernández de Oviedo y Valdés, Gonzalo:
    11–15
Díaz del Castillo, Bernal: **17–21**
Ercilla y Zúñiga, Don Alonso de: **23–31**
González de Eslava, Fernán: **33–37**
Garcilaso de la Vega, El Inca: **39–45**
Acosta, Father Joseph de: **47–51**
Balbuena, Bernardo de: **53–57**
Oña, Pedro de: **59–63**
Mattos, Gregório de: **65–69**
Sigüenza y Góngora, Carlos de: **71–77**
Valle y Caviedes, Juan del: **79–83**
Juana Inéz de La Cruz, Sor: **85–106**
Carrió de la Vandera, Alonso: **107–111**
Costa, Cláudio Manuel da: **113–117**
Fernández de Lizardi, José Joaquín: **119–128**
Bello, Andrés: **129–134**
Heredia, José Mariá: **135–140**
Echeverría, Esteban: **141–145**

Ascasubi, Hilario: **147–151**
Alberdi, Juan Bautista: **153–158**
Sarmiento, Domingo Faustino: **159–167**
Villaverde, Cirilo: **169–174**
Gómez de Avellaneda, Gertrudis: **175–180**
Mármol, José: **181–184**
Gonçalves Dias, Antônio: **185–193**
Alencar, José de: **195–203**
Blest Gana, Alberto: **205–213**
Montalvo, Juan: **215–220**
Palma, Ricardo: **221–228**
Campo, Estanislao del: **229–233**
Hernández, José: **235–246**
Isaacs, Jorge: **247–251**
Machado de Assis, Joaquim Maria: **253–268**
Cambaceres, Eugenio: **269–276**
Caro, Miguel Antonio: **277–281**
González Prada, Manuel: **283–288**
Castro Alves, Antônio de: **289–297**
Acevedo Díaz, Eduardo: **299–303**
Matto de Turner, Clorinda: **305–309**
Martí, José: **311–320**
Zeno Gandía, Manuel: **321–326**
Zorrilla de San Martín, Juan: **327–331**
Azevedo, Aluísio: **333–341**
Carrasquilla, Tomás: **343–350**
Gutiérrez Nájera, Manuel: **351–357**
Cruz e Sousa, João: **359–363**
Casal, Julián del: **365–370**
Gamboa, Federico: **371–375**
Silva, José Asunción: **377–385**
Cunha, Euclides da: **387–395**
Darío, Rubén: **397–412**
Payró, Roberto Jorge: **413–417**
Jaimes Freyre, Ricardo: **419–423**
Nervo, Amado: **425–429**
Díaz Rodríguez, Manuel: **431–439**
Tablada, José Juan: **441–446**

VOLUME 2

Rodó, José Enrique: **447–455**
Azuela, Mariano: **457–464**
Gómez Carillo, Enrique: **465–469**
Larreta, Enrique: **471–476**
Valencia, Guillermo: **477–482**

Fernández, Macedonio: **483–491**
Lugones, Leopoldo: **493–502**
Blanco Fombona, Rufino: **503–511**
Eguren, José María: **513–518**
Herrera y Reissig, Julio: **519–530**
Sánchez, Florencio: **531–538**
Molina, Juan Ramón: **539–542**
Chocano, José Santos: **543–549**
Quiroga, Horacio: **551–558**
Lynch, Benito: **559–563**
Lima Barreto, Afonso Henriques de: **565–573**
Vasconcelos, José: **575–584**
Gálvez, Manuel: **585–589**
Rojas, Ricardo: **591–596**
Henríquez Ureña, Pedro: **597–601**
Gallegos, Rómulo: **603–610**
Barrios, Eduardo: **611–618**
Güiraldes, Ricardo: **619–627**
Bandeira, Manuel: **629–641**
Prado, Pedro: **643–647**
Agustini, Delmira: **649–654**
Guzmán, Martín Luis: **655–662**
Lopez Velarde, Ramon: **663–670**
Rivera, José Eustasio: **671–675**
Mistral, Gabriela: **677–692**
Reyes, Alfonso: **693–703**
Ocampo, Victoria: **705–710**
Romero, José Rubén: **711–715**
Parra Sanojo, Ana Teresa de la: **717–720**
Valle, Rafael Heliodoro: **721–725**
Vallejo, César: **727–738**
Storni, Alfonsina: **739–743**
Ramos, Graciliano: **745–754**
Huidobro, Vicente: **755–764**
Lima, Jorge de: **765–770**
Andrade, Mário de: **771–780**
Amoroso Lima, Alceu: **781–790**
Mariátegui, José Carlos: **791–796**
Eichelbaum, Samuel: **797–801**
Ibarbourou, Juana de: **803–807**
Martínez Estrada, Ezequiel: **809–813**
Rojas, Manuel: **815–820**
Palés Matos, Luis: **821–830**
Mañach Robato, Jorge: **831–836**
Molinari, Ricardo E.: **837–844**
Borges, Jorge Luis: **845–864**

Asturias, Miguel Ángel: **865–873**
Salazar Arrué, Salvador (Salarrué): **875–879**
Arlt, Roberto: **881–886**
Marechal, Leopoldo: **887–896**
Arciniegas, Germán: **897–901**
Picón Salas, Mariano: **903–908**
Lins do Rego, José: **909–913**
Meireles, Cecília: **915–922**
Gorostiza, José: **923–931**
Torres Bodet, Jaime: **933–939**
Sinán, Rogelio: **941–946**
Guillén, Nicolás: **947–955**
Drummond de Andrade, Carlos: **957–974**

VOLUME 3

Villaurrutia, Xavier: **975–980**
Mallea, Eduardo: **981–989**
Marín Cañas, José: **991–994**
Yáñez, Agustín: **995–999**
Neruda, Pablo: **1001–1018**
Carpentier, Alejo: **1019–1031**
Usigli, Rodolfo: **1033–1042**
Veríssimo, Érico: **1043–1048**
Laguerre, Enrique A.: **1049–1055**
Uslar Pietri, Arturo: **1057–1062**
Icaza, Jorge: **1063–1067**
Guimarães Rosa, João: **1069–1080**
Ballagas, Emilio: **1081–1087**
Onetti, Juan Carlos: **1089–1097**
Alegría, Ciro: **1099–1103**
Anderson Imbert, Enrique: **1105–1110**
Bombal, María Luisa: **1111–1117**
Queiroz, Rachel de: **1119–1123**
Lezama Lima, José: **1125–1130**
Arguedas, José María: **1131–1138**
Sábato, Ernesto: **1139–1143**
Silveira de Queiroz, Dinah: **1145–1151**
Amado, Jorge: **1153–1162**
Paz, Octavio: **1163–1176**
Cortázar, Julio: **1177–1194**
Parra, Nicanor: **1195–1200**
Bioy Casares, Adolfo: **1201–1208**
Roa Bastos, Augusto: **1209–1213**
Rulfo, Juan: **1215–1228**
Arreola, Juan José: **1229–1236**

Marqués, René: **1237–1246**
Cabral de Melo Neto, João: **1247–1253**
Benedetti, Mario: **1255–1263**
Denevi, Marco: **1265–1269**
Fagundes Telles, Lygia: **1271–1275**
Donoso, José: **1277–1288**
Carballido, Emilio: **1289–1294**
Castellanos, Rosario: **1295–1302**
Lispector, Clarice: **1303–1309**
Wolff, Egon: **1311–1315**
Suassuna, Ariano Vilar: **1317–1321**
Gambaro, Griselda: **1323–1328**
García Márquez, Gabriel: **1329–1346**
Heiremans, Luis Alberto: **1347–1352**
Fuentes, Carlos: **1353–1376**
Dragún, Osvaldo: **1377–1382**
Cabrera Infante, Guillermo: **1383–1391**
Díaz, Jorge: **1393–1397**
Edwards, Jorge: **1399–1403**
Puig, Manuel: **1405–1413**
Triana, José: **1415–1419**
Vargas Llosa, Mario: **1421–1436**
Sarduy, Severo: **1437–1444**
Valenzuela, Luisa: **1445–1449**
Arenas, Reinaldo: **1451–1458**

Science Fiction Writers

I. Early Science Fiction
Shelley, Mary Wollstonecraft: **3–9**
Poe, Edgar Allan: **11–18**
Haggard, H. Rider: **19–24**
Wells, H. G.: **25–30**
Shiel, M. P.: **31–37**
Serviss, Garrett P.: **39–44**
Doyle, Sir Arthur Conan: **45–50**

*II. Primitive Science Fiction: The American
Dime Novel and Pulp Magazines*
Senarens, Luis Philip: **53–58**
Burroughs, Edgar Rice: **59–64**
Merritt, A.: **65–71**

III. Mainstream Georgian Authors
Taine, John: **75–82**
Wright, S. Fowler: **83–89**
Stapledon, Olaf: **91–100**
Huxley, Aldous: **101–108**

*IV. American Science Fiction:
The Formative Period*
Leinster, Murray: **111–117**
Keller, David H.: **119–123**
Smith, E. E.: **125–130**
Lovecraft, H. P.: **131–137**
Smith, Clark Ashton: **139–144**
Weinbaum, Stanley G.: **145–149**
Campbell, John W., Jr.: **151–159**
Moore, C. L., and Henry Kuttner: **161–167**
Kuttner, Henry: **161–167**

V. The Circumbellum Period
Bradbury, Ray: **171–178**
De Camp, L. Sprague: **179–184**
Heinlein, Robert A.: **185–196**
Russell, Eric Frank: **197–202**
Sturgeon, Theodore: **203–208**
Van Vogt, A. E.: **209–217**
Wyndham, John: **219–224**
Williamson, Jack: **225–231**
Orwell, George: **233–241**
Lewis, C. S.: **243–248**

VI. The Moderns
Aldiss, Brian W.: **251–258**
Anderson, Poul: **259–265**
Asimov, Isaac: **267–276**
Ballard, J. G.: **277–282**
Bester, Alfred: **283–290**
Blish, James: **291–296**
Brunner, John: **297–304**
Budrys, Algis: **305–311**
Clarke, Arthur C.: **313–320**
Clement, Hal: **321–327**
Delany, Samuel R.: **329–336**
Dick, Philip K.: **337–343**
Dickson, Gordon R.: **345–350**
Disch, Thomas M.: **351–356**
Ellison, Harlan: **357–368**
Farmer, Philip José: **369–375**
Herbert, Frank: **377–385**
Hoyle, Fred: **387–392**
Knight, Damon: **393–400**
Kornbluth, C. M.: **401–407**
Le Guin, Ursula K.: **409–417**
Leiber, Fritz: **419–424**
Matheson, Richard: **425–431**

Merril, Judith: **433–439**
Miller, Walter M., Jr.: **441–448**
Moorcock, Michael: **449–457**
Niven, Larry: **459–465**
Oliver, Chad: **467–473**
Pohl, Frederik: **475–482**
Russ, Joanna: **483–490**
St. Clair, Margaret: **491–495**
Sheckley, Robert: **497–503**
Silverberg, Robert: **505–511**
Simak, Clifford D.: **513–518**
Smith, Cordwainer: **519–524**
Tenn, William: **525–530**
Tiptree, James, Jr.: **531–541**
Vance, Jack: **543–549**
Vonnegut, Kurt: **551–561**
Zelazny, Roger: **563–570**

VII. Continental Science Fiction
Verne, Jules: **573–582**
Čapek, Karel: **583–589**
Łem, Stanisław: **591–598**

Supernatural Fiction Writers

VOLUME 1

I. Early Writers
Apuleius: **3–9**
Arthurian Romances: **11–18**
Arabian Nights: **19–26**

II. French Writers
Cazotte, Jacques: **29–35**
Balzac, Honoré de: **37–44**
Gautier, Théophile: **45–50**
Mérimée, Prosper: **51–57**
Maupassant, Guy de: **59–65**
France, Anatole: **67–72**

III. German Writers
Musaeus, J. K.: **75–81**
Tieck, Ludwig: **83–89**
Chamisso, Adelbert von: **91–95**
Fouqué, Friedrich de la Motte: **97–105**
Hauff, William: **107–110**
Hoffmann, E. T. A.: **111–119**
Meinhold, Wilhelm: **121–127**

IV. British Gothic and Romantic Writers
Walpole, Horace: **131–137**
Beckford, William: **139–144**
Radcliffe, Ann: **145–151**
Lewis, M. G.: **153–160**
Maturin, Charles Robert: **161–168**
Scott, Sir Walter: **169–176**
Hogg, James: **177–183**

V. British Victorian Writers
Ainsworth, William Harrison: **187–193**
Bulwer-Lytton, Edward: **195–204**
Reynolds, G. W. M.: **205–211**
Dickens, Charles: **213–218**
Le Fanu, J. S.: **219–231**
Collins, Wilkie: **233–238**
MacDonald, George: **239–246**
Carroll, Lewis: **247–253**
Edwards, Amelia B.: **255–260**
Oliphant, Mrs.: **261–268**
Riddell, Mrs. J. H.: **269–277**
Wood, Mrs. Henry: **279–286**
Anstey, F.: **287–292**
Corelli, Marie: **293–297**
Morris, William: **299–306**
Stevenson, Robert Louis: **307–313**

VI. British Fin-de-Siècle Writers
Garnett, Richard: **317–320**
Haggard, H. Rider: **321–327**
Lee, Vernon: **329–335**
James, Henry: **337–344**
Wilde, Oscar: **345–350**
Machen, Arthur: **351–359**
Shiel, M. P.: **361–367**
Macleod, Fiona: **369–374**
Stoker, Bram: **375–381**
Jacobs, W. W.: **383–387**
Quiller-Couch, Arthur: **389–395**
Wells, H. G.: **397–402**

VII. British Early-Twentieth-Century Writers
Barrie, J. M.: **405–410**
Chesterton, G. K.: **411–414**
Hichens, Robert: **415–420**
Hodgson, William Hope: **421–428**
James, M. R.: **429–436**

Kipling, Rudyard: **437–442**
Pain, Barry: **443–448**
Saki: **449–455**
Beresford, J. D.: **457–461**
Blackwood, Algernon: **463–470**
Dunsany, Lord: **471–478**
Forster, E. M.: **479–484**
Stephens, James: **485–490**
Benson, E. F.: **491–496**
De la Mare, Walter: **497–503**
Onions, Oliver: **505–511**
Sinclair, May: **513–519**

VOLUME 2

*VIII. British Writers of the
Interbellum Period*
Coppard, A. E.: **523–528**
Eddison, E. R.: **529–534**
Garnett, David: **535–539**
Lindsay, David: **541–547**
Phillpotts, Eden: **549–553**
Rohmer, Sax: **555–560**
Baker, Frank: **561–567**
Bowen, Elizabeth: **569–575**
Collier, John: **577–583**
Fortune, Dion: **585–590**
Harvey, William Fryer: **591–596**
Metcalfe, John: **597–602**
Mirrlees, Hope: **603–607**
Powys, T. F.: **609–616**
Powys, John Cowper: **609–616**
Wakefield, H. Russell: **617–622**
Wheatley, Dennis: **623–629**
Williams, Charles: **631–638**
Hartley, L. P.: **639–644**
Wall, Mervyn: **645–650**
White, T. H.: **651–657**

IX. British Postwar Writers
Lewis, C. S.: **661–666**
Sarban: **667–673**
Tolkien, J. R. R.: **675–682**

*X. American Early-Nineteenth-Century
and Victorian Writers*
Irving, Washington: **685–691**
Austin, William: **693–696**

Poe, Edgar Allan: **697–705**
Hawthorne, Nathaniel: **707–715**
O'Brien, Fitz-James: **717–722**

XI. American Fin-de-Siècle Writers
Bangs, J. K.: **725–729**
Bierce, Ambrose: **731–737**
Chambers, Robert W.: **739–745**
Crawford, F. Marion: **747–751**
Stockton, Frank R.: **753–759**
Twain, Mark: **761–768**
Freeman, Mary Wilkins: **769–773**

*XII. American Mainstream Writers of the
Early to Middle Twentieth Century*
Atherton, Gertrude: **777–781**
Wharton, Edith: **783–788**
Cabell, James Branch: **789–796**
Benét, Stephen Vincent: **797–803**
Smith, Thorne: **805–811**
Nathan, Robert: **813–819**
Finney, Charles: **821–826**
Thurber, James: **827–831**

XIII. Early American Pulp Writers
Merritt, A.: **835–843**
Mundy, Talbot: **845–851**
Lovecraft, H. P.: **853–859**
Howard, Robert E.: **861–868**
Long, Frank Belknap: **869–874**
Smith, Clark Ashton: **875–881**
Derleth, August: **883–890**
Moore, C. L.: **891–898**

*XIV. American Pulp Writers of the
Circumbellum Period*
Bloch, Robert: **901–907**
Brackett, Leigh: **909–915**
Bradbury, Ray: **917–923**
De Camp, L. Sprague, and Fletcher Pratt:
925–931
Leiber, Fritz: **933–939**
Sturgeon, Theodore: **941–945**
Wellman, Manly Wade: **947–954**

XV. British and American Modern Writers
Aickman, Robert: **957–964**
Alexander, Lloyd: **965–971**
Anderson, Poul: **973–980**

Anthony, Piers: **981–986**
Beagle, Peter S.: **987–991**
Campbell, Ramsey: **993–999**
Davidson, Avram: **1001–1008**
Donaldson, Stephen R.: **1009–1013**
Ellison, Harlan: **1015–1021**
Garner, Alan: **1023–1029**
Jackson, Shirley: **1031–1036**
King, Stephen: **1037–1044**
Lafferty, R. A.: **1045–1052**
Lee, Tanith: **1053–1058**
Le Guin, Ursula K.: **1059–1066**
McKillip, Patricia: **1067–1072**
Matheson, Richard: **1073–1080**
Moorcock, Michael: **1081–1089**
Norton, Andre: **1091–1096**
Swann, Thomas Burnett: **1097–1103**
Vance, Jack: **1105–1111**
Zelazny, Roger: **1113–1119**

Writers for Children

Alcott, Louisa May: **1–6**
Andersen, Hans Christian: **7–13**
Ardizzone, Edward: **15–20**
Asbjørnsen and Moe (Peter Christen
    Asbjørnsen and Jørgen Moe): **21–28**
Barrie, J. M.: **29–35**
Baum, L. Frank: **37–48**
Belloc, Hilaire: **49–54**
Bemelmans, Ludwig: **55–61**
Bianco, Margery Williams: **63–67**
Blake, William: **69–76**
Bontemps, Arna: **77–83**
Brink, Carol Ryrie: **85–90**
Brunhoff, Jean de: **91–96**
Bunyan, John: **97–102**
Burnett, Frances Hodgson: **103–109**
Burton, Virginia Lee: **111–115**
Carroll, Lewis: **117–127**
Collodi, C.: **129–137**
Colum, Padraic: **139–146**
Cooper, James Fenimore: **147–153**
Daugherty, James Henry: **155–161**
Defoe, Daniel: **163–171**

De la Mare, Walter: **173–180**
Dickens, Charles: **181–191**
Dodge, Mary Mapes: **193–199**
Doyle, Sir Arthur Conan: **201–207**
Dumas, Alexandre (Père): **209–213**
Enright, Elizabeth: **215–220**
Ewing, Juliana Horatia: **221–226**
Farjeon, Eleanor: **227–234**
Field, Rachel Lyman: **235–240**
Gág, Wanda: **241–246**
Grahame, Kenneth: **247–254**
Grimm, Jacob and Wilhelm: **255–263**
Hale, Lucretia P.: **265–268**
Harris, Joel Chandler: **269–275**
Hawthorne, Nathaniel: **277–282**
Hoffmann, E. T. A.: **283–288**
Hoffmann, Heinrich: **289–294**
Hughes, Langston: **295–301**
Irving, Washington: **303–307**
Jacobs, Joseph: **309–316**
Kästner, Erich: **317–322**
Kingsley, Charles: **323–327**
Kipling, Rudyard: **329–336**
Lang, Andrew: **337–343**
Lawson, Robert: **345–349**
Lear, Edward: **351–356**
Lewis, C. S.: **357–364**
Lofting, Hugh: **365–371**
MacDonald, George: **373–380**
Marryat, Frederick: **381–387**
Meigs, Cornelia: **389–395**
Milne, A. A.: **397–405**
Molesworth, M. L. S.: **407–413**
Montgomery, L. M.: **415–422**
Nesbit, E.: **423–430**
Perrault, Charles: **431–437**
Potter, Beatrix: **439–446**
Pyle, Howard: **447–454**
Ransome, Arthur: **455–461**
Rawlings, Marjorie Kinnan: **463–467**
Richards, Laura E.: **469–475**
Roberts, Elizabeth Madox: **477–481**
Rossetti, Christina: **483–491**
Ruskin, John: **493–496**
Salten, Felix: **497–501**
Sandburg, Carl: **503–510**

Sawyer, Ruth: **511–517**
Seredy, Kate: **519–524**
Sewell, Anna: **525–528**
Spyri, Johanna: **529–533**
Stevenson, Robert Louis: **535–543**
Stockton, Frank R.: **545–554**
Swift, Jonathan: **555–559**
Tolkien, J. R. R.: **561–571**
Twain, Mark: **573–582**
Van Loon, Hendrik Willem: **583–589**
Verne, Jules: **591–598**
Wells, H. G.: **599–603**
Wiggin, Kate Douglas: **605–609**
Wilde, Oscar: **611–616**
Wilder, Laura Ingalls: **617–623**
Yonge, Charlotte Mary: **625–631**

Writers for Young Adults

VOLUME 1

Aiken, Joan: **1–9**
Alcott, Louisa May: **11–20**
Alexander, Lloyd: **21–33**
Angell, Judie: **35–42**
Angelou, Maya: **43–52**
Asher, Sandy: **53–61**
Avi: **63–72**
Bauer, Joan: **73–80**
Bauer, Marion Dane: **81–88**
Bennett, Jay: **89–97**
Bethancourt, T. Ernesto: **99–109**
Block, Francesca Lia: **111–119**
Blume, Judy: **121–131**
Bograd, Larry: **133–141**
Brancato, Robin F.: **143–152**
Branscum, Robbie: **153–161**
Bridgers, Sue Ellen: **163–172**
Brooks, Bruce: **173–182**
Bunting, Eve: **183–189**
Burns, Olive Ann: **191–198**
Byars, Betsy: **199–207**
Carter, Alden R.: **209–218**
Chambers, Aidan: **219–227**
Childress, Alice: **229–240**

Cleaver, Vera and Bill: **241–248**
Cole, Brock: **249–256**
Collier, Christopher and James Lincoln: **257–269**
Colman, Hila: **271–280**
Cooney, Caroline B.: **281–290**
Cormier, Robert: **291–301**
Crane, Stephen: **303–312**
Crutcher, Chris: **313–322**
Daly, Maureen: **323–333**
Danziger, Paula: **335–344**
Davis, Terry: **345–352**
Dickens, Charles: **353–364**
Dickinson, Emily: **365–372**
Dickinson, Peter: **375–383**
Doyle, Sir Arthur Conan: **385–392**
Duncan, Lois: **393–402**
Eyerly, Jeannette: **403–411**
Fox, Paula: **413–422**
Frank, Anne: **423–431**

VOLUME 2

Freedman, Russell: **1–9**
French, Michael: **11–20**
Frost, Robert: **21–31**
Garfield, Leon: **33–45**
George, Jean Craighead: **47–57**
Greene, Bette: **59–68**
Hall, Lynn: **69–77**
Hamilton, Virginia: **79–92**
Hemingway, Ernest: **93–102**
Hentoff, Nat: **103–112**
Hinton, S. E.: **113–120**
Hobbs, Will: **121–129**
Holland, Isabelle: **131–140**
Hughes, Monica: **141–148**
Hunter, Mollie: **149–159**
Irwin, Hadley: **161–166**
Johnston, Norma: **167–176**
Kerr, M. E.: **177–185**
Klein, Norma: **187–197**
Korman, Gordon: **199–206**
Lasky, Kathryn: **207–216**
Lee, Harper: **217–225**
Le Guin, Ursula K.: **227–236**

L'Engle, Madeleine: **237–246**
Lewis, C. S.: **247–255**
Lipsyte, Robert: **257–266**
London, Jack: **267–278**
Lowry, Lois: **279–287**
Lynch, Chris: **289–297**
McCaffrey, Anne: **299–306**
Mahy, Margaret (May): **307–315**
Major, Kevin: **317–326**
Mazer, Harry: **327–336**
Mazer, Norma Fox: **337–346**
Meltzer, Milton: **347–358**
Miklowitz, Gloria D.: **359–368**
Mohr, Nicholasa: **369–378**
Montgomery, L. M.: **379–386**
Myers, Walter Dean: **387–396**
Naylor, Phyllis Reynolds: **397–409**
Nixon, Joan Lowery: **411–419**
O'Dell, Scott: **421–431**
Oneal, Zibby: **433–442**
Paterson, Katherine: **443–454**
Paulsen, Gary: **455–463**

VOLUME 3

Peck, Richard: **1–14**
Peck, Robert Newton: **15–26**
Pevsner, Stella: **27–34**
Peyton, K. M.: **35–42**
Pfeffer, Susan Beth: **43–52**
Platt, Kin: **53–60**
Poe, Edgar Allan: **61–73**
Rinaldi, Ann: **75–85**

Rodowsky, Colby: **87–93**
Sachs, Marilyn: **95–104**
Salinger, J. D.: **105–112**
Salisbury, Graham: **113–121**
Sandburg, Carl: **123–133**
Scoppettone, Sandra: **135–143**
Sebestyen, Ouida: **145–153**
Shakespeare, William: **155–172**
Sleator, William: **173–182**
Soto, Gary: **183–191**
Spinelli, Jerry: **193–201**
Steinbeck, John: **203–214**
Stevenson, Robert Louis: **215–224**
Strasser, Todd: **225–236**
Stratemeyer, Edward: **237–249**
Sutcliff, Rosemary: **251–261**
Talbert, Marc: **263–272**
Taylor, Mildred Delois: **273–282**
Taylor, Theodore: **283–292**
Thomas, Joyce Carol: **293–301**
Thompson, Julian F.: **303–310**
Tolkien, J. R. R.: **311–320**
Twain, Mark: **321–328**
Voigt, Cynthia: **329–338**
Walsh, Jill Paton: **339–347**
Wersba, Barbara: **349–357**
Westall, Robert Atkinson: **359–369**
Wilder, Laura Ingalls: **371–380**
Wilkinson, Brenda: **381–390**
Wolff, Virginia Euwer: **391–398**
Yep, Laurence: **399–408**
Yolen, Jane: **409–420**
Zindel, Paul: **421–430**